PHILIP'S

STREET ATLAS

Warwickshire and Coventry

First published in 1992 by

Philip's, a division of
Octopus Publishing Group Ltd
2-4 Heron Quays, London E14 4JP

Third colour edition 2006
First impression 2006
WARCA

ISBN-10 0-540-08758-0 (spiral)
ISBN-13 978-0-540-08758-7 (spiral)

Printed by Toppan, China

Contents

III **Key to map symbols**

IV **Key to map pages**

VI **Route planning**

X **Administrative and Postcode boundaries**

1 **Street maps** at 3½ inches to 1 mile

112 **Street maps** at 1¾ inches to 1 mile

143 **Street maps** at 3½ inches to 1 mile

151 **Street map of Coventry city centre** at 7 inches to 1 mile

152 **Index** of towns and villages

154 **Index** of streets, hospitals, industrial estates, railway stations, schools, shopping centres, universities and places of interest

Digital Data

The exceptionally high-quality mapping found in this atlas is available as digital data in TIFF format, which is easily convertible to other bitmapped (raster) image formats.

The index is also available in digital form as a standard database table. It contains all the details found in the printed index together with the National Grid reference for the map square in which each entry is named.

For further information and to discuss your requirements, please contact Philip's on 020 7644 6932 or james.mann@philips-maps.co.uk

Key to map symbols

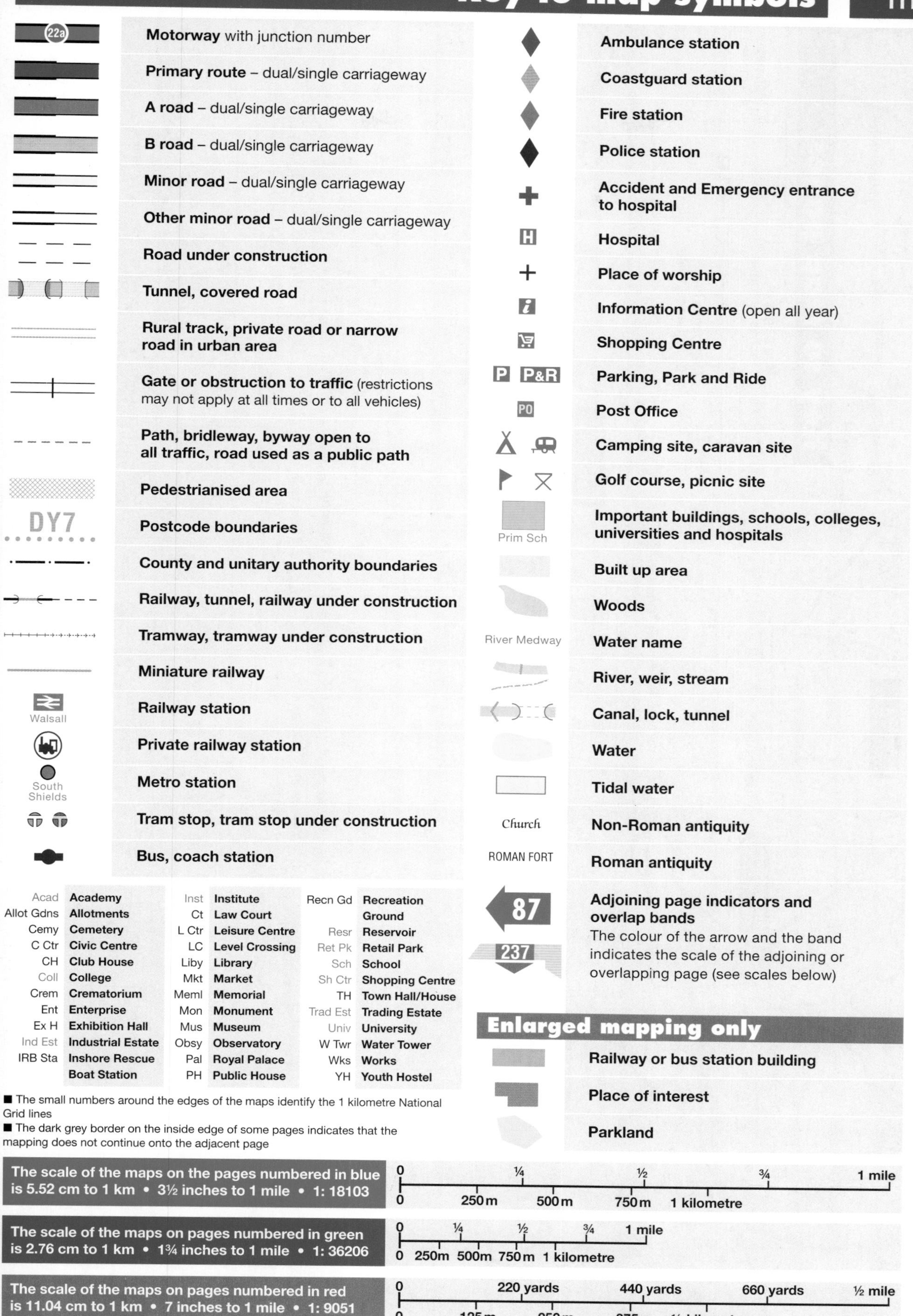

Motorway with junction number

Primary route – dual/single carriageway

A road – dual/single carriageway

B road – dual/single carriageway

Minor road – dual/single carriageway

Other minor road – dual/single carriageway

Road under construction

Tunnel, covered road

Rural track, private road or narrow road in urban area

Gate or obstruction to traffic (restrictions may not apply at all times or to all vehicles)

Path, bridleway, byway open to all traffic, road used as a public path

Pedestrianised area

DY7 Postcode boundaries

County and unitary authority boundaries

Railway, tunnel, railway under construction

Tramway, tramway under construction

Miniature railway

Walsall Railway station

Private railway station

South Shields Metro station

Tram stop, tram stop under construction

Bus, coach station

Ambulance station

Coastguard station

Fire station

Police station

Accident and Emergency entrance to hospital

Hospital

Place of worship

Information Centre (open all year)

Shopping Centre

P P&R Parking, Park and Ride

PO Post Office

Camping site, caravan site

Golf course, picnic site

Prim Sch Important buildings, schools, colleges, universities and hospitals

Built up area

Woods

River Medway Water name

River, weir, stream

Canal, lock, tunnel

Water

Tidal water

Church Non-Roman antiquity

ROMAN FORT Roman antiquity

87 237 Adjoining page indicators and overlap bands
The colour of the arrow and the band indicates the scale of the adjoining or overlapping page (see scales below)

Acad	Academy	Inst	Institute	Recn Gd	Recreation Ground
Allot Gdns	Allotments	Ct	Law Court	Resr	Reservoir
Cemy	Cemetery	L Ctr	Leisure Centre	Ret Pk	Retail Park
C Ctr	Civic Centre	LC	Level Crossing	Sch	School
CH	Club House	Liby	Library	Sh Ctr	Shopping Centre
Coll	College	Mkt	Market	TH	Town Hall/House
Crem	Crematorium	Meml	Memorial	Trad Est	Trading Estate
Ent	Enterprise	Mon	Monument	Univ	University
Ex H	Exhibition Hall	Mus	Museum	W Twr	Water Tower
Ind Est	Industrial Estate	Obsy	Observatory	Wks	Works
IRB Sta	Inshore Rescue Boat Station	Pal	Royal Palace	YH	Youth Hostel
		PH	Public House		

Enlarged mapping only

Railway or bus station building

Place of interest

Parkland

- The small numbers around the edges of the maps identify the 1 kilometre National Grid lines
- The dark grey border on the inside edge of some pages indicates that the mapping does not continue onto the adjacent page

The scale of the maps on the pages numbered in blue is 5.52 cm to 1 km • 3½ inches to 1 mile • 1: 18103

0 ¼ ½ ¾ 1 mile
0 250 m 500 m 750 m 1 kilometre

The scale of the maps on pages numbered in green is 2.76 cm to 1 km • 1¾ inches to 1 mile • 1: 36206

0 ¼ ½ ¾ 1 mile
0 250m 500m 750m 1 kilometre

The scale of the maps on pages numbered in red is 11.04 cm to 1 km • 7 inches to 1 mile • 1: 9051

0 220 yards 440 yards 660 yards ½ mile
0 125 m 250 m 375 m ½ kilometre

Key to map pages

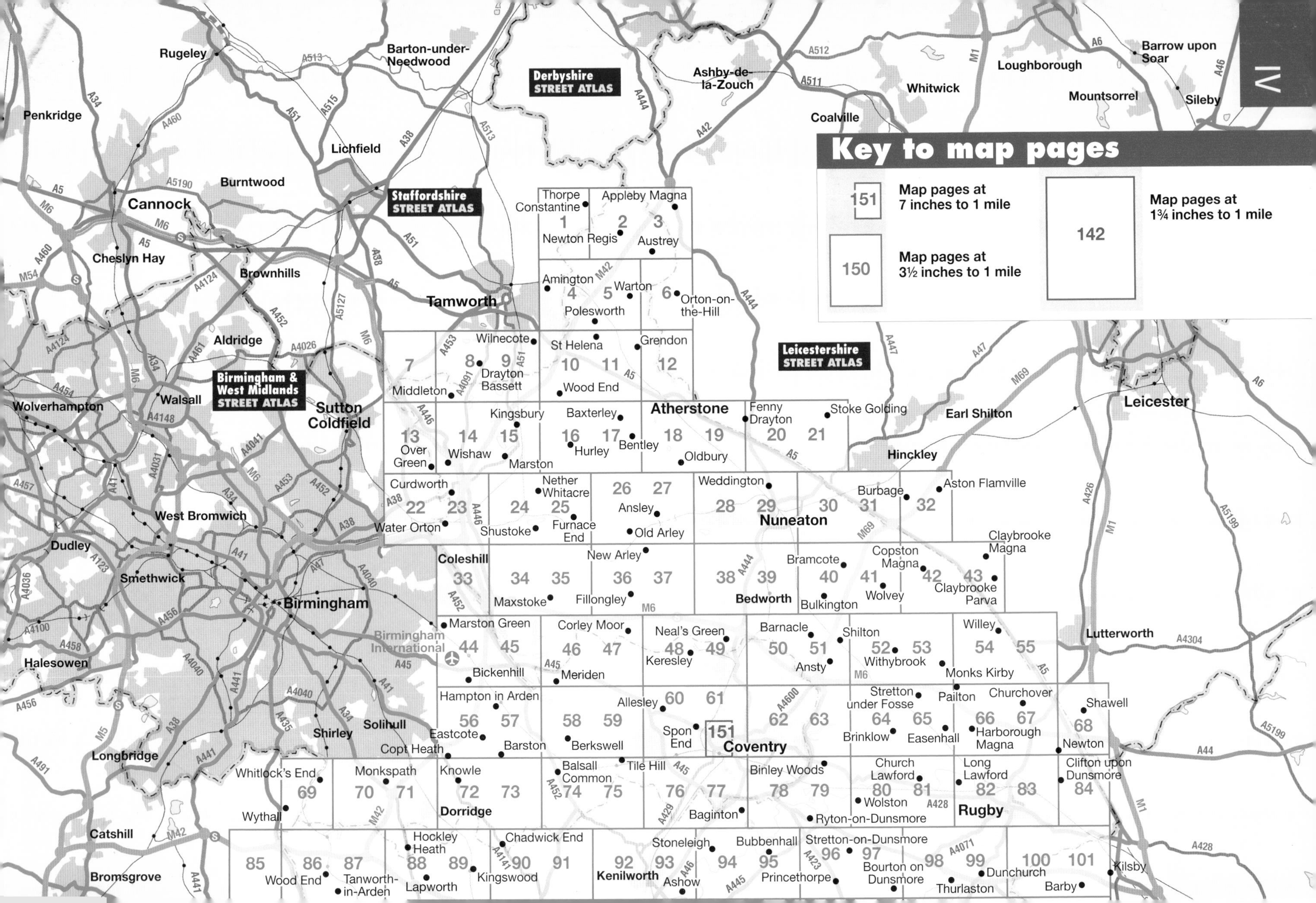

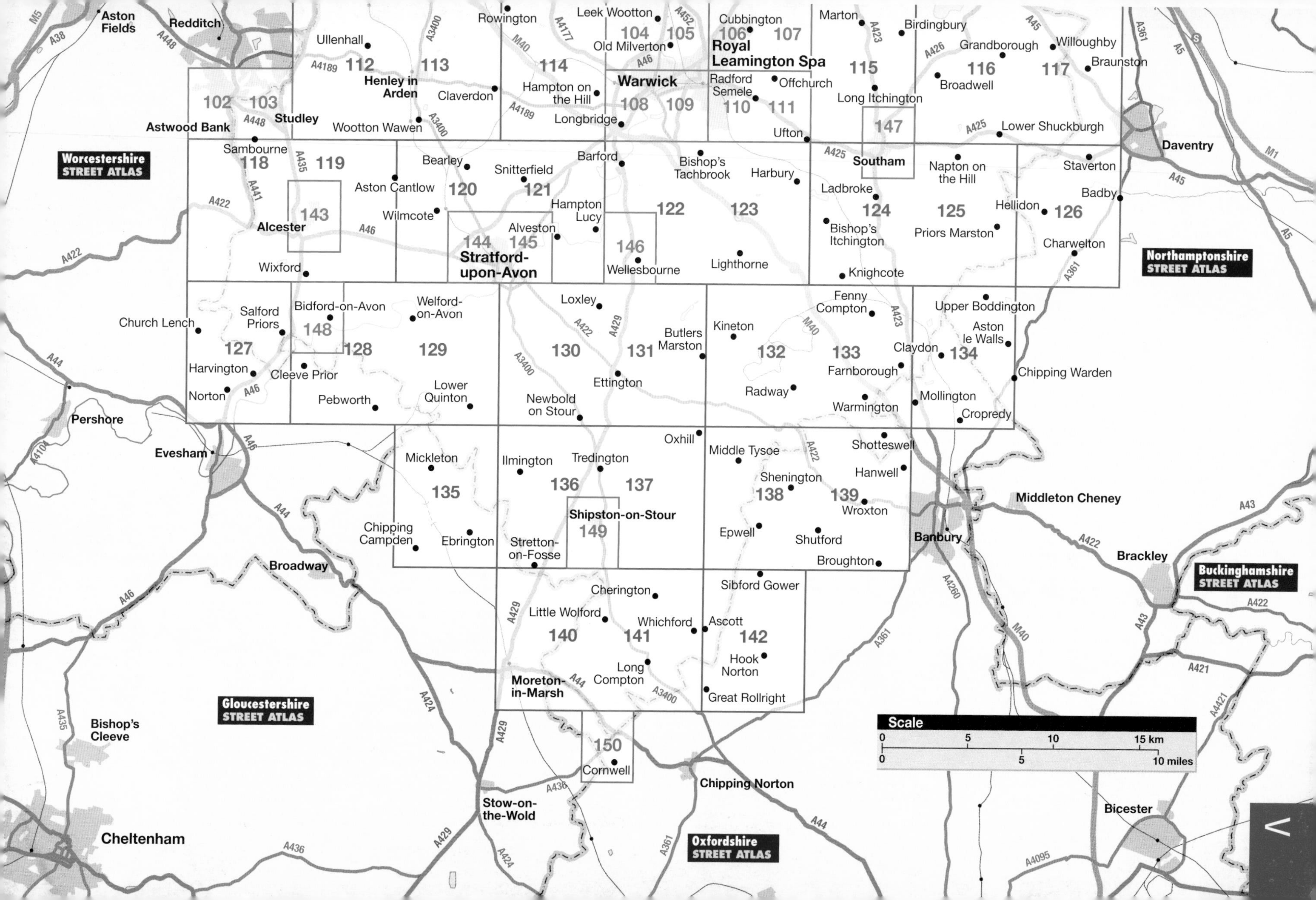

V
Worcestershire STREET ATLAS
Northamptonshire STREET ATLAS
Buckinghamshire STREET ATLAS
Gloucestershire STREET ATLAS
Oxfordshire STREET ATLAS
Scale
0 5 10 15 km
0 5 10 miles
Aston Fields
Redditch
Astwood Bank
Studley
Ullenhall
Henley in Arden
Claverdon
Wootton Wawen
Rowington
Hampton on the Hill
Longbridge
Leek Wootton
Old Milverton
Warwick
Cubbington
Royal Leamington Spa
Radford Semele
Offchurch
Ufton
Marton
Birdingbury
Long Itchington
Southam
Grandborough
Broadwell
Willoughby
Braunston
Lower Shuckburgh
Daventry
Staverton
Badby
Napton on the Hill
Hellidon
Charwelton
Priors Marston
Ladbroke
Bishop's Itchington
Knightcote
Harbury
Bishop's Tachbrook
Lighthorne
Wellesbourne
Barford
Hampton Lucy
Alveston
Snitterfield
Bearley
Aston Cantlow
Wilmcote
Stratford-upon-Avon
Sambourne
Alcester
Wixford
Church Lench
Salford Priors
Bidford-on-Avon
Welford-on-Avon
Harvington
Cleeve Prior
Norton
Pebworth
Lower Quinton
Loxley
Ettington
Butlers Marston
Newbold on Stour
Kineton
Radway
Fenny Compton
Farnborough
Warmington
Upper Boddington
Aston le Walls
Claydon
Chipping Warden
Mollington
Cropredy
Pershore
Evesham
Mickleton
Chipping Campden
Ebrington
Ilmington
Tredington
Shipston-on-Stour
Stretton-on-Fosse
Oxhill
Middle Tysoe
Shenington
Epwell
Shutford
Broughton
Shotteswell
Hanwell
Wroxton
Banbury
Middleton Cheney
Brackley
Broadway
Cherington
Little Wolford
Whichford
Long Compton
Moreton-in-Marsh
Sibford Gower
Ascott
Hook Norton
Great Rollright
Cornwell
Chipping Norton
Stow-on-the-Wold
Bishop's Cleeve
Cheltenham
Bicester
102 103 104 105 106 107 108 109 110 111 112 113 114 115 116 117 118 119 120 121 122 123 124 125 126 127 128 129 130 131 132 133 134 135 136 137 138 139 140 141 142 143 144 145 146 147 148 149 150
M5 A38 A448 A4189 A3400 M40 A4177 A452 A46 A423 A426 A45 A361 A5 M1 A425 A435 A441 A422 A4104 A44 A429 A4260 A43 A421 A4421 A4095 A435 A436 A424

Route planning

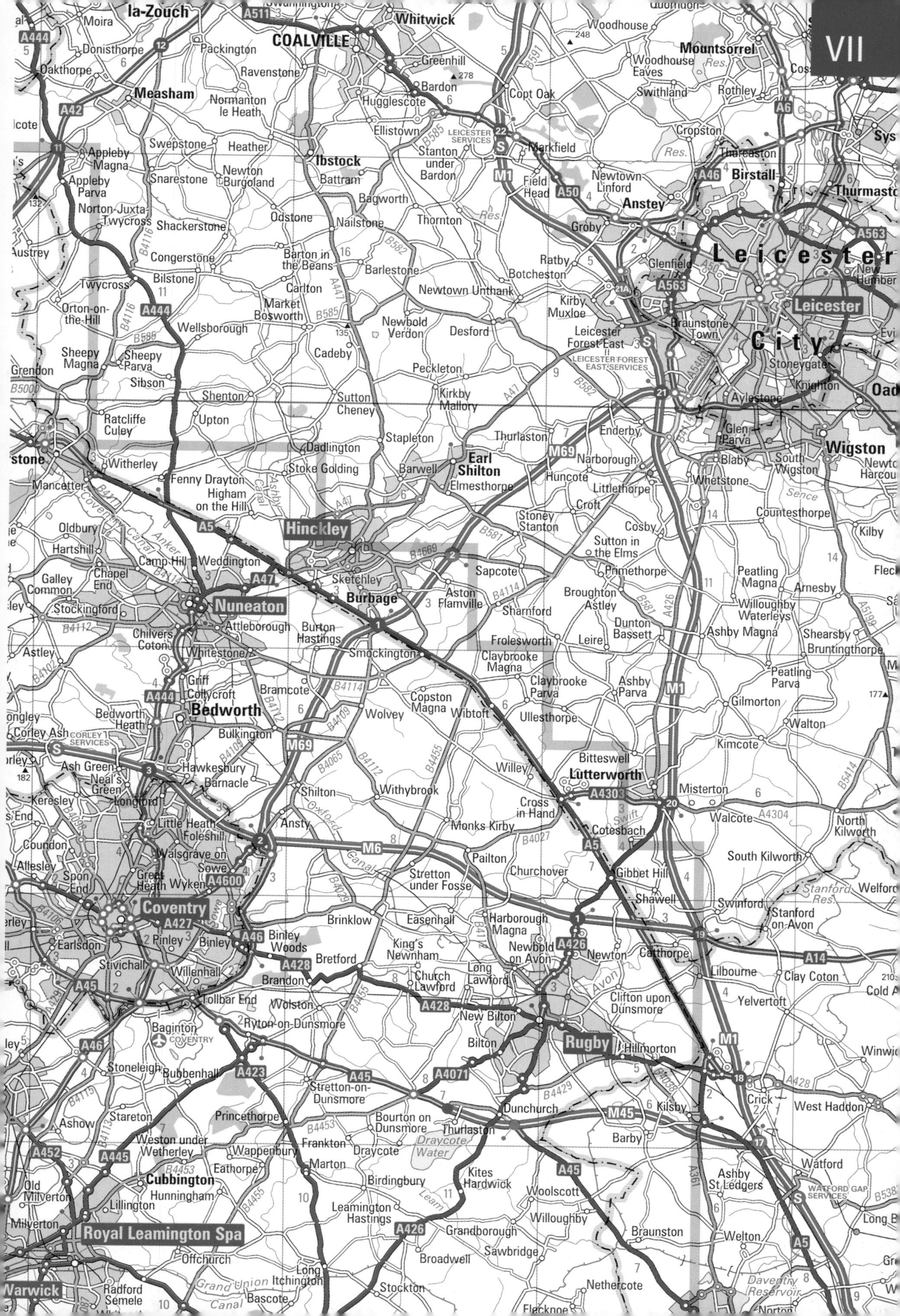

COALVILLE
Whitwick
Moira
Donisthorpe
Oakthorpe
Packington
Ravenstone
Greenhill
Bardon
Hugglescote
Ellistown
Measham
Normanton le Heath
Swepstone
Heather
Appleby Magna
Appleby Parva
Snarestone
Newton Burgoland
Ibstock
Battram
Bagworth
Stanton under Bardon
Leicester Services
Markfield
Field Head
Copt Oak
Woodhouse
Woodhouse Eaves
Mountsorrel
Swithland
Rothley
Cropston
Thurcaston
Birstall
Thurmaston
Newtown Linford
Anstey
Groby
Glenfield
Ratby
Botcheston
Leicester
Leicester City
Kirby Muxloe
Braunstone Town
Leicester Forest East
Leicester Forest East Services
Stoneygate
Knighton
Aylestone
Glen Parva
Wigston
South Wigston
Blaby
Whetstone
Enderby
Narborough
Thurlaston
Huncote
Littlethorpe
Croft
Cosby
Countesthorpe
Kilby
Stoney Stanton
Sutton in the Elms
Primethorpe
Peatling Magna
Arnesby
Broughton Astley
Willoughby Waterleys
Dunton Bassett
Leire
Ashby Magna
Shearsby
Bruntingthorpe
Peatling Parva
Gilmorton
Walton
Kimcote
Norton-Juxta-Twycross
Shackerstone
Odstone
Nailstone
Thornton
Barton in the Beans
Barlestone
Congerstone
Bilstone
Twycross
Carlton
Market Bosworth
Newtown Unthank
Newbold Verdon
Desford
Orton-on-the-Hill
Wellsborough
Cadeby
Peckleton
Sheepy Magna
Sheepy Parva
Sibson
Grendon
Shenton
Upton
Sutton Cheney
Kirkby Mallory
Ratcliffe Culey
Stapleton
Dadlington
Witherley
Mancetter
Fenny Drayton
Stoke Golding
Higham on the Hill
Barwell
Earl Shilton
Elmesthorpe
Oldbury
Hartshill
Hinckley
Sketchley
Burbage
Sapcote
Aston Flamville
Sharnford
Chapel End
Galley Common
Camp Hill
Weddington
Nuneaton
Stockingford
Attleborough
Chilvers Coton
Burton Hastings
Smockington
Frolesworth
Claybrooke Magna
Claybrooke Parva
Ullesthorpe
Ashby Parva
Astley
Whitestone
Griff
Collycroft
Bedworth
Bramcote
Copston Magna
Wibtoft
Wolvey
Bedworth Heath
Corley Ash
Corley Services
Bulkington
Hawkesbury
Barnacle
Ash Green
Neal's Green
Keresley
Longford
Shilton
Withybrook
Willey
Bitteswell
Lutterworth
Misterton
Walcote
North Kilworth
Cross in Hand
Monks Kirby
Little Heath
Foleshill
Ansty
Coundon
Allesley
Walsgrave on Sowe
Spon End
Great Heath
Wyken
Coventry
Pailton
Churchover
Cotesbach
Gibbet Hill
South Kilworth
Welford
Shawell
Swinford
Stanford on-Avon
Stretton under Fosse
Brinklow
Easenhall
Harborough Magna
Earlsdon
Pinley
Binley
Binley Woods
Stivichall
Willenhall
Bretford
Brandon
King's Newnham
Church Lawford
Long Lawford
Newbold on Avon
Newton
Catthorpe
Lilbourne
Clay Coton
Yelvertoft
Clifton upon Dunsmore
Tollbar End
Wolston
Ryton-on-Dunsmore
New Bilton
Bilton
Rugby
Hillmorton
Baginton
Stoneleigh
Bubbenhall
Stretton-on-Dunsmore
Crick
West Haddon
Kilsby
Ashow
Stareton
Princethorpe
Bourton on Dunsmore
Thurlaston
Dunchurch
Barby
Weston under Wetherley
Wappenbury
Frankton
Draycote
Draycote Water
Cubbington
Eathorpe
Marton
Kites Hardwick
Ashby St Ledgers
Watford
Watford Gap Services
Old Milverton
Hunningham
Lillington
Birdingbury
Woolscott
Milverton
Royal Leamington Spa
Leamington Hastings
Willoughby
Grandborough
Braunston
Welton
Long Buckby
Offchurch
Sawbridge
Broadwell
Long Itchington
Warwick
Radford Semele
Bascote
Stockton
Nethercote
Flecknoe
Daventry Reservoir
Grand Union Canal
Oxford Canal
Coventry Canal
Ashby Canal
M1
M6
M69
M45
A5
A6
A14
A42
A444
A511
A50
A46
A47
A426
A428
A45
A423
A4071
A427
A4600
A563
A4303
A452
A445

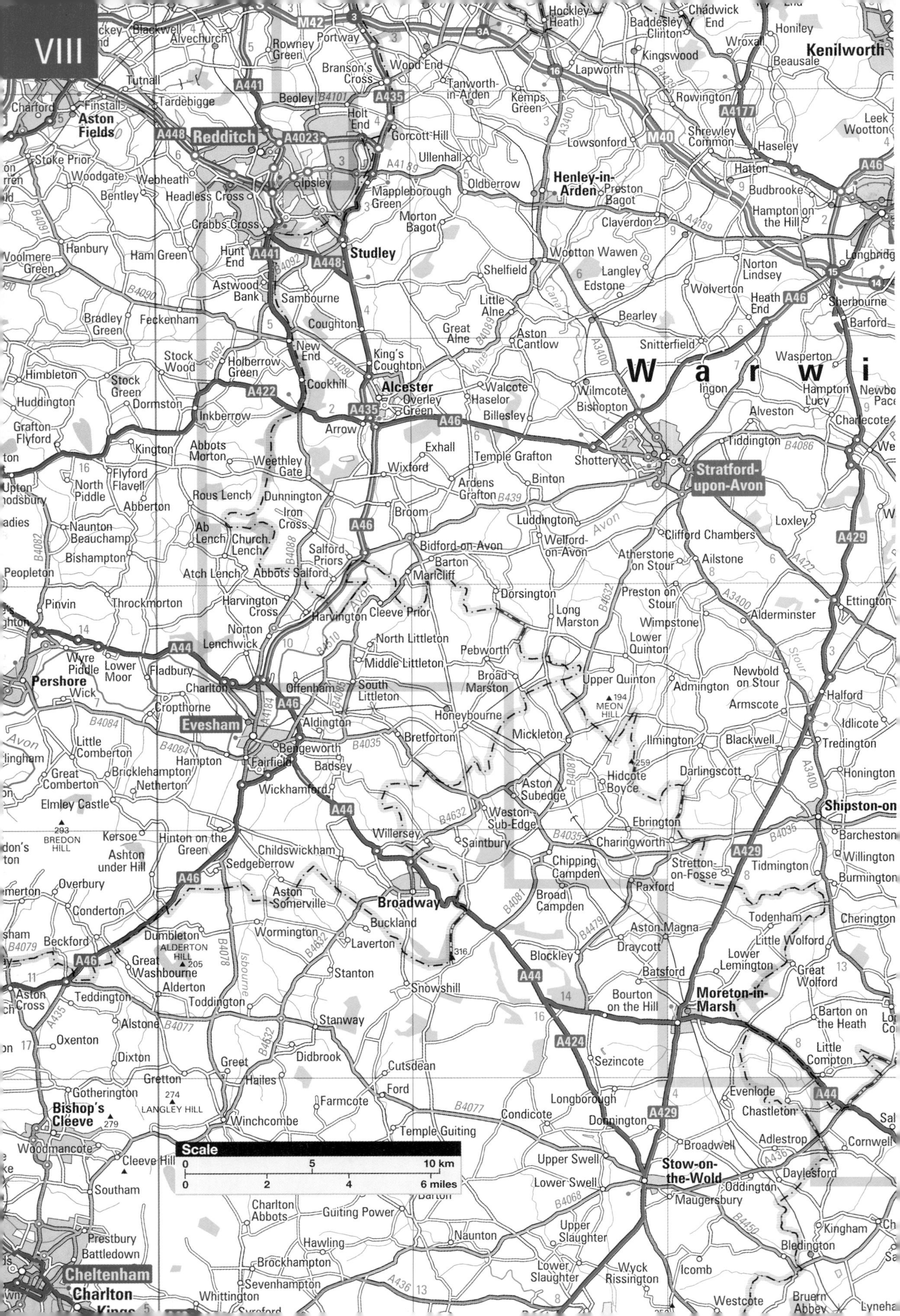
Blackwell
Alvechurch
M42
Rowney Green
Portway
Hockley Heath
Chadwick End
Baddesley Clinton
Honiley
Wroxall
Kenilworth
Beausale
Kingswood
Lapworth
Branson's Cross
Wood End
Tanworth-in-Arden
Tutnall
A441
Tardebigge
Beoley
B4101
Holt End
A435
Kemps Green
Rowington
A4177
Charford
Finstall
Aston Fields
A448
Redditch
A4023
Gorcott Hill
Lowsonford
M40
Shrewley Common
Leek Wootton
Stoke Prior
Ullenhall
Haseley
Woodgate
Webheath
Ipsley
Oldberrow
Henley-in-Arden
Preston Bagot
Hatton
A46
Budbrooke
Bentley
Headless Cross
Mappleborough Green
Hampton on the Hill
Crabbs Cross
Morton Bagot
Claverdon
A4189
B4091
Woolmere Green
Hanbury
Ham Green
Hunt End
A441
B4092
A448
Studley
Wootton Wawen
Longbridge
Norton Lindsey
Shelfield
Langley
Edstone
Astwood Bank
Sambourne
Wolverton
B4090
Little Alne
Heath End
Sherbourne
Bradley Green
Feckenham
Coughton
Great Alne
Bearley
Barford
Aston Cantlow
New End
Snitterfield
Stock Wood
Holberrow Green
King's Coughton
B4089
A3400
Wasperton
Himbleton
Stock Green
Cookhill
Alcester
Walcote
Warwi
Huddington
Dormston
A422
Overley Green
Haselor
Wilmcote
Ingon
Hampton Lucy
Newbold Pacey
Grafton Flyford
Inkberrow
A435
Arrow
A46
Billesley
Bishopton
Alveston
Charlecote
Kington
Abbots Morton
Exhall
Tiddington
B4086
Weethley Gate
Temple Grafton
Shottery
Flyford Flavell
Wixford
Stratford-upon-Avon
North Piddle
Upton
Ardens Grafton
Binton
Abberton
Rous Lench
Dunnington
B439
Loxley
Naunton Beauchamp
Ab Lench
Church Lench
Iron Cross
Broom
Luddington
A46
Avon
Welford-on-Avon
Clifford Chambers
A429
Bishampton
Salford Priors
Bidford-on-Avon
B4088
B4082
Barton
Atherstone on Stour
Ailstone
Peopleton
Atch Lench
Abbots Salford
Marlcliff
A422
Dorsington
Preston on Stour
Pinvin
Throckmorton
Harvington Cross
Harvington
Cleeve Prior
Long Marston
B4632
A3400
Alderminster
Ettington
Norton
Wimpstone
North Littleton
Lower Quinton
Lenchwick
B4510
Pebworth
A44
Middle Littleton
Stour
Wyre Piddle
Lower Moor
Fladbury
Broad Marston
Upper Quinton
Newbold on Stour
Halford
Pershore
Charlton
Offenham
South Littleton
Admington
Wick
Cropthorne
A46
MEON HILL
Armscote
B4084
Evesham
A4184
Honeybourne
Idlicote
Aldington
Bretforton
Mickleton
Ilmington
Blackwell
Tredington
Little Comberton
B4085
Bengeworth
B4035
Hampton
Fairfield
Badsey
Hidcote Boyce
Darlingscott
Honington
Great Comberton
Bricklehampton
Netherton
Aston Subedge
B4081
A3400
Wickhamford
Weston-Sub-Edge
Shipston-on
Elmley Castle
A44
Ebrington
B4632
BREDON HILL
Kersoe
Hinton on the Green
Willersey
B4035
Charingworth
Barcheston
B4035
Ashton under Hill
Childswickham
Saintbury
Willington
Sedgeberrow
Chipping Campden
A429
Stretton-on-Fosse
Tidmington
Overbury
A46
Burmington
Aston Somerville
Paxford
Conderton
Broadway
Broad Campden
B4081
Todenham
Cherington
Beckford
Dumbleton
Wormington
Buckland
B4479
Aston Magna
B4079
ALDERTON HILL
B4078
Laverton
Draycott
Little Wolford
A46
Great Washbourne
Isbourne
B4632
Blockley
Lower Lemington
Great Wolford
Stanton
Batsford
Aston Cross
Teddington
Alderton
Toddington
Snowshill
A44
Bourton on the Hill
Moreton-in-Marsh
Barton on the Heath
A435
Alstone
B4077
Stanway
Oxenton
B4632
A424
Little Compton
Dixton
Didbrook
Sezincote
Greet
Cutsdean
Gretton
Hailes
Gotherington
Ford
Evenlode
LANGLEY HILL
A44
Bishop's Cleeve
Farmcote
B4077
Longborough
Chastleton
Winchcombe
Condicote
Donnington
A429
Temple Guiting
Woodmancote
Broadwell
Adlestrop
Cornwell
Scale
Cleeve Hill
0
5
10 km
0
2
4
6 miles
Upper Swell
Stow-on-the-Wold
A436
Daylesford
Southam
Lower Swell
Oddington
B4068
Maugersbury
Charlton Abbots
Guiting Power
B4450
Prestbury
Upper Slaughter
Kingham
Naunton
Battledown
Hawling
Bledington
Brockhampton
Lower Slaughter
Wyck Rissington
Icomb
Cheltenham
Sevenhampton
A436
Charlton Kings
Whittington
Westcote
Bruern Abbey

Stoneleigh
Bubbenhall
A423
A45
Stretton-on-Dunsmore
A4071
Dunchurch
B4429
Kilsby
Crick
M45
Ashow
Stareton
Princethorpe
B4453
Bourton on Dunsmore
Frankton
Thurlaston
Draycote Water
Barby
Weston under Wetherley
Wappenbury
Draycote
A452
A445
Eathorpe
Marton
Watford
B4453
Cubbington
Birdingbury
Kites Hardwick
A45
Ashby St Ledgers
Old Milverton
Hunningham
Leam
Woolscott
WATFORD GAP SERVICES
Lillington
Leamington Hastings
Willoughby
Long
Milverton
Royal Leamington Spa
A426
Grandborough
Braunston
Welton
Sawbridge
A5
Offchurch
Broadwell
Long Itchington
Grand Union Canal
Nethercote
Daventry Reservoir
Warwick
Radford Semele
Bascote
Stockton
Whitnash
Flecknoe
Norton
B4087
A425
Lower Shuckburgh
Ufton
Southam
A425
Staverton
Daventry
Napton on the Hill
B4452
Itchen
Bishop's Tachbrook
Dodford
Chapel Green
Upper Catesby
A45
Upper Weedon
Harbury
Badby
Newnham
Ladbroke
Nene
Chesterton
WARWICK SERVICES
Hellidon
Church Stowe
Marston Doles
Ashorne
Cross Green
Bishop's Itchington
Everdon
Priors Marston
Moreton Morrell
B4100
M40
B4451
A361
Charwelton
Priors Hardwick
Lighthorne
222
Knightcote
Oxford Canal
Preston Capes
Farthingstone
Gaydon
A423
Wormleighton
Upper Boddington
Litchborough
Byfield
Chadshunt
B4086
Northend
Boddington Reservoir
Hinton
Maidford
Woodford Halse
Temple Herdewyke
Fenny Compton
203
Lower Boddington
Kineton
Combrook
Burton Dassett
Adstone
Aston le Walls
Eydon
Canons Ashby
Blakesley
Little Kineton
Claydon
Avon Dassett
Farnborough
Moreton Pinkney
Woodend
Butlers Marston
Chipping Warden
Cherwell
B4100
Pillerton Hersey
Radway
Woodend Green
Warmington
Mollington
Ratley
Pillerton Priors
Culworth
Weston
Slapton
Wardington
182
Oxhill
Cropredy
Upper Wardington
Weedon Lois
Shotteswell
Sulgrave
A361
Lower Tysoe
Great Bourton
Williamscott
Wappenham
Whatcote
Hornton
Thorpe Mandeville
Middle Tysoe
Upper Tysoe
Horley
Helmdon
Hanwell
Chacombe
Alkerton
227
B4525
Marston St Lawrence
A422
Middleton Cheney
Syresham
Shenington
B4100
Wroxton
Greatworth
Drayton
Crowfield
Thenford
Balscott
Grimsbury
Neithrop
Winderton
Overthorpe
-Stour
Radstone
Banbury
Halse
Warkworth
Epwell
A422
Upper Brailes
Shutford
Whitfield
North Newington
Farthinghoe
Easington
B4035
Lower Brailes
232
Sibford Gower
Sutton under Brailes
Broughton
M40
Upper Astrop
Turweston
Tadmarton
Bodicote
Swalcliffe
Newbottle
Brackley
B4035
Sor Brook
A4260
Sibford Ferris
Stourton
Astrop
Hinton-in-the-Hedges
A422
Bloxham
A361
King's Sutton
West Adderbury
Charlton
East Adderbury
Great Ouse
Westbury
Ascott
Evenley
Milcombe
Milton
B4100
Whichford
Croughton
Barford St John
B4031
A43
Mixbury
Hook Norton
A421
Barford St Michael
Wigginton
South Newington
Aynho
Great Rollright
Clifton
Swerford
Souldern
Cottisford
Newton Purcell
B4031
Hempton
Deddington
Nether Worton
B4100
A3400
Baynard's Green
Hardwick
Great Tew
Over Worton
North Aston
Fritwell
Duns Tew
Hethe
Over Norton
A361
Little Tew
Somerton
221
Fringford
Fewcott
Stoke Lyne
Ledwell
Middle Aston
CHERWELL VALLEY SERVICES
Heythrop
Chipping Norton
Sandford St Martin
Ardley
B4022
A4260
Upper Heyford
Middle Barton
Westcott Barton
Stratton Audley
A4421
Church Enstone
Steeple Aston
Bucknell
Lidstone
B4030
Gagingwell
B4030
B430
Caversfield
Steeple Barton
Lower Heyford
Caulcott
Enstone
A361
Cleveley
B4026
Highfield
Woodfield
Middleton Stoney
Bicester
Kiddington
A44
Taston
Oxford Canal
Launton
Chadlington
Spelsbury
Over Kiddington
A4095
Chesterton
Glympton
B4022
Dorn
A41
Tackley

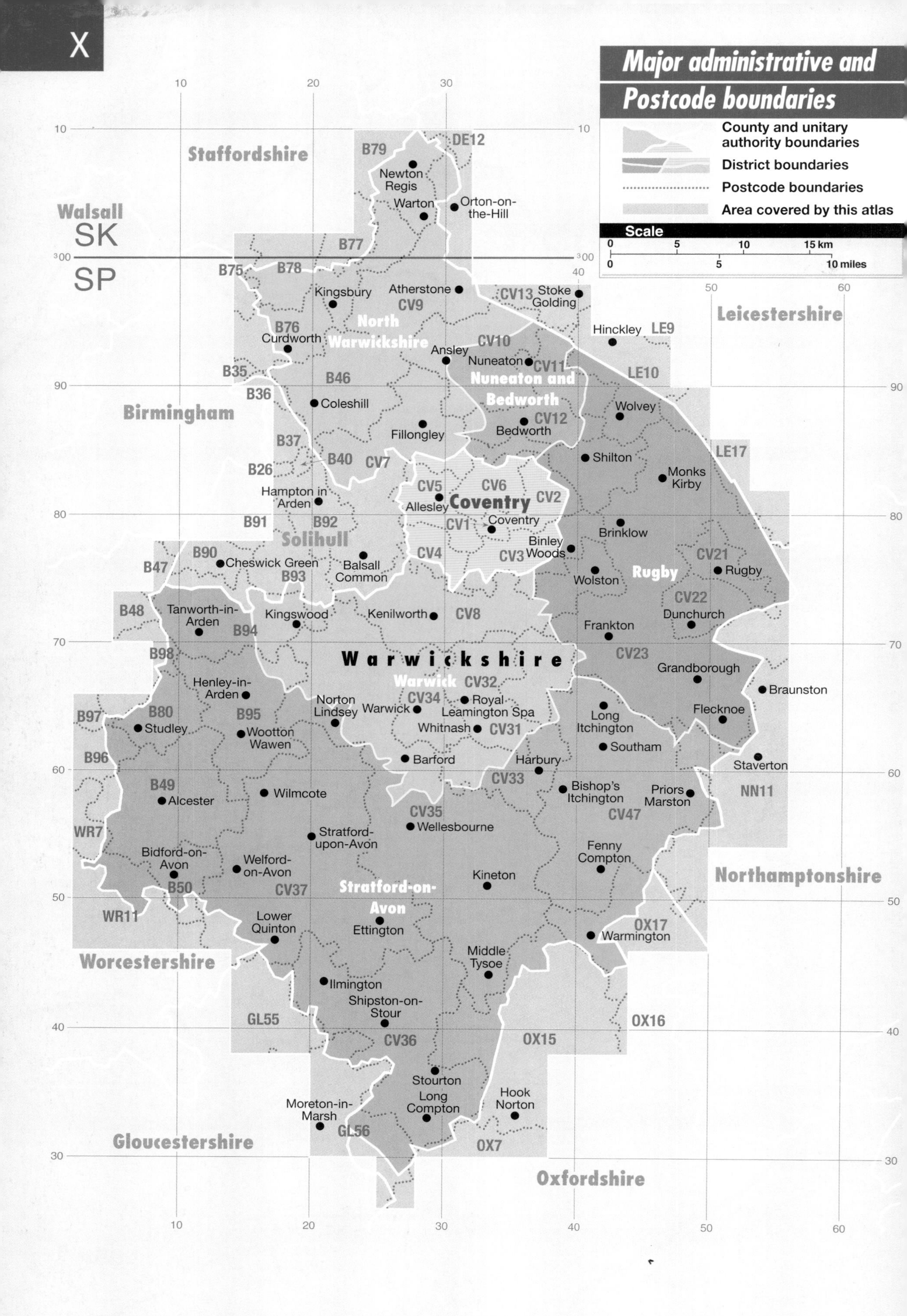

Major administrative and Postcode boundaries
County and unitary authority boundaries
District boundaries
Postcode boundaries
Area covered by this atlas
Scale
0 5 10 15 km
0 5 10 miles
SK
SP
Staffordshire
Walsall
Birmingham
Solihull
Leicestershire
Northamptonshire
Worcestershire
Gloucestershire
Oxfordshire
North Warwickshire
Nuneaton and Bedworth
Coventry
Rugby
Warwickshire
Warwick
Stratford-on-Avon
B79
DE12
Newton Regis
Warton
Orton-on-the-Hill
B77
B75
B78
Kingsbury
Atherstone
CV9
CV13
Stoke Golding
B76
Curdworth
Hinckley
LE9
CV10
Ansley
Nuneaton
CV11
LE10
B35
B46
B36
Coleshill
Wolvey
CV12
Bedworth
Fillongley
B37
B40
CV7
Shilton
LE17
B26
Monks Kirby
Hampton in Arden
CV5
CV6
CV2
Allesley
B91
B92
CV1
Coventry
Brinklow
Binley Woods
B90
CV4
CV3
CV21
B47
Cheswick Green
Balsall Common
B93
Wolston
Rugby
CV22
B48
Tanworth-in-Arden
Kingswood
Kenilworth
CV8
Dunchurch
B94
Frankton
CV23
B98
Grandborough
Henley-in-Arden
CV32
Braunston
B97
B80
B95
Norton Lindsey
CV34
Royal Leamington Spa
Long Itchington
Fleckney
Studley
Wootton Wawen
Warwick
Whitnash
CV31
Southam
B96
Barford
Harbury
Staverton
B49
CV33
Bishop's Itchington
Priors Marston
NN11
Alcester
Wilmcote
CV47
WR7
CV35
Wellesbourne
Stratford-upon-Avon
Fenny Compton
Bidford-on-Avon
Welford-on-Avon
Kineton
B50
CV37
WR11
Lower Quinton
Ettington
OX17
Warmington
Middle Tysoe
Ilmington
Shipston-on-Stour
GL55
CV36
OX15
OX16
Stourton
Long Compton
Hook Norton
Moreton-in-Marsh
GL56
OX7

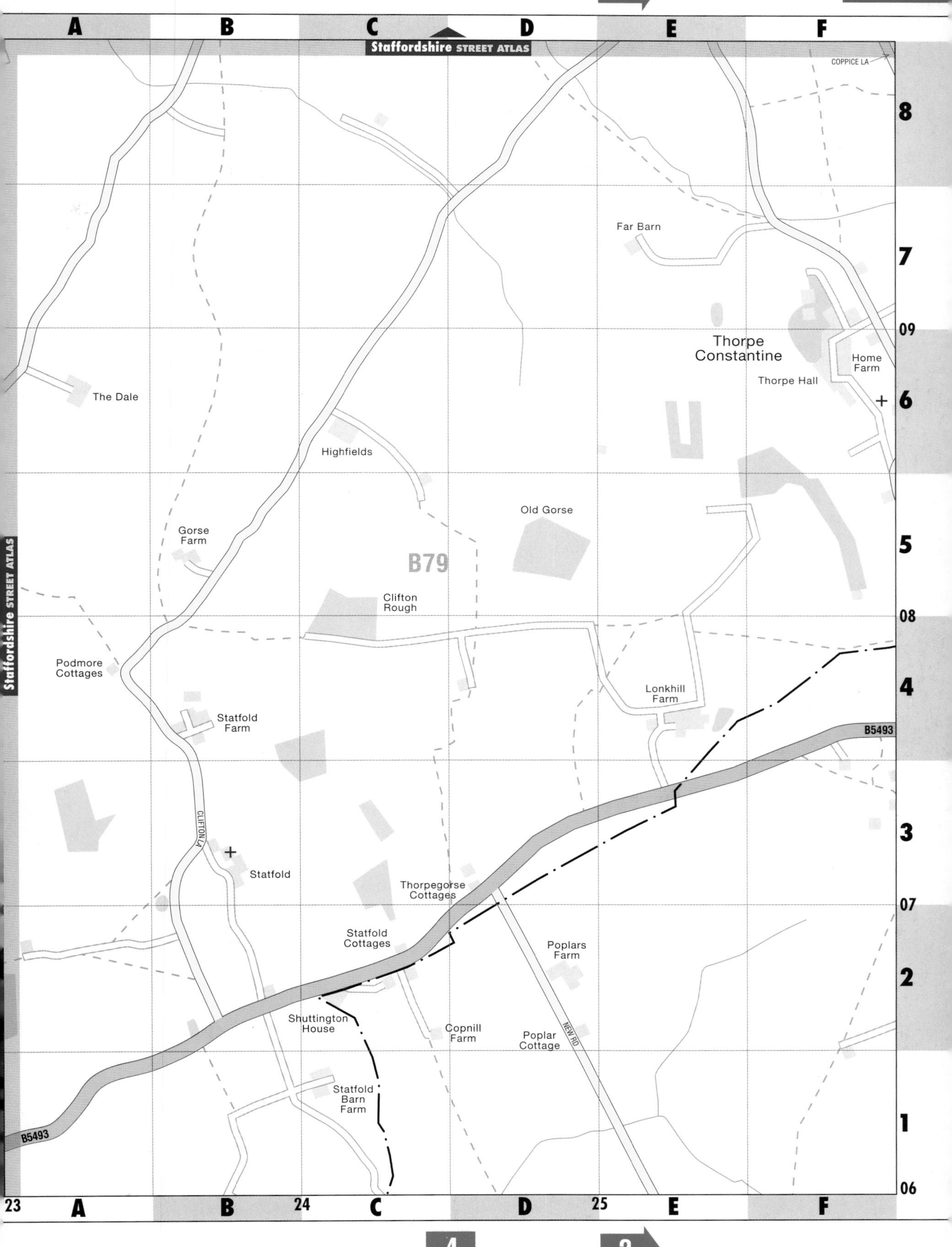
Staffordshire STREET ATLAS
A
B
C
D
E
F
COPPICE LA
8
7
09
6
5
08
4
3
07
2
1
06
23
24
25
Far Barn
Thorpe
Constantine
Home
Farm
Thorpe Hall
The Dale
Highfields
Old Gorse
Gorse
Farm
B79
Clifton
Rough
Podmore
Cottages
Lonkhill
Farm
Statfold
Farm
B5493
CLIFTON LA
Statfold
Thorpegorse
Cottages
Statfold
Cottages
Poplars
Farm
Shuttington
House
Copnill
Farm
Poplar
Cottage
NEW RD
Statfold
Barn
Farm
B5493
4
2

1

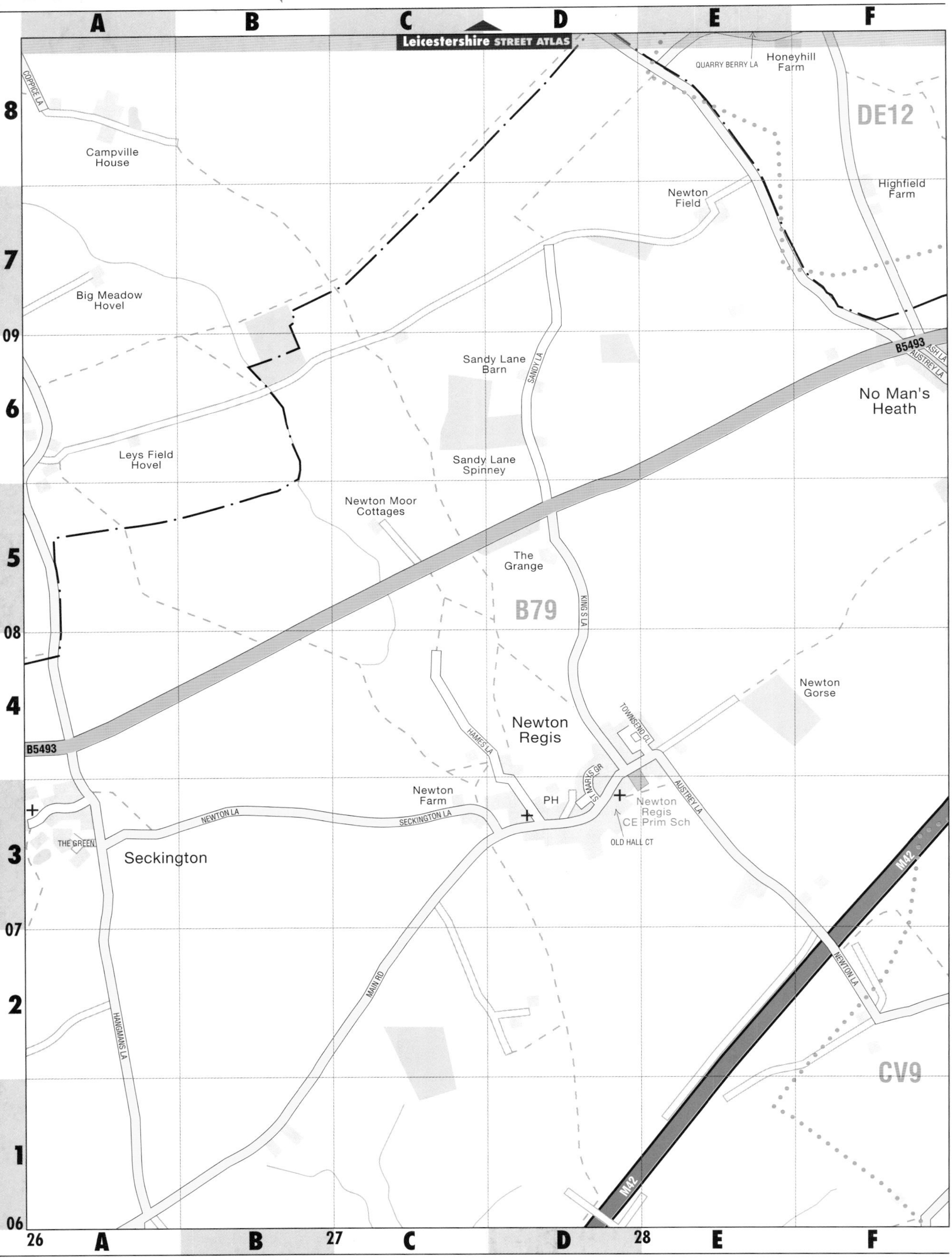

A B C D E F

Leicestershire STREET ATLAS

COPPICE LA
QUARRY BERRY LA
Honeyhill Farm
DE12
Campville House
Newton Field
Highfield Farm
Big Meadow Hovel
Sandy Lane Barn
SANDY LA
B5493
ASH LA
AUSTREY LA
No Man's Heath
Leys Field Hovel
Sandy Lane Spinney
Newton Moor Cottages
The Grange
B79
KING S LA
Newton Gorse
TOWNSEND CL
Newton Regis
HAMES LA
ST MARY'S GR
AUSTREY LA
Newton Farm
PH
Newton Regis CE Prim Sch
NEWTON LA
SECKINGTON LA
OLD HALL CT
THE GREEN
Seckington
M42
NEWTON LA
MAIN RD
HANGMANS LA
CV9

8 7 09 6 5 08 4 3 07 2 1 06

26 A B 27 C D 28 E F

1

5

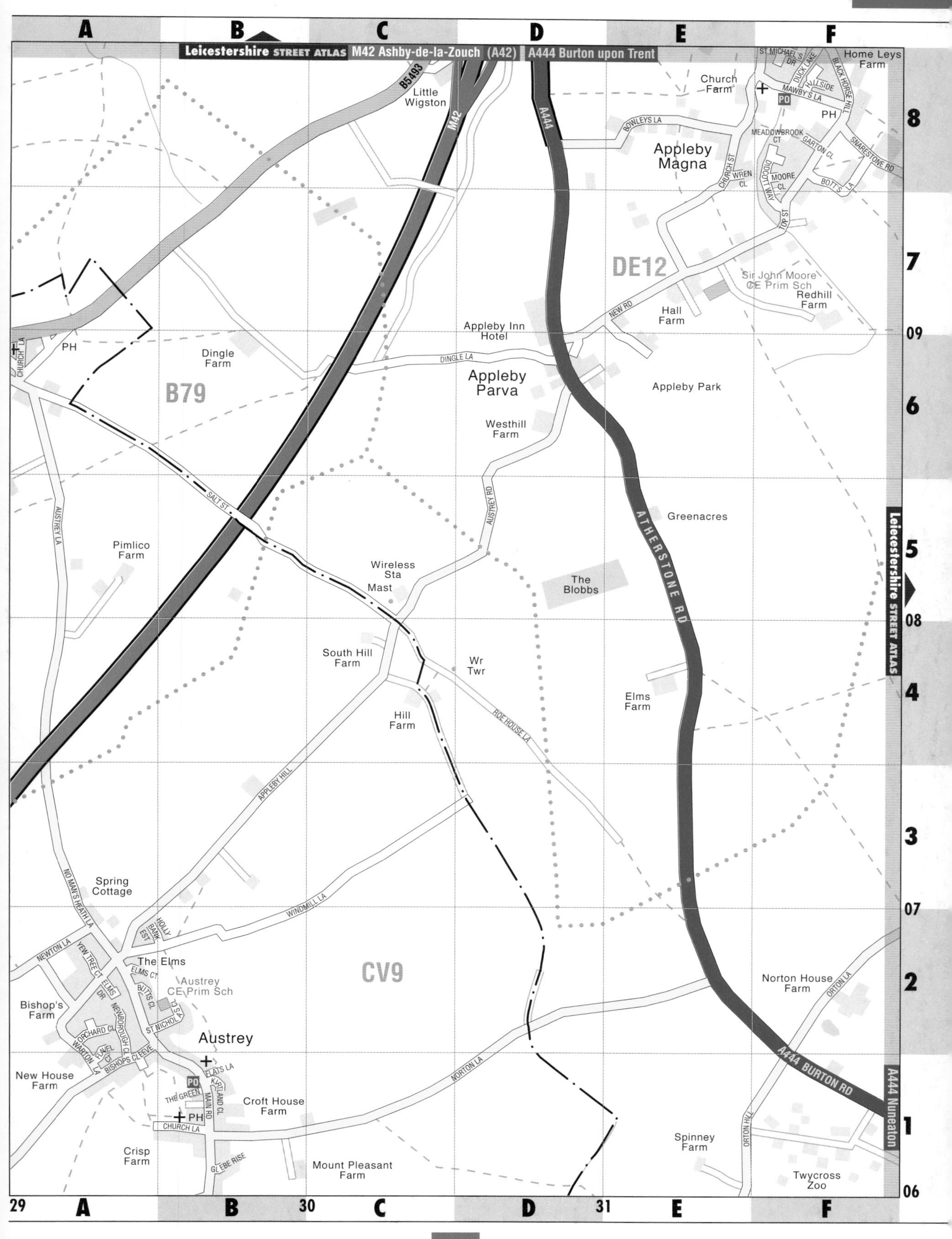

Leicestershire STREET ATLAS
M42 Ashby-de-la-Zouch (A42)
A444 Burton upon Trent
Little Wigston
Church Farm
Home Leys Farm
Appleby Magna
DE12
Sir John Moore CE Prim Sch
Redhill Farm
Hall Farm
Appleby Inn Hotel
Dingle Farm
Appleby Parva
Appleby Park
B79
Westhill Farm
Greenacres
Pimlico Farm
Wireless Sta
Mast
The Blobbs
South Hill Farm
Wr Twr
Hill Farm
Elms Farm
Spring Cottage
The Elms
Austrey CE Prim Sch
CV9
Norton House Farm
Bishop's Farm
Austrey
New House Farm
Croft House Farm
Crisp Farm
Mount Pleasant Farm
Spinney Farm
Twycross Zoo
ATHERSTONE RD
A444 BURTON RD
A444 Nuneaton

6

1

A
B
C
D
E
F
8
7
05
6
5
04
4
3
03
2
1
02
23
24
25
Staffordshire STREET ATLAS
AMINGTON HALL
Cow Barn
The Decoy
Amington Old Hall
Shuttington Bridge
Wolferstan Arms (PH)
Shuttington
Church Farm
NEW RD
PEAR TREE CL
MILNER DR
WESSEX CT
CORONATION CRES
SCHOOL LA
CHURCH LA
EAST VIEW
The Pretty Pigs (PH)
SHUTTINGTON RD
AMINGTON PK
MOOR LA
B79
Alvecote
Alvecote Pools Nature Reserve
Cvn Pk
ALVECOTE LA
ALVECOTE COTTS
BRACKLESHAM WAY
CAISTER
LANGDALE CT
TAMWORTH RD (AMINGTON)
HODGE LA
DOG LA
THE GREEN
BRANCASTER CL
Askew Bridge
DURLSTON CL
BY PASS RD
REPINGTON RD N
LEVETT RD
Greenacres Prim Sch
GREENACRE CL
CHANDLERS DR
Coventry Canal
River Anker
TAMWORTH RD (AMINGTON)
THE OLD SCHOOL YD
REPINGTON RD S
CHAPEL MEWS
Cemy
TAMWORTH
Hodge La
MERCIAN WAY
TILIA RD
TREFOIL
RIDGEWOOD RISE
WOODHOUSE LA
TURNBERRY
LYTHAM
GLENEAGLES
Marina
Alvecote Priory
FLORENDINE ST
INGRAM PIT LA
SHARPE ST
HIGHFIELD AVE
CRESTWOOD
SORREL
CARNOUSTIE
1 SUNNINGDALE
2 MUIRFIELD
LINDERA
HOYLAKE
HAREBELL
JASMINE RD
WOODLAND RD
HORNBEAM
SPRUCE
Amington
MADRONA
Sch
JUNIPER
MAPLE RISE
MAGNOLIA
SORBUS
ST ANDREWS
TROON
B77
GREENHEART
Kerria Ctr
ROBINIA
NEMESIA
SAFFRON
KERRIA RD
FOXGLOVE
CH
CORNEL
EAGLE DR
CLEMATIS
Amington Heath Com Sch
MERCIAN WAY
Amber Bsns Village
PEBBLE CL
QUINCE
Quince Tree Sch
Tamworth Bsns Pk
ROBEY'S LA
Alvecote Wood
ABELIA
BROOKWEED
SANDY WAY
AMBER CT
THE PAVILION
FAIRWAY CT
MERCURY PK
AMBER CL
Woodhouse Farm
Works
BRIAR
B78
Tamworth Bsns Ctr
FELSPAR RD
Amington Ind Est
SANDY WAY
B5000
Mercian Pk
War Meml
Sch
M42
PULLMAN CL
BEYER CL
SILICA RD
SIGNAL WLK
BRAIN ST
STEPHENSON CL
GALENA CL
Pooley Hall and remains of Hall
CARISBROOKE
ENGINE LA
GLASCOTE RD
B5000
MICA CL
CARADOC
CAMBRIAN
CASTLEHALL
CARLCROFT
Darwell Pk
Priory Farm
ABBERLEY
CROMDALE
POOLEY LA
River Anker
CHAPELON
SILVER LINK RD
CALDER
B5080
CORREEN
CHEVIOT
CRIGDON
DERRHILL
DOVESTONE
DEEPDALE
COLLETT
CROWDEN RD
CRAVEN
CAMHOUSES
EALINGHAM
BLACKDOWN
AMICOMBE
DARNBROOK
FARINGDON
CLEASBY
BIRDHOPE
BELLINGHAM
TAMWORTH RD
Sports Gd
DEELEY
DUNEDIN
COLLETT
Playing Field
CROSSFELL
PENNINE WAY
EDALE
CHILTERN RD
BROADLEE
TAMWORTH RD
THE LYNCH
ELLERBECK
EDENFIELD PL
BREDON
BUCKDEN
MENDIP WAY
BROADLEE
HERMITAGE CL
Stoneydelph Prim Sch
ANNANDALE
ELLERBECK
GREEN LA
B5000
DELTIC
LOUGHSHAW
The Hermitage
Mast
HERMITAGE LA
PADDOCKS CL
KILN WAY
MINERS WLK
ENSOR DR
SAXON CL
MILLERS WHARF
GOLDSBOROUGH
GAYLE
FOSSDALE RD
GARRIGILL
FRINGDEN
Stonydelph La
LITTON
LOWDHAM
MALHAM RD
MALDALE
MARRICK
LOWFORCE
LINTLY
LINTLY
THE GULLET
FOXWOOD RD
DELTIC
B5080

5
2
6
A
B
C
D
E
F
8
7
05
6
5
04
4
3
03
2
1
02
M42
Shuttington Fields
Farm
Bramcote
Covert
Bramcote Brook
Austrey Meadows
Lodge
Farm
WARTON LA
Meadow
Farm
New
Covert
Furlong Barn
Bentley
Farm
B79
Bramcote
Hall
Bramcote Brook
The Elms
Potford
Bridge
AUSTREY RD
CURLEW CL
WAVERTON AVE
WILLIS CROFT
THE CROFT
Warton
HILL CREST FARM CL
CHURCH VIEW
PO
MAYPOLE RD
Warton
Nethersole's
CE Prim Sch
River Anker
Hatters Arms
(PH)
TRINITY CL
IVYCROFT RD
LITTLE WARTON RD
Warren House
CHURCH RD
COPELAND CL
BARN END RD
WINDMILL CL
Donative
Farm
ORTON RD
Polesworth
Pooley Fields
Heritage Ctr
ROWLAND AVE
WINDSOR RD
ORCHARD CL
GREENWAY
Station Road
Farm
Longfield
Farm
Linden
Lodge
Little Warton
BRUNEL WLK
ANKERSIDE
POOLEY VIEW
GOODERE DR
BEAR LANE CL
STATION RD
PRINCE'S RD
ELIZABETH AVE
CORONATION AVE
STIPER'S HILL
FRANCIS CL
THE GABLES
NETHERSOLE ST
ABBEY CROFT
ROFS CROFT
HIGH ST
Stiper's Hill
Farm
Inn
The
Nethersole
CE Prim Sch
Stiper's Hill
Plantation
RICKYARD CL
PO
Liby
HALL CT
B78
BRIDGE ST
P
Kisses'
Barn
CV9
River Anker
B5000
Polesworth
Bridge
Polesworth
Coventry Canal
MARKET ST
GRENDON RD
1 MILLERS WHARF
2 FAIRFIELDS HILL
ABBEY GREEN CT
WATERSIDE
Limekiln
Bridge
Bassett's
Bridge
The Mount
26
27
28
11
6

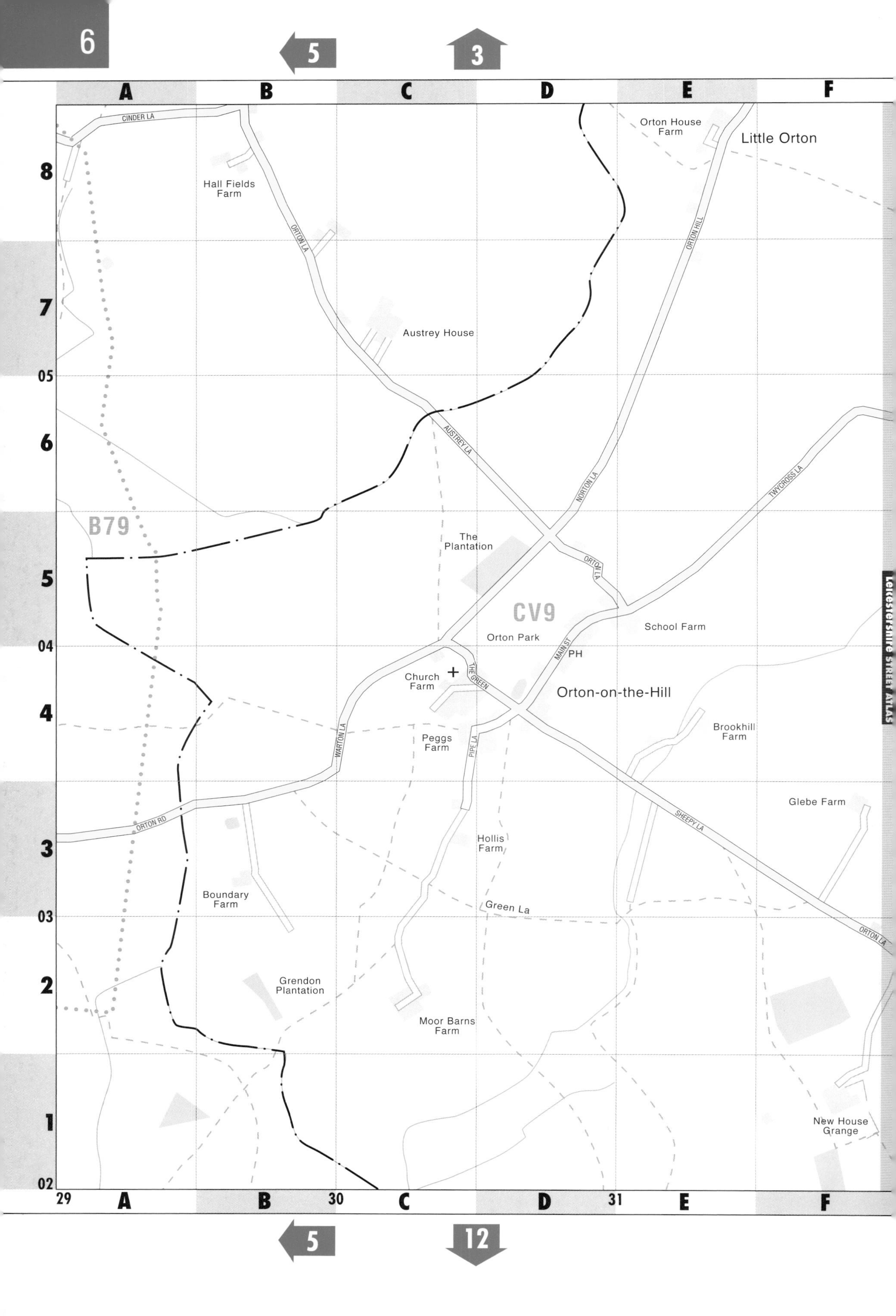
5
3
A B C D E F
8
7
05
6
5
04
4
3
03
2
1
02
29 30 31
CINDER LA
Hall Fields Farm
ORTON LA
Austrey House
Orton House Farm
Little Orton
ORTON HILL
AUSTREY LA
NORTON LA
TWYCROSS LA
B79
The Plantation
ORTON LA
CV9
Orton Park
School Farm
MAIN ST
PH
Church Farm
THE GREEN
Orton-on-the-Hill
Brookhill Farm
WARTON LA
Peggs Farm
PIPE LA
ORTON RD
Glebe Farm
SHEEPY LA
Hollis Farm
Boundary Farm
Green La
ORTON LA
Grendon Plantation
Moor Barns Farm
New House Grange
Leicestershire STREET ATLAS
12

8

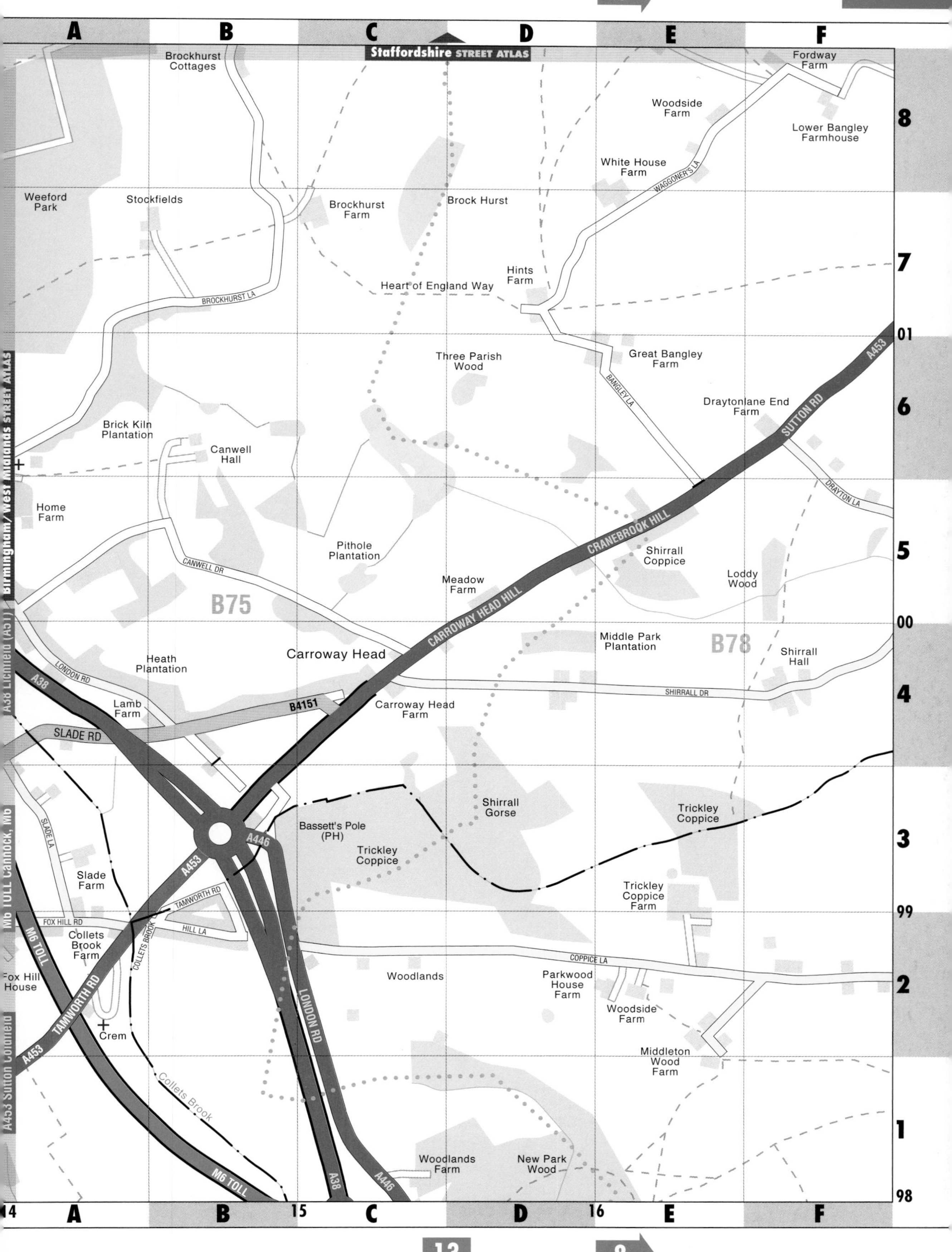
Staffordshire STREET ATLAS
A B C D E F
8 7 01 6 5 00 4 3 99 2 1 98
14 15 16
Brockhurst Cottages
Fordway Farm
Woodside Farm
Lower Bangley Farmhouse
White House Farm
WAGGONER'S LA
Weeford Park
Stockfields
Brockhurst Farm
Brock Hurst
Hints Farm
Heart of England Way
BROCKHURST LA
Three Parish Wood
Great Bangley Farm
BANGLEY LA
Draytonlane End Farm
A453
SUTTON RD
Brick Kiln Plantation
Canwell Hall
DRAYTON LA
Home Farm
CRANEBROOK HILL
Pithole Plantation
Shirrall Coppice
CANWELL DR
Loddy Wood
Meadow Farm
B75
CARROWAY HEAD HILL
Middle Park Plantation
B78
Shirrall Hall
Heath Plantation
Carroway Head
LONDON RD
A38
SHIRRALL DR
Lamb Farm
B4151
Carroway Head Farm
SLADE RD
Shirrall Gorse
Trickley Coppice
Bassett's Pole (PH)
Trickley Coppice
A446
SLADE LA
Slade Farm
A453
TAMWORTH RD
Trickley Coppice Farm
FOX HILL RD
HILL LA
Collets Brook Farm
COLLETS BROOK
COPPICE LA
M6 TOLL
Fox Hill House
Woodlands
Parkwood House Farm
LONDON RD
TAMWORTH RD
Woodside Farm
A453
Crem
Middleton Wood Farm
Collets Brook
M6 TOLL
Woodlands Farm
New Park Wood
A38
A446
Birmingham/West Midlands STREET ATLAS
A38 Lichfield (A51)
M6 TOLL Cannock, M6
A453 Sutton Coldfield

13

8

7

A
B
C
D
E
F
A453 Tamworth
Birmingham/West Midlands STREET ATLAS
New House Farm
BANGLEY LA
CAISTOR CL
GAINSBOROUGH DR
CRANWELL RISE
KIRKLAND WAY
Mile Oak
A453
Bourne Bridge
SUTTON RD
Alder Wood
Bourne Brook
Bourne Brook Cut
Seventeen Acre
Duck Decoy
YORKSAND RD
REINDEER RD
DAMA RD
MAYAMA RD
DRAYTON MANOR DR
Fazeley
Longwood House
SWISS LODGE DR
Works
Drayton Manor Park
CH
DRAYTON MANOR DR
Lodge Farm
Hill Farm
COLESHILL RD
A4091
Longwood Stables
Heathley Farm
HEATHLEY LA
Bullocks End Farm
Edden's Wood
Drayton Bassett
OLD MANOR CL
MOAT DR
CHURCH CL
PEEL CL
NEW ROW
PO
EDDENS WOOD CL
Manor Prim Sch
Sewage Works
Oak Farm Craft Ctr
SHIRRAL DR
Stone House
Heart of England Way
DRAYTON LA
RECTORY CL
SALTS LA
Ashdene Farm
B78
PORTLEYS LA
Drayton Brick Bridge
Brook End Farm
Brook Farm
Heart of England Way
Birmingham and Fazeley Canal
Upper House Farm
Gallows Brook
COPPICE LA
Quarry
Mill Plantation
Middleton Park
Newhouse Farm
Middleton
CHURCH ROW
SIMMONS CL
Highfields Farm
Park-gate Farm
CHURCH LA
Walker's Spinney
Sewage Works
Middleton Pool
The Green Man (PH)
VICARAGE HILL
Langley Brook
CROWBERRY LA
A4091
Middleton Hall
8
7
01
6
5
00
4
3
99
2
1
98
17
18
19

7
14

F6
1 BAKERS WLK
2 CALLIS WLK
3 LINTHOUSE WLK
4 COTTAGE WLK
5 STONEHILL WLK
6 IVYHOUSE WLK
7 LEISURE WLK

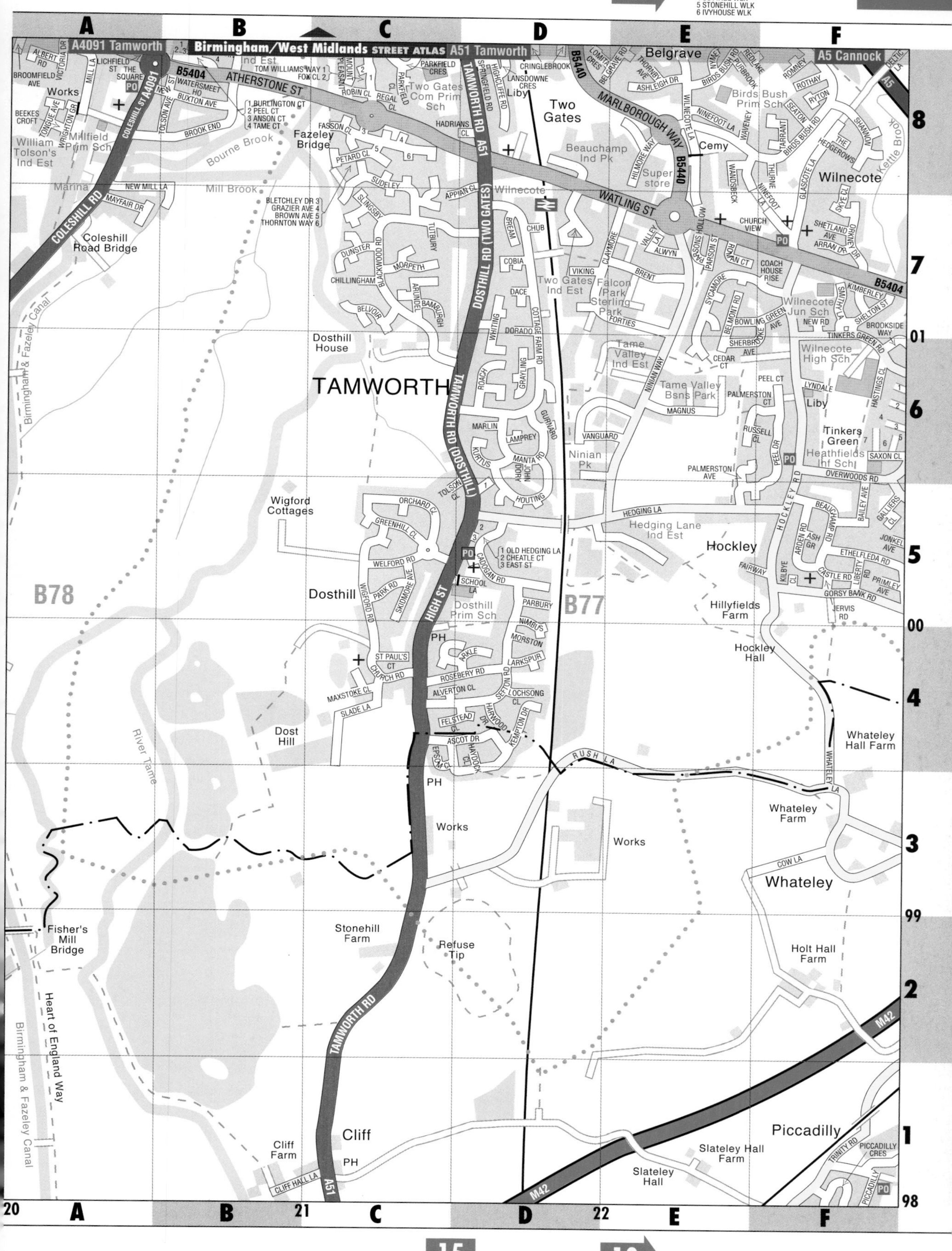

15
10

9
4

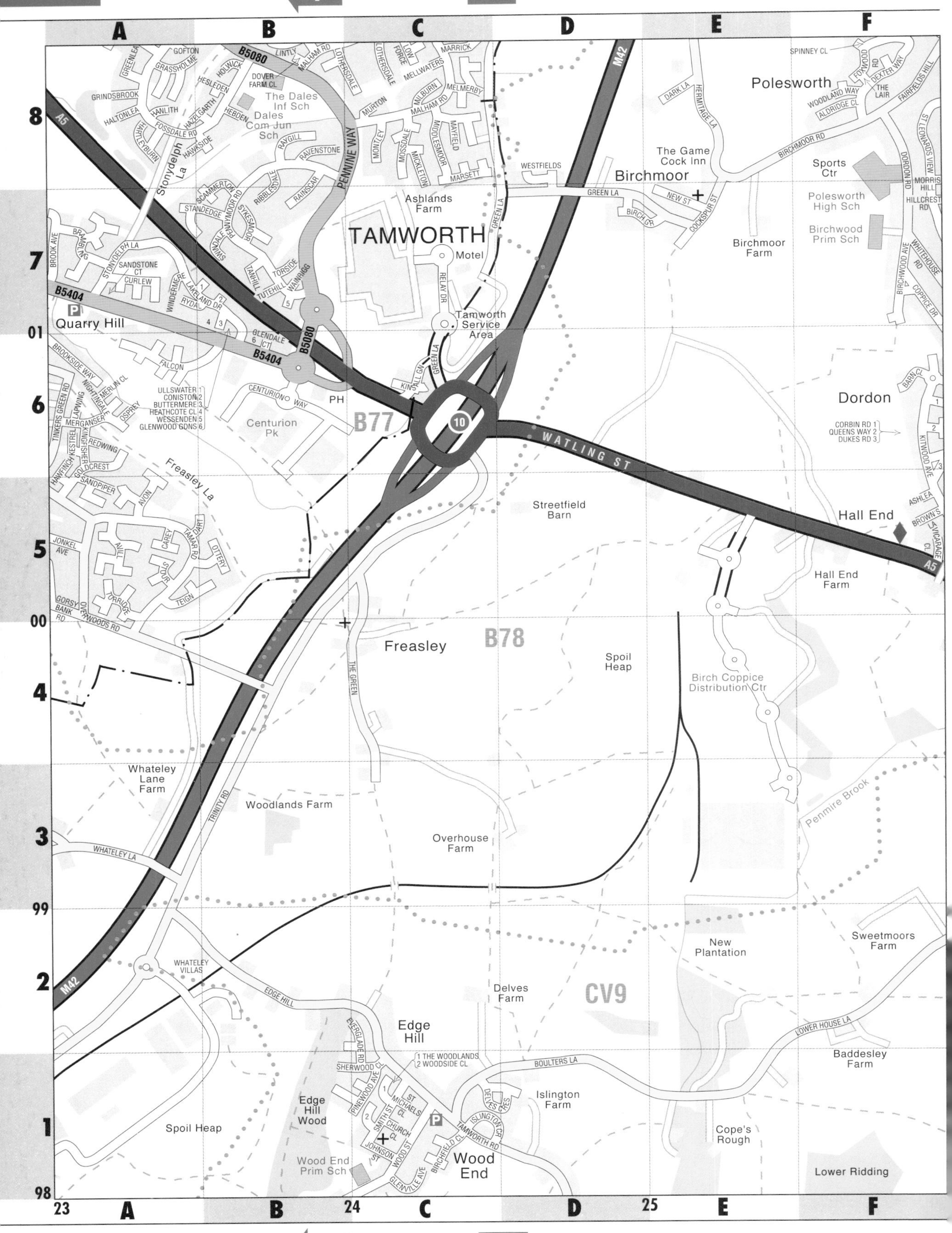
A
B
C
D
E
F
8
7
01
6
5
00
4
3
99
2
1
98
23
24
25
TAMWORTH
Polesworth
Birchmoor
Dordon
Hall End
Freasley
Edge Hill
Wood End
Quarry Hill
The Dales Inf Sch
Dales Com Jun Sch
Ashlands Farm
Motel
Tamworth Service Area
The Game Cock Inn
Birchmoor Farm
Sports Ctr
Polesworth High Sch
Birchwood Prim Sch
Centurion Pk
PH
B77
B78
CV9
WATLING ST
M42
A5
B5080
B5404
PENNINE WAY
Stonydelph La
Freasley La
Streetfield Barn
Hall End Farm
Spoil Heap
Birch Coppice Distribution Ctr
Whateley Lane Farm
Woodlands Farm
Overhouse Farm
Penmire Brook
New Plantation
Sweetmoors Farm
Delves Farm
Baddesley Farm
Islington Farm
Edge Hill Wood
Spoil Heap
Wood End Prim Sch
Cope's Rough
Lower Ridding
WHATELEY LA
WHATELEY VILLAS
EDGE HILL
TRINITY RD
THE GREEN
BOULTERS LA
LOWER HOUSE LA
TAMWORTH RD
GREEN LA
RELAY DR
BIRCHMOOR RD
COCKSPUR ST
HERMITAGE LA
DARK LA
WESTFIELDS
ULLSWATER 1
CONISTON 2
BUTTERMERE 3
HEATHCOTE CL 4
WESSENDEN 5
GLENWOOD GDNS 6
CORBIN RD 1
QUEENS WAY 2
DUKES RD 3
1 THE WOODLANDS
2 WOODSIDE CL

9
16

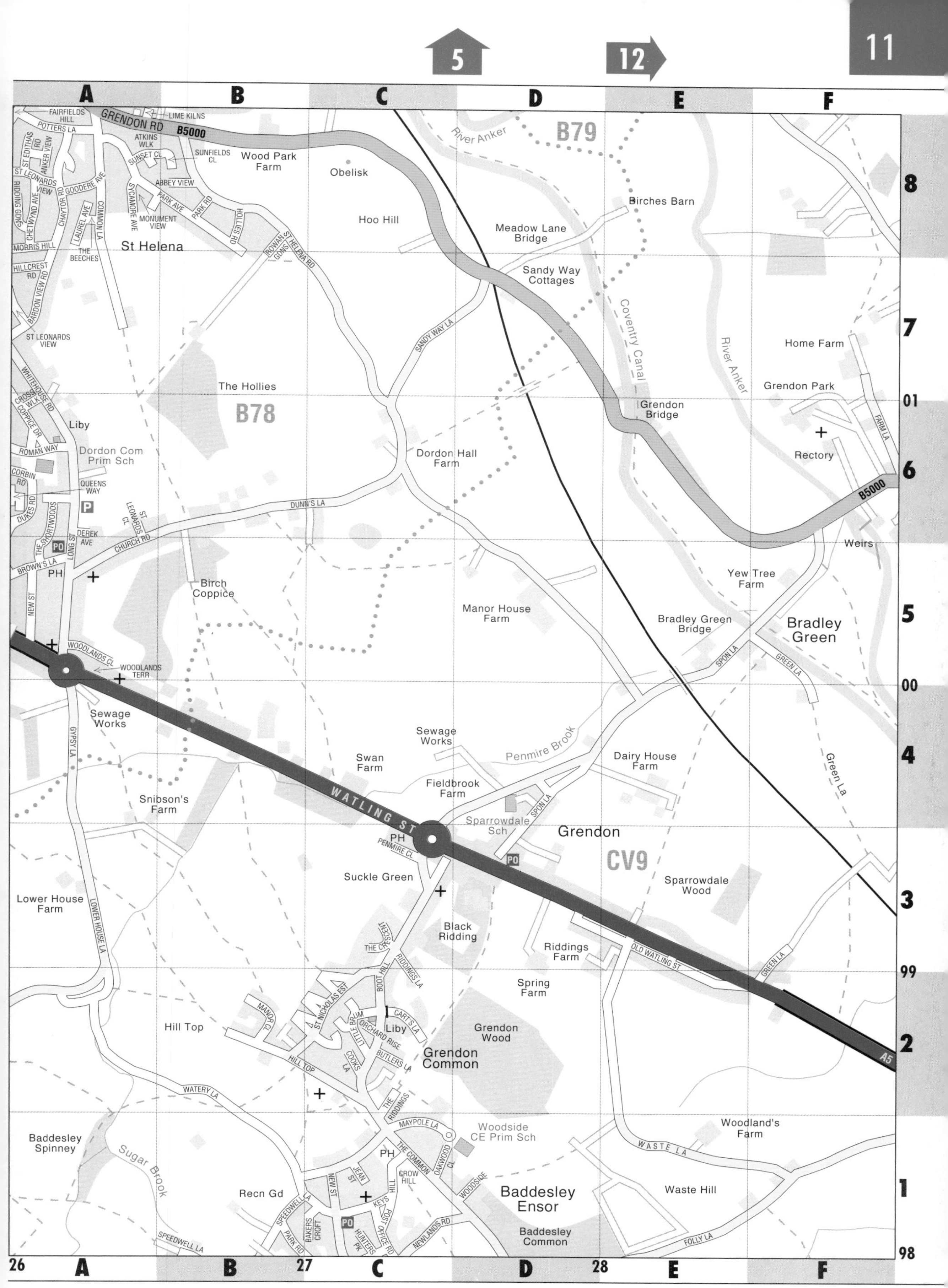
5
12
A
B
C
D
E
F
8
7
01
6
5
00
4
3
99
2
1
98
26
27
28
17
GRENDON RD
B5000
B79
River Anker
Wood Park Farm
Obelisk
Birches Barn
Hoo Hill
Meadow Lane Bridge
St Helena
Sandy Way Cottages
Coventry Canal
River Anker
Home Farm
Grendon Park
The Hollies
B78
Grendon Bridge
Liby
Dordon Com Prim Sch
Dordon Hall Farm
Rectory
B5000
DUNN'S LA
CHURCH RD
Weirs
Yew Tree Farm
Birch Coppice
Manor House Farm
Bradley Green Bridge
Bradley Green
SPON LA
GREEN LA
WOODLANDS CL
WOODLANDS TERR
Sewage Works
Sewage Works
Penmire Brook
Swan Farm
Dairy House Farm
Green La
Snibson's Farm
Fieldbrook Farm
WATLING ST
Sparrowdale Sch
Grendon
CV9
PH
PENMIRE CL
Suckle Green
Sparrowdale Wood
Lower House Farm
LOWER HOUSE LA
GYPSY LA
Black Ridding
Riddings Farm
OLD WATLING ST
Spring Farm
Hill Top
Liby
Grendon Wood
Grendon Common
A5
HILL TOP
WATERY LA
Baddesley Spinney
Sugar Brook
Woodside CE Prim Sch
MAYPOLE LA
THE COMMON
Woodland's Farm
WASTE LA
Recn Gd
Baddesley Ensor
Waste Hill
Baddesley Common
SPEEDWELL LA
NEWLANDS RD
FOLLY LA
PO
PH
PO
PO

11
6

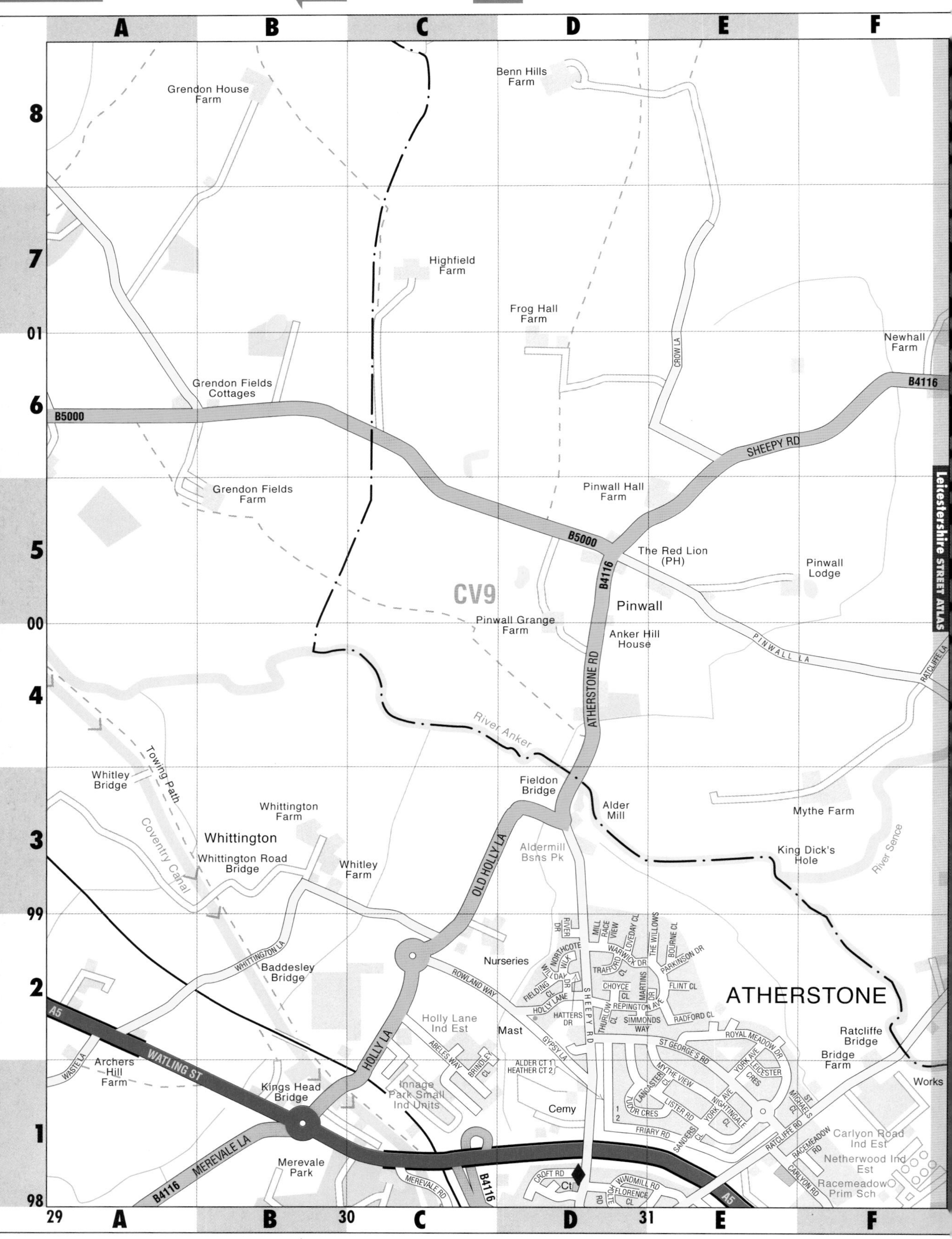
A
B
C
D
E
F
8
7
01
6
5
00
4
3
99
2
1
98
29
30
31
Grendon House Farm
Benn Hills Farm
Highfield Farm
Frog Hall Farm
Newhall Farm
CROW LA
B4116
Grendon Fields Cottages
B5000
SHEEPY RD
Grendon Fields Farm
Pinwall Hall Farm
B5000
The Red Lion (PH)
Pinwall Lodge
B4116
CV9
Pinwall
Pinwall Grange Farm
Anker Hill House
PINWALL LA
RATCLIFFE LA
ATHERSTONE RD
River Anker
Towing Path
Whitley Bridge
Fieldon Bridge
Alder Mill
Mythe Farm
Whittington Farm
Coventry Canal
Whittington
Aldermill Bsns Pk
King Dick's Hole
River Sence
Whittington Road Bridge
Whitley Farm
OLD HOLLY LA
WHITTINGTON LA
Baddesley Bridge
Nurseries
ROWLAND WAY
ATHERSTONE
A5
WATLING ST
Holly Lane Ind Est
Mast
HOLLY LA
Archers Hill Farm
WASTE LA
ABELES WAY
BRINDLEY CL
ALDER CT 1
HEATHER CT 2
GYPSY LA
Kings Head Bridge
Innage Park Small Ind Units
Cemy
Ratcliffe Bridge
Bridge Farm
Works
Carlyon Road Ind Est
Netherwood Ind Est
Racemeadow Prim Sch
MEREVALE LA
Merevale Park
MEREVALE RD
B4116
CROFT RD
Ct
WINDMILL RD
FLORENCE CL
HOLTE RD
RIVER DR
MILL RACE VIEW
LOVEDAY CL
THE WILLOWS
BOURNE CL
PARKINSON DR
WARWICK DR
TRAFFORD CL
NORTHCOTE WLK
WILDAY CL
FIELDING CL
HOLLY LANE
HATTERS DR
SHEEPY RD
CHOYCE CL
MARTINS DR
FLINT CL
REPINGTON AVE
THURLOW CL
SIMMONDS WAY
RADFORD CL
ROYAL MEADOW DR
ST GEORGE'S RD
YORK AVE
LEICESTER CRES
MYTHE VIEW
LANCASTER CL
TUDOR CRES
LISTER RD
YORK AVE
NIGHTINGALE CL
FRIARY RD
SANDERS CL
RATCLIFFE RD
ST MICHAELS CL
RACEMEADOW RD
CARLYON RD
Leicestershire STREET ATLAS

11
18

7
14

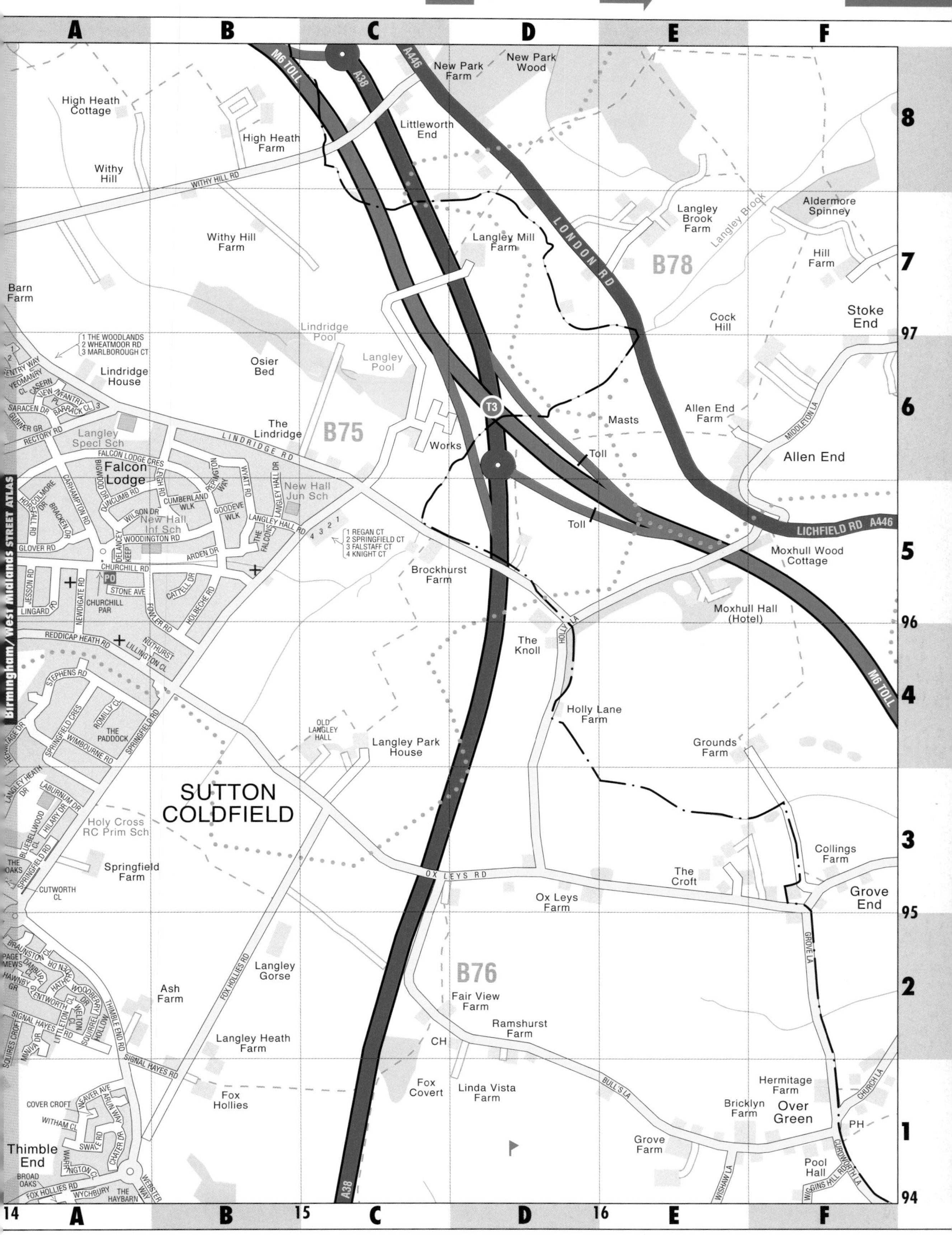

A
B
C
D
E
F
8
7
97
6
5
96
4
3
95
2
1
94
14
15
16
M6 TOLL
A38
A446
New Park Farm
New Park Wood
High Heath Cottage
High Heath Farm
Littleworth End
Withy Hill
WITHY HILL RD
Withy Hill Farm
Langley Mill Farm
LONDON RD
Langley Brook Farm
Langley Brook
Aldermore Spinney
Hill Farm
B78
Barn Farm
Cock Hill
Stoke End
1 THE WOODLANDS
2 WHEATMOOR RD
3 MARLBOROUGH CT
Lindridge Pool
Langley Pool
Osier Bed
Lindridge House
T3
Allen End Farm
Masts
The Lindridge
B75
Langley Specl Sch
LINDRIDGE RD
Works
Toll
MIDDLETON LA
Allen End
Falcon Lodge
New Hall Jun Sch
New Hall Inf Sch
LICHFIELD RD A446
1 REGAN CT
2 SPRINGFIELD CT
3 FALSTAFF CT
4 KNIGHT CT
Moxhull Wood Cottage
Brockhurst Farm
Moxhull Hall (Hotel)
The Knoll
HOLLY LA
Holly Lane Farm
OLD LANGLEY HALL
Langley Park House
Grounds Farm
SUTTON COLDFIELD
Holy Cross RC Prim Sch
Collings Farm
Springfield Farm
The Croft
OX LEYS RD
Ox Leys Farm
Grove End
GROVE LA
Langley Gorse
B76
Ash Farm
FOX HOLLIES RD
Fair View Farm
Ramshurst Farm
Langley Heath Farm
CH
SIGNAL HAYES RD
BULL'S LA
Hermitage Farm
Fox Hollies
Fox Covert
Linda Vista Farm
Bricklyn Farm
Over Green
CHURCH LA
PH
Thimble End
Grove Farm
Pool Hall
WISHAW LA
CURDWORTH LA
WIGGINS HILL RD
COVER CROFT
WITHAM CL
BROAD OAKS
FOX HOLLIES RD
WYCHBURY
THE HAYBARN
WEBSTER WAY
THIMBLE END RD
Birmingham/West Midlands STREET ATLAS

22
14

13
8

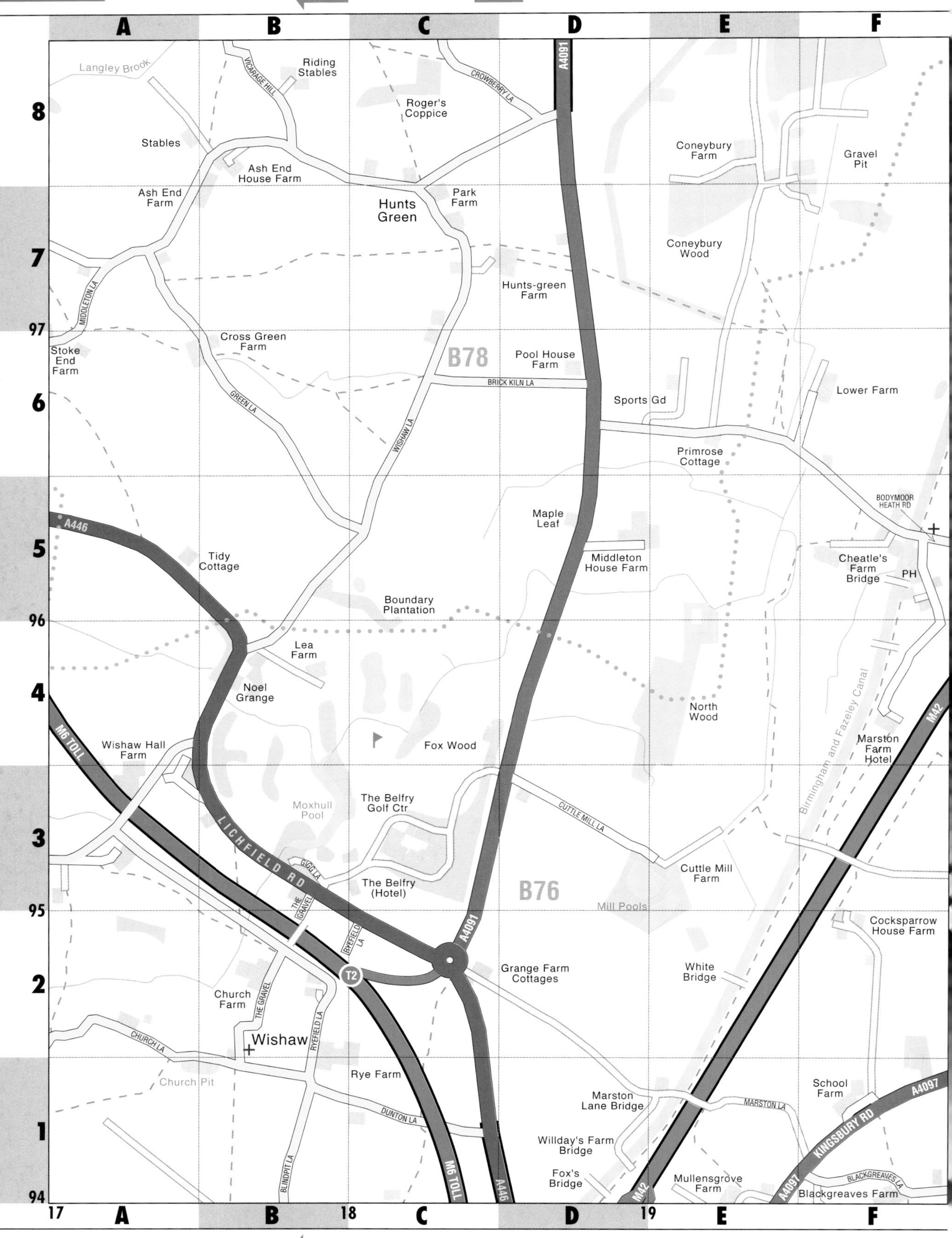
A
B
C
D
E
F
8
7
97
6
5
96
4
3
95
2
1
94
17
18
19
Langley Brook
Riding Stables
VICARAGE HILL
Roger's Coppice
CROWBERRY LA
A4091
Stables
Ash End House Farm
Ash End Farm
Hunts Green
Park Farm
Coneybury Farm
Gravel Pit
Coneybury Wood
MIDDLETON LA
Hunts-green Farm
Cross Green Farm
Stoke End Farm
B78
Pool House Farm
BRICK KILN LA
GREEN LA
WISHAW LA
Sports Gd
Lower Farm
Primrose Cottage
BODYMOOR HEATH RD
Maple Leaf
A446
Tidy Cottage
Middleton House Farm
Cheatle's Farm Bridge
PH
Boundary Plantation
Lea Farm
Noel Grange
North Wood
M6 TOLL
Wishaw Hall Farm
Fox Wood
Birmingham and Fazeley Canal
Marston Farm Hotel
M42
Moxhull Pool
The Belfry Golf Ctr
CUTTLE MILL LA
LICHFIELD RD
GIGG LA
Cuttle Mill Farm
The Belfry (Hotel)
THE GRAVEL
B76
Mill Pools
RYEFIELD LA
Cocksparrow House Farm
T2
Grange Farm Cottages
White Bridge
Church Farm
Wishaw
CHURCH LA
Church Pit
Rye Farm
Marston Lane Bridge
MARSTON LA
School Farm
A4097
KINGSBURY RD
DUNTON LA
Willday's Farm Bridge
BLINDPIT LA
Fox's Bridge
Mullensgrove Farm
BLACKGREAVES LA
Blackgreaves Farm

13
23

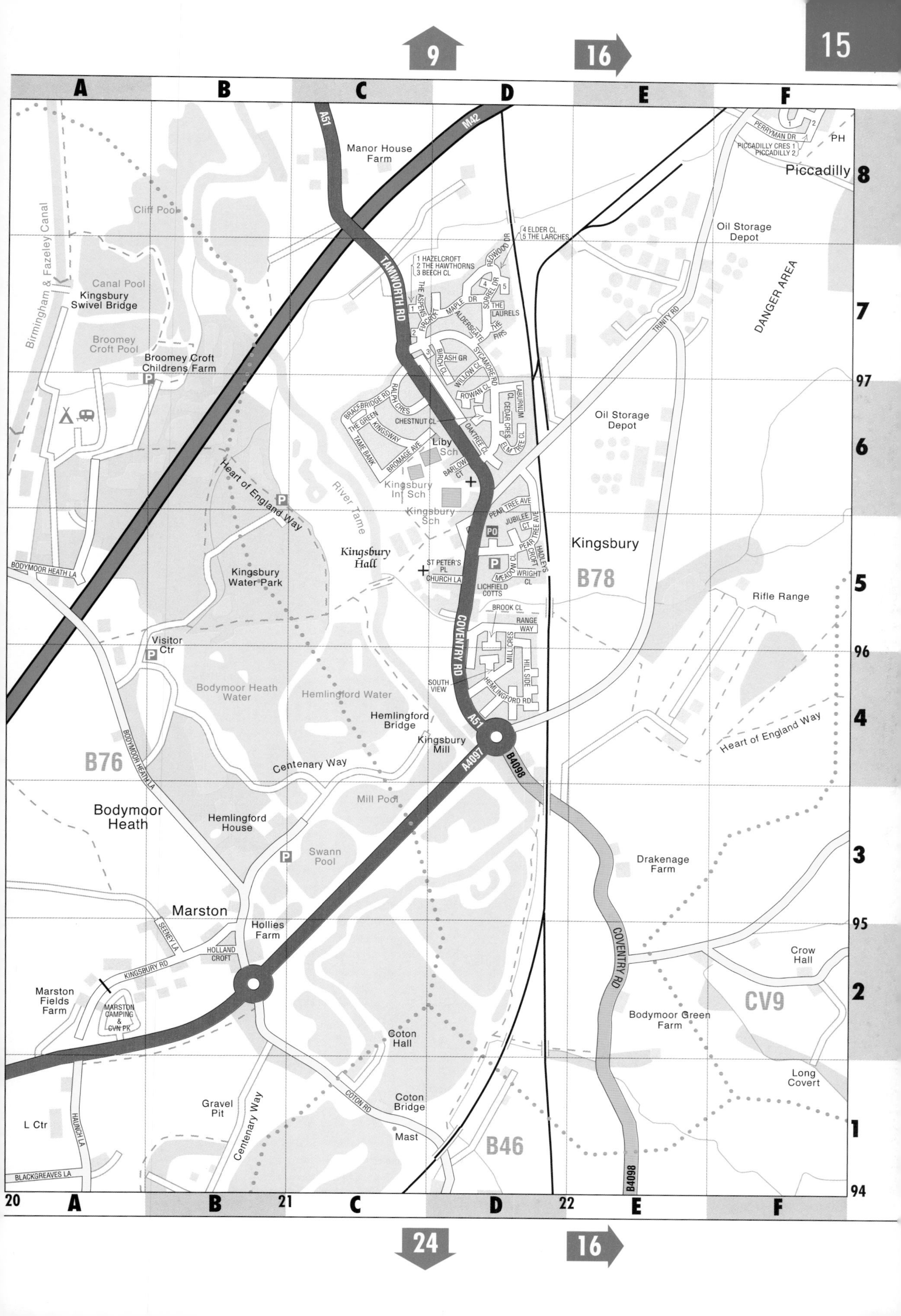
9
16
A
B
C
D
E
F
A51
M42
Manor House Farm
PERRYMAN DR
PICCADILLY CRES 1
PICCADILLY 2
PH
Piccadilly
8
Cliff Pool
Birmingham & Fazeley Canal
Canal Pool
Kingsbury Swivel Bridge
Broomey Croft Pool
Broomey Croft Childrens Farm
4 ELDER CL
5 THE LARCHES
1 HAZELCROFT
2 THE HAWTHORNS
3 BEECH CL
TAMWORTH RD
REDWOOD DR
Oil Storage Depot
DANGER AREA
THE ASPENS
FIRCROFT
MAPLE DR
SORREL DR
THE LAURELS
ALDERSGATE
THE FIRS
7
TRINITY RD
BIRCH CL
ASH GR
SYCAMORE RD
WILLOW CL
97
ROWAN CL
LABURNUM CL
CEDAR CRES
ELM TREE CL
BRACEBRIDGE RD
RALPH CRES
THE GREEN
KINGSWAY
CHESTNUT CL
OAKTREE CL
TAME BANK
BROMAGE AVE
Liby
Sch
BARLOW CT
Oil Storage Depot
6
Heart of England Way
River Tame
Kingsbury Inf Sch
Kingsbury Sch
PEAR TREE AVE
JUBILEE CT
PEAR TREE CROFT
HADLEYS CL
PO
Kingsbury
Kingsbury Hall
BODYMOOR HEATH LA
Kingsbury Water Park
ST PETER'S PL
CHURCH LA
MEADOW CL
WRIGHT CL
LICHFIELD COTTS
B78
5
Rifle Range
BROOK CL
RANGE WAY
COVENTRY RD
Visitor Ctr
MILLCRES
HILL SIDE
96
Bodymoor Heath Water
Hemlingford Water
SOUTH VIEW
HEMLINGFORD RD
Hemlingford Bridge
A51
Kingsbury Mill
4
Heart of England Way
B76
Centenary Way
A4097
B4098
Mill Pool
Bodymoor Heath
Hemlingford House
Swann Pool
Drakenage Farm
3
Marston
SEENEY LA
Hollies Farm
COVENTRY RD
95
HOLLAND CROFT
KINGSBURY RD
Crow Hall
Marston Fields Farm
MARSTON CAMPING & CVN PK
CV9
2
Bodymoor Green Farm
Coton Hall
Long Covert
Gravel Pit
Centenary Way
COTON RD
Coton Bridge
L Ctr
HAUNCH LA
Mast
B46
1
BLACKGREAVES LA
B4098
94
20
21
22
24
16

15
10

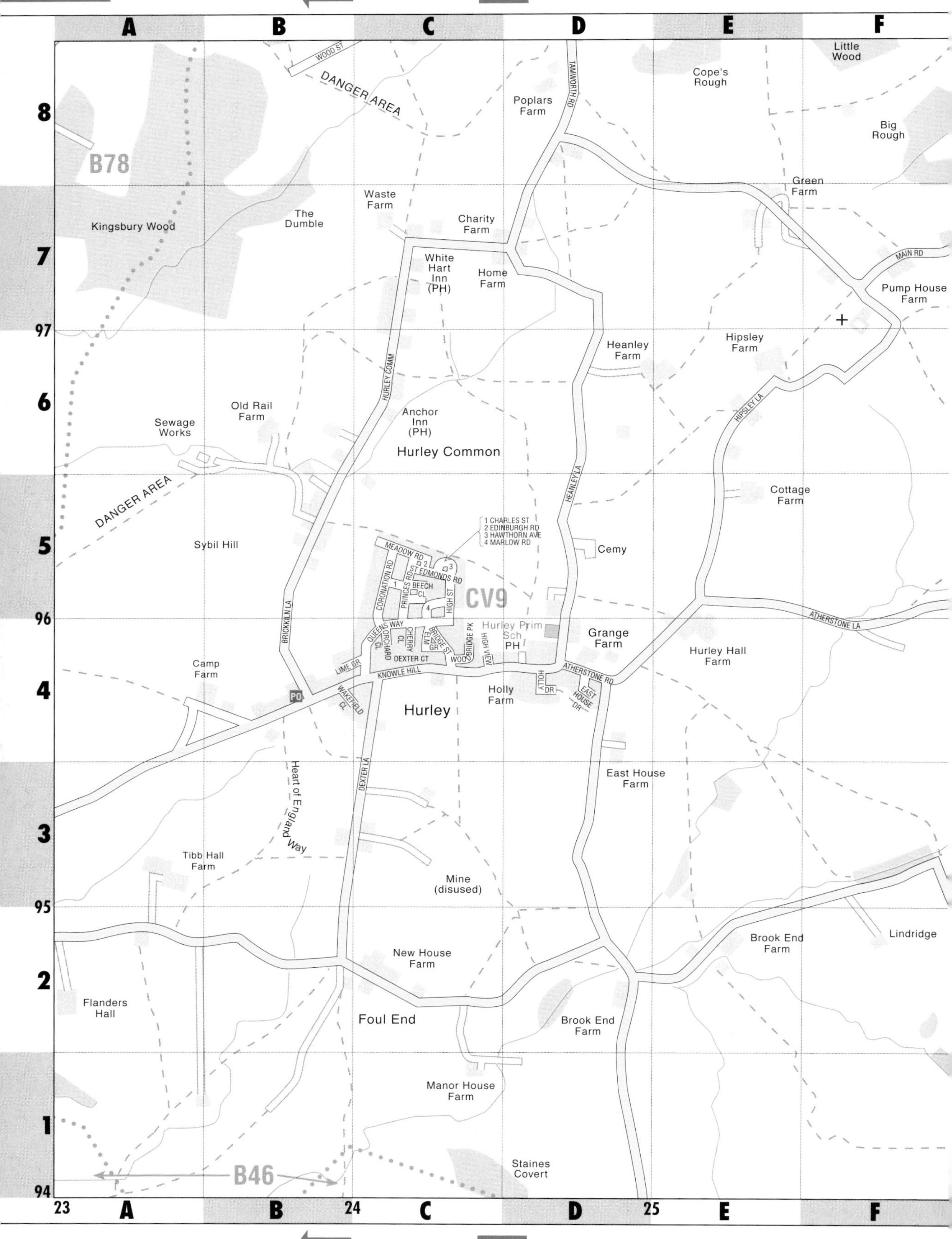
A
B
C
D
E
F
8
7
97
6
5
96
4
3
95
2
1
94
23
24
25
WOOD ST
DANGER AREA
TAMWORTH RD
Little Wood
Cope's Rough
Poplars Farm
Big Rough
B78
Green Farm
Kingsbury Wood
The Dumble
Waste Farm
Charity Farm
MAIN RD
White Hart Inn (PH)
Home Farm
Pump House Farm
Heanley Farm
Hipsley Farm
HURLEY COMM
Old Rail Farm
Sewage Works
Anchor Inn (PH)
Hurley Common
HIPSLEY LA
Cottage Farm
HEANLEY LA
DANGER AREA
1 CHARLES ST
2 EDINBURGH RD
3 HAWTHORN AVE
4 MARLOW RD
Sybil Hill
MEADOW RD
EDMONDS RD
Cemy
CORONATION RD
PRINCES RD
ST
BEECH CL
HIGH ST
CV9
BRICKKILN LA
QUEENS WAY
ORCHARD CL
CHERRY CL
ELM GR
BRIDGE ST
BRIDGE PK
HIGH VIEW
Hurley Prim Sch
PH
Grange Farm
ATHERSTONE LA
Hurley Hall Farm
Camp Farm
LIME GR
DEXTER CT
WOOD
KNOWLE HILL
HOLLY DR
ATHERSTONE RD
EAST HOUSE DR
PO
WAKEFIELD CL
Hurley
Holly Farm
Heart of England Way
DEXTER LA
East House Farm
Tibb Hall Farm
Mine (disused)
Lindridge
Brook End Farm
New House Farm
Flanders Hall
Foul End
Brook End Farm
Manor House Farm
Staines Covert
B46

15
25

11

18

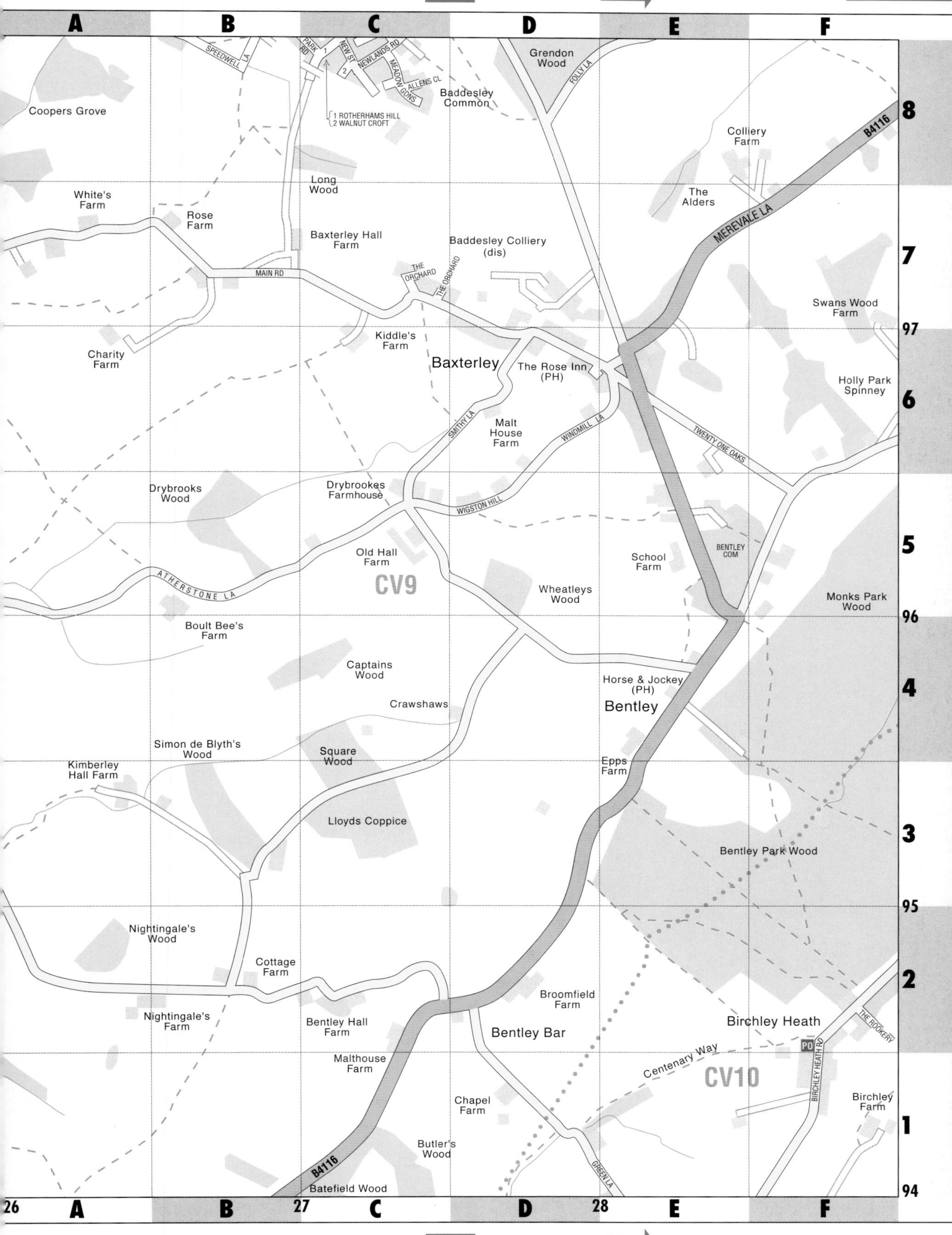
A
B
C
D
E
F
SPEEDWELL LA
PARK RD
NEW ST
NEWLANDS RD
MEADOW GDNS
ALLENS CL
1 ROTHERHAMS HILL
2 WALNUT CROFT
Grendon Wood
FOLLY LA
Baddesley Common
Coopers Grove
Colliery Farm
B4116
Long Wood
The Alders
White's Farm
Rose Farm
Baxterley Hall Farm
Baddesley Colliery (dis)
MEREVALE LA
MAIN RD
THE ORCHARD
Swans Wood Farm
Kiddle's Farm
Charity Farm
Baxterley
The Rose Inn (PH)
Holly Park Spinney
SMITHY LA
Malt House Farm
WINDMILL LA
TWENTY ONE OAKS
Drybrooks Wood
Drybrookes Farmhouse
WIGSTON HILL
Old Hall Farm
School Farm
BENTLEY COM
ATHERSTONE LA
CV9
Wheatleys Wood
Monks Park Wood
Boult Bee's Farm
Captains Wood
Horse & Jockey (PH)
Bentley
Crawshaws
Simon de Blyth's Wood
Square Wood
Kimberley Hall Farm
Epps Farm
Lloyds Coppice
Bentley Park Wood
Nightingale's Wood
Cottage Farm
Broomfield Farm
Nightingale's Farm
Bentley Hall Farm
Bentley Bar
Birchley Heath
THE ROOKERY
PO
Centenary Way
Malthouse Farm
CV10
BIRCHLEY HEATH RD
Chapel Farm
Birchley Farm
Butler's Wood
GREEN LA
Batefield Wood
8
7
97
6
5
96
4
3
95
2
1
94
26
27
28

17
12

A
B
C
D
E
F
8
7
97
6
5
96
4
3
95
2
1
94
29
30
31
B4116
MEREVALE LA
Abbey Farm
Abbey Pool
Black Pool
Merevale Hall
Merevale Park
Atherstone
Locks
Superstore
Liby
ATHERSTONE
LONG ST
WITHERLEY RD
A5
Queen Elizabeth Sch
Carlyon Rd Ind Est
Arden Hill Inf Sch
Oakfield Jun Sch
St Benedict's RC Prim Sch
Manor Rd Ind Est
Innage Brook
Ward's Hill
Merevale Lake
Outwoods
COLESHILL RD
CV9
CH
Rawn Hill
Mancetter
Rose Hill Farm
Mancetter Farm
Coventry Canal
WOODSIDE COTTAGES
Outwoods Farm
Purley Quarries (dis)
Purley Park
QUARRY LA
Monks Park Wood
QUARRY RD
Quarry Farm
The Premises
Stoneleigh Quarry Farm
Upper Coal Spinney
Mancetter Hill Farm
Purley Chase
PURLEY CHASE LA
Works
Bentley Park Wood
Bratts Waste
Oldbury Resr
Oldbury Farm
Masts
Ridge Lane
ARDEN FOREST EST
BIRCHLEY HEATH RD
PH
Glebe Farm
Mast
RIDGE LA
CH
The Belt
Oldbury Camp
Oldbury
CV10
Oldbury Grange
Hartshill Hayes Country Park
Hartshill Hayes Visitors Centre
OLDBURY RD
Lady Wood Farm
Centenary Way
Moor Wood Farm
PIPERS LA

20

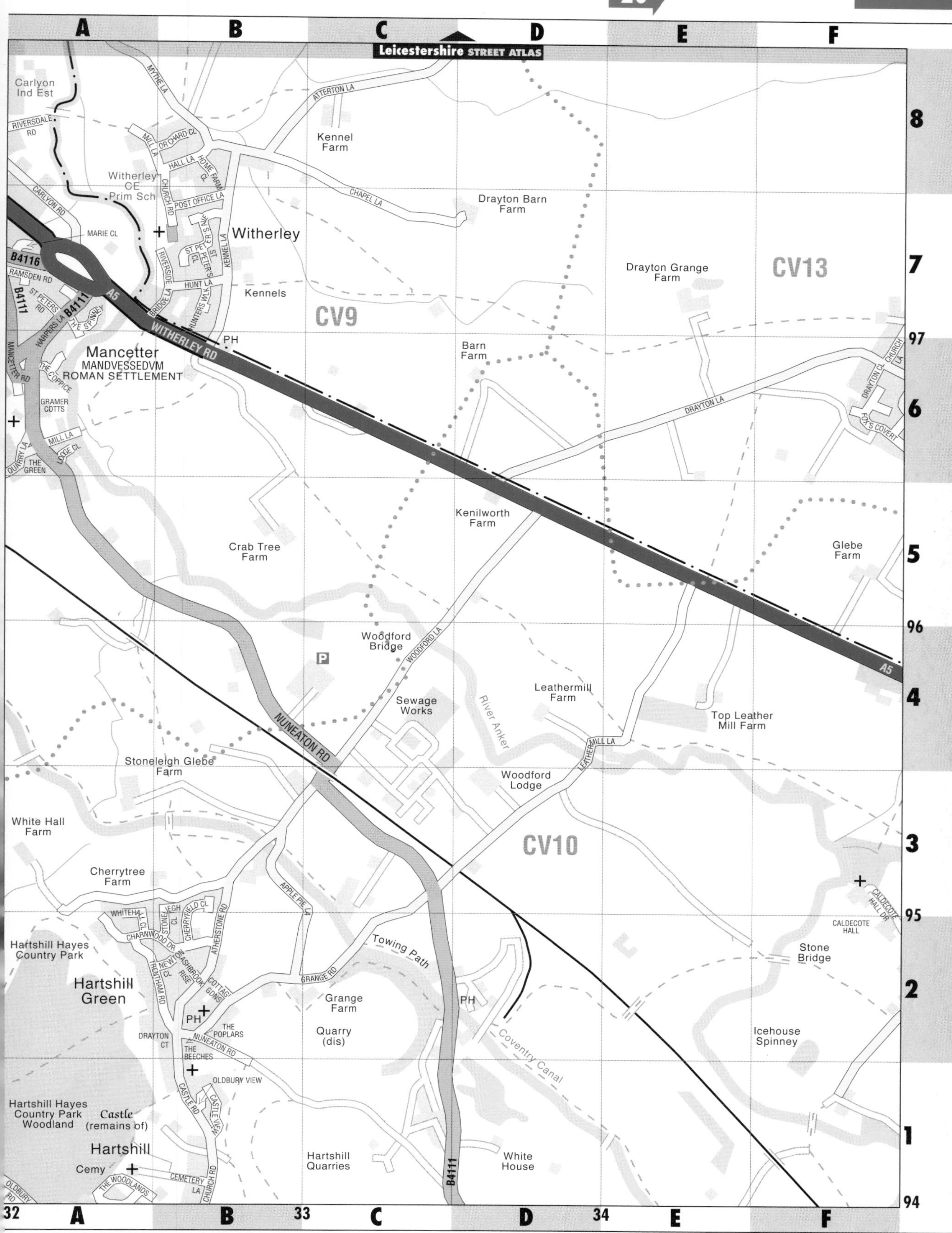
Leicestershire STREET ATLAS
A B C D E F
8 7 6 5 4 3 2 1
97 96 95 94
32 33 34
Carlyon Ind Est
RIVERSDALE RD
MYTHE LA
ATHERTON LA
Kennel Farm
MILL LA
ORCHARD CL
HALL LA
HOME FARM CL
Witherley CE Prim Sch
CHURCH RD
POST OFFICE LA
CHAPEL LA
Drayton Barn Farm
CARLYON RD
MARIE CL
Witherley
ST PETER'S AV
ST PETER'S CL
KENNEL LA
RIVERSIDE
HUNT LA
HUNTERS WLK
BRIDGE LA
Kennels
CV9
B4116
RAMSDEN RD
B4111
ST PETERS RD
HARPERS LA
THE SPINNEY
A5
WITHERLEY RD
PH
Drayton Grange Farm
CV13
Barn Farm
Mancetter
MANDVESSEDVM
ROMAN SETTLEMENT
MANCETTER RD
THE COPPICE
GRAMER COTTS
MILL LA
LODGE CL
QUARRY LA
THE GREEN
DRAYTON LA
DRAYTON CL
CHURCH LA
FOX'S COVERT
Kenilworth Farm
Crab Tree Farm
Glebe Farm
Woodford Bridge
WOODFORD LA
Sewage Works
Leathermill Farm
River Anker
Top Leather Mill Farm
NUNEATON RD
LEATHERMILL LA
Stoneleigh Glebe Farm
Woodford Lodge
White Hall Farm
CV10
Cherrytree Farm
APPLE PIE LA
CALDECOTE HALL DR
CALDECOTE HALL
WHITEHALL CL
STONELEIGH CL
CHERRYFIELD CL
ATHERSTONE RD
CHARNWOOD DR
Towing Path
Hartshill Hayes Country Park
NEWTON CL
ASHBROOK RISE
TRENTHAM RD
COTTAGE GDNS
GRANGE RD
Stone Bridge
Hartshill Green
Grange Farm
PH
Quarry (dis)
DRAYTON CT
THE POPLARS
NUNEATON RD
THE BEECHES
Coventry Canal
Icehouse Spinney
OLDBURY VIEW
CASTLE RD
CASTLE VIEW
Hartshill Hayes Country Park Woodland
Castle (remains of)
Hartshill
Cemy
CEMETERY LA
CHURCH RD
THE WOODLANDS
OLDBURY RD
Hartshill Quarries
B4111
White House

28

20

19

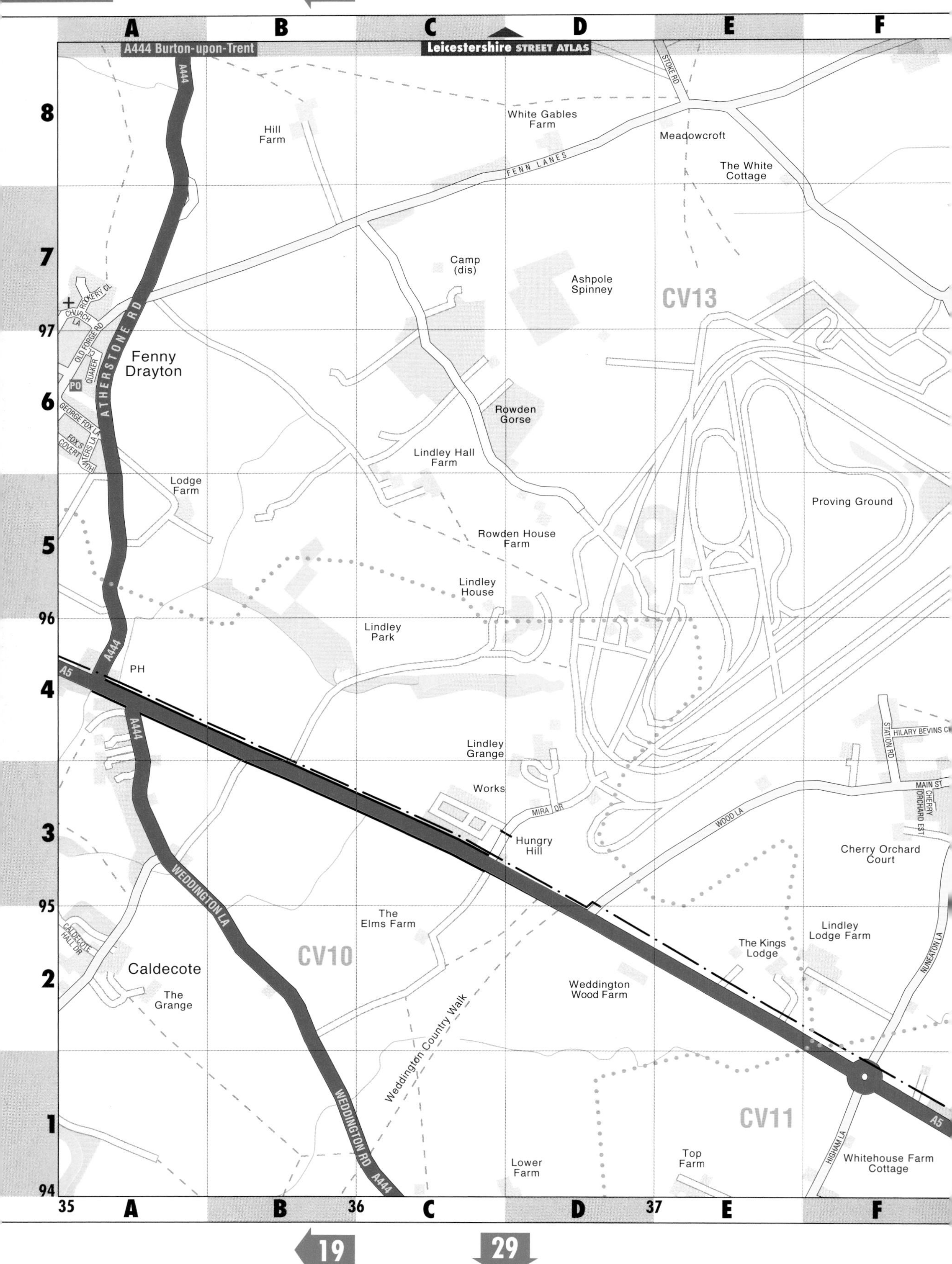

A444 Burton-upon-Trent
Leicestershire STREET ATLAS
A B C D E F
8 7 97 6 5 96 4 3 95 2 1 94
35 36 37
Hill Farm
White Gables Farm
Meadowcroft
The White Cottage
FENN LANES
STOKE RD
Camp (dis)
Ashpole Spinney
CV13
ROOKERY CL
CHURCH LA
OLD FORGE RD
QUAKER CL
ATHERSTONE RD
Fenny Drayton
PO
GEORGE FOX LA
FOX'S COVERT
Rowden Gorse
Lindley Hall Farm
Lodge Farm
Proving Ground
Rowden House Farm
Lindley House
Lindley Park
A444
A5
PH
Lindley Grange
Works
MIRA DR
Hungry Hill
STATION RD
HILARY BEVINS CL
MAIN ST
CHERRY ORCHARD EST
WOOD LA
Cherry Orchard Court
WEDDINGTON LA
The Elms Farm
CV10
Lindley Lodge Farm
The Kings Lodge
CALDECOTE HALL DR
Caldecote
The Grange
Weddington Wood Farm
NUNEATON LA
Weddington Country Walk
WEDDINGTON RD
CV11
HIGHAM LA
Lower Farm
Top Farm
Whitehouse Farm Cottage

19
29

Leicestershire STREET ATLAS
A
B
C
D
E
F
Dadlington
Grange Farm
Marina
Ivy House Farm
Stoke Golding
Fox Covert Farm
Willow Park Ind Est
Crown Hill
PH
St Martin's Convent
St Margaret's CE Prim Sch
St Martin's RC Sch
Brook Farm
Cemy
Stokefields Farm
HIGHAM FIELDS CT
Willow Farm
Brook House
Brook Farm
Millfield Farm
CV13
Highfield Farm
Cuckoo's Nest Farm
Oaklands
Oak Tree Farm
Basin Bridge Farm
Compass Fields Farm
Basin Bridge
Higham Fields
Vale Farm
Wykin Fields
Hall Farm
The Hollow
Wykin
Higham on the Hill CE Prim Sch
Spring Hill Farm
Higham on the Hill
Higham Hall
Wykin House Farm
Wykin Hall
Grange Farm
Higham Thorns
Hijaz Coll
Harper's Hill
LE10
Hollow Farm
CV11
Ashby de la Zouch Canal
Change Brook
WATLING ST
A5
A47 Leicester
NORMANDY WAY
A47
STAPLETON LA
STOKE LA
THE GREEN
FOXCOVERT LA
UPTON LA
STATION RD
HINCKLEY RD
STOKE RD
HIGHAM FIELDS LA
HIGHAM LA
STOKE LA
BASIN BRIDGE LA
HINCKLEY LA
MAIN ST
NUNEATON LA
BARR LA
HIGHAM LA
WYKIN LA
WYKIN RD
8
7
97
6
5
96
4
3
95
2
1
94
38
39
40

13

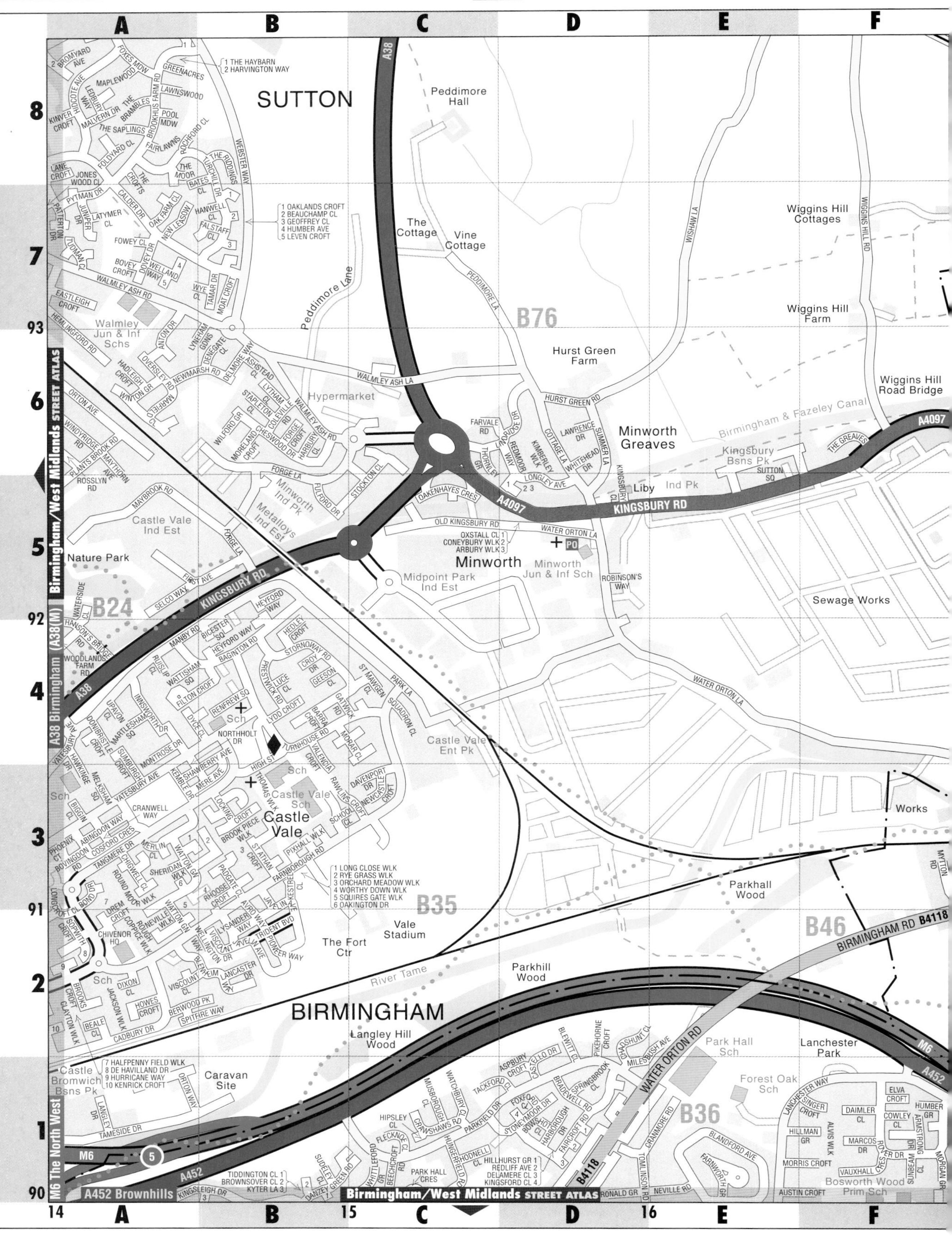

A B C D E F
8 7 93 6 5 92 4 3 91 2 1 90
14 15 16

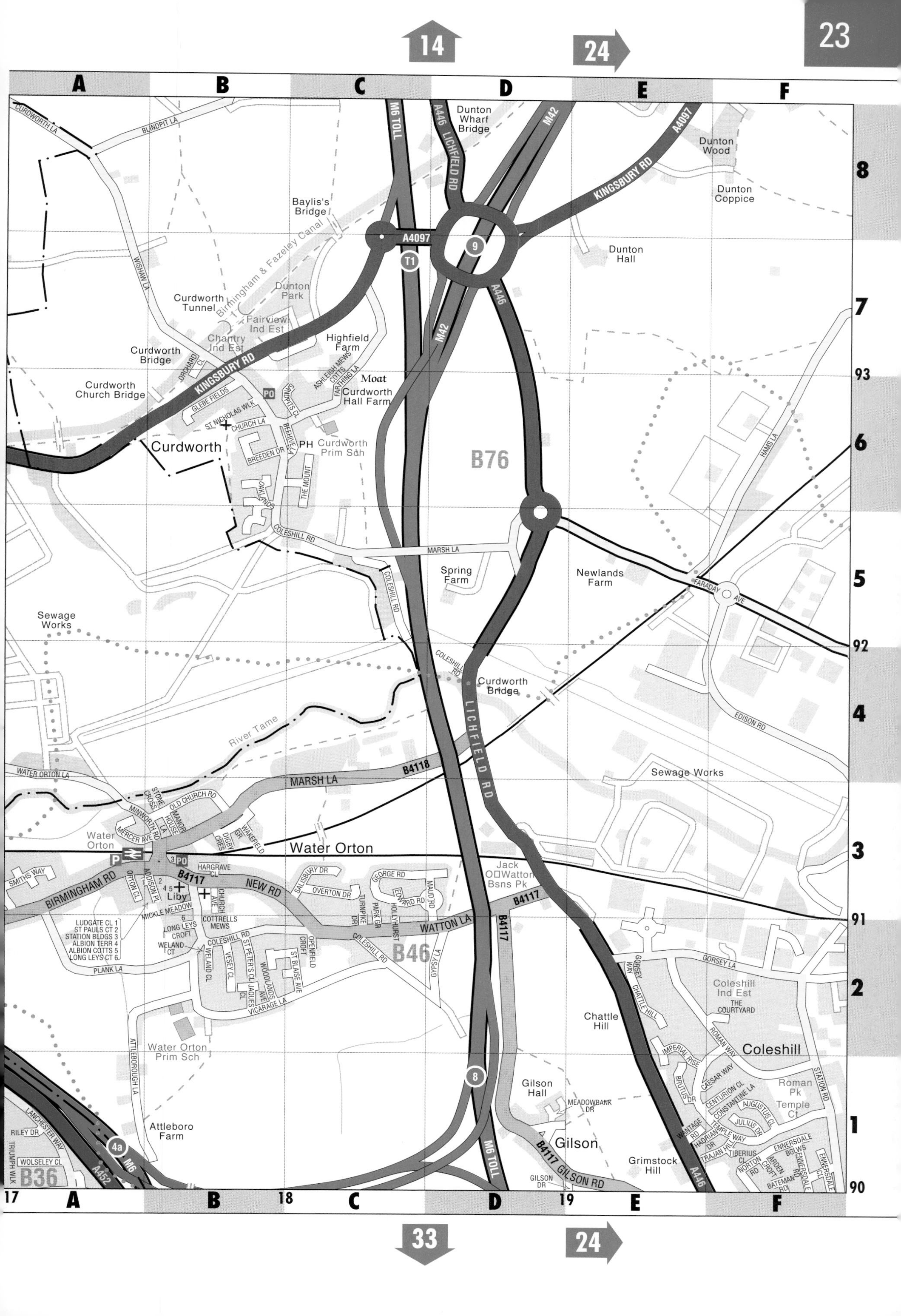
14
24
A
B
C
D
E
F
8
7
93
6
5
92
4
3
91
2
1
90
17
18
19
Dunton Wharf Bridge
Dunton Wood
Dunton Coppice
Dunton Hall
Baylis's Bridge
Birmingham & Fazeley Canal
Dunton Park
Curdworth Tunnel
Fairview Ind Est
Chantry Ind Est
Highfield Farm
Curdworth Bridge
Curdworth Church Bridge
Moat
Curdworth Hall Farm
Curdworth
PH
Curdworth Prim Sch
B76
Spring Farm
Newlands Farm
Sewage Works
Curdworth Bridge
River Tame
Sewage Works
Water Orton
Water Orton
Jack O'Watton Bsns Pk
Liby
B46
Chattle Hill
Coleshill Ind Est
THE COURTYARD
Coleshill
Roman Pk
Temple Ct
Water Orton Prim Sch
Gilson Hall
Gilson
Grimstock Hill
Attleboro Farm
B36
M6 TOLL
M42
A446
A4097
A452
B4118
B4117
M6
LICHFIELD RD
KINGSBURY RD
CURDWORTH LA
BLINDPIT LA
WISHAW LA
ORCHARD CL
GLEBE FIELDS
ST NICHOLAS WLK
CHURCH LA
BREEDEN DR
BEEHIVE LA
OAKLANDS
THE MOUNT
ASHLEIGH MEWS COTTS
FARTHING LA
COLESHILL RD
MARSH LA
HAMS LA
FARADAY AVE
EDISON RD
WATER ORTON LA
STONE CROSS
OLD CHURCH RD
MINWORTH RD
MANOR HOUSE LA
MERCER AVE
DIGBY CRES
WAKEFIELD
HARGRAVE CL
BIRMINGHAM RD
SMITHS WAY
ORTON CL
ADDISON PL
NEW RD
SALISBURY DR
OVERTON DR
GEORGE RD
EDWARD RD
MAUD RD
TURNPIKE DR
PARK GR
HOLLYHURST
WATTON LA
GYPSY LA
CHURCH AVE
MICKLE MEADOW
COTTRELLS MEWS
LONG LEYS CROFT
WELAND CT
WELAND CL
VESEY CL
ST PETER'S CL
JAQUES CL
WOODLANDS AVE
OPENFIELD CROFT
ST BLAISE AVE
VICARAGE LA
PLANK LA
LUDGATE CL 1
ST PAULS CT 2
STATION BLDGS 3
ALBION TERR 4
ALBION COTTS 5
LONG LEYS CT 6
ATTLEBOROUGH LA
LANCHESTER WAY
RILEY DR
WOLSELEY CL
TRIUMPH WLK
MEADOWBANK DR
GILSON DR
GILSON RD
GORSEY WAY
GORSEY LA
CHATTLE HILL
ROMAN WAY
IMPERIAL RISE
CAESAR WAY
BRUTUS DR
CENTURION CL
CONSTANTINE LA
AUGUSTUS CL
JULIUS DR
WANTAGE RD
HADRIAN DR
TEMPLE WAY
TRAJAN HILL
TIBERIUS CL
NORTON RD
ARDEN CROFT
BATEMAN RD
ENNERSDALE RD
ENNERSDALE BGLWS
ENNERSDALE CL
STATION RD
33
24

23
15

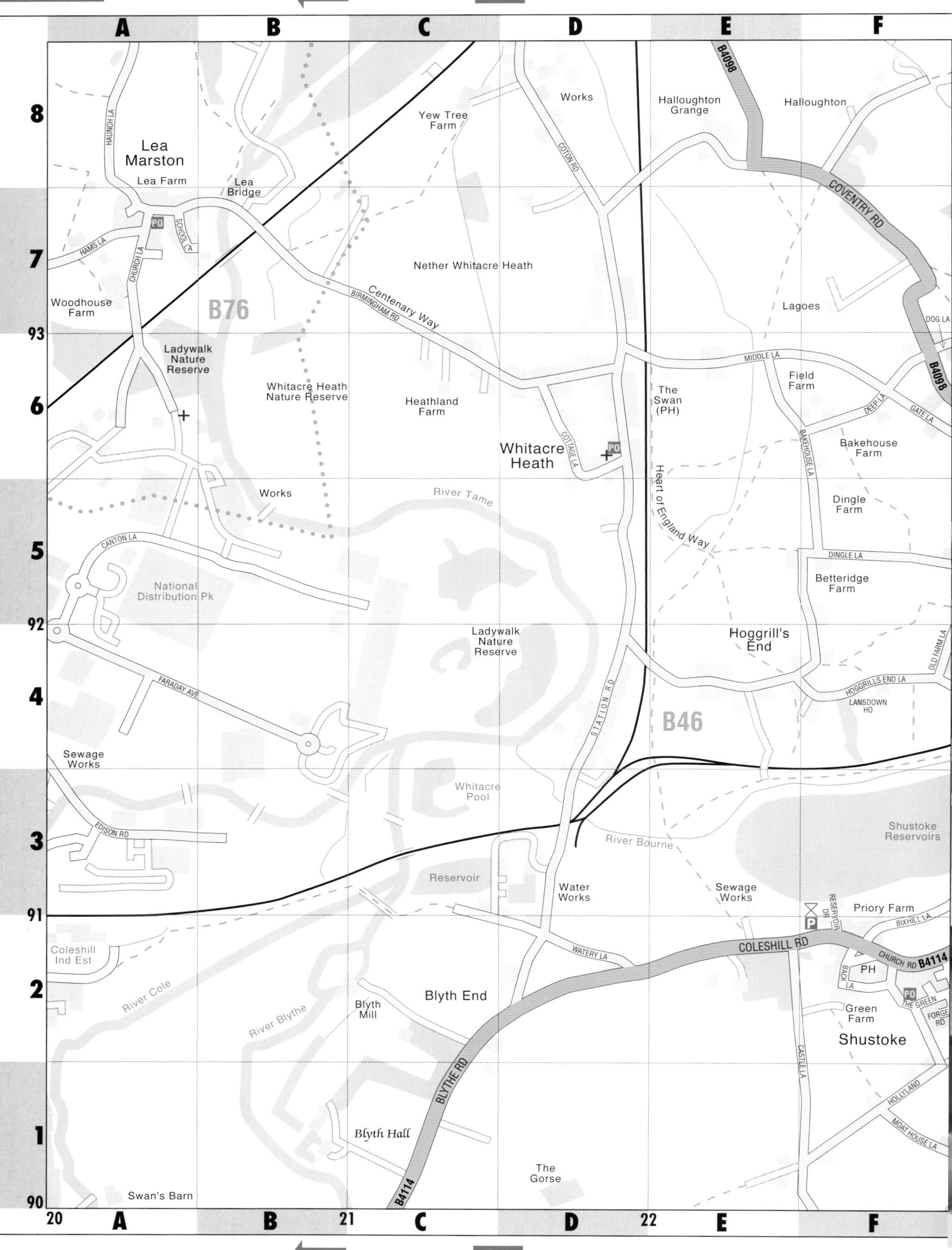
A
B
C
D
E
F
8
7
93
6
5
92
4
3
91
2
1
90
20
21
22
Lea Marston
Lea Farm
Lea Bridge
HAUNCH LA
HAMS LA
CHURCH LA
SCHOOL LA
PO
Woodhouse Farm
B76
Ladywalk Nature Reserve
Yew Tree Farm
Works
COTON RD
Halloughton Grange
Halloughton
B4098
COVENTRY RD
Nether Whitacre Heath
Centenary Way
BIRMINGHAM RD
Lagoes
DOG LA
MIDDLE LA
Field Farm
DEEP LA
GATE LA
Whitacre Heath Nature Reserve
Heathland Farm
The Swan (PH)
Whitacre Heath
COTTAGE LA
BAKEHOUSE LA
Bakehouse Farm
Works
River Tame
Heart of England Way
Dingle Farm
CANTON LA
DINGLE LA
Betteridge Farm
National Distribution Pk
Ladywalk Nature Reserve
Hoggrill's End
OLD FARM LA
FARADAY AVE
HOGGRILLS END LA
LANSDOWN HO
STATION RD
B46
Sewage Works
Whitacre Pool
EDISON RD
River Bourne
Shustoke Reservoirs
Reservoir
Water Works
Sewage Works
RESERVOIR DR
Priory Farm
BIXHILL LA
Coleshill Ind Est
WATERY LA
COLESHILL RD
CHURCH RD
B4114
PH
BACK LA
River Cole
River Blythe
Blyth Mill
Blyth End
THE GREEN
FORGE RD
Green Farm
Shustoke
BLYTHE RD
CASTLE LA
HOLLYLAND
MOAT HOUSE LA
Blyth Hall
The Gorse
Swan's Barn
B4114

23
34

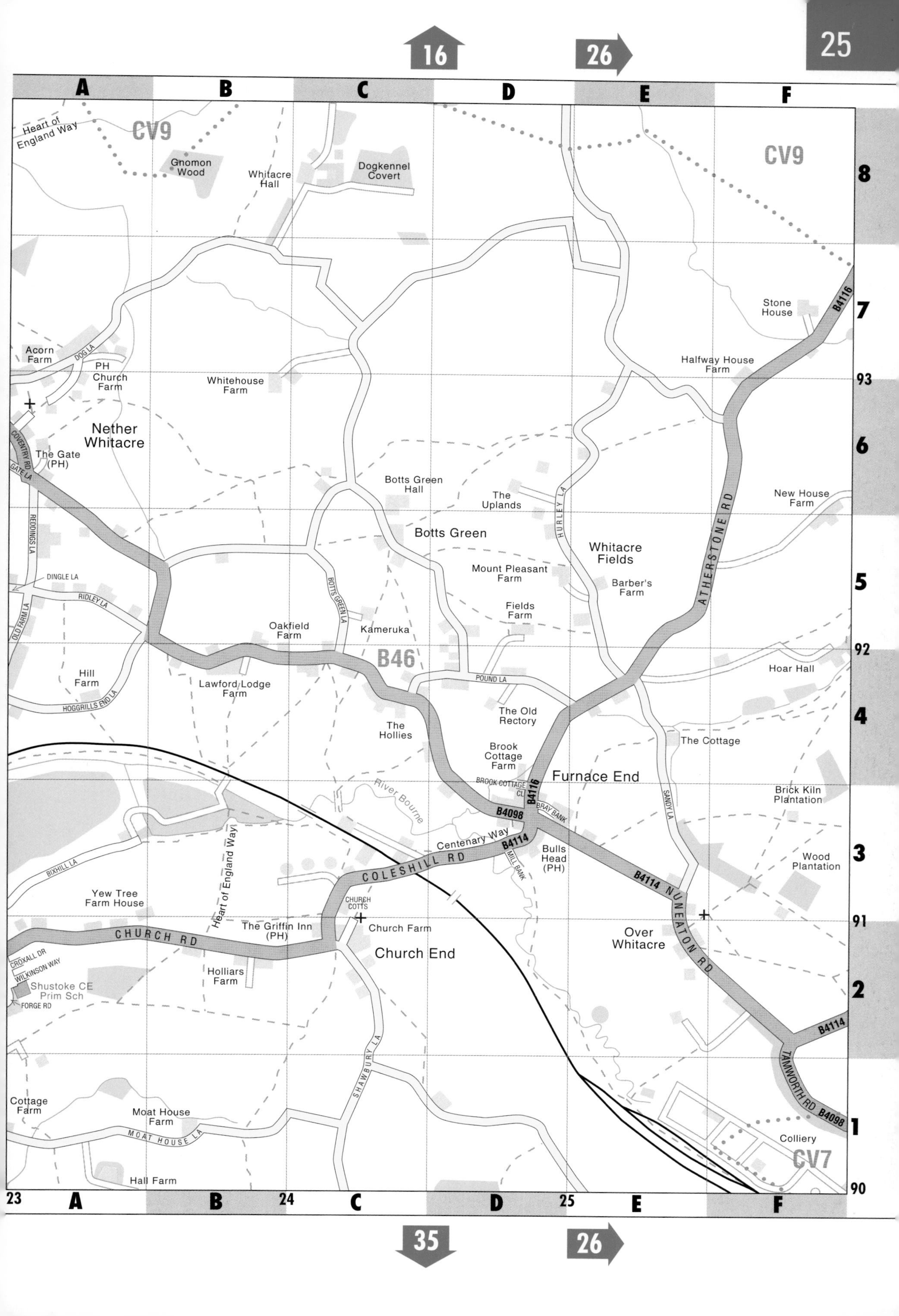

16
26
A
B
C
D
E
F
8
7
93
6
5
92
4
3
91
2
1
90
23
24
25
35
26
Heart of England Way
CV9
Gnomon Wood
Whitacre Hall
Dogkennel Covert
CV9
Stone House
B4116
Acorn Farm
DOG LA
PH
Church Farm
Whitehouse Farm
Halfway House Farm
Nether Whitacre
COVENTRY RD
The Gate (PH)
GATE LA
Botts Green Hall
The Uplands
HURLEY LA
New House Farm
REDDINGS LA
Botts Green
Whitacre Fields
ATHERSTONE RD
Mount Pleasant Farm
Barber's Farm
DINGLE LA
RIDLEY LA
BOTTS GREEN LA
Fields Farm
OLD FARM LA
Oakfield Farm
Kameruka
B46
Hill Farm
Lawford Lodge Farm
POUND LA
Hoar Hall
HOGGRILLS END LA
The Old Rectory
The Hollies
The Cottage
Brook Cottage Farm
Furnace End
BROOK COTTAGE CL
B4116
River Bourne
SANDY LA
Brick Kiln Plantation
B4098
BRAY BANK
Centenary Way
B4114
BIXHILL LA
Heart of England Way
COLESHILL RD
MILL BANK
Bulls Head (PH)
Wood Plantation
B4114
NUNEATON RD
Yew Tree Farm House
CHURCH COTTS
CHURCH RD
The Griffin Inn (PH)
Church Farm
Over Whitacre
Church End
CROXALL DR
WILKINSON WAY
Holliars Farm
Shustoke CE Prim Sch
FORGE RD
B4114
SHAWBURY LA
TAMWORTH RD
B4098
Cottage Farm
Moat House Farm
MOAT HOUSE LA
Colliery
CV7
Hall Farm

25
17

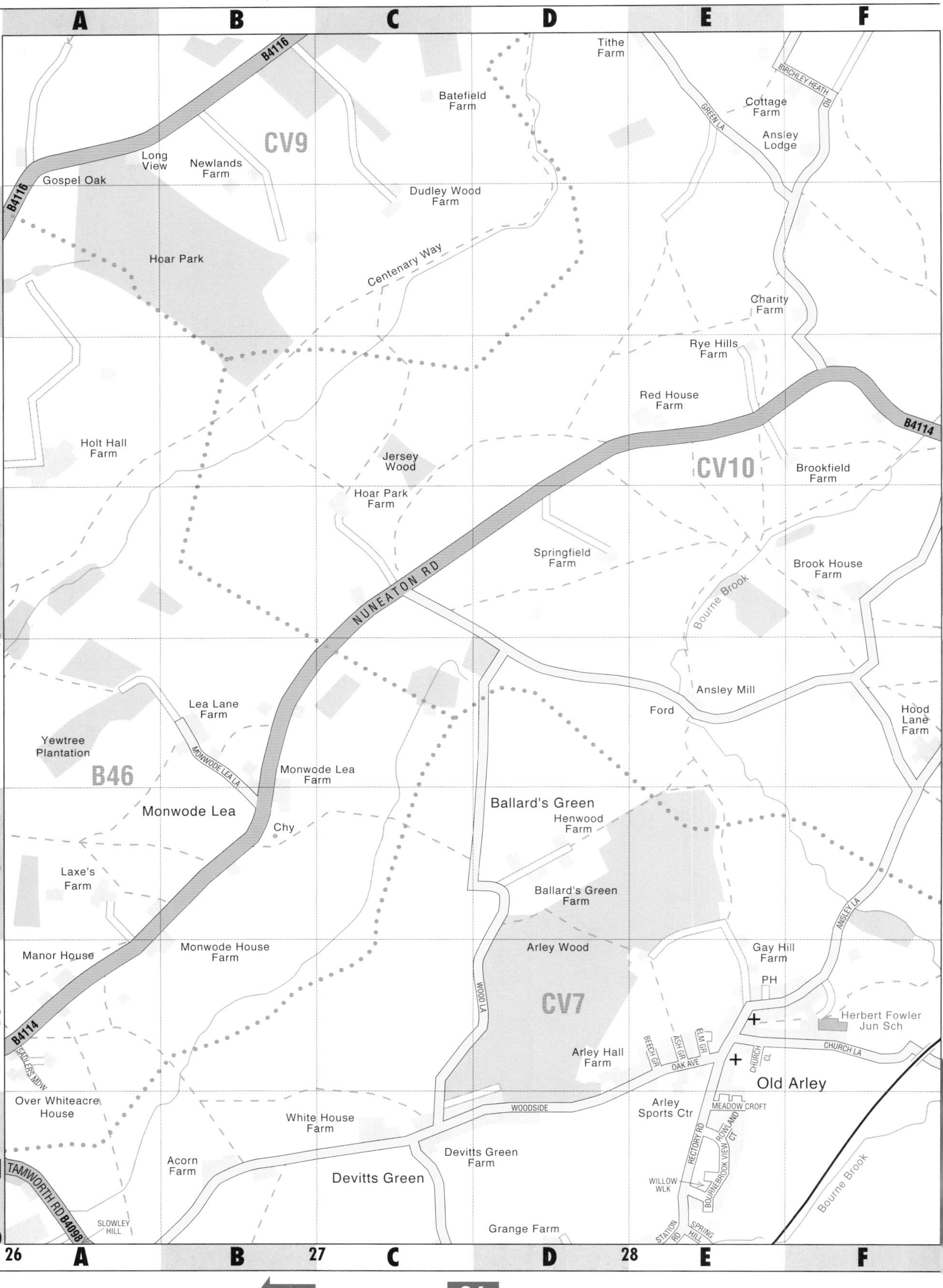

A B C D E F

8 7 93 6 5 92 4 3 91 2 1 90

B4116
Tithe Farm
Batefield Farm
CV9
BIRCHLEY HEATH RD
GREEN LA
Cottage Farm
Ansley Lodge
Long View
Newlands Farm
Gospel Oak
Dudley Wood Farm
B4116
Hoar Park
Centenary Way
Charity Farm
Rye Hills Farm
Red House Farm
B4114
Holt Hall Farm
Jersey Wood
CV10
Brookfield Farm
Hoar Park Farm
Springfield Farm
Brook House Farm
NUNEATON RD
Bourne Brook
Ansley Mill
Ford
Hood Lane Farm
Lea Lane Farm
Yewtree Plantation
B46
MONWODE LEA LA
Monwode Lea Farm
Monwode Lea
Ballard's Green
Henwood Farm
Chy
Laxe's Farm
Ballard's Green Farm
ANSLEY LA
Manor House
Monwode House Farm
Arley Wood
Gay Hill Farm
PH
WOOD LA
CV7
Herbert Fowler Jun Sch
B4114
SADLERS MDW
BEECH GR
ASH GR
ELM GR
CHURCH CL
CHURCH LA
Arley Hall Farm
OAK AVE
Old Arley
Over Whiteacre House
WOODSIDE
Arley Sports Ctr
MEADOW CROFT
White House Farm
RECTORY RD
ROWLAND CT
Acorn Farm
Devitts Green Farm
Devitts Green
TAMWORTH RD B4098
WILLOW WLK
BOURNEBROOK VIEW
Bourne Brook
SLOWLEY HILL
Grange Farm
STATION RD
SPRING HILL

26 A B 27 C D 28 E F

25
36

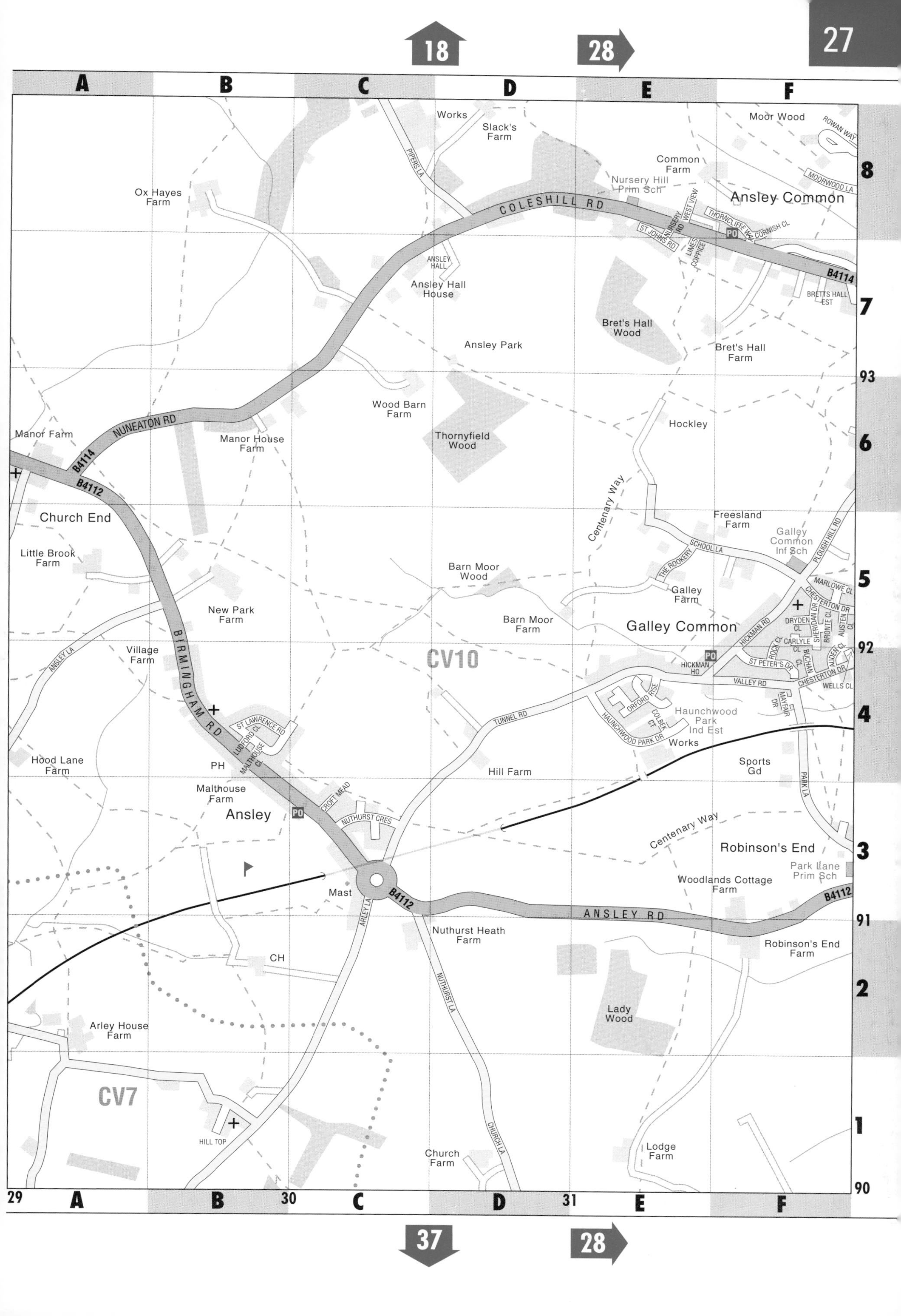
18
28
A
B
C
D
E
F
Works
Slack's Farm
Moor Wood
ROWAN WAY
Common Farm
Nursery Hill Prim Sch
MOORWOOD LA
Ox Hayes Farm
PIPERS LA
COLESHILL RD
Ansley Common
THORNCLIFFE WAY
CORNISH CL
ST JOHNS RD
NURSERY RD
WEST VIEW
LIMES COPPICE
PO
B4114
ANSLEY HALL
Ansley Hall House
BRETTS HALL EST
Bret's Hall Wood
Bret's Hall Farm
Ansley Park
Wood Barn Farm
Hockley
Manor Farm
NUNEATON RD
Manor House Farm
Thornyfield Wood
B4114
B4112
Centenary Way
Church End
Freesland Farm
Galley Common Inf Sch
PLOUGH HILL RD
SCHOOL LA
Little Brook Farm
THE ROOKERY
Barn Moor Wood
MARLOWE CL
Galley Farm
CHESTERTON DR
New Park Farm
Barn Moor Farm
Galley Common
HICKMAN RD
DRYDEN CL
SHERIDAN DR
BRONTE CL
AUSTEN CL
CARLYLE CL
ROCK CL
AUDEN CL
BIRMINGHAM RD
Village Farm
ANSLEY LA
CV10
HICKMAN HO
ST PETER'S DR
BUCHAN CL
CHESTERTON DR
VALLEY RD
WELLS CL
ORFORD RISE
MAYFAIR DR
ST LAWRENCE RD
LUDFORD CL
MALTHOUSE CL
TUNNEL RD
COLBEK CT
Haunchwood Park Ind Est
HAUNCHWOOD PARK DR
Works
Hood Lane Farm
PH
Hill Farm
Sports Gd
Malthouse Farm
CROFT MEAD
PARK LA
Ansley
NUTHURST CRES
Centenary Way
Robinson's End
Park Lane Prim Sch
Mast
Woodlands Cottage Farm
B4112
ANSLEY RD
B4112
ARLEY LA
Nuthurst Heath Farm
Robinson's End Farm
CH
NUTHURST LA
Lady Wood
Arley House Farm
CV7
HILL TOP
CHURCH LA
Church Farm
Lodge Farm
8
7
93
6
5
92
4
3
91
2
1
90
29
30
31
37
28

27
19

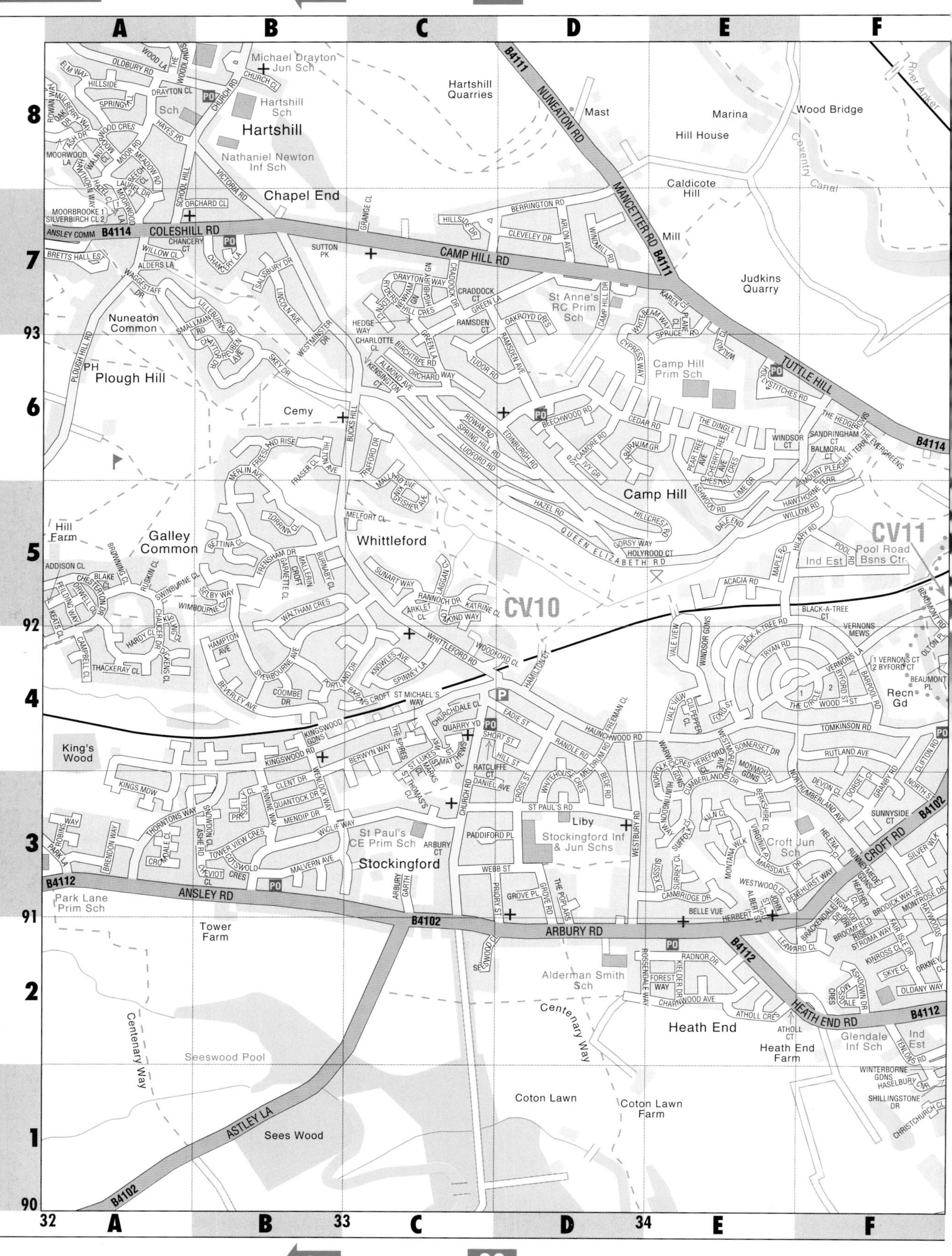
A
B
C
D
E
F
8
7
93
6
5
92
4
3
91
2
1
90
32
33
34
Hartshill
Michael Drayton Jun Sch
Hartshill Sch
Nathaniel Newton Inf Sch
Chapel End
Hartshill Quarries
Mast
Marina
Wood Bridge
Hill House
Caldicote Hill
Coventry Canal
River Anker
Mill
Judkins Quarry
St Anne's RC Prim Sch
Camp Hill Prim Sch
Camp Hill
Nuneaton Common
Plough Hill
PH
Cemy
Whittleford
Galley Common
Hill Farm
CV10
CV11
Pool Road Bsns Ctr
Ind Est
Recn Gd
King's Wood
St Paul's CE Prim Sch
Stockingford
Liby
Stockingford Inf & Jun Schs
Croft Jun Sch
Park Lane Prim Sch
Tower Farm
Alderman Smith Sch
Heath End
Heath End Farm
Glendale Inf Sch
Ind Est
Seeswood Pool
Centenary Way
Coton Lawn
Coton Lawn Farm
Sees Wood
B4111
NUNEATON RD
MANCETTER RD
B4114
COLESHILL RD
CAMP HILL RD
TUTTLE HILL
B4112
ANSLEY RD
B4102
ARBURY RD
HEATH END RD
CROFT RD
ASTLEY LA
QUEEN ELIZABETH RD
WHITTLEFORD RD
BUCKS HILL
CHURCH RD
OLDBURY RD
WOOD LA
HILLSIDE
DRAYTON CL
CHURCH CL
SPRINGHILL
HAYES RD
SCHOOL HILL
VICTORIA RD
ORCHARD CL
GRANGE CL
BERRINGTON RD
CLEVELEY DR
ARLON AVE
WINDMILL RD
HILLSIDE DR
ANSLEY COMM
WILLOW CL
ALDERS LA
BRETTS HALL EST
CHANCERY CT
CHANCERY LA
SALISBURY DR
LINCOLN AVE
WESTMINSTER DR
SUTTON PK
SKEY DR
WAGGESTAFF DR
PLOUGH HILL RD
DRAYTON WAY
CRADDOCK DR
GREEN LA
RAMSDEN CT
RAMSDEN AVE
OAKROYD CRES
TUDOR RD
ORCHARD WAY
BIRCHTREE RD
KENSINGTON CT
HEDGE WAY
CHARLOTTE CL
ROWAN RD
SPRING HILL RD
LUDFORD RD
EDINBURGH RD
BEECHWOOD RD
SYCAMORE RD
IVY GR
CEDAR RD
LABURNUM GR
PEAR TREE AVE
CHERRY TREE AVE
CHESTNUT CRES
ASHWOOD RD
LIME GR
THE DINGLE
WINDSOR CT
SANDRINGHAM CT
BALMORAL CT
THE HEDGEROWS
THE EVERGREENS
MOUNT PLEASANT TERR
HAWTHORNE TERR
WILLOW RD
DALE END
HILLCREST RD
HAZEL RD
GORSY WAY
HOLYROOD CT
CAMP HILL DR
WHITEBEAM WAY
CYPRESS WAY
SPRUCE RD
KAREN CL
PLANE
HOLYSTITCHES RD
FREESLAND RISE
HILTON AVE
FRASER CL
TRAFFORD DR
MALLARD AVE
KINGFISHER AVE
MERLIN AVE
ZORRINA CL
MELFORT CL
BETTINA CL
FRENSHAM DR
GARNETTE CL
CROFT
MALLERIN
BURNABY CL
SUNART WAY
LAGGAN CL
RANNOCH DR
ARKLET CL
KATRINE CL
LOMOND WAY
WALTHAM CRES
SELBY WAY
WIMBOURNE CL
SWINBURNE CL
HAMPTON AVE
SHERBOURNE AVE
BEVERLEY AVE
COOMBE DR
PORTLAND DR
KNOWLES AVE
SPINNEY LA
WOODFORD CL
HAMILTON CT
BARONS CROFT
ST MICHAEL'S WAY
BROWNING CL
RUSKIN CL
ADDISON CL
BLAKE CL
CHESTERTON DR
ORWELL CL
FIELDING WAY
KEATS CL
HARDY CL
CHAUCER DR
DICKENS CL
CAMPBELL CL
THACKERAY CL
KINGSWOOD GDNS
KINGSWOOD RD
KINGS MDW
BERWYN WAY
THE SPIRES
ST LUKE'S CL
ST MARKS CL
ST MATTHEWS CL
ST THOMAS'S CL
CHURCHDALE CL
QUARRY YD
EADIE ST
SHORT ST
HILL ST
RATCLIFFE CT
DANIEL AVE
CROSS ST
WHITEHOUSE CRES
MELDRUM RD
BEDE RD
RANDLE RD
HAUNCHWOOD RD
FREEMAN CL
ST PAUL'S RD
PADDIFORD PL
WEBB ST
GROVE PL
GROVE RD
PRIORY ST
THE POPLARS
WESTBURY RD
ARBURY GARTH
ARBURY CT
THORNTONS WAY
SNOWDON CL
ASHE RD
PRESCELLY CL
PENNINE WAY
CLENT DR
QUANTOCK DR
MENDIP DR
WENLOCK WAY
WICLIF WAY
MALVERN AVE
TOWER VIEW CRES
COTSWOLD CRES
CHEVIOT CL
CRODALE CL
BRENDON WAY
ROBINS WAY
PARK LA
VALE VIEW
WINDSOR GDNS
CULPEPPER CL
FORD ST
BLACK-A-TREE RD
BLACK-A-TREE CT
ACACIA RD
MAPLE RD
HILARY RD
POOL RD
VERNONS MEWS
TRYAN RD
VERNONS LA
1 VERNONS CT
2 BYFORD CT
BYFORD ST
BARPOOL RD
BEAUMONT RD
BEAUMONT PL
OLTON PL
THE CIRCLE
WOOD ST
TOMKINSON RD
RUTLAND AVE
CLIFTON RD
NORTH ST
GRANBY RD
DORSET CL
DEVON CL
SUNNYSIDE CT
SILVER WLK
NORTHUMBERLAND AVE
SOMERSET DR
MONMOUTH GDNS
WESTMORELAND AVE
HEREFORD CL
CUMBERLAND DR
NORFOLK CRES
WARWICK GDNS
HUNTINGDON WAY
SUFFOLK CL
SUSSEX CL
SURREY CL
CAMBRIDGE DR
BERKSHIRE CL
VIRGINIA RD
MONTANA WLK
MARSDALE DR
HELENA CL
RUNNYMEDE GDNS
DEMEHURST WAY
WESTWOOD CL
ALBERT ST
JOHN ST
HERBERT
BELLE VUE
HEATHER CL
BRACKENDALE DR
LINGWOOD DR
BROOMFIELD RISE
STROMA WAY
BRODICK WAY
MONTROSE DR
THE HAYWOODS
FAIR ISLE DR
KINROSS CL
SKYE CL
ORKNEY CL
OLDANY WAY
ASHDOWN DR
LEAWARD CL
RADNOR DR
KIELDER DR
FOREST WAY
CHARNWOOD AVE
ROSEDALE WAY
ATHOLL CRES
ATHOLL CT
SEESWOOD CL
TENLONS RD
WINTERBORNE GDNS
HASELBURY
SHILLINGSTONE DR
CHRISTCHURCH CL
PO
P

27
38

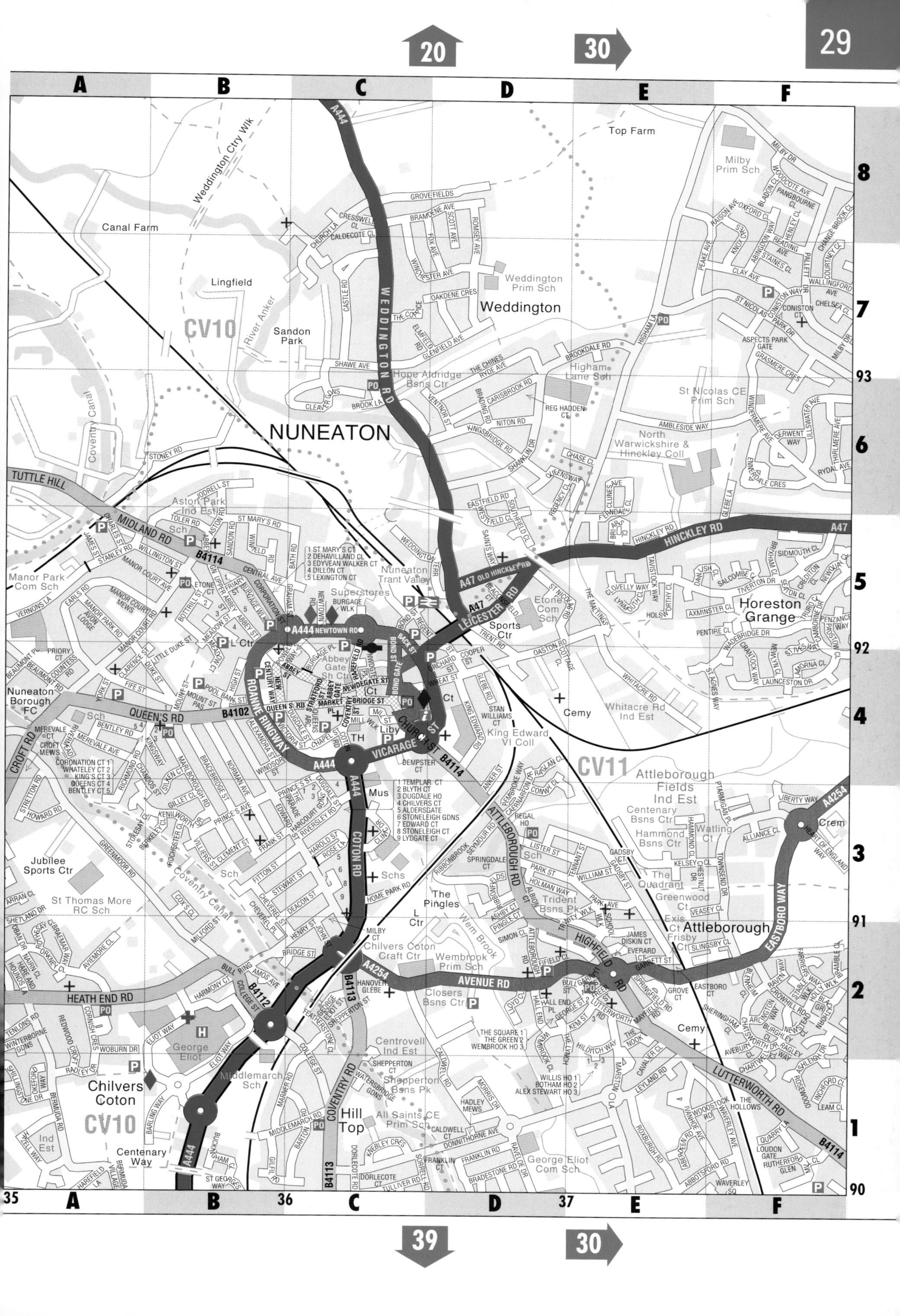
20
30
A
B
C
D
E
F
8
7
93
6
5
92
4
3
91
2
1
90
Top Farm
Milby Prim Sch
Canal Farm
Weddington Ctry Wlk
Lingfield
Sandon Park
CV10
River Anker
Weddington Prim Sch
Weddington
WEDDINGTON RD
A444
GROVE FIELDS
SHAWE AVE
Hope Aldridge Bsns Ctr
BROOK LA
CLEAVER GDNS
NUNEATON
Coventry Canal
STONEY RD
TUTTLE HILL
Higham Lane Sch
HIGHAM LA
St Nicolas CE Prim Sch
AMBLESIDE WAY
North Warwickshire & Hinckley Coll
CHASE CL
QUEENSWAY
HINCKLEY RD
A47
Aston Park Ind Est
MIDLAND RD
B4114
Manor Park Com Sch
1 ST MARY'S CT
2 DEHAVILLAND CL
3 EDYVEAN WALKER CT
4 DILLON CT
5 LEXINGTON CT
Nuneaton Trant Valley
Superstores
A47 OLD HINCKLEY RD
LEICESTER RD
Etone Com Sch
Sports Ctr
Horeston Grange
A444 NEWTOWN RD
Abbey Gate Sh Ctr
L Ctr
Nuneaton Borough FC
QUEEN'S RD
B4102
ROANNE RINGWAY
VICARAGE ST
CHURCH ST
B4114
Liby
TH
Mus
Cemy
Whitacre Rd Ind Est
Stan Williams Ct
King Edward VI Coll
CV11
Attleborough Fields Ind Est
Centenary Bsns Ctr
Hammond Bsns Ctr
Watling Ct
Crem
A4254
1 TEMPLAR CT
2 BLYTH CT
3 DUGDALE HO
4 CHILVERS CT
5 ALDERSGATE
6 STONELEIGH GDNS
7 EDWARD CT
8 STONELEIGH CT
9 LYDGATE CT
COTON RD
Schs
Jubilee Sports Ctr
St Thomas More RC Sch
ATTLEBOROUGH RD
The Pingles
Trident Bsns Pk
The Quadrant
Greenwood Ct
Exis Ct
Frisby Ct
Attleborough
EASTBORO WAY
HIGHFIELD RD
Wem Brook
Chilvers Coton Craft Ctr
Wembrook Prim Sch
AVENUE RD
HEATH END RD
Closers Bsns Ctr
George Eliot
Middlemarch Sch
Centrovell Ind Est
Shepperton Bsns Pk
THE SQUARE 1
THE GREEN 2
WEMBROOK HO 3
WILLIS HO 1
BOTHAM HO 2
ALEX STEWART HO 3
LUTTERWORTH RD
Cemy
Chilvers Coton
CV10
Ind Est
Centenary Way
Hill Top
All Saints CE Prim Sch
COVENTRY RD
B4113
George Eliot Com Sch
B4114
35
36
37
39
30

29
21

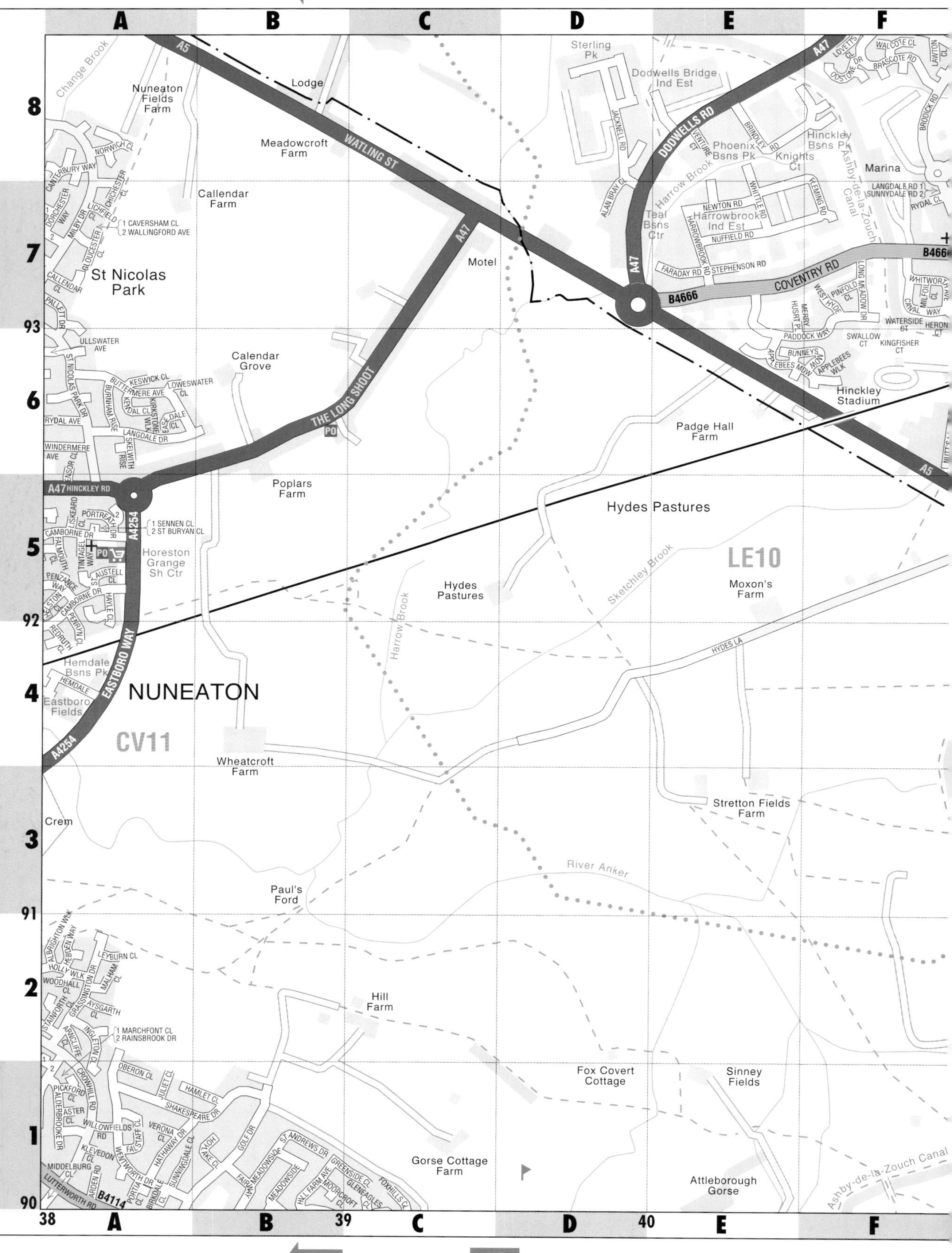
A
B
C
D
E
F
8
7
93
6
5
92
4
3
91
2
1
90
38
39
40
Change Brook
A5
Lodge
Nuneaton
Fields
Farm
Meadowcroft
Farm
WATLING ST
Callendar
Farm
NORWICH CL
CANTERBURY WAY
CHICHESTER CL
DORCHESTER WAY
MILBY DR
LICHFIELD CL
GLOUCESTER CL
1 CAVERSHAM CL
2 WALLINGFORD AVE
CALLENDAR CL
St Nicolas
Park
PALLETT DR
A47
Motel
Sterling
Pk
Dodwells Bridge
Ind Est
JACKNELL RD
DODWELLS RD
VENTURE CT
BRINDLEY RD
Phoenix
Bsns Pk
Knights
Ct
Hinckley
Bsns Pk
Ashby-de-la-Zouch
Canal
Marina
LANGDALE RD 1
SUNNYDALE RD 2
RYDAL CL
WALCOTE CL
BRASCOTE RD
LOVETTS CL
COSTONE DR
LAWTON CL
BRODICK RD
Harrow Brook
ALAN BRAY CL
NEWTON RD
WHITTLE RD
FLEMING RD
Teal
Bsns
Ctr
Harrowbrook
Ind Est
HARROWBROOK RD
NUFFIELD RD
FARADAY RD
STEPHENSON RD
COVENTRY RD
B4666
LONG MEADOW DR
WEST HYDE
PINFOLD CL
MERRY
HUSKIT PL
WHITWORTH AVE
MILFOIL CL
CANAL WAY
WATERSIDE CT
HERON CT
PADDOCK WAY
SWALLOW CT
KINGFISHER CT
BUNNEYS
APPLEBEES MDW
APPLEBEES WLK
Hinckley
Stadium
ULLSWATER
AVE
ST NICOLAS PARK DR
KESWICK CL
BUTTERMERE AVE
LOWESWATER CL
KENDAL CL
KIRKSTONE WLK
EASEDALE CL
BURNHAM RISE
RYDAL AVE
LANGDALE DR
WINDERMERE AVE
SKELWITH RISE
Calendar
Grove
THE LONG SHOOT
PO
Padge Hall
Farm
Poplars
Farm
A47 HINCKLEY RD
A4254
PORTREATH DR
LISKEARD CL
CAMBORNE DR
1 SENNEN CL
2 ST BURYAN CL
Horeston
Grange
Sh Ctr
FALMOUTH CL
TINTAGEL WAY
PENZANCE WAY
ST AUSTELL CL
HELSTON CL
CAMBORNE DR
PENRYN CL
HAYLE CL
REDRUTH CL
Hydes Pastures
LE10
Sketchley Brook
Hydes
Pastures
Moxon's
Farm
Harrow Brook
HYDES LA
Hemdale
Bsns Pk
HEMDALE
Eastboro
Fields
EASTBORO WAY
NUNEATON
CV11
Wheatcroft
Farm
Stretton Fields
Farm
Crem
River Anker
Paul's
Ford
ALBRIGHTON WLK
KEBSEN WAY
LEYBURN CL
HOLLY WLK
WOODHALL CL
GRASSINGTON DR
MALHAM CL
AYSGARTH CL
STAINFORTH CL
1 MARCHFONT CL
2 RAINSBROOK DR
ARNCLIFFE CL
INGLETON CL
Hill
Farm
OBERON CL
JULIET CL
HAMLET CL
SHAKESPEARE DR
CROWHILL RD
PICKFORD CL
ALDERBROOKE DR
ASTER CL
WILLOWFIELDS RD
VERONA CL
FALSTAFF CL
KLEVEDON CL
WENTWORTH DR
HATHAWAY DR
SUNNINGDALE CL
MIDDELBURG CL
ARDEN RD
PORTIA CL
BIRKDALE CL
LUTTERWORTH RD
B4114
GOLF DR
FAIRWAY
MEADOWSIDE
ST ANDREWS DR
GREENSIDE CL
GLENEAGLES CL
MOORCROFT CL
HILL FARM AVE
FOXHILLS CL
Fox Covert
Cottage
Sinney
Fields
Gorse Cottage
Farm
Attleborough
Gorse
Ashby-de-la-Zouch Canal

29
40

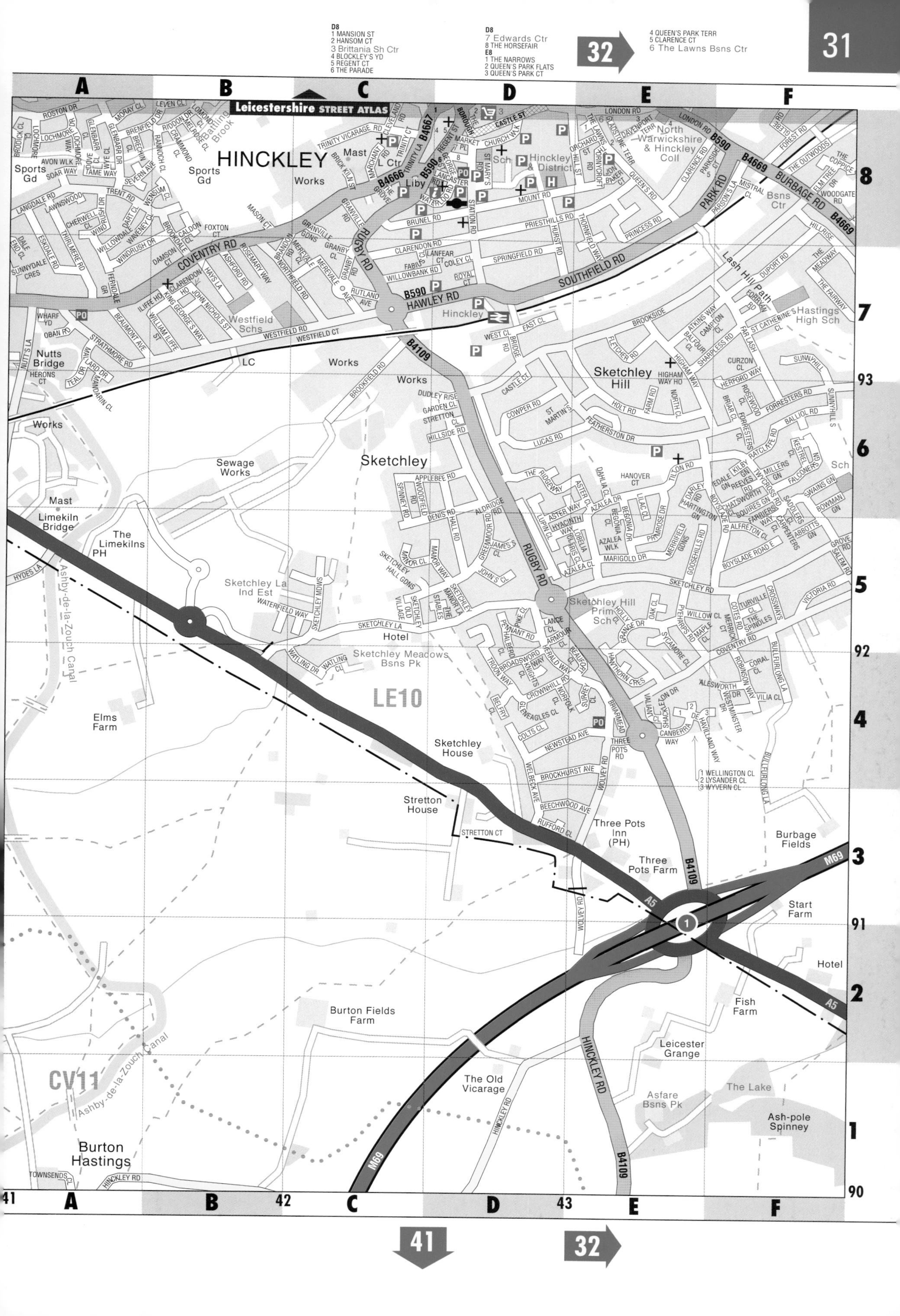
D8
1 MANSION ST
2 HANSOM CT
3 Brittania Sh Ctr
4 BLOCKLEY'S YD
5 REGENT CT
6 THE PARADE
D8
7 Edwards Ctr
8 THE HORSEFAIR
E8
1 THE NARROWS
2 QUEEN'S PARK FLATS
3 QUEEN'S PARK CT
32
4 QUEEN'S PARK TERR
5 CLARENCE CT
6 The Lawns Bsns Ctr
Leicestershire STREET ATLAS
HINCKLEY
Sports Gd
Sports Gd
Works
Mast
L Ctr
Liby
Sch
Hinckley & District
North Warwickshire & Hinckley Coll
Bsns Ctr
Westfield Schs
Hinckley
Hastings High Sch
Nutts Bridge
LC
Works
Works
Works
Sketchley Hill
Sewage Works
Sketchley
Sch
Mast
Limekiln Bridge
The Limekilns PH
Sketchley La Ind Est
Hotel
Sketchley Meadows Bsns Pk
Sketchley Hill Prim Sch
LE10
Elms Farm
Sketchley House
Stretton House
Three Pots Inn (PH)
Three Pots Farm
Burbage Fields
Start Farm
Hotel
Fish Farm
Burton Fields Farm
Leicester Grange
The Old Vicarage
The Lake
Asfare Bsns Pk
Ash-pole Spinney
CV11
Burton Hastings
Ashby-de-la-Zouch Canal
COVENTRY RD
HAWLEY RD
SOUTHFIELD RD
RUGBY RD
BURBAGE RD
PARK RD
LONDON RD
WESTFIELD RD
HINCKLEY RD
B590
B4666
B4667
B4669
B4109
A5
M69
1 WELLINGTON CL
2 LYSANDER CL
3 WYVERN CL
A
B
C
D
E
F
8
7
93
6
5
92
4
3
91
2
1
90
41
42
43
41
32

31

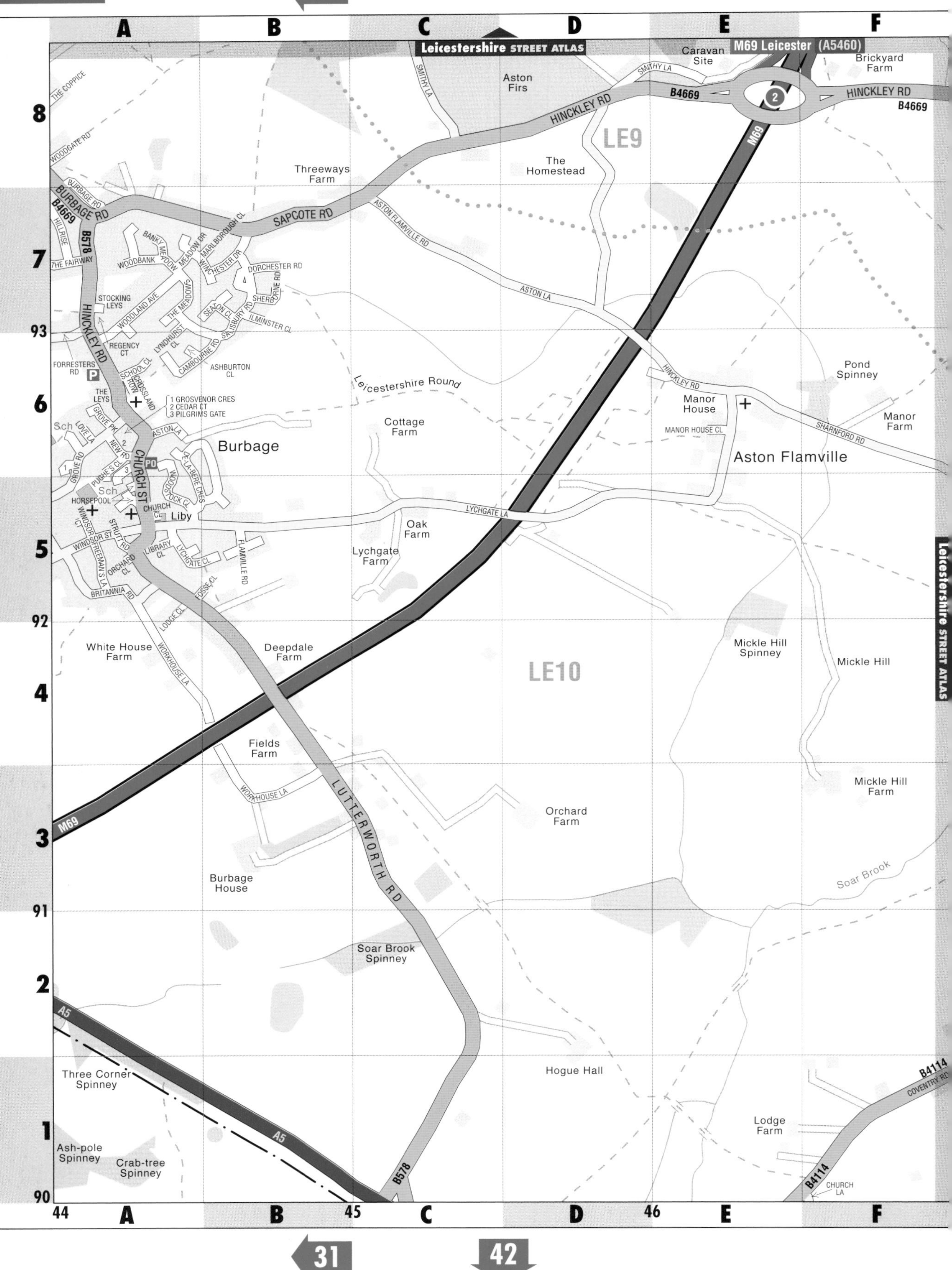

Leicestershire STREET ATLAS
M69 Leicester (A5460)
Caravan Site
Brickyard Farm
Aston Firs
SMITHY LA
HINCKLEY RD
B4669
LE9
The Homestead
Threeways Farm
SAPCOTE RD
BURBAGE RD
ASTON FLAMVILLE RD
ASTON LA
M69
THE COPPICE
WOODGATE RD
HILLRISE
THE FAIRWAY
B578
WOODBANK
BANKY MEADOW
MEADOW DR
MARLBOROUGH CL
WINCHESTER DR
DORCHESTER RD
SHERBORNE RD
STOCKING LEYS
WOODLAND AVE
THE MEADOWS
SEATON CL
SALISBURY RD
ILMINSTER CL
REGENCY CT
LYNDHURST CL
CAMBOURNE RD
ASHBURTON CL
FORRESTERS RD
SCHOOL CL
CROSSLAND ROW
THE LEYS
1 GROSVENOR CRES
2 CEDAR CT
3 PILGRIMS GATE
GROVE PK
LOVE LA
ASTON LA
Sch
Burbage
NEW RD
CHURCH ST
PO
GROVE RD
PUGHE'S CL
Sch
HORSEPOOL
CHURCH CL
Liby
DE-LA-BERE CRES
WINDSOR CT
WINDSOR ST
STRUTT RD
FREEMAN'S LA
ORCHARD CL
LIBRARY CL
LYCHGATE CL
FLAMVILLE RD
BRITANNIA RD
FOSSE CL
LODGE CL
WORKHOUSE LA
Leicestershire Round
Cottage Farm
Oak Farm
Lychgate Farm
LYCHGATE LA
Pond Spinney
HINCKLEY RD
Manor House
MANOR HOUSE CL
SHARNFORD RD
Manor Farm
Aston Flamville
White House Farm
Deepdale Farm
LE10
Mickle Hill Spinney
Mickle Hill
Fields Farm
WORKHOUSE LA
LUTTERWORTH RD
Mickle Hill Farm
Orchard Farm
Burbage House
Soar Brook
Soar Brook Spinney
A5
Three Corner Spinney
Hogue Hall
B4114
COVENTRY RD
Lodge Farm
Ash-pole Spinney
Crab-tree Spinney
CHURCH LA
A B C D E F
8 7 6 5 4 3 2 1
93 92 91 90
44 45 46

31

42

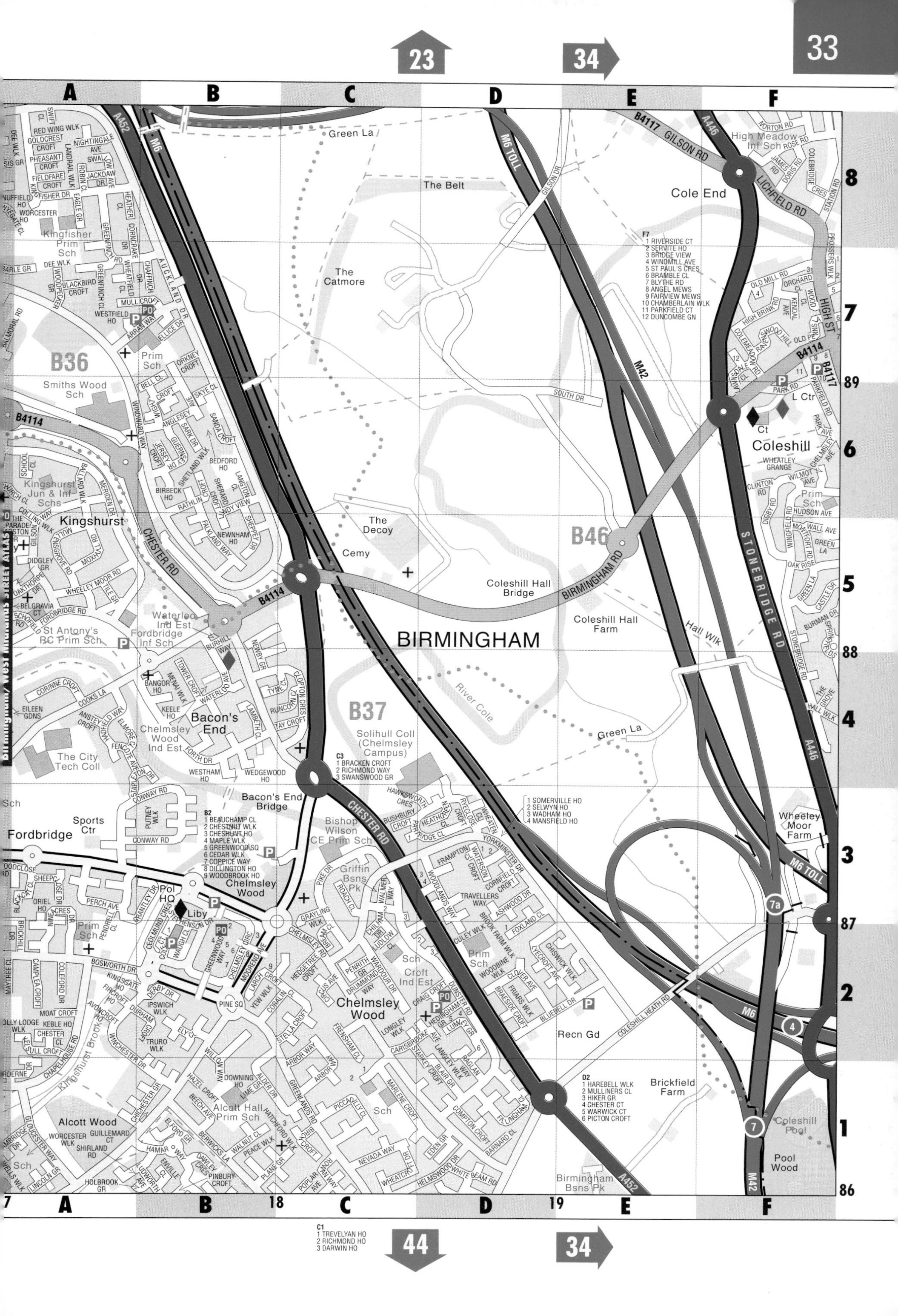
33
23
34
44
34
A
B
C
D
E
F
8
7
89
6
5
88
4
3
87
2
1
86
18
19
BIRMINGHAM
B36
B37
B46
Green La
The Belt
The Catmore
The Decoy
Cemy
Coleshill Hall Bridge
Coleshill Hall Farm
BIRMINGHAM RD
River Cole
Hall Wlk
Cole End
Coleshill
High Meadow Inf Sch
GILSON RD
LICHFIELD RD
STONEBRIDGE RD
HIGH ST
PARK RD
L Ctr
Ct
Prim Sch
Wheeley Moor Farm
Brickfield Farm
Coleshill Pool
Pool Wood
Recn Gd
COLESHILL HEATH RD
Birmingham Bsns Pk
Kingfisher Prim Sch
Smiths Wood Sch
Kingshurst Jun & Inf Schs
Kingshurst
CHESTER RD
Waterloo Ind Est
St Antony's RC Prim Sch
Fordbridge Inf Sch
Bacon's End
Bacon's End Bridge
Chelmsley Wood Ind Est
The City Tech Coll
Fordbridge
Sports Ctr
Pol HQ
Liby
Chelmsley Wood
Solihull Coll (Chelmsley Campus)
Bishop Wilson CE Prim Sch
Griffin Bsns Pk
Croft Ind Est
Alcott Hall Prim Sch
Alcott Wood
Kingshurst Brook
M6
M6 TOLL
M42
A452
A446
B4114
B4117
F7
1 RIVERSIDE CT
2 SERVITE HO
3 BRIDGE VIEW
4 WINDMILL AVE
5 ST PAUL'S CRES
6 BRAMBLE CL
7 BLYTHE RD
8 ANGEL MEWS
9 FAIRVIEW MEWS
10 CHAMBERLAIN WLK
11 PARKFIELD CT
12 DUNCOMBE GN
C3
1 BRACKEN CROFT
2 RICHMOND WAY
3 SWANSWOOD GR
1 SOMERVILLE HO
2 SELWYN HO
3 WADHAM HO
4 MANSFIELD HO
B2
1 BEAUCHAMP CL
2 CHESTNUT WLK
3 CHESHUNT HO
4 MAPLE WLK
5 GREENWOOD SQ
6 CEDAR WLK
7 COPPICE WAY
8 DILLINGTON HO
9 WOODBROOK HO
D2
1 HAREBELL WLK
2 MULLINERS CL
3 HIKER GR
4 CHESTER CT
5 WARWICK CT
6 PICTON CROFT
C1
1 TREVELYAN HO
2 RICHMOND HO
3 DARWIN HO

33
24
A
B
C
D
E
F
8
7
89
6
5
88
4
3
87
2
1
86
20
21
22
B4114
Blyth Bridge
River Cole
BLYTHE RD
CHESTNUT GR
1 MANSARD CT
2 BRAMBLE CL
3 ST PAUL'S CRES
4 BLYTHE CT
B4114
MORNINGTON CT
CHURCH HILL
ST PHILIP'S CT
Cemy
B4117
HIGH ST
SUMNER RD
COLEHAVEN
TH
PARKFIELD RD
WYNDSHIELS
THE CLOSE
WALKERS WAY
THE DRIVE
The Cottage
A6
1 DE MONTFORT MEWS
MAXSTOKE LA
WINGFIELD RD
GREEN LA
Father Hudson's Society
MOTT'S WAY
PRIORY CL
Coleshill
1 CASTLE DR
2 FERNDALE MEWS
3 FERNDALE CT
FERNDALE RD
BURMAN DR
SPRING FIELDS
COVENTRY RD
BRENDAN CL
SOUTH FIELDS CL
POUND LA
MAXSTOKE CT
Southfields Farm
HALL WLK
SHERBORNE CL
Blythe Sch
KEEPERS CL
The Coleshill Sch
St Edward's RC Prim Sch
Mast
Cooper's Farm
HAWKESWELL LA
Packington Lane Farm
M6 TOLL
A446
PACKINGTON LA
Hawkeswell Farm
Pool Farm
STONEBRIDGE RD
M6
The Bogs
Bannerley Pool
A446
Round Wood
Old Park Plantation
Birch Wood
Castle Farm
River Blythe
Maxstoke Mill (disused)
Mill Farm
Duke Bridge
Duke End
COLESHILL RD
B46
Duke End Farm
ARNOLDS LA
Maxstoke Farm
The Dairy Farm
Dairy Farm Cottages
M6 TOLL
CV7
Moat House Farm
M6
The Butt Ground
CASTLE LA
Maxstoke Castle
CH
Pooltail Plantation
33
45

25
36
A
B
C
D
E
F
Withy Wood
Mast
Hill Farm
CV7
8
Dew Mill Cottage
The Metlins
The Elms
Wagstaff Farm
Shawberry Farm
Metlins Rough
SHAWBURY LA
Hillside
7
Dandy's Farm
SHAWBURY COTTS
Manrod Rough
Dove House
89
SHAWBURY VILLAGE
Dumble Wood
Dumble Farm
Mordic's Wood
6
Mawdykes Farm
Heart of England Way
Shawbury Wood
CASTLE LA
Brock Hall Farm
B46
Hill Plantation
Packsaddle Wood
5
Maxstoke School Farm
Parsons Wood
COLESHILL RD
Hill Farm
Heach Wood
88
Packsaddle
Maxstoke Hall Farm
FILLONGLEY RD
Butler's Wood
4
Collier's Oak Farm
BROAD LA
NEW END RD
High House
Kimberley's Grove
BENTLEY LA
Bentley's Farm
Cooper's Grove
3
HARDINGWOOD LA
ARNOLDS LA
87
Water Wood
CHURCH LA
Broadmoor Wood
Wood Corner Farm
Priory Farm
Maxstoke
CV7
2
Priory (rems of)
Church End Farm
Mast
Blabers Hall Farm
PACKINGTON LA
1
Priory Wood
Quarry Wood
CV7
86
23
A
B
24
C
D
25
E
F
46
36

35
26

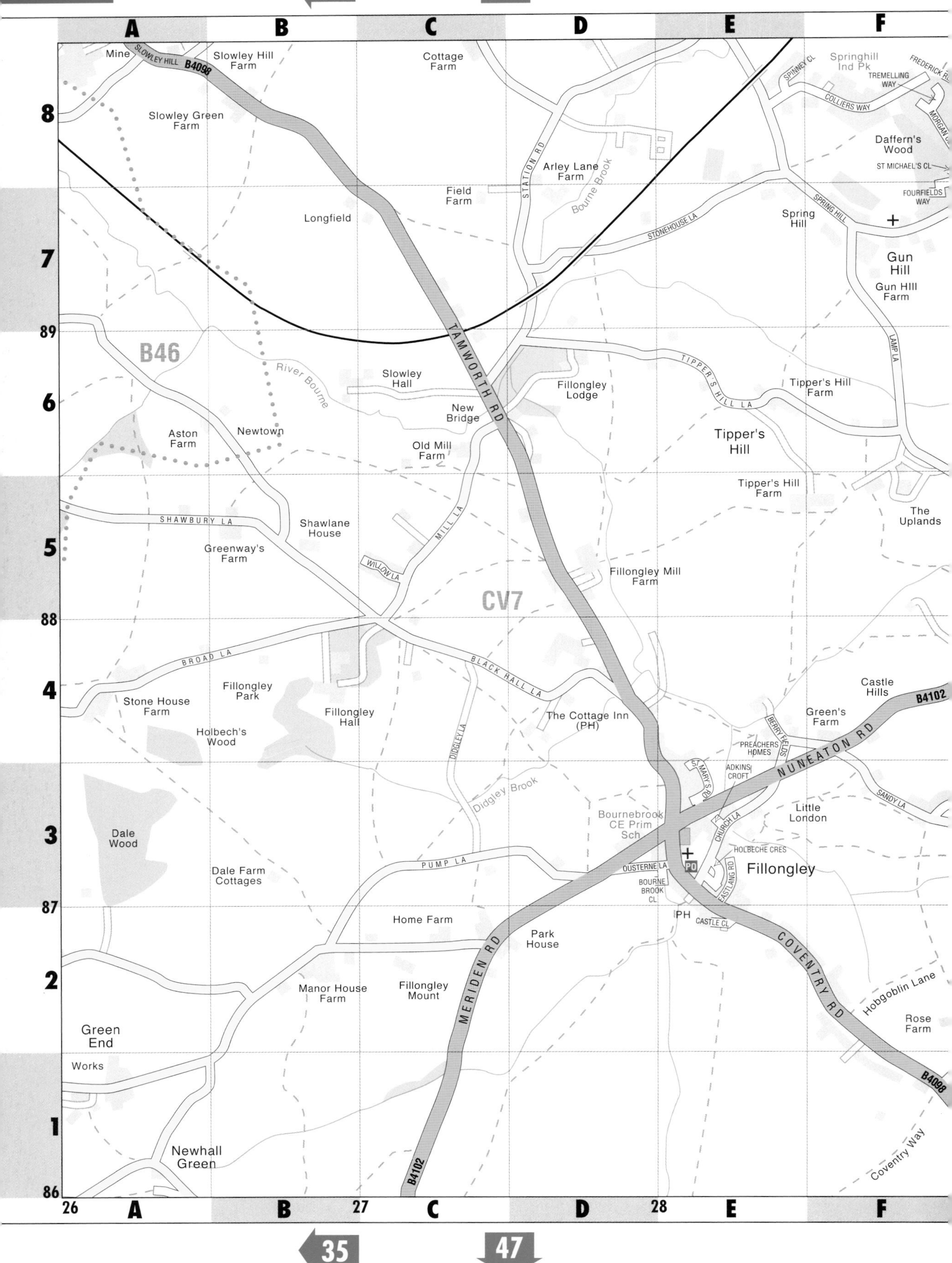
A
B
C
D
E
F
Mine
SLOWLEY HILL
B4098
Slowley Hill Farm
Cottage Farm
SPINNEY CL
Springhill Ind Pk
FREDERICK RD
TREMELLING WAY
COLLIERS WAY
MORGAN CL
8
Slowley Green Farm
Daffern's Wood
Arley Lane Farm
STATION RD
Bourne Brook
ST MICHAEL'S CL
Field Farm
FOURFIELDS WAY
Longfield
STONEHOUSE LA
SPRING HILL
Spring Hill
7
Gun Hill
Gun Hill Farm
89
B46
LAMP LA
River Bourne
Slowley Hall
TIPPER'S HILL LA
Fillongley Lodge
Tipper's Hill Farm
6
TAMWORTH RD
New Bridge
Aston Farm
Newtown
Old Mill Farm
Tipper's Hill
Tipper's Hill Farm
The Uplands
SHAWBURY LA
Shawlane House
MILL LA
5
Greenway's Farm
WILLOW LA
Fillongley Mill Farm
CV7
88
BROAD LA
BLACK HALL LA
Castle Hills
4
Fillongley Park
Stone House Farm
Fillongley Hall
The Cottage Inn (PH)
B4102
Green's Farm
Holbech's Wood
BERRY FIELDS
PREACHERS HOMES
NUNEATON RD
DIDGLEY LA
ST MARY'S RD
ADKINS CROFT
Didgley Brook
SANDY LA
Little London
Bournebrook CE Prim Sch
CHURCH LA
3
Dale Wood
HOLBECHE CRES
PUMP LA
Fillongley
OUSTERNE LA
PO
EASTLANG RD
Dale Farm Cottages
BOURNE BROOK CL
87
PH
CASTLE CL
Home Farm
Park House
COVENTRY RD
MERIDEN RD
2
Manor House Farm
Fillongley Mount
Hobgoblin Lane
Rose Farm
Green End
Works
B4098
1
Coventry Way
Newhall Green
B4102
86
26
27
28

35
47

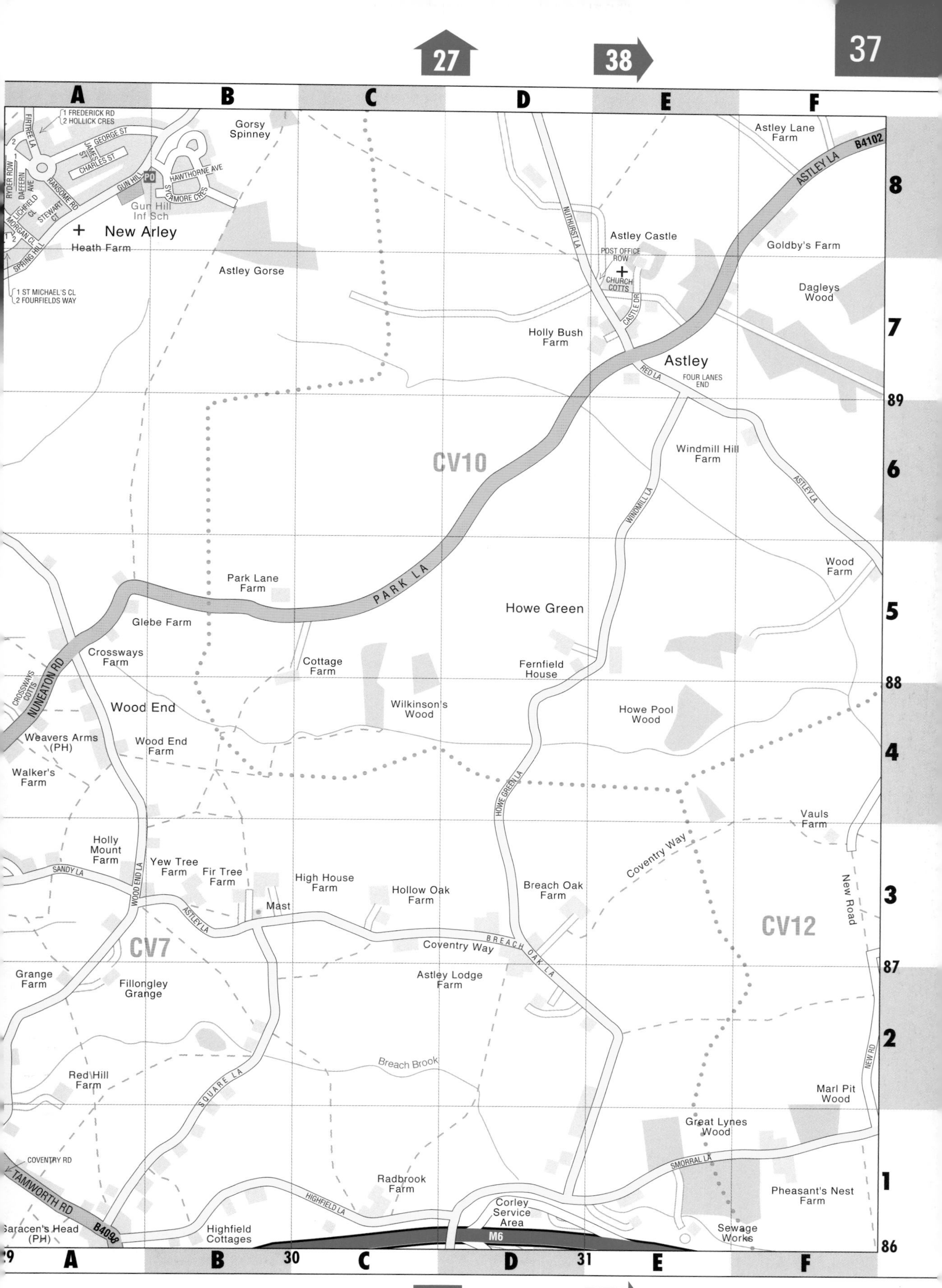
27
38
A
B
C
D
E
F
1 FREDERICK RD
2 HOLLICK CRES
FIRTREE LA
GEORGE ST
JAMES ST
CHARLES ST
RYDER ROW
DAFFERN AVE
LICHFIELD CL
RANSOME RD
STEWART CT
MORGAN CL
SPRING HILL
GUN HILL
PO
HAWTHORNE AVE
SYCAMORE CRES
Gun Hill Inf Sch
New Arley
Heath Farm
1 ST MICHAEL'S CL
2 FOURFIELDS WAY
Gorsy Spinney
Astley Gorse
Astley Lane Farm
B4102
ASTLEY LA
NUTHURST LA
Astley Castle
POST OFFICE ROW
CHURCH COTTS
CASTLE DR
Goldby's Farm
Dagleys Wood
Holly Bush Farm
Astley
RED LA
FOUR LANES END
Windmill Hill Farm
CV10
WINDMILL LA
ASTLEY LA
Wood Farm
Park Lane Farm
PARK LA
Howe Green
Glebe Farm
Crossways Farm
Cottage Farm
Fernfield House
CROSSWAYS COTTS
NUNEATON RD
Wood End
Wilkinson's Wood
Howe Pool Wood
Weavers Arms (PH)
Wood End Farm
Walker's Farm
HOWE GREEN LA
Vauls Farm
Coventry Way
Holly Mount Farm
SANDY LA
WOOD END LA
Yew Tree Farm
Fir Tree Farm
High House Farm
Hollow Oak Farm
Breach Oak Farm
New Road
Mast
ASTLEY LA
CV12
CV7
Coventry Way
BREACH OAK LA
Grange Farm
Fillongley Grange
Astley Lodge Farm
Breach Brook
NEW RD
Red Hill Farm
SQUARE LA
Marl Pit Wood
Great Lynes Wood
COVENTRY RD
SMORRAL LA
TAMWORTH RD
Radbrook Farm
Pheasant's Nest Farm
HIGHFIELD LA
Corley Service Area
Saracen's Head (PH)
B4098
Highfield Cottages
M6
Sewage Works
8
7
89
6
5
88
4
3
87
2
1
86
29
30
31

37
28

D2
1 WILDEY RD
2 HIMLEY RD
3 CAMPION WAY
4 DAFFODIL DRIVE
5 LARKSPUR GR
6 SPEEDWELL CL

F2
1 SYDNEY CT
2 CANBERRA CT
3 MELBOURNE CT
4 QUEENSLAND GDNS

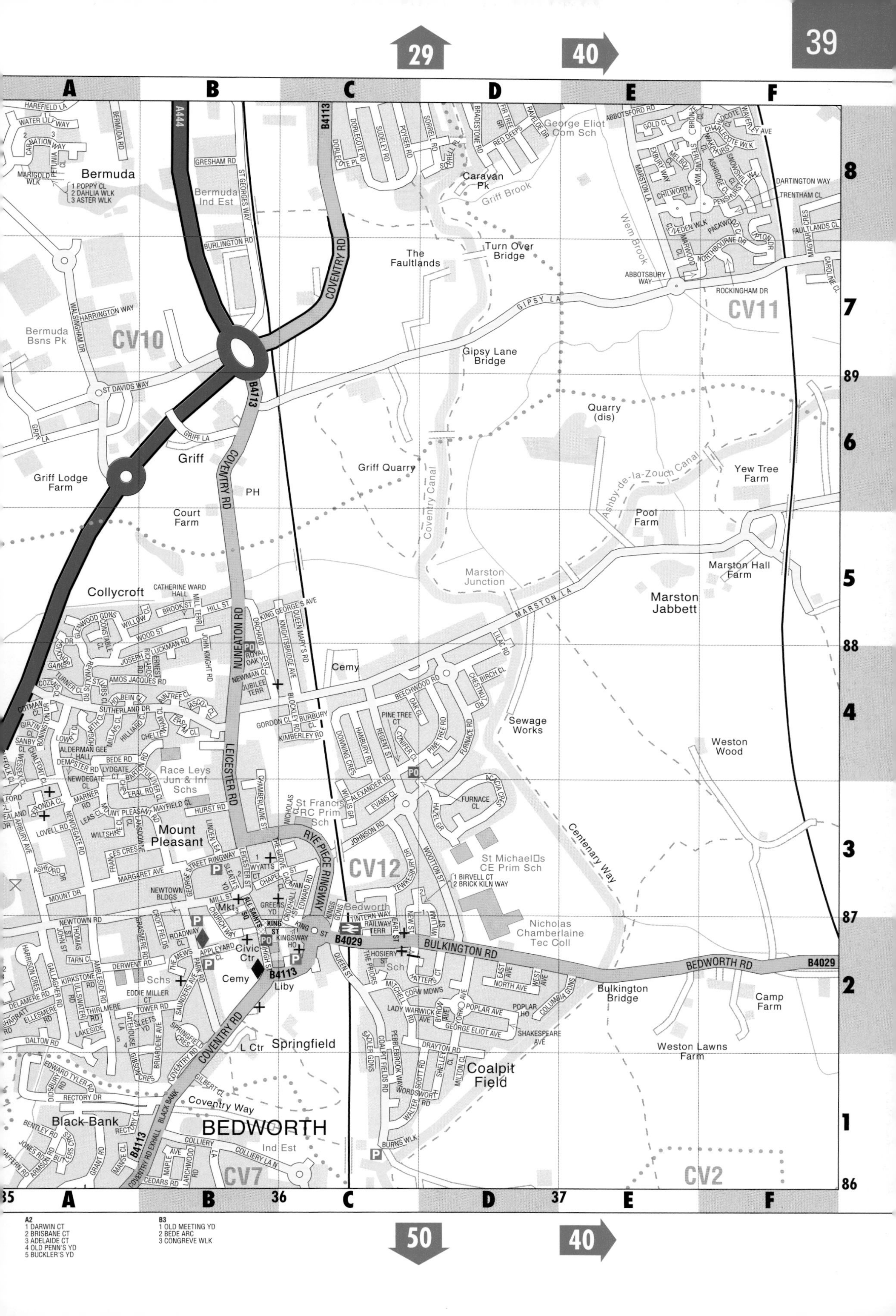

39
29
40
50
40
A
B
C
D
E
F
8
7
6
5
4
3
2
1
89
88
87
86
35
36
37
A444
B4113
B4029
Bermuda
Bermuda Ind Est
Bermuda Bsns Pk
CV10
CV11
CV12
CV7
CV2
Caravan Pk
Griff Brook
George Eliot Com Sch
The Faultlands
Turn Over Bridge
Wem Brook
GIPSY LA
Gipsy Lane Bridge
Quarry (dis)
Griff
Griff Lodge Farm
Griff Quarry
PH
Court Farm
Coventry Canal
Ashby-de-la-Zouch Canal
Yew Tree Farm
Pool Farm
Marston Junction
Marston Hall Farm
Marston Jabbett
Collycroft
CATHERINE WARD HALL
MARSTON LA
Cemy
Sewage Works
Weston Wood
Race Leys Jun & Inf Schs
St Francis RC Prim Sch
Mount Pleasant
St Michael's CE Prim Sch
Centenary Way
RYE PIECE RINGWAY
NUNEATON RD
LEICESTER RD
COVENTRY RD
Bedworth
Mkt
Civic Ctr
Liby
Sch
Schs
Nicholas Chamberlaine Tec Coll
BULKINGTON RD
BEDWORTH RD
Bulkington Bridge
Camp Farm
Weston Lawns Farm
Springfield
L Ctr
Coalpit Field
Coventry Way
Black Bank
BEDWORTH
Ind Est
A2
1 DARWIN CT
2 BRISBANE CT
3 ADELAIDE CT
4 OLD PENN'S YD
5 BUCKLER'S YD
B3
1 OLD MEETING YD
2 BEDE ARC
3 CONGREVE WLK

39
30
A
B
C
D
E
F
8
7
89
6
5
88
4
3
87
2
1
86
38
39
40
51
MIDDELBURG CL
B4114
GOLF DR
B4112
FAIRWAY
GREENWAY
MEADOWSIDE
EAGLE CL
FOXHILLS CL
MUIRFIELDS CL
CH
MOORPARK CL
HOLLINWELL CL
CARNOUSTIE CL
TURNBERRY DR
THORNHILL DR
DORCAS CL
CAVENDISH WLK
SLADE CL
Burton Mill
MILL LA
Whitestone Inf Sch
STONEWELL CRES
WHITESTONE RD
LUTTERWORTH RD
GIPSY LA
BULKINGTON LA
Whitestone
WALTON CL
BRITTEN CL
COPSEWOOD AVE
HOARESTONE AVE
ROSS WAY
CHETWYND DR
Chetwynd Jun Sch
Gorse Farm
Bramcote
Bramcote Wharf
BURTON LA
B4114
MILL FARM PK
Ashby-de-la-Zouch Canal
CV11
PH
Marston House
MARSTON LA
AVON CL
WILLIAM BEESLEY CRES
ADMIRALS WAY
ALDERNEY CL
HEREFORD RD
BAZZARD RD
Bramcote
WOOLWICH RD
ALMA CT
PO
Gamecock Barracks
Bramcote Fields Farm
Eastland Fields Farm
SILVER TREES DR
THE BIRCHES
NUNEATON RD
Weston Hill Farm
CLAREMONT CL
CV12
Weston Hall (Hotel)
WESTON HALL STABLES
MILL LA
WESTON LA
Weston in Arden
Arden Forest Inf Sch
THE PADDOCKS
FARNDON CL
AMELIA CL
CONISTON CL
CARLTON CL
KINGSLEY CRES
BRAMPTON WAY
CLEVELAND RD
GLENDON GDNS
STAPLES CL
ARUNDEL RD
FINDON CL
LANCING RD
AMBERLEY AVE
Bramcote Mains
M69
B4109
SEVERN RD
THAMES CL
CLYDE RD
TRENT RD
MERSEY RD
RIBBLE CL
TAMAR RD
CALDER CL
WYE CL
LARKIN CL
HEMSWORTH DR
BARBRIDGE RD
BARBRIDGE CL
St James CE Jun Sch
Ryton
FIRLEIGH DR
LONG ST
MILNER CL
BRAMCOTE CL
BEDWORTH RD
THE CROFT
PHILLIP DOCKER CT
ST JAMES GDNS
Liby
SCHOOL RD
RUGBY RD
ARDEN RD
OAKHAM CRES
WOLVEY RD
B4109
BENN RD
CAMPLING CL
DINGLEY RD
LEYLAND RD
BEDWORTH CL
CHURCH ST
CHEQUER ST
THE SANDPITS
LEICESTER ST
NEW ST
B4029
WINTERTON RD
ELM TREE RD
BREWER RD
EUSTACE RD
MORLAND CL
The Elms
WITHYBROOK RD
Sewage Works
VILLA CL
VILLA CRES
WARWICK GN
NEALE CL
BARNACLE LA
LEONARD PARKINS HO
Bulkington
SHILTON LA
B4029
Arbury Bungalow Farm
B4112
COVENTRY RD
Arbury House Farm
Well Green Farm
Bulkington Fields Farm

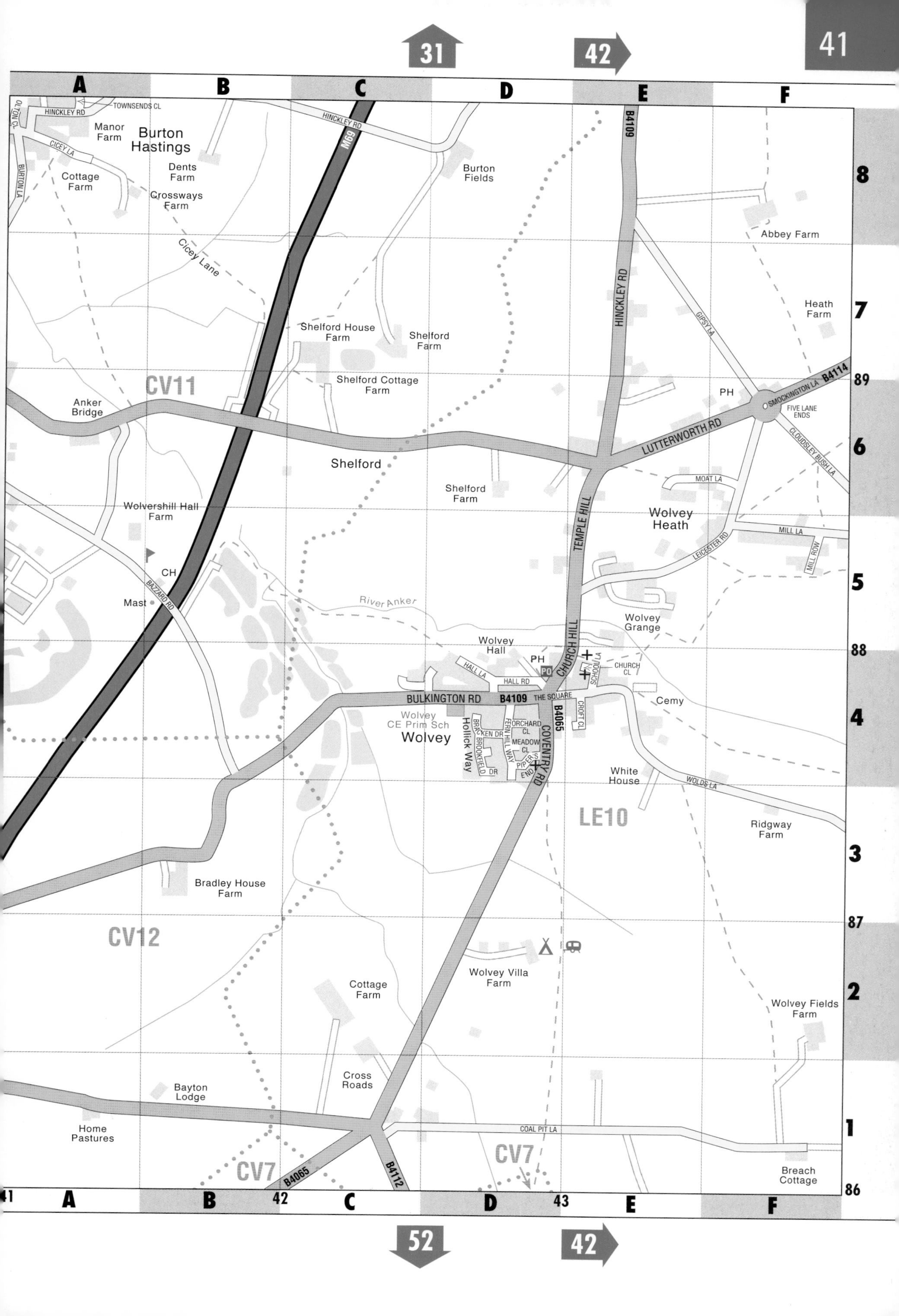
31
42
A
B
C
D
E
F
HINCKLEY RD
TOWNSENDS CL
OLTON CL
Manor Farm
Burton Hastings
CICEY LA
BURTON LA
Cottage Farm
Dents Farm
Crossways Farm
M69
HINCKLEY RD
Burton Fields
B4109
8
Abbey Farm
Cicey Lane
HINCKLEY RD
7
Heath Farm
GIPSY LA
Shelford House Farm
Shelford Farm
Shelford Cottage Farm
B4114
89
CV11
PH
SMOCKINGTON LA
FIVE LANE ENDS
Anker Bridge
LUTTERWORTH RD
CLOUDSLEY BUSH LA
6
Shelford
Shelford Farm
MOAT LA
TEMPLE HILL
Wolversill Hall Farm
Wolvey Heath
MILL LA
LEICESTER RD
MILL ROW
CH
5
Mast
BAZZARD RD
River Anker
Wolvey Grange
CHURCH HILL
Wolvey Hall
88
PH
PO
HALL LA
SCHOOL LA
CHURCH CL
HALL RD
BULKINGTON RD
B4109
THE SQUARE
Cemy
B4065
Wolvey CE Prim Sch
CROFT CL
4
Wolvey
Hollick Way
BRACKEN DR
ORCHARD CL
FERN HILL WAY
MEADOW CL
BROOKFIELD DR
PIPER'S END
COVENTRY RD
White House
WOLDS LA
LE10
Ridgway Farm
3
Bradley House Farm
87
CV12
Wolvey Villa Farm
2
Cottage Farm
Wolvey Fields Farm
Cross Roads
Bayton Lodge
1
Home Pastures
COAL PIT LA
CV7
CV7
B4065
B4112
Breach Cottage
86
41
A
B
42
C
D
43
E
F
52
42

41
32

A B C D E F

8 7 89 6 5 88 4 3 87 2 1 86

A5
Red Lion Farm
Smockington
Watling Street Farm
B4114
Pear Tree Farm
COVENTRY RD
THE GREEN
CHURCH LA
Wigston Parva
Smockington House
SMOCKINGTON LA
Smockington Hollow Farm
Copston Spinney
Copston Farm
The Hollies Farm
Orchard Farm
CLOUDESLEY BUSH LA
MILL LA
GREEN LA
Copston Magna
COPSTON LA
LE17
LE10
Copston Fields Farm
Wolvey Lodge Farm
MERE LA
FOSSE WAY
WOLDS LA
Grove Farm
CV23
PENN LA
Cloudesley Bush
Wolvey Fields
COAL PIT LA
MONKS KIRBY LA
B4455
CV7

44 A B 45 C D 46 E F

41
53

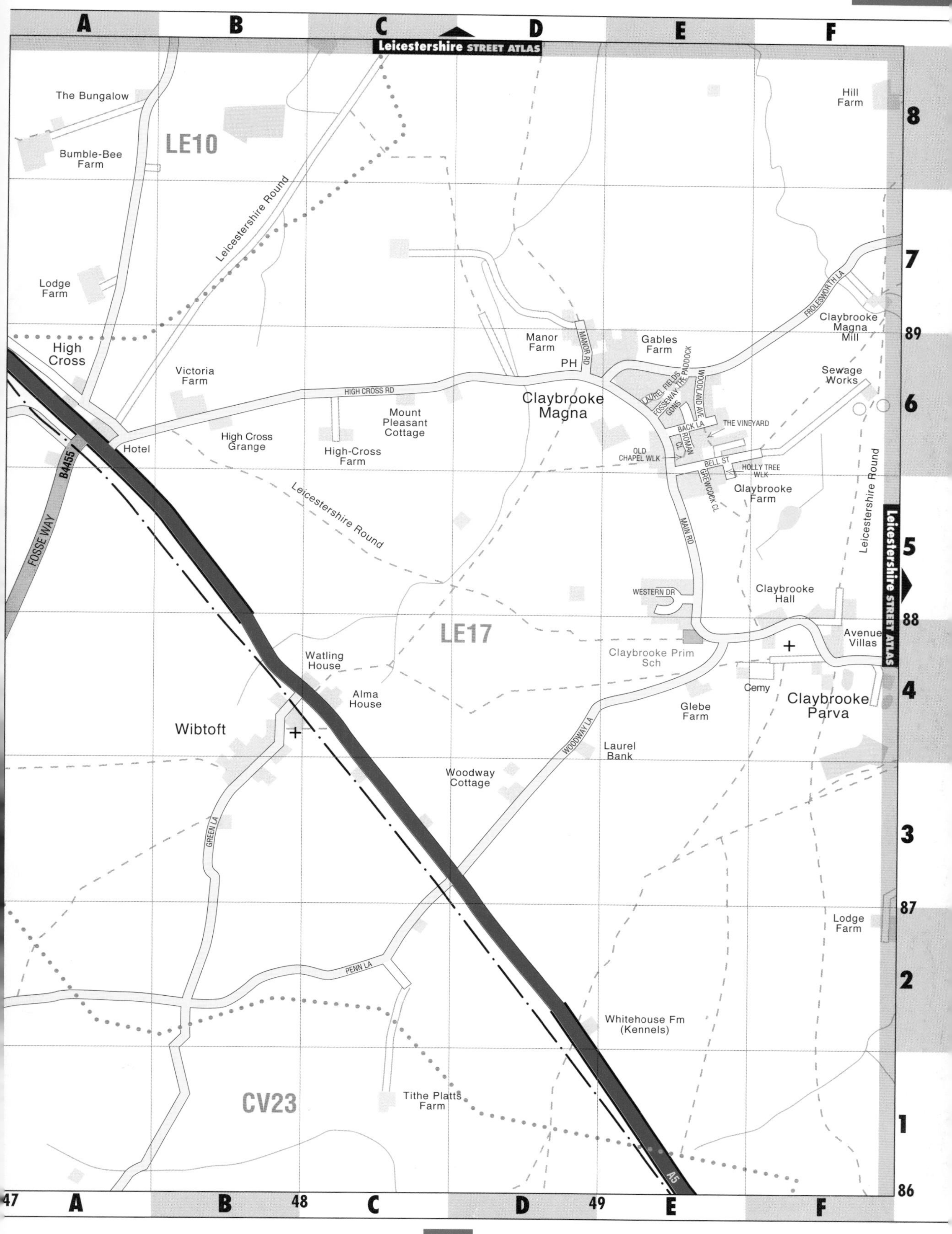
Leicestershire STREET ATLAS
The Bungalow
Bumble-Bee Farm
LE10
Leicestershire Round
Lodge Farm
High Cross
Victoria Farm
Hotel
High Cross Grange
B4455
FOSSE WAY
HIGH CROSS RD
Mount Pleasant Cottage
High-Cross Farm
Manor Farm
MANOR RD
PH
Gables Farm
Claybrooke Magna
LAUREL FIELDS
FOSSEWAY GDNS
THE PADDOCK
WOODLAND AVE
BACK LA
ROMAN CL
THE VINEYARD
OLD CHAPEL WLK
BELL ST
HOLLY TREE WLK
GREWCOCK CL
Claybrooke Farm
FROLESWORTH LA
Claybrooke Magna Mill
Sewage Works
Hill Farm
MAIN RD
WESTERN DR
Claybrooke Hall
LE17
Claybrooke Prim Sch
Avenue Villas
Cemy
Claybrooke Parva
Glebe Farm
Watling House
Alma House
Wibtoft
WOODWAY LA
Laurel Bank
Woodway Cottage
GREEN LA
Lodge Farm
PENN LA
Whitehouse Fm (Kennels)
Tithe Platts Farm
CV23
A5

Marston Green
Coleshill Heath
Sports Ctr
Heath Farm
Birmingham Bsns Pk
Pinewood Bsns Pk
Marston Green Jun & Inf Schs
Liby
B37
School Rough
Cemy
Century Pk
Elmdon Trad Est
Bickenhill Plantations
Hotel
B46
B40
National Exhibition Ctr (The NEC)
Birmingham International
Pendigo Lake
Birmingham International Airport
Low Brook
B26
Mast
Hotels
Depot
CH
Dunston Farm
The Clock Inn (PH)
Trinity Pk
Wyckhams Close
B92
The Jungle
Castle Hills
Grange Farm
Bickenhill
COVENTRY RD
A45
M42
A452
CHESTER RD
B4438
BICKENHILL PARKWAY
BICKENHILL LA
CATHERINE DE BARNES LA
COLESHILL RD
COLESHILL HEATH RD
BLACKFIRS LA
STARLEY WAY
AIRPORT WAY
PERIMETER RD
PENDIGO WAY
EASTWAY
NORTHWAY
SOUTH WAY
AMBASSADOR RD 1
VANGUARD RD 2
STATION LINK RD 3
1 ROTHERBY GR
2 WOLVERTON RD
1 NEWINGTON RD
2 FULWELL MEWS
1 EXETER DR
2 WELLS WLK
Birmingham/West Midlands STREET ATLAS
A45 Birmingham

34

46

A
B
C
D
E
F
The Bogs Farm
B37
Bannerley Rough
Depot
Todd's Rough
Mulliner's Rough
M6
A446
8
Nursery Farm
Broadwater
7
Ford
SCHOOL LA
Golf & Country Club
Nursery
STONEBRIDGE RD
B46
Brook Farm
Foxes Den
85
Refuse Tip
Fish Breeding Farm
The Ash Beds
PACKINGTON LA
6
DENBIGH CNR
Little Packington
Butler's Moors
Packington Park
Park Meadow
A446
FISHPOOL LA
Church Farm
Denbigh Spinney
River Blythe
Deer Park
5
Garden Spinney
CHESTER RD
84
CV7
Park Farm
Siding Wood
Packington Hall
MIDDLE BICKENHILL LA
Hall Pool
4
Great Pool
The Wilderness
Mill Shrubbery
Middle Bickenhill
Beech Lodge
B92
The Mill Farm
Little Dayhouse Wood
3
PH
Dials Pool
EAST WAY
COVENTRY RD
COVENTRY RD
BIRMINGHAM RD
Stonebridge
83
Works
The National Motorcycle Mus
A45
Geary's Heath
B4102
Pasture Farm
2
Mills Gorse
Diddington Hill
KENILWORTH RD
DIDDINGTON LA
Diddington Hall
P
CH
Shadow Brook
SOMERS RD
OLD STATION RD
1
The Somers
Mouldings Green Farm
A452
Molands Bridge
THE GROVE
B4102
82
20
21
22

57
46

45
35

A
B
C
D
E
F
M6
B46
PACKINGTON LA
Daniels Wood
Green End Farm
Barrat's Farm
8
Rutters Hall
Hermitage Farm
Parsonage Farm
Burnt Iron Leys Wood
Flints Wood
Kinwalsey
7
New Plantation
Kinwalsey Farm
85
Warren Farm
Outwoods Farm
6
Old Hall
KINWALSEY LA
Boultbee's Wood
Intake Coppice
Spring Pools
Close Wood
Mast
Outwoods
Butler's End
5
B4102
84
Church Wood
Wood End Farm
High Ash Farm
Church Wood
Keatley's Pool
CV7
4
The Decoy
Sparrow's Grove
Chantry Wood
SHAFT LA
Grovenear Farm
The Dairy Farm
White Stitch
Lodge Green Farm
Harding's Wood
Whitestitch Farm
LODGE GREEN LA N
Lodge Green
3
SHEPHEARDS LA
MAXSTOKE LA
Whitestitch House
FILLONGLEY RD
Grange Farm
WHITESTITCH LA
Old Hall Farm
Tudor Lodge
83
A45
LODGE GREEN LA
EAVES GREEN MOBILE HOME PK
2
Brailes Farm
Lodge Green Farmhouse
Walsh Hall
WALSH LA
Eaves Green
Forest Hall
Meriden CE Prim Sch
BIRMINGHAM RD
THE FIRS
MAXSTOKE LA
KITTERMASTER RD
ARCHERY RD
Coventry Way
EAVES GREEN LA
Heart of England Way
HIGHFIELD
MAXSTOKE CL
ARDEN CL
ALSPATH RD
LEYMERE CL
HAMPTON GRANGE
Cross
Liby
FAIRFIELD RISE
DIGBY PL
LEYS LA
Meriden
Village Farm
1
PO
MAIN RD
THE CROFT
WATERFALL CL
WHICHCOTE AVE
Queen's Head (PH)
HAMPTON LA
DARLSTON ROW 1
THE GREEN 2
WINSPEAR CL 3
STRAWBERRY FIELDS
GLOVERS CL
Hotel
BIRMINGHAM RD
Mast
DARLASTON CT
OLD RD
SHOWELL LA
82
B4102
23
24
25
45
58

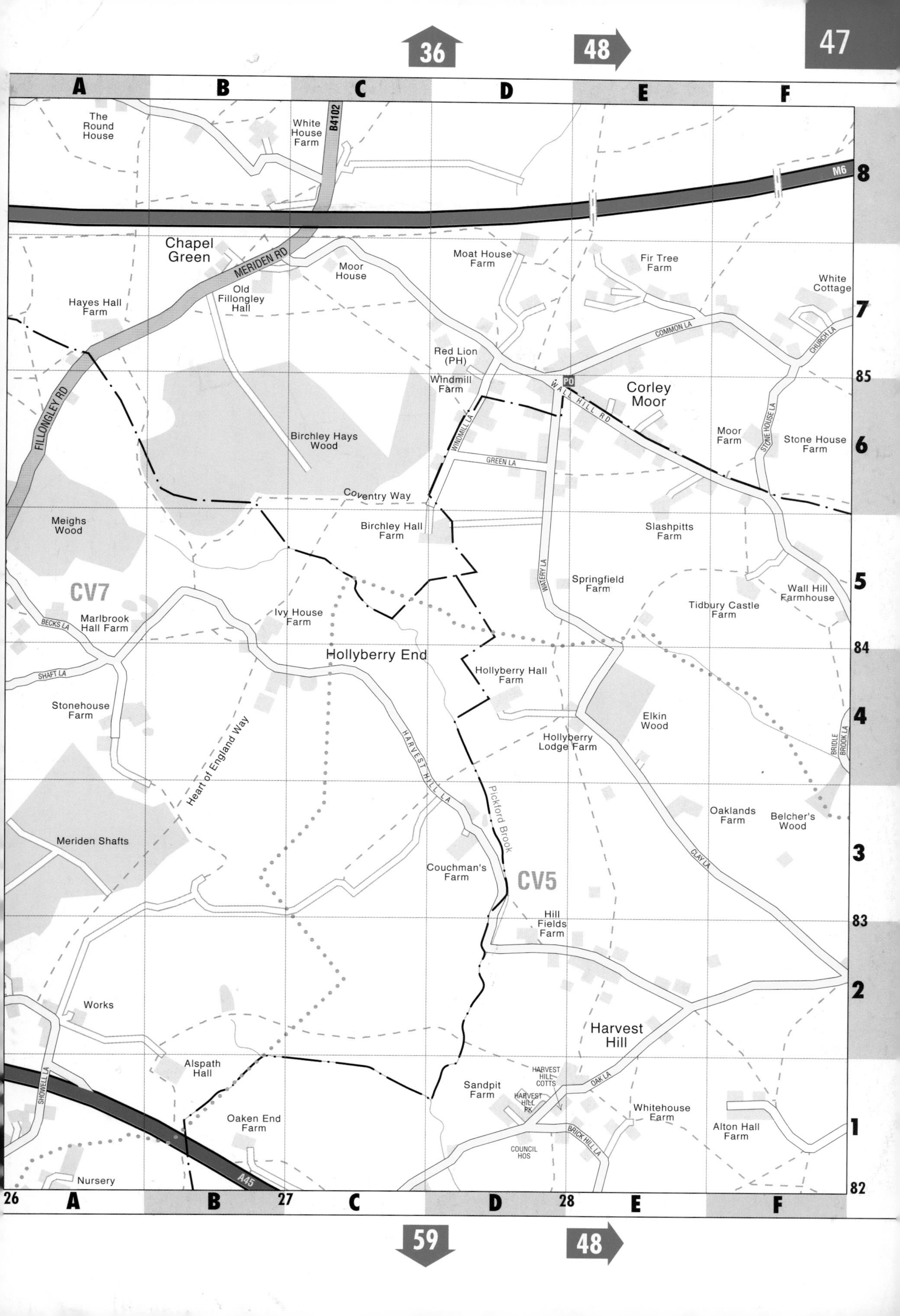

36
48
A
B
C
D
E
F
The Round House
White House Farm
B4102
M6
8
Chapel Green
MERIDEN RD
Moor House
Old Fillongley Hall
Moat House Farm
Fir Tree Farm
White Cottage
Hayes Hall Farm
7
COMMON LA
CHURCH LA
Red Lion (PH)
Windmill Farm
PO
WALL HILL RD
Corley Moor
85
FILLONGLEY RD
Birchley Hays Wood
WINDMILL LA
GREEN LA
Moor Farm
STONE HOUSE LA
Stone House Farm
6
Coventry Way
Meighs Wood
Birchley Hall Farm
Slashpitts Farm
CV7
WATERY LA
Springfield Farm
5
Wall Hill Farmhouse
Tidbury Castle Farm
Marlbrook Hall Farm
BECKS LA
Ivy House Farm
Hollyberry End
84
SHAFT LA
Hollyberry Hall Farm
Stonehouse Farm
Elkin Wood
4
Hollyberry Lodge Farm
BRIDLE BROOK LA
Heart of England Way
HARVEST HILL LA
Pickford Brook
Oaklands Farm
Belcher's Wood
Meriden Shafts
3
CLAY LA
Couchman's Farm
CV5
Hill Fields Farm
83
2
Works
Harvest Hill
Alspath Hall
HARVEST HILL COTTS
OAK LA
Sandpit Farm
HARVEST HILL PK
Whitehouse Farm
SHOWELL LA
Oaken End Farm
BRICK HILL LA
Alton Hall Farm
1
COUNCIL HOS
Nursery
A45
82
26
27
28
59

47
37

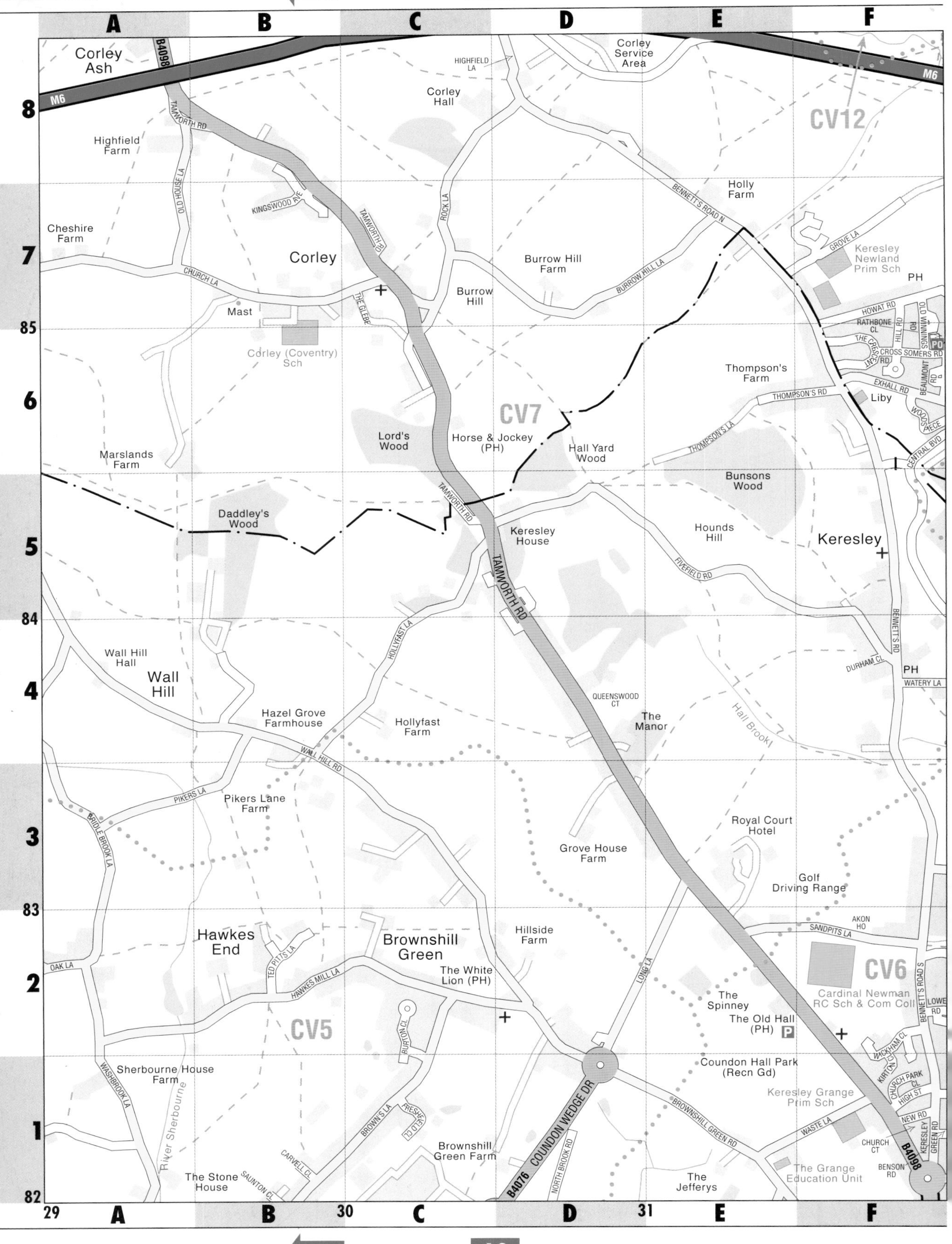
A
B
C
D
E
F
8
7
85
6
5
84
4
3
83
2
1
82
29
30
31
Corley Ash
B4098
M6
HIGHFIELD LA
Corley Service Area
Corley Hall
CV12
TAMWORTH RD
Highfield Farm
OLD HOUSE LA
KINGSWOOD AVE
ROCK LA
BENNETT'S ROAD N
Holly Farm
Cheshire Farm
Corley
Burrow Hill Farm
GROVE LA
Keresley Newland Prim Sch
PH
CHURCH LA
THE GLEBE
Burrow Hill
BURROW HILL LA
HOWAT RD
RATHBONE CL
HILL RD
THE CRESCENT
CROSS SOMERS RD
PO
Mast
Corley (Coventry) Sch
Thompson's Farm
EXHALL RD
BEAUMONT RD
THOMPSON'S RD
Liby
CV7
THOMPSON'S LA
Lord's Wood
Horse & Jockey (PH)
Hall Yard Wood
Marslands Farm
CENTRAL BVD
Bunsons Wood
Daddley's Wood
Keresley House
Hounds Hill
Keresley
FIVEFIELD RD
BENNETT'S RD
HOLLYFAST LA
Wall Hill Hall
Wall Hill
DURHAM CL
PH
WATERY LA
QUEENSWOOD CT
Hazel Grove Farmhouse
Hollyfast Farm
The Manor
Hall Brook
WALL HILL RD
PIKERS LA
Pikers Lane Farm
BRIDLE BROOK LA
Royal Court Hotel
Grove House Farm
Golf Driving Range
AKON HO
SANDPITS LA
Hawkes End
Brownshill Green
Hillside Farm
OAK LA
TED PITTS LA
HAWKES MILL LA
The White Lion (PH)
LONG LA
CV6
The Spinney
Cardinal Newman RC Sch & Com Coll
BENNETT'S ROAD S
The Old Hall (PH)
P
CV5
BURTON CL
WICKHAM CL
Sherbourne House Farm
Coundon Hall Park (Recn Gd)
KIRTON CL
CHURCH PARK CL
WASHBROOK LA
Keresley Grange Prim Sch
HIGH ST
BROWN'S LA
FRESHFIELD CL
COUNDON WEDGE DR
BROWNSHILL GREEN RD
NEW RD
River Sherbourne
Brownshill Green Farm
NORTH BROOK RD
WASTE LA
CHURCH CT
KERESLEY GREEN RD
CARVELL CL
B4076
The Grange Education Unit
The Stone House
SAUNTON CL
The Jefferys
BENSON RD

47
60

38

50

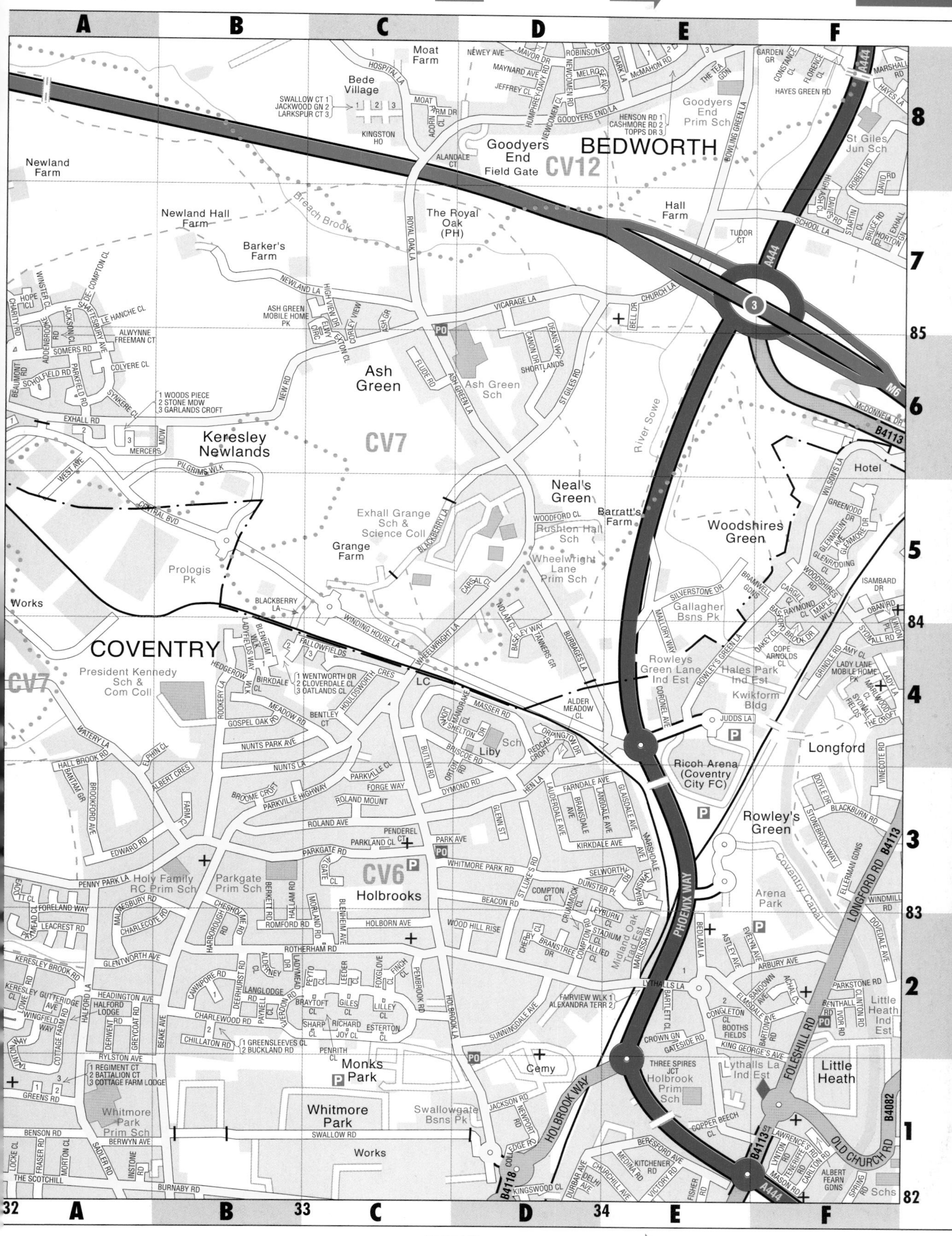
A
B
C
D
E
F
8
7
85
6
5
84
4
3
83
2
1
82
32
33
34
Moat Farm
Bede Village
HOSPITAL LA
SWALLOW CT 1
JACKWOOD GN 2
LARKSPUR CT 3
KINGSTON HO
MOAT FARM DR
ACORN CL
ALANDALE CT
NEWEY AVE
MAYNARD AVE
JEFFREY CL
MAVOR DR
HUMPHREY-DAVY RD
NEWCOMEN RD
NEWCOMEN CL
ROBINSON RD
MELROSE AVE
DARK LA
McMAHON RD
GOODYERS END LA
HENSON RD 1
CASHMORE RD 2
TOPPS DR 3
THE TEA GDN
Goodyers End Prim Sch
Goodyers End Field Gate
BEDWORTH
CV12
BOWLING GREEN LA
GARDEN GR
CONSTANCE CL
FLORENCE CL
HAYES GREEN RD
MARSHALL RD
HAYES LA
A444
St Giles Jun Sch
ROBERT RD
DAVID RD
HIGH ASH CL
DAVIS RD
STARTIN CL
BRUCE RD
HORTON GN
EXHALL GN
SCHOOL LA
Hall Farm
TUDOR CT
Newland Farm
Newland Hall Farm
Breach Brook
Barker's Farm
The Royal Oak (PH)
ROYAL OAK LA
NEWLAND LA
HIGH VIEW DR
ELWY CIRC
LEXTON CL
CORLEY VIEW
ASH GR
ASH GREEN MOBILE HOME PK
VICARAGE LA
CHURCH LA
BELL DR
PO
WINSTER CL
DE COMPTON CL
HOPE CL
CHARITY RD
SHAFTESBURY AVE
JACKSON CL
ADDENBROOKE RD
LE HANCHE CL
ALWYNNE FREEMAN CT
SOMERS RD
BEAUMONT RD
SCHOFIELD RD
PARKFIELD RD
COLYERE CL
SYNKERE CL
1 WOODS PIECE
2 STONE MDW
3 GARLANDS CROFT
NEW RD
Ash Green
FLUDE RD
ASH GREEN LA
Ash Green Sch
CANON DR
DEANS WAY
SHORTLANDS
ST GILES RD
River Sowe
3
M6
McDONNELL DR
B4113
EXHALL RD
MERCERS
MDW
Keresley Newlands
CV7
WEST AVE
PILGRIMS WLK
CENTRAL BVD
Exhall Grange Sch & Science Coll
Grange Farm
BLACKBERRY LA
Neal's Green
WOODFORD CL
Rushton Hall Sch
Barratt's Farm
Wheelwright Lane Prim Sch
Hotel
WILSON'S LA
GREENODD DR
GLENMOUNT AVE
GLENMORE DR
GLENRIDDING CL
Woodshires Green
ISAMBARD DR
Prologis Pk
Works
BLACKBERRY LA
WINDING HOUSE LA
CARSAL CL
NOLAN CL
BASELEY WAY
TANNERS GR
BURBAGES LA
SILVERSTONE DR
BRAMWELL GDNS
CARGILL CL
WOODSHIRES RD
RAYMOND CL
MAPLE WLK
BASFORD BROOK DR
OBAN RD
SYDNALL RD
UNION PL
Gallagher Bsns Pk
MALLORY WAY
OAKEY CL
COPE ARNOLDS CL
AMY CL
GRINDLE RD
LADY LANE MOBILE HOME PK
LADY LA
MARLWOOD CL
SYDNALL FIELDS
THE CROFT
COVENTRY
President Kennedy Sch & Com Coll
CV7
LADYFIELDS WAY
BLENHEIM WLK
HEDGEROW WLK
FALLOWFIELDS
BIRKDALE CL
1 WENTWORTH DR
2 CLOVERDALE CL
3 OATLANDS CL
HOULDSWORTH CRES
WHEELWRIGHT LA
LC
Rowleys Green Lane Ind Est
ROWLEY'S GREEN LA
Hales Park Ind Est
Kwikform Bldg
CORONEL AVE
ALDER MEADOW CL
ROOKERY LA
GOSPEL OAK RD
MEADOW RD
BENTLEY CT
MANDRAKE CL
JOHN SHELTON DR
MASSER RD
Sch
Liby
ORPINGTON DR
REDCAP CROFT
BRISCOE RD
JUDDS LA
Longford
WATERY LA
ELPHIN CL
NUNTS PARK AVE
NUNTS LA
BUTLIN RD
ORTON RD
DYMOND RD
HEN LA
HALL BROOK RD
BANTAM GR
ALBERT CRES
BROOKFORD AVE
FARM CL
BROOME CROFT
PARKVILLE HIGHWAY
PARKVILLE CL
FORGE WAY
ROLAND MOUNT
ROLAND AVE
Ricoh Arena (Coventry City FC)
FARNDALE AVE
LAUDERDALE AVE
BRANSDALE AVE
LANGDALE AVE
GLAISDALE AVE
MARSHDALE AVE
KIRKDALE AVE
GLENN ST
VINECOTE RD
DOYLE DR
BLACKBURN RD
STONEBROOK WAY
Rowley's Green
EDWARD RD
PENDEREL CT
PARKLAND CL
PARK AVE
PARKGATE RD
PO
CV6
Holbrooks
WHITMORE PARK RD
SELWORTHY RD
DUNSTER PL
BRUNSWICK CL
ST LUKE'S RD
COMPTON CT
BEACON RD
Coventry Canal
Arena Park
ELLERMAN GDNS
LONGFORD RD
B4113
WINDMILL RD
PENNY PARK LA
Holy Family RC Prim Sch
Parkgate Prim Sch
GATE CL
FORELAND WAY
MALMESBURY RD
CHESHOLME RD
BERKETT RD
HALLAM RD
MORLAND RD
BLENHEIM AVE
HOLBORN AVE
WOOD HILL RISE
CRUMMOCK CL
LEYBURN CL
STADIUM CL
ALLIED CL
CHERRY CL
BRANSTREE DR
COMPTON RD
Midland Oak Trad Est
MARLISSA DR
PHOENIX WAY
BEDLAM LA
ASTLEY AVE
EVELYN AVE
DOVEDALE AVE
LEACREST RD
CHARLECOTE RD
HARBOROUGH RD
ROMFORD RD
ROTHERHAM RD
KERESLEY BROOK RD
GLENTWORTH AVE
ALDERNEY CL
LADYMEAD
PEYTO CL
LEEDER CL
FOXGLOVE CL
FINCH CL
PEMBROOK RD
LYTHALLS LA
BARTLETT CL
SANDOWN AVE
ACHAL CL
ARBURY AVE
PARKSTONE RD
KERESLEY GUTTERIDGE AVE
LOWE RD
HALFORD LA
HEADINGTON AVE
HALFORD LODGE
CAWNPORE RD
DEERHURST RD
LANGLODGE RD
PAYNELL CL
BRAYTOFT CL
GILES CL
LILLEY CL
FAIRVIEW WLK 1
ALEXANDRA TERR 2
CONGLETON CL
ELMSDALE AVE
BOOTHS FIELDS
BARTON RD
BENTHALL RD
CLINTON RD
IVOR RD
Little Heath Ind Est
WINGFIELD WAY
COTTAGE FARM RD
DERWENT RD
GREYCOAT RD
BEAKE AVE
CHARLEWOOD RD
SHARP CL
RICHARD ST
JOY CL
ESTERTON CL
HOLBROOK LA
SUNNINGDALE AVE
CROWN GN
GATESIDE RD
KING GEORGE'S AVE
FOLESHILL RD
CHILLATON RD
1 GREENSLEEVES CL
2 BUCKLAND RD
PENRITH CL
RYLSTON AVE
Monks Park
PO
Cemy
THREE SPIRES JCT
Holbrook Prim Sch
Lythalls La Ind Est
Little Heath
1 REGIMENT CT
2 BATTALION CT
3 COTTAGE FARM LODGE
GREENS RD
Whitmore Park Prim Sch
Whitmore Park
Swallowgate Bsns Pk
JACKSON RD
NEWPORT RD
HOLBROOK WAY
COPPER BEECH CL
B4082
BENSON RD
BERWYN AVE
SWALLOW RD
Works
COLLEGE RD
BERESFORD AVE
KITCHENER RD
MEDINA RD
ST LAWRENCE'S RD
LYNTON RD
TENERIFFE RD
CARLTON RD
OLD CHURCH RD
B4113
LOCKE CL
FRASER RD
MORTON CL
SADLER RD
INSTONE RD
THE SCOTCHILL
BURNABY RD
B4118
KINGSWOOD CL
DURBAR AVE
DELHI AVE
CHURCHILL AVE
VICTORY RD
FISHER RD
MASON RD
ALBERT FEARN GDNS
SPRING RD
Schs
A444

61

50

49
39

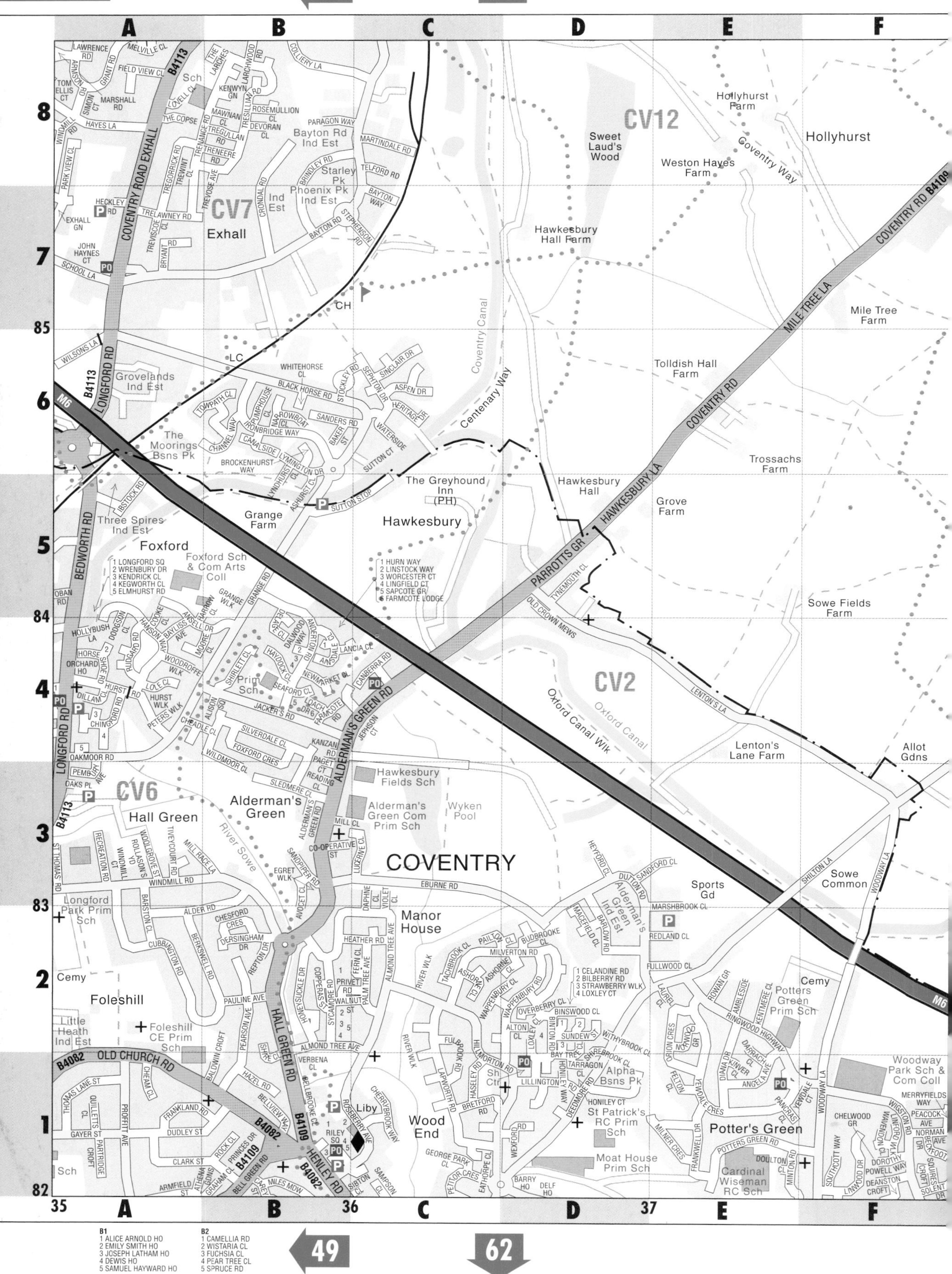

B1
1 ALICE ARNOLD HO
2 EMILY SMITH HO
3 JOSEPH LATHAM HO
4 DEWIS HO
5 SAMUEL HAYWARD HO

B2
1 CAMELLIA RD
2 WISTARIA CL
3 FUCHSIA CL
4 PEAR TREE CL
5 SPRUCE RD

49
62

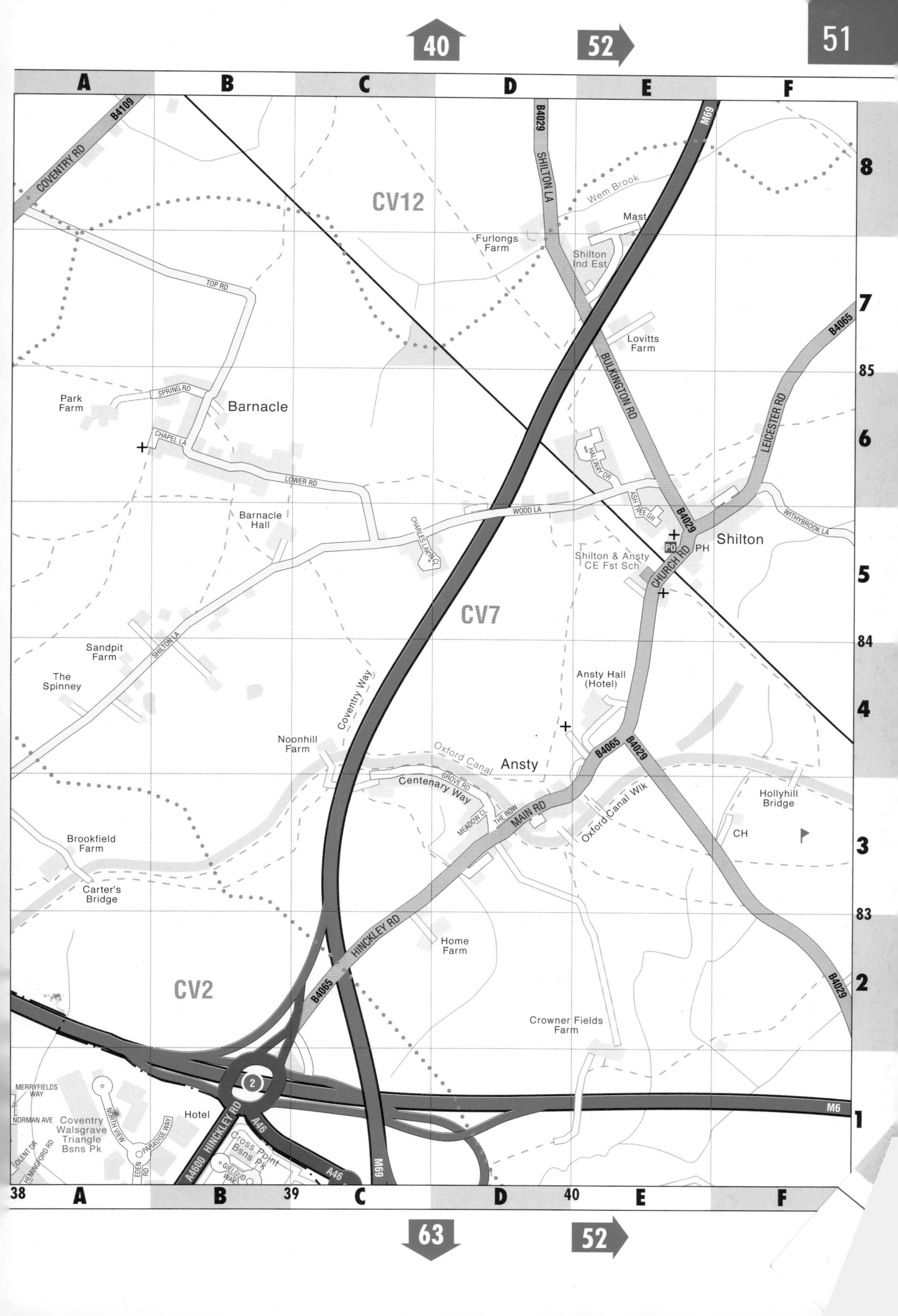
40
52
A
B
C
D
E
F
8
7
85
6
5
84
4
3
83
2
1
38
39
40
63
52
B4109
COVENTRY RD
TOP RD
SPRING RD
Park Farm
Barnacle
CHAPEL LA
LOWER RD
Barnacle Hall
Sandpit Farm
The Spinney
SHILTON LA
CV12
CV7
CV2
B4029
SHILTON LA
Wem Brook
Mast
Furlongs Farm
Shilton Ind Est
M69
Lovitts Farm
BULKINGTON RD
B4065
LEICESTER RD
HALLWAY DR
WOOD LA
CHARLES LAKIN CL
ASH TREE GR
B4029
Shilton
PO
PH
WITHYBROOK LA
Shilton & Ansty CE Fst Sch
CHURCH RD
Ansty Hall (Hotel)
Coventry Way
Noonhill Farm
Oxford Canal
Ansty
B4065
B4029
GROVE RD
Centenary Way
MEADOW CL
THE ROW
MAIN RD
Oxford Canal Wlk
Hollyhill Bridge
CH
Brookfield Farm
Carter's Bridge
HINCKLEY RD
B4065
Home Farm
Crowner Fields Farm
B4029
M6
2
MERRYFIELDS WAY
NORMAN AVE
Coventry Walsgrave Triangle Bsns Pk
NORTH VIEW
PARADISE WAY
Hotel
SOLENT DR
HEMINGFORD RD
EDEN RD
A4600 HINCKLEY RD
A46
Cross Point Bsns Pk
GIELGUD WAY
A46
M69

51
41

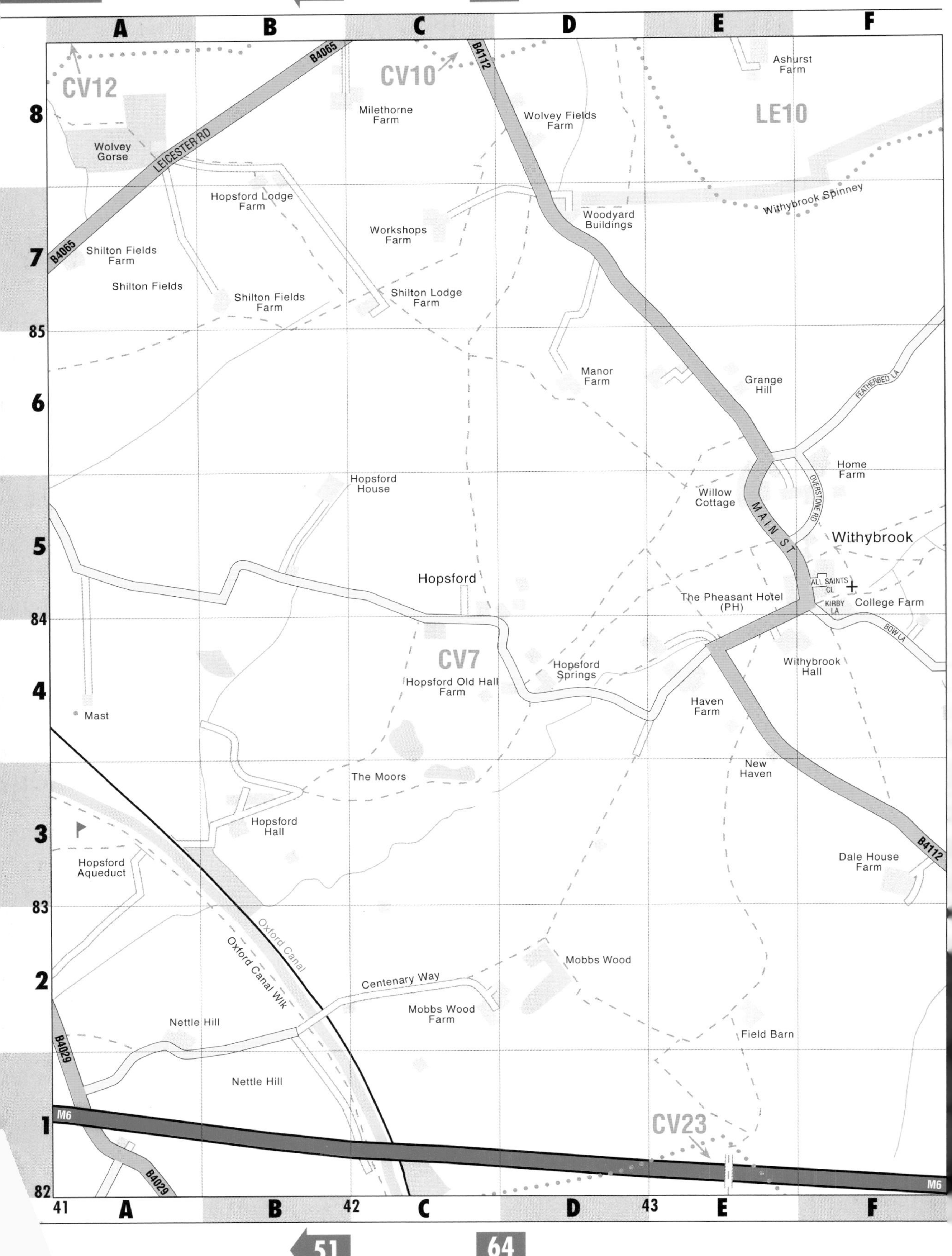
A
B
C
D
E
F
CV12
CV10
LE10
B4065
B4112
Ashurst Farm
Milethorne Farm
Wolvey Fields Farm
Wolvey Gorse
LEICESTER RD
Hopsford Lodge Farm
Workshops Farm
Woodyard Buildings
Withybrook Spinney
Shilton Fields Farm
Shilton Fields
Shilton Fields Farm
Shilton Lodge Farm
Manor Farm
Grange Hill
FEATHERBED LA
Home Farm
Willow Cottage
OVERSTONE RD
MAIN ST
Withybrook
Hopsford House
Hopsford
ALL SAINTS CL
KIRBY LA
College Farm
The Pheasant Hotel (PH)
BOW LA
CV7
Hopsford Springs
Withybrook Hall
Hopsford Old Hall Farm
Haven Farm
Mast
New Haven
The Moors
Hopsford Hall
Hopsford Aqueduct
Dale House Farm
Oxford Canal
Oxford Canal Wlk
Mobbs Wood
Centenary Way
Mobbs Wood Farm
Nettle Hill
Field Barn
B4029
Nettle Hill
CV23
M6
8
7
85
6
5
84
4
3
83
2
1
82
41
42
43

51
64

42
54
A
B
C
D
E
F
LE10
Withybrook Spinney
B4455
COAL PIT LA
Cloudesley Farm
Hobley Furze
FOSSE WAY
8
Lodge Farm
7
Grange Farm
Grounds Farm
85
MONKS KIRBY LA
Withybrook Spinney
6
Fosse Farm
Kirby Lane Cottage
Brickyard Cottages
5
Elmhurst Farm
Monks Kirby Lodge
84
CV7
BROCKHURST LA
Barn Farm
CV23
4
BOW LA
SANDY LA
Cemy
FOXON'S CNR
Manor Farm
Bond End
Brockhurst
Stave Hall Farm
MILLERS LA
ST EDITH'S CL
BOND END
GATE FARM
Brockhurst Farm
STOCKING MDW
DR
3
The Butts
BUSBYS PIECE
PO
The Old Vicarage
MAIN ST
SMITE CL
The Denbigh Arms Inn
83
The Revel CE Prim Sch
BELL LA
Monks Kirby
The Bell Inn
2
Sewage Works
Street Ashton House
College Farm
Fosse Farm
Street Ashton Farm
Hotel
Street Ashton
1
COVENTRY RD
B4112
Lodge Farm
B4027
Pailton House
B4455
M6
82
44
45
46
65
54

53
43

A B C D E F

8 7 85 6 5 84 4 3 83 2 1 82

Spring Farm
Wood Farm
Willey Fields Farm
LE17
A5
GREEN LA
Cottons Furze
Norwood Farm
Sewage Works
Manor Farm
BROCKHURST LA
Newnham Lodge Farm
COAL PIT LA
PH
CHURCH LA
MAIN ST
PARSONS CL
Willey
Larch Covert (Fox Covert)
The Old Kennels
Kennel Spinney
Allot Gdns
Long Spinney
The Nursery
CV23
Garden Spinney
Home Farm
The Grove
Burton Pool Wood
Newnham Fields Farm
Muswell Leys
Park Cottage
The Pinetum
Newnham Paddock
Newnham Paddock Park
The Kennels
Cabbage Clump
Fox Covert
Pinch Furlong
Railway Covert (Fox Covert)

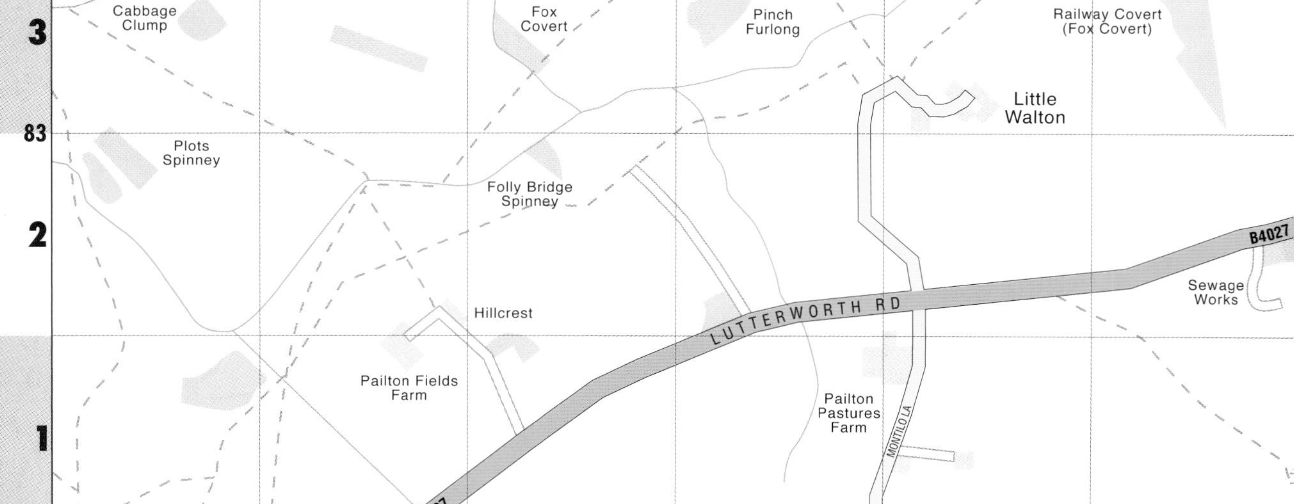

47 A B 48 C D 49 E F

53
66

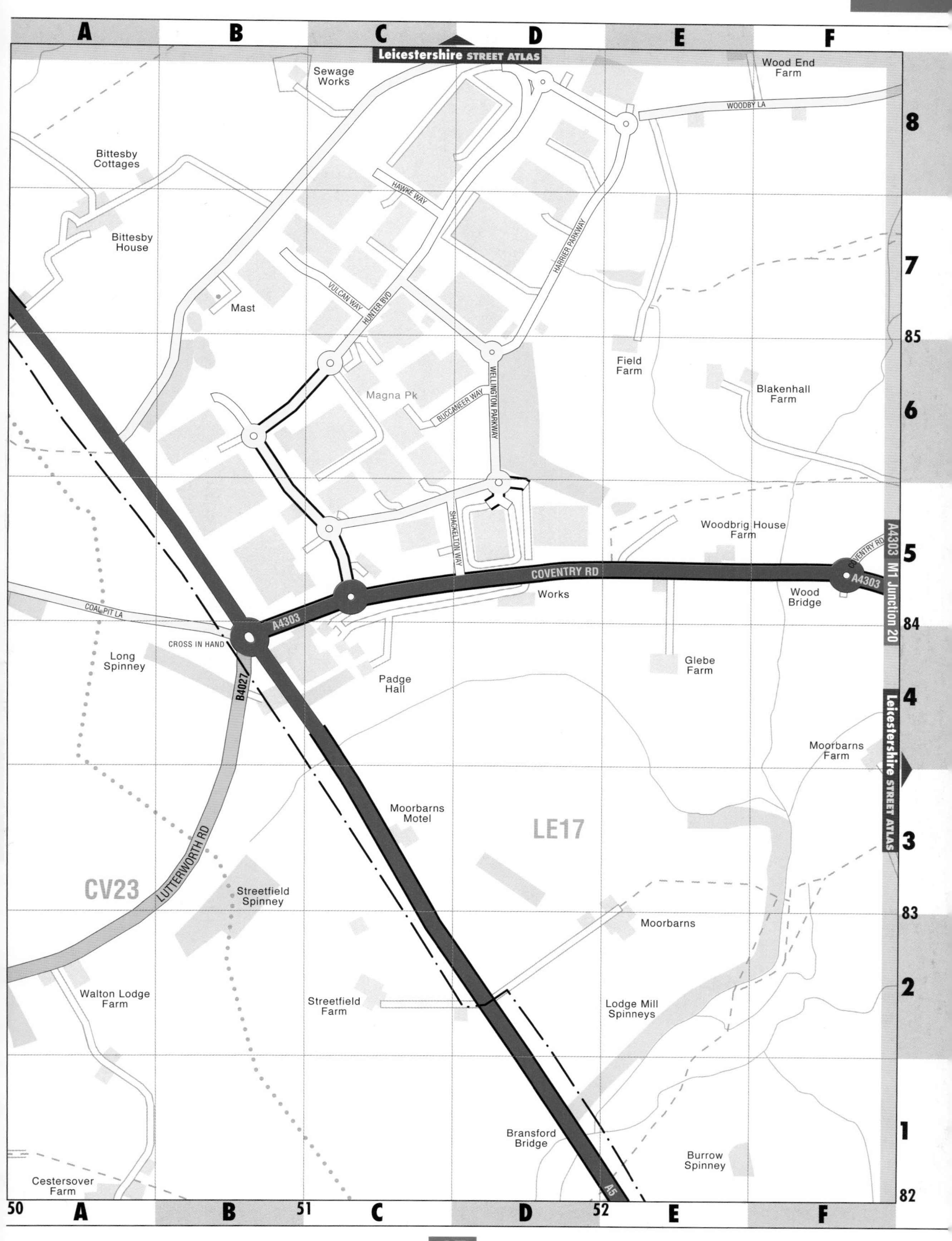

A
B
C
D
E
F
Leicestershire STREET ATLAS
Sewage Works
Wood End Farm
WOODBY LA
Bittesby Cottages
HAWKE WAY
Bittesby House
HARRIER PARKWAY
VULCAN WAY
HUNTER BVD
Mast
Field Farm
Blakenhall Farm
Magna Pk
BUCCANEER WAY
WELLINGTON PARKWAY
Woodbrig House Farm
SHACKELTON WAY
COVENTRY RD
A4303 M1 Junction 20
Works
Wood Bridge
A4303
COAL PIT LA
CROSS IN HAND
Long Spinney
B4027
Glebe Farm
Padge Hall
Leicestershire STREET ATLAS
Moorbarns Farm
Moorbarns Motel
LE17
CV23
LUTTERWORTH RD
Streetfield Spinney
Moorbarns
Walton Lodge Farm
Streetfield Farm
Lodge Mill Spinneys
Bransford Bridge
Burrow Spinney
Cestersover Farm
A5
8
7
85
6
5
84
4
3
83
2
1
82
50
51
52

44

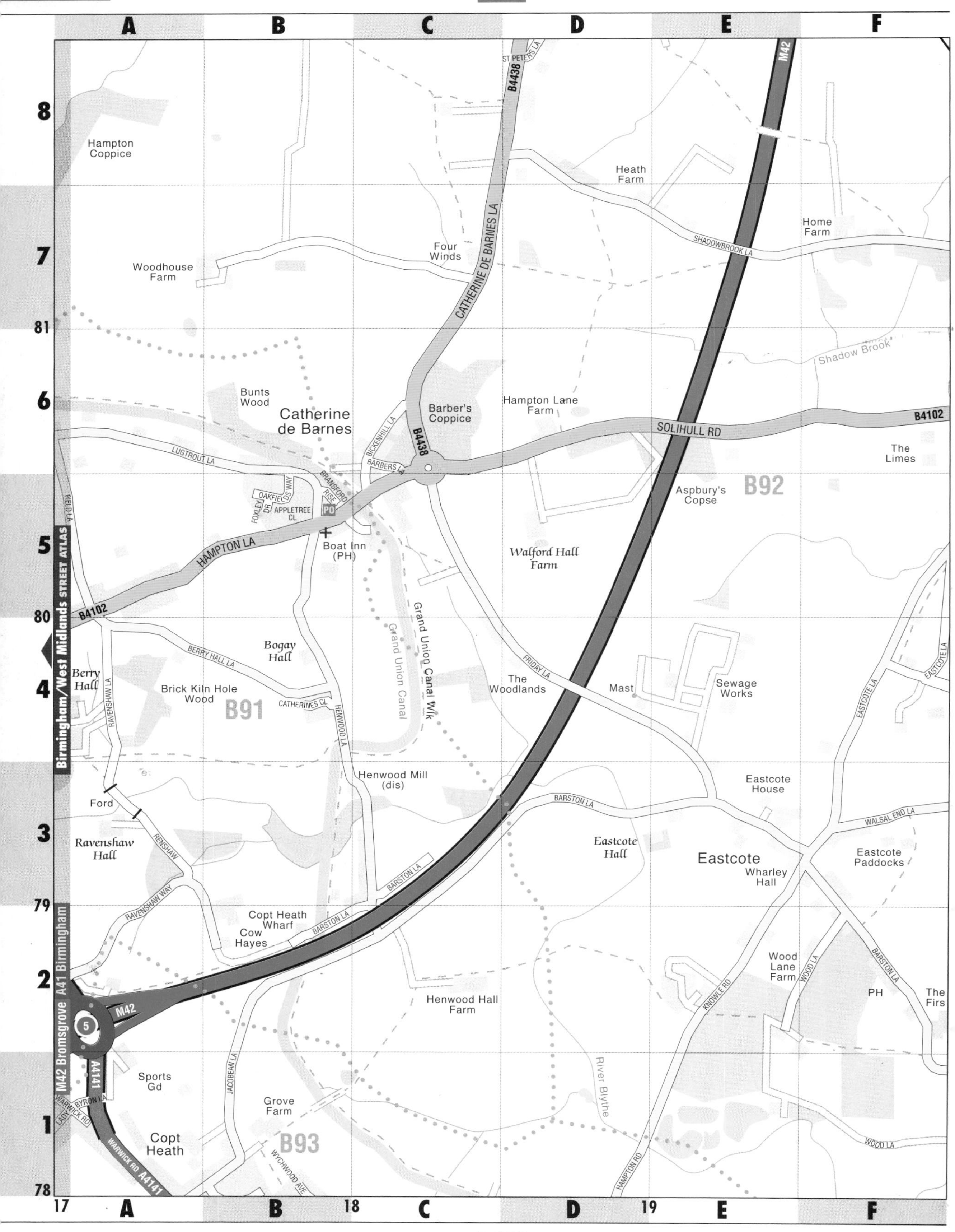

Hampton Coppice
Woodhouse Farm
Four Winds
Heath Farm
Home Farm
Shadowbrook La
Catherine de Barnes La
B4438
M42
Shadow Brook
Bunts Wood
Catherine de Barnes
Barber's Coppice
Hampton Lane Farm
Solihull Rd
B4102
The Limes
Lugtrout La
Bickenhill La
Barbers La
Bransford Rise
Oakfield Dr
Appletree Cl
Foxley Dr
PO
Aspbury's Copse
B92
Hampton La
Boat Inn (PH)
Walford Hall Farm
Field La
Grand Union Canal Wlk
Grand Union Canal
Berry Hall La
Bogay Hall
Berry Hall
Ravenshaw La
Brick Kiln Hole Wood
B91
Catherines Cl
Henwood La
Friday La
The Woodlands
Mast
Sewage Works
Eastcote La
Henwood Mill (dis)
Barston La
Eastcote House
Ford
Walsal End La
Ravenshaw Hall
Renshaw
Eastcote Hall
Eastcote
Eastcote Paddocks
Whaley Hall
Ravenshaw Way
Copt Heath Wharf
Cow Hayes
Wood Lane Farm
Wood La
Knowle Rd
PH
The Firs
Henwood Hall Farm
A4141
Sports Gd
Jacobean La
River Blythe
Byron La
Warwick Rd
Lady Byron La
Grove Farm
Copt Heath
B93
Wychwood Ave
Hampton Rd
Birmingham/West Midlands STREET ATLAS
A41 Birmingham
M42 Bromsgrove
5

72

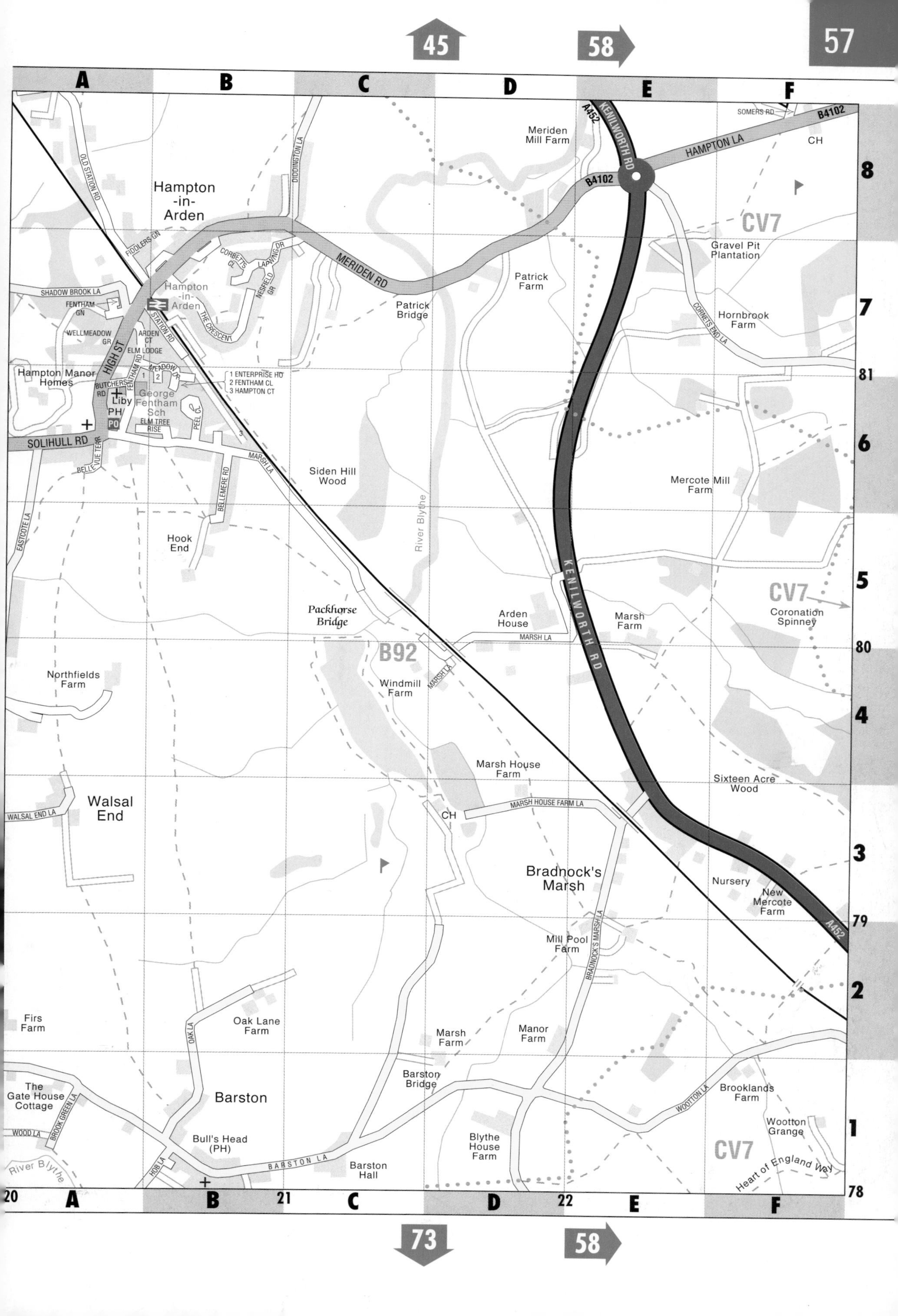
45
58
A
B
C
D
E
F
Hampton
-in-
Arden
OLD STATION RD
DIDDINGTON LA
Meriden
Mill Farm
A452
KENILWORTH RD
SOMERS RD
B4102
HAMPTON LA
CH
B4102
CV7
Gravel Pit
Plantation
FIDDLERS GN
CORBETTS CL
LAPWING DR
NESFIELD GR
MERIDEN RD
Patrick
Farm
SHADOW BROOK LA
FENTHAM GN
Hampton
-in-
Arden
THE CRESCENT
STATION RD
Patrick
Bridge
CORNETS END LA
Hornbrook
Farm
WELLMEADOW GR
ARDEN CT
HIGH ST
ELM LODGE
MEADOW DR
Hampton Manor
Homes
BUTCHERS RD
FENTHAM RD
1 ENTERPRISE HO
2 FENTHAM CL
3 HAMPTON CT
Liby
PH
PO
George
Fentham
Sch
ELM TREE RISE
PEEL CL
SOLIHULL RD
BELLE VUE TERR
MARSH LA
Siden Hill
Wood
BELLEMERE RD
Mercote Mill
Farm
EASTCOTE LA
Hook
End
River Blythe
KENILWORTH RD
CV7
Coronation
Spinney
Packhorse
Bridge
Arden
House
Marsh
Farm
MARSH LA
B92
Northfields
Farm
Windmill
Farm
MARSH LA
Marsh House
Farm
Sixteen Acre
Wood
Walsal
End
WALSAL END LA
MARSH HOUSE FARM LA
CH
Bradnock's
Marsh
Nursery
New
Mercote
Farm
A452
Mill Pool
Farm
BRADNOCK'S MARSH LA
Firs
Farm
Oak Lane
Farm
OAK LA
Marsh
Farm
Manor
Farm
The
Gate House
Cottage
Barston
Barston
Bridge
Brooklands
Farm
WOOTTON LA
BROOK GREEN LA
WOOD LA
Bull's Head
(PH)
Blythe
House
Farm
Wootton
Grange
CV7
River Blythe
HOB LA
BARSTON LA
Barston
Hall
Heart of England Way
8
7
81
6
5
80
4
3
79
2
1
78
20
21
22
73
58

57
46

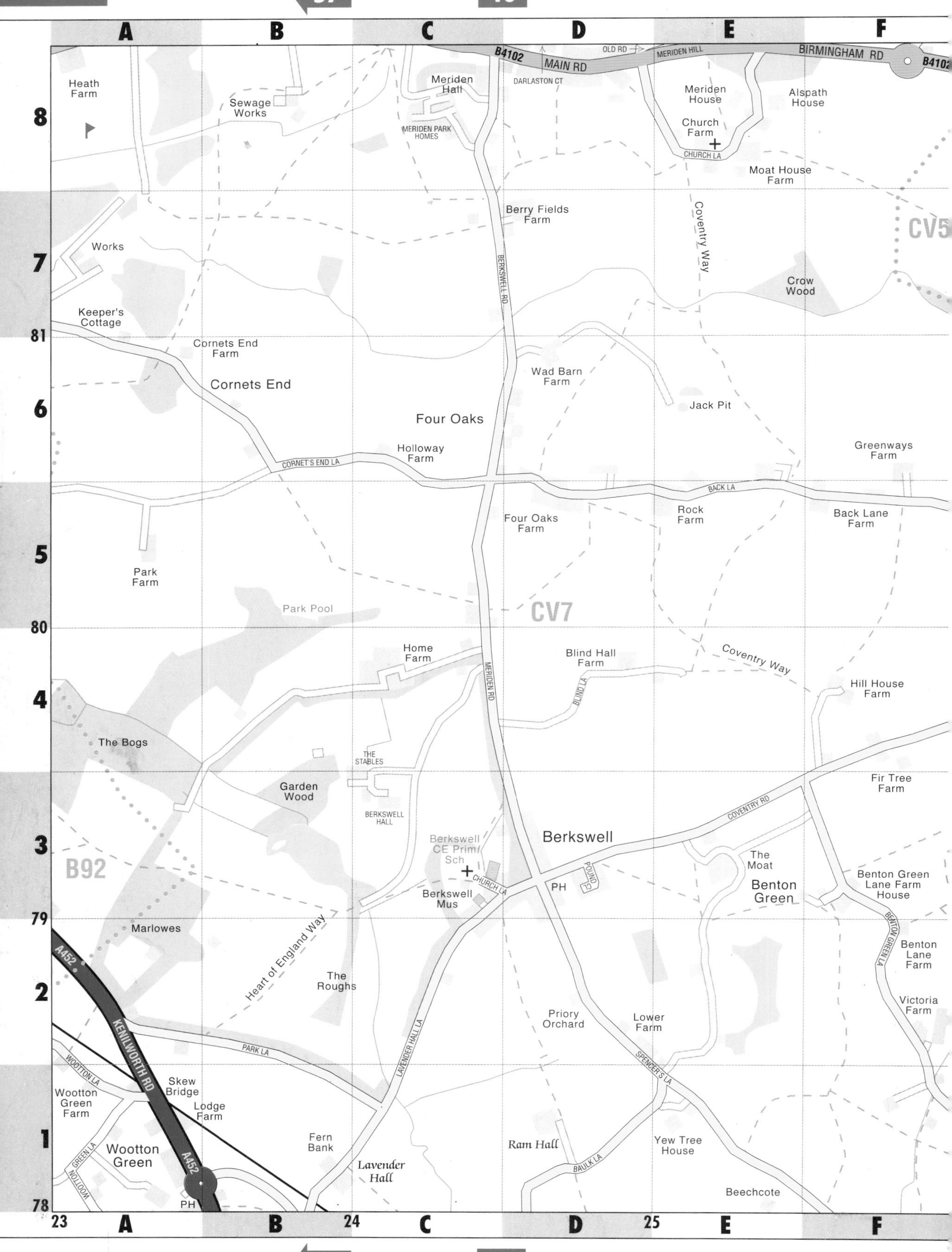
A
B
C
D
E
F
8
7
81
6
5
80
4
3
79
2
1
78
23
24
25
B4102
MAIN RD
OLD RD
MERIDEN HILL
BIRMINGHAM RD
B4102
DARLASTON CT
Heath Farm
Sewage Works
Meriden Hall
MERIDEN PARK HOMES
Meriden House
Alspath House
Church Farm
CHURCH LA
Moat House Farm
Berry Fields Farm
Coventry Way
CV5
Works
BERKSWELL RD
Crow Wood
Keeper's Cottage
Cornets End Farm
Cornets End
Wad Barn Farm
Jack Pit
Four Oaks
Holloway Farm
Greenways Farm
CORNET'S END LA
BACK LA
Rock Farm
Four Oaks Farm
Back Lane Farm
Park Farm
Park Pool
CV7
Home Farm
Blind Hall Farm
Coventry Way
MERIDEN RD
BLIND LA
Hill House Farm
The Bogs
THE STABLES
Garden Wood
Fir Tree Farm
BERKSWELL HALL
COVENTRY RD
Berkswell CE Prim Sch
Berkswell
The Moat
B92
CHURCH LA
POUND CL
PH
Benton Green
Benton Green Lane Farm House
Berkswell Mus
Marlowes
BENTON GREEN LA
Benton Lane Farm
A452
Heart of England Way
The Roughs
Victoria Farm
KENILWORTH RD
Priory Orchard
Lower Farm
PARK LA
LAVENDER HALL LA
SPENCER'S LA
WOOTTON LA
Skew Bridge
Wootton Green Farm
Lodge Farm
Fern Bank
Ram Hall
Yew Tree House
GREEN LA
Wootton Green
A452
Lavender Hall
BAULK LA
WOOTTON
Beechcote
PH

57
74

47
60

A
B
C
D
E
F
8
7
6
5
4
3
2
1
81
80
79
78
26
27
28
B4102
BIRMINGHAM RD
A45
Pinkett's Booth
Merjden Bsns Pk
COPSE DR
ELM CT
OAK LA
Pinkett's Wood
GRACE RD
ALBERT RD
DAYTONA DR
BONNEVILLE CL
OLYMPUS CL
ARMARNA DR
DAWSON DR
LUXOR LA
THEBES CL
JAMES
Millison's Wood
PICKFORD GRANGE LA
Pickford Green
Pickford Bridge
BRICK HILL LA
Pickford
Pickford Farm
BIRMINGHAM RD
Pickford Brook
Windmill Ind Est
SYCAMORE CT
Hotel
Spring Wood
Pickford Grange Farm
PICKFORD GREEN LA
CH
Hotel
Brook Farm
CV5
Shirley Farm
Woodlands
SHIRLEY LA
New Home Farm
Larges Farm
CHURCH LA
St Andrew's CE Inf Sch
GARDEN FLATS
COVENTRY
Oak Farm
BACK LA
Flint's Green
PH
MELLOWSHIP RD
ROSE COTTAGE FLATS
POND FARM MEWS
Pond Farm
MANDERLEY CL
WILLIAM BREE RD
MAGPIE HO
Jun Sch
HOLMES DR
DESPARD RD
DRAYTON CRES
UPPER EASTERN GREEN LA
HOCKLEY LA
MORGANS RD
ORCHARD DR
Barnacles Farm
Hockley
Upper Eastern Green
FREDERICK NEAL AVE
HOWARD CL
KIMBERLEY
LOWER EASTERN GREEN LA
PINE CT
LYNDHURST CROFT
GARRICK CL
THORNTON CL
KENTHURST CL
CONISTON DR
PO
RODWAY DR
MOYLE CRES
MARTIN CL
OSBASTON CL
DERWENT CL
WINDERMERE AVE
UNICORN AVE
TILEWOOD AVE
JENKINS AVE
LUTHER WAY
COVENTRY RD
NOVA CROFT
HARWOOD CL
SUTTON AVE
GOLDTHORN CL
CHILTERN HO
MALVERN HO
FARCROFT AVE
HOVE AVE
STONEBURY AVE
ALANDALE AVE
OLTON AVE
FAULCONBRIDGE AVE
HANDSWORTH CRES
BROAD LA
EASTERN GREEN RD
TROUTBECK RD
TREDINGTON RD
TUDOR AVE
CV7
Works
The Woodlands Sch
ROSEMARY CL
THIRLMERE CL
HAWTHORN LA
DYSON ST
The Meadows Sch
BURY HO 1
THOMAS NAUL CROFT 2
ACTON HO 3
GEORGE HODGKINSON CL 4
ASHCOMBE DR 5
Limbrick Wood Sch
BUSH CL
LODER CL
DUNHILL AVE
BLISS CL
GURNEY CL
COLEMAN ST
DELIUS ST
KEW HO
SHEPHERD CL
PEPYS CNR
ALDRICH AVE
Tilehill Wood (Nature Reserve)
CAVENDISH RD
FASEMAN AVE
GIBBONS CL
JARDINE CRES
Liby
BANNER LA
WICKMANS DR
FOW OAK
GLENDALE WAY
FEIN BANK
GREENWAYS
PHEASANT OAK
EMPIRE RD
BANTOCK RD
BERNERS CL
Rough Close
Tile Hill Wood Sch & Language Coll
ROOSEVELT DR
BRAZIL ST
HERONBANK
BEECHNUT CL
OAK WAY
BROCKHURST DR
WHEATE CROFT
BOAR CROFT
Limbrick Wood
Conway Farm
NUTBROOK AVE
FRISBY RD
HOWLETTE RD
BUSHBERY AVE
JELIFF ST
JAMES GREEN RD
HOLROYD HO
TILEHURST DR
HOLYWELL CL
HAWTHORN LA
HAWTHORN CT
FALSTAFF RD
BOHUN ST
DEVEREUX CL
MAUREEN CL
GOODMAN WAY
ENSIGN CL
CROMES WOOD
ASHFIELD AVE
Pig Wood
PINNOCK PL
BLUEBELL WLK
LIMBRICK AVE
EDGEHILL PL
RC Prim Sch
Glebe Farm
PATRICIA CL
LOWE PL
WINCEBY PL
ASPEN CL
RODHOUSE CL
WHITEBEAM CL
HORNBEAM DR
CV4
B4101
TANYARD CL
SAMMONS WAY
TILE HILL LA
GRAVEL HILL
BRAMSTON CRES
BENTON GREEN LA
IRETON CL
FRANKLIN GR
Hereward Coll
Tile Hill
BULLFIELD AVE
GRESWOLD CL
Plants Hill Wood
TANNERS' LA
NAILCOTE AVE
GRENDON CL
CONWAY AVE
STATION AVE
PO
HATHAWAY RD
NICKSON RD
LESINGHAM DR
COPLAND PL
BRADNICK AVE
DORMER HARRIS
PENN HO
HEDGE FIELD WAY
City Coll
PLANTS HILL CRES
B4101

75
60

59
48

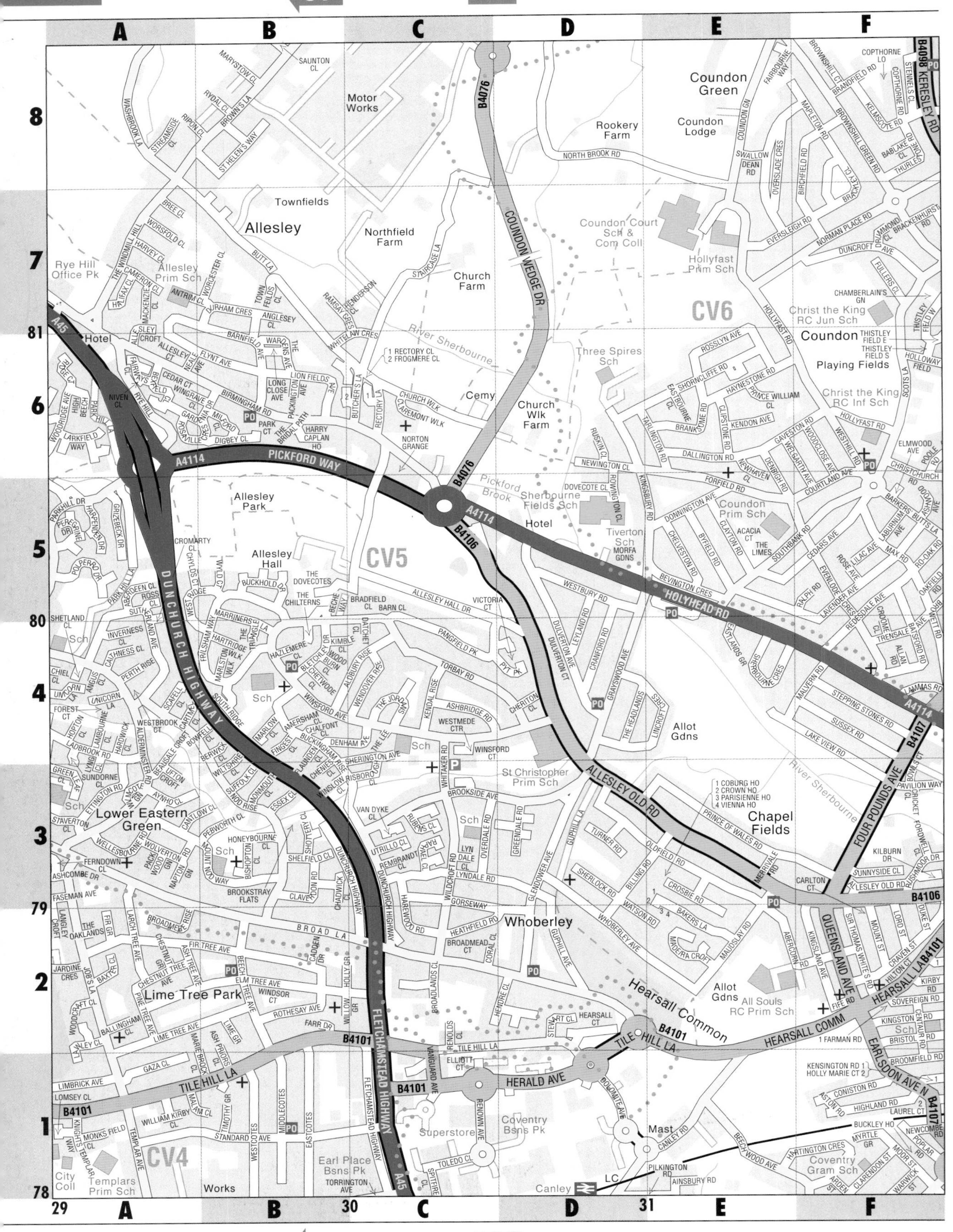
A
B
C
D
E
F
8
7
81
6
5
80
4
3
79
2
1
78
29
30
31
Coundon Green
Motor Works
Rookery Farm
Coundon Lodge
Townfields
Allesley
Northfield Farm
Church Farm
Coundon Court Sch & Com Coll
Hollyfast Prim Sch
Rye Hill Office Pk
Allesley Prim Sch
CV6
Christ the King RC Jun Sch
Coundon
Playing Fields
Three Spires Sch
Christ the King RC Inf Sch
River Sherbourne
Hotel
Cemy
Church Wlk Farm
PICKFORD WAY
A4114
A45
B4076
COUNDON WEDGE DR
Allesley Park
Pickford Brook
Sherbourne Fields Sch
Coundon Prim Sch
Tiverton Sch
Allesley Hall
CV5
B4106
HOLYHEAD RD
DUNCHURCH HIGHWAY
Sch
Allot Gdns
St Christopher Prim Sch
ALLESLEY OLD RD
Chapel Fields
FOUR POUNDS AVE
B4107
Lower Eastern Green
Whoberley
QUEENSLAND AVE
Hearsall Common
Lime Tree Park
Allot Gdns
All Souls RC Prim Sch
B4101
TILE HILL LA
HEARSALL COMM
FLETCHAMSTEAD HIGHWAY
HERALD AVE
EARLSDON AVE N
Coventry Bsns Pk
Superstore
Mast
CV4
Earl Place Bsns Pk
Coventry Gram Sch
City Coll
Templars Prim Sch
Works
Canley
LC
B4098
KERESLEY RD

59
76

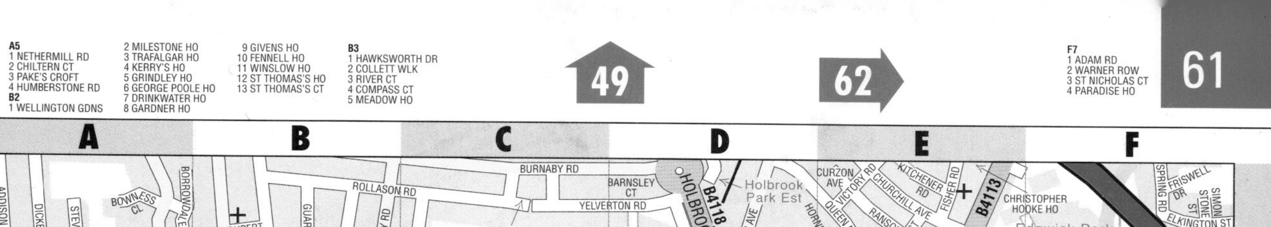

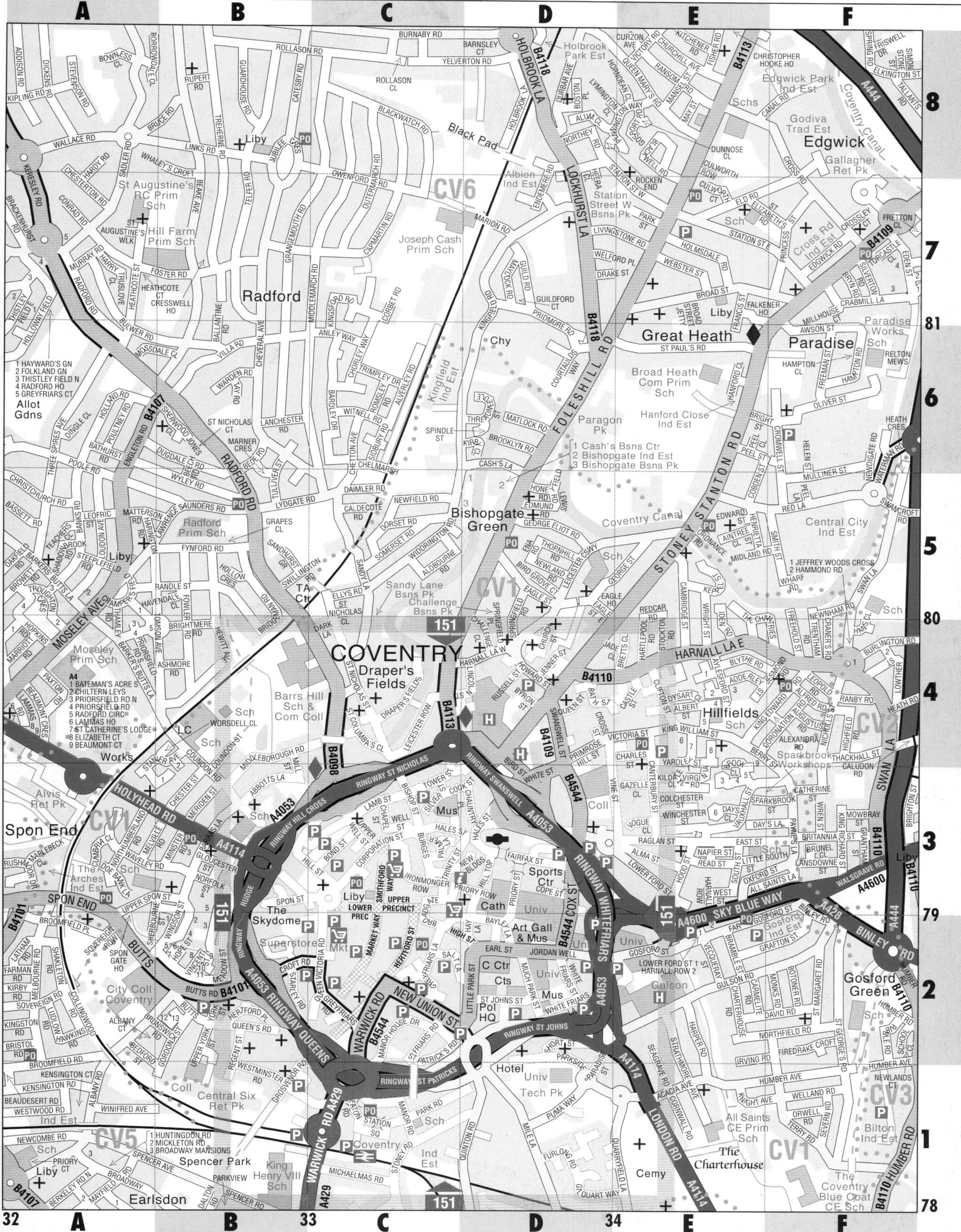

For full street detail of the highlighted area see page 151.

77

62

E3
1 HILLFIELDS HO
2 JEPHCOTT HO
3 GILBERT CL
4 VAUXHALL CL
5 VERNON CL
6 SPRING CL
7 RAGLAN CT

E4
1 CAWTHORNE CL
2 PENSILVA WAY
3 JACQUARD HO
4 LEIGH ST
5 CLARENCE ST
6 THOMAS KING HO
7 NELSON ST
8 WATERLOO ST
9 VERNON CT

61
50
D8
1 LYNE HO
2 HARRY EDWARDS HO
3 FRISWELL HO

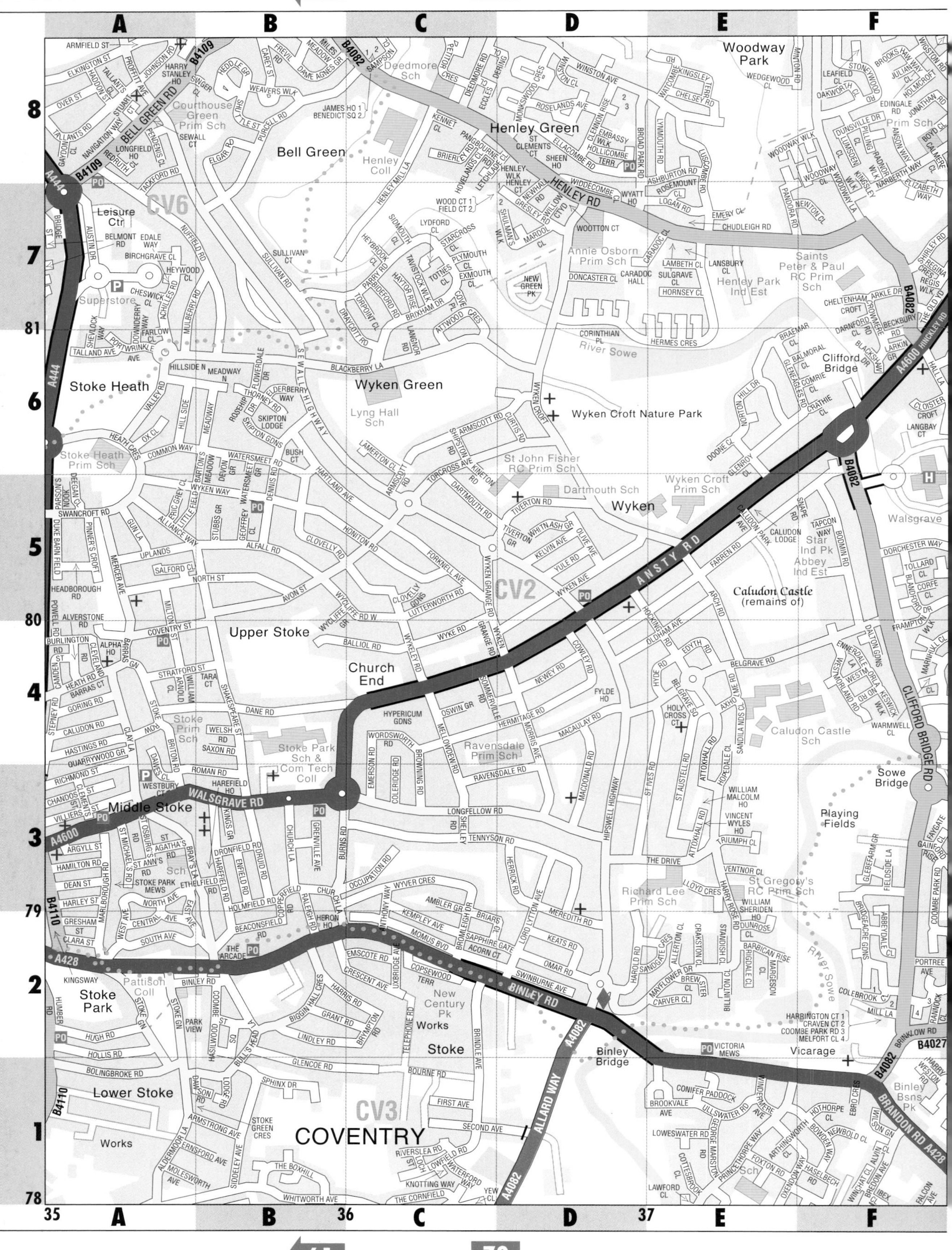

61
78

Mount Pleasant
Coventry Walsgrave Triangle
Cross Point Bsns Pk
HINCKLEY RD
A4600
A46
M69
Hotel
Walsgrave Ret Pk
Walsgrave on Sowe
CV2
Walsgrave CE Prim Sch
High Bridge
Walsgrave Hill
University Hospital-Walsgrave (under construction opens summer 2006)
Pearl Hyde Com Prim Sch
River Sowe
Superstore
Hungerley Hall Farm
B4082
Coombe Pool
The Woodlands
Clifford Bridge Prim Sch
BRINKLOW RD
Oak Farm Nurseries
Binley Bsns Pk
A428
Little Rough
Hill Park Wood
Walsgrave Hill Farm
Hill Fields Farm
Centenary Way
CV7
Works
PETER HALL LA
Smite Brook
CV2
Little Wrautam
Wrautam
Coombe Abbey Farm
Coombe Abbey Hotel
COMBE FIELDS RD
Visitor Ctr
Coombe Abbey Country Park
CV3
B4027
COVENTRY RD
Centenary Way
Old Pools
Old Lodge Farm
Birchley Wood
The Grove
CV8
A7
1 BRACKNELL WLK
2 STEVENAGE WLK
3 BASILDON WLK
4 REDDITCH WLK
5 WALSGRAVE GDNS
6 PETERLEE WLK
7 CUMBERNAULD WLK
8 HARLOW WLK
9 DAWLEY WLK
10 RUNCORN WLK
1 HEMINGFORD RD
2 DOWNTON CL
3 ASHCROFT CL
4 CASPIAN WAY
5 GILLIANS WLK
6 SHARPLEY CT
1 SWANAGE GN
2 BRYANSTON CL
1 SOREDALE CROFT
2 GAULBY WLK
3 UPPERFIELD WAY
4 BULWICK CL
5 MURRAYFIELD WAY
6 DONNYBROOK DR
7 FRANKLINS GDNS
8 STRADEY CL
9 KINGSHOLM CL
10 THE STOOP
A B C D E F
8 7 81 6 5 80 4 3 79 2 1 78
38 39 40

63
52

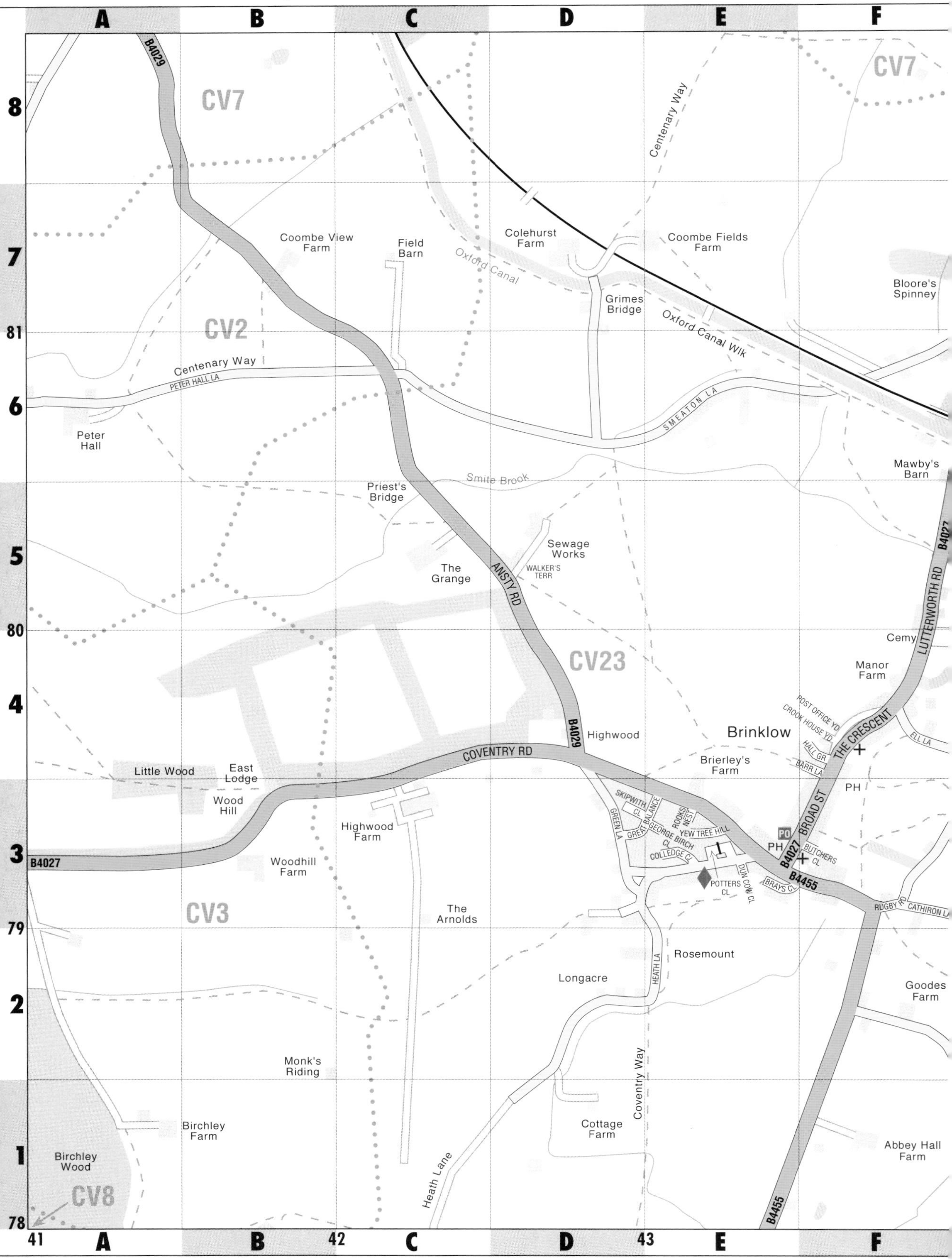

A B C D E F

8
7
81
6
5
80
4
3
79
2
1
78

B4029
CV7
CV7
Centenary Way
Coombe View Farm
Field Barn
Colehurst Farm
Coombe Fields Farm
Oxford Canal
CV2
Grimes Bridge
Oxford Canal Wlk
Bloore's Spinney
Centenary Way
PETER HALL LA
SMEATON LA
Peter Hall
Mawby's Barn
Priest's Bridge
Smite Brook
Sewage Works
The Grange
WALKER'S TERR
ANSTY RD
B4027
LUTTERWORTH RD
Cemy
CV23
Manor Farm
B4029
Highwood
Brinklow
POST OFFICE YD
CROOK HOUSE YD
THE CRESCENT
ELL LA
HALL GR
BARR LA
Brierley's Farm
COVENTRY RD
Little Wood
East Lodge
Wood Hill
PH
SKIPWITH CL
GREEN LA
GREAT BALANCE
ROOKS NEST
GEORGE BIRCH CL
YEW TREE HILL
BROAD ST
PO
Highwood Farm
PH
B4027
BUTCHERS CL
B4027
Woodhill Farm
COLLEDGE CL
POTTERS CL
DUN COW CL
BRAYS CL
B4455
RUGBY RD
CATHIRON LA
CV3
The Arnolds
HEATH LA
Rosemount
Longacre
Goodes Farm
Monk's Riding
Coventry Way
Birchley Farm
Cottage Farm
Abbey Hall Farm
Birchley Wood
Heath Lane
CV8
B4455

41 A B 42 C D 43 E F

63
80

53
66
A
B
C
D
E
F
CV7
M6
B4455
B4027
Campbell Farm
8
Stretton under Fosse
Manor House
ANNS LA
FARRIERS CT
Malt Kiln Farm
FOSSE WAY
Bloore's Spinney
Hill Crest
PH
Dog Kennel Spinney
7
The Wharf Ind Est
Stretton Wharf
Tower Cottages
Smite Brook
The Grove
MAIN ST
SMEATON LA
81
Keeper's Spinney
Newbold Revel Coll
6
Conery Spinney
Black Hovel Spinney
Brick Kiln Spinney
5
Hare Spinney
Tumley Wood
80
Wood Way Spinney
CV23
Little Gorse
Tumley Hill
Bottom Barn
Welkin Farm
Apple Tree Farm
CORD LA
Slang Spinney
Town Thorns Wood
Larch Spinney
4
FARM LA
Manor Farm
PH
BRINKLOW RD
MAIN ST
RICKYARD
THE
ELL LA
The Hill
Easenhall
Town Thorns
RUGBY RD
Oxford Canal Wlk
3
Keeper's Lodge
Adderley Spinney
Crabtree Spinney
79
Oxford Canal
Cathiron Spinneys
Town Thorns Farm
Hungerfield Bridge
Brickyard Spinney
2
Hungerfield
Cathiron Bridge
All Oaks Wood
CATHIRON LA
Cattles Covert
Cathiron Farm
1
Walton's Bridge
78
44
45
46
81
66

65
54

A B C D E F

8
7
81
6
5
80
4
3
79
2
1
78

COVENTRY RD
B4112
FOXFIELD
BROOKSIDE AVE
B4027 LUTTERWORTH RD B4027
Yews Farm
PO
HOME FARM CL
B4112
ST DENIS VIEW
Pailton
POST HOUSE GDNS
RUGBY RD
Greenway Farm
Pailton Pastures
Tythe Farm
Masts
Thwaite Farm
CORD LA
M6
Montilo Farm
Fieldgate Farm
MONTILO LA
Glebe Farm
CV23
Hospital Farm
Harborough Magna
BACK LA
PAILTON RD
THE GREEN
THE CRESCENT
CHURCH CL
PH
MEADOW WAY
Church Farm
MAIN ST
PRIMROSE CT
HAWTHORN TERR
Spike Lane
M6
Cosford
Grange Farm
Cosford Hall Farm
Harborough Parva
EASENHALL RD
Lodge Farm
Manor Farm
Cosford Grounds
Chestnut Farm
RUGBY RD
Tuckey's Farm
CATHIRON LA
Cathiron
VALLEY DR
Oxford Canal
Tuckey's Bridge
Oxford Canal Wlk
CV21
Swift Valley Ind Est
SWIFT POINT
CATHIRON LA
High Oaks
CATHIRON LA
B4112

47 A B 48 C D 49 E F

65
82

55
68
A
B
C
D
E
F
Cestersover Farm
Bransford Spinney
A5
8
River Swift
Ryehill Spinney
Black Spinney
Hill Farm
A426
7
LE17
RUGBY RD
81
THE CHARITY HOS
Churchover
PH
OLD RECTORY CL
THE 5 HOUSES
SCHOOL ST
THE GREEN
Harborough Fields Farm
CHURCH ST
GREEN'S CL
TRUSTEEL HOS
GIBBET HILL
GIBBET LA
6
Heath Farm
CV23
LUTTERWORTH RD
5
COTON RD
80
Newton Spinney
4
Smith's Spinney
Ashtree Farm Top Barn
Coton Farm
Coton House
Icehouse Spinney
Fish Pond
3
Oak Spinney
1
Grange Farm
M6
79
Mitchell Ct 1
Davy Ct 2
CASTLE MOUND WAY
2
COSFORD LA
CV21
CENTRAL PARK DR
Great Central Walk
Lower Lodge Farm
1 STONECHAT RD
2 BENCHES FURLONG
3 MILL FURLONG
4 LONGSTOCK RD
5 ELSTOP AVE
6 CRACKTHORNE DR
VALLEY DR
PIPIT WLK
AVOCET CL
CROWS FURLONG
LANCUT HILL
LONG HASSOCKS
1
Swift Valley Ind Est
A426
TUTHILL FURLONG
THE HOLMES
THE ORCHARDS
GRIMS LA
BRAMBLING CL
78
A
B
51
C
D
52
E
F
83
68

A B C D E F
A426 Leicester
Leicestershire STREET ATLAS M1 Leicester (A5460)
Town End Farm
Lodge Plantations
Home Farm
Spinney Farm
Shawell Wood
SHAWELL RD
SWINFORD RD
RUGBY RD
A426
M1
West Cottages
Cotesbach Fields Farm
Hill Farm
South Lodge
Shawell Lodge Farm
LUTTERWORTH RD
GIBBET LA
Holme Close Farm
Barn Farm
Middle Barn Farm
LE17
Works
Shawell
PH
MAIN ST
SWINFORD RD
Shawell Manor
Hill Top Farm
Mast
Tripontium Bsns Ctr
BULLACES LA
CHURCH LA
Shawell Hall
CATTHORPE RD
SHAWELL RD
Grange Farm
Works
Tomley Hall Farm
M1 Northampton (A45)
NEWTON LA
Europark Ind Est
M6
A14
M6 M1 Junction 19
CV23
Old Barn Farm
THE LEYS
Catthorpe
ELM LA
Newton
Depot
WATLING CRES
Manor Farm
HERMITAGE CL
CATTHORPE MANOR
PH
MAIN ST
LITTLE LONDON LA
SILVER ST
1 NEWTON RD
2 THE PADDOCK
PH
A5
Northamptonshire STREET ATLAS
8 7 81 6 5 80 4 3 79 2 1 78
53 54 55

70

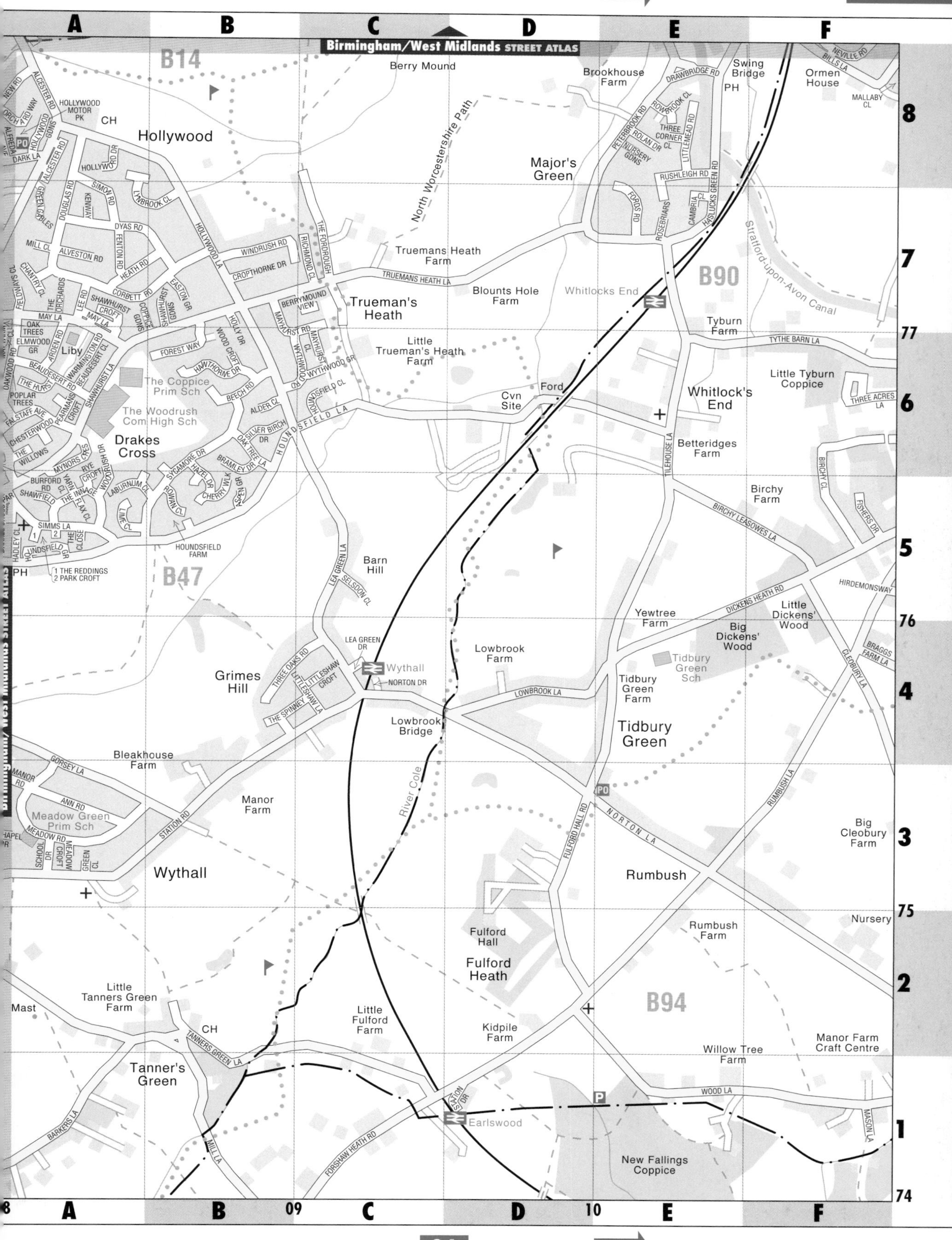
Birmingham/West Midlands STREET ATLAS
B14
Berry Mound
Brookhouse Farm
Swing Bridge
PH
Ormen House
Hollywood
CH
Major's Green
North Worcestershire Path
Truemans Heath Farm
Trueman's Heath
Blounts Hole Farm
Whitlocks End
B90
Stratford-upon-Avon Canal
Tyburn Farm
Little Trueman's Heath Farm
Little Tyburn Coppice
Liby
The Coppice Prim Sch
The Woodrush Com High Sch
Ford
Cvn Site
Whitlock's End
Drakes Cross
Betteridges Farm
Birchy Farm
B47
Barn Hill
Yewtree Farm
Little Dickens' Wood
Big Dickens' Wood
Lowbrook Farm
Tidbury Green Sch
Grimes Hill
Wythall
Tidbury Green Farm
Lowbrook Bridge
Tidbury Green
Bleakhouse Farm
Manor Farm
River Cole
Meadow Green Prim Sch
Big Cleobury Farm
Wythall
Rumbush
Rumbush Farm
Nursery
Fulford Hall
Fulford Heath
B94
Little Tanners Green Farm
Mast
CH
Little Fulford Farm
Kidpile Farm
Manor Farm Craft Centre
Willow Tree Farm
Tanner's Green
Earlswood
New Fallings Coppice
A
B
C
D
E
F
8
7
77
6
5
76
4
3
75
2
1
74
09
10

86
70

69

C8
1 HARWOOD GR
2 SHIRLEYDALE
3 CHELTONDALE
4 HENLEYDALE
5 QUINTONDALE
6 ARDENDALE
7 YARNINGDALE
A34 Birmingham
Birmingham/West Midlands STREET ATLAS
A
B
C
D
E
F
8
7
77
6
5
76
4
3
75
2
1
74
11
12
13
B90
B94
B91
A34
B4102
M42
Light Hall Sch
Sch
Solihull Ret Pk
Our Lady of the Wayside RC Prim Sch
Whitlock's End Farm
Shirley Heath
PH
The Swallows Ind Est
Sports Ctr
Focus Pk
Stirling Pk
Radway Ind Est
Monkspath Bsns Pk
Parish Poles
Research Ctr
Light Hall Farm
Three Maypoles
Three Maypoles Farm
Dickens Heath
Wharf Farm
Baroda Farm
Hotel
Monkspath Street
The Plough (PH)
High Leas Farm
Jerrings Hall Farm
Square Acre Farm
Cheswick Green Prim Sch
Cheswick Green Farm
Mount Dairy Farm
Braggs Farm
Lady Lane Farm
Cheswick Green
River Blythe
Brook House
Little Cleobury Farm
Stratford-upon-Avon Canal
Bedsworth Farm
Winterton Farm
L Ctr
Blythe Valley Park
St Patrick's CE Jun & Inf Sch
Lodge Paddocks
Salter Street
Woodfield Farm
Canal Feeder
Brook Farm Ind Est
Manor Farm Craft Centre
Earlswood
Engine Pool
Earlswood Lakes
Model Railway Club
Illshaw Heath
Waring's Green
Blue Bell Inn (PH)
CH
STRATFORD RD
BLACKFORD RD
TANWORTH LA
SALTER ST
SHUTT LA
DOG KENNEL LA
DICKENS HEATH RD
TYTHE BARN LA
MONKSPATH HALL RD
BRAGGS FARM LA
LADY LA
CLEOBURY LA
VICARAGE RD
ILLSHAW HEATH RD
WARINGS GREEN RD
LIMEKILN LA
KINETON LA
NORTON LA
WOOD LA
VALLEY RD
EARLSMERE
MALTHOUSE LA
BLYTHE GATE
CENTRAL BVD
WATERDALE
1 SPINDLE LA
2 IVY WAY
3 CALCUTT WAY
4 CLARKS LA
1 BROCKHURST LA
2 HARESFIELD
3 BUCKRIDGE LA
4 WADBARN
5 TRUNDALLS LA
6 OLD DICKENS HEATH RD
7 LEDWELL
8 BACK LA
9 TIBBLESTONE
1 HENSBOROUGH
2 WILLOWHERB WAY
3 PRIMROSE LA
4 CAMPION WAY
5 DICKENS HEATH RD
MEERHILL AVE 1
SHERDMORE CROFT 2
STONEHILL CROFT 3
COLEHURST CROFT 4
SLATELEY CRES 5
WREN'S NEST CL

69
87

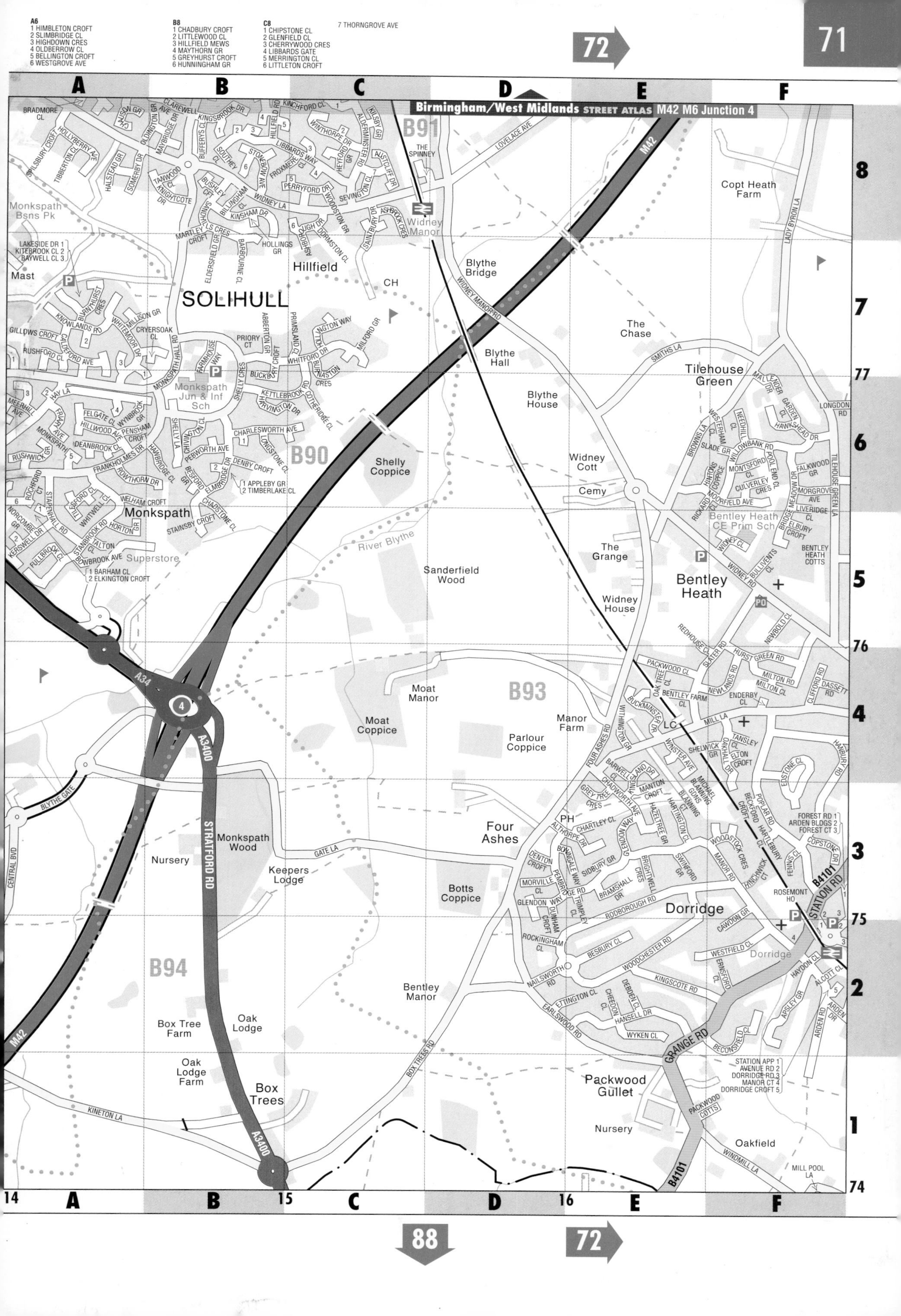
A6
1 HIMBLETON CROFT
2 SLIMBRIDGE CL
3 HIGHDOWN CRES
4 OLDBERROW CL
5 BELLINGTON CROFT
6 WESTGROVE AVE
B8
1 CHADBURY CROFT
2 LITTLEWOOD CL
3 HILLFIELD MEWS
4 MAYTHORN GR
5 GREYHURST CROFT
6 HUNNINGHAM GR
C8
1 CHIPSTONE CL
2 GLENFIELD CL
3 CHERRYWOOD CRES
4 LIBBARDS GATE
5 MERRINGTON CL
6 LITTLETON CROFT
7 THORNGROVE AVE
72
Birmingham/West Midlands STREET ATLAS M42 M6 Junction 4
A
B
C
D
E
F
8
7
77
6
5
76
4
3
75
2
1
74
14
15
16
B91
B90
B93
B94
SOLIHULL
Hillfield
Monkspath
Monkspath Bsns Pk
Mast
Monkspath Jun & Inf Sch
Superstore
Widney Manor
THE SPINNEY
Blythe Bridge
Blythe Hall
Blythe House
The Chase
Copt Heath Farm
Tilehouse Green
Widney Cott
Cemy
The Grange
Widney House
Bentley Heath
Bentley Heath CE Prim Sch
Shelly Coppice
River Blythe
Sanderfield Wood
Moat Manor
Moat Coppice
Manor Farm
Parlour Coppice
Four Ashes
Monkspath Wood
Nursery
Keepers Lodge
Botts Coppice
Dorridge
Bentley Manor
Box Tree Farm
Oak Lodge
Oak Lodge Farm
Box Trees
Packwood Gullet
Nursery
Oakfield
ROSEMONT HO
M42
A34
A3400
STRATFORD RD
B4101
STATION RD
GRANGE RD
LAKESIDE DR 1
KITEBROOK CL 2
BAYWELL CL 3
1 APPLEBY GR
2 TIMBERLAKE CL
1 BARHAM CL
2 ELKINGTON CROFT
FOREST RD 1
ARDEN BLDGS 2
FOREST CT 3
STATION APP 1
AVENUE RD 2
DORRIDGE RD 3
MANOR CT 4
DORRIDGE CROFT 5
WIDNEY LA
WIDNEY MANOR RD
SMITHS LA
LOVELACE AVE
LADY BYRON LA
LONGDON RD
TILEHOUSE GREEN LA
MONKSPATH HALL RD
GATE LA
BLYTHE GATE
CENTRAL BLVD
KINETON LA
BOX TREES RD
FOUR ASHES RD
MILL LA
WINDMILL LA
MILL POOL LA
PACKWOOD COTTS
NAILSWORTH RD
EARLSWOOD RD
RODBOROUGH RD
WOODCHESTER RD
KINGSCOTE RD
HAVDON CL
CH
PH
LC
P
PO

88
72

71
56

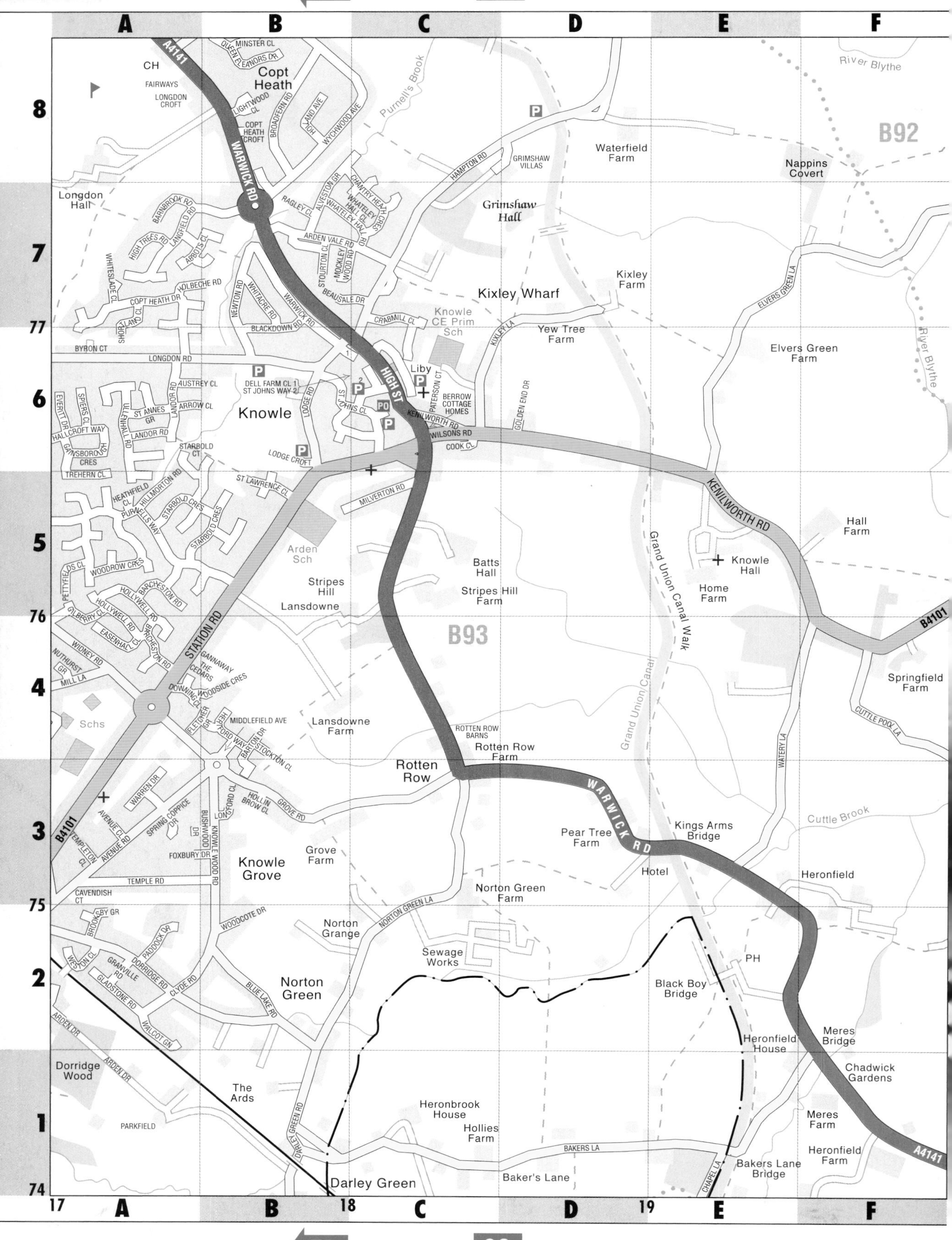
A
B
C
D
E
F
8
7
77
6
5
76
4
3
75
2
1
74
17
18
19
A4141
CH
FAIRWAYS
LONGDON CROFT
Copt Heath
MINSTER CL
QUEEN ELEANORS DR
LIGHTWOOD CL
COPT HEATH CROFT
BROADFERN RD
LAND AVE
WYCHWOOD AVE
Purnell's Brook
WARWICK RD
Longdon Hall
BARNBROOK RD
ANGIFIELD RD
ABBOTS CL
HIGH TREES RD
WHITESLADE CL
HOLBECHE RD
COPT HEATH DR
RAGLEY CL
ALVESTON GR
CHANTRY HEATH CRES
WHATELEY HALL CL
WHATELEY HALL RD
ARDEN VALE RD
STOURTON CL
MOCKLEY WOOD RD
BEAUSALE DR
NEWTON RD
WHITACRE RD
BLACKDOWN RD
CRABMILL CL
HAMPTON RD
GRIMSHAW VILLAS
Grimshaw Hall
Waterfield Farm
River Blythe
B92
Nappins Covert
Kixley Wharf
Kixley Farm
Knowle CE Prim Sch
KIXLEY LA
Yew Tree Farm
ELVERS GREEN LA
Elvers Green Farm
BYRON CT
LONGDON RD
AUSTREY CL
DELL FARM CL
ST JOHNS WAY
LODGE RD
HIGH ST
Liby
PATERSON CT
BERROW COTTAGE HOMES
GOLDEN END DR
ARROW CL
Knowle
ST JOHNS CL
PO
KENILWORTH RD
WILSONS RD
COOK CL
EVERITT DR
SPIERS CL
ULLENHALL RD
ST ANNES GR
LANDOR RD
HALLCROFT WAY
GAINSBOROUGH CRES
TREHERN CL
STARBOLD CT
LODGE CROFT
ST LAWRENCE CL
MILVERTON RD
HEATHFIELD CL
HILLMORTON RD
PURNELLS WAY
STARBOLD CRES
Arden Sch
Batts Hall
Stripes Hill
Stripes Hill Farm
Lansdowne
Grand Union Canal Walk
Hall Farm
Knowle Hall
Home Farm
PETTYFIELDS CL
WOODROW CRES
HOLLYWELL RD
BARCHESTON RD
GILBERRY CL
EASENHALL CL
STATION RD
B93
B4101
Springfield Farm
WIDNEY RD
NUTHURST GR
MILL LA
GANNAWAY
THE CEDARS
WOODSIDE CRES
DOWNING CL
Schs
FLETCHER GR
MIDDLEFIELD AVE
Lansdowne Farm
ROTTEN ROW BARNS
Rotten Row Farm
Grand Union Canal
CUTTLE POOL LA
WATERY LA
BARTON DR
STOCKTON CL
Rotten Row
WARREN DR
HOLLIN BROW CL
GROVE RD
LOWSFORD CL
SPRING COPPICE DR
BUSHWOOD DR
KNOWLE WOOD RD
AVENUE CL
AVENUE RD
TEMPLETON CL
Pear Tree Farm
Kings Arms Bridge
Cuttle Brook
FOXBURY DR
Knowle Grove
Grove Farm
Hotel
Heronfield
TEMPLE RD
CAVENDISH CT
Norton Green Farm
NORTON GREEN LA
WOODCOTE DR
Norton Grange
BROOKSBY GR
PADDOCK DR
WESTON CL
GRANVILLE RD
DORRIDGE RD
GLADSTONE RD
CLYDE RD
Sewage Works
PH
Norton Green
BLUE LAKE RD
Black Boy Bridge
ARDEN DR
WALCOT GN
Heronfield House
Meres Bridge
Dorridge Wood
Chadwick Gardens
The Ards
Heronbrook House
Hollies Farm
Meres Farm
PARKFIELD
DARLEY GREEN RD
BAKERS LA
Heronfield Farm
CHAPEL LA
Bakers Lane Bridge
Darley Green
Baker's Lane

A
B
C
D
E
F
River Blythe
Barston Farm
ELVERS GREEN LA
HOB LA
Barston Park
B92
Barston Park Spinney
BARSTON LA
Sewage Works
CV7
BALSALL ST
The Elms
Grange Farm
PH
GRANGE RD 1
NEEDLERS END LA 2
TEMPLE AVE 3
GREENBANK RD 4
Piercil End
Balsall Farm
MAGPIE LA
SARACEN DR
NEEDLERS END LA
FERN DALE RD
B4101
Magpie Farm
Balsall Street
Springfield House Com Specl Sch
River Blythe
Heart of England Way
Howletts Farm
Fern Hill Farm
FERNHILL LA
Temple Balsall
Lady Katherine Leveson CE Sch
THE COURT OF LADY KATHERINE LEVESON
KENILWORTH RD
Templars Hall
Temple Farm
Cemy
LONG BROOK LA
Gate Farm
Sedgemere
FEN END RD
Ravensbridge
TEMPLE LA
CUTTLE POOL LA
Cuttle Pool
Fen End House
Temple Farm
Frogmore Farm
Park Corner
B93
Balsall Lodge Farm
CV8
Fen End
FROGMORE LA
Woodside
Frogmore Wood
TABLE OAK LA
HONILEY RD
CHADWICK LA
Manor Farm
Chadwick Grange
Fen End Farm
CHADWICK MANOR
OLD GREEN LA
SPARROW COCK LA
Chadwick Cottage Farm
Oldwich House Farm
Balsall Cottage Farm
OLDWICH LANE W
OLDWICH LANE E
COLLEGE LA
OLDWICH LANE E
OAKLEY
PO
Oldwich Lane
Works
A4141
WARWICK RD
8
7
77
6
5
76
4
3
75
2
1
74
20
21
22

73
58

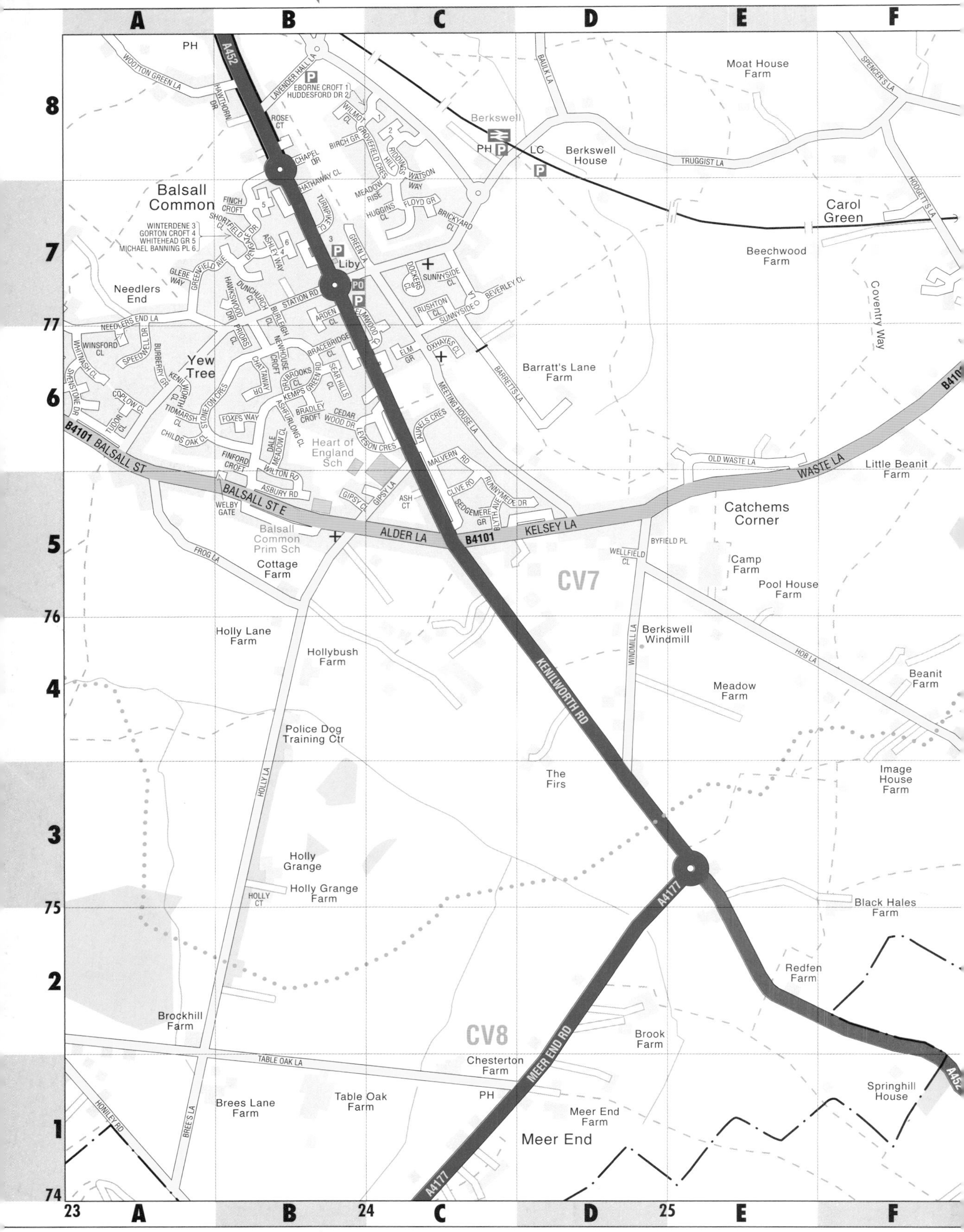

Balsall Common
Needlers End
Yew Tree
Berkswell
Berkswell House
Moat House Farm
Carol Green
Beechwood Farm
Coventry Way
Barratt's Lane Farm
Little Beanit Farm
Catchems Corner
Camp Farm
Pool House Farm
Berkswell Windmill
Beanit Farm
Meadow Farm
Heart of England Sch
Balsall Common Prim Sch
Cottage Farm
Holly Lane Farm
Hollybush Farm
Police Dog Training Ctr
The Firs
Image House Farm
Holly Grange
Holly Grange Farm
Black Hales Farm
Redfen Farm
Brockhill Farm
Brook Farm
Chesterton Farm
Springhill House
Brees Lane Farm
Table Oak Farm
Meer End Farm
Meer End
CV7
CV8
A452
B4101
A4177
BALSALL ST
BALSALL ST E
ALDER LA
KELSEY LA
WASTE LA
OLD WASTE LA
KENILWORTH RD
MEER END RD
TABLE OAK LA
HOLLY LA
HOB LA
WINDMILL LA
FROG LA
TRUGGIST LA
STATION RD
NEEDLERS END LA
MEETING HOUSE LA
BARRETTS LA
HONILEY RD
BREE'S LA
SPENCER'S LA
HODGETTS LA
BAULK LA
WOOTTON GREEN LA
Liby
PH
LC

73
91

59
76
A B C D E F
Cedar Wood Farm
TANNERS LA
B4101
Reeves Green
SPENCER'S LA
Heronbank Farm
DUGGINS LA
LANT CL
Tile Hill
ALAN HIGGS WAY
Leigh CE Prim Sch
Works
Sports Ctr
THE PINES
FALKLAND CL
CURRIERS CL
CHARTER AVE
TORRINGTON AVE
PORTWAY CL
PARBROOK CL
WOODEND CROFT 1
SORREL CL 2
PORTER CL 3
RIDGLEY RD
ROBERT CRAMB AVE
MEADOWCROFT CL
West Side Bsns Ctr
Maguire Ind Est
PAPENHAM GN
HANCOCK GN
FOUNDER CL
WHITCHURCH WAY
SCARBOROUGH WAY
PRESTON CL
YARMOUTH GN
HAYTON GN
KEBULL GN
HOWCOTTE GN
DILCOCK WAY
PAGE RD
CH
Nailcote Hall Hotel
CV7
NAILCOTE LA
Nailcote Farm
Beechwood
WASTE LA
Park Wood
COVENTRY
Charter Prim Sch (Harris Site)
CV4
COPT OAK CL
COLEBY CL
PARK WOOD LA
DALMENY RD
BARN LEIGH DR
ROUGHKNOWLES RD
THRUPPENCE CL
GUINEA CRES
FARTHING WLK
TEN SHILLING DR
LONGWOOD CL
TORWOOD CL
WESTWOOD WAY
Mercia Bsns Village
Westwood Heath
Westwood Bsns Pk
Ensign Bsns Ctr
Cable & Wireless Training & Confrence Ctr
HEATH GREEN WAY
APPLECROSS CL
SANDRINGHAM CL
WESTWOOD HEATH RD
WOODLEIGH RD
HIGHGROVE
BROADWELLS CRES
PH
CROMWELL LA
HODGETTS LA
Lodge Farm
Wr Twr
Beanit Spinney
BOCKENDON RD
Black Waste Wood
Burton Green
Bockendon Grange
Big Poors Wood
Burton Green Farm
Hob Farm
HOB LA
Burton Green CE Prim Sch
Wr Twr
Broadwells Wood
Hurst Farm
South Hurst Farm
CRACKLEY LA
Coventry Way
CV8
RED LA
Roughknowles Wood
Long Meadow Wood
Long Meadow Barn Farm
BLIND LA
HOLLIS LA
Crackley Wood
Redfern Manor
BIRMINGHAM RD
A452
Dunns Pitts Farm
8 7 77 6 5 76 4 3 75 2 1 74
26 27 28
92
76

75
60

A
B
C
D
E
F
8
7
77
6
5
76
4
3
75
2
1
74
29
30
31
TEMPLAR AVE
TORRINGTON AVE
WESTCOTES
EASTCOTES
WOLFE RD
A45
SPITFIRE CL
Coventry Bsns Pk
Works
Fletchworth Gate Ind Est
Charter Prim Sch (Parkes Site)
PILKINGTON RD
Beechwood Gardens
Allot Gdns
LYNBROOK RD
INGRAM RD
KARLINGFORD CL
ROCHESTER RD
RAVEN CRAGG RD
BOW CT
BURNSALL RD
BOTT RD
Westwood Gardens
Canley Gardens
NIGHTINGALE LA
CV5
THE RIDDINGS
BEECHWOOD AVE
AYLESDENE CT 1
WEDGE-WOODS 2
BEECHWOOD CT 3
LEALHOLME CT 4
CH
PAPENHAM GN
FOUNDER CL
KELE RD
PRESTON CL
QUEEN MARGARET'S RD
GERARD AVE
Liby
PRIOR DERAM WLK
TEMPLARS' FIELDS
GRAFTON CT
MAYOR'S CROFT
Canley
WENDIBURGH ST
WALSALL ST
JOHN ROUS AVE
HENRY BOTELER RD
SHERIFF AVE
FREEBURN CSWY
THIMBLER RD
MOAT HOUSE LA
ONLEY TERR
SIR HENRY PARKES RD
CENTENARY RD
FLETCHAMSTEAD HIGHWAY
CANLEY FORD
Ford
GLENROSA WLK 1
CHARTER HO 2
MITCHELL HO 3
Ten Shilling Wood
Alderman Callow Sch & Com Coll
MITCHELL AVE
HUNT TERR
CHARTER AVE
NORTHFOLK TERR
EASTLEIGH AVE
WESTLEIGH AVE
STONELEIGH AVE
WOODLAND AVE
SOUTHLEIGH AVE
Playing Fields
Univ of Warwick (Westwood)
AVON RD
Cemy & Crem
ORLESCOTE RD
CANNON CL
STARETON CL
TORWOOD CL
WESTWOOD WAY
Westwood Bsns Pk
Ensign Bsns Ctr
KIRBY CORNER RD
LYNCHGATE CT & HO
AVON HO
PO
VANGUARD CTR
SIR WILLIAM LYONS RD
Cannon Park District Ctr
SHULTERN LA
JACOB DR
SWALEDALE
THE CHEVIOT
RAVENSHOLT
ATHERSTON PL
HILARY RD
SEFTON RD
TUTBURY AVE
CANNOCKS LA
CANNES CT
BUTTERWORTH DR
BROADWELLS CRES
MILBURN HILL RD
ADVANCED TECHNOLOGY UNIT
LEEMING CL
SQUIRES WAY
BRILL CL
STARE GN
CLOUD GN
LEAM GN
LILACVALE WAY
MERYNTON AVE
CANNON PARK RD
FAIRLANDS PK
THE LAURELS
A45
KENPAS HIGHWAY
A429
KIRBY CNR
WESTWOOD HEATH RD
FEATHERBED LA
Univ of Warwick Science Pk
LICHEN GN
BRANSFORD AVE
CANNON HILL RD
REGENCY DR
WOODSIDE AVE S
WAINBODY AVE S
Country Club
CV4
EVESHAM WLK
DE MONTFORT WAY
BLACKTHORN CL
LUNAR CL
COLLINS GR
HIGHWAYMANS CROFT
Cannon Park Prim Sch
SCARMAN RD
LIBRARY RD
UNIVERSITY RD
OLD MILL AVE
TOLL CROFT
CHANCELLORS CL
THE SHRUBBERIES
MOAT AVE
MEDLAND AVE
BEANFIELD AVE
LEASOWE'S AVE
GRETNA RD
HEALTH CENTRE RD
Old Brickyard Plantation
CRYFIELD VILLAGE
Univ of Warwick
THE GALLIARDS
HEYCROFT
RIVERFORD CROFT
PIPERS CT
Bishop Ullathorne RC Sch
Whitefield Coppice
Cryfield House
GIBBET HILL RD
Tocil Wood
Univ of Warwick (Gibbet Hill)
ABBERTON WAY
HERITAGE CT
POPPYFIELD CT
KENILWORTH RD
MOREALL MDWS
CASSANDRA CL
THE ARBORETUM
RUSSET GR
CV3
THE SPINNEY
LITTLE CRYFIELD
CRYFIELD HTS
LEIGHTON CL
Wainbody Wood
Wainbody Wood Sch
CRYFIELD GRANGE RD
Cryfield Grange
CV8
MARSHFIELD DR
BEVERLY DR
STONELEIGH RD
Gibbet Hill
Wainbody Wood Farm
KING'S HILL LA
Newera Farm
Crackley Wood
A429

75
93

61
78

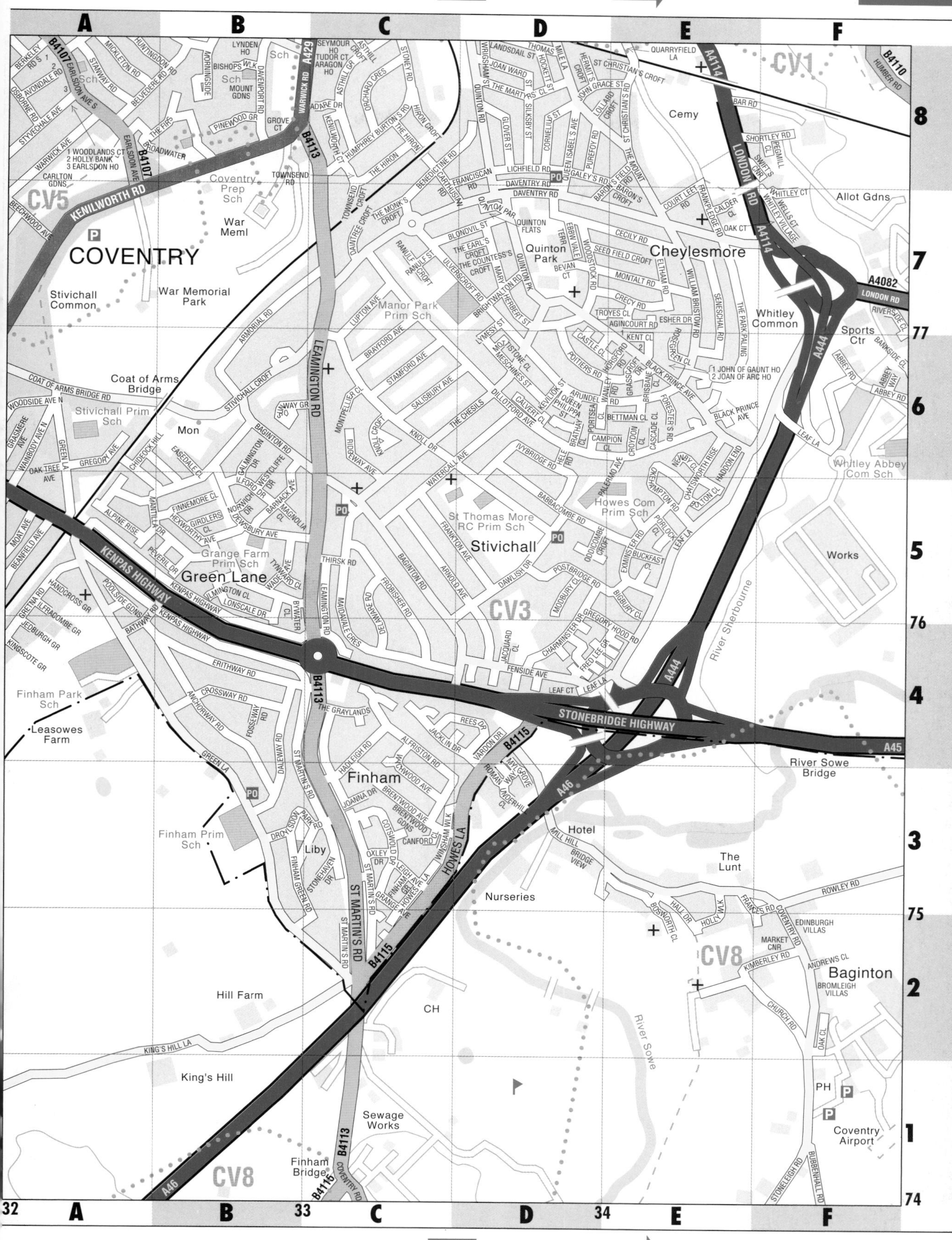
A
B
C
D
E
F
8
7
77
6
5
76
4
3
75
2
1
74
32
33
34
COVENTRY
CV5
CV1
CV3
CV8
Cheylesmore
Quinton Park
Stivichall
Green Lane
Finham
Baginton
Stivichall Common
War Memorial Park
War Meml
Coventry Prep Sch
Coat of Arms Bridge
Stivichall Prim Sch
Mon
Manor Park Prim Sch
St Thomas More RC Prim Sch
Howes Com Prim Sch
Grange Farm Prim Sch
Whitley Common
Whitley Abbey Com Sch
Allot Gdns
Sports Ctr
Cemy
Works
River Sherbourne
Finham Park Sch
Leasowes Farm
Finham Prim Sch
Liby
Hotel
The Lunt
Nurseries
River Sowe Bridge
River Sowe
Hill Farm
King's Hill
CH
Sewage Works
Finham Bridge
PH
Coventry Airport
KENILWORTH RD
KENPAS HIGHWAY
STONEBRIDGE HIGHWAY
LEAMINGTON RD
LONDON RD
ST MARTIN'S RD
HOWES LA
COVENTRY RD
A46
A45
A444
A4114
A4082
A429
B4113
B4115
B4107
B4110
1 WOODLANDS CT
2 HOLLY BANK
3 EARLSDON HO
1 JOHN OF GAUNT HO
2 JOAN OF ARC HO

94
78

77
62

F8
1 CARDALE CROFT
2 KESTREL CROFT
3 RUTLAND CROFT
4 JIM FORREST CL
5 WILLOWHERB CL
6 WASPERTON CL
7 JOE WILLIAMS CL
8 DEERDALE TERR

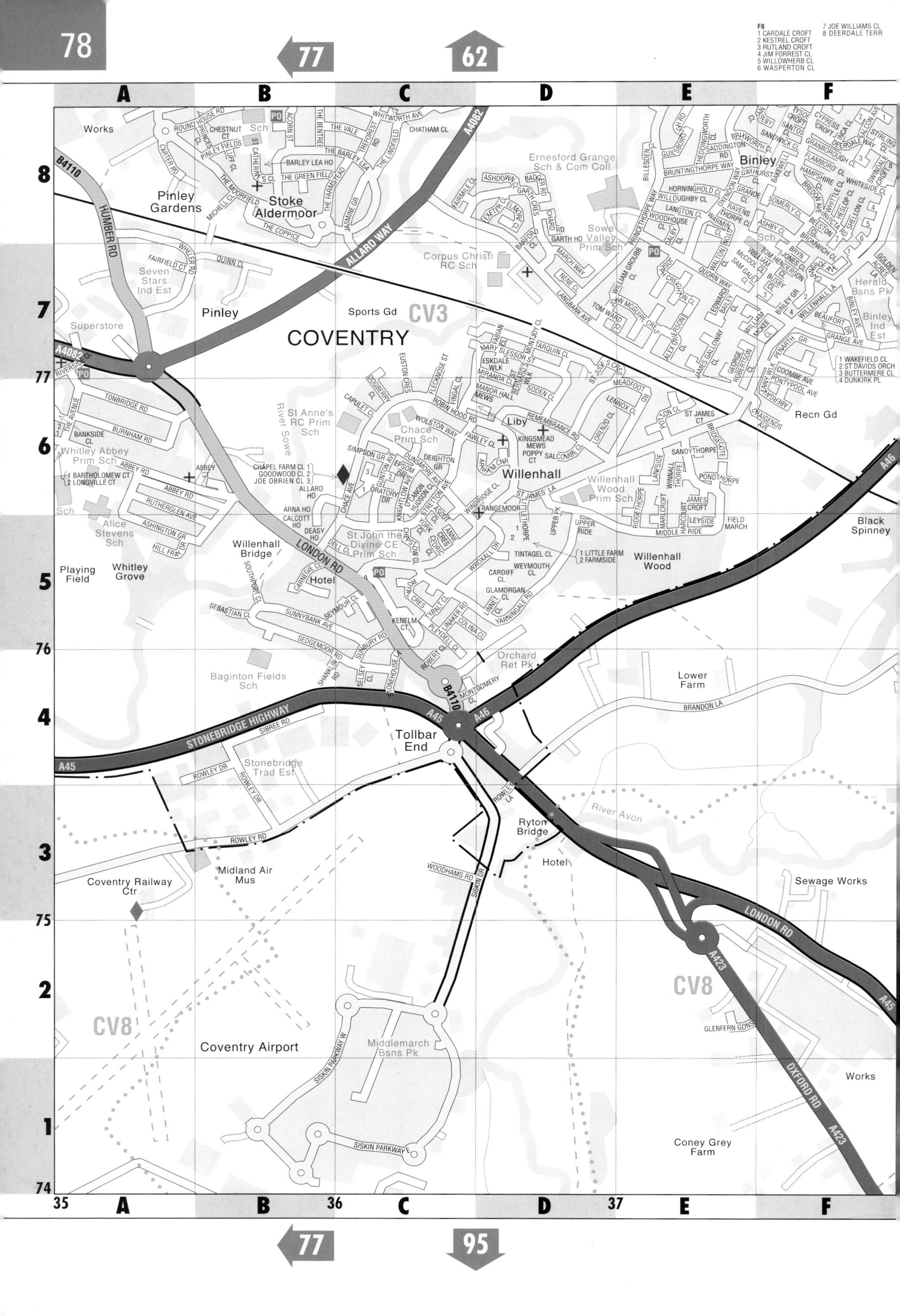

77
95

63
80
Big Rough
Roseycombe Cottages
New Close Wood
One O'clock Ride
Twelve O'clock Ride
Centenary Way
Merton Hall Farm
Superstore
Binley Ind Est
Hotel
BRANDON RD
RUGBY RD
Sherwood Farm
Coventry Stadium
Binley Woods
Liby
Binley Woods Prim Sch
The Bogs
Piles Coppice
Brandon Little Wood
CV3
Brandon Wood
The Pools
Works
Hotel
Brandon
Brandon Wood Farm
Long Spinney
BRANDON LA
Mast
CH
Brandon Marsh Visitor Ctr
New Hare Covert
Brandon Marsh Nature Reserve
River Avon
Wolston Fields Farm
The Plantation
Old Hare Covert
CV8
Allot Gdns
Wolston
Coventry Way
Sewage Works
Centenary Way
Fields House
The Cottage
Grounds Farm
Ryton-on-Dunsmore
Church Farm
LONDON RD
WOLSTON LA
Ryton Organic Gdns
Provost Williams CE Prim Sch
LEAMINGTON RD
The Barbellows
CV23
96
80

79
64

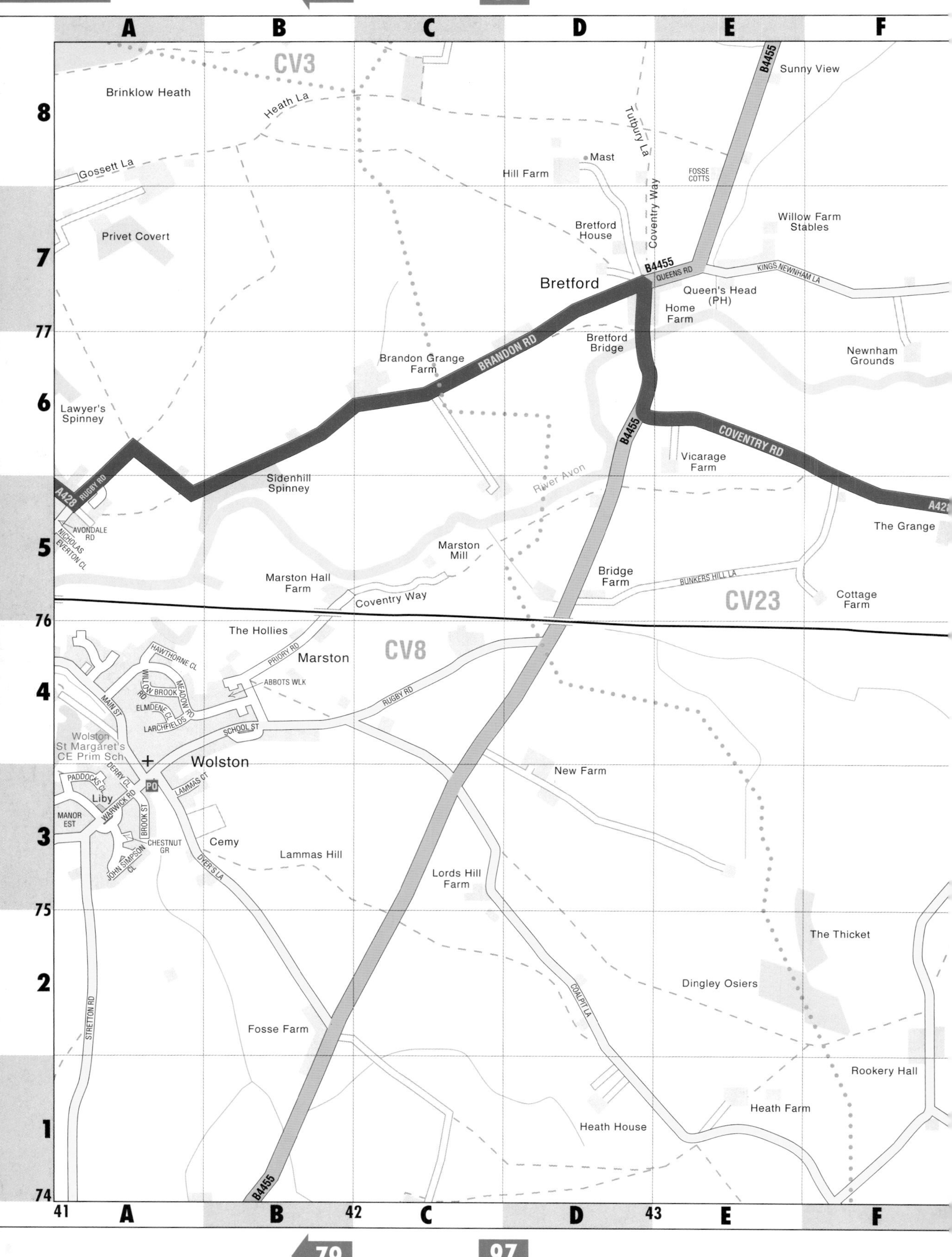
A B C D E F
8 7 6 5 4 3 2 1
77 76 75 74
41 42 43
CV3
Brinklow Heath
Heath La
Gossett La
Privet Covert
Lawyer's Spinney
A428 RUGBY RD
Sidenhill Spinney
AVONDALE RD
NICHOLAS
EVERTON CL
Marston Hall Farm
Coventry Way
Marston Mill
Brandon Grange Farm
BRANDON RD
Bretford
Hill Farm
Mast
Tutbury La
Coventry Way
Bretford House
B4455
QUEENS RD
FOSSE COTTS
Sunny View
Willow Farm Stables
KINGS NEWNHAM LA
Queen's Head (PH)
Home Farm
Bretford Bridge
Newnham Grounds
COVENTRY RD
Vicarage Farm
River Avon
The Grange
A428
Bridge Farm
BUNKERS HILL LA
CV23
Cottage Farm
The Hollies
HAWTHORNE CL
PRIORY RD
Marston
CV8
ABBOTS WLK
WILLOW RD
BROOK
MEADOW RD
ELMDENE CL
LARCHFIELDS
MAIN ST
SCHOOL ST
RUGBY RD
Wolston St Margaret's CE Prim Sch
Wolston
PO
PADDOCKS CL
DERRY CL
LAMMAS CT
Liby
MANOR EST
WARWICK RD
BROOK ST
CHESTNUT GR
JOHN SIMPSON CL
Cemy
DYER'S LA
Lammas Hill
New Farm
Lords Hill Farm
STRETTON RD
The Thicket
Dingley Osiers
COALPIT LA
Fosse Farm
Rookery Hall
Heath Farm
Heath House

79
97

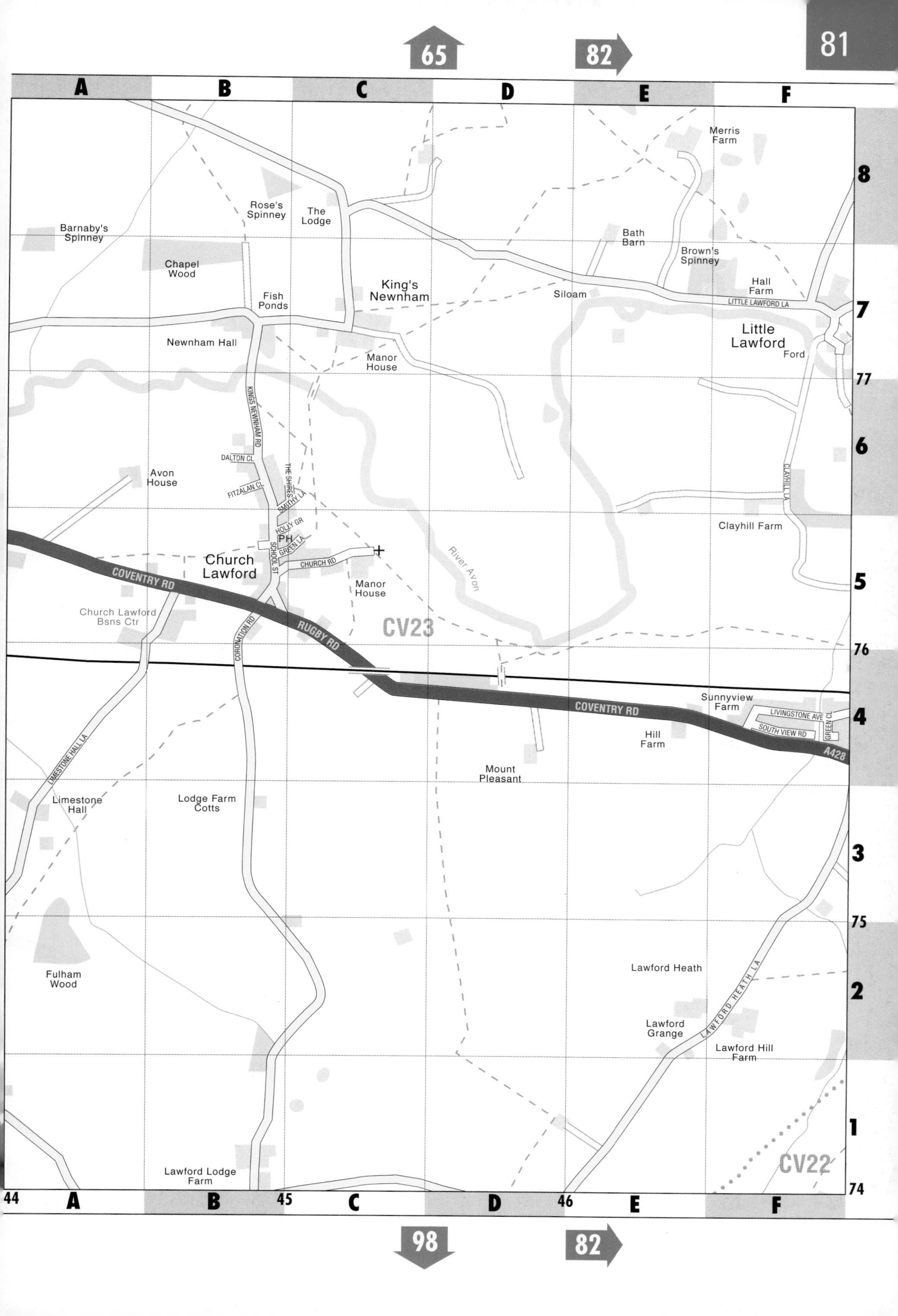
65
82
A
B
C
D
E
F
8
7
77
6
5
76
4
3
75
2
1
74
44
45
46
Merris Farm
Rose's Spinney
The Lodge
Barnaby's Spinney
Bath Barn
Brown's Spinney
Chapel Wood
Hall Farm
Fish Ponds
King's Newnham
Siloam
LITTLE LAWFORD LA
Little Lawford
Newnham Hall
Manor House
Ford
KINGS NEWNHAM RD
DALTON CL
THE SHIRES
Avon House
FITZALAN CL
SMITHY LA
CLAYHILL LA
HOLLY GR
PH
GREEN LA
Clayhill Farm
SCHOOL ST
Church Lawford
CHURCH RD
River Avon
COVENTRY RD
Manor House
Church Lawford Bsns Ctr
CORONATION RD
RUGBY RD
CV23
Sunnyview Farm
COVENTRY RD
LIVINGSTONE AVE
SOUTH VIEW RD
GREEN CL
Hill Farm
A428
LIMESTONE HALL LA
Mount Pleasant
Limestone Hall
Lodge Farm Cotts
Fulham Wood
Lawford Heath
LAWFORD HEATH LA
Lawford Grange
Lawford Hill Farm
CV22
Lawford Lodge Farm
98
82

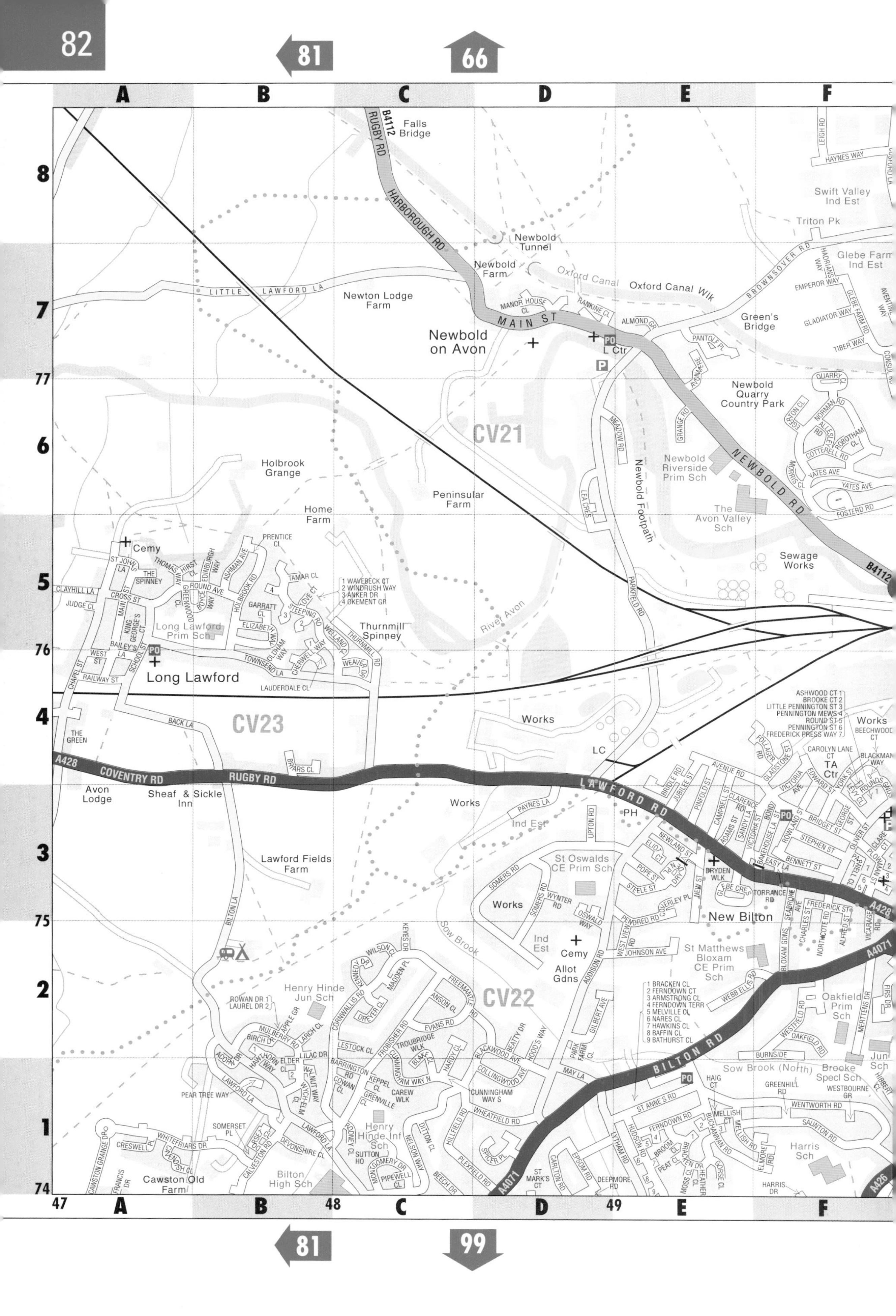
A
B
C
D
E
F
8
7
77
6
5
76
4
3
75
2
1
74
47
48
49
Falls Bridge
B4112
RUGBY RD
HARBOROUGH RD
Newbold Tunnel
Newbold Farm
Oxford Canal
Oxford Canal Wlk
LITTLE LAWFORD LA
Newton Lodge Farm
MAIN ST
Newbold on Avon
L Ctr
Swift Valley Ind Est
Triton Pk
Glebe Farm Ind Est
BROWNSOVER RD
Green's Bridge
Newbold Quarry Country Park
CV21
Holbrook Grange
Home Farm
Peninsular Farm
Newbold Riverside Prim Sch
NEWBOLD RD
The Avon Valley Sch
Newbold Footpath
Sewage Works
Cemy
1 WAVEBECK CT
2 WINDRUSH WAY
3 ANKER DR
4 OKEMENT GR
Thurnmill Spinney
River Avon
Long Lawford Prim Sch
Long Lawford
CV23
Works
LC
A428
COVENTRY RD
RUGBY RD
LAWFORD RD
Avon Lodge
Sheaf & Sickle Inn
Works
Ind Est
Lawford Fields Farm
St Oswalds CE Prim Sch
Works
New Bilton
St Matthews Bloxam CE Prim Sch
Cemy
Allot Gdns
ASHWOOD CT 1
BROOKE CT 2
LITTLE PENNINGTON ST 3
PENNINGTON MEWS 4
ROUND ST 5
PENNINGTON ST 6
FREDERICK PRESS WAY 7
TA Ctr
Henry Hinde Jun Sch
ROWAN DR 1
LAUREL DR 2
CV22
Sow Brook
1 BRACKEN CL
2 FERNDOWN CT
3 ARMSTRONG CL
4 FERNDOWN TERR
5 MELVILLE CL
6 NARES CL
7 HAWKINS CL
8 BAFFIN CL
9 BATHURST CL
Oakfield Prim Sch
BILTON RD
Sow Brook (North)
Brooke Specl Sch
Jun Sch
Henry Hinde Inf Sch
Bilton High Sch
Cawston Old Farm
Harris Sch
A4071
A426

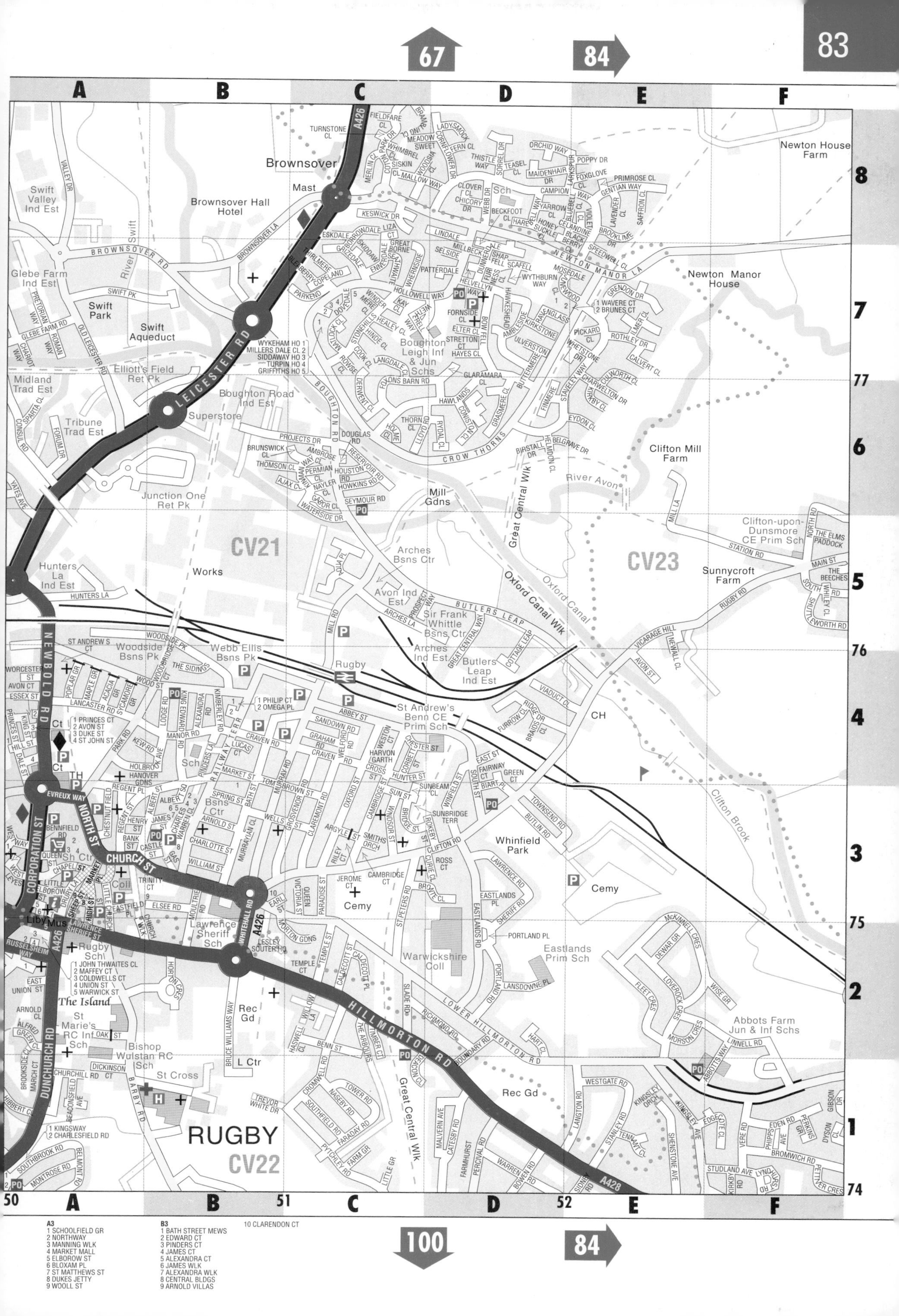

83
67
84
100
84
A
B
C
D
E
F
8
7
77
6
5
76
4
3
75
2
1
74
50
51
52
Brownsover
Mast
Brownsover Hall Hotel
Swift Valley Ind Est
Glebe Farm Ind Est
Swift Park
Swift Aqueduct
River Swift
Elliott's Field Ret Pk
Midland Trad Est
Tribune Trad Est
Boughton Road Ind Est
Superstore
Junction One Ret Pk
Works
CV21
Hunters La Ind Est
Woodside Bsns Pk
Webb Ellis Bsns Pk
Rugby
Arches Bsns Ctr
Avon Ind Est
Sir Frank Whittle Bsns Ctr
Arches Ind Est
Butlers Leap Ind Est
Mill Gdns
River Avon
Great Central Wlk
Oxford Canal Wlk
Oxford Canal
CV23
Newton House Farm
Newton Manor House
Clifton Mill Farm
Clifton-upon-Dunsmore CE Prim Sch
Sunnycroft Farm
Clifton Brook
Boughton Leigh Inf & Jun Schs
St Andrew's Benn CE Prim Sch
Whinfield Park
Cemy
Warwickshire Coll
Eastlands Prim Sch
Abbots Farm Jun & Inf Schs
Lawrence Sheriff Sch
Rugby Sch
The Island
St Marie's RC Inf Sch
Bishop Wulstan RC Sch
St Cross
Rec Gd
L Ctr
RUGBY
CV22
LEICESTER RD
NEWBOLD RD
CORPORATION ST
NORTH ST
CHURCH ST
EVREUX WAY
HILLMORTON RD
LOWER HILLMORTON RD
DUNCHURCH RD
BOUGHTON RD
NEWTON MANOR LA
CROW THORNS
BUTLERS LEAP
RUGBY RD
CLIFTON RD
WHITEHALL RD
A426
A428
A3
1 SCHOOLFIELD GR
2 NORTHWAY
3 MANNING WLK
4 MARKET MALL
5 ELBOROW ST
6 BLOXAM PL
7 ST MATTHEWS ST
8 DUKES JETTY
9 WOOLL ST
B3
1 BATH STREET MEWS
2 EDWARD CT
3 PINDERS CT
4 JAMES CT
5 ALEXANDRA CT
6 JAMES WLK
7 ALEXANDRA WLK
8 CENTRAL BLDGS
9 ARNOLD VILLAS
10 CLARENDON CT

83
68

A1
1 BROMWICH RD
2 PETTIVER CRES
3 THE MEWS

83
101

86

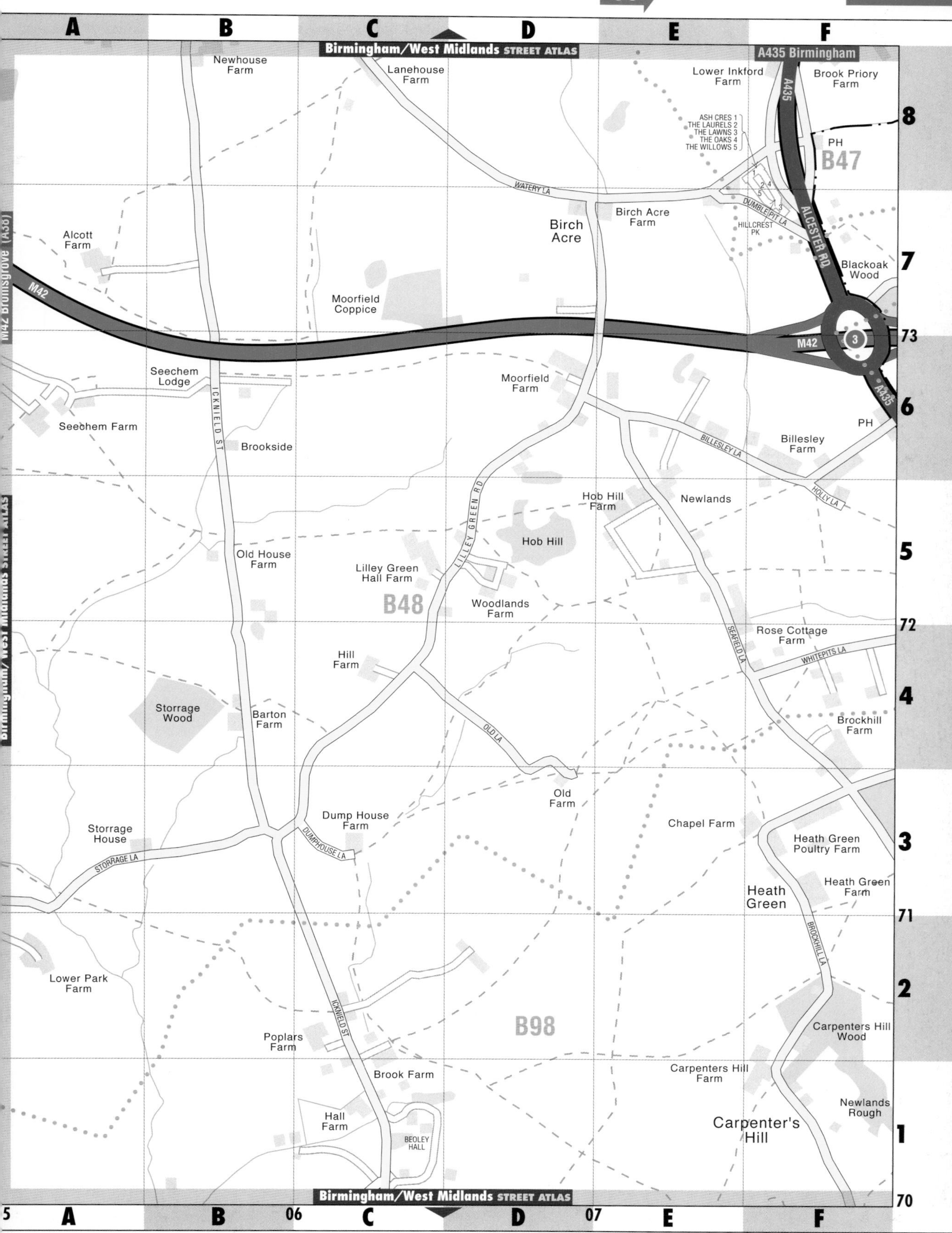
A
B
C
D
E
F
Birmingham/West Midlands STREET ATLAS
A435 Birmingham
Newhouse Farm
Lanehouse Farm
Lower Inkford Farm
Brook Priory Farm
ASH CRES 1
THE LAURELS 2
THE LAWNS 3
THE OAKS 4
THE WILLOWS 5
PH
B47
WATERY LA
DUMBLE PIT LA
HILLCREST PK
ALCESTER RD
A435
Birch Acre
Birch Acre Farm
Alcott Farm
Blackoak Wood
M42 Bromsgrove (A38)
M42
Moorfield Coppice
Seechem Lodge
Seechem Farm
Moorfield Farm
Brookside
ICKNIELD ST
BILLESLEY LA
Billesley Farm
PH
HOLLY LA
Hob Hill Farm
Newlands
Hob Hill
LILLEY GREEN RD
Old House Farm
Lilley Green Hall Farm
B48
Woodlands Farm
Rose Cottage Farm
WHITEPITS LA
SEAFIELD LA
Hill Farm
Storrage Wood
Barton Farm
OLD LA
Brockhill Farm
Old Farm
Dump House Farm
DUMPHOUSE LA
Chapel Farm
Storrage House
STORRAGE LA
Heath Green Poultry Farm
Heath Green
Heath Green Farm
BROCKHILL LA
Lower Park Farm
B98
Poplars Farm
Carpenters Hill Wood
Brook Farm
Carpenters Hill Farm
Hall Farm
BEOLEY HALL
Carpenter's Hill
Newlands Rough
8
7
73
6
5
72
4
3
71
2
1
70
05
06
07
Birmingham/West Midlands STREET ATLAS

86

85
69

A
B
C
D
E
F
River Cole
MILL LA
FORSHAW HEATH RD
The Poplars
Terry's Pool
8
B47
Clowes Wood
Pound Close Farm
CLOWESWOOD LA
The Lakes
Terry's Green
Forshaw Heath
B48
Graves Coppice
POOLHEAD LA
White House Farm
MALTHOUSE LA
SPRINGBROOK LA
7
FORSHAW HEATH LA
JUGGINS LA
OAKTREE FARM MOBILE HOMES PK
Yew Tree Farm
Forshaw Park Farm
Glebe Farm
Springbrook Farm
Checkley's Coppice
WOODSIDE PK MOBILE HOMES PK
73
M42
The Plantation
The Lyndons
Small Lane Farm
SMALL LA
FORSHAW HEATH LA
Earlswood Trad Est
BIDDLES HILL
Spring Brook
6
A435
Rugby Football Ground
Sewage Works
M42
Tyler's Grove
Windmill Naps
B48
Portway
POOLHEAD LA
5
Pool House Farm
Ladbrookpark Coppice
Poolhead Farm
WOOD END LA
B94
Holly Farm
72
WHITEPITS LA
PENN LA
ALCESTER RD
Cottage Farm
Ladbrooke Hall Farm
PH
Little Ladbrooke Farm
Ladbrooke Hall
Wood End
B4101
4
Lion Wood
PENN LA
ALCESTER RD
CH
BROCKHILL LA
Wood End
Hill Barn
Brockhill Wood
WOODCOCK CL
3
RUSHBROOK LA
Rushbrook
High Park Farm
Rushbrook Farm
BROAD LA
VICARAGE HILL
Gilbert's Green
71
Highpark Wood
Spring Brook
B98
SEAFIELD LA
2
ARDEN LEYS
ASPLEY HEATH LA
Park Farm
Aspley Heath
River Alne
PH
ASPLEY HEATH
Branson's Cross
Baylis Green
BEOLEY LA
BROAD LA
BLIND LA
CHERRY PIT LA
1
Pinkfield Wood
Branson's Cross Farm
Aspley Farm
BATES LA
Alderhanger Wood
B4101
A435
70
08
A
B
09
C
D
10
E
F

85
112

70
88
A
B
C
D
E
F
VALLEY RD
SHUTT LA
PH
PO
B4102
MALTHOUSE LA
WARREN CL
Windmill Pool
Earlswood Court
Waring's Green Farm
Waring's Green
M42
SALTER ST
WARINGS GREEN RD
DYERS LA
TINKERS LA
SCHOOL RD
Stratford-upon-Avon Canal
Rotheram's Oak Farm
The Old Moathouse
Terry's Green
Flower Knott Cottage
High Chimneys Farm
Clay Bank Farm
Acorn Coppice
CUT THROAT LA
Woodlands Farm
Cottage Farm
Mast
ROTHERHAMS OAK LA
SPRINGBROOK LA
UMBERSLADE RD
Old Grove Wood
Heathfield Farm
EARLSWOOD COMM
Wychpitts Farm
Arnold's Wood
Old Grove
The Beeches
TITHE BARN LA
3a
Three Gables Wood Farm
Abbey Farm
The Priory
Chamber's Coppice
Chalcot Wood
Jonathan's Farm
Wood's Coppice
Bissell's Coppice
M42
M40
Clarksland Coppice
B94
Birchy Cross
M40
BROAD LA
Beaumont Hill Farm
Birchy Cross Farm
Brown's Green
POUND HOUSE LA
B4101
Works
Brown's Green House
Tom Hill
Brook House Farm
Brown's Green Wood
Umberslade Hall
TOM HILL
UMBERSLADE RD
South Lodge
Knowlebury Cross
VICARAGE HILL
DOCTORS HILL
MILE END
BELLFIELD
The Vicarage
DOCTORS CL
BUTTS LA
Tanworth-in-Arden
Umberslade Children's Farm
PO PH
Tanworth-in-Arden CE Prim Sch
BATES LA
THE GREEN
OVERBARE CL
WELL LA
Dairy House Farm
Cank Farm
Sewage Works
DANZEY GREEN LA
Robin Hood Farm
KEMPS GREEN RD
8
7
73
6
5
72
4
3
71
2
1
70
1
12
13

87

71

A B C D E F

8

7

73

6

5

72

4

3

71

2

1

70

Ivy House Farm

B4101

MILL POOL LA

WINDMILL LA

B93

Packwood Towers

GRANGE RD

A3400

HOCKLEY CT

Cheedon Farm

Motel

Aylesbury House (Hotel)

ASHFORD LA

AYLESBURY RD

VICARAGE RD

SCHOOL RD

RASHWOOD CL

UTNALL DR

ORCHARD RD

AYLESBURY CL

B4101

HAZEL GR

PH

PARK VIEW

MEADOW CL

Hockley Heath

SADLERSWELL LA

2

1

ARDEN MEADS

3

FIELD WAY

CUT THROAT LA

Hockley Heath Prim Sch

PO

Packwood Hall

BLACKBERRY AVE

MUNTZ CRES

TYSOE CL

PH

1 PORTMANTEAU MEWS
2 BLACKSMITHS LA
3 SHELFIELD CL

Big Spring Coppice

LINDHURST DR

B4439

GLASSHOUSE LA

Home Farm

SPRING LA

BELTON CL

B4101

FETHERSTON GRANGE

Stratford-upon-Avon Canal

Drawbridge

Sands Farm

Fetherston House

Malthouse Farm

Little Spring Coppice

STRATFORD RD

OLD WARWICK RD

BELLE COTTS

B94

B4101

M40

Nuthurst

WHARF LA

Lapworth Hall

GROVE LA

Obelisk Farm

NUTHURST GRANGE LA

Drawbridge Farm Bridge

POUND HOUSE LA

Obelisk

Spring Cottage

Drawbridge Farm

Lapworth Farm

Mountford Farm

Pool's Wood

B4439

Umberslade Park

PH

SPRING LA

Lapworth

Nuthurst Grange (Hotel)

Lapworth Hill Farm

CHURCH LA

Far Croft

Lapworth Croft

Lapworth Grange

Green Acres

16

Harrisons Farm

NUTHURST RD

TAPSTER LA

Kemps Green Farm

Lapworth Bridge

M40

Kemps Green

Nuthurst Farm

KEMPS GREEN RD

MOWS HILL RD

The Birches

TINKERS LA

A3400

Hole House Farm

HOLE HOUSE LA

14 A B 15 C D 16 E F

87

72
90

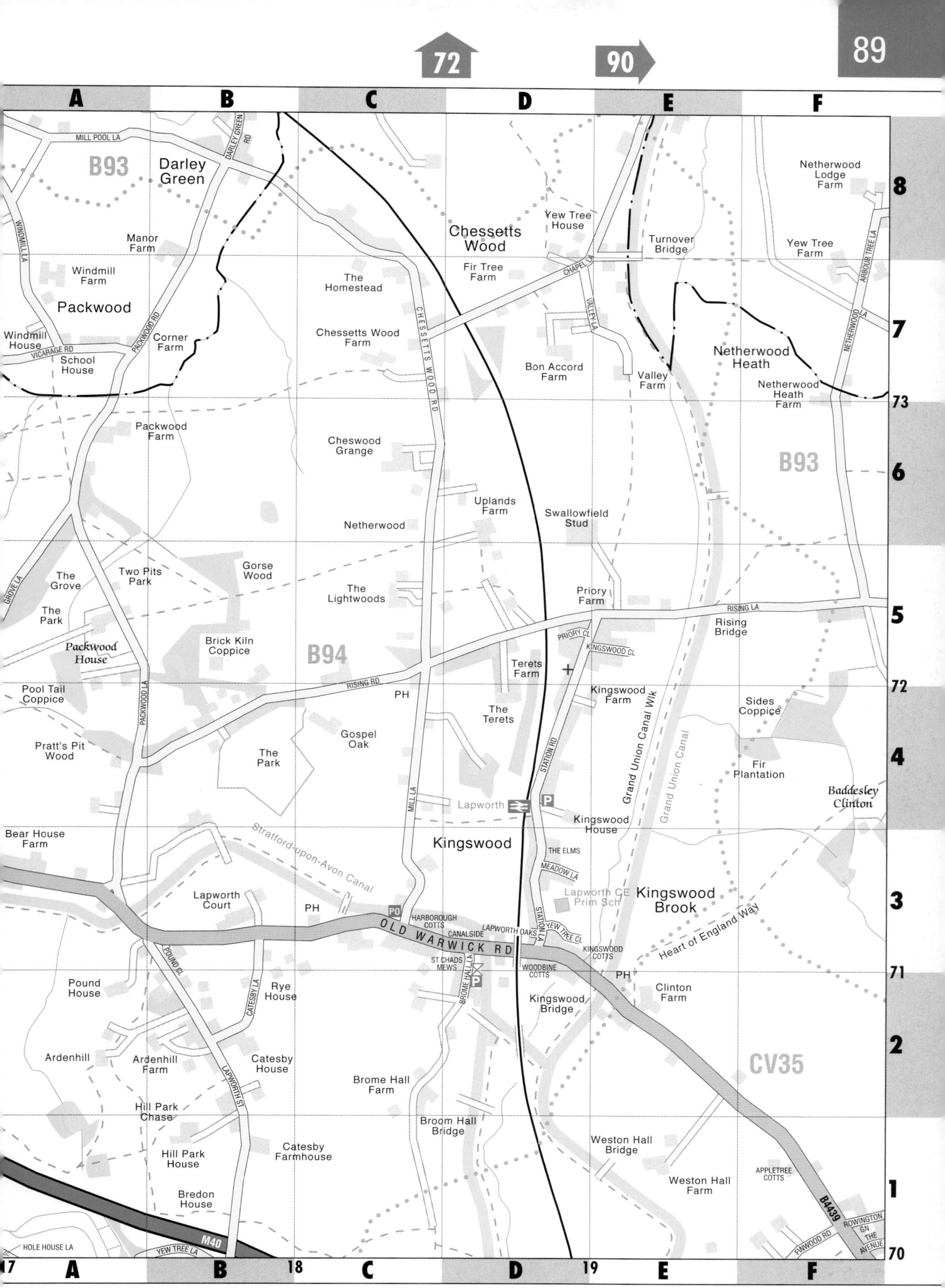
Darley Green
Packwood
Chessetts Wood
Netherwood Heath
Kingswood
Kingswood Brook
Lapworth
B93
B94
CV35
Manor Farm
Windmill Farm
Windmill House
School House
Corner Farm
The Homestead
Chessetts Wood Farm
Fir Tree Farm
Yew Tree House
Turnover Bridge
Netherwood Lodge Farm
Yew Tree Farm
Bon Accord Farm
Valley Farm
Netherwood Heath Farm
Packwood Farm
Cheswood Grange
Uplands Farm
Swallowfield Stud
Netherwood
The Grove
Two Pits Park
Gorse Wood
The Lightwoods
Priory Farm
Rising Bridge
The Park
Packwood House
Brick Kiln Coppice
Terets Farm
Pool Tail Coppice
Kingswood Farm
Sides Coppice
The Terets
Pratt's Pit Wood
Gospel Oak
Fir Plantation
Baddesley Clinton
Kingswood House
Bear House Farm
Lapworth Court
Lapworth CE Prim Sch
Pound House
Rye House
Kingswood Bridge
Clinton Farm
Ardenhill
Ardenhill Farm
Catesby House
Brome Hall Farm
Hill Park Chase
Broom Hall Bridge
Weston Hall Bridge
Hill Park House
Catesby Farmhouse
Weston Hall Farm
Bredon House
Stratford-upon-Avon Canal
Grand Union Canal
Grand Union Canal Wlk
Heart of England Way
MILL POOL LA
DARLEY GREEN RD
WINDMILL LA
VICARAGE RD
PACKWOOD RD
CHESSETTS WOOD RD
CHAPEL LA
VALLEY LA
NETHERWOOD LA
ARBOUR TREE LA
GROVE LA
RISING LA
RISING RD
PRIORY CL
KINGSWOOD CL
PACKWOOD LA
STATION RD
MILL LA
THE ELMS
MEADOW LA
OLD WARWICK RD
HARBOROUGH COTTS
CANALSIDE
LAPWORTH OAKS
STATION LA
YEW TREE CL
KINGSWOOD COTTS
ST CHADS MEWS
BROME HALL LA
WOODBINE COTTS
POUND CL
CATESBY LA
LAPWORTH ST
APPLETREE COTTS
B4439
ROWINGTON GN
THE AVENUE
FINWOOD RD
HOLE HOUSE LA
YEW TREE LA
M40
PH
PO
P
A
B
C
D
E
F
17
18
19
8
7
73
6
5
72
4
3
71
2
1
70

113
90

89
73

A B C D E F
8
7
73
6
5
72
4
3
71
2
1
70
20 21 22
A4141
WARWICK RD
BIRMINGHAM RD
Arbour Tree Farm
ARBOUR TREE LA
CHADWICK LA
Chadwick End Farm
OLDWICH LA W
Rosemary Farm
SPARROW COCK LA
Brookside Grange
Dadkin Farm
Sewage Works
OLDWICH LA E
HILLTOP CL
CV8
Hill Farm
Chadwick End
Priests Park Wood
Heart of England Way
Nunley Farm
Proving Ground
Works
NETHERWOOD LA
WHEELER CL
BAKEHOUSE LA
PH
Bedlam's End
THISTLEWOOD GR
Priests Park Farm
CHADWICK MEWS
B93
BAKERS MEWS
Baddesley Clinton
Nunley Pit
Breach Wood
Convent
Warren Farm
RISING LA
Manor Park Farm
Haywood Farm
Manor Wood
Nunnery Coppice
Brome's Park
SCHOOL LA
Cemy
Glendale
Abbey Farm
CV35
LAUNDRY COTTS
MANOR LA
SCHOOL COTTS
Wroxall
Old Keeper's Lodge
HAY WOOD LA
Hay Wood
Wood Corner Farm
Heart of England Way
Wroxall Abbey
Priory (rems of)
The Park
Rowington Coppice
Gilbert's Coppice
Rowington Green
Lyons Farm
Rowington Mill
QUARRY LA
Quarry Farm
ROWINGTON GN
QUEEN'S DR
THE AVENUE
1 BEECH CL
2 ALMSHOUSES
Shrewley Lodge Farm
CASE LA
PH
FIVE WAYS
FIVE WAYS RD
A4177

89
114

74
92
A
B
C
D
E
F
8
7
73
6
5
72
4
3
71
2
1
70
23
24
25
114
92
Proving Ground
Honiley Rd
Meer End Rd
A4177
Pear Tree Farm
Blenheim Farm
Rudfyn Manor
Runway Farm
Croft Farm
Black Hill Wood
Poors Wood
Holly Farm Bsns Pk
Wattcote Farm
Honiley Rd
Warriors Lodge Farm
Chase La
Chase Wood
CV8
Honiley Boot (PH)
Yew Tree Cottage
Church Farm
Honiley
Honiley Hall
Featherstons Grove
Manor La
Thorny Coppice
Grove Farm
Clattyland Wood
Grove Cottage
Wakefield Wood
PO
Haseley Knob
CV35
Hill Farm Cottage
Cheyneys Farm
School Croft
Hill Farm
Fernwood Farm
Heath Terr
Butlers End
Barracks La
Rouncil La
The Glade
Haseleygreen Farm
Beausale
Lyon Farm
Elmwood Farm
Holly Farm
Beausale La
Kites Nest La
Camphill Farm

91
75

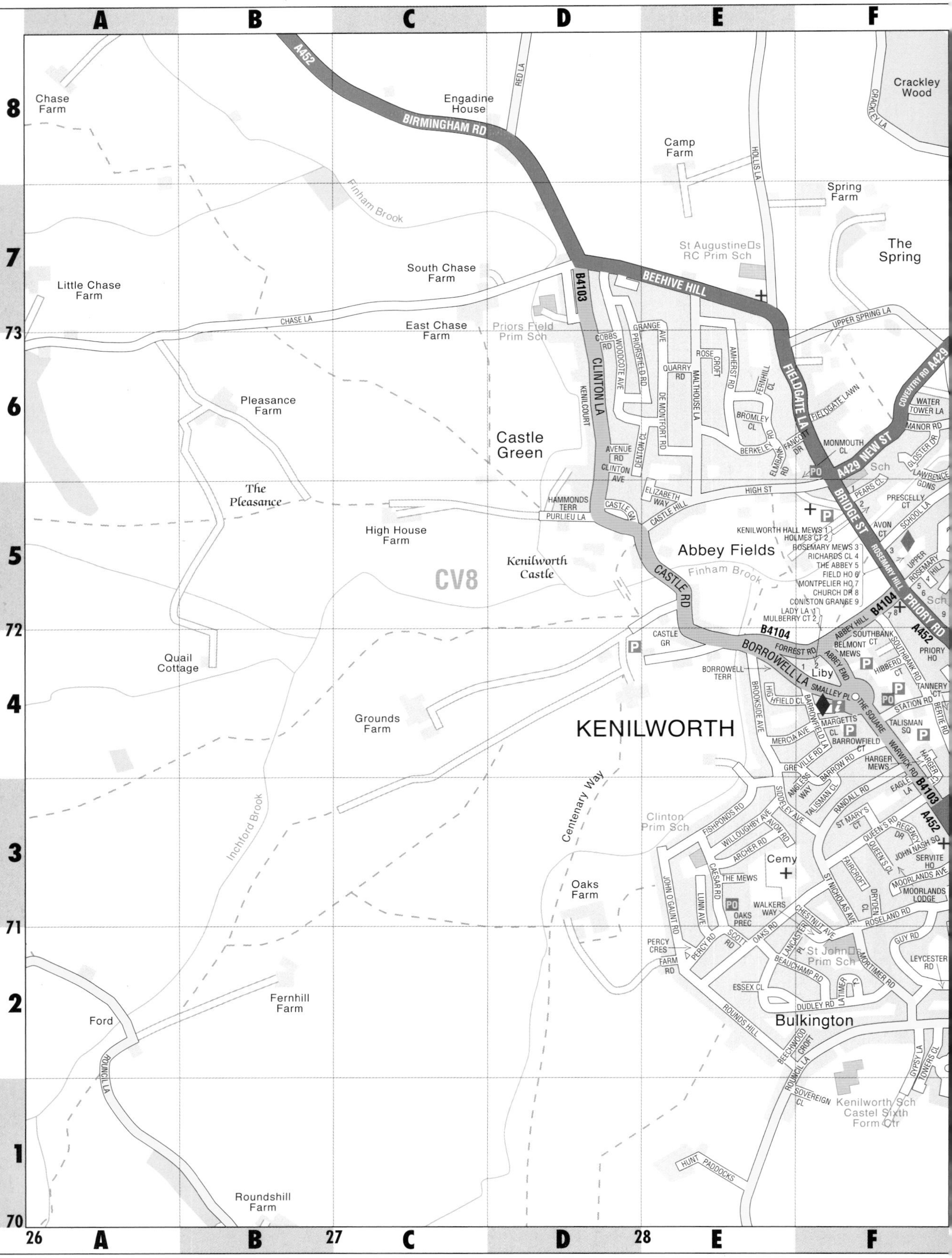

A B C D E F

8
7
73
6
5
72
4
3
71
2
1
70

Chase Farm
Engadine House
BIRMINGHAM RD
A452
RED LA
Crackley Wood
CRACKLEY LA
Camp Farm
HOLLIS LA
Spring Farm
Finham Brook
The Spring
St Augustine's RC Prim Sch
South Chase Farm
BEEHIVE HILL
Little Chase Farm
B4103
CHASE LA
East Chase Farm
Priors Field Prim Sch
UPPER SPRING LA
COBBS RD
GRANGE AVE
PRIORSFIELD RD
WOODCOTE AVE
QUARRY RD
ROSE CROFT
AMHERST RD
FERNHILL CL
FIELDGATE LA
COVENTRY RD A429
WATER TOWER LA
MANOR RD
FIELDGATE LAWN
Pleasance Farm
CLINTON LA
KENILCOURT
DE MONTFORT RD
MALTHOUSE LA
BROMLEY CL
BERKELEY RD
FANCOTT DR
ELMBANK RD
MONMOUTH CL
A429 NEW ST
GLOSTER DR
LAWRENCE GDNS
Castle Green
AVENUE RD
DENCER CT
CLINTON AVE
Sch
PO
The Pleasance
HAMMONDS TERR
PURLIEU LA
ELIZABETH WAY
CASTLE GN
CASTLE HILL
HIGH ST
BRIDGE ST
PEARS CL
PRESCELLY CT
SCHOOL LA
AVON CT
High House Farm
Abbey Fields
KENILWORTH HALL MEWS 1
HOLMES CT 2
ROSEMARY MEWS 3
RICHARDS CL 4
THE ABBEY 5
FIELD HO 6
MONTPELIER HO 7
CHURCH DR 8
CONISTON GRANGE 9
LADY LA 1
MULBERRY CT 2
ROSEMARY HILL
UPPER ROSEMARY HILL
Kenilworth Castle
CV8
CASTLE RD
Finham Brook
B4104
PRIORY RD
A452
ABBEY HILL
SOUTHBANK CT
BELMONT MEWS
SOUTHBANK RD
PRIORY HO
Quail Cottage
CASTLE GR
P
FORREST RD
BORROWELL LA
ABBEY END
Liby
HIBBERD CT
BORROWELL TERR
TANNERY CT
SMALLEY PL
THE SQUARE
STATION RD
BERTIE RD
HIGHFIELD CL
BARROWFIELD LA
BROOKSIDE AVE
Grounds Farm
KENILWORTH
MARGETTS CL
TALISMAN SQ
MERCIA AVE
BARROWFIELD CT
WARWICK RD
GREVILLE RD
HARGER MEWS
HARGER CT
ANGLESEY WAY
BARROW RD
TALISMAN CL
RANDALL RD
EAGLE LA
B4103
Centenary Way
Inchford Brook
Clinton Prim Sch
FISHPONDS RD
WILLOUGHBY AVE
SIDDELEY AVE
AVON RD
ST MARY'S CT
QUEEN'S RD
REGENCY DR
A452
JOHN NASH SQ
ARCHER RD
Cemy
QUEEN'S CL
SERVITE HO
MOORLANDS AVE
FAIRCROFT
Oaks Farm
JOHN O'GAUNT RD
CAESAR RD
THE MEWS
ST NICHOLAS AVE
DRYDEN CL
MOORLANDS LODGE
LUNN AVE
PO
OAKS PREC
WALKERS WAY
CHESTNUT AVE
ROSELAND RD
SCOTT RD
OAKS RD
LANCASTER PL
GUY RD
PERCY CRES
PERCY RD
St John's Prim Sch
MORTIMER RD
LEYCESTER RD
FARM RD
BEAUCHAMP RD
ESSEX CL
LATIMER CL
Fernhill Farm
DUDLEY RD
Ford
ROUNDS HILL
Bulkington
BEECHWOOD CROFT
GYPSY LA
TOWERS CL
ROUNCIL LA
ROUNCIL LA
SOVEREIGN CL
Kenilworth Sch
Castel Sixth Form Ctr
HUNT PADDOCKS
Roundshill Farm

26 A B 27 C D 28 E F

91
104

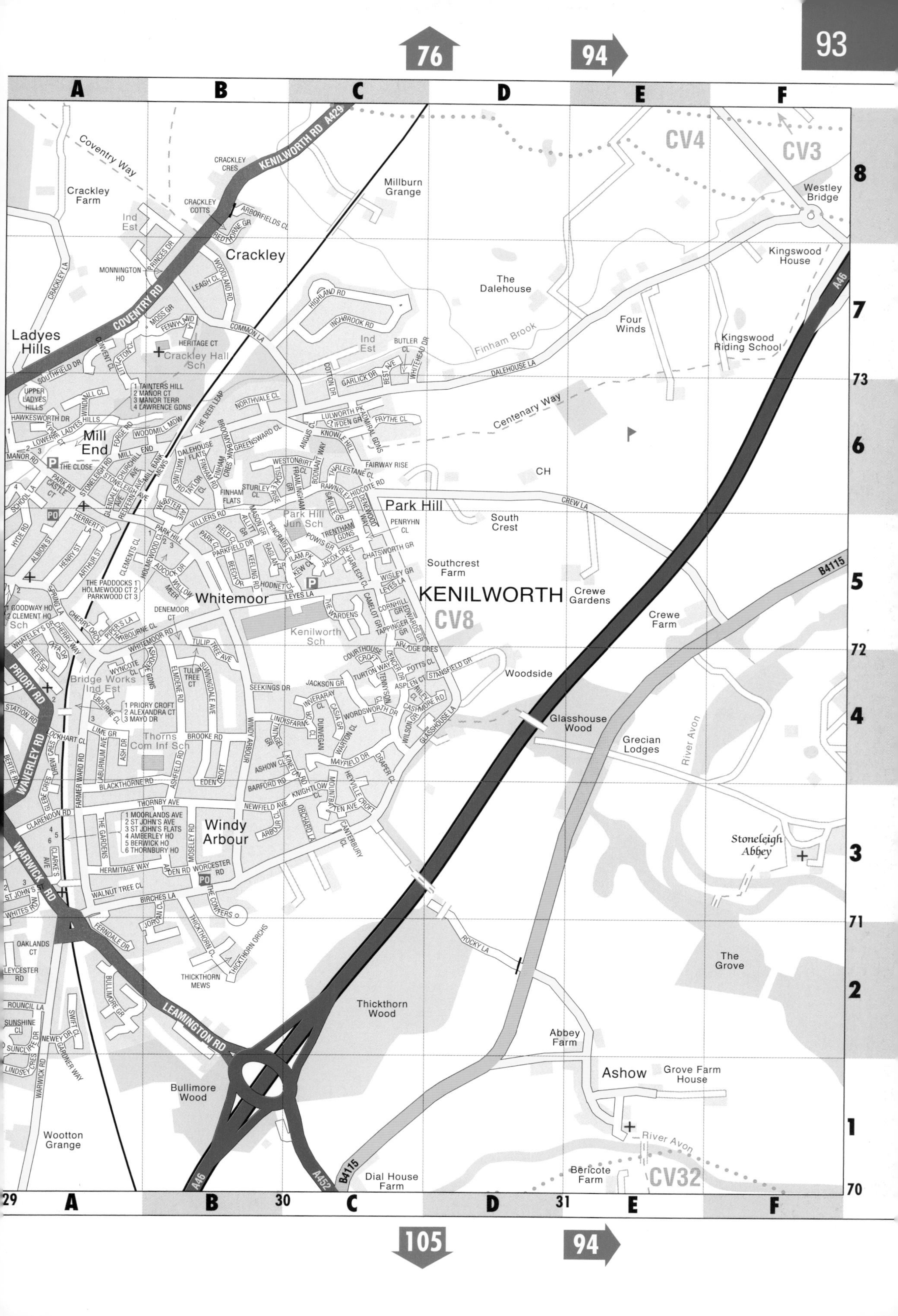
76
94
105
94
KENILWORTH
CV8
CV4
CV3
CV32
Crackley
Ladyes Hills
Mill End
Park Hill
Whitemoor
Windy Arbour
Ashow
Crackley Farm
Millburn Grange
Westley Bridge
Kingswood House
The Dalehouse
Four Winds
Kingswood Riding School
Southcrest Farm
South Crest
Crewe Gardens
Crewe Farm
Woodside
Glasshouse Wood
Grecian Lodges
Stoneleigh Abbey
The Grove
Thickthorn Wood
Abbey Farm
Grove Farm House
Bullimore Wood
Wootton Grange
Dial House Farm
Bericote Farm
Coventry Way
Centenary Way
Finham Brook
River Avon
KENILWORTH RD A429
COVENTRY RD
LEAMINGTON RD
A46
A452
B4115
Kenilworth Sch
Park Hill Jun Sch
Crackley Hall Sch
Thorns Com Inf Sch
Bridge Works Ind Est

93
77
A
B
C
D
E
F
8
7
73
6
5
72
4
3
71
2
1
70
32
33
34
A46
B4115
B4113
CV3
CV4
Pypes Mill House
Sewage Works
The Rough
Manor Fields
COVENTRY RD
Gospel Oak
Chantry Heath Wood
Stoneleigh Grange
River Sowe
Kings Wood
ACORN CL
HALL CL
DUDLEY TERR
STONELEIGH CL
BIRMINGHAM RD
THE BANK
Stoneleigh Bridge
Stoneleigh
WALKERS ORCH
THE GREEN
ALMSHOUSES
CHURCH LA
VICARAGE RD
SCHOOL BELL MEWS
Chantry Heath Cottages
Motslow Hill
Sowe Mouth
CH
Cloud Bridge
Motslowhill Spinney
Coach Bridge
River Avon
Tantara Lodge
CV8
Gilbert's Spinney
Centenary Way
Coventry Way
Sewage Works
Stoneleigh Deer Park Bsns Village
Stoneleigh Park National Agricultural Ctr
weir
Stare Bridge
Waverley Farm
Stareton
Park Farm
STONELEIGH RD
HOME FARM
THE CUNNERY
Ticknell Spinney
Hares Parlour
GROVEHURST PK
River Avon
A445
Brick Kiln Spinney
Decoy Spinney
CV32
LEICESTER LA
Stone House Farm
COVENTRY RD
Furzen Hill Farm
Leicester Lane Cotts
Bericote Wood
B4113
A445
93
106

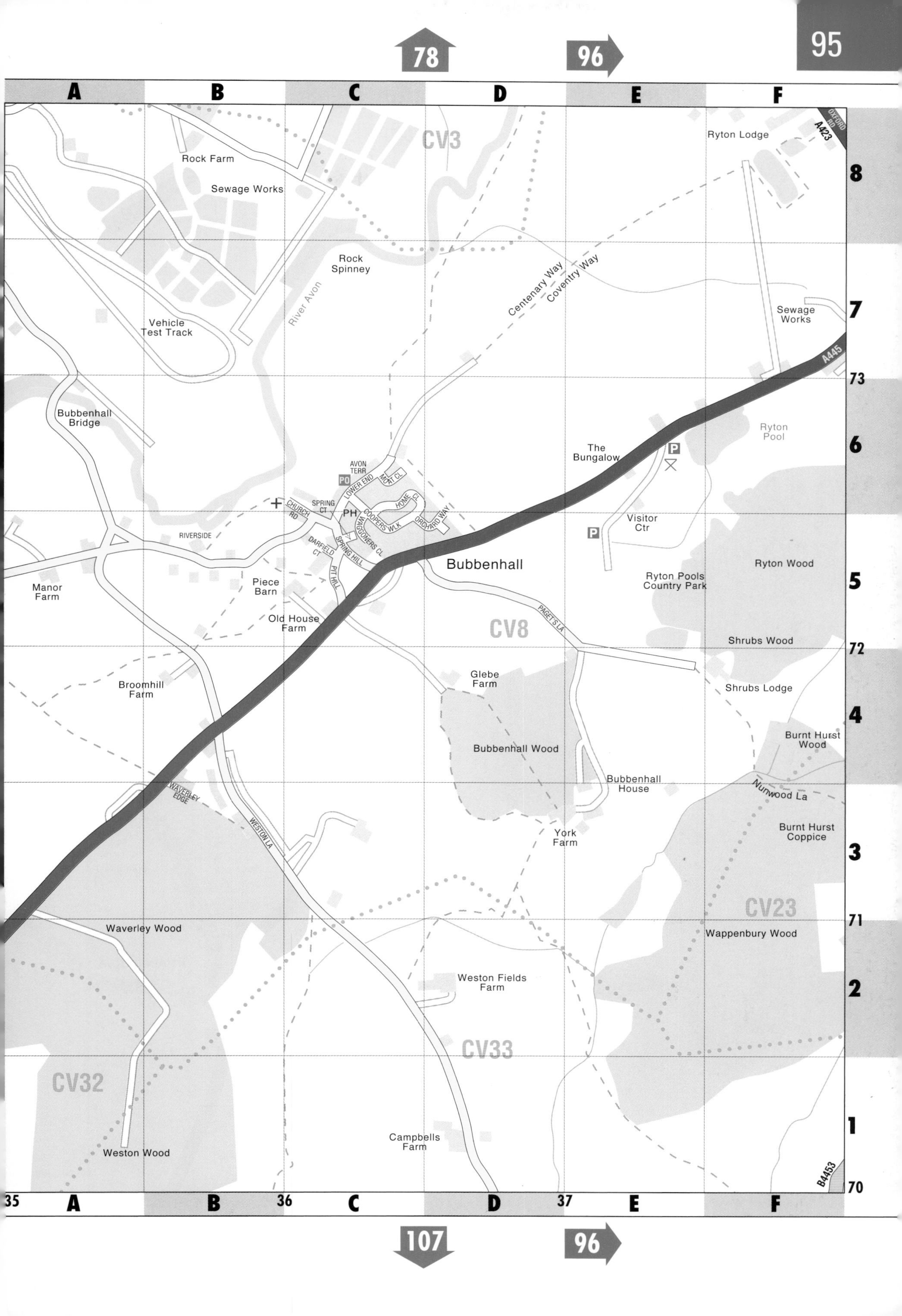
78
96
A
B
C
D
E
F
CV3
Rock Farm
Sewage Works
Ryton Lodge
A423
OXFORD RD
8
Rock Spinney
River Avon
Centenary Way
Coventry Way
Vehicle Test Track
Sewage Works
7
A445
73
Bubbenhall Bridge
Ryton Pool
6
The Bungalow
AVON TERR
PO
LOWER END
MOAT CL
HOME CL
CHURCH RD
SPRING CT
PH
COOPERS WLK
ORCHARD WAY
WAGGONERS CL
RIVERSIDE
DARFIELD CT
SPRING HILL
PIT HILL
Visitor Ctr
Bubbenhall
Ryton Wood
Manor Farm
Piece Barn
Ryton Pools Country Park
5
Old House Farm
CV8
PAGET'S LA
Shrubs Wood
72
Glebe Farm
Broomhill Farm
Shrubs Lodge
4
Burnt Hurst Wood
Bubbenhall Wood
Bubbenhall House
WAVERLEY EDGE
Nunwood La
WESTON LA
York Farm
Burnt Hurst Coppice
3
CV23
71
Waverley Wood
Wappenbury Wood
Weston Fields Farm
2
CV33
CV32
1
Campbells Farm
Weston Wood
B4453
70
35
36
37
107
96

95
79

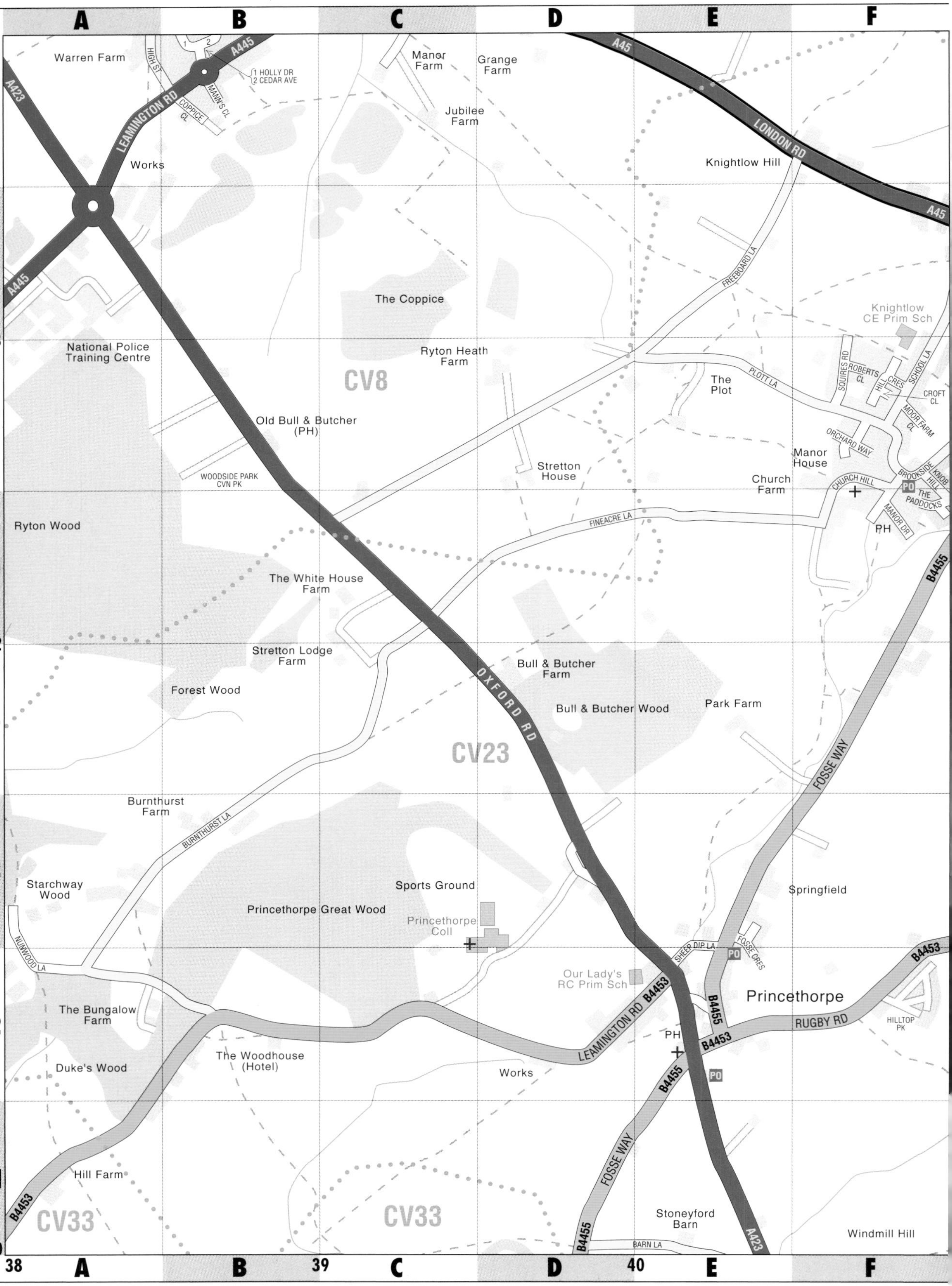

A B C D E F

8 7 73 6 5 72 4 3 71 2 1 70

Warren Farm
HIGH ST
A423
A445
LEAMINGTON RD
COPPICE CL
MANN'S CL
1 HOLLY DR
2 CEDAR AVE
Manor Farm
Grange Farm
Jubilee Farm
A45
LONDON RD
Knightlow Hill
Works
FREEBOARD LA
The Coppice
Knightlow CE Prim Sch
National Police Training Centre
Ryton Heath Farm
CV8
The Plot
PLOTT LA
SQUIRES RD
ROBERTS CL
HILL CRES
SCHOOL LA
CROFT CL
MOOR FARM CL
ORCHARD WAY
Old Bull & Butcher (PH)
Manor House
Stretton House
Church Farm
CHURCH HILL
BROOKSIDE
KNOB HILL
PO
THE PADDOCKS
MANOR DR
PH
WOODSIDE PARK CVN PK
Ryton Wood
FINEACRE LA
B4455
The White House Farm
Stretton Lodge Farm
Bull & Butcher Farm
OXFORD RD
Forest Wood
Bull & Butcher Wood
Park Farm
CV23
FOSSE WAY
Burnthurst Farm
BURNTHURST LA
Starchway Wood
Sports Ground
Springfield
Princethorpe Great Wood
Princethorpe Coll
SHEEP DIP LA
FOSSE CRES
PO
NUNWOOD LA
Our Lady's RC Prim Sch
B4453
Princethorpe
LEAMINGTON RD
B4455
The Bungalow Farm
RUGBY RD
HILLTOP PK
PH
B4453
The Woodhouse (Hotel)
Duke's Wood
Works
B4455
PO
FOSSE WAY
Hill Farm
B4453
CV33
CV33
Stoneyford Barn
A423
Windmill Hill
B4455
BARN LA

38 39 40

95
115

80
98
A
B
C
D
E
F
Barn Cottage Farm
Mickle Hill Farm
CV8
Wilcox's Gorse
B4455
FOSSE WAY
STRETTON RD
COALPIT LA
Frog Hall
Denchwood Farm
Ferry Farm
Manor Farm
The Holdings
LONDON RD
Avenue House
Home Farm
Well Head
MEADOW CL
BROOKSIDE
RUGBY LA
Beech Tree Farm
The Hollies
Deep Meadow
A45
Kiln La
Dunsmore Heath
Stretton-on-Dunsmore
Limekiln Farm
Broomhill Farm
FRANKTON LA
CV23
Lemon's Wood
Hill Farm
Ash Grove
Heath Farm
Bourton Heath
Grove Farm
Boots Spinney
Boots Farm
B4453
STRAIGHT MILE
Woodside Farm
Larch Spinney
Tile Barn
Highfield Cottages
Sunnycrest
Bourton on Dunsmore
Bog Spinney
Gate Farm
Highfield Farm
FRANKTON RD
CHERRY TREE LA
SHUCKBURGH CRES
PO
ACHRAY COTTS
Friendly Inn (PH)
BOURTON RD
MAIN ST
Bourton Hall
Frankton
FAIR CL
Nursery
Badgers Spinney
COOKS LA
BIDDULPH TERR
Manor House
BIRDINGBURY LA
BIRDINGBURY RD
Home Farm
8
7
73
6
5
72
4
3
71
2
1
70
42
43
115
98

97
81

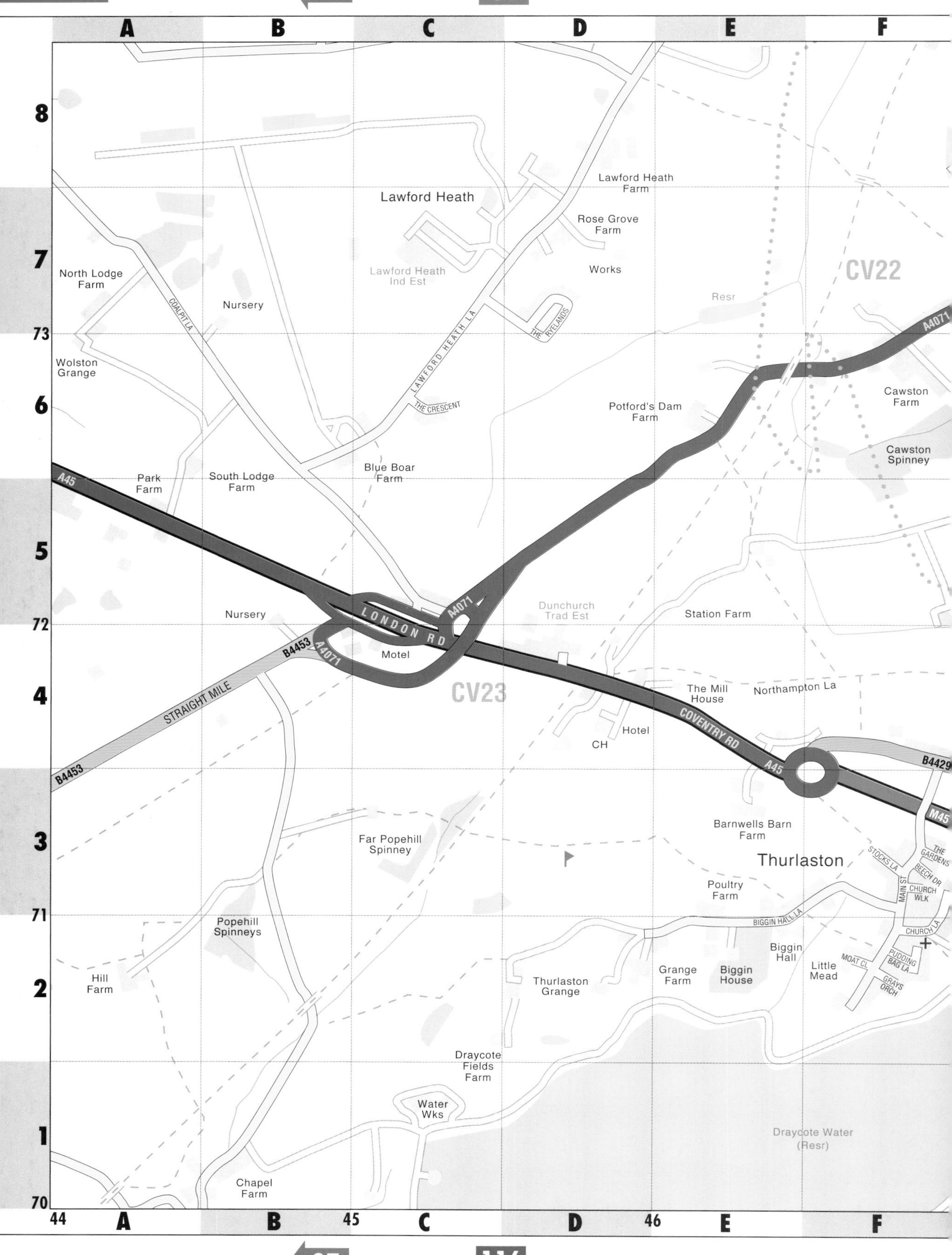
A
B
C
D
E
F
8
7
73
6
5
72
4
3
71
2
1
70
44
45
46
Lawford Heath
Lawford Heath Farm
Rose Grove Farm
Works
Lawford Heath Ind Est
North Lodge Farm
Nursery
COALPIT LA
CV22
Resr
THE RYELANDS
LAWFORD HEATH LA
A4071
Wolston Grange
Cawston Farm
THE CRESCENT
Potford's Dam Farm
Cawston Spinney
Blue Boar Farm
A45
Park Farm
South Lodge Farm
Dunchurch Trad Est
Station Farm
Nursery
LONDON RD
B4453
Motel
CV23
STRAIGHT MILE
The Mill House
Northampton La
Hotel
CH
COVENTRY RD
B4429
M45
Barnwells Barn Farm
Far Popehill Spinney
Thurlaston
STOCKS LA
THE GARDENS
BEECH DR
Poultry Farm
MAIN ST
CHURCH WLK
BIGGIN HALL LA
CHURCH LA
Popehill Spinneys
Biggin Hall
MOAT CL
PUDDING BAG LA
Hill Farm
Thurlaston Grange
Grange Farm
Biggin House
Little Mead
GRAYS ORCH
Draycote Fields Farm
Water Wks
Draycote Water (Resr)
Chapel Farm

97
116

A8
1 GARARD PL
2 GARARD ROW
3 GARARD CT
4 SAXON CL
82
100
A
B
C
D
E
F
Cawston Grange Prim Sch
1 SCHOLARS DR
2 PRIMARY WLK
3 THE CRESCENT
4 CALVESTONE SQ
Bilton High Sch
Cawston
Brooke Sch
Overslade
RUGBY
Bilton
Bilton Common
Bilton Inf Sch
Crescent Sch
Recn Gd
Bawnmore Inf Sch
Bilton CE Jun Sch
Rugby High Sch
Little Scotland Farm
1 CAWSTON HO
2 SALEMORTON CT
3 COMPTON CT
4 NAPTON CT
Fox Covert
Cawston Spinney
Boat House Spinney
Dunkleys Farm
Cherry Tree Farm
CV22
Superstore
Bilton Fields
Cock Robin Plantation
Lion Farm
Windmill Farm
Northampton Lane
Homestead Farm
The Elms
Heath
Bilton Grange Park
Bilton Grange Sch
Dunchurch Lodge Farm
Dunchurch Boughton CE Jun Sch
Dunchurch Inf Sch
Ryefield Farm
Liby
Dunchurch
Dunchurch Lodge
DUNCHURCH HALL
PH
Toft
Toft House
Ox House
CV23
Cut-Throat La
Laurel Farm
Rains Brook
Wolscott Bridge
Sewage Works
COVENTRY RD
MAIN ST
BILTON RD
A4071
A426
DUNCHURCH RD
B4429
ASHLAWN RD
CAWSTON LA
NORTHAMPTON LA
RUGBY RD
SOUTHAM RD
TOFT HILL
DAVENTRY RD
A45
M45
8
7
73
6
5
72
4
3
71
2
1
70
47
48
49
116
100

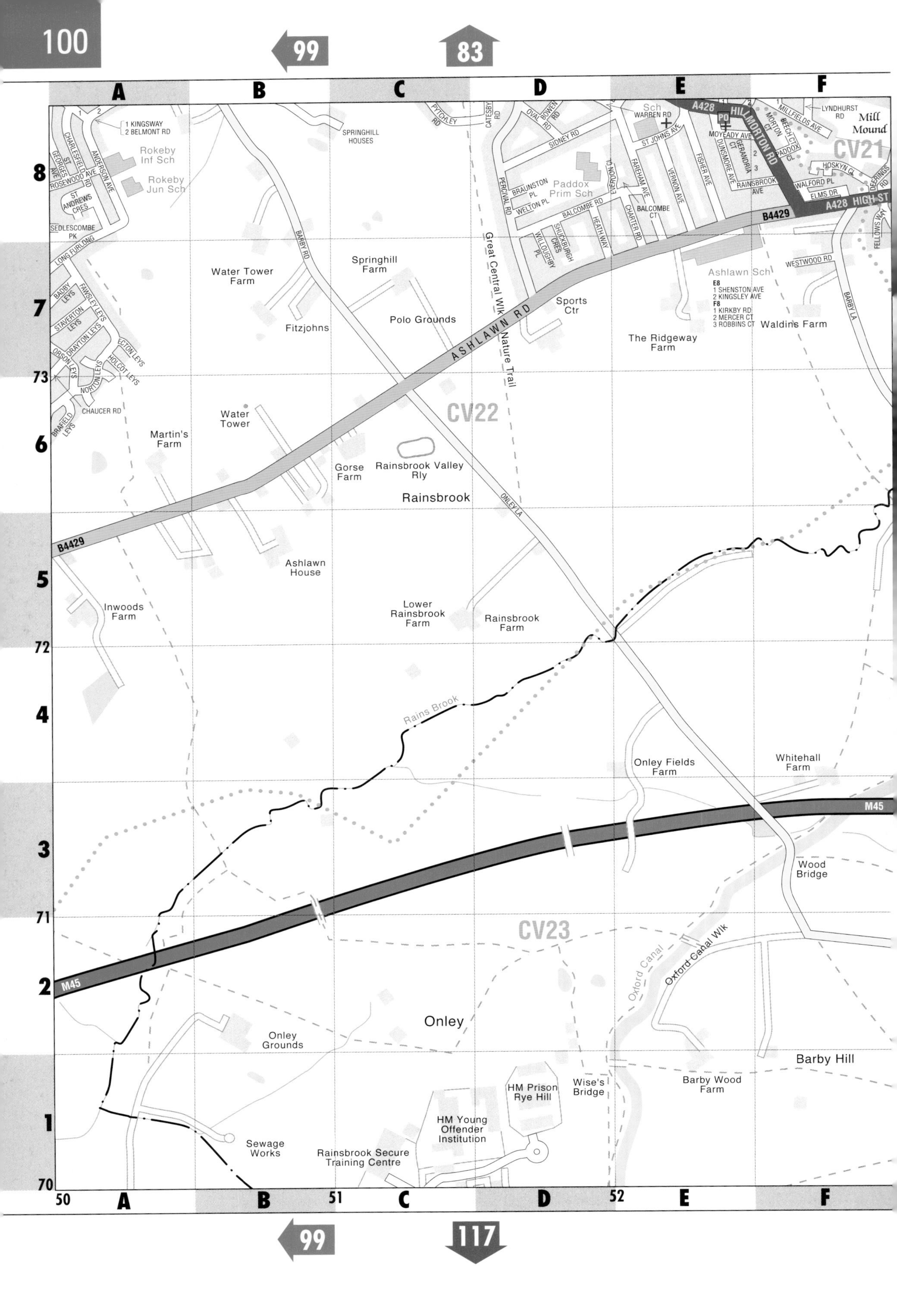
99
83
A
B
C
D
E
F
8
7
73
6
5
72
4
3
71
2
1
70
50
51
52
1 KINGSWAY
2 BELMONT RD
Rokeby Inf Sch
Rokeby Jun Sch
SPRINGHILL HOUSES
PYTCHLEY RD
CATESBY RD
OVAL RD
BOWEN RD
SIDNEY RD
Sch
WARREN RD
ST JOHNS AVE
A428
HILLMORTON RD
PO
MOYEADY AVE
DUNSMORE AVE
GERANDRIA CT
MORTON CT
BEECH CT
PADDOX CL
MILLFIELDS AVE
LYNDHURST RD
Mill Mound
CV21
HOSKYN CL
WALFORD PL
ELMS DR
DERINGS RD
A428 HIGH ST
B4429
FELLOWS WAY
CHARLESFIELD RD
ST GEORGES AVE
ANDERSON AVE
ROSEWOOD AVE
ST ANDREWS CRES
SEDLESCOMBE PK
LONG FURLONG
BADBY LEYS
FAWSLEY LEYS
STAVERTON LEYS
DRAYTON LEYS
ORSON LEYS
ECTON LEYS
HOLCOT LEYS
NORTON LEYS
CHAUCER RD
BRAFIELD LEYS
PERCIVAL RD
BRAUNSTON PL
WELTON PL
Paddox Prim Sch
BALCOMBE RD
WILLOUGHBY PL
SHUCKBURGH CRES
HEATH WAY
CHARTER RD
FAREHAM AVE
BALCOMBE CT
VERNON AVE
FISHER AVE
RAINSBROOK AVE
BARBY RD
Water Tower Farm
Springhill Farm
Fitzjohns
Polo Grounds
Great Central Wlk Nature Trail
ASHLAWN RD
Sports Ctr
Ashlawn Sch
WESTWOOD RD
E8
1 SHENSTON AVE
2 KINGSLEY AVE
F8
1 KIRKBY RD
2 MERCER CT
3 ROBBINS CT
Waldins Farm
BARBY LA
The Ridgeway Farm
Water Tower
Martin's Farm
CV22
Gorse Farm
Rainsbrook Valley Rly
Rainsbrook
ONLEY LA
Ashlawn House
Inwoods Farm
Lower Rainsbrook Farm
Rainsbrook Farm
Rains Brook
Onley Fields Farm
Whitehall Farm
M45
Wood Bridge
CV23
Oxford Canal
Oxford Canal Wlk
Onley
Onley Grounds
Barby Hill
Barby Wood Farm
Wise's Bridge
HM Prison Rye Hill
HM Young Offender Institution
Sewage Works
Rainsbrook Secure Training Centre
99
117

84

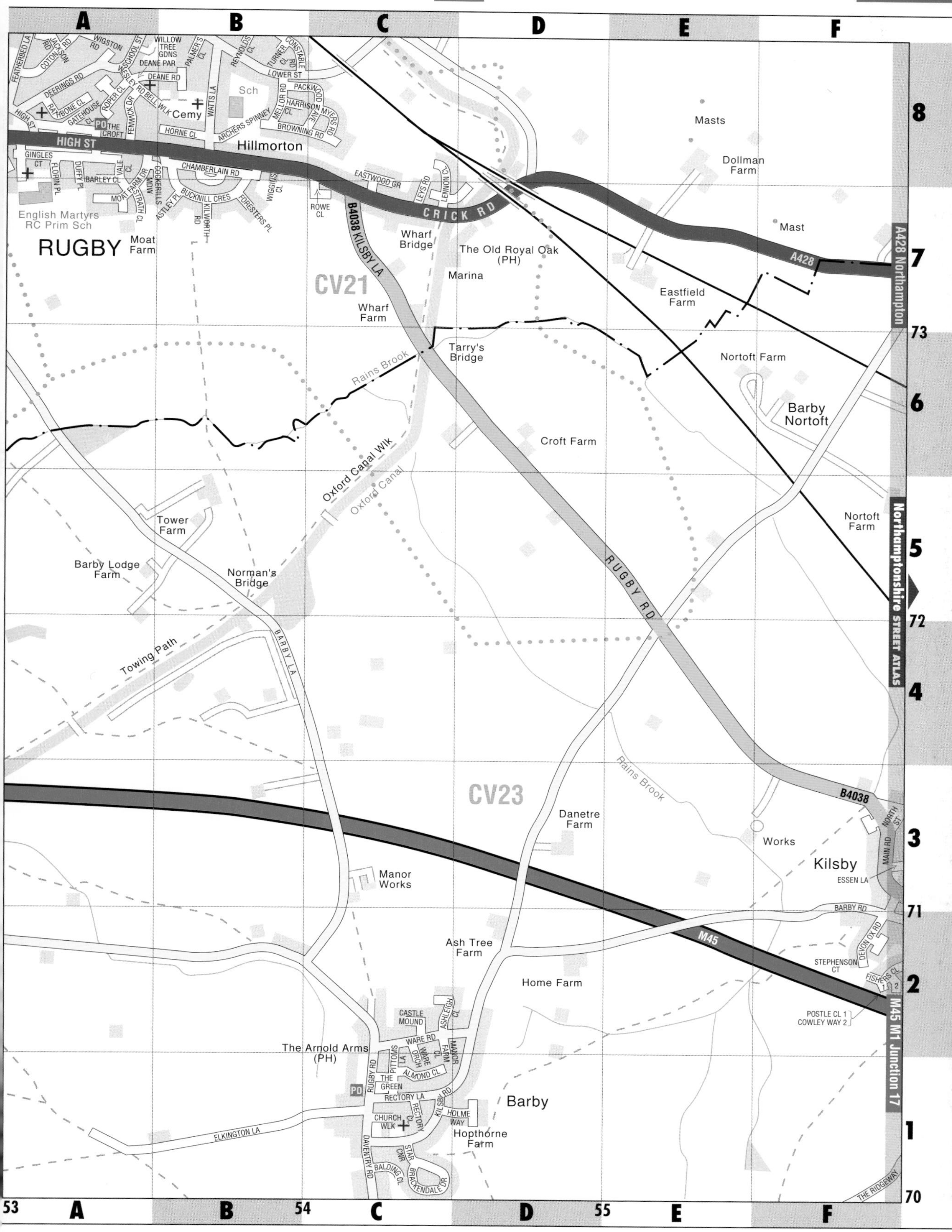

RUGBY
Hillmorton
HIGH ST
CRICK RD
B4038 KILSBY LA
RUGBY RD
A428
A428 Northampton
M45
B4038
CV21
CV23
English Martyrs RC Prim Sch
Moat Farm
Sch
Cemy
Wharf Bridge
The Old Royal Oak (PH)
Marina
Wharf Farm
Tarry's Bridge
Rains Brook
Masts
Dollman Farm
Mast
Eastfield Farm
Nortoft Farm
Barby Nortoft
Croft Farm
Oxford Canal Wlk
Oxford Canal
Tower Farm
Barby Lodge Farm
Norman's Bridge
Northoft Farm
Towing Path
BARBY LA
Danetre Farm
Works
Kilsby
Manor Works
Ash Tree Farm
Home Farm
The Arnold Arms (PH)
Barby
Hopthorne Farm
ELKINGTON LA
BARBY RD
ESSEN LA
MAIN RD
NORTH ST
STEPHENSON CT
POSTLE CL 1
COWLEY WAY 2
THE RIDGEWAY
Northamptonshire STREET ATLAS
M45 M1 Junction 17
CASTLE MOUND
WARE RD
RECTORY LA
CHURCH WLK
HOLME WAY
DAVENTRY RD
BALDING CL
BRACKENDALE DR
CHAMBERLAIN RD
BUCKNILL CRES
EASTWOOD GR
LEYS RD
LENNON CL
ROWE CL
BROWNING RD
HARRISON CL
LOWER ST
HORNE CL
ARCHERS SPINNEY
WATTS LA
DEANE RD
DEANE PAR
GATEHOUSE CL
DEERINGS RD
WIGSTON RD
A B C D E F
1 2 3 4 5 6 7 8
53 54 55
70 71 72 73

117

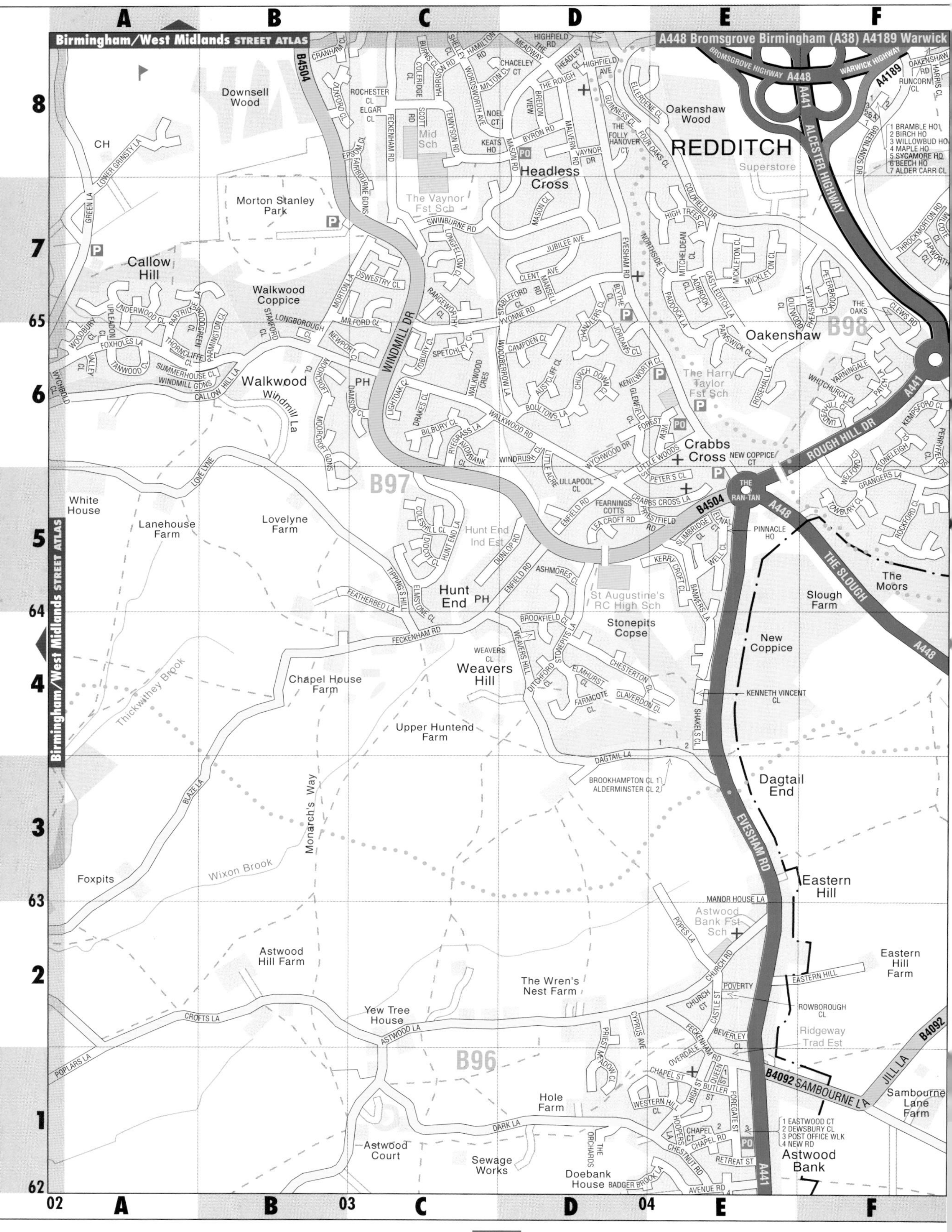
Birmingham/West Midlands STREET ATLAS
A448 Bromsgrove Birmingham (A38) A4189 Warwick
REDDITCH
Headless Cross
Oakenshaw
Crabbs Cross
Callow Hill
Walkwood
Hunt End
Weavers Hill
Dagtail End
Eastern Hill
Astwood Bank
Downsell Wood
Morton Stanley Park
Walkwood Coppice
Oakenshaw Wood
White House
Lanehouse Farm
Lovelyne Farm
Chapel House Farm
Upper Huntend Farm
Stonepits Copse
New Coppice
Slough Farm
The Moors
Foxpits
Astwood Hill Farm
The Wren's Nest Farm
Yew Tree House
Eastern Hill Farm
Hole Farm
Astwood Court
Sewage Works
Doebank House
Sambourne Lane Farm
B97
B98
B96
WINDMILL DR
EVESHAM RD
ALCESTER HIGHWAY
ROUGH HILL DR
THE SLOUGH
B4092 SAMBOURNE LA
Monarch's Way
Wixon Brook
Thickwithey Brook
1 BRAMBLE HO
2 BIRCH HO
3 WILLOWBUD HO
4 MAPLE HO
5 SYCAMORE HO
6 BEECH HO
7 ALDER CARR CL
1 EASTWOOD CT
2 DEWSBURY CL
3 POST OFFICE WLK
4 NEW RD
BROOKHAMPTON CL 1
ALDERMINSTER CL 2

112

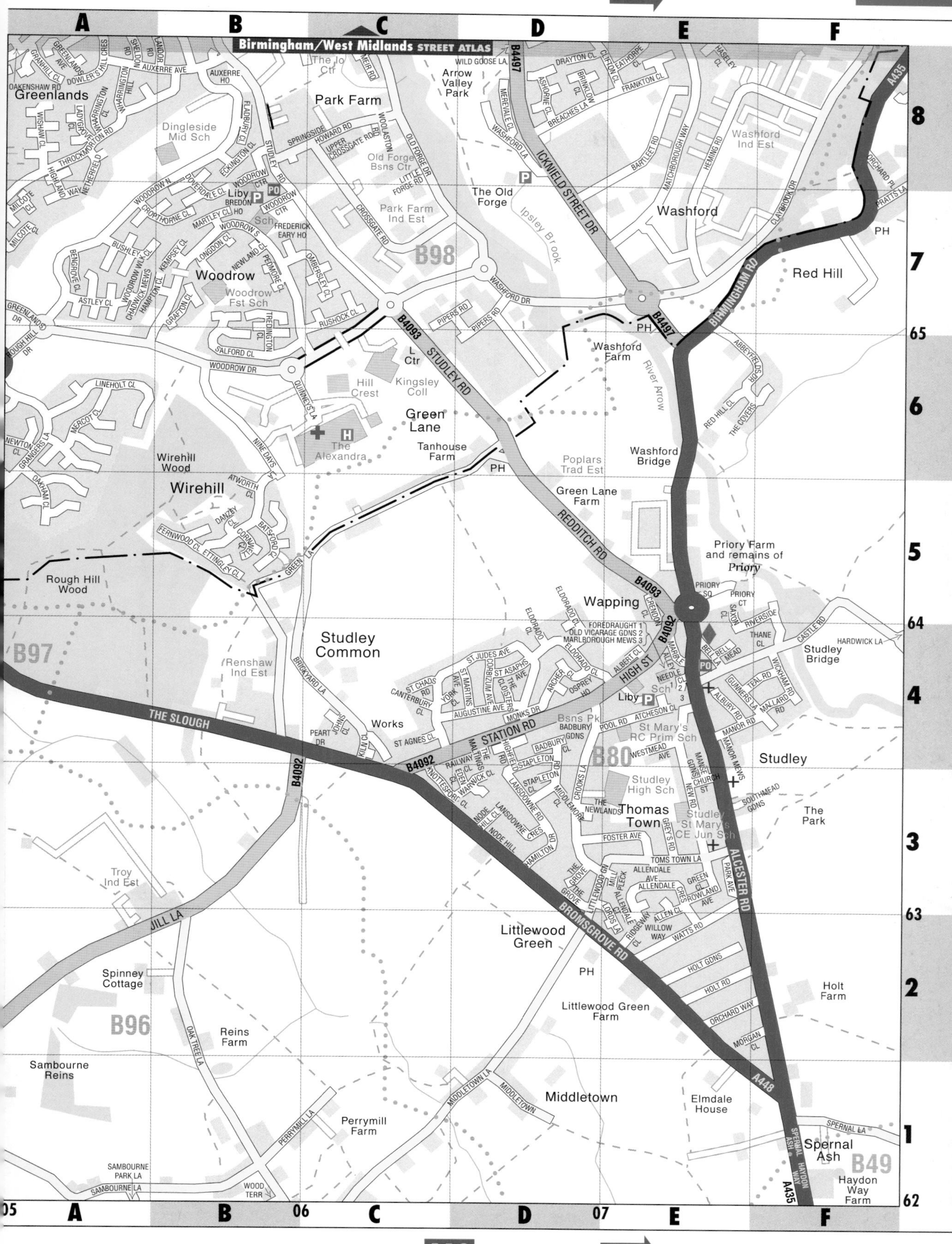
Birmingham/West Midlands STREET ATLAS
Greenlands
Park Farm
Arrow Valley Park
Dingleside Mid Sch
Old Forge Bsns Ctr
Park Farm Ind Est
The Old Forge
Washford Ind Est
Washford
Red Hill
Woodrow
Woodrow Fst Sch
Washford Farm
Hill Crest
Kingsley Coll
Green Lane
The Alexandra
Tanhouse Farm
Wirehill Wood
Wirehill
Poplars Trad Est
Green Lane Farm
Washford Bridge
Priory Farm and remains of Priory
Rough Hill Wood
Wapping
Studley Common
Renshaw Ind Est
Studley Bridge
Works
Studley
St Mary's RC Prim Sch
Studley High Sch
Thomas Town
Studley St Mary's CE Jun Sch
The Park
Troy Ind Est
Littlewood Green
Spinney Cottage
Littlewood Green Farm
Holt Farm
Reins Farm
Sambourne Reins
Middletown
Elmdale House
Perrymill Farm
Spernal Ash
Haydon Way Farm
THE SLOUGH
STUDLEY RD
REDDITCH RD
ICKNIELD STREET DR
BIRMINGHAM RD
ALCESTER RD
BROMSGROVE RD
STATION RD
HIGH ST
JILL LA
B97
B98
B80
B96
B49

118

112

A B C D E F
8 7 69 6 5 68 4 3 67 2 1 66
26 27 28

E1
1 NEWSHOLME CL
2 ADDINGHAM CL
3 WATSON CL
4 RYLSTONE WAY
5 KILDWICK WAY

F1
1 HETTON CL
2 BUCKDEN CL
3 LEYBURN CL
4 ARNCLIFFE WAY
5 HUDDISDON CL
6 PHILLIPPES RD

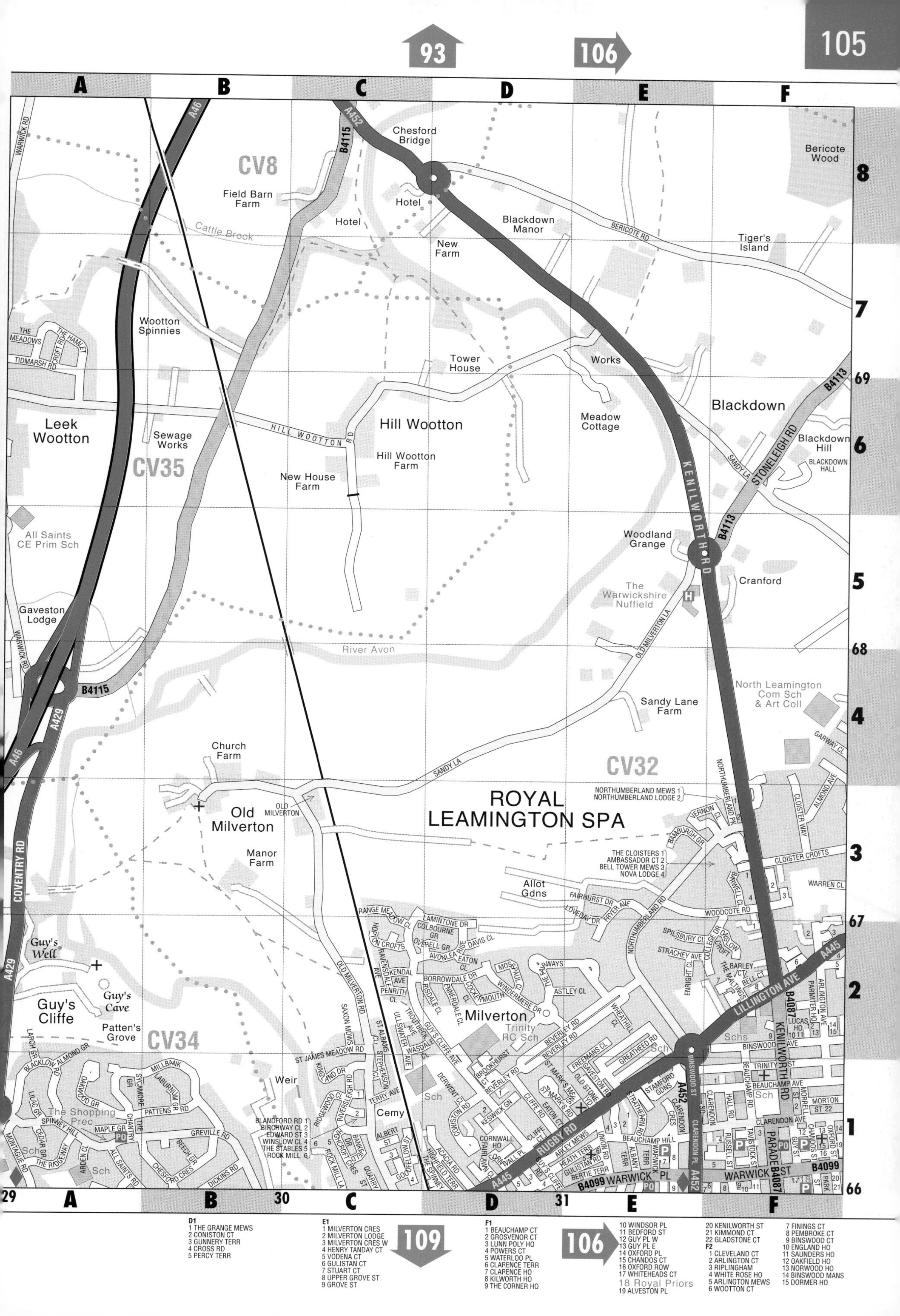
93
106
A
B
C
D
E
F
8
7
69
6
5
68
4
3
67
2
1
66
29
30
31
CV8
CV35
CV34
CV32
Chesford Bridge
Field Barn Farm
Hotel
Hotel
New Farm
Blackdown Manor
BERICOTE RD
Tiger's Island
Bericote Wood
Cattle Brook
Wootton Spinnies
THE MEADOWS
THE HAMLET
CROFT RD
TIDMARSH RD
Tower House
Works
Leek Wootton
Sewage Works
HILL WOOTTON RD
Hill Wootton
Hill Wootton Farm
New House Farm
Meadow Cottage
Blackdown
Blackdown Hill
BLACKDOWN HALL
SANDY LA
STONELEIGH RD
KENILWORTH RD
All Saints CE Prim Sch
Woodland Grange
Cranford
The Warwickshire Nuffield
Gaveston Lodge
WARWICK RD
River Avon
OLD MILVERTON LA
B4115
A429
A46
A452
B4113
North Leamington Com Sch & Art Coll
Sandy Lane Farm
GARWAY CL
Church Farm
SANDY LA
ROYAL LEAMINGTON SPA
Old Milverton
OLD MILVERTON
NORTHUMBERLAND MEWS 1
NORTHUMBERLAND LODGE 2
NORTHUMBERLAND PK
VERNON CL
CLOISTER WAY
ALMOND AVE
BAMBURGH GR
THE CLOISTERS 1
AMBASSADOR CT 2
BELL TOWER MEWS 3
NOVA LODGE 4
CLOISTER CROFTS
Manor Farm
Allot Gdns
COVENTRY RD
FAIRHURST DR
FRYER AVE
LOVEDAY DR
WARREN CL
WOODCOTE RD
NORTHUMBERLAND RD
RANGE MEADOW CL
LAMINTONE DR
COLBOURNE GR
HOPTON CROFTS
OVERELL GR
DAVIS CL
AVONLEA RISE
EATON CL
SPILSBURY CL
COLLEGE DR
ONSLOW CROFT
STRACHEY AVE
Guy's Well
Guy's Cave
Guy's Cliffe
Patten's Grove
KENDAL AVE
RAVENSDALE AVE
PENRITH CL
BORROWDALE DR
MOSSPAUL CL
THE FAIRWAYS
WINDERMERE DR
ASTLEY CL
ENRIGHT CL
THE MALTINGS
BARLEY CT
BELL CT
LILLINGTON AVE
A445
PARMITER HO
ARLINGTON AVE
LUCAS HO
KENILWORTH RD
B4087
RYSDALE CL
ENNERDALE CL
COCKERMOUTH CL
Milverton
Trinity RC Sch
BEVERLEY RD
WHEATHILL CL
GREATHEED RD
Sch
Schs
BINSWOOD AVE
BINSWOOD ST
TRINITY ST
BEAUCHAMP AVE
BEAUCHAMP RD
MORRELL ST
MORTON ST
LARCH GR
BLACKLOW RD
ALMOND GR
MILLBANK
LABURNUM GR
SYCAMORE GR
OAKWOOD GR
LILAC GR
The Shopping Prec
PATTENS RD
SPINNEY HILL
CEDAR GR
MAPLE GR
PO
CHANTRY
THE RIDGEWAY
Sch
ARDEN CL
ALL SAINTS RD
GREVILLE RD
BEECH CL
CHESFORD CRES
DICKINS RD
MONTAGUE RD
SAXON MDWS
OLD MILVERTON RD
ST ALBANS CL
STEPHENSON CL
ULLSWATER AVE
TROUTBECK AVE
WASDALE CL
GUY'S CLIFFE AVE
ST JAMES MEADOW RD
KINGLAND DR
Weir
RIDGEWOOD CL
RIVERSLEIGH RD
TERRY AVE
Cemy
BLANDFORD RD 1
BIRCHWAY CL 2
EDWARD ST 3
WINSLOW CL 4
THE STABLES 5
ROCK MILL 6
RYECROFT CRES
BANKER DR
ROCK MILL LA
QUARRY ST
ALBERT ST
GOODFELLOW ST
DERWENT CL
Sch
CONISTON RD
KESWICK GN
BROOKHURST CT
HIGHFIELD TERR
THE SPINNEY
ACACIA RD
FAIRLAWN CL
CORNWALL HO
RUGBY RD
CLIFFE RD
EATON CT
ST MARK'S RD
ST MARK'S MEWS
OLD STONE CL
GAVESTON RD
FREEMANS CL
STAMFORD GDNS
CLARENDON CRES
STRATHEARN RD
BEAUCHAMP HILL
ARLEY MEWS
HEATH TERR
GULISTAN RD
BERTIE TERR
UNION RD
ALBANY TERR
WARWICK PL
B4099
CLARENDON PL
CLARENDON SQ
HALL RD
RUSSELL ST
TAVISTOCK ST
PARADE
GUY ST
CHANDOS ST
OXFORD ST
CLARENDON AVE
WARWICK ST
PARK ST
P
PO
D1
1 THE GRANGE MEWS
2 CONISTON CT
3 GUNNERY TERR
4 CROSS RD
5 PERCY TERR
E1
1 MILVERTON CRES
2 MILVERTON LODGE
3 MILVERTON CRES W
4 HENRY TANDEY CT
5 VODENA CT
6 GULISTAN CT
7 STUART CT
8 UPPER GROVE ST
9 GROVE ST
109
F1
1 BEAUCHAMP CT
2 GROSVENOR CT
3 LUNN POLY HO
4 POWERS CT
5 WATERLOO PL
6 CLARENCE TERR
7 CLARENCE HO
8 KILWORTH HO
9 THE CORNER HO
106
10 WINDSOR PL
11 BEDFORD ST
12 GUY PL W
13 GUY PL E
14 OXFORD PL
15 CHANDOS CT
16 OXFORD ROW
17 WHITEHEADS CT
18 Royal Priors
19 ALVESTON PL
20 KENILWORTH ST
21 KIMMOND CT
22 GLADSTONE CT
F2
1 CLEVELAND CT
2 ARLINGTON CT
3 RIPLINGHAM
4 WHITE ROSE HO
5 ARLINGTON MEWS
6 WOOTTON CT
7 FININGS CT
8 PEMBROKE CT
9 BINSWOOD CT
10 ENGLAND HO
11 SAUNDERS HO
12 OAKFIELD HO
13 NORWOOD HO
14 BINSWOOD MANS
15 DORMER HO

105
94

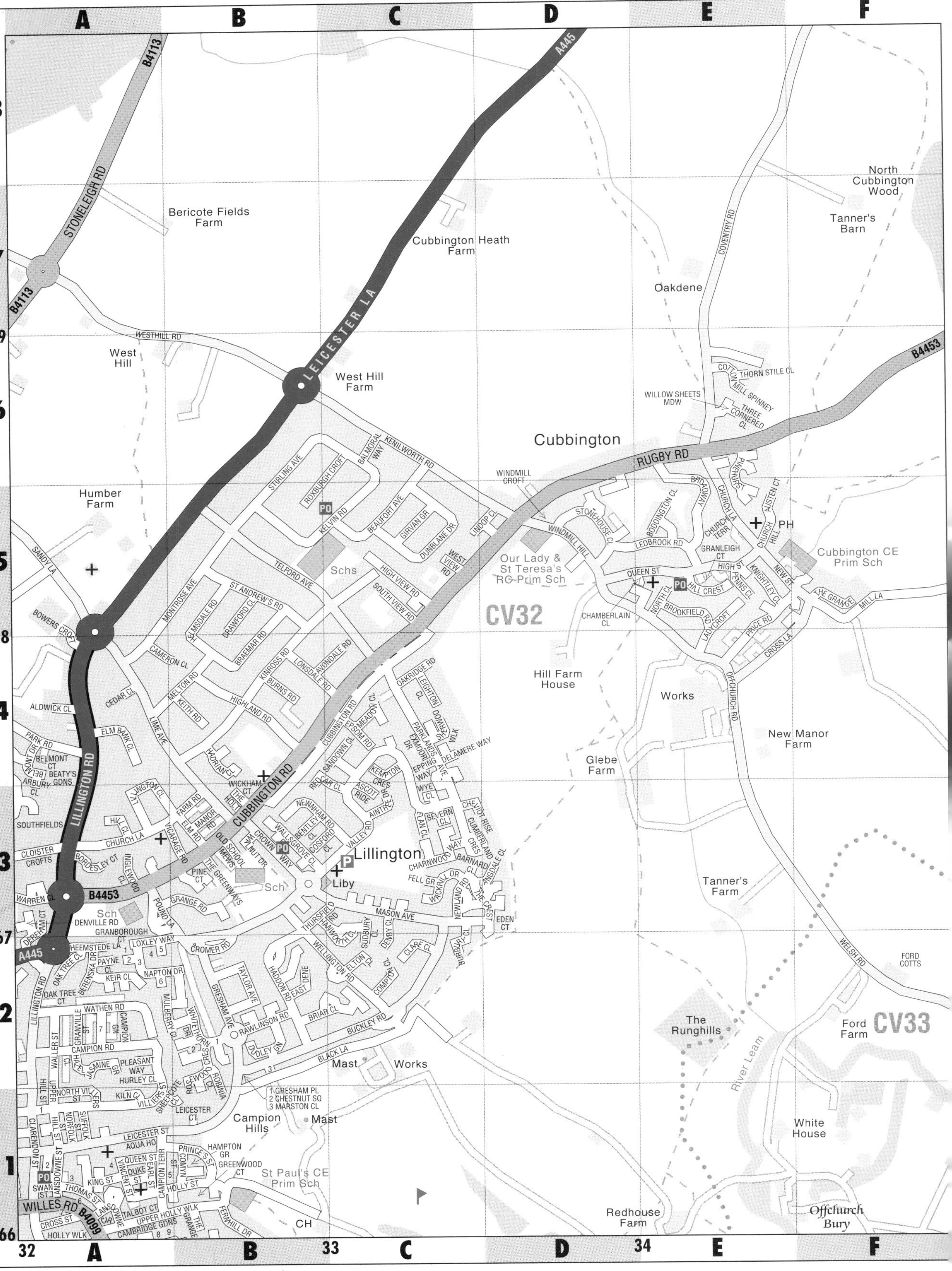

A B C D E F

8
7
69
6
5
68
4
3
67
2
1
66

B4113
STONELEIGH RD
A445
LEICESTER LA
Bericote Fields Farm
Cubbington Heath Farm
North Cubbington Wood
Tanner's Barn
COVENTRY RD
Oakdene
WESTHILL RD
West Hill
West Hill Farm
B4453
COTTON MILL SPINNEY
THORN STILE CL
WILLOW SHEETS MDW
THREE CORNERED CL
Cubbington
RUGBY RD
KENILWORTH RD
BALMORAL WAY
STIRLING AVE
ROXBURGH CROFT
KELVIN RD
BEAUFORT AVE
GIRVAN GR
DUNBLANE DR
WEST VIEW RD
WINDMILL CROFT
LINDOP CL
WINDMILL HILL
STONEHOUSE CL
BODDINGTON CL
BROADWAY
PINEHURST
CHURCH LA
CHURCH TERR
AUSTEN CT
CHURCH HILL
PH
LEDBROOK RD
GRANLEIGH CT
HIGH ST
PEWINS CL
KNIGHTLEY CL
NEW ST
Cubbington CE Prim Sch
THE GRANGE
MILL LA
Humber Farm
SANDY LA
Schs
TELFORD AVE
HIGH VIEW RD
SOUTH VIEW RD
Our Lady & St Teresa's RC Prim Sch
QUEEN ST
NORTH CL
HILL CREST
BROOKFIELD RD
LADYCROFT
PRICE RD
CROSS LA
CV32
CHAMBERLAIN CL
BOWERS CROFT
MONTROSE AVE
ST ANDREW'S RD
ELMSDALE RD
CRAWFORD CL
BRAEMAR RD
CAMERON CL
KINROSS RD
LONSDALE RD
AVONDALE RD
BURNS RD
MELTON RD
KEITH RD
HIGHLAND RD
CEDAR CL
ALDWICK CL
LIME AVE
ELM BANK CL
Hill Farm House
Works
OFFCHURCH RD
OAKRIDGE RD
LEIGHTON CL
MEADOW CL
CUBBINGTON RD
EPSOM RD
SANDOWN CL
PARKLANDS AVE
EXMOOR DR
OXFORD WLK
DELAMERE WAY
EPPING WAY
WYE CL
New Manor Farm
Glebe Farm
PARK RD
BELMONT DR
BELMONT CT
BEATY'S GDNS
ARBURY CL
LILLINGTON RD
LILLINGTON CL
HADRIAN CL
WICKHAM CT
THE HOLT
REDCAR CL
KEMPTON CRES
ASCOT RIDE
AINTREE DR
NEWNHAM RD
BENTLEY CL
COSFORD CL
WALLSGROVE CL
SEVERN CL
ELAN CL
CHEVIOT RISE
CUMBERLAND CRES
SOUTHFIELDS
HILL CL
FARM RD
MANOR RD
ELM RD
CHURCH LA
CLOISTER CROFTS
BORDESLEY CT
VICARAGE RD
OLD SCHOOL MEWS
WALNUT DR
CROWN WAY
VALLEY RD
CHARNWOOD WAY
BARNARD CL
LANGDALE CL
Lillington
Liby
INGLEWOOD CL
PINE CT
THE GREENWAYS
Sch
FELL GR
WICKRILL DR
NEWLAND RD
THE CREST
WARREN CL
B4453
POUND LA
GRANGE RD
THURSFIELD RD
HAWORTH CL
SUDBURY CL
DENBY CL
MASON AVE
EDEN CT
DENVILLE RD
GRANBOROUGH CT
DEERHAM CT
HEEMSTEDE LA
LOXLEY WAY
CROMER RD
WELLINGTON RD
ELTON CL
COMPTON CL
CLARE CL
BURBURY CL
Tanner's Farm
A445
OAK TREE CL
BERENSKA DR
PAYNE CL
KEIR CL
NAPTON DR
OAK TREE CT
MULBERRY CL
WHITETHORN DR
GRESHAM AVE
TAYLOR AVE
HADDON RD
EAST DENE
BRIAR CL
WELSH RD
FORD COTTS
WATHEN RD
GRANVILLE ST
CAMPION GN
CAMPION RD
RAWLINSON RD
DUDLEY GN
BUCKLEY RD
The Runghills
Ford Farm
CV33
WALLER ST
HAZEL CL
JASMINE GR
PLEASANT WAY
HURLEY CL
ROSEWOOD CRES
ROBINIA CL
BLACK LA
Mast
Works
River Leam
UPPER HILL ST
NORTH VILLIERS ST
KILN CL
VILLIERS ST
SHEEPCOTE CL
LEICESTER CT
1 GRESHAM PL
2 CHESTNUT SQ
3 MARSTON CL
Campion Hills
Mast
White House
CLARENDON ST
HILL ST
NORFOLK ST
SUFFOLK ST
LEICESTER ST
AQUA HO
QUEEN ST
PRINCE'S ST
HAMPTON GR
GREENWOOD CT
St Paul's CE Prim Sch
KING ST
VINCENT ST
DUKE ST
EARL ST
CAMPION TERR
COMYN ST
HOLLY ST
SWAN ST
LANSDOWNE ST
THOMAS ST
WILLES RD
B4099
LANSDOWNE CIR
TALBOT CT
UPPER HOLLY WLK
THE GRANGE
FERNHILL DR
CROSS ST
HOLLY WLK
CAMBRIDGE GDNS
CH
Redhouse Farm
Offchurch Bury

32 A B 33 C D 34 E F

A1
1 LOWER VILLIERS ST
2 LANSDOWNE RD
3 KENNEDY SQ
4 ST PAUL'S SQ
5 MERCHANTS CT
6 LANSDOWNE CRES
7 WILLIAM THOMAS HO
8 HANOVER GDNS
9 WHITTLE CT

A2
1 ACORN CT
2 STOCKTON GR
3 WHITACRE RD
4 CHARLES WATSON CT
5 SHUCKBURGH GR
6 HELLIDON CL
7 BROWNLOW ST

105
110

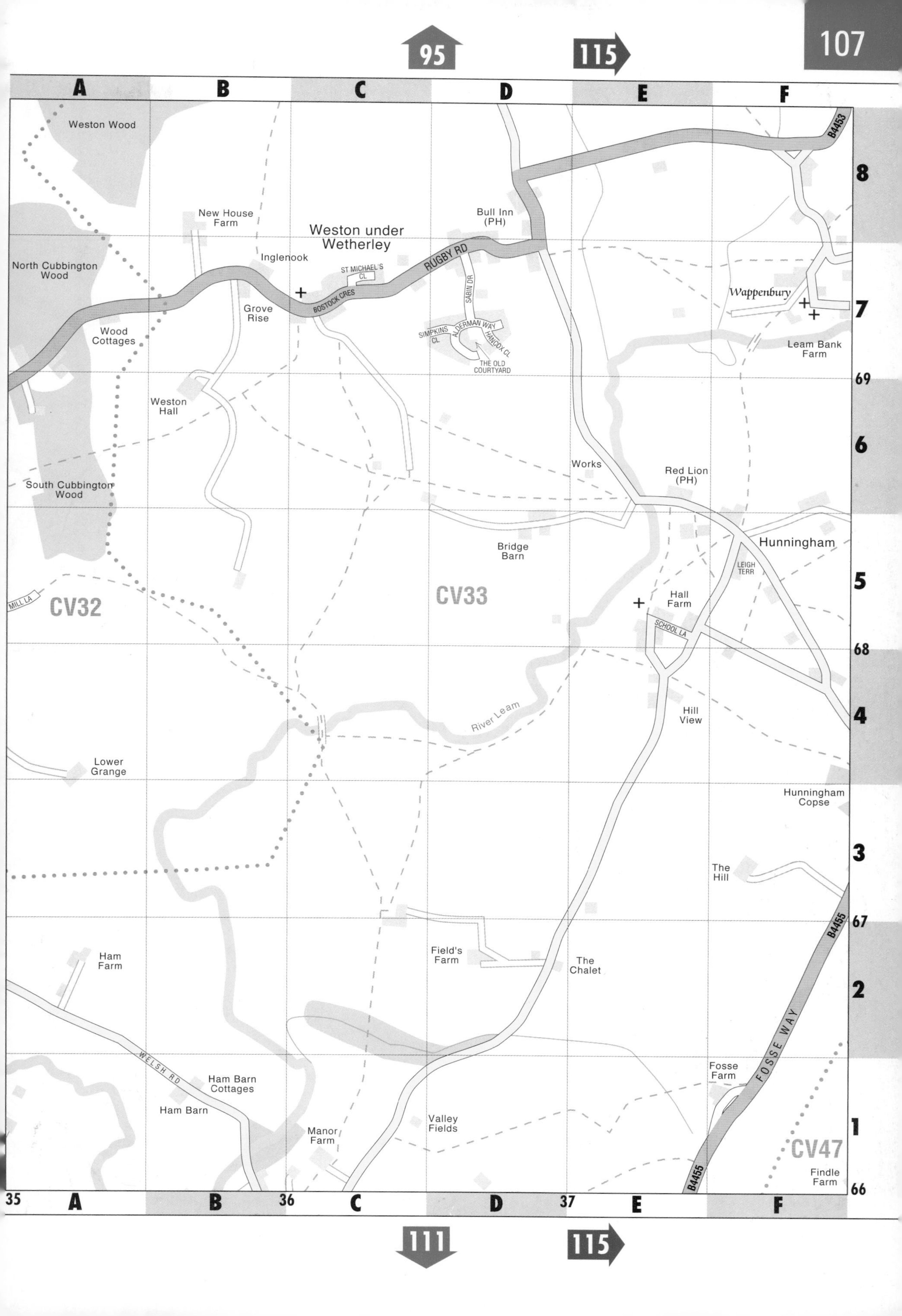
95
115
A
B
C
D
E
F
8
7
69
6
5
68
4
3
67
2
1
66
35
36
37
Weston Wood
New House Farm
Weston under Wetherley
Bull Inn (PH)
North Cubbington Wood
Inglenook
ST MICHAEL'S CL
RUGBY RD
BOSTOCK CRES
SABIN DR
ALDERMAN WAY
SIMPKINS CL
HANCOX CL
THE OLD COURTYARD
Grove Rise
Wood Cottages
Weston Hall
Wappenbury
Leam Bank Farm
B4453
Works
Red Lion (PH)
South Cubbington Wood
Bridge Barn
Hunningham
LEIGH TERR
MILL LA
CV32
CV33
Hall Farm
SCHOOL LA
Hill View
River Leam
Lower Grange
Hunningham Copse
The Hill
B4455
Ham Farm
Field's Farm
The Chalet
FOSSE WAY
WELSH RD
Ham Barn Cottages
Ham Barn
Fosse Farm
Valley Fields
Manor Farm
CV47
Findle Farm
B4455
111
115

114
104

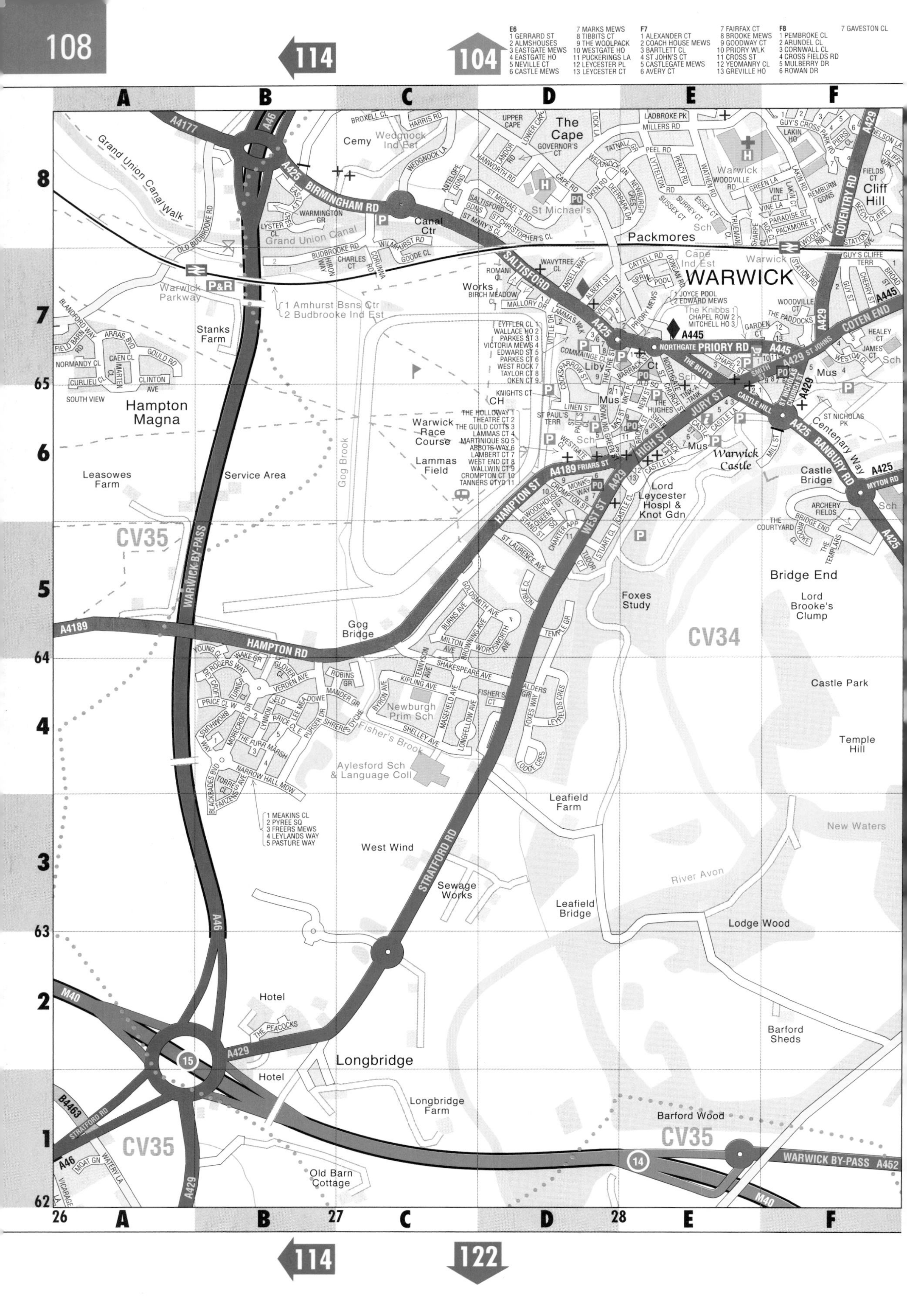

114
122

B8
1 CHARLES CT
2 ST EDITH'S HO
3 ST EDITH'S GN
4 WHITTINGTON CL
5 PACKWOOD MEWS
6 HERALDS CT
D8
1 WESTGROVE TERR
2 CROSS RD
3 THE CEDARS MEWS
4 PENDINE CT
5 GOODWAY HO
6 BEECH HO
7 OAK HO
8 BROOKLANDS HO
9 LEAM SIDE HO
10 SOUTHBANK HO
11 WILLOW HO
12 ALDER HO
E8
1 WOODBINE ST
2 WOODBINE COTTS
3 NEW BROOK ST
4 SOMERS PL
5 PORTLAND PL W
6 RIVERSDALE
7 CEDAR HO
F7
1 CHURCH WLK
2 SMITH ST
3 BATH PL
4 ABBOTTS ST
5 VICTORIA COLONNADE
105
F8
1 EUSTON SQ
2 ROSEFIELD ST
3 ROSEFIELD WLK
4 ROSEFIELD PL
5 BEDFORD PL
6 Regency Arc
110
F8
7 ST PETER'S RD
8 CARLTON HO
9 PORTLAND CT
10 PORTLAND MEWS
11 CHURCHILL HO
12 WINDSOR CT
13 CHAPEL CT
14 Royal Priors
15 SATCHWELL CT
16 SATCHWELL WLK
17 DENBY BLDGS
18 KENILWORTH ST
109
Emscote
CV32
RUGBY RD
EMSCOTE RD
Grand Union Canal Wlk
Centenary Way
Jephson's Farm
River Leam
River Avon
PARK DR
AVENUE RD
ADELAIDE RD
OLD WARWICK RD
MYTON RD
Coten End Prim Sch
Myton Sch
The Trinity RC Sch
Brook Farm
King Henry VIII Farm
Myton
Warwick Sch
ROYAL LEAMINGTON SPA
CV31
Shires Gate Ret Pk
Shires Gate Trad Est
Queensway Trad Est
Shires Ret Pk
Hermes Ct
Schs
Mus & Liby
Leamington Spa
EUROPA WAY
Sports Ctr
Warwick Tech Pk
Heathcote Hill Farm
CV34
HEATHCOTE LA
GALLOWS HILL
Heathcote Ind Est
Titan Bsns Ctr
Royal Leamington Spa Rehabilitation
Turnbulls Garden
Hawkes Farm
Heathcote
BANBURY RD
TACHBROOK RD
Nursery Wood
The Stews
The Asps
Lower Heathcote Farm
Asps Cottages
Sewage Works
Heathcote Pk
Grove Farm
Park Farm
New House Farm
CV33
WARWICK BY-PASS
OAKLEY WOOD RD
The Grove
A B C D E F
29 30 31
62 63 64 65
122
110
F5
1 YEW TREE CT
2 GINKGO WLK
3 CONIFER GR
4 SPRUCE GR
5 SILVER BIRCH GR
6 WYCH ELM DR
7 BONNIKSEN CL
8 LOCKHEED CL
F6
1 PHILIP CT
2 FRANCES HAVERGAL CL
3 PRINCE REGENT CT
4 FETHERSTON CT
5 TATCHBROOK CT
6 CHARLES GARDNER RD
7 MARKET CNR

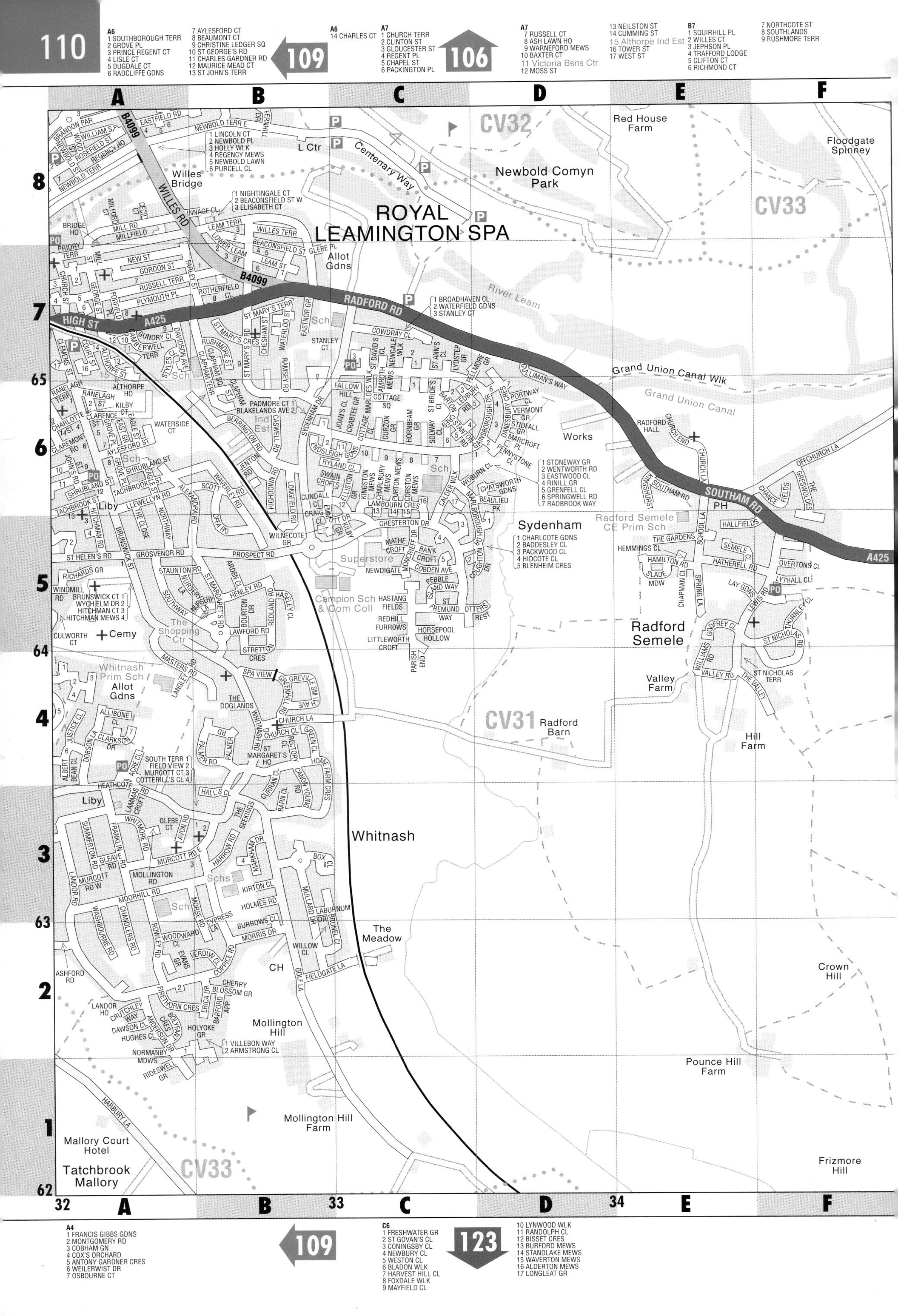

110
A6
1 SOUTHBOROUGH TERR
2 GROVE PL
3 PRINCE REGENT CT
4 LISLE CT
5 DUGDALE CT
6 RADCLIFFE GDNS
7 AYLESFORD CT
8 BEAUMONT CT
9 CHRISTINE LEDGER SQ
10 ST GEORGE'S RD
11 CHARLES GARDNER RD
12 MAURICE MEAD CT
13 ST JOHN'S TERR
109
A6
14 CHARLES CT
A7
1 CHURCH TERR
2 CLINTON ST
3 GLOUCESTER ST
4 REGENT PL
5 CHAPEL ST
6 PACKINGTON PL
106
A7
7 RUSSELL CT
8 ASH LAWN HO
9 WARNEFORD MEWS
10 BAXTER CT
11 Victoria Bsns Ctr
12 MOSS ST
13 NEILSTON ST
14 CUMMING ST
15 Althorpe Ind Est
16 TOWER ST
17 WEST ST
B7
1 SQUIRHILL PL
2 WILLES CT
3 JEPHSON PL
4 TRAFFORD LODGE
5 CLIFTON CT
6 RICHMOND CT
7 NORTHCOTE ST
8 SOUTHLANDS
9 RUSHMORE TERR
ROYAL LEAMINGTON SPA
Newbold Comyn Park
Red House Farm
Floodgate Spinney
CV32
CV33
CV31
Willes Bridge
L Ctr
Centenary Way
River Leam
Grand Union Canal Wlk
Grand Union Canal
RADFORD RD
SOUTHAM RD
HIGH ST
A425
B4099
WILLES RD
Sydenham
Radford Semele
Radford Semele CE Prim Sch
Valley Farm
Radford Barn
Hill Farm
Whitnash
Whitnash Prim Sch
The Meadow
Mollington Hill
Mollington Hill Farm
Crown Hill
Pounce Hill Farm
Frizmore Hill
Mallory Court Hotel
Tatchbrook Mallory
Campion Sch & Com Coll
Superstore
The Shopping Ctr
Works
Cemy
32
33
34
62
63
64
65
A
B
C
D
E
F
1
2
3
4
5
6
7
8
A4
1 FRANCIS GIBBS GDNS
2 MONTGOMERY RD
3 COBHAM GN
4 COX'S ORCHARD
5 ANTONY GARDNER CRES
6 WEILERWIST DR
7 OSBOURNE CT
109
C6
1 FRESHWATER GR
2 ST GOVAN'S CL
3 CONINGSBY CL
4 NEWBURY CL
5 WESTON CL
6 BLADON WLK
7 HARVEST HILL CL
8 FOXDALE WLK
9 MAYFIELD CL
123
10 LYNWOOD WLK
11 RANDOLPH CL
12 BISSET CRES
13 BURFORD MEWS
14 STANDLAKE MEWS
15 WAVERTON MEWS
16 ALDERTON MEWS
17 LONGLEAT GR

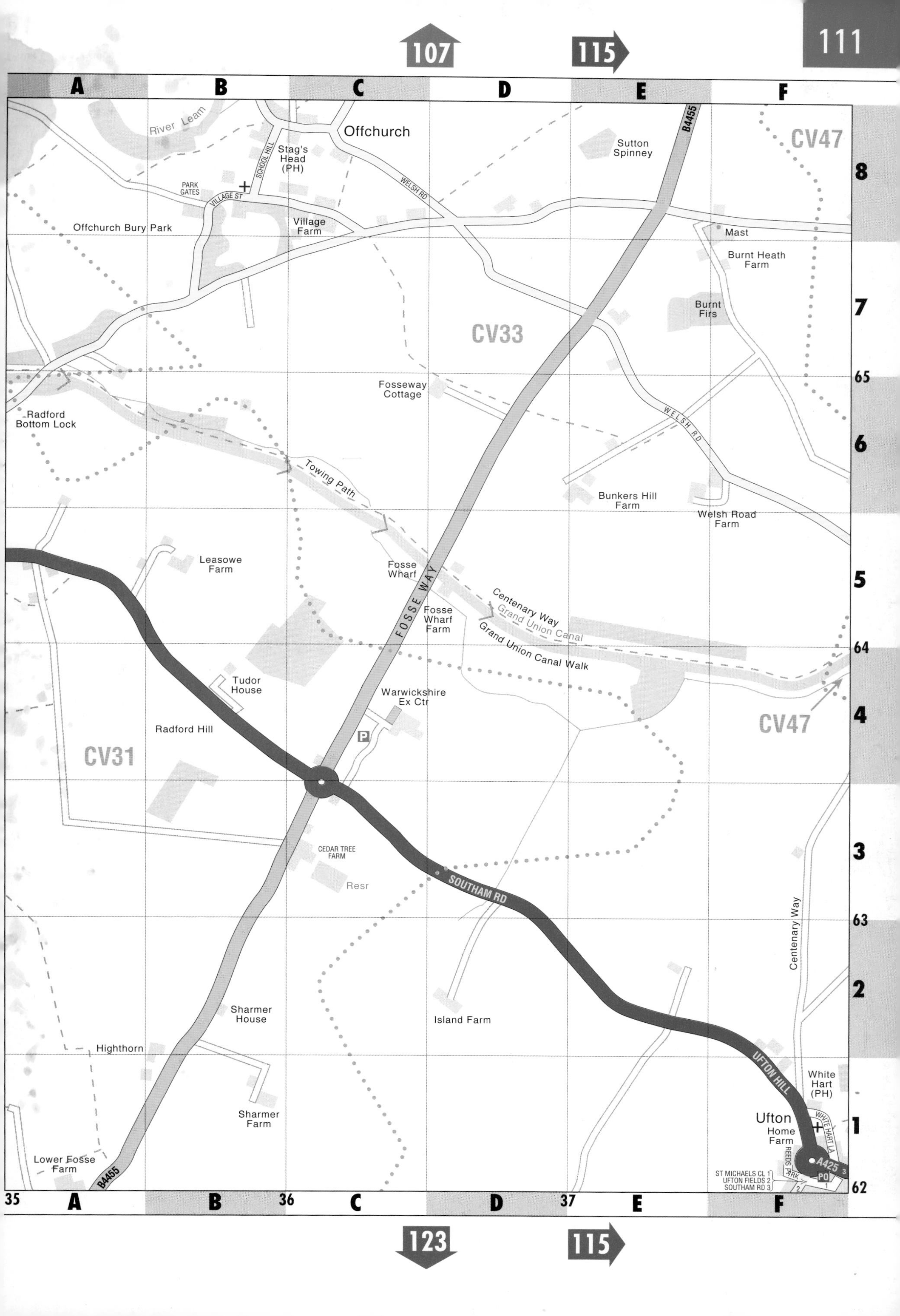
A
B
C
D
E
F
River Leam
Offchurch
Stag's Head (PH)
SCHOOL HILL
PARK GATES
VILLAGE ST
WELSH RD
Sutton Spinney
B4455
CV47
8
Offchurch Bury Park
Village Farm
Mast
Burnt Heath Farm
Burnt Firs
7
CV33
65
Fosseway Cottage
Radford Bottom Lock
WELSH RD
6
Towing Path
Bunkers Hill Farm
Welsh Road Farm
Leasowe Farm
Fosse Wharf
FOSSE WAY
5
Fosse Wharf Farm
Centenary Way
Grand Union Canal
Grand Union Canal Walk
64
Tudor House
Warwickshire Ex Ctr
CV47
4
Radford Hill
P
CV31
CEDAR TREE FARM
3
Resr
SOUTHAM RD
63
Centenary Way
2
Sharmer House
Island Farm
Highthorn
UFTON HILL
White Hart (PH)
Sharmer Farm
Ufton
Home Farm
WHITE HART LA
1
Lower Fosse Farm
REEDS PARK
A425
PO
ST MICHAELS CL 1
UFTON FIELDS 2
SOUTHAM RD 3
B4455
62
35
36
37

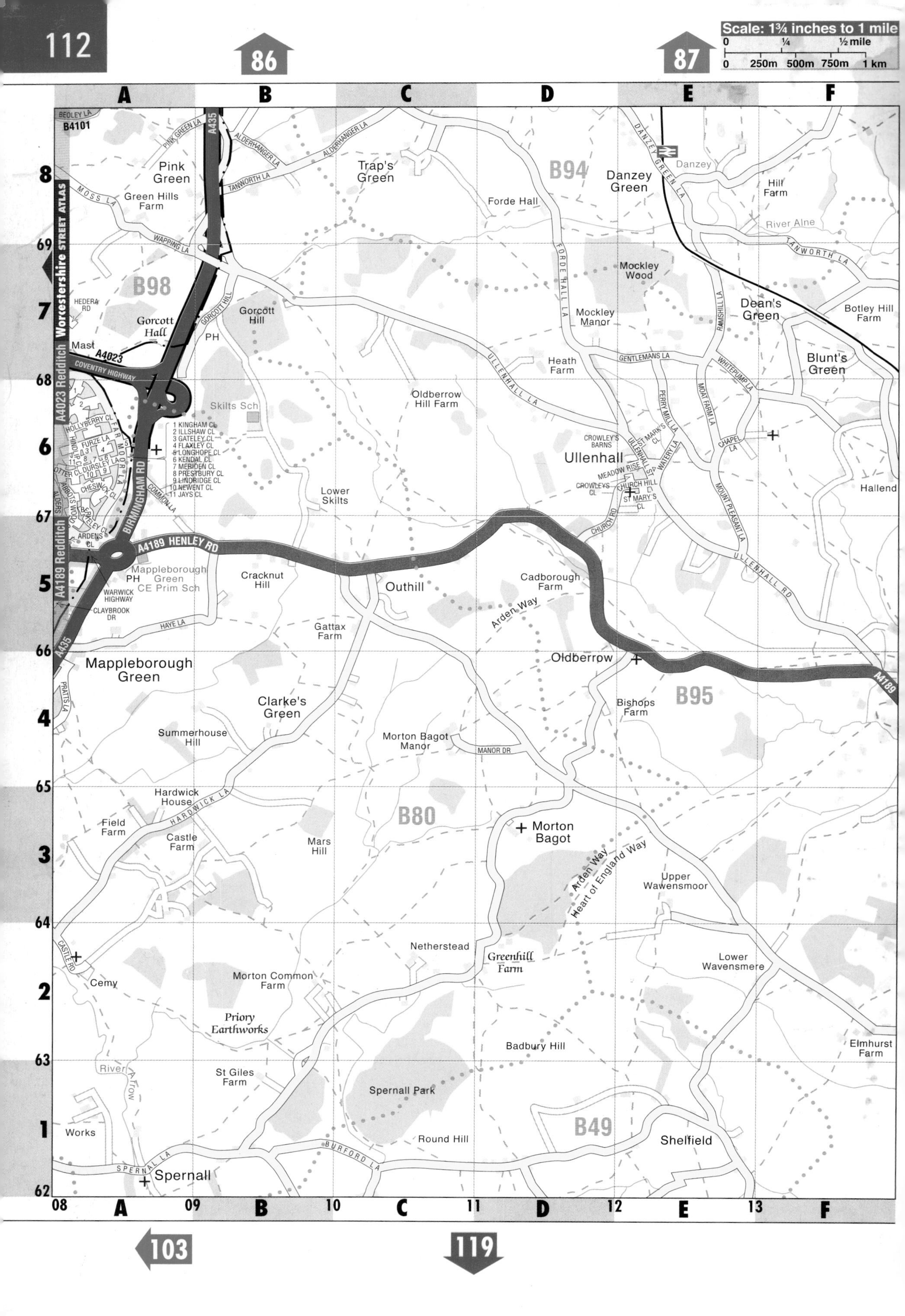
86
87
Scale: 1¾ inches to 1 mile
0 ¼ ½ mile
0 250m 500m 750m 1 km
A B C D E F
Pink Green
Green Hills Farm
Trap's Green
Forde Hall
Danzey Green
Danzey
Hill Farm
River Alne
B94
B98
Gorcott Hall
Gorcott Hill
PH
Mast
Mockley Wood
Mockley Manor
Dean's Green
Botley Hill Farm
Blunt's Green
Heath Farm
Oldberrow Hill Farm
Skilts Sch
Ullenhall
Hallend
Lower Skilts
Cracknut Hill
Outhill
Cadborough Farm
Arden Way
Mappleborough Green
Mappleborough Green CE Prim Sch
Gattax Farm
Oldberrow
Bishops Farm
B95
Clarke's Green
Summerhouse Hill
Morton Bagot Manor
Hardwick House
Field Farm
Castle Farm
Mars Hill
B80
Morton Bagot
Heart of England Way
Upper Wawensmoor
Netherstead
Greenhill Farm
Lower Wavensmere
Cemy
Morton Common Farm
Priory Earthworks
Badbury Hill
Elmhurst Farm
River Arrow
St Giles Farm
Spernall Park
Works
Round Hill
B49
Shelfield
Spernall
A435
A4023
A4189
B4101
A4023 Redditch
A4189 Redditch
Worcestershire STREET ATLAS
1 KINGHAM CL
2 ILLSHAW CL
3 GATELEY CL
4 FLAXLEY CL
5 LONGHOPE CL
6 KENDAL CL
7 MERIDEN CL
8 PRESTBURY CL
9 LINDRIDGE CL
10 NEWENT CL
11 JAYS CL
8 69 7 68 6 67 5 66 4 65 3 64 2 63 1 62
08 09 10 11 12 13
103
119

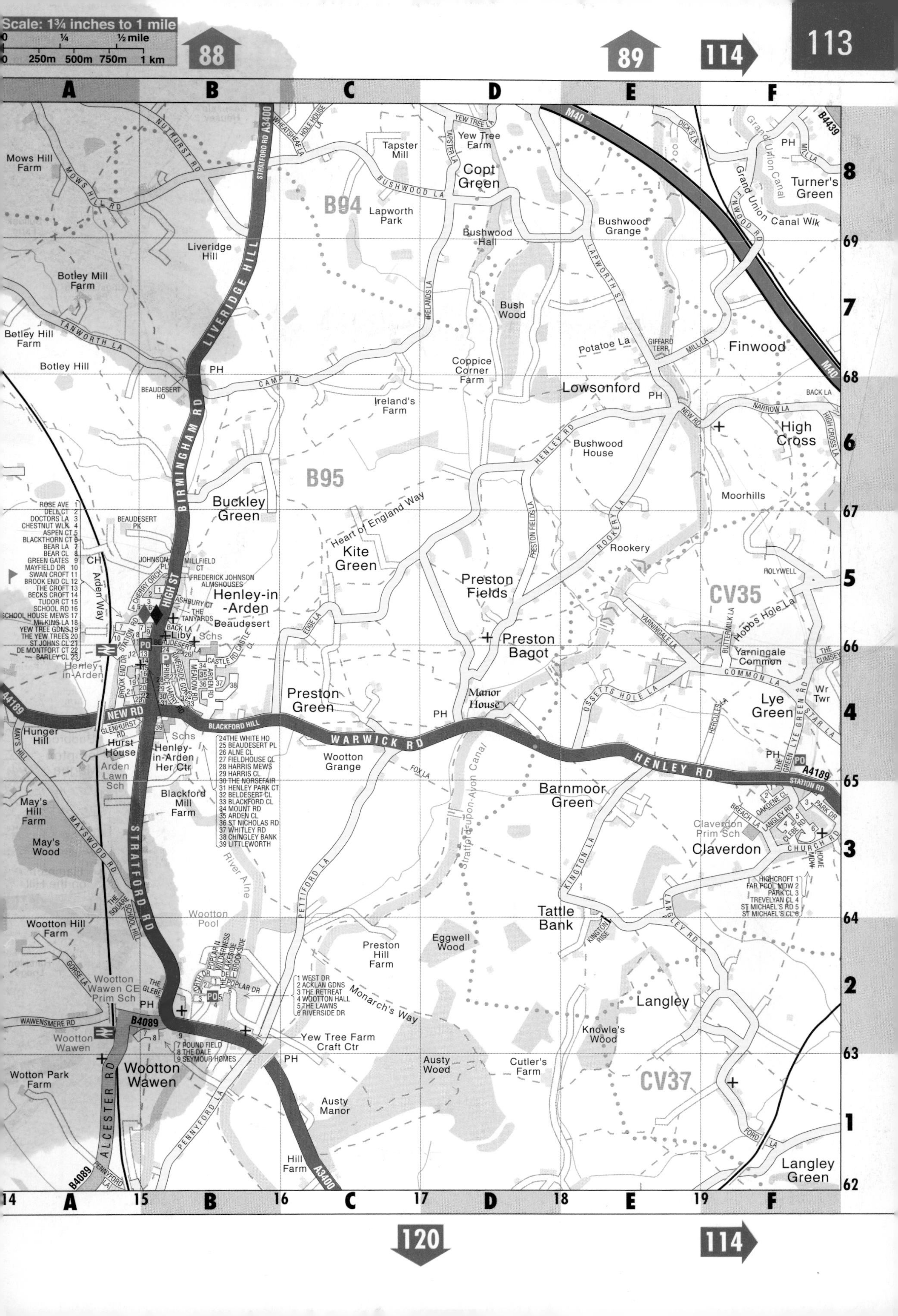
113
Scale: 1¾ inches to 1 mile
0
¼
½ mile
0
250m
500m
750m
1 km
88
89
114
A
B
C
D
E
F
Mows Hill Farm
MOWS HILL RD
NUTHURST RD
STRATFORD RD A3400
WHEATSHEAF LA
HOLE HOUSE LA
YEW TREE LA
TAPSTER LA
Yew Tree Farm
Tapster Mill
Copt Green
BUSHWOOD LA
B94
Lapworth Park
M40
DICK'S LA
B4439
PH
Grand Union Canal
MILL LA
Turner's Green
Grand Union Canal Wlk
FINWOOD RD
Bushwood Hall
Bushwood Grange
Liveridge Hill
LIVERIDGE HILL
Botley Mill Farm
IRELANDS LA
LAPWORTH ST
Bush Wood
TANWORTH LA
Botley Hill Farm
Botley Hill
Potatoe La
GIFFARD TERR
MILL LA
Finwood
Coppice Corner Farm
PH
CAMP LA
BEAUDESERT HO
Lowsonford
PH
BACK LA
Ireland's Farm
NEW RD
NARROW LA
High Cross
HIGH CROSS LA
BIRMINGHAM RD
HENLEY RD
Bushwood House
B95
Moorhills
Buckley Green
ROSE AVE 1
DELL CT 2
DOCTORS LA 3
CHESTNUT WLK 4
ASPEN CT 5
BLACKTHORN CT 6
BEAR LA 7
BEAR CL 8
GREEN GATES 9
MAYFIELD DR 10
SWAN CROFT 11
BROOK END CL 12
THE CROFT 13
BECKS CROFT 14
TUDOR CT 15
SCHOOL RD 16
SCHOOL HOUSE MEWS 17
MILKINS LA 18
YEW TREE GDNS 19
THE YEW TREES 20
ST JOHNS CL 21
DE MONTFORT CT 22
BARLEY CL 23
BEAUDESERT PK
Heart of England Way
PRESTON FIELDS LA
ROOKERY LA
Rookery
Kite Green
CH
JOHNSON PL
MILLFIELD CT
FREDERICK JOHNSON ALMSHOUSES
HOLYWELL
Arden Way
CHERRY ORCH
HIGH ST
ASHBURY CT
THE TANYARDS
Henley-in-Arden
Beaudesert
Preston Fields
CV35
BACK LA
Liby
Schs
EDGE LA
YARNINGALE LA
BUTTERMILK LA
Hobbs Hole La
PO
BEAUDESERT LA
CASTLE CL
CASTLE RD
Preston Bagot
Yarningale Common
THE CUMSEY
Henley-in-Arden
BROOK END DR
STATION RD
MEADOW RD
ARDEN RD
COMMON LA
OSSETTS HOLE LA
Lye Green
Wr Twr
A4189
NEW RD
Preston Green
Manor House
HERCULES LA
LYE GREEN RD
STAR LA
PH
GLENHURST RD
BLACKFORD HILL
Hunger Hill
MAYS HILL
Hurst House
Schs
24 THE WHITE HO
25 BEAUDESERT PL
26 ALNE CL
27 FIELDHOUSE CL
28 HARRIS MEWS
29 HARRIS CL
30 THE NORSEFAIR
31 HENLEY PARK CT
32 BELDESERT CL
33 BLACKFORD CL
34 MOUNT RD
35 ARDEN CL
36 ST NICHOLAS RD
37 WHITLEY RD
38 CHINGLEY BANK
39 LITTLEWORTH
WARWICK RD
Wootton Grange
Henley-in-Arden Her Ctr
Arden Lawn Sch
FOX LA
HENLEY RD
PH
PO
THE GREEN
A4189
STATION RD
May's Hill Farm
MAYSWOOD RD
Blackford Mill Farm
Barnmoor Green
OAKDENE CL
PARK DR
BREACH LA
LANGLEY RD
Claverdon Prim Sch
CLEBE RD
May's Wood
STRATFORD RD
River Alne
Stratford-upon-Avon Canal
KINGTON LA
Claverdon
CHURCH RD
HOME MDW
PETTIFORD LA
HIGHCROFT 1
FAR POOL MDW 2
PARK CL 3
TREVELYAN CL 4
ST MICHAEL'S RD 5
ST MICHAEL'S CL 6
THE SQUARE
SCHOOL HILL
Wootton Pool
Tattle Bank
Wootton Hill Farm
POPLAR LN
WILDERNESS LA
LAKESIDE
BROOKSIDE
Eggwell Wood
Preston Hill Farm
KINGTON RISE
LANGLEY RD
GORSE LA
Wootton Wawen CE Prim Sch
THE GLEBE
SMITH DR
DELL
POPLAR DR
1 WEST DR
2 ACKLAN GDNS
3 THE RETREAT
4 WOOTTON HALL
5 THE LAWNS
6 RIVERSIDE DR
Monarch's Way
Langley
PH
WAWENSMERE RD
B4089
Wootton Wawen
7 POUND FIELD
8 THE DALE
9 SEYMOUR HOMES
Yew Tree Farm Craft Ctr
Knowle's Wood
PH
Wotton Park Farm
Wootton Wawen
Austy Wood
Cutler's Farm
CV37
ALCESTER RD
PENNYFORD LA
Austy Manor
FORD LA
B4089
PENNYFORD LA
Hill Farm
A3400
Langley Green
8
69
7
68
6
67
5
66
4
65
3
64
2
63
1
62
14
15
16
17
18
19
120
114

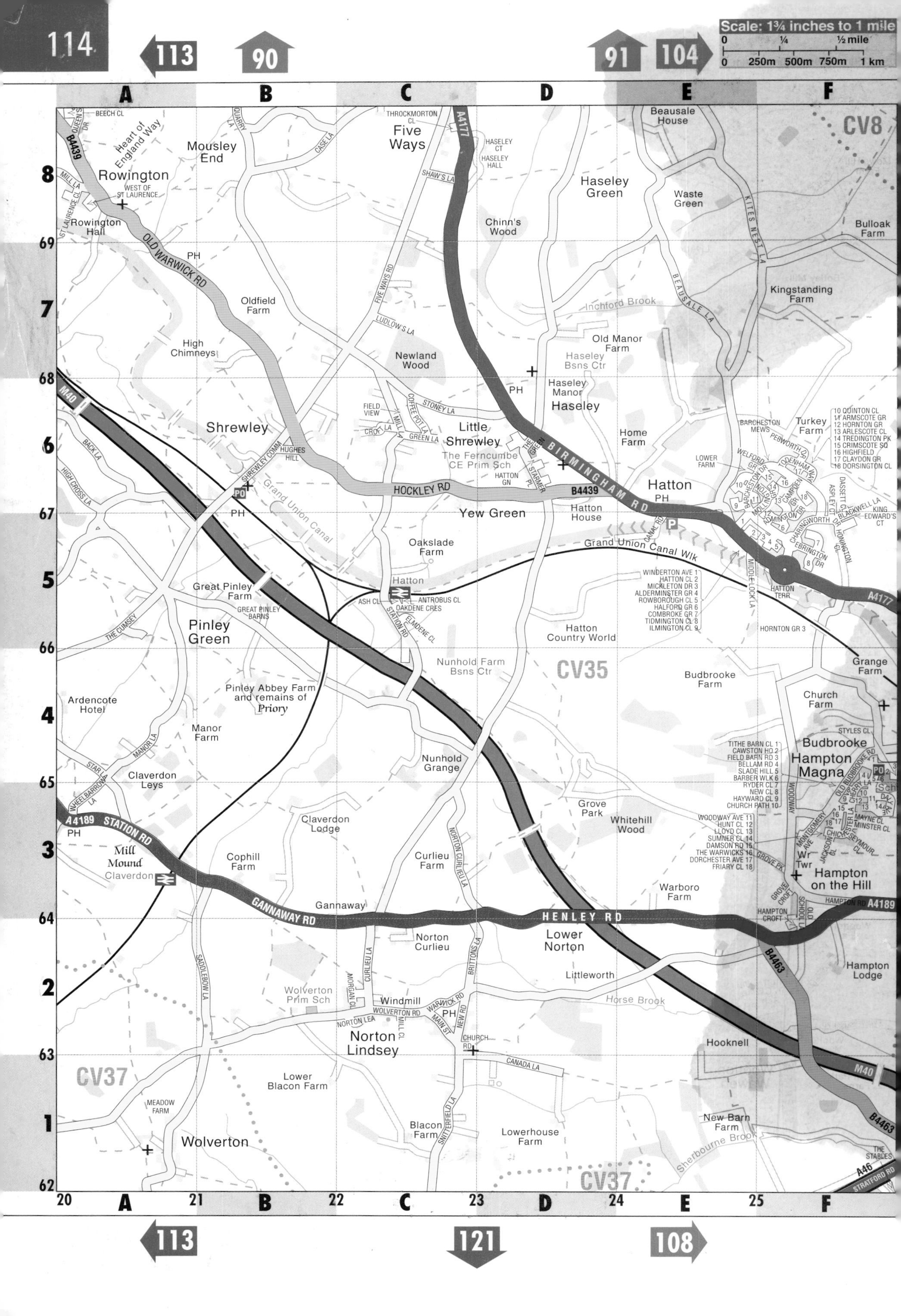

114
113
90
91
104
Scale: 1¾ inches to 1 mile
0
¼
½ mile
0
250m
500m
750m
1 km
A
B
C
D
E
F
8
69
7
68
6
67
5
66
4
65
3
64
2
63
1
62
20
21
22
23
24
25
BEECH CL
Heart of England Way
B4439
Rowington
WEST OF ST LAURENCE
MILL LA
ST LAURENCE CL
Rowington Hall
Mousley End
QUARRY LA
CASE LA
THROCKMORTON CL
Five Ways
A4177
HASELEY CT
HASELEY HALL
SHAW'S LA
Haseley Green
Beausale House
Waste Green
KITES NEST LA
CV8
Bulloak Farm
Chinn's Wood
OLD WARWICK RD
PH
Oldfield Farm
FIVE WAYS RD
Inchford Brook
BEAUSALE LA
Kingstanding Farm
LUDLOW'S LA
Newland Wood
High Chimneys
Old Manor Farm
Haseley Bsns Ctr
M40
PH
Haseley Manor
Haseley
FIELD VIEW
COFFEE POT LA
STONEY LA
MILL LA
CROFT LA
GREEN LA
Little Shrewley
Shrewley
BACK LA
HIGH CROSS LA
SHREWLEY COMM
HUGHES HILL
The Ferncumbe CE Prim Sch
THE GREEN
BIRMINGHAM RD
Home Farm
HATTON GN
STARMER PL
Hatton
PH
BARCHESTON MEWS
Turkey Farm
PEBWORTH
WELFORD
LOWER FARM
10 QUINTON CL
11 ARMSCOTE GR
12 HORNTON GR
13 ARLESCOTE CL
14 TREDINGTON PK
15 CRIMSCOTE SQ
16 HIGHFIELD
17 CLAYDON GR
18 DORSINGTON CL
HOCKLEY RD
B4439
Grand Union Canal
PO
PH
Yew Green
Hatton House
CANAL RD
P
ASPLEY CT
DASSETT CL
BLACKWELL LA
KING EDWARD'S CT
CHARINGWORTH
EBRINGTON
HONINGTON CL
Oakslade Farm
Grand Union Canal Wlk
Hatton
ASH CL
ANTROBUS CL
OAKDENE CRES
STATION RD
ELMDENE CL
Great Pinley Farm
GREAT PINLEY BARNS
WINDERTON AVE 1
HATTON CL 2
MICKLETON DR 3
ALDERMINSTER GR 4
ROWBOROUGH CL 5
HALFORD GR 6
COMBROKE GR 7
TIDMINGTON CL 8
ILMINGTON CL 9
MIDDLE LOCK LA
HATTON TERR
A4177
HORNTON GR 3
THE CUMSEY
Pinley Green
Hatton Country World
Nunhold Farm Bsns Ctr
CV35
Budbrooke Farm
Grange Farm
Ardencote Hotel
Pinley Abbey Farm and remains of Priory
Church Farm
Manor Farm
STYLES CL
TITHE BARN CL 1
CAWSTON HO 2
FIELD BARN RD 3
BELLAM RD 4
SLADE HILL 5
BARBER WLK 6
RYDER CL 7
NEW CL 8
HAYWARD CL 9
CHURCH PATH 10
Budbrooke
Hampton Magna
OLD BUDBROOKE RD
WOODWAY
MANOR LA
STAR LA
WHEELBARROW LA
Claverdon Leys
Nunhold Grange
Grove Park
Whitehill Wood
A4189
STATION RD
PH
Claverdon Lodge
NORTON CURLIEU LA
WOODWAY AVE 11
HUNT CL 12
LLOYD CL 13
SUMNER CL 14
DAMSON RD 15
THE WARWICKS 16
DORCHESTER AVE 17
FRIARY CL 18
GROVE PK
MAYNE CL
MINSTER CL
SEYMOUR CL
MONTGOMERY AVE
JACKSON CL
Mill Mound
Claverdon
Cophill Farm
Curlieu Farm
Wr Twr
Hampton on the Hill
Warboro Farm
GROVE CROFT
SCHOOL LA
HAMPTON RD
A4189
GANNAWAY RD
Gannaway
HENLEY RD
HAMPTON CROFT
Norton Curlieu
Lower Norton
B4463
Hampton Lodge
SADDLEBOW LA
CURLIEU LA
BRITTONS LA
Littleworth
MORGAN CL
Wolverton Prim Sch
Windmill
WARWICK RD
Horse Brook
WOLVERTON RD
PH
NORTON LEA
MILL CL
MAIN ST
NEW RD
Norton Lindsey
CHURCH RD
Hooknell
CANADA LA
CV37
Lower Blacon Farm
M40
MEADOW FARM
B4463
New Barn Farm
Blacon Farm
Lowerhouse Farm
SNITTERFIELD LA
Sherbourne Brook
Wolverton
THE STABLES
A46
STRATFORD RD
CV37
113
121
108

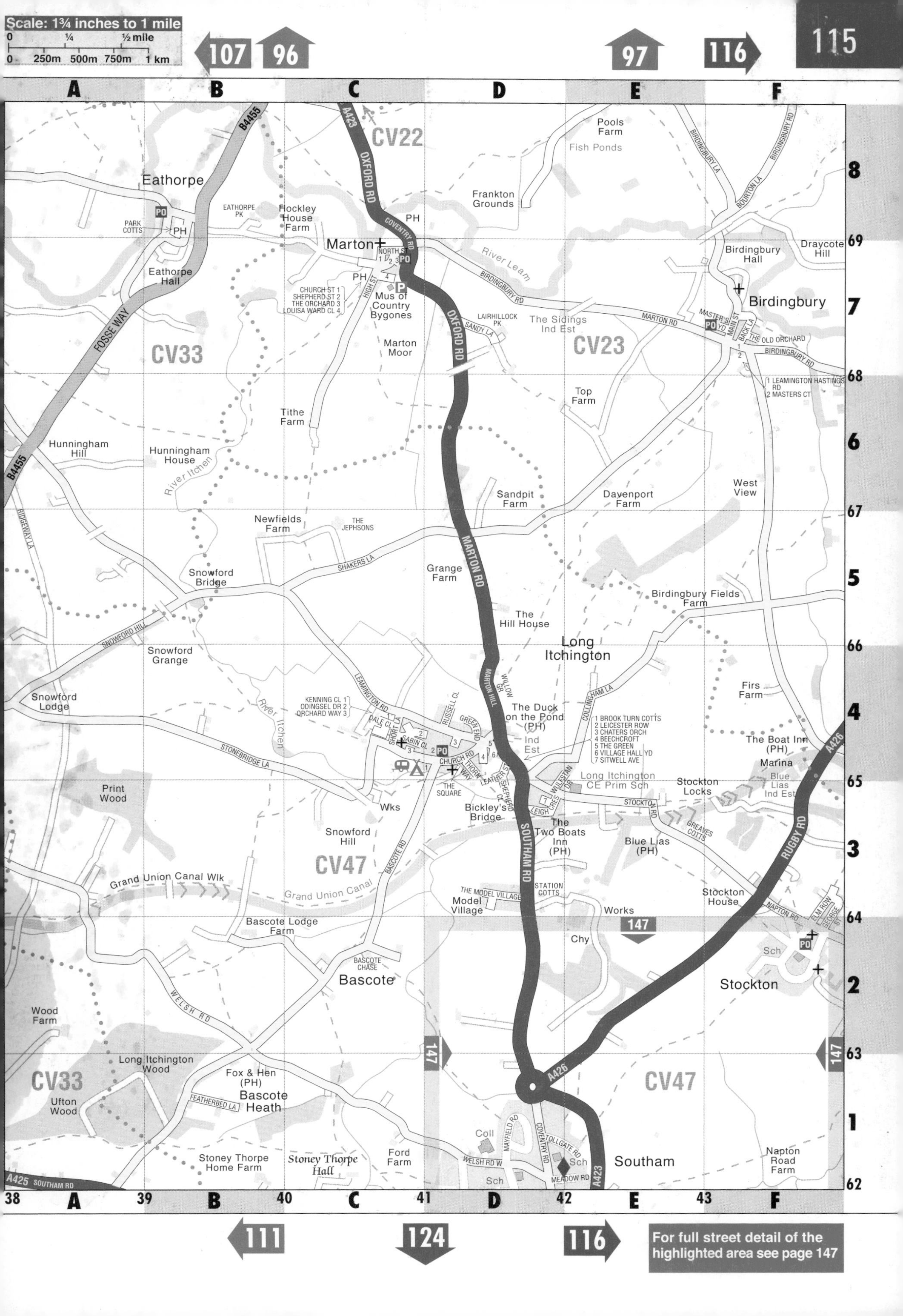
Scale: 1¾ inches to 1 mile
0 ¼ ½ mile
0 250m 500m 750m 1 km
107
96
97
116
A B C D E F
8 69 7 68 6 67 5 66 4 65 3 64 2 63 1 62
38 39 40 41 42 43
Eathorpe
PARK COTTS
PH
EATHORPE PK
Eathorpe Hall
B4455
FOSSE WAY
Hockley House Farm
Marton
NORTH ST
PH
PO
CHURCH ST 1
SHEPHERD ST 2
THE ORCHARD 3
LOUISA WARD CL 4
HIGH ST
Mus of Country Bygones
Marton Moor
OXFORD RD
A423
CV22
COVENTRY RD
Frankton Grounds
Pools Farm
Fish Ponds
River Leam
BIRDINGBURY RD
LAIRHILLOCK PK
SANDY LA
The Sidings Ind Est
CV23
CV33
MARTON RD
BIRDINGBURY LA
BOURTON LA
Birdingbury Hall
Draycote Hill
Birdingbury
MASTER'S YD
MAIN ST
BACK LA
THE OLD ORCHARD
1 LEAMINGTON HASTINGS RD
2 MASTERS CT
Top Farm
Tithe Farm
Hunningham Hill
Hunningham House
River Itchen
Sandpit Farm
Davenport Farm
West View
Newfields Farm
THE JEPHSONS
RIDGEWAY LA
SHAKERS LA
Grange Farm
MARTON RD
Snowford Bridge
Birdingbury Fields Farm
The Hill House
SNOWFORD HILL
Snowford Grange
Long Itchington
MARTON HILL
WILLOW GR
Firs Farm
Snowford Lodge
KENNING CL 1
ODINGSEL DR 2
ORCHARD WAY 3
LEAMINGTON RD
RUSSELL CL
GREEN END
The Duck on the Pond (PH)
COLLINGHAM LA
1 BROOK TURN COTTS
2 LEICESTER ROW
3 CHATERS ORCH
4 BEECHCROFT
5 THE GREEN
6 VILLAGE HALL YD
7 SITWELL AVE
The Boat Inn (PH)
A426
STONEBRIDGE LA
DALE CL
SHORT LA
SABIN CL
CHURCH RD
THORN WAY
LEATHER ST
SHEPHERD CL
Ind Est
WILLESTAN DR
Long Itchington CE Prim Sch
Stockton Locks
Marina
Blue Lias Ind Est
Print Wood
THE SQUARE
Wks
Bickley's Bridge
LEIGH CRES
STOCKTON RD
The Two Boats Inn (PH)
GREAVES COTTS
Blue Lias (PH)
RUGBY RD
Snowford Hill
CV47
BASCOTE RD
SOUTHAM RD
Grand Union Canal Wlk
Grand Union Canal
THE MODEL VILLAGE
STATION COTTS
Model Village
Works
Stockton House
NAPTON RD
ELM ROW
GEORGE ST
Bascote Lodge Farm
147
Chy
Sch
PO
BASCOTE CHASE
Bascote
Stockton
WELSH RD
Wood Farm
Long Itchington Wood
CV33
Ufton Wood
Fox & Hen (PH)
Bascote Heath
FEATHERBED LA
CV47
Coll
MAYFIELD RD
COVENTRY RD
TOLLGATE RD
Sch
Southam
WELSH RD W
MEADOW RD
Napton Road Farm
Stoney Thorpe Home Farm
Stoney Thorpe Hall
Ford Farm
A425 SOUTHAM RD
A423
111
124
116
For full street detail of the highlighted area see page 147

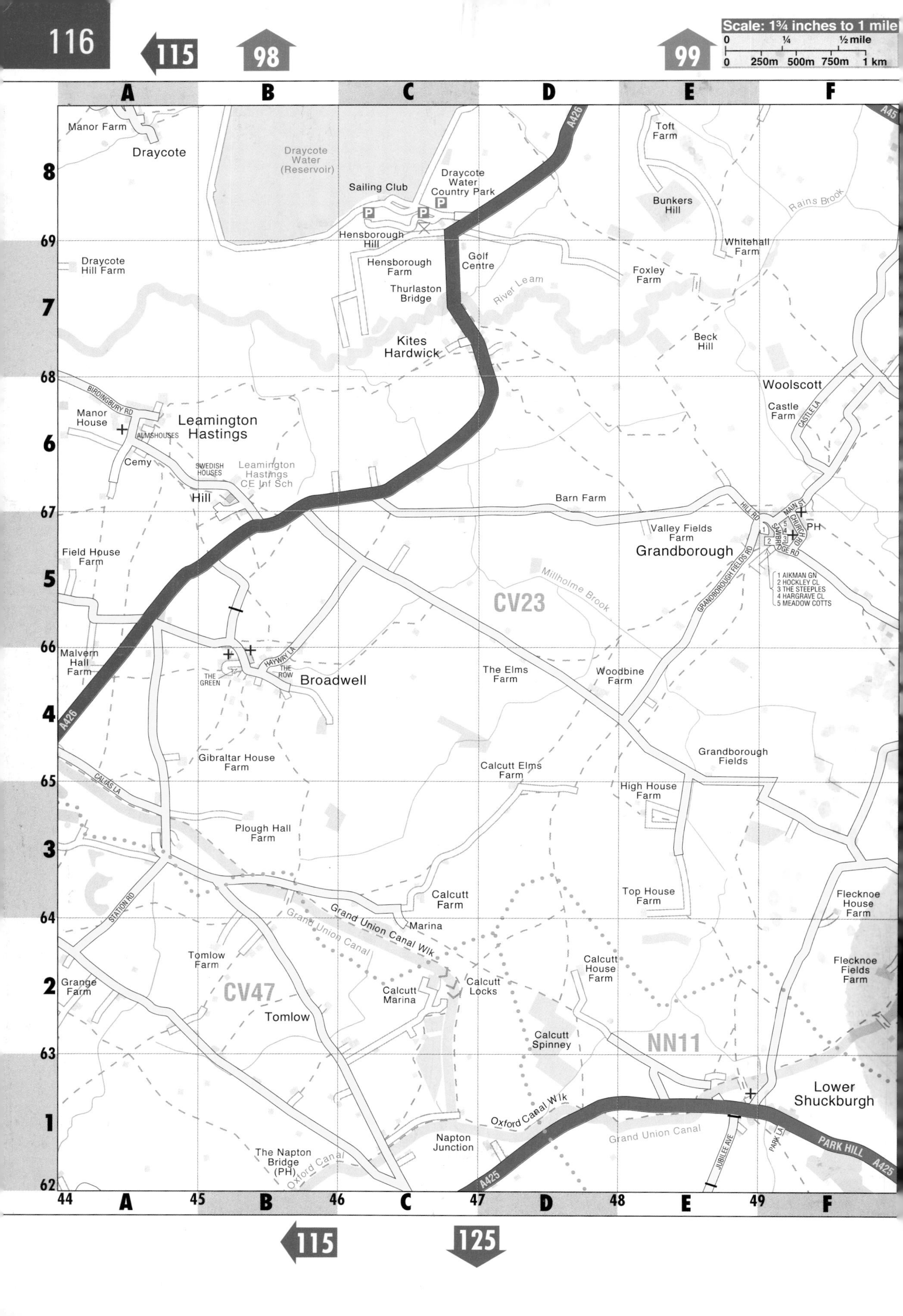
115
98
99
Scale: 1¾ inches to 1 mile
0 ¼ ½ mile
0 250m 500m 750m 1 km
A B C D E F
8 69 7 68 6 67 5 66 4 65 3 64 2 63 1 62
44 45 46 47 48 49
Manor Farm
Draycote
Draycote Water (Reservoir)
Sailing Club
Draycote Water Country Park
Hensborough Hill
Hensborough Farm
Golf Centre
Thurlaston Bridge
River Leam
Kites Hardwick
Toft Farm
Bunkers Hill
Rains Brook
Whitehall Farm
Foxley Farm
Beck Hill
Draycote Hill Farm
Woolscott
Castle Farm
CASTLE LA
BIRDINGBURY RD
Manor House
ALMSHOUSES
Leamington Hastings
Cemy
SWEDISH HOUSES
Leamington Hastings CE Inf Sch
Hill
Barn Farm
HILL RD
MAIN ST
CHURCH RD
SAWBRIDGE RD
PH
Valley Fields Farm
Grandborough
GRANDBOROUGH FIELDS RD
1 AIKMAN GN
2 HOCKLEY CL
3 THE STEEPLES
4 HARGRAVE CL
5 MEADOW COTTS
Field House Farm
Millholme Brook
CV23
Malvern Hall Farm
HAYWAY LA
THE ROW
THE GREEN
Broadwell
The Elms Farm
Woodbine Farm
A426
Grandborough Fields
Gibraltar House Farm
Calcutt Elms Farm
High House Farm
CALIAS LA
Plough Hall Farm
STATION RD
Calcutt Farm
Top House Farm
Flecknoe House Farm
Marina
Grand Union Canal Wlk
Grand Union Canal
Tomlow Farm
Calcutt House Farm
Flecknoe Fields Farm
Grange Farm
CV47
Calcutt Marina
Calcutt Locks
Tomlow
Calcutt Spinney
NN11
Lower Shuckburgh
Oxford Canal Wlk
JUBILEE AVE
PARK LA
PARK HILL
A425
A45
Napton Junction
The Napton Bridge (PH)
Oxford Canal
125

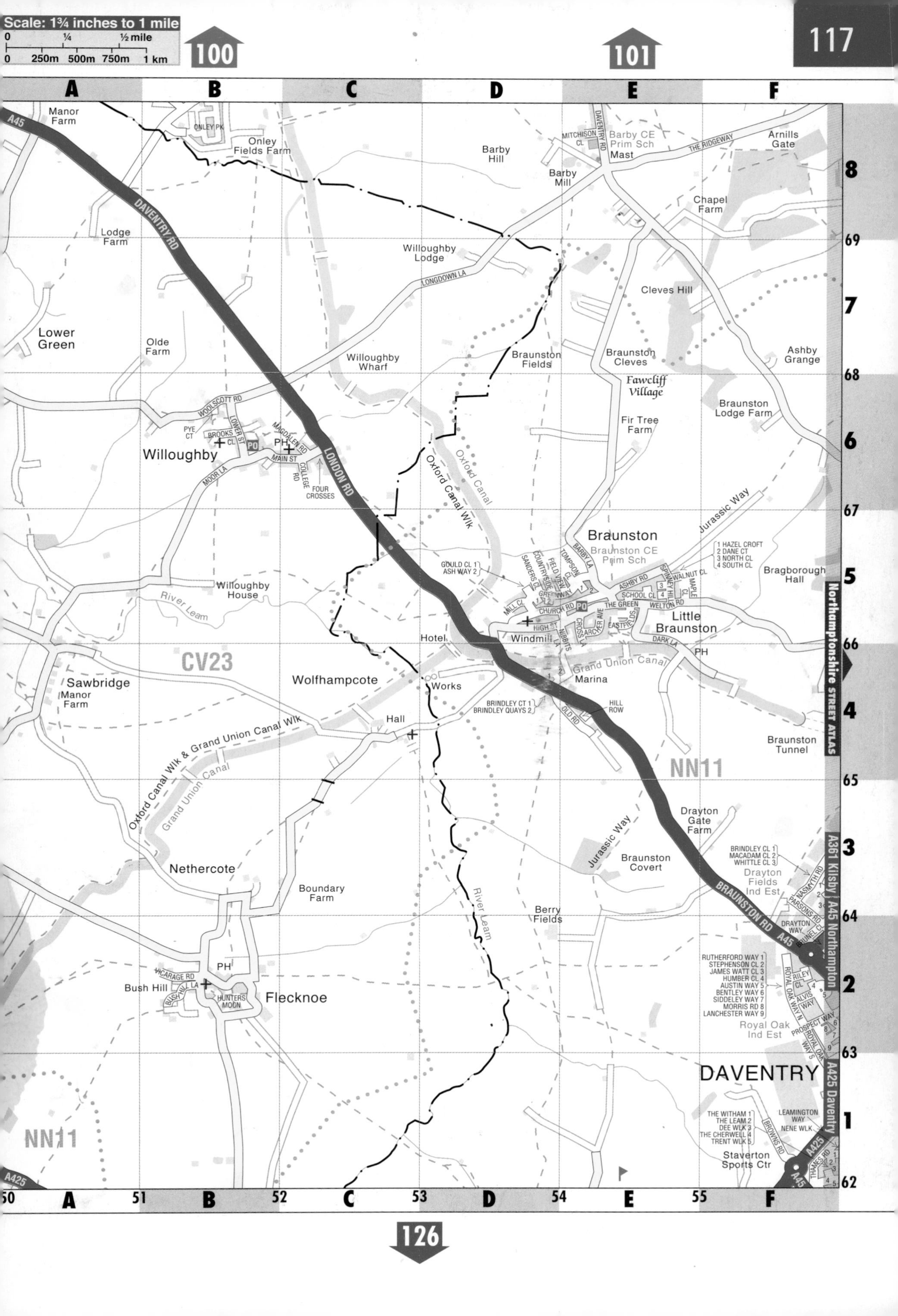
Scale: 1¾ inches to 1 mile
100
101
126
Manor Farm
Onley Fields Farm
ONLEY PK
Barby Hill
Barby Mill
MITCHISON CL
Barby CE Prim Sch
Mast
THE RIDGEWAY
Arnills Gate
Chapel Farm
DAVENTRY RD
Lodge Farm
Willoughby Lodge
LONGDOWN LA
Cleves Hill
Lower Green
Olde Farm
Willoughby Wharf
Braunston Fields
Braunston Cleves
Ashby Grange
Fawcliff Village
Braunston Lodge Farm
Fir Tree Farm
WOOLSCOTT RD
PYE CT
BROOKS CL
LOWER ST
MAGDALEN RD
PH
PO
Willoughby
MAIN ST
MOOR LA
COLLEGE RD
FOUR CROSSES
LONDON RD
Oxford Canal Wlk
Oxford Canal
Jurassic Way
Braunston
Braunston CE Prim Sch
1 HAZEL CROFT
2 DANE CT
3 NORTH CL
4 SOUTH CL
Bragborough Hall
GOULD CL 1
ASH WAY 2
Willoughby House
River Leam
ASHBY RD
SCHOOL CL
WALNUT CL
MAPLE CL
SPINNEY HILL
THE GREEN
WELTON RD
Little Braunston
CHURCH RD
HIGH ST
MILL CL
Windmill
NIBBITS LA
CROSS LA
ARCHER AVE
EASTFIELDS
DARK LA
Hotel
CV23
Sawbridge Manor Farm
Wolfhampcote
Works
Grand Union Canal
Marina
BRINDLEY CT 1
BRINDLEY QUAYS 2
OLD RD
HILL ROW
Hall
Oxford Canal Wlk & Grand Union Canal Wlk
Grand Union Canal
NN11
Braunston Tunnel
Drayton Gate Farm
Jurassic Way
Braunston Covert
Nethercote
BRINDLEY CL 1
MACADAM CL 2
WHITTLE CL 3
Drayton Fields Ind Est
NASMYTH RD
PARSONS RD
DRAYTON WAY
BRUNEL CL
BRAUNSTON RD
A45
Boundary Farm
Berry Fields
River Leam
RUTHERFORD WAY 1
STEPHENSON CL 2
JAMES WATT CL 3
HUMBER CL 4
AUSTIN WAY 5
BENTLEY WAY 6
SIDDELEY WAY 7
MORRIS RD 8
LANCHESTER WAY 9
ROYAL OAK WAY N
RILEY CL
ALVIS WAY
PROSPECT WAY
ROYAL OAK WAY S
Royal Oak Ind Est
PH
VICARAGE RD
Bush Hill
BUSH HILL LA
HUNTERS MOON
Flecknoe
DAVENTRY
THE WITHAM 1
THE LEAM 2
DEE WLK 3
THE CHERWELL 4
TRENT WLK 5
BROWNS RD
LEAMINGTON WAY
NENE WLK
Staverton Sports Ctr
THAMES RD
A425
NN11
Northamptonshire STREET ATLAS
A361 Kilsby | A45 Northampton
A425 Daventry
A B C D E F
8 69 7 68 6 67 5 66 4 65 3 64 2 63 1 62
50 51 52 53 54 55

102

103

Scale: 1¾ inches to 1 mile

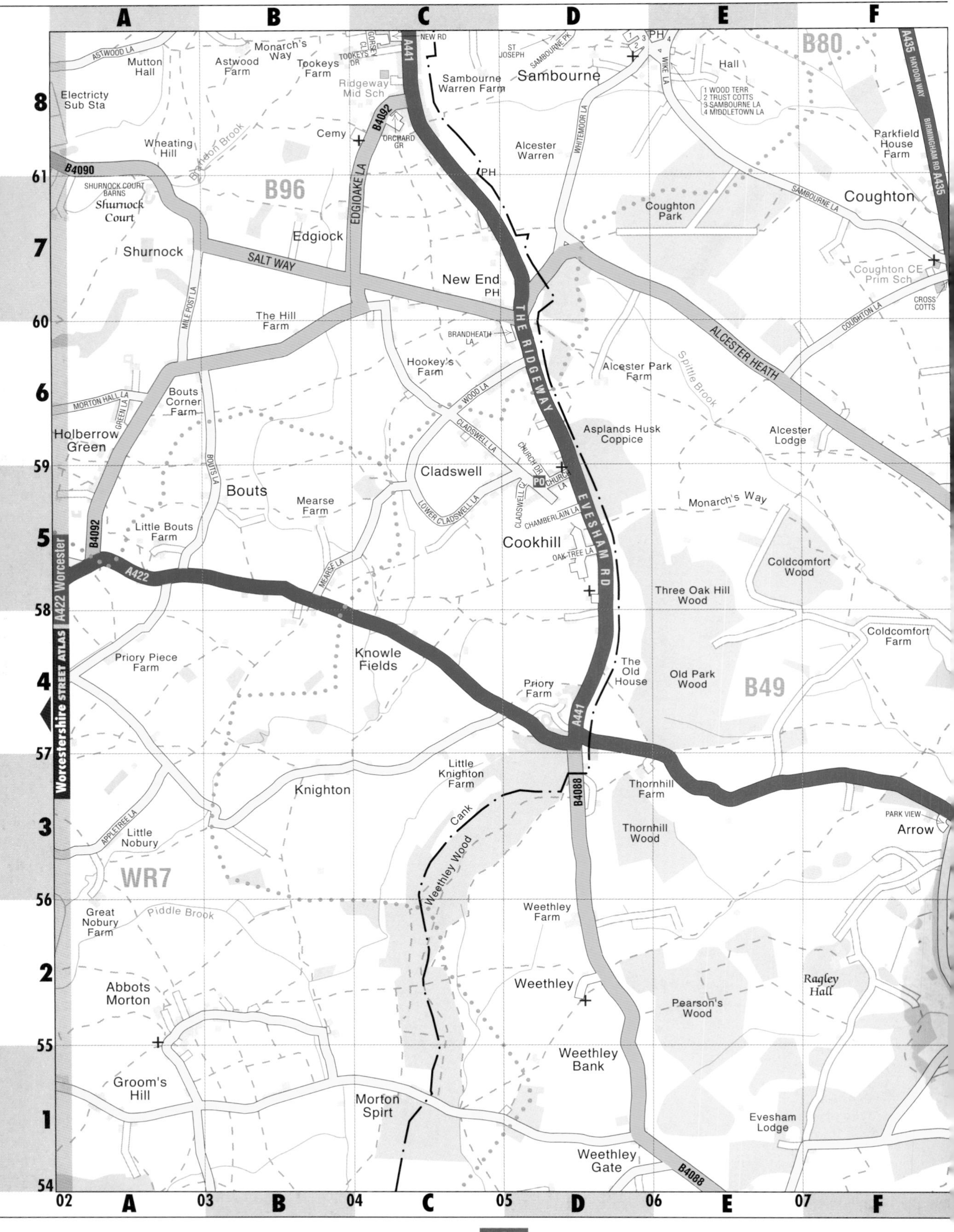

127

112
120

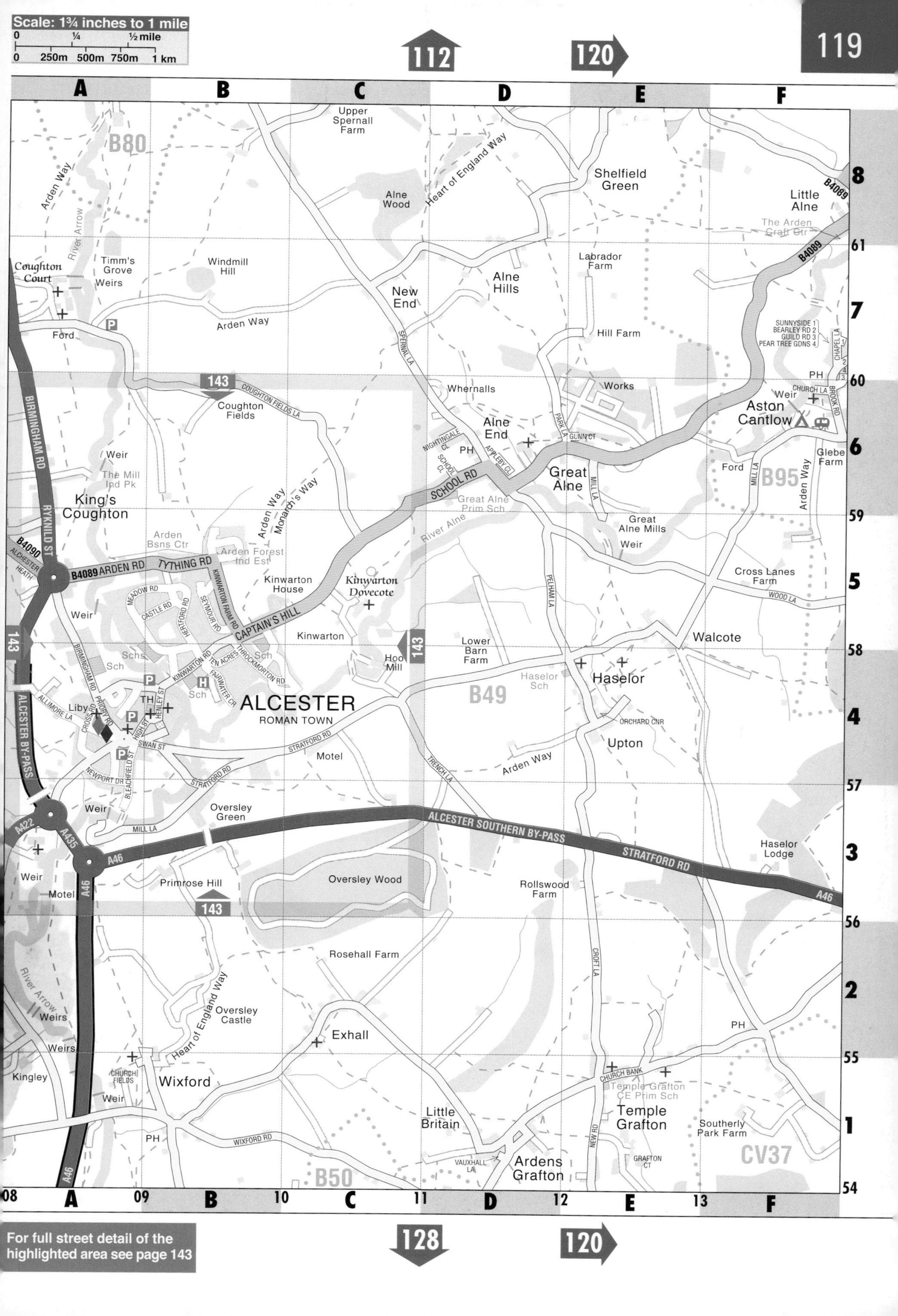

128
120
For full street detail of the highlighted area see page 143

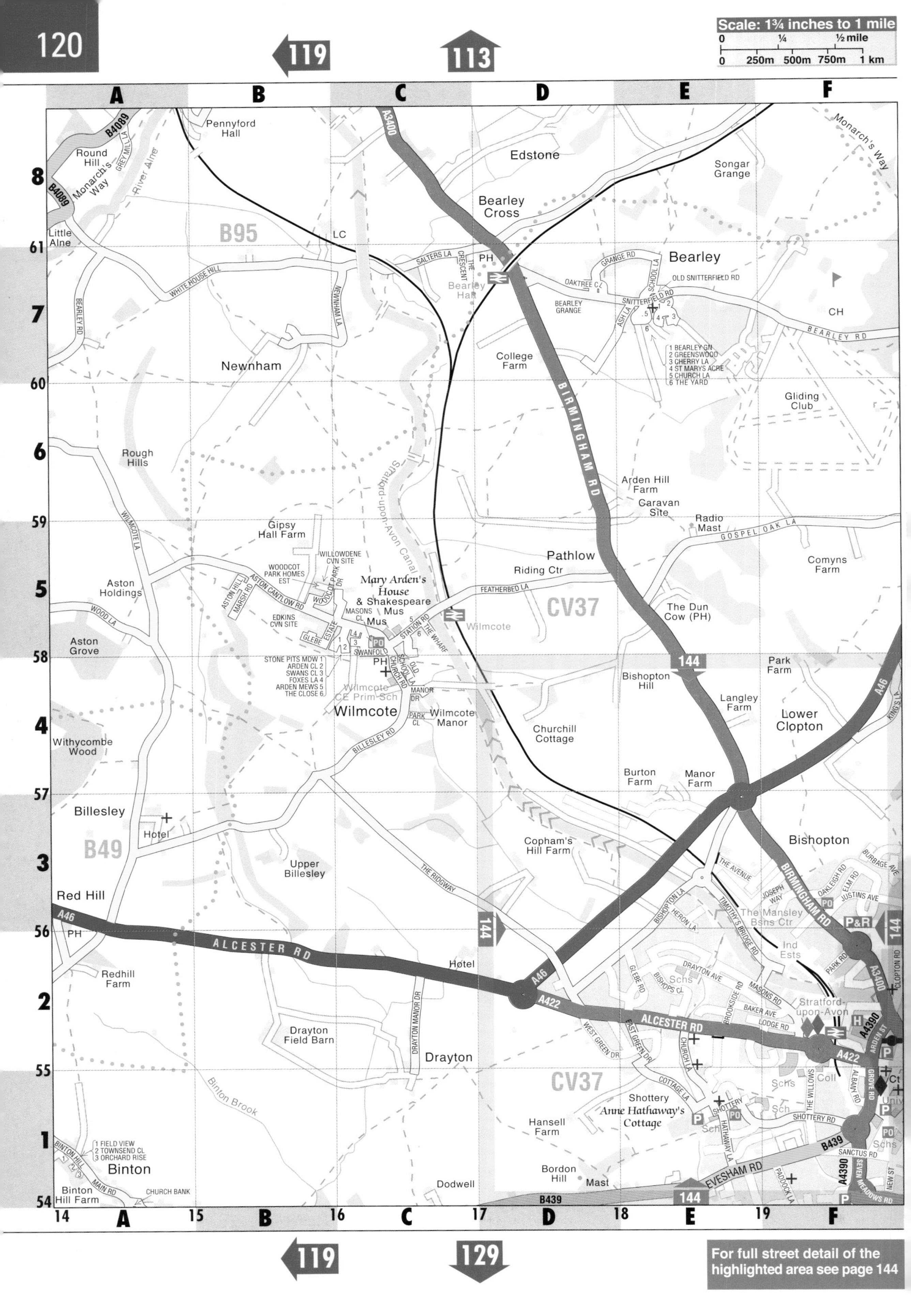

For full street detail of the highlighted area see page 144

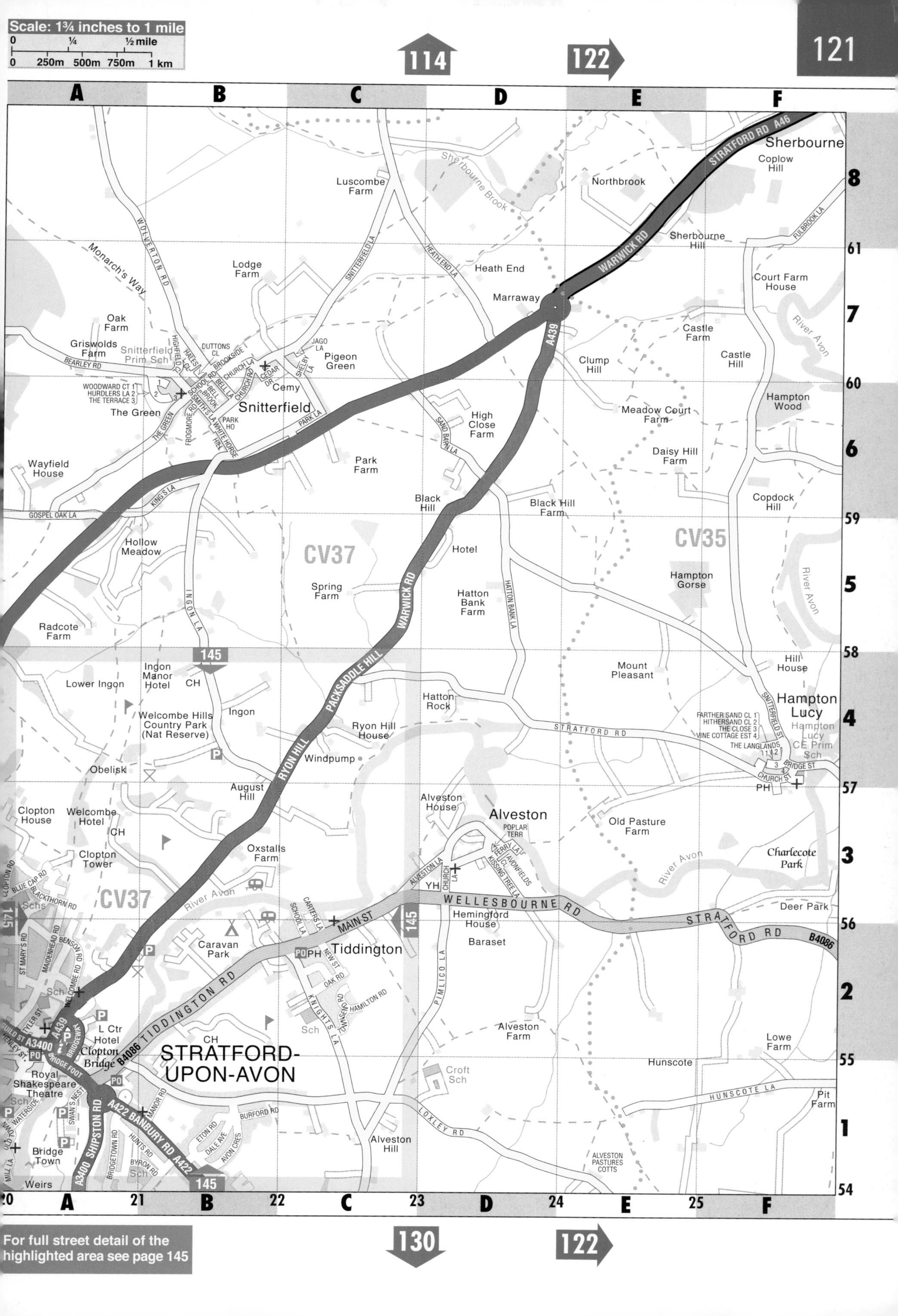
Scale: 1¾ inches to 1 mile
0 ¼ ½ mile
0 250m 500m 750m 1 km
114
122
Sherbourne
Coplow Hill
Northbrook
Luscombe Farm
Sherbourne Brook
Sherbourne Hill
Monarch's Way
Lodge Farm
Heath End
Marraway
Court Farm House
Oak Farm
Griswolds Farm
Snitterfield Prim Sch
Pigeon Green
Castle Farm
Clump Hill
Castle Hill
Cemy
Snitterfield
The Green
Hampton Wood
Meadow Court Farm
High Close Farm
Park Farm
Daisy Hill Farm
Wayfield House
Black Hill
Black Hill Farm
Copdock Hill
Hollow Meadow
CV37
CV35
Hotel
Spring Farm
Hatton Bank Farm
Hampton Gorse
River Avon
Radcote Farm
Mount Pleasant
Hill House
Ingon Manor Hotel
Lower Ingon
Hatton Rock
Hampton Lucy
Welcombe Hills Country Park (Nat Reserve)
Ingon
Ryon Hill House
Windpump
Hampton Lucy CE Prim Sch
Obelisk
August Hill
Alveston House
Alveston
Clopton House
Welcombe Hotel
Old Pasture Farm
Clopton Tower
Oxstalls Farm
Charlecote Park
Deer Park
Hemingford House
Baraset
Caravan Park
Tiddington
L Ctr
Hotel
Clopton Bridge
Alveston Farm
Lowe Farm
Royal Shakespeare Theatre
STRATFORD-UPON-AVON
Hunscote
Croft Sch
Pit Farm
Bridge Town
Alveston Hill
ALVESTON PASTURES COTTS
Weirs
145
For full street detail of the highlighted area see page 145
130
122

121 108 109

Scale: 1¾ inches to 1 mile

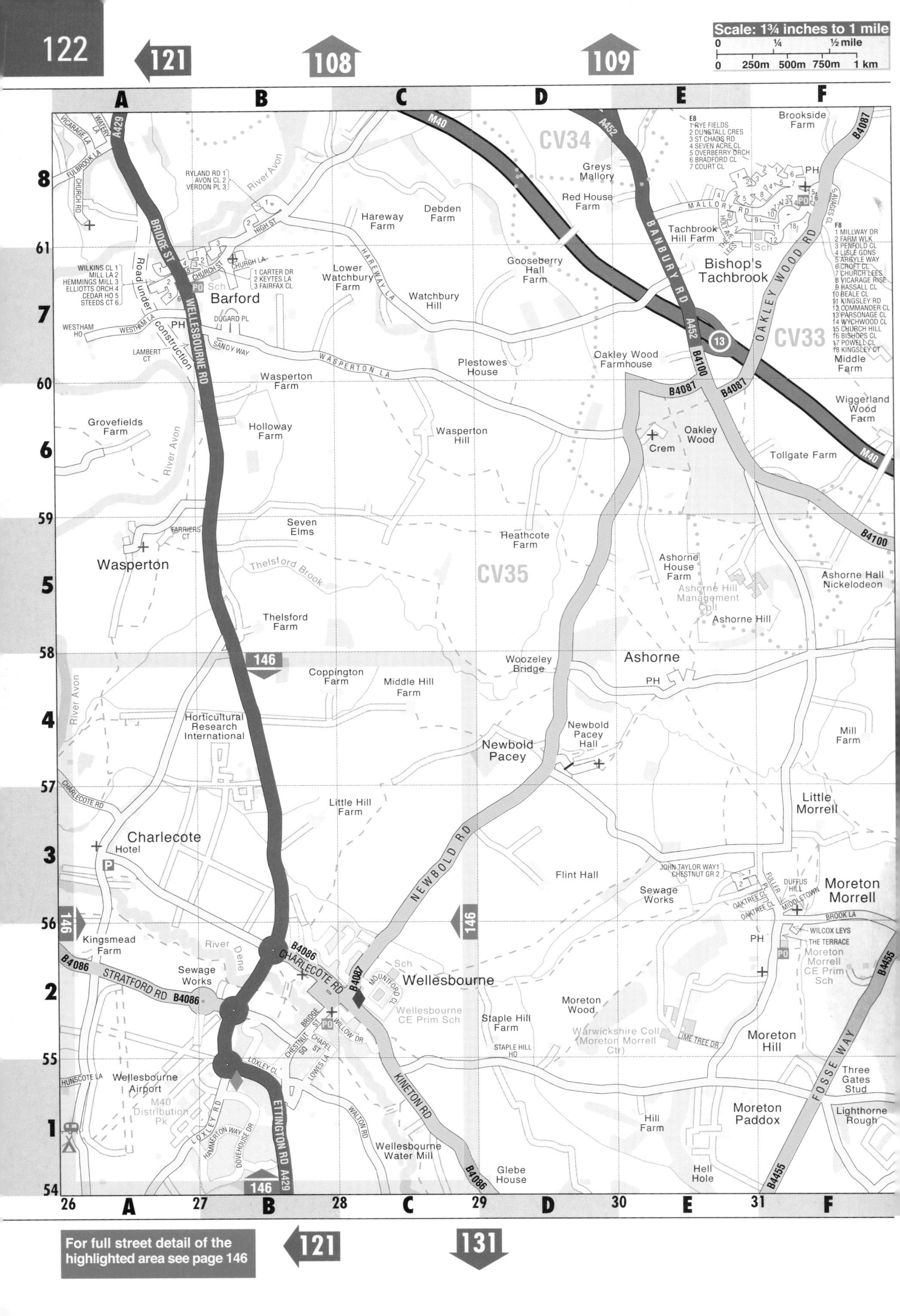

For full street detail of the highlighted area see page 146

121 131

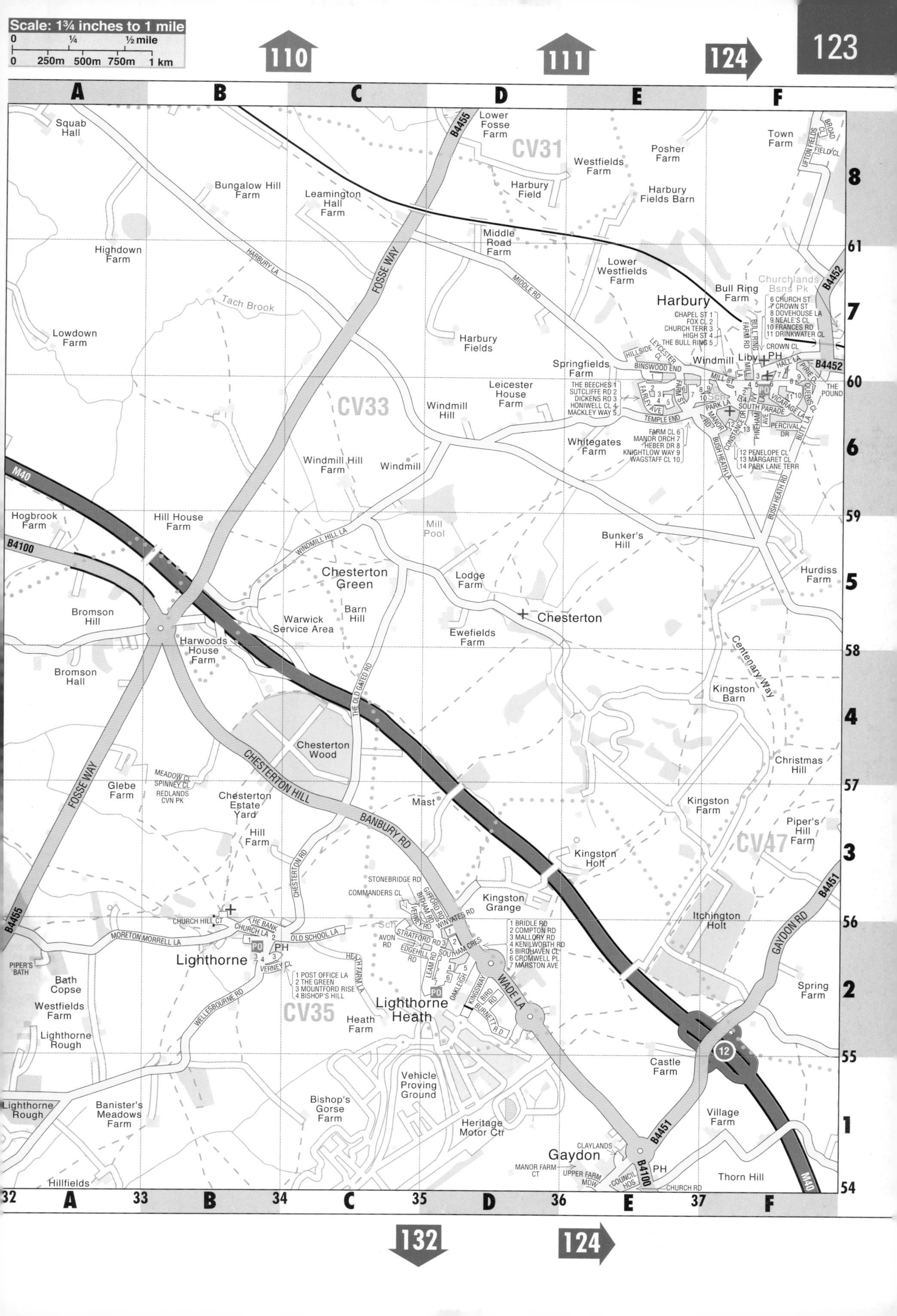
Scale: 1¾ inches to 1 mile
110
111
124
Squab Hall
Lower Fosse Farm
CV31
Westfields Farm
Posher Farm
Town Farm
Bungalow Hill Farm
Leamington Hall Farm
Harbury Field
Harbury Fields Barn
Highdown Farm
Middle Road Farm
Lower Westfields Farm
Churchlands Bsns Pk
Bull Ring Farm
Harbury
Tach Brook
Lowdown Farm
Harbury Fields
Springfields Farm
Windmill
Leicester House Farm
CV33
Windmill Hill
Whitegates Farm
Windmill Hill Farm
Windmill
Hogbrook Farm
Hill House Farm
Mill Pool
Bunker's Hill
Chesterton Green
Lodge Farm
Hurdiss Farm
Bromson Hill
Warwick Service Area
Barn Hill
Chesterton
Harwoods House Farm
Ewefields Farm
Bromson Hall
Centenary Way
Kingston Barn
Chesterton Wood
Christmas Hill
Glebe Farm
Chesterton Estate Yard
Mast
Kingston Farm
Piper's Hill Farm
CV47
Hill Farm
Kingston Holt
Kingston Grange
Itchington Holt
Lighthorne
Bath Copse
Westfields Farm
Lighthorne Rough
CV35
Heath Farm
Lighthorne Heath
Spring Farm
Castle Farm
Lighthorne Rough
Banister's Meadows Farm
Bishop's Gorse Farm
Vehicle Proving Ground
Heritage Motor Ctr
Village Farm
Gaydon
Thorn Hill
Hillfields
132
124

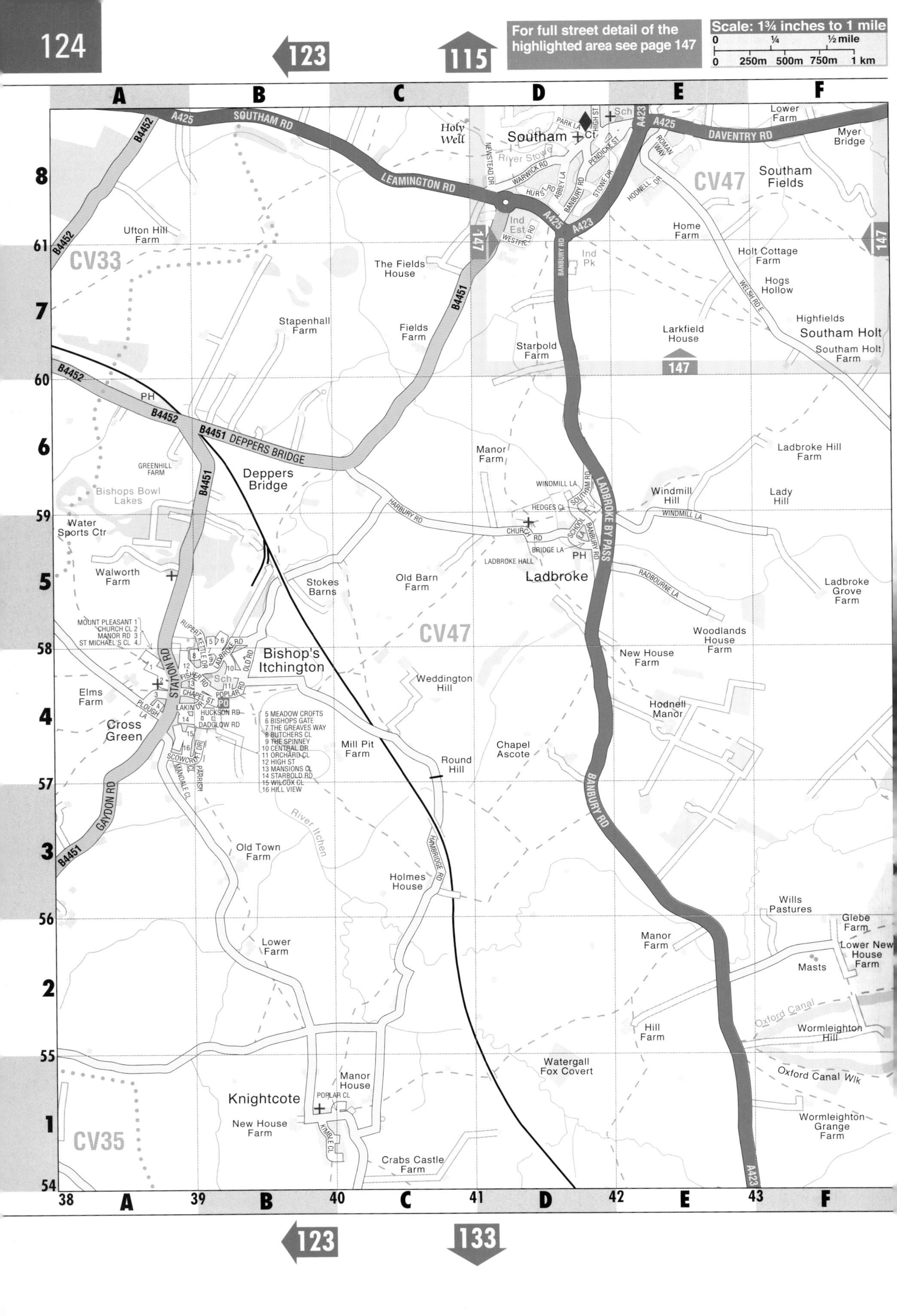
124
123
115
For full street detail of the highlighted area see page 147
Scale: 1¾ inches to 1 mile
0 ¼ ½ mile
0 250m 500m 750m 1 km
A B C D E F
8 7 6 5 4 3 2 1
61 60 59 58 57 56 55 54
38 39 40 41 42 43
A425 SOUTHAM RD
B4452
Holy Well
Southam
PARK LA
HIGH ST
Sch
Ct
A423
A425
DAVENTRY RD
Lower Farm
Myer Bridge
River Stowe
NEWSTEAD DR
WARWICK RD
PENDICKE ST
ROMAN WAY
LEAMINGTON RD
HURST RD
ABBEY LA
BANBURY RD
STONE DR
HODNELL DR
CV47
Southam Fields
Ind Est
WESTFIELD RD
147
Ufton Hill Farm
CV33
Home Farm
Holt Cottage Farm
Ind Pk
The Fields House
Hogs Hollow
B4451
WELSH RD E
Stapenhall Farm
Fields Farm
Highfields
Southam Holt
Larkfield House
Starbold Farm
Southam Holt Farm
PH
B4451 DEPPERS BRIDGE
Manor Farm
Ladbroke Hill Farm
GREENHILL FARM
Deppers Bridge
Bishops Bowl Lakes
WINDMILL LA
SOUTHAM RD
LADBROKE BY PASS
Windmill Hill
Lady Hill
HARBURY RD
HEDGES CL
WINDMILL LA
Water Sports Ctr
CHURCH RD
SCHOOL LA
BRIDGE LA
LADBROKE HALL
Walworth Farm
Stokes Barns
Old Barn Farm
Ladbroke
RADBOURNE LA
Ladbroke Grove Farm
MOUNT PLEASANT 1
CHURCH CL 2
MANOR RD 3
ST MICHAEL'S CL 4
RUPERT KETTLE DR
LADBROKE RD
OLD RD
Bishop's Itchington
Woodlands House Farm
New House Farm
Weddington Hill
STATION RD
FISHER RD
CHAPEL ST
POPLAR RD
PO
Elms Farm
PLOUGH LA
LAKIN
HUCKSON RD
DADGLOW RD
Hodnell Manor
Cross Green
5 MEADOW CROFTS
6 BISHOPS GATE
7 THE GREAVES WAY
8 BUTCHERS CL
9 THE SPINNEY
10 CENTRAL DR
11 ORCHARD CL
12 HIGH ST
13 MANSIONS CL
14 STARBOLD RD
15 WILCOX CL
16 HILL VIEW
Mill Pit Farm
Chapel Ascote
Round Hill
SCOWCROFT DR
MANDALE CL
PARRISH
GAYDON RD
River Itchen
HAMBRIDGE RD
BANBURY RD
Old Town Farm
Holmes House
Wills Pastures
Glebe Farm
Manor Farm
Lower Farm
Lower New House Farm
Masts
Oxford Canal
Hill Farm
Wormleighton Hill
Watergall Fox Covert
Oxford Canal Wlk
Manor House
Knightcote
POPLAR CL
New House Farm
KIMBLE CL
Wormleighton Grange Farm
CV35
Crabs Castle Farm
133

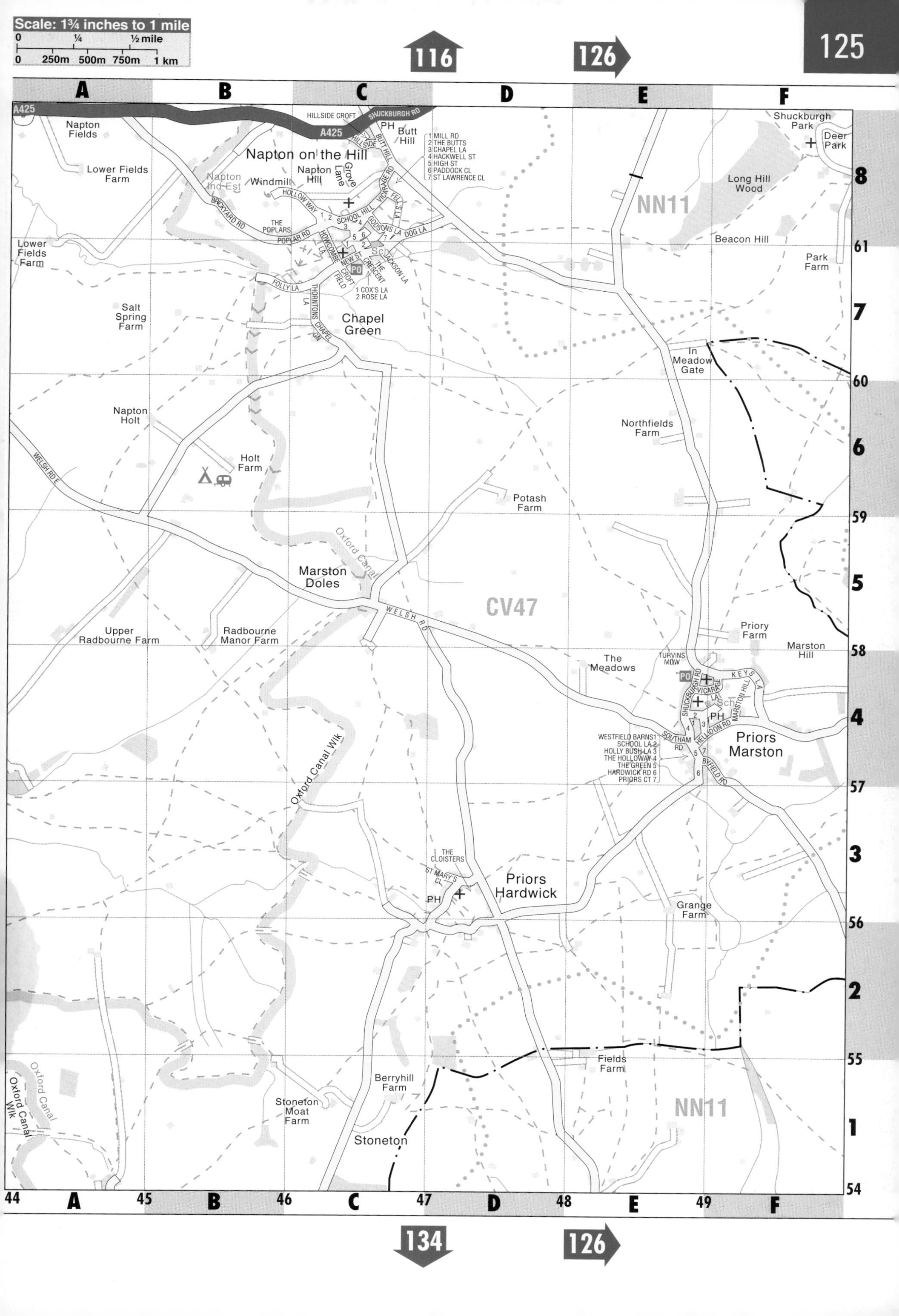
Scale: 1¾ inches to 1 mile
0 ¼ ½ mile
0 250m 500m 750m 1 km
116
126
A B C D E F
A425
Napton Fields
Lower Fields Farm
Napton Ind Est
Windmill
Napton on the Hill
Napton Hill
Grove Lane
HILLSIDE CROFT
SHUCKBURGH RD
PH
Butt Hill
1 MILL RD
2 THE BUTTS
3 CHAPEL LA
4 HACKWELL ST
5 HIGH ST
6 PADDOCK CL
7 ST LAWRENCE CL
BRICKYARD RD
HOLLOW WAY
SCHOOL HILL
VICARAGE RD
FELLS LA
DOG LA
THE POPLARS
POPLAR RD
HOWCOMBE LA
NEW ST
CROFT FIELD
THE CRESCENT
JACKSON LA
FOLLY LA
1 COX'S LA
2 ROSE LA
THORNTONS LA
CHAPEL GN
Chapel Green
Lower Fields Farm
Salt Spring Farm
NN11
Shuckburgh Park
Deer Park
Long Hill Wood
Beacon Hill
Park Farm
In Meadow Gate
Northfields Farm
Napton Holt
Holt Farm
Potash Farm
WELSH RD E
Oxford Canal
Marston Doles
CV47
WELSH RD
Upper Radbourne Farm
Radbourne Manor Farm
Priory Farm
Marston Hill
The Meadows
TURVINS MDW
KEYS LA
VICARAGE
MARSTON HILL
SHUCKBURGH RD
SOUTHAM RD
HELLIDON RD
BYFIELD RD
Priors Marston
WESTFIELD BARNS 1
SCHOOL LA 2
HOLLY BUSH LA 3
THE HOLLOWAY 4
THE GREEN 5
HARDWICK RD 6
PRIORS CT 7
Oxford Canal Wlk
THE CLOISTERS
ST MARY'S CL
PH
Priors Hardwick
Grange Farm
Fields Farm
Berryhill Farm
Stoneton Moat Farm
Stoneton
NN11
Oxford Canal
Oxford Canal Wlk
8 61 7 60 6 59 5 58 4 57 3 56 2 55 1 54
44 45 46 47 48 49
134
126

125
117

Scale: 1¾ inches to 1 mile

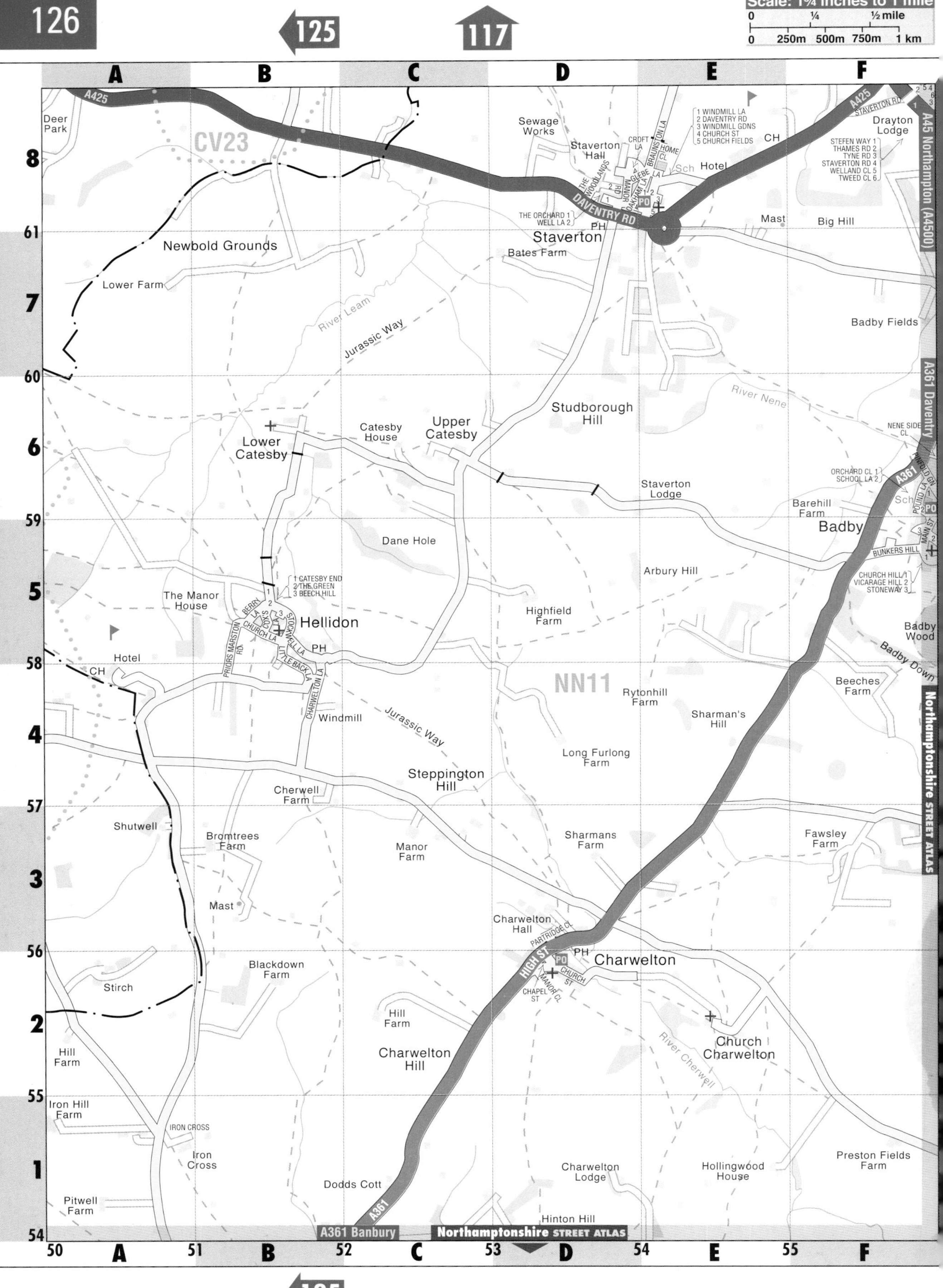

125

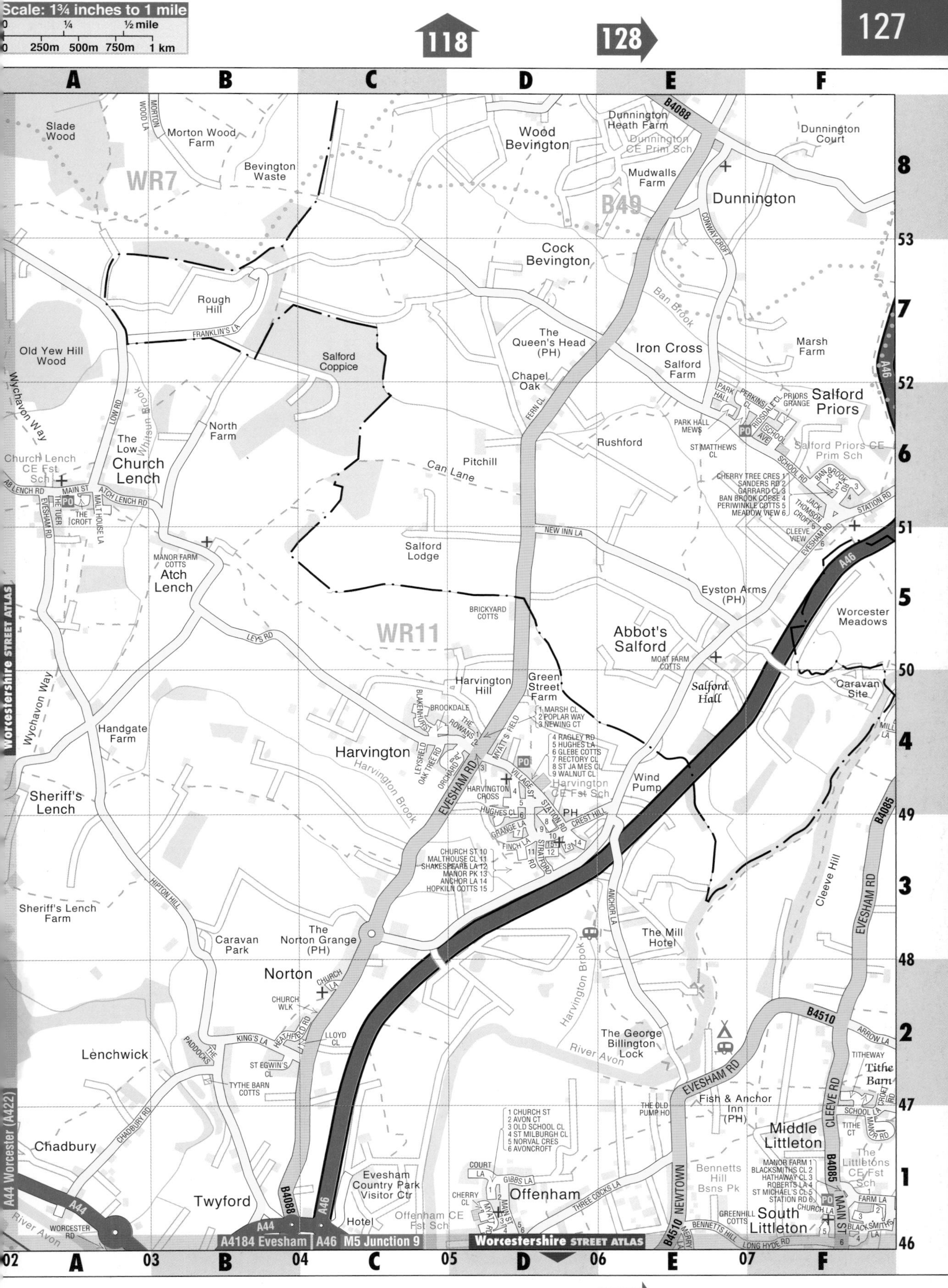

Scale: 1¾ inches to 1 mile
0 ¼ ½ mile
0 250m 500m 750m 1 km
118
128
A B C D E F
Slade Wood
MORTON WOOD LA
Morton Wood Farm
Bevington Waste
WR7
Wood Bevington
Dunnington Heath Farm
Dunnington CE Prim Sch
B4088
Dunnington Court
Mudwalls Farm
B49
Dunnington
8
53
Cock Bevington
CONWAY CROFT
Ban Brook
Rough Hill
FRANKLIN'S LA
7
Old Yew Hill Wood
Salford Coppice
The Queen's Head (PH)
Iron Cross
Salford Farm
Marsh Farm
A46
Chapel Oak
52
Wychavon Way
FERN CL
PARK HALL
PERKINS CL
RIDSDALE CL
PRIORS GRANGE
Salford Priors
SCHOOL AVE
PARK HALL MEWS
North Farm
LOW RD
Whitsun Brook
The Low
Church Lench
Rushford
ST MATTHEWS CL
Salford Priors CE Prim Sch
Church Lench CE Fst Sch
Pitchill
Can Lane
6
SCHOOL RD
BAN BROOK RD
AB LENCH RD
MAIN ST
THE TUER
EVESHAM RD
THE CROFT
MALT HOUSE LA
ATCH LENCH RD
CHERRY TREE CRES 1
SANDERS RD 2
GARRARD CL 3
BAN BROOK COPSE 4
PERIWINKLE COTTS 5
MEADOW VIEW 6
JACK THOMSON CROFT
STATION RD
51
NEW INN LA
CLEEVE VIEW
EVESHAM RD
MANOR FARM COTTS
Atch Lench
Salford Lodge
Eyston Arms (PH)
5
Worcestershire STREET ATLAS
BRICKYARD COTTS
Worcester Meadows
WR11
LEYS RD
Abbot's Salford
MOAT FARM COTTS
50
Wychavon Way
Harvington Hill
Green Street Farm
Salford Hall
Caravan Site
BROOKDALE
BLAKENHURST
THE ROWANS
MYATT'S FIELD
1 MARSH CL
2 POPLAR WAY
3 NEWING CT
MILL LA
Handgate Farm
4
4 RAGLEY RD
5 HUGHES LA
6 GLEBE COTTS
7 RECTORY CL
8 ST JAMES CL
9 WALNUT CL
Harvington
LEYSFIELD
OAK TREE RD
ORCHARD
Harvington Brook
VILLAGE ST
Harvington CE Fst Sch
Wind Pump
Sheriff's Lench
HARVINGTON CROSS
EVESHAM RD
HUGHES CL
STATION RD
GRANGE LA
FINCH LA
STRATFORD RD
CREST HILL
PH
49
B4085
CHURCH ST 10
MALTHOUSE CL 11
SHAKESPEARE LA 12
MANOR PK 13
ANCHOR LA 14
HOPKILN COTTS 15
Cleeve Hill
HIPTON HILL
3
ANCHOR LA
Sheriff's Lench Farm
The Mill Hotel
Caravan Park
The Norton Grange (PH)
48
Harvington Brook
Norton
CHURCH LA
CHURCH WLK
EVESHAM RD
B4510
2
HEATHFIELD RD
LLOYD CL
KING'S LA
THE PADDOCKS
The George Billington Lock
ARROW LA
Lenchwick
River Avon
TITHEWAY
ST EGWIN'S CL
Tithe Barn
TYTHE BARN COTTS
EVESHAM RD
THE OLD PUMP HO
Fish & Anchor Inn (PH)
CLEEVE RD
CROFT RD
47
1 CHURCH ST
2 AVON CT
3 OLD SCHOOL CL
4 ST MILBURGH CL
5 NORVAL CRES
6 AVONCROFT
SCHOOL LA
MANOR RD
TITHE CT
Middle Littleton
CHADBURY RD
Chadbury
The Littletons CE Fst Sch
A44 Worcester (A422)
COURT LA
GIBBS LA
Evesham Country Park Visitor Ctr
Bennetts Hill Bsns Pk
MANOR FARM 1
BLACKSMITHS CL 2
HATHAWAY CL 3
ROBERTS LA 4
ST MICHAEL'S CL 5
STATION RD 6
B4085
MAIN ST
1
Twyford
CHERRY CL
MYATT RD
MAIN ST
Offenham
THREE COCKS LA
NEWTOWN
GREENHILL COTTS
South Littleton
CHURCH LA
FARM LA
BLACKSMITHS LA
A44
B4088
A46
Hotel
Offenham CE Fst Sch
B4510
BENNETTS HILL
LONG HYDE RD
River Avon
WORCESTER RD
A44
A4184 Evesham
A46
M5 Junction 9
Worcestershire STREET ATLAS
46
02 03 04 05 06 07

128

For full street detail of the highlighted area see page 148.

127

119

Scale: 1¾ inches to 1 mile

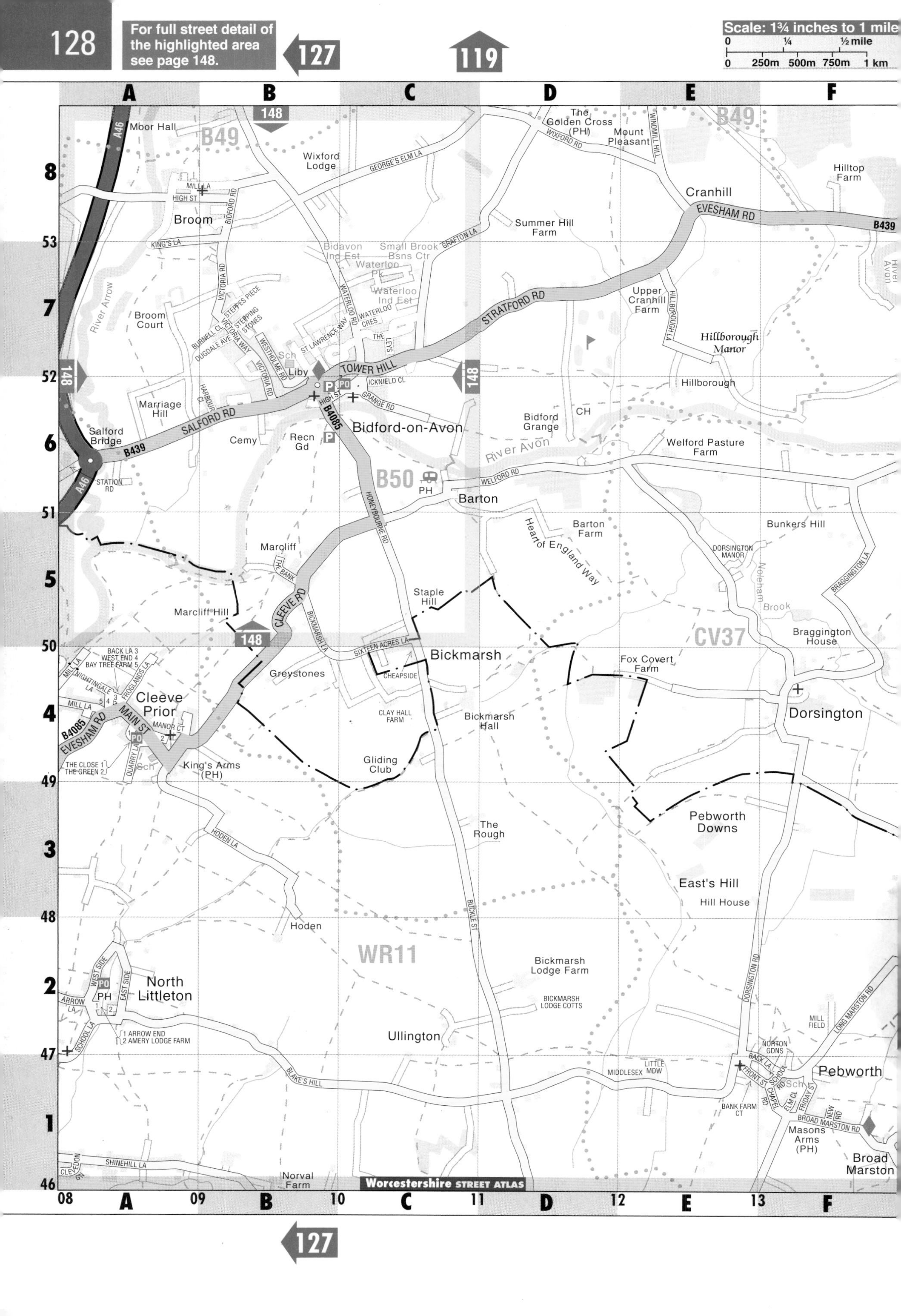

127

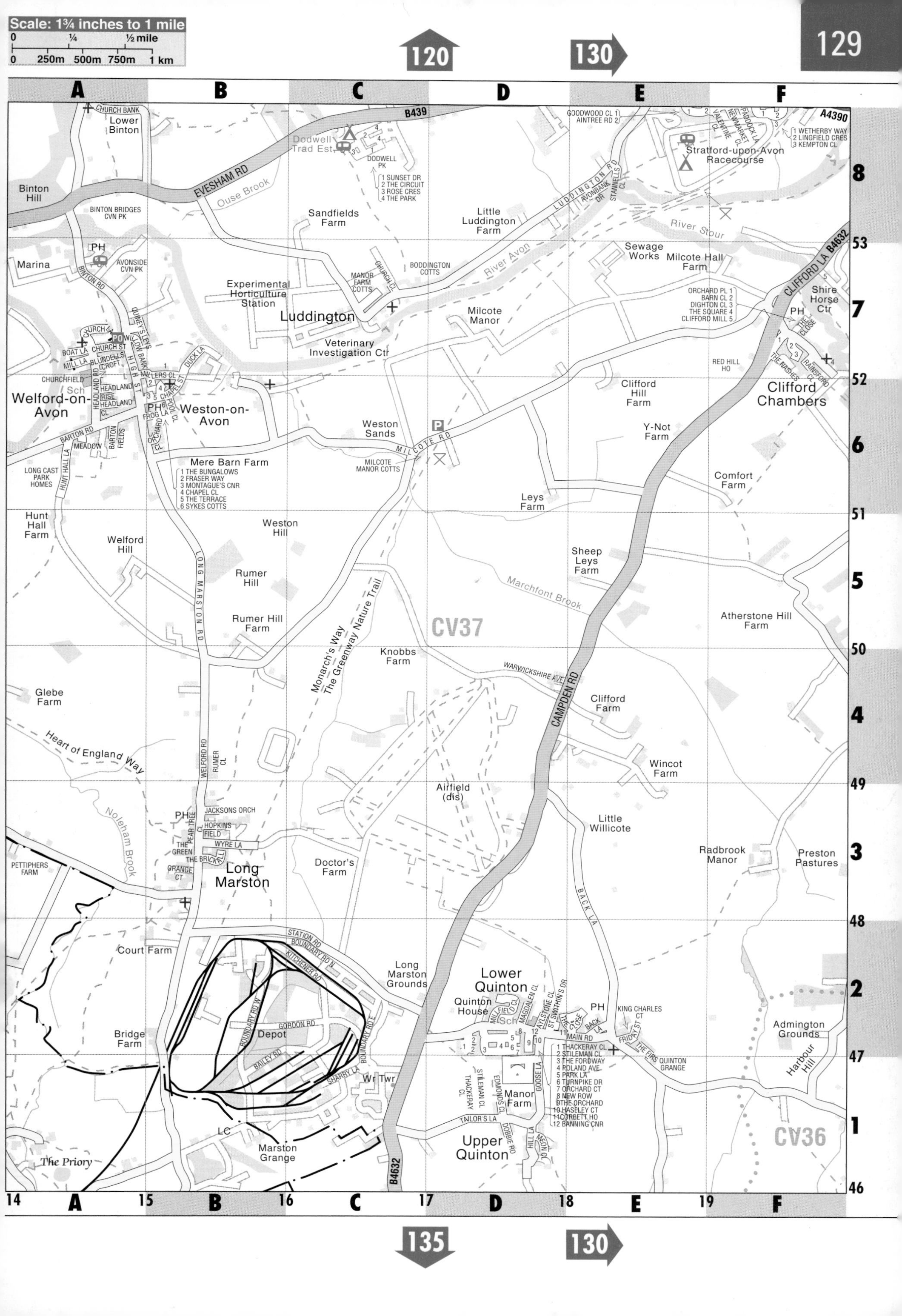

Scale: 1¾ inches to 1 mile
120
130
135
Welford-on-Avon
Weston-on-Avon
Luddington
Long Marston
Lower Quinton
Upper Quinton
Clifford Chambers
Stratford-upon-Avon Racecourse
CV37
CV36
Airfield (dis)
Depot
Heart of England Way
Monarch's Way
The Greenway Nature Trail
River Avon
Marchfont Brook
Noleham Brook
Ouse Brook
River Stour
EVESHAM RD
CAMPDEN RD
LUDDINGTON RD
MILCOTE RD
LONG MARSTON RD
WARWICKSHIRE AVE
BACK LA
CLIFFORD LA B4632
B439
A4390
B4632

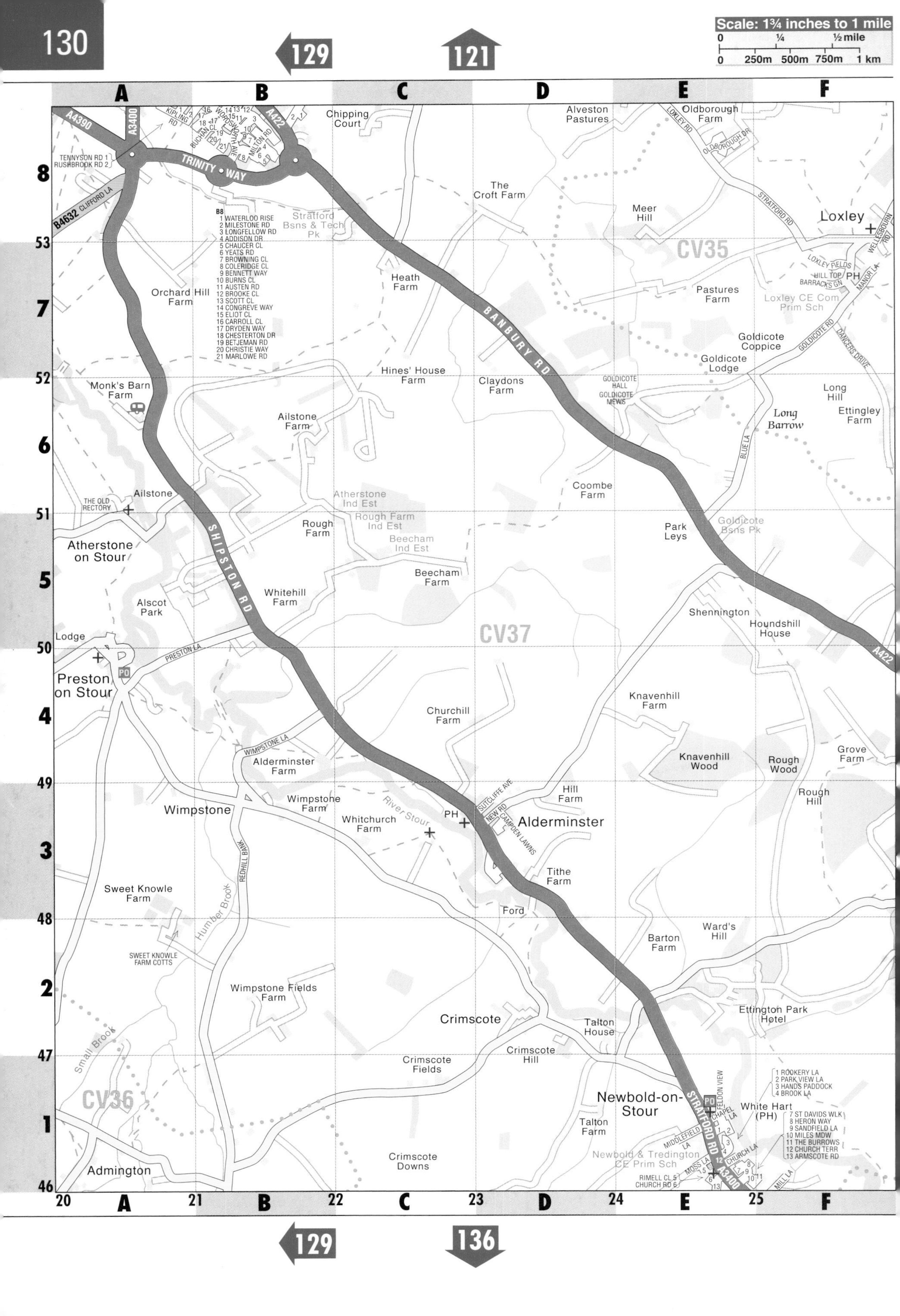
129
121
Scale: 1¾ inches to 1 mile
Chipping Court
Alveston Pastures
Oldborough Farm
The Croft Farm
Meer Hill
Loxley
Stratford Bsns & Tech Pk
B8
1 WATERLOO RISE
2 MILESTONE RD
3 LONGFELLOW RD
4 ADDISON DR
5 CHAUCER CL
6 YEATS RD
7 BROWNING CL
8 COLERIDGE CL
9 BENNETT WAY
10 BURNS CL
11 AUSTEN RD
12 BROOKE CL
13 SCOTT CL
14 CONGREVE WAY
15 ELIOT CL
16 CARROLL CL
17 DRYDEN WAY
18 CHESTERTON DR
19 BETJEMAN RD
20 CHRISTIE WAY
21 MARLOWE RD
TENNYSON RD 1
RUSHBROOK RD 2
TRINITY WAY
CV35
Heath Farm
Orchard Hill Farm
Pastures Farm
Loxley CE Com Prim Sch
BANBURY RD
Goldicote Coppice
Goldicote Lodge
Hines' House Farm
Claydons Farm
Monk's Barn Farm
Long Hill
Ettingley Farm
Long Barrow
Ailstone Farm
Coombe Farm
Ailstone
THE OLD RECTORY
Atherstone Ind Est
Rough Farm Ind Est
Beecham Ind Est
Rough Farm
Park Leys
Goldicote Bsns Pk
Atherstone on Stour
SHIPSTON RD
Beecham Farm
Alscot Park
Whitehill Farm
Shennington
Houndshill House
Lodge
CV37
Preston on Stour
PRESTON LA
Churchill Farm
Knavenhill Farm
Alderminster Farm
Knavenhill Wood
Rough Wood
Grove Farm
Wimpstone
Wimpstone Farm
Whitchurch Farm
River Stour
PH
Alderminster
Hill Farm
Rough Hill
Tithe Farm
Sweet Knowle Farm
Ford
Barton Farm
Ward's Hill
SWEET KNOWLE FARM COTTS
Humber Brook
REDHILL BANK
Wimpstone Fields Farm
Crimscote
Talton House
Ettington Park Hotel
Crimscote Fields
Crimscote Hill
Small Brook
CV36
Newbold-on-Stour
White Hart (PH)
1 ROOKERY LA
2 PARK VIEW LA
3 HANDS PADDOCK
4 BROOK LA
7 ST DAVIDS WLK
8 HERON WAY
9 SANDFIELD LA
10 MILES MDW
11 THE BURROWS
12 CHURCH TERR
13 ARMSCOTE RD
Talton Farm
Newbold & Tredington CE Prim Sch
RIMELL CL 5
CHURCH RD 6
Crimscote Downs
Admington
STRATFORD RD
A3400
A4390
A422
B4632
136

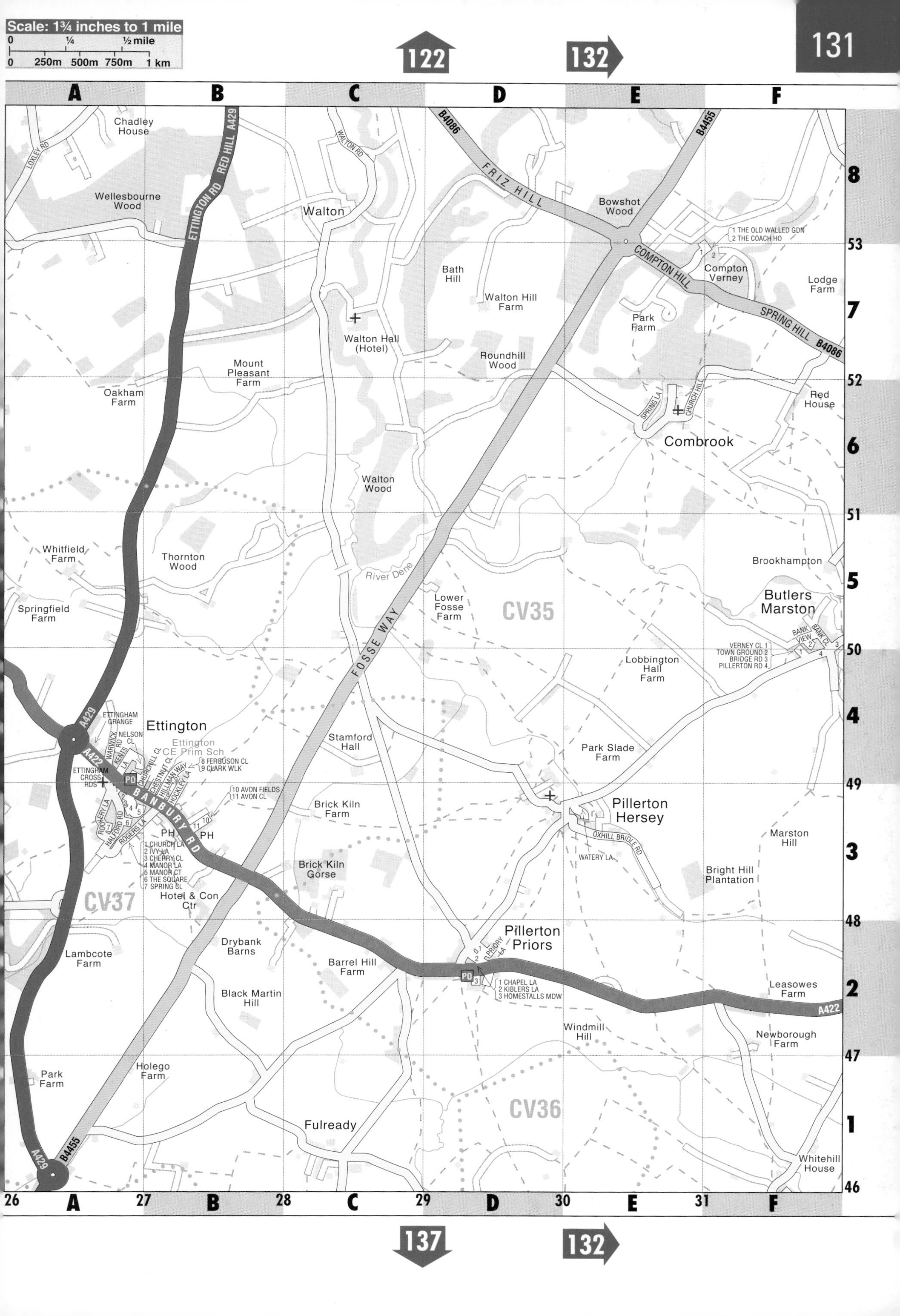
Scale: 1¾ inches to 1 mile
0 ¼ ½ mile
0 250m 500m 750m 1 km
122
132
A B C D E F
8 53 7 52 6 51 5 50 4 49 3 48 2 47 1 46
26 27 28 29 30 31
Chadley House
LOXLEY RD
RED HILL A429
ETTINGTON RD
Wellesbourne Wood
WALTON RD
Walton
B4086
FRIZ HILL
B4455
Bowshot Wood
1 THE OLD WALLED GDN
2 THE COACH HO
COMPTON HILL
Compton Verney
Lodge Farm
Bath Hill
Walton Hill Farm
Park Farm
SPRING HILL
Walton Hall (Hotel)
Roundhill Wood
Mount Pleasant Farm
Oakham Farm
SPRING LA
CHURCH HILL
Red House
Combrook
Walton Wood
Whitfield Farm
Thornton Wood
River Dene
Brookhampton
Springfield Farm
Lower Fosse Farm
CV35
Butlers Marston
FOSSE WAY
BANK VIEW
BANK CL
VERNEY CL 1
TOWN GROUND 2
BRIDGE RD 3
PILLERTON RD 4
Lobbington Hall Farm
A429
ETTINGHAM GRANGE
Ettington
Ettington CE Prim Sch
Stamford Hall
Park Slade Farm
A422
WARWICK RD
KENTS LA
NELSON CL
CHURCHILL CL
CHESTNUT CL
HILLMAN WAY
HOCKLEY LA
8 FERGUSON CL
9 CLARK WLK
ETTINGHAM CROSS RDS
PO
BANBURY RD
10 AVON FIELDS
11 AVON CL
Brick Kiln Farm
Pillerton Hersey
ROOKERY LA
HALFORD RD
ROGERS LA
PH
OXHILL BRIDLE RD
WATERY LA
Marston Hill
1 CHURCH LA
2 IVY LA
3 CHERRY CL
4 MANOR LA
5 MANOR CT
6 THE SQUARE
7 SPRING CL
Brick Kiln Gorse
Bright Hill Plantation
CV37
Hotel & Con Ctr
Pillerton Priors
PRIORY LA
Lambcote Farm
Drybank Barns
Barrel Hill Farm
1 CHAPEL LA
2 KIBLERS LA
3 HOMESTALLS MDW
Leasowes Farm
A422
Black Martin Hill
Windmill Hill
Newborough Farm
Park Farm
Holego Farm
CV36
Fulready
Whitehill House
B4455
137
132

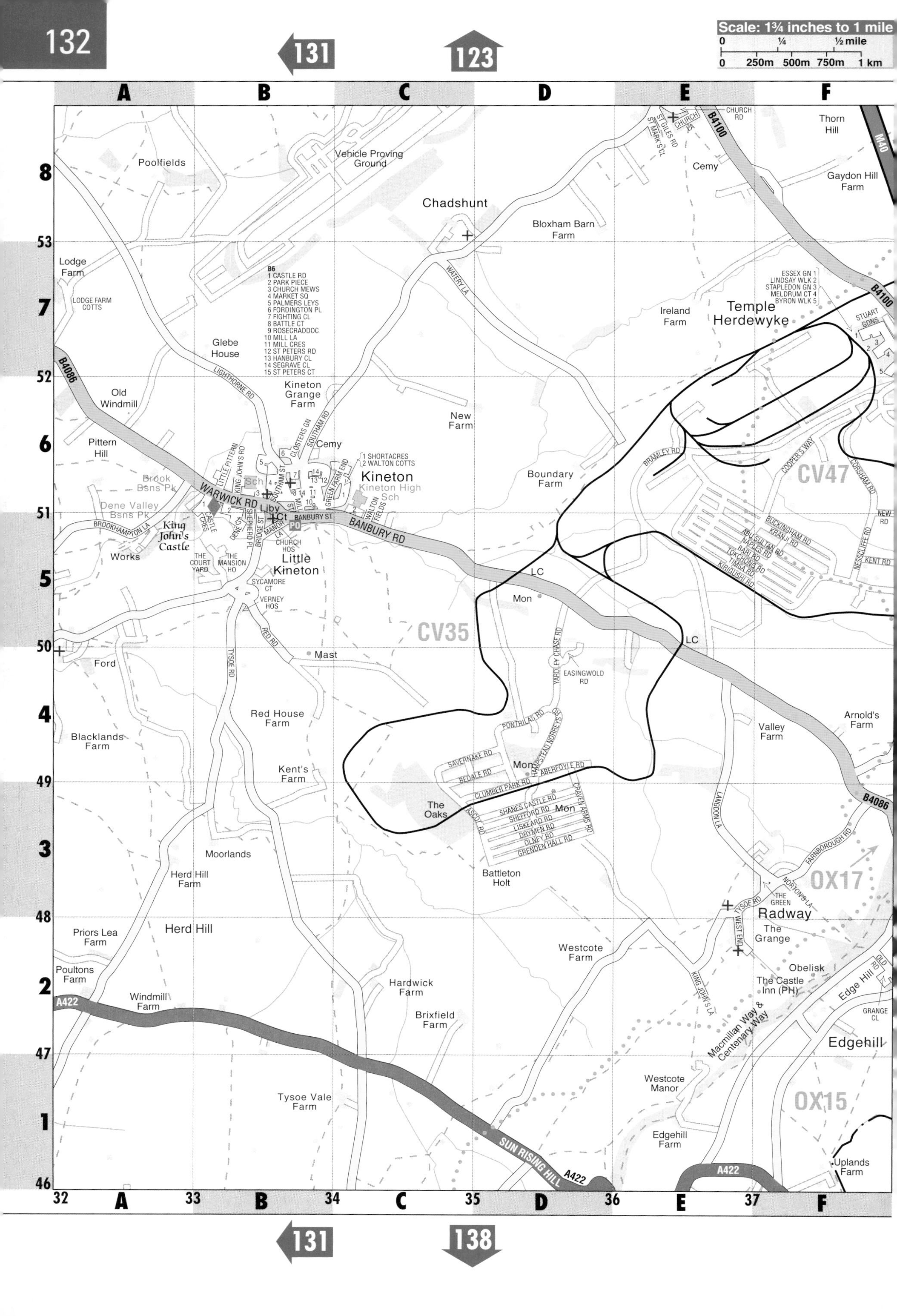

131
123
Scale: 1¾ inches to 1 mile
0 ¼ ½ mile
0 250m 500m 750m 1 km
A B C D E F
8 53 7 52 6 51 5 50 4 49 3 48 2 47 1 46
32 33 34 35 36 37
Poolfields
Vehicle Proving Ground
Chadshunt
Bloxham Barn Farm
Cemy
Thorn Hill
Gaydon Hill Farm
B4100
M40
CHURCH RD
CHURCH LA
ST GILES RD
ST MARK'S CL
Lodge Farm
LODGE FARM COTTS
B6
1 CASTLE RD
2 PARK PIECE
3 CHURCH MEWS
4 MARKET SQ
5 PALMERS LEYS
6 FORDINGTON PL
7 FIGHTING CL
8 BATTLE CT
9 ROSECRADDOC
10 MILL LA
11 MILL CRES
12 ST PETERS RD
13 HANBURY CL
14 SEGRAVE CL
15 ST PETERS CT
WATERY LA
Ireland Farm
Temple Herdewyke
ESSEX GN 1
LINDSAY WLK 2
STAPLEDON GN 3
MELDRUM CT 4
BYRON WLK 5
STUART GDNS
Glebe House
B4086
LIGHTHORNE RD
Kineton Grange Farm
Old Windmill
New Farm
Pittern Hill
CLOSTERS GN
SOUTHAM RD
Cemy
1 SHORTACRES
2 WALTON COTTS
Kineton
Kineton High Sch
BRAMLEY RD
COOPER'S WAY
CV47
CORSHAM RD
Brook Bsns Pk
Dene Valley Bsns Pk
LITTLE PITTERN
KING JOHN'S RD
Sch
SOUTHAM ST
GREEN FARM END
WALTON FIELDS
WARWICK RD
Liby
Ct
BANBURY ST
PO
BANBURY RD
Boundary Farm
BUCKINGHAM RD
KRANJI RD
ABU SULTAN RD
NAPLES RD
BARI RD
TOKCHONG RD
TIMSA RD
KIRIGUSHI RD
NESSCLIFFE RD
NEW RD
KENT RD
BROOKHAMPTON LA
King John's Castle
CASTLE CRES
DENE CL
SHEPHERD PL
BRIDGE ST
MANOR LA
CHURCH HOS
Works
THE COURT YARD
THE MANSION HO
Little Kineton
LC
Mon
SYCAMORE CT
VERNEY HOS
CV35
LC
Ford
RED RD
TYSOE RD
Mast
YARDLEY CHASE RD
EASINGWOLD RD
Blacklands Farm
Red House Farm
PONTRILAS RD
HAMPSTEAD NORREYS RD
Valley Farm
Arnold's Farm
Kent's Farm
SAVERNAKE RD
BEDALE RD
Mon
ABERFOYLE RD
CLUMBER PARK RD
The Oaks
ASCOT RD
SHANES CASTLE RD
SHEFFORD RD
LISKEARD RD
DRYMEN RD
OLNEY RD
GRENDEN HALL RD
Mon
CRAVEN ARMS RD
LANGDON LA
B4086
FARNBOROUGH RD
Moorlands
Herd Hill Farm
Battleton Holt
NORTON'S LA
OX17
TYSOE RD
THE GREEN
Radway
Priors Lea Farm
Herd Hill
WEST END
The Grange
Westcote Farm
Obelisk
KING JOHN'S LA
The Castle Inn (PH)
Edge Hill
OLD RD
Poultons Farm
Hardwick Farm
Windmill Farm
A422
Brixfield Farm
Macmillan Way & Centenary Way
GRANGE CL
Edgehill
Westcote Manor
OX15
Tysoe Vale Farm
SUN RISING HILL
Edgehill Farm
A422
A422
Uplands Farm
131
138

Scale: 1¾ inches to 1 mile
¼
½ mile
250m 500m 750m 1 km
124
134
A B C D E F
8 53 7 52 6 51 5 50 4 49 3 48 2 47 1 46
39 40 41 42 43
CV35
CV47
OX17
OX15
Hammonds Barn
LC
PH
Wharf
Shrine Hill
Sewage Works
Northend
NORTHEND RD
BLACKSMITHS LA
TOP ST
MALT HOUSE CL
THE PREBEND HILL CL
1 MELDRUM CT
2 HAMPDEN CT
3 ASTLEY WLK
4 BEAUMONT CL
5 BYRON WLK
1 NORTONS CL
2 LEYS CL
3 PEARTREES
4 MALT HOUSE LA
5 BOTTOM ST
Burton Hills
Burton Dassett Hills Cty Pk
Marlborough Barracks
Sch
COTTERS CROFT 1
MANOR CT 2
BROOK ST 3
MEMORIAL RD 4
SQUIRE PL 5
CHURCH ST 6
DOG LA 7
GRANTS CL 8
Fenny Compton
Sewage Works
Works
Marina
Oxford Canal
STATION RD
1 FIELDGATE LA
2 THE READINGS
3 MEADOW WAY
4 BERRY MDW
HIGH ST
MILL LA
THE LANKETT
BRIDGE ST
AVON DASSETT RD
The Tunnel
Mill Hill
Gredenton Hill
Burton Dassett
Church Hill
THE SLADE
Fenny Compton Hill
Farnborough Barn
1 PRINCE RUPERT CL
2 WENTWORTH AVE
3 VERNEY RD
Centenary Way
Bitham Hill
BITHAM HALL
Shooter's Hill
Hall's Hill
Windmill Hill
Avon Dassett
PARK CL
LOWER END COTTS
AVON CARROW
Farnborough
HAY POOL
PH
Sourland Pool
DASSET RD
FORGE LA
HEYDONS TERR
Burton Hill Farm
Splash Leys Farm
Farnborough Hall
Farnborough Park
Macmillan Way
Obelisk
A423
SOUTHAM RD
Knowle End
Arlescote
College Farm
Nadbury
Edgehill Cty Pk
Nadbury House
CAMP LA
VILLAGE RD
SCHOOL LA
SOOT LA
Mast
MOLLINGTON LA
Warmington
1 RECTORY CL
2 CHAPEL ST
3 COURT CL
4 CHURCH HILL
ROUNDHILL RD 1
SCHOOL HILL 2
TINKERS LA 3
THE PADDOCKS 4
THE HOLT 5
THE ROW 6
WHITEWAY
MAIN ST
LOWER FARM
THE MEAD
MARCH RD
MARCH RD
1 OLD RD
2 TOWN HILL
2 CHAPEL LA
HIGH ST
Ratley
PH
B4086
Fir Tree Farm
Deddington Hill
National Herb Ctr
BANBURY RD
PH
Bush Hill
Hornton Hill Farm
Mast
Valley Farm
B4100
M40

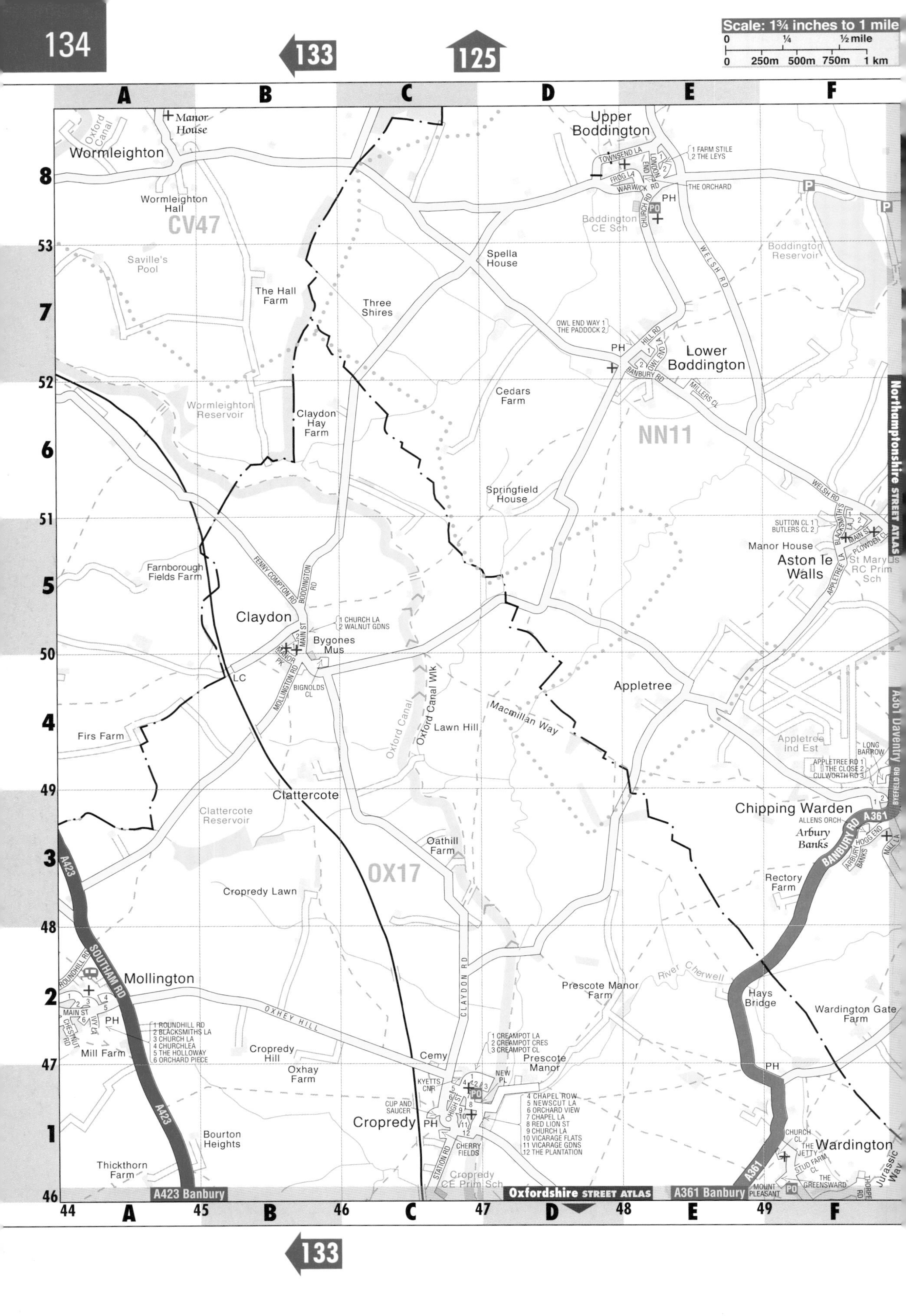
134
133
125
Scale: 1¾ inches to 1 mile
0 ¼ ½ mile
0 250m 500m 750m 1 km
A B C D E F
8 53 7 52 6 51 5 50 4 49 3 48 2 47 1 46
44 45 46 47 48 49
Manor House
Oxford Canal
Wormleighton
Wormleighton Hall
CV47
Saville's Pool
The Hall Farm
Three Shires
Upper Boddington
TOWNSEND LA
FROG LA
WARWICK RD
LONDON END
CHURCH RD
1 FARM STILE
2 THE LEYS
THE ORCHARD
PH
PO
Boddington CE Sch
Spella House
WELSH RD
Boddington Reservoir
OWL END WAY 1
THE PADDOCK 2
HILL RD
OWL END LA
BANBURY RD
MILLERS CL
Lower Boddington
Cedars Farm
Wormleighton Reservoir
Claydon Hay Farm
NN11
Springfield House
Northamptonshire STREET ATLAS
SUTTON CL 1
BUTLERS CL 2
BLACKSMITHS LA
MAIN ST
PLOWDEN CL
Manor House
Aston le Walls
St Mary's RC Prim Sch
APPLETREE LA
Farnborough Fields Farm
FENNY COMPTON RD
BODDINGTON RD
Claydon
1 CHURCH LA
2 WALNUT GDNS
Bygones Mus
MANOR PK
MOLLINGTON RD
BIGNOLDS CL
LC
Appletree
Macmillan Way
Oxford Canal Wlk
Oxford Canal
Lawn Hill
Firs Farm
Appletree Ind Est
A361 Daventry
LONG BARROW
APPLETREE RD 1
THE CLOSE 2
CULWORTH RD 3
BYFIELD RD
Clattercote
Clattercote Reservoir
Chipping Warden
ALLENS ORCH
Arbury Banks
A361
BANBURY RD
HOGG END
ARBURY BANKS
MILL LA
Oathill Farm
OX17
A423
Rectory Farm
Cropredy Lawn
SOUTHAM RD
ROUNDHILL RD
Mollington
CLAYDON RD
River Cherwell
Prescote Manor Farm
Hays Bridge
Wardington Gate Farm
MAIN ST
CHESTNUT RD
IVY LA
1 ROUNDHILL RD
2 BLACKSMITHS LA
3 CHURCH LA
4 CHURCHLEA
5 THE HOLLOWAY
6 ORCHARD PIECE
OXHEY HILL
Mill Farm
Cropredy Hill
Oxhay Farm
Cemy
1 CREAMPOT LA
2 CREAMPOT CRES
3 CREAMPOT CL
Prescote Manor
NEW PL
KYETTS CNR
CUP AND SAUCER
HIGH ST
Cropredy
4 CHAPEL ROW
5 NEWSCUT LA
6 ORCHARD VIEW
7 CHAPEL LA
8 RED LION ST
9 CHURCH LA
10 VICARAGE FLATS
11 VICARAGE GDNS
12 THE PLANTATION
CHERRY FIELDS
STATION RD
Cropredy CE Prim Sch
Bourton Heights
Thickthorn Farm
A423 Banbury
Oxfordshire STREET ATLAS
A361 Banbury
CHURCH CL
THE JETTY
STUD FARM CL
Wardington
THE GREENSWARD
MOUNT PLEASANT
THORPE RD
Jurassic Way

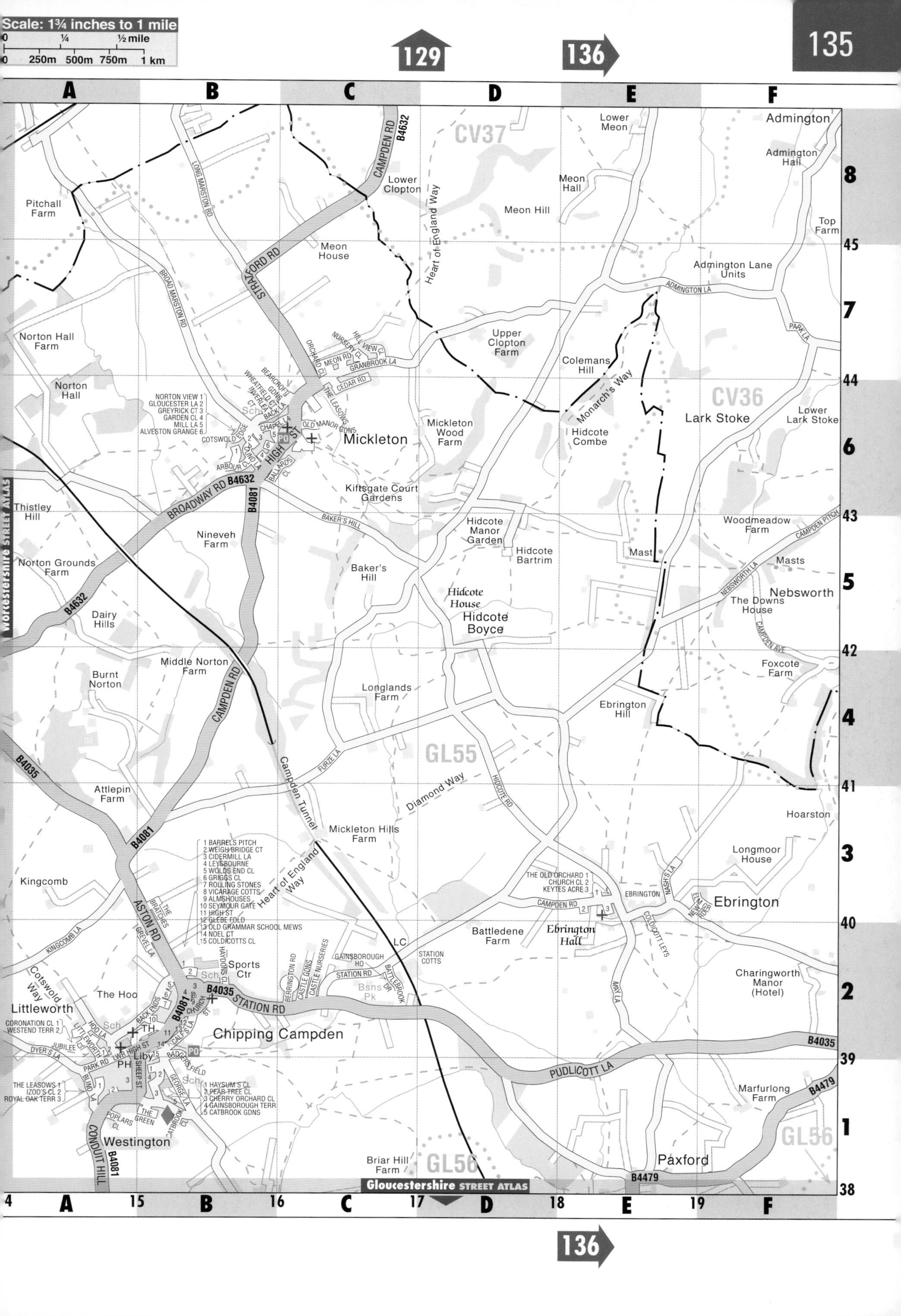
Scale: 1¾ inches to 1 mile
0 ¼ ½ mile
0 250m 500m 750m 1 km
129
136
A B C D E F
8 7 6 5 4 3 2 1
45 44 43 42 41 40 39 38
15 16 17 18 19
CV37
CV36
GL55
GL56
Lower Meon
Admington
Admington Hall
Lower Clopton
Meon Hall
Meon Hill
Pitchall Farm
Top Farm
Meon House
Admington Lane Units
ADMINGTON LA
Norton Hall Farm
Upper Clopton Farm
Colemans Hill
Norton Hall
Lark Stoke
Lower Lark Stoke
Mickleton Wood Farm
Hidcote Combe
Mickleton
Kiftsgate Court Gardens
Thistley Hill
Nineveh Farm
Hidcote Manor Garden
Hidcote Bartrim
Woodmeadow Farm
Norton Grounds Farm
Baker's Hill
Mast
Masts
Nebsworth
Hidcote House
Hidcote Boyce
The Downs House
Dairy Hills
Middle Norton Farm
Foxcote Farm
Burnt Norton
Longlands Farm
Ebrington Hill
Attlepin Farm
Diamond Way
Hoarston
Mickleton Hills Farm
Longmoor House
Kingcomb
Ebrington
Battledene Farm
Ebrington Hall
Charingworth Manor (Hotel)
The Hoo
Sports Ctr
Littleworth
Chipping Campden
Marfurlong Farm
Westington
Briar Hill Farm
Paxford
Heart of England Way
Monarch's Way
Campden Tunnel
Cotswold Way
CAMPDEN RD
B4632
STRATFORD RD
LONG MARSTON RD
BROAD MARSTON RD
BROADWAY RD
B4081
BAKER'S HILL
FURZE LA
HIDCOTE RD
NEBSWORTH LA
CAMPDEN PITCH
CAMPDEN AVE
PARK LA
B4035
ASTON RD
KINGCOMB LA
GREVEL LA
THE BRAICHES
STATION RD
PUDLICOTT LA
B4479
NASH'S LA
ELM GR
NEW RD
COLDICOTT LEYS
MAY LA
EBRINGTON
CAMPDEN RD
STATION COTTS
GAINSBOROUGH HO
BATTLEBROOK DR
BERRINGTON RD
CASTLE GDNS
CASTLE NURSERIES
Bsns Pk
LC
CONDUIT HILL
POPLARS CL
THE GREEN
CATBROOK
GEORGE LA
BADGERS FIELD
SHEEP ST
PARK RD
BLIND LA
DYER'S LA
JUBILEE CL
HOO LA
BACK ENDS
CALF'S LA
CHURCH ST
HAYDONS CL
HIGH ST
LWR HIGH ST
Liby
PH
TH
PO
Sch
NORTON VIEW 1
GLOUCESTER LA 2
GREYRICK CT 3
GARDEN CL 4
MILL LA 5
ALVESTON GRANGE 6
COTSWOLD EDGE
ARBOUR CL
BALLARDS CL
CHAPEL LA
BACK LA
INVERLEA CT
WHEATFIELD CL
BEARCROFT GDNS
OLD MANOR GDNS
THE LEASOWS
CEDAR RD
GRANBROOK LA
MEON RD
NURSERY CL
HILL VIEW
ORCHARD CL
1 BARRELS PITCH
2 WEIGHBRIDGE CT
3 CIDERMILL LA
4 LEYSBOURNE
5 WOLDS END CL
6 GRIGGS CL
7 ROLLING STONES
8 VICARAGE COTTS
9 ALMSHOUSES
10 SEYMOUR GATE
11 HIGH ST
12 GLEBE FOLD
13 OLD GRAMMAR SCHOOL MEWS
14 NOEL CT
15 COLDICOTTS CL
THE OLD ORCHARD 1
CHURCH CL 2
KEYTES ACRE 3
CORONATION CL 1
WESTEND TERR 2
THE LEASOWS 1
IZOD'S CL 2
ROYAL OAK TERR 3
1 HAYSUM'S CL
2 PEAR TREE CL
3 CHERRY ORCHARD CL
4 GAINSBOROUGH TERR
5 CATBROOK GDNS
Worcestershire STREET ATLAS
Gloucestershire STREET ATLAS

136
135
130
Scale: 1¾ inches to 1 mile
0 ¼ ½ mile
0 250m 500m 750m 1 km
A B C D E F
8 45 7 44 6 43 5 42 4 41 3 40 2 39 1 38
20 21 22 23 24 25
Berryfield Farm
CV37
York Farm
STRATFORD RD
Caley Fields
BERRYFIELDS LA
Manor House
PH
Armscote
MIDDLE ST
ARMSCOTE RD
NEWBOLD RD
A3400
MILL LA
ROMAN WAY
PH
A429
Mansill Farm
Sewage Works
ILMINGTON RD
MICKLETON RD
CROSS LEYS
ARMSCOTE RD
OLD FOSSE WAY
PH
MANOR BARNS
Ilmington CE Prim Sch
BACK ST
BENNETT PL
KEYTE RD
PO
PH
1 WINDMILL CL
2 BALLARDS LA
FRONT ST
ELM CL
WASHBROOK PL
VALANDERS LA
NELLANDS CL
New Bridges Farm
Tredington
Sch
Blackwell
BLACKWELL RD
Centenary Way
ILMINGTON RD
ARMSCOTE RD
CAMPDEN PITCH
CAMPDEN HILL
FROG LA
GRUMP ST
FOXCOTE HILL
Ilmington
SHAKESFIELD CL 1
COTSWOLD CL 2
FOSSEWAY CRES 3
QUEENS RD 4
MANOR FARM RD 5
River Stour
Harolds Farm
El Sub Sta
Tredington Hills
A3400
POTTERS LA
Darlingscott
Windmill Hill
Southfield Farm
149
Cathole
Longdon Manor
CV36
FOSSE WAY
DARLINGSCOTE RD
Whaddon Farm
Ind Est
TILEMANS LA
MAYO RD
Sch
Sch
HAY MDW
Shipston-on-Stour
Compton Scorpion Manor
Holt Farm
P
PO
PITTWAY AVE
BERRY AVE
Far Longdon
Works
CAMPDEN RD
B4035
GREEN LA
NEW ST
HANSON AVE
GL55
Portobello Farm
149
Middlehurst Farm
BANISTER WAY
FURZE HILL RD
Goose Hill
Charingworth
Furze Hill
Braxfield House
Pig Brook
Charingworth Grange
B4035
B4479
GL56
Rowborough Farm
Ditchford Farm
Horseleys Farm
Cottage Farm
COTTAGE FARM CT 1
THE SHARRIES 2
HAROLD'S ORCH 3
Sewage Works
SHOULDERWAY LA
TANKARDS HILL
4 MANOR COTTS
5 CARSON CL
6 CHAPEL GDNS
PH
BELCONY
OLD TREE COTTS
Stretton-on-Fosse
Blackdowns
MANOR FARM COTTS 7
MANOR CT 8
A429
Tidmington
149
135
140
For full street detail of the highlighted area see page 149.

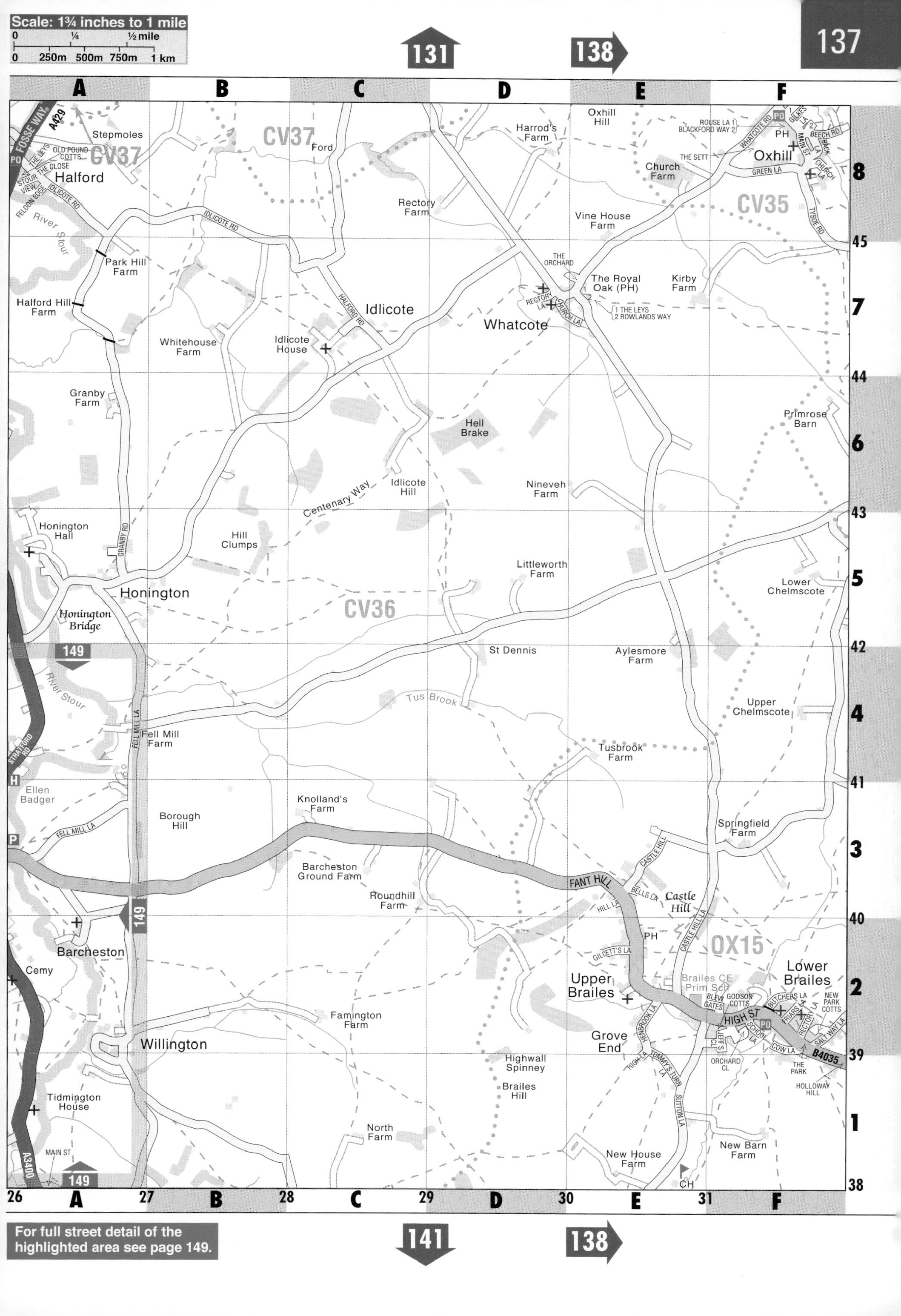

For full street detail of the highlighted area see page 149.

137
132

Scale: 1¾ inches to 1 mile

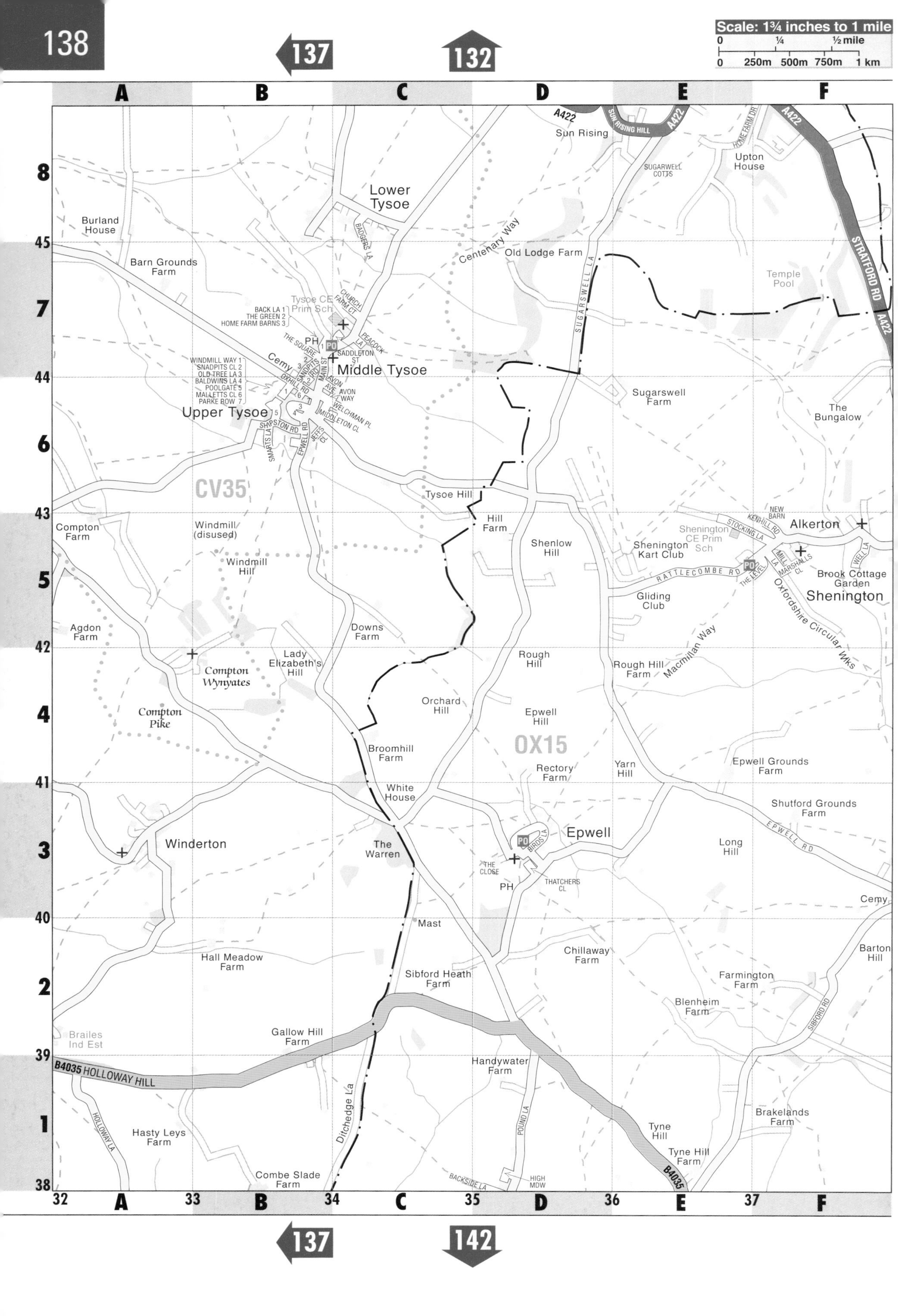

137
142

Scale: 1¾ inches to 1 mile

0 ¼ ½ mile

0 250m 500m 750m 1 km

133

F5
1 WINTER GARDENS WAY
2 SAGE CL
3 WINCHELSEA CL
4 HEREFORD WAY
5 GUERNSEY WAY
6 JERSEY RD
7 BARCOMBE CL
8 ROTHER RD
9 RYE CL
10 PITMASTON CL
11 USHER DR
12 MELROSE CT
13 ASHMEAD RD
14 LAXTON WAY
15 WINSTON DR
16 ELLISON DR
17 FIRTREE CL
18 HARDWICK PK
19 HIGHLANDS
20 HORSHAM CL
21 SUSSEX DR
22 CHEVIOT WAY
23 ROMNEY RD

A B C D E F

Hornton Hall
Hornton
Horley Fields Farm
Savee Farm
Shotteswell
BACK HILL 1
SNUFF LA 2
CORONATION LA 3
CHAPEL LA 4
CHURCH LA 5
BURY COURT LA 6
PERKINS CL
MILLERS LA
CHURCH LA
WEST END
THE GREEN
EASTGATE
PAGES LA
BELL ST
PH
PO
Sch
Sor Brook
Oxfordshire Circular Wlk
Hornton Grounds
OX17
B4100
M40
Hanwell
LANE CL
MANOR ORCH 1
THE OLD COUNCIL HOS 2
GULLIVER'S CL
Horley
New Inn (PH)
Ragnell Bottom
THE COUNCIL HOS
SACKVILLE CT
GULLICOTE LA
SPRINGFIELD AVE
MAIN ST
CHURCH LA
PARK CL
WARWICK RD
FRIARS HILL
STRATFORD RD
Drayton Lodge
CH
Cemy
Southfields Farm
OX15
Wroxton
HORLEY PATH RD
THE FIRS
Balscote
MIDDLE LA
THE HEDGES
QUEEN'S CRES
METCALFE CL
ARDEN CL
RED POLL CL
LUDLOW DR
Drayton
MAIN ST
MILLS LA
DARK LA
CHURCH ST
SILVER ST
Guide Post
Wroxton Abbey
Wroxton Coll
1 DRIFT LA
2 LEYS CL
3 THE LEY'S
4 WROXTON CT
5 LAMPITTS GN
6 WROXTON HO
Obelisk
MILL LA
RECTORY GDNS
A422
Alkerton Hill Farm
THE GREEN 1
MALTHOUSE LA 2
WEAVERS ROW 3
SIBFORD RD 4
CHURCH LA 5
Balscote Mill
Castle Bank Enclosure
BANBURY
HASTINGS RD
EDINBURGH WAY
APPLEBY CL
Shutford
COOK'S HILL
LOWER END
PLOT RD
DAIRYGROUND
THE PLAIN RD
Tythe Farm
Newington Grounds Farm
HIGHCLERE GDNS
DOVER AVE
PRESCOTT AVE
EDMUNDS RD
Cemy
EPWELL RD
HIGH ST
IVY LA
BANBURY RD
FIVE WAYS
THE RICKYARD
Claydon Hill
Sor Brook
Withycombe Farm
THORNBURY RISE
BALMORAL AVE
Round Hill
Bishop Carpenter CE Prim Sch
SHUTFORD RD
MAIN ST
SCHOOL LA
THE POUND
PARK LA
Wr Twr
Mast
BALMORAL AVE 1
BRIGGS CL 2
DORCHESTER GR 3
DENBIGH CL
Jester's Hill
Welshcroft Hill
North Newington
B4035
BROUGHTON RD
OX16
Broughton Grounds Farm
The Bretch
BANBURY RD
Crouch Hill
Salt Way
Madmarston Hill
Woadmill Farm
Crouch Farm
Upper Lea Farm
Swalcliffe Lea
SANDFINE RD
Broughton
MAIN RD
DANVERS RD
SWALCLIFFE LEA
SHUTFORD RD
Broughton Park
Fulling Mill Farm
Broughton Castle
PH DANVERS CL
WYKHAM LA
A361
BLOXHAM RD
GREEN LA
B4035
Cemy

M40 Banbury
Oxfordshire STREET ATLAS
A422 Banbury, M40
A361 Banbury
A361 Chipping Norton

45 44 43 42 41 40 39 38
8 7 6 5 4 3 2 1

38 39 40 41 42 43

A B C D E F

F3
1 HASTING CL
2 GLAMIS PL
3 CAERNARVON WAY
4 STIRLING CT
5 CHESTER WAY
6 MARLOWE CL
7 CONWAY DR
8 KENILWORTH WAY
9 CHEPSTOW GDNS
10 HARLECH CL
11 HAMPDEN CL
12 Bradley Arc

F4
1 ALVIS GATE
2 BENTLEY CL
3 RICHMAN GDNS
4 MORGAN CL
5 DAIMLER AVE
6 TALBOT CL
7 BEDFORD CL
8 HUMBER WLK
9 LANCHESTER DR
10 MORRIS DR
11 SINCLAIR AVE
12 WILLIAM CL
13 BRAMBER CL
14 PENRHYN CL
15 FERNDALE RD
16 THE FAIRWAY
17 CHERRY RD

136

Scale: 1¾ inches to 1 mile
0 ¼ ½ mile
0 250m 500m 750m 1 km

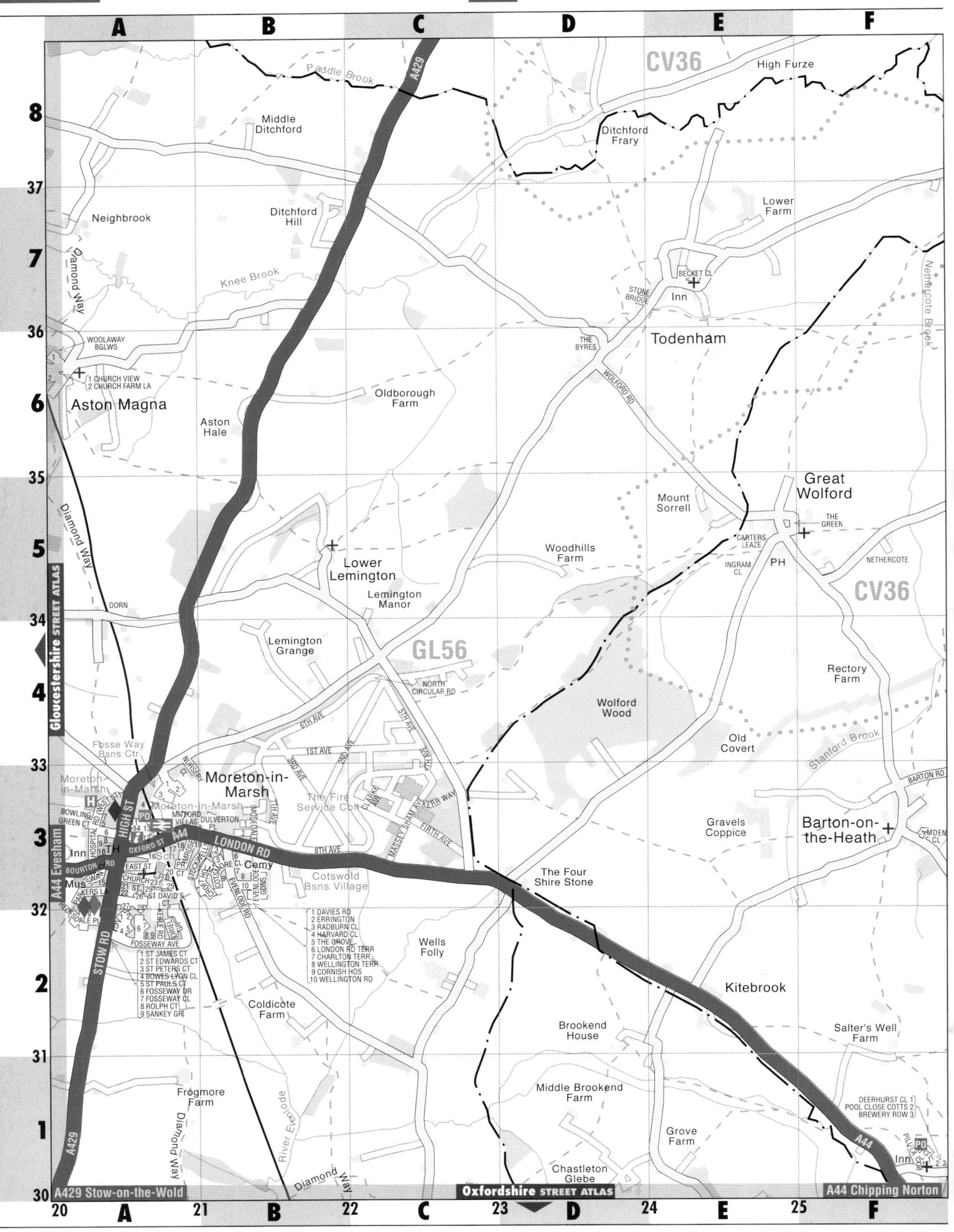

A3
1 BLENHEIM WAY
2 BECESHORE CL
3 ROUNDHOUSE MEWS
4 THE GRANGE
5 MARSH CT
6 CORDER'S LA
7 DEVONSHIRE TERR
8 MANCHESTER CT
9 CORDERS CL
10 REDESDALE MEWS
11 NEW RD
12 STATION RD
13 THE GREEN
14 OLD MARKET WAY
15 UNIVERSITY FARM
16 OXFORD ST
17 ODDFELLOWS' TERR
18 TURNPIKE CL
19 CICESTER TER
20 MEAD CL
21 STONEFERN CT
22 DUNSTALL HO
23 GRAY'S LA
24 ST GEORGE'S CL
25 WARNEFORD PL
26 COTSWOLD GDNS
27 JAMESON CT
28 TINKER'S CL
29 OLD TOWN

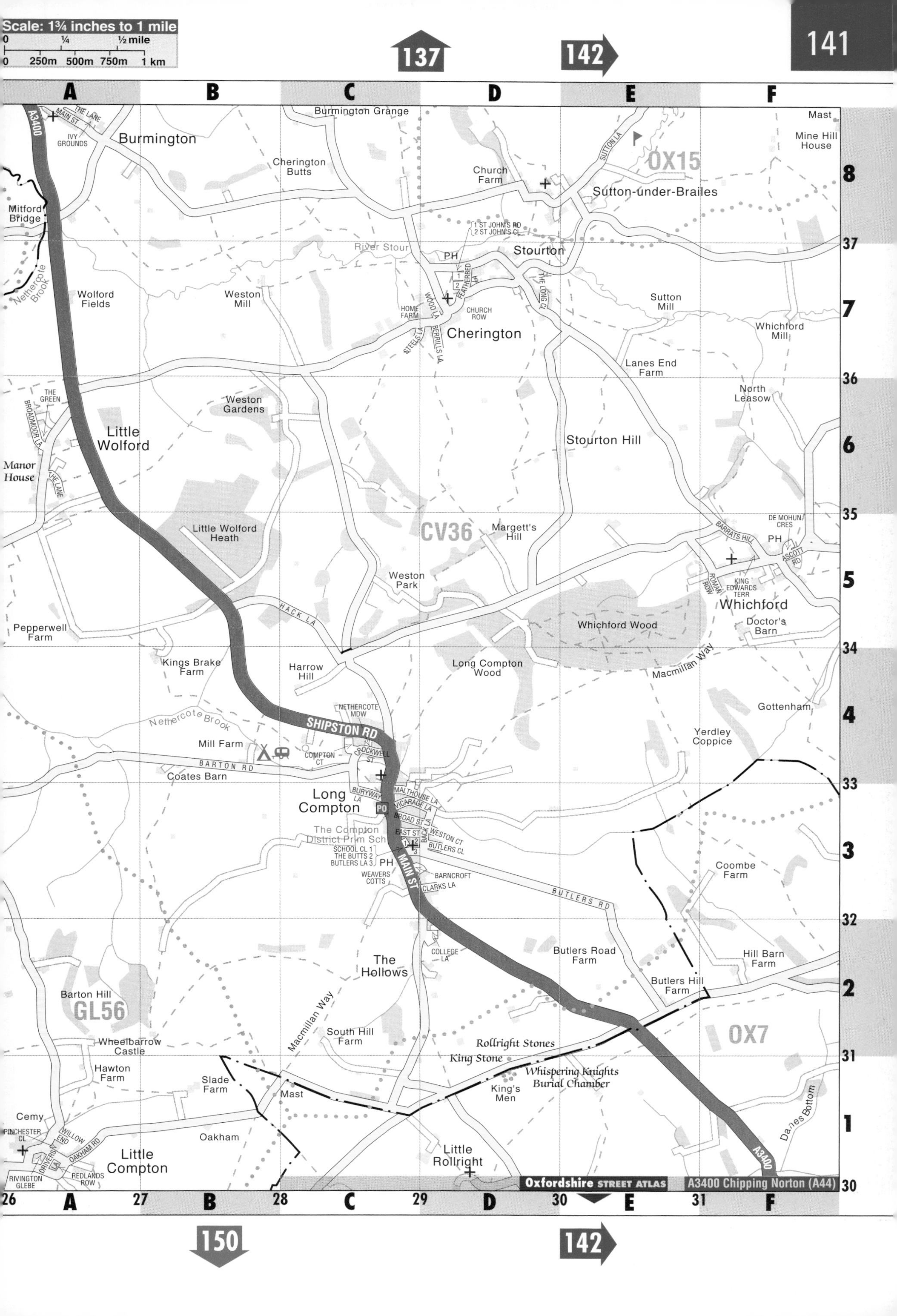
Scale: 1¾ inches to 1 mile
137
142
Burmington
Burmington Grange
Cherington Butts
Church Farm
Sutton-under-Brailes
OX15
Mine Hill House
Mast
Mitford Bridge
River Stour
Stourton
Wolford Fields
Weston Mill
Cherington
Sutton Mill
Whichford Mill
Lanes End Farm
North Leasow
Weston Gardens
Little Wolford
Manor House
Stourton Hill
Little Wolford Heath
CV36
Margett's Hill
Weston Park
Whichford
Whichford Wood
Doctor's Barn
Pepperwell Farm
Kings Brake Farm
Harrow Hill
Long Compton Wood
Macmillan Way
Gottenham
Nethercote Brook
SHIPSTON RD
Mill Farm
Coates Barn
Yerdley Coppice
Long Compton
The Compton District Prim Sch
MAIN ST
Coombe Farm
BUTLERS RD
The Hollows
Butlers Road Farm
Hill Barn Farm
Barton Hill
GL56
Butlers Hill Farm
South Hill Farm
Wheelbarrow Castle
Rollright Stones
King Stone
Whispering Knights Burial Chamber
King's Men
OX7
Hawton Farm
Slade Farm
Mast
Cemy
Oakham
Little Compton
Little Rollright
Dane's Bottom
A3400

Scale: 1¾ inches to 1 mile
0 ¼ ½ mile
0 250m 500m 750m 1 km

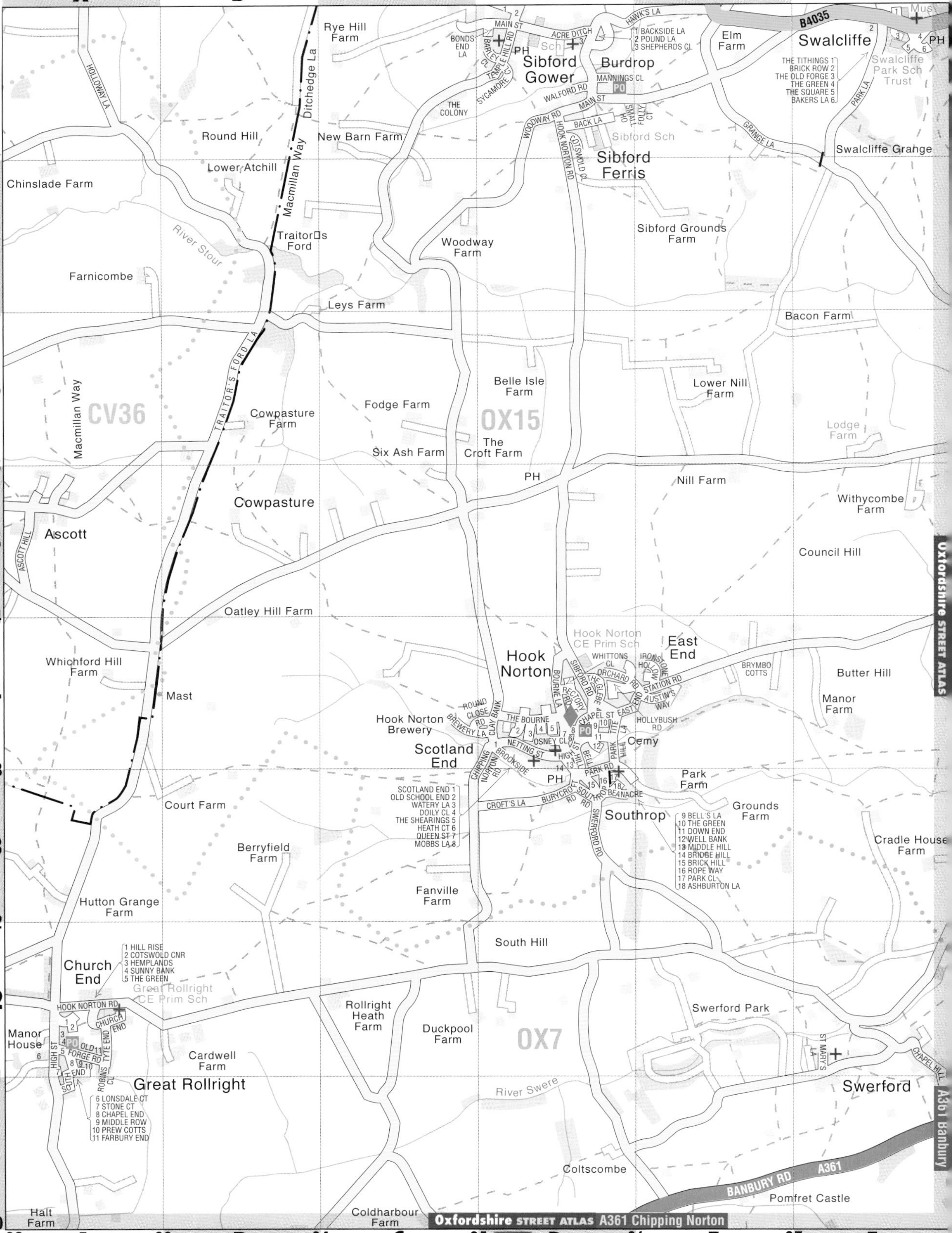

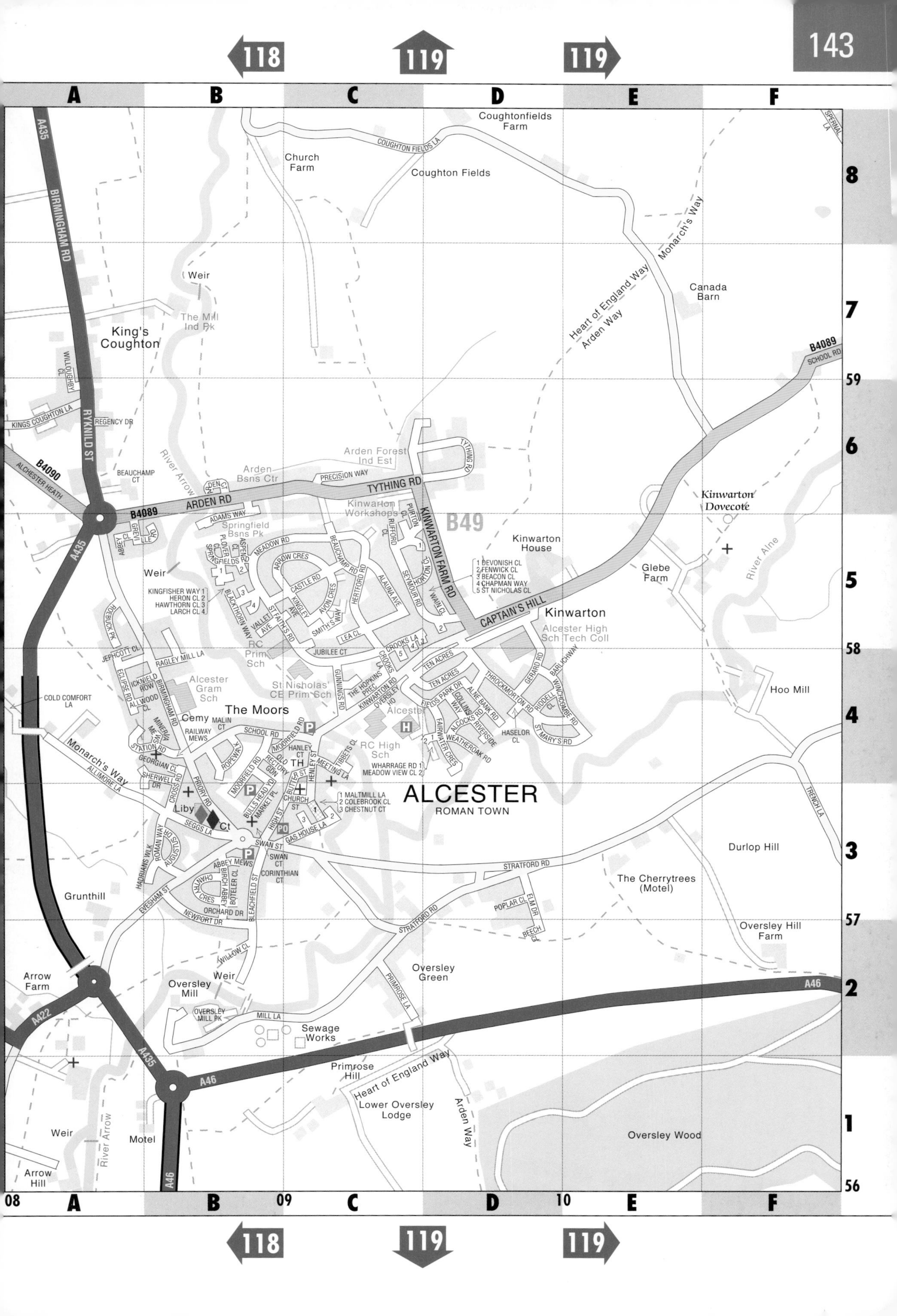
118
119
119
ALCESTER
ROMAN TOWN
King's Coughton
Coughtonfields Farm
Church Farm
Coughton Fields
Weir
The Mill Ind Pk
Arden Forest Ind Est
Arden Bsns Ctr
Kinwarton Workshops
Springfield Bsns Pk
Kinwarton House
Kinwarton Dovecote
Kinwarton
Glebe Farm
Canada Barn
Alcester High Sch Tech Coll
Alcester Gram Sch
RC Prim Sch
St Nicholas' CE Prim Sch
The Moors
Cemy
RC High Sch
Hoo Mill
Durlop Hill
The Cherrytrees (Motel)
Oversley Hill Farm
Oversley Green
Oversley Mill
Sewage Works
Grunthill
Arrow Farm
Arrow Hill
Motel
Primrose Hill
Lower Oversley Lodge
Oversley Wood
Heart of England Way
Monarch's Way
Arden Way
River Arrow
River Alne
BIRMINGHAM RD
RYKNILD ST
A435
A46
A422
B4089
B4090
B49
ARDEN RD
TYTHING RD
KINWARTON FARM RD
CAPTAIN'S HILL
SCHOOL RD
STRATFORD RD
EVESHAM ST
COUGHTON FIELDS LA
KINGS COUGHTON LA
ALCESTER HEATH
1 DEVONISH CL
2 FENWICK CL
3 BEACON CL
4 CHAPMAN WAY
5 ST NICHOLAS CL
KINGFISHER WAY 1
HERON CL 2
HAWTHORN CL 3
LARCH CL 4
1 MALTMILL LA
2 COLEBROOK CL
3 CHESTNUT CT
WHARRAGE RD 1
MEADOW VIEW CL 2
COLD COMFORT LA
A B C D E F
8 7 6 5 4 3 2 1
59 58 57 56
08 09 10

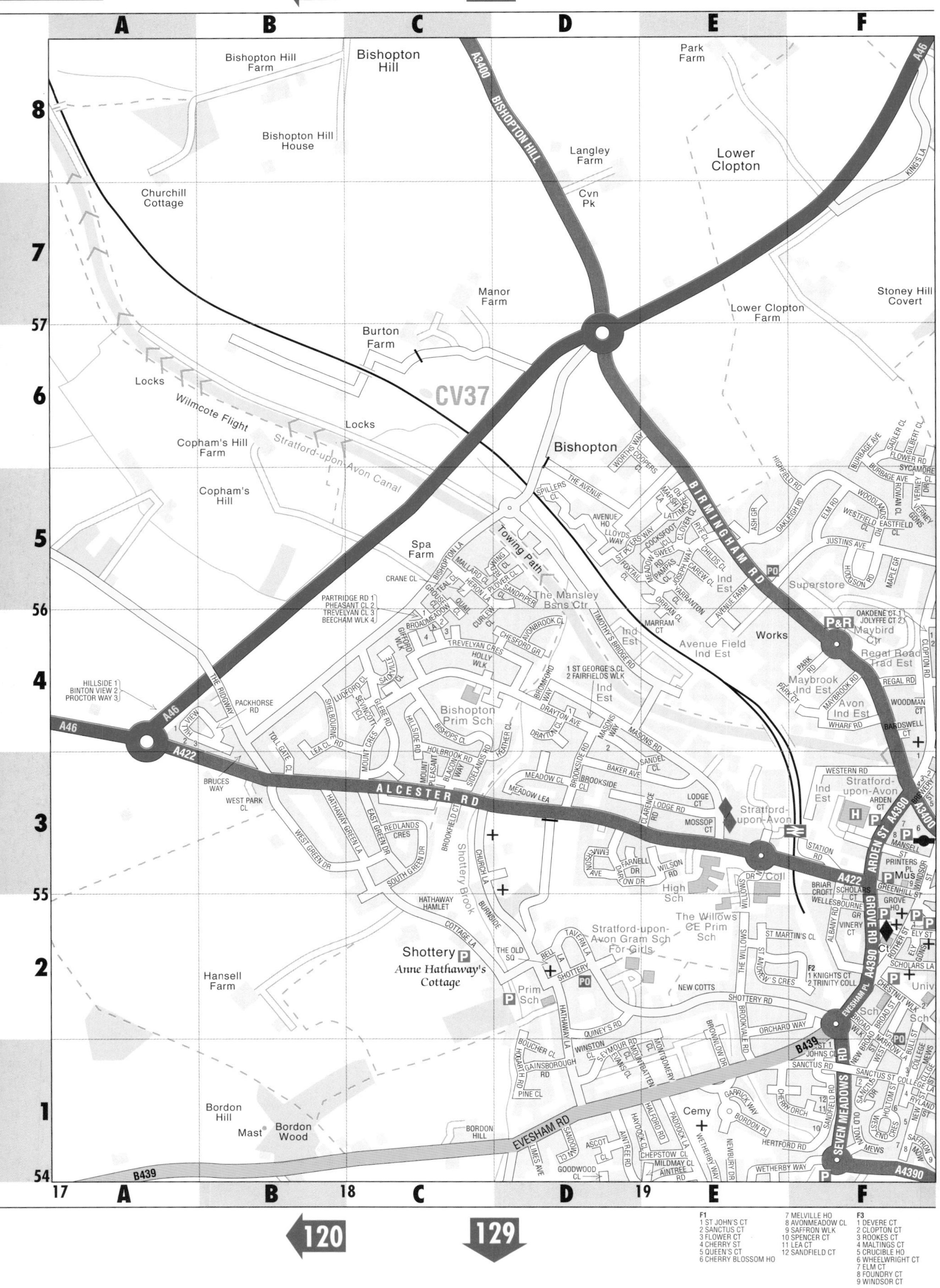
120
120
A
B
C
D
E
F
Bishopton Hill Farm
Bishopton Hill
A3400
BISHOPTON HILL
Park Farm
A46
Bishopton Hill House
Langley Farm
Lower Clopton
Churchill Cottage
Cvn Pk
KING'S LA
Manor Farm
Stoney Hill Covert
Lower Clopton Farm
Burton Farm
Locks
CV37
Wilmcote Flight
Locks
Copham's Hill Farm
Stratford-upon-Avon Canal
Bishopton
Copham's Hill
THE AVENUE
BIRMINGHAM RD
Spa Farm
Towing Path
CRANE CL
The Mansley Bsns Ctr
Superstore
PARTRIDGE RD 1
PHEASANT CL 2
TREVELYAN CL 3
BEECHAM WLK 4
Ind Est
Works
Avenue Field Ind Est
P&R
Maybird Ctr
Regal Road Trad Est
Maybrook Ind Est
Avon Ind Est
HILLSIDE 1
BINTON VIEW 2
PROCTOR WAY 3
1 ST GEORGE'S CL
2 FAIRFIELDS WLK
PACKHORSE RD
Bishopton Prim Sch
A46
A422
BRUCES WAY
WEST PARK CL
ALCESTER RD
Stratford-upon-Avon
Ind Est
ARDEN ST
A3400
A4390
Stratford-upon-Avon
Shottery Brook
High Sch
The Willows CE Prim Sch
Coll
Mus
Stratford-upon-Avon Gram Sch For Girls
HATHAWAY HAMLET
COTTAGE LA
Shottery
Anne Hathaway's Cottage
Hansell Farm
Prim Sch
THE OLD SQ
SHOTTERY RD
ORCHARD WAY
Univ
Sch
B439
SEVEN MEADOWS RD
Cemy
EVESHAM RD
Bordon Hill
Mast
Bordon Wood
BORDON HILL
WETHERBY WAY
A4390
B439
54
17
18
19
8
7
57
6
5
56
4
3
55
2
1

F1
1 ST JOHN'S CT
2 SANCTUS CT
3 FLOWER CT
4 CHERRY ST
5 QUEEN'S CT
6 CHERRY BLOSSOM HO
7 MELVILLE HO
8 AVONMEADOW CL
9 SAFFRON WLK
10 SPENCER CT
11 LEA CT
12 SANDFIELD CT

F3
1 DEVERE CT
2 CLOPTON CT
3 ROOKES CT
4 MALTINGS CT
5 CRUCIBLE HO
6 WHEELWRIGHT CT
7 ELM CT
8 FOUNDRY CT
9 WINDSOR CT

120
129

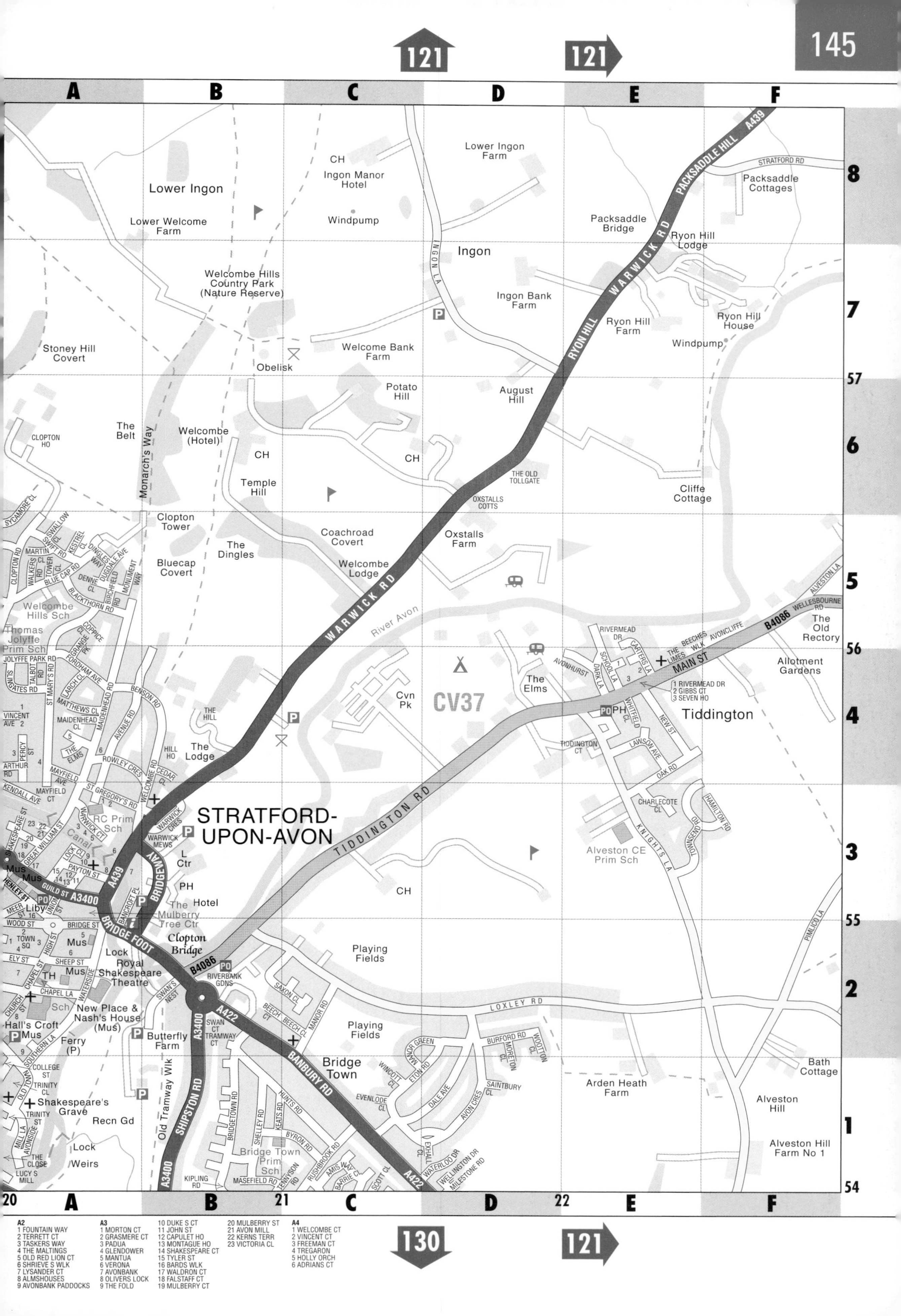
121
121
Lower Ingon
Lower Welcome Farm
Ingon Manor Hotel
Windpump
Lower Ingon Farm
Ingon
INGON LA
Packsaddle Bridge
PACKSADDLE HILL
STRATFORD RD
Packsaddle Cottages
Ryon Hill Lodge
Welcombe Hills Country Park (Nature Reserve)
Ingon Bank Farm
Ryon Hill Farm
Ryon Hill House
Windpump
Stoney Hill Covert
Obelisk
Welcome Bank Farm
Potato Hill
August Hill
RYON HILL
WARWICK RD
The Belt
Monarch's Way
Welcombe (Hotel)
CLOPTON HO
Temple Hill
THE OLD TOLLGATE
OXSTALLS COTTS
Cliffe Cottage
Clopton Tower
Bluecap Covert
The Dingles
Coachroad Covert
Welcombe Lodge
Oxstalls Farm
River Avon
Welcombe Hills Sch
Thomas Jolyffe Prim Sch
WELLESBOURNE RD
ALVESTON LA
The Old Rectory
B4086
MAIN ST
Allotment Gardens
Cvn Pk
CV37
The Elms
Tiddington
1 RIVERMEAD DR
2 GIBBS CT
3 SEVEN HO
THE HILL
The Lodge
HILL HO
TIDDINGTON RD
TIDDINGTON CT
CHARLECOTE CL
HAMILTON RD
KNIGHTS LA
STRATFORD-UPON-AVON
Alveston CE Prim Sch
RC Prim Sch
Canal
A439
BRIDGEWAY
L Ctr
PH
Hotel
The Mulberry Tree Ctr
Clopton Bridge
GUILD ST A3400
BRIDGE FOOT
Mus
Liby
Lock
Royal Shakespeare Theatre
New Place & Nash's House (Mus)
Hall's Croft
Ferry (P)
Butterfly Farm
Playing Fields
LOXLEY RD
A422
BANBURY RD
Bridge Town
Playing Fields
Arden Heath Farm
Bath Cottage
Alveston Hill
Alveston Hill Farm No 1
Shakespeare's Grave
Recn Gd
Old Tramway Wlk
SHIPSTON RD
A3400
Lock
Weirs
THE CLOSE
LUCY S MILL
Bridge Town Prim Sch
KIPLING RD
MASEFIELD RD
TENNYSON RD
20
21
22
A
B
C
D
E
F
54
55
56
57
1
2
3
4
5
6
7
8
A2
1 FOUNTAIN WAY
2 TERRETT CT
3 TASKERS WAY
4 THE MALTINGS
5 OLD RED LION CT
6 SHRIEVE S WLK
7 LYSANDER CT
8 ALMSHOUSES
9 AVONBANK PADDOCKS
A3
1 MORTON CT
2 GRASMERE CT
3 PADUA
4 GLENDOWER
5 MANTUA
6 VERONA
7 AVONBANK
8 OLIVERS LOCK
9 THE FOLD
10 DUKE S CT
11 JOHN ST
12 CAPULET HO
13 MONTAGUE HO
14 SHAKESPEARE CT
15 TYLER ST
16 BARDS WLK
17 WALDRON CT
18 FALSTAFF CT
19 MULBERRY CT
20 MULBERRY ST
21 AVON MILL
22 KERNS TERR
23 VICTORIA CL
A4
1 WELCOMBE CT
2 VINCENT CT
3 FREEMAN CT
4 TREGARON
5 HOLLY ORCH
6 ADRIANS CT
130
121

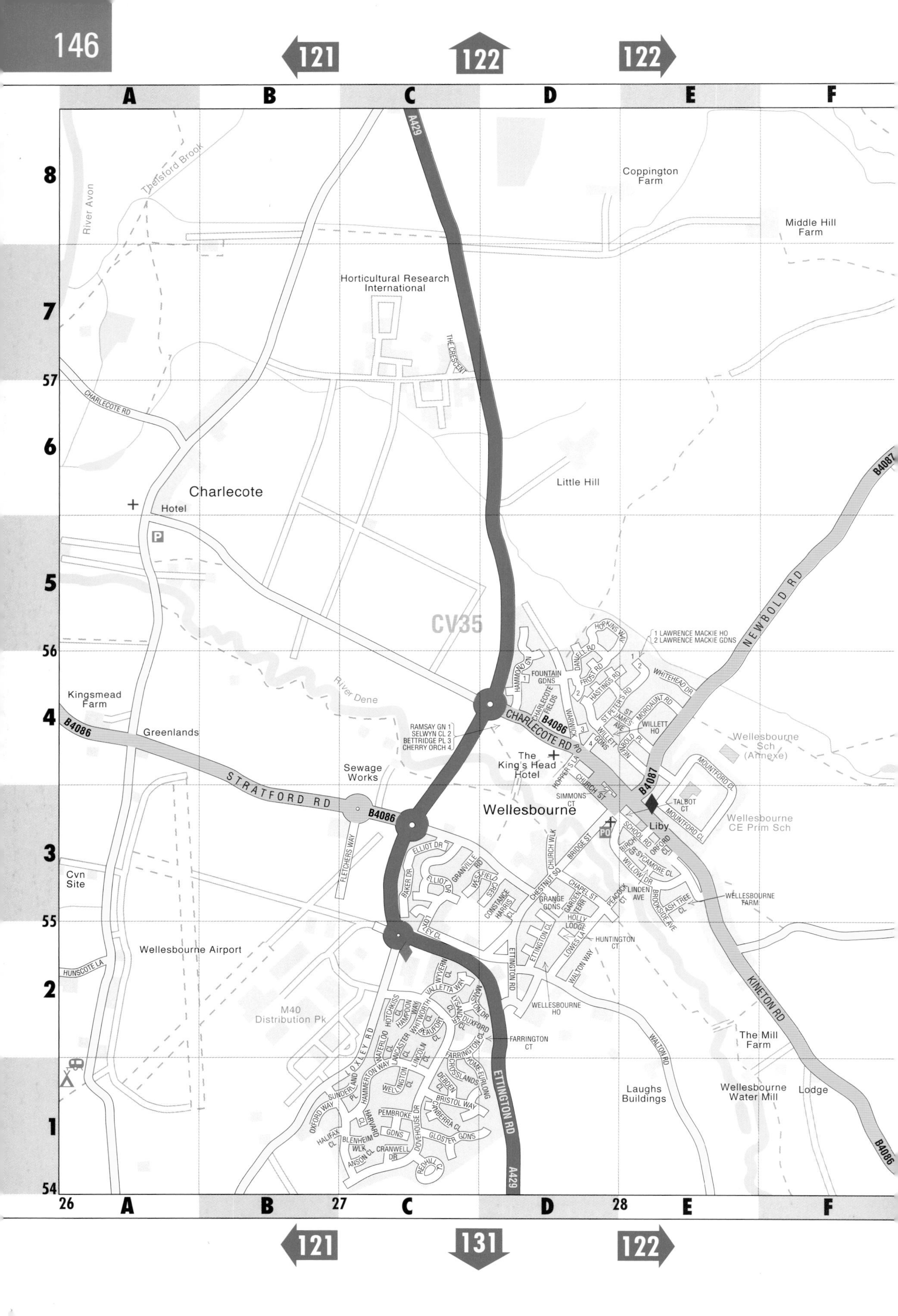
A
B
C
D
E
F
8
7
57
6
5
56
4
3
55
2
1
54
26
27
28
A429
Thelsford Brook
River Avon
Coppington Farm
Middle Hill Farm
Horticultural Research International
THE CRESCENT
CHARLECOTE RD
Charlecote
Hotel
Little Hill
B4087
NEWBOLD RD
CV35
River Dene
Kingsmead Farm
B4086
Greenlands
STRATFORD RD
Sewage Works
1 LAWRENCE MACKIE HO
2 LAWRENCE MACKIE GDNS
HOPKINS WAY
DANELL RD
HAMMOND GN
FOUNTAIN GDNS
FROST RD
HASTINGS RD
WHITEHEAD DR
CHARLECOTE FIELDS
ST PETER'S RD
ST JAMES AVE
MORDAUNT RD
WARWICK RD
WILLETT GDNS
WILLETT HO
NEWBOLD PL
CHARLECOTE RD
RAMSAY GN 1
SELWYN CL 2
BETTRIDGE PL 3
CHERRY ORCH 4
The King's Head Hotel
Wellesbourne Sch (Annexe)
MOUNTFORD CL
HOPPER'S LA
CHURCH ST
SIMMONS CT
TALBOT CT
Wellesbourne
Liby
PO
SCHOOL RD
Wellesbourne CE Prim Sch
ELLIOT DR
GRANVILLE RD
WESTFIELD CRES
FLETCHERS WAY
BAKER DR
CHURCH WLK
BRIDGE ST
BIRCH GR
SYCAMORE CL
OXFORD CL
WILLOW DR
CHESTNUT SQ
CHAPEL ST
Cvn Site
CONSTANCE HARRIS CL
GRANGE GDNS
GARDEN TERR
PEACOCK CT
LINDEN AVE
BROOKSIDE AVE
ASH TREE CL
WELLESBOURNE FARM
OXLEY CL
HOLLY LODGE
ETTINGTON CL
LOWES LA
HUNTINGTON CT
Wellesbourne Airport
HUNSCOTE LA
WYVERN CL
VALLETTA WAY
MANSTON DR
ETTINGTON RD
WALTON WAY
KINETON RD
M40 Distribution Pk
HOTCHKISS CL
HAMPDEN WAY
WHITWORTH
LYSANDER CL
DUXFORD
BEAUFORT CL
WELLESBOURNE HO
FARRINGTON CT
WALTON RD
The Mill Farm
OXLEY RD
WATERLOO
LANCASTER CL
LINCOLN CL
FARRINGTON CL
HOME FURLONG
CROSSLANDS
SUNDERLAND PL
HAMMERTON WAY
WELLINGTON
DEBDEN CL
BRISTOL WAY
Laughs Buildings
Wellesbourne Water Mill
Lodge
OXFORD WAY
HARVARD CL
PEMBROKE GDNS
DOVEHOUSE DR
CANBERRA CL
HALIFAX CL
BLENHEIM WLK
GLOSTER GDNS
ANSON CL
CRANWELL DR
REDHILL CL
A429

115
115
116
A
B
C
D
E
F
A423
A426
A425
A423
Chy
Stockton
The Grey House
SOUTHAM RD
Southam Fields Farm
Quarry
Griffin's Farm
Rectory Farm
COVENTRY RD
MOUNT PLEASANT
TUCKWELL CL
HIGH ST
ELM ROW
GEORGE ST
VICTORIA TERR
NAPTON RD
POST OFFICE LA
ORCHARD GR
GRANGE FARM DR
THE SQUARE
SYCAMORE CL
LAUREL DR
BECK'S LA
SCHOOL ST
MANOR RD
CHURCH ST
RECTORY CL
ST MICHAEL'S CRES
GLEBE CL
EARLES CL
Stockton Prim Sch
Recn Gd
Cemy
PLOUGHMANS HOLT
LINLEY RD
MERESTOWE CL
SYCAMORE GR
CHERRY TREE WLK
ORCHARD WAY
LIME RD
PINE TREE CRES
TOLL GATE RD
ASH GR
THE FURROWS
SPRINGFIELD GR
MAYFIELD RD
Southam Coll
L Ctr
SPRINGS CRES
GRANGE CL
Sch
1 HEATHER CL
2 RED LION CL
OLD FORD AVE
BASCOTE RISE
WINDMILL WAY
WELSH RD W
HILLTOP CL
MILL RD
GORSE LEA
GLEBE RD
HILLYARD RD
MILL CRES
MILL CL
ST JAMES CRES
ST JAMES RD
TOMWELL CL
CHESTNUT PL
COVENTRY ST
MEADOW RD
ST MARY'S CL
ST WULSTAN WAY
CV47
Glebe Farm
HERDWYCKE CL
CALCUTT MDW
Napton Road Farm
Lower Farm
Myer Bridge
Myer-Bridge Farm
River Stowe
DAVENTRY RD
HOLYWELL RD
WATTON'S LODGE
PARKFIELDS
LITTLE PARK
PARK LA
Ct
THE CLOISTERS
WOOD ST
Sch
Liby
Sewage Works
Southam
River Stowe
WARWICK ST
MARKET HILL
OXFORD ST
PENDICKE ST
SCHOOL ST
POUND WAY
HOLT LEYS
ROMAN WAY
DROVERS WAY
SHEPHERDS HILL
NAPTON RISE
WELSH RD E
MILLHOLME CL
LIVING FIELDS RD
BARKUS CL
RAINSBROOK CL
PRIORS MDW
WILLOW GDNS
TATTLE BANK
BRIDGE END
SPIRE BANK
STOWE DR
BROWN'S BRIDGE RD
ELMBANK
BANBURY RD
BRIDGE CT
The Bailiffs House
Southam Fields
WATERGALL CL
HODNELL DR
ASCOTE WAY
STONETON CL
RADBOURNE CL
BERRY LA
NEWSTEAD DR
WARWICK RD
KINETON RD
BEECH CL
TUDOR LA
ELM CL
ABBEY LA
ABBEY CL
HURST RD
OLD RD
LEAMINGTON RD
A425
NORTHFIELD RD
B4451
Gainsborough Trad Est
BOURNE END
Kineton Road Ind Est
WESTFIELD RD
Cobalt Ctr
KINETON RD
SOUTHAM DR
SOUTHFIELD RD
Home Farm
Holt Cottage Farm
Warwick House Ind Pk
Hogs Hollow
WELSH RD E
BANBURY RD
Larkfield House
Highfields
Southam Holt
Starbold Farm
Southam Holt Farm
8
7
63
6
5
62
4
3
61
2
1
60
A
B
42
C
D
43
E
F
B4
1 HORSEWELL
2 VICTOR HODGES HO
3 DAVENTRY ST
4 MOUNTFIELD GDNS
5 THE BULL YD
6 FALCON CT
7 CRAVEN CT
8 PENDICKE CT
9 SOVEREIGN CT
10 CHICKABIDDY LA
11 JAMES MOORE HO
124
124
125

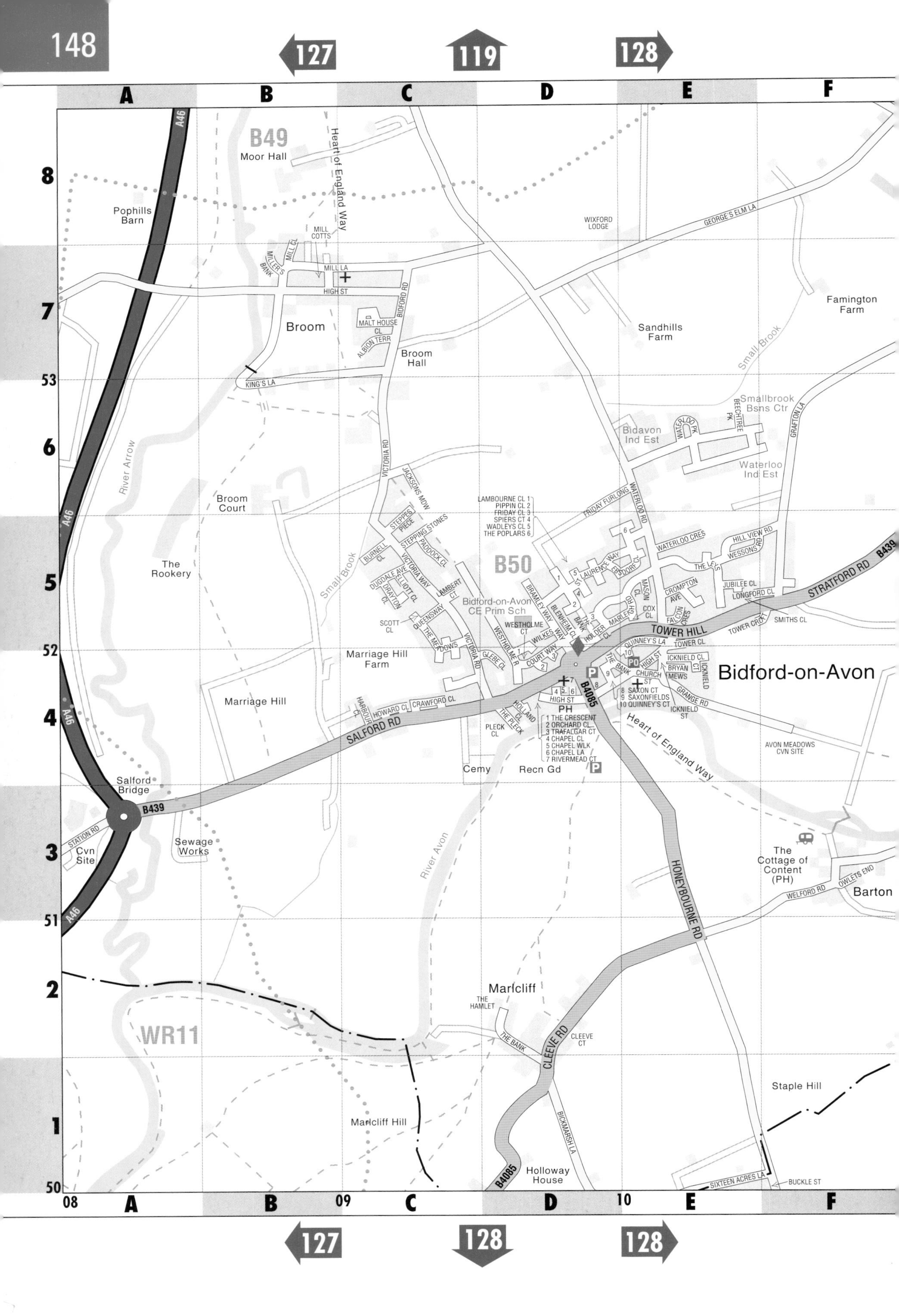
127
119
128
A B C D E F
8 7 53 6 5 52 4 3 51 2 1 50
08 09 10
B49
Moor Hall
Heart of England Way
Pophills Barn
MILL COTTS
MILL CL
MILLER'S BANK
MILL LA
HIGH ST
BIDFORD RD
Broom
MALT HOUSE CL
ALBION TERR
Broom Hall
KING'S LA
WIXFORD LODGE
GEORGE'S ELM LA
Sandhills Farm
Famington Farm
Small Brook
Smallbrook Bsns Ctr
BEECHTREE PK
GRAFTON LA
WATERLOO PK
Bidavon Ind Est
Waterloo Ind Est
River Arrow
A46
VICTORIA RD
JACKSONS MDW
Broom Court
STEPPES PIECE
STEPPING STONES
PADDOCK CL
BURNELL CL
DUGDALE AVE
ELLIOTT CL
DRAYTON CL
VICTORIA WAY
LAMBERT CT
QUEENSWAY
SCOTT CL
THE MEADOWS
LAMBOURNE CL 1
PIPPIN CL 2
FRIDAY CL 3
SPIERS CT 4
WADLEYS CL 5
THE POPLARS 6
FRIDAY FURLONG
WATERLOO RD
WATERLOO CRES
HILL VIEW RD
WESSONS RD
B50
LAURENCE WAY
FOSDORF CL
THE LEYS
JUBILEE CL
LONGFORD CL
STRATFORD RD
B439
The Rookery
Bidford-on-Avon CE Prim Sch
BRAMLEY WAY
BLENHEIM CL
MASON CL
CROMPTON AVE
FALCON CRES
COX CL
MARLEY
TOWER HILL
TOWER CROFT
SMITHS CL
WESTHOLME CT
WESTHOLME RD
WILKES WAY
BANK
HOLDER CL
QUINNEY'S LA
TOWER CL
ICKNIELD CL
BRYAN MEWS
ICKNIELD CT
THE BANK
CHURCH ST
HIGH ST
PO
P
Bidford-on-Avon
Marriage Hill Farm
GLEBE CL
COURT WAY
Marriage Hill
HARBOUR CL
HOWARD CL
CRAWFORD CL
SALFORD RD
HOLLAND CL
THE PLECK
PLECK CL
B4085
PH
1 THE CRESCENT
2 ORCHARD CL
3 TRAFALGAR CT
4 CHAPEL CL
5 CHAPEL WLK
6 CHAPEL LA
7 RIVERMEAD CT
8 SAXON CT
9 SAXONFIELDS
10 QUINNEY'S CT
ICKNIELD ST
GRANGE RD
AVON MEADOWS CVN SITE
Cemy
Recn Gd
Salford Bridge
B439
STATION RD
Cvn Site
Sewage Works
River Avon
HONEYBOURNE RD
The Cottage of Content (PH)
WELFORD RD
OWLETS END
Barton
Marlcliff
THE HAMLET
WR11
THE BANK
CLEEVE RD
CLEEVE CT
Staple Hill
Marlcliff Hill
BICKMARSH LA
Holloway House
SIXTEEN ACRES LA
BUCKLE ST

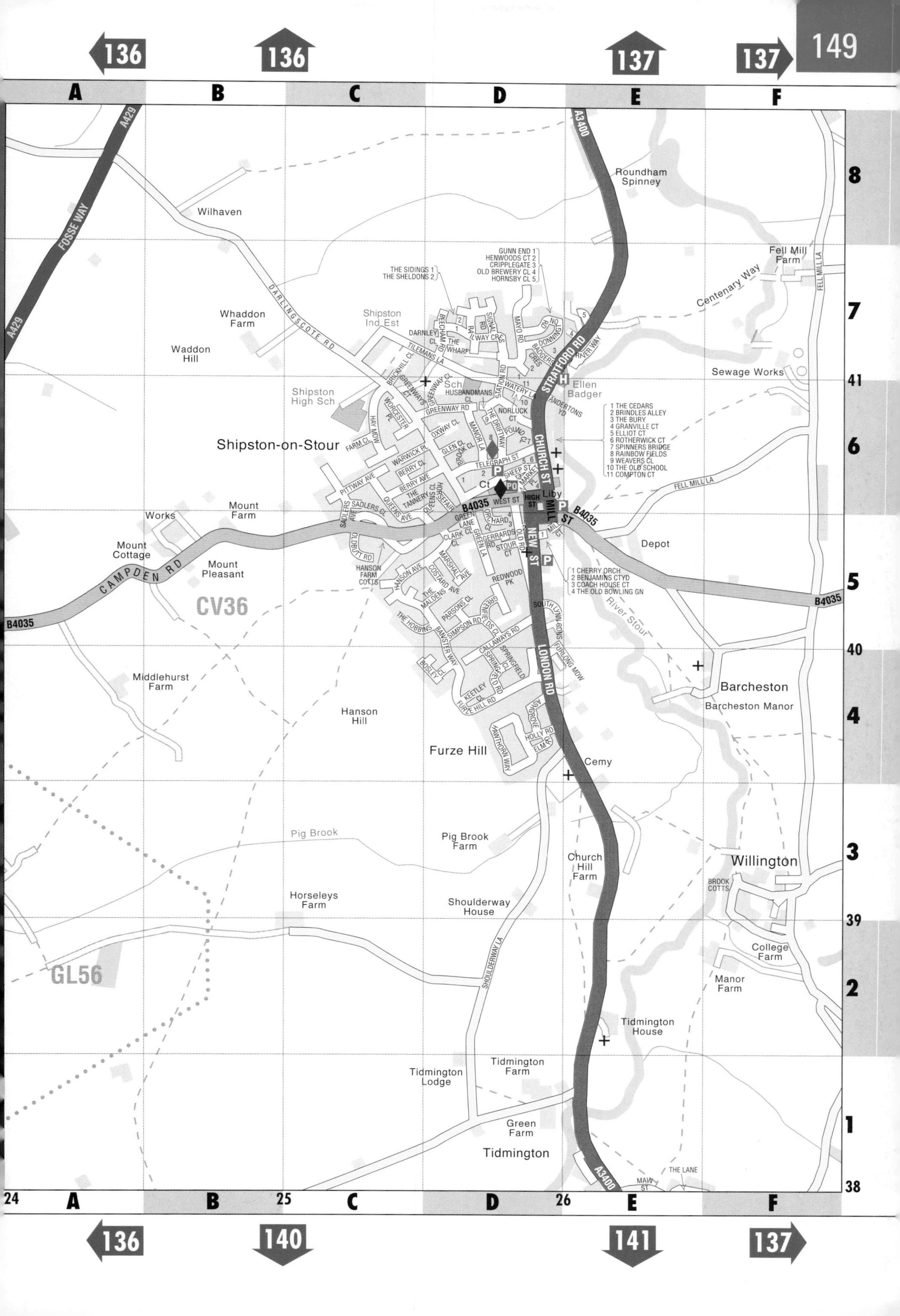
136
136
137
137
A
B
C
D
E
F
8
7
41
6
5
40
4
3
39
2
1
38
24
25
26
A429
FOSSE WAY
A3400
Roundham Spinney
Wilhaven
Fell Mill Farm
FELL MILL LA
Centenary Way
Whaddon Farm
Waddon Hill
DARLINGSCOTE RD
Shipston Ind Est
GUNN END 1
HENWOODS CT 2
CRIPPLEGATE 3
OLD BREWERY CL 4
HORNSBY CL 5
THE SIDINGS 1
THE SHELDONS 2
BEECHAM RD
DARNLEY CL
THE WHARF
RAILWAY CRES
SIGNAL RD
MAYO RD
DONNING RD
BADGERS CRES
STRATFORD RD
RIVER WAY
TILEMANS LA
Sewage Works
Shipston High Sch
BRICKHILL CL
GREENWAYS CT
GREENWAY CL
Sch
HUSBANDMANS CL
STATION RD
WATERY LA
Ellen Badger
ANDERTONS YD
1 THE CEDARS
2 BRINDLES ALLEY
3 THE BURY
4 GRANVILLE CT
5 ELLIOT CT
6 ROTHERWICK CT
7 SPINNERS BRIDGE
8 RAINBOW FIELDS
9 WEAVERS CL
10 THE OLD SCHOOL
11 COMPTON CT
Shipston-on-Stour
WORCESTER PL
HAY MDW
FARM CL
GREENWAY RD
NORLUCK CT
POUND CL
MANOR LA
THE DRIFTWAY
OXWAY CL
GLEN CL
BROOK CL
WARWICK PL
BERRY CL
BERRY AVE
TELEGRAPH ST
SHEEP ST
MARKET PL
CHURCH ST
Ct
PO
PITTWAY AVE
THE TANNERY
QUEENS CL
HORSEFAIR
SADLERS CL
QUEENS AVE
WEST ST
HIGH ST
Liby
FELL MILL LA
Works
Mount Farm
SADLERS AVE
B4035
GREEN LANE
ORCHARD CL
MILL ST
Depot
OLDBUTT RD
CLARK CL
GREEN LA
GERRARDS RD
OLD RD
STOUR CT
MILL CT
Mount Cottage
CAMPDEN RD
Mount Pleasant
HANSON FARM COTTS
HANSON AVE
COSTARD AVE
MARSHALL AVE
REDWOOD PK
NEW ST
1 CHERRY ORCH
2 BENJAMINS CTYD
3 COACH HOUSE CT
4 THE OLD BOWLING GN
CV36
THE MALDENS
PARSONS CL
GREENFIELDS CL
SOUTH LYNN GDNS
River Stour
THE HOBBINS
SIMPSON RD
CALLAWAYS RD
LONDON RD
BANNISTER WAY
SPRINGFIELD
SPRING CL
FURLONG MDW
Middlehurst Farm
BOSLEY CL
KEETLEY CL
FURZE HILL RD
Barcheston
Barcheston Manor
Hanson Hill
ASH GROVE
HAWTHORN WAY
HOLLY RD
ELM RD
Furze Hill
Cemy
Pig Brook
Pig Brook Farm
Church Hill Farm
Willington
BROOK COTTS
Horseleys Farm
Shoulderway House
College Farm
GL56
SHOULDERWAY LA
Manor Farm
Tidmington House
Tidmington Farm
Tidmington Lodge
Green Farm
Tidmington
THE LANE
MAW ST
136
140
141
137

140
141

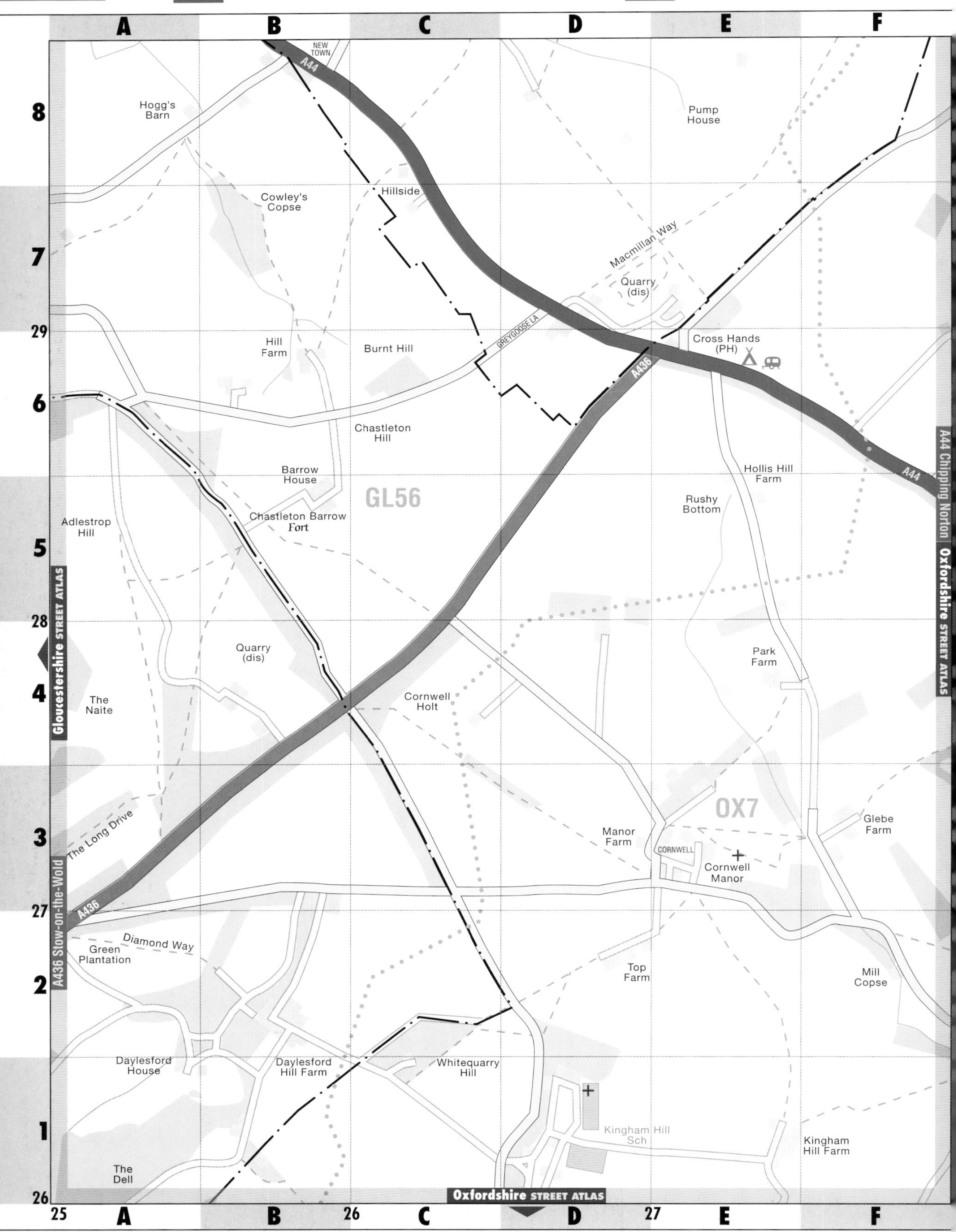
A
B
C
D
E
F
8
7
29
6
5
28
4
3
27
2
1
26
25
26
27
NEW TOWN
A44
Hogg's Barn
Pump House
Cowley's Copse
Hillside
Macmillan Way
Quarry (dis)
GREYGOOSE LA
Hill Farm
Burnt Hill
Cross Hands (PH)
A436
Chastleton Hill
Barrow House
Hollis Hill Farm
A44
GL56
Rushy Bottom
Chastleton Barrow Fort
Adlestrop Hill
A44 Chipping Norton
Oxfordshire STREET ATLAS
Gloucestershire STREET ATLAS
Quarry (dis)
Park Farm
The Naite
Cornwell Holt
OX7
The Long Drive
Manor Farm
CORNWELL
Cornwell Manor
Glebe Farm
A436
A436 Stow-on-the-Wold
Diamond Way
Green Plantation
Top Farm
Mill Copse
Daylesford House
Daylesford Hill Farm
Whitequarry Hill
Kingham Hill Sch
Kingham Hill Farm
The Dell
Oxfordshire STREET ATLAS

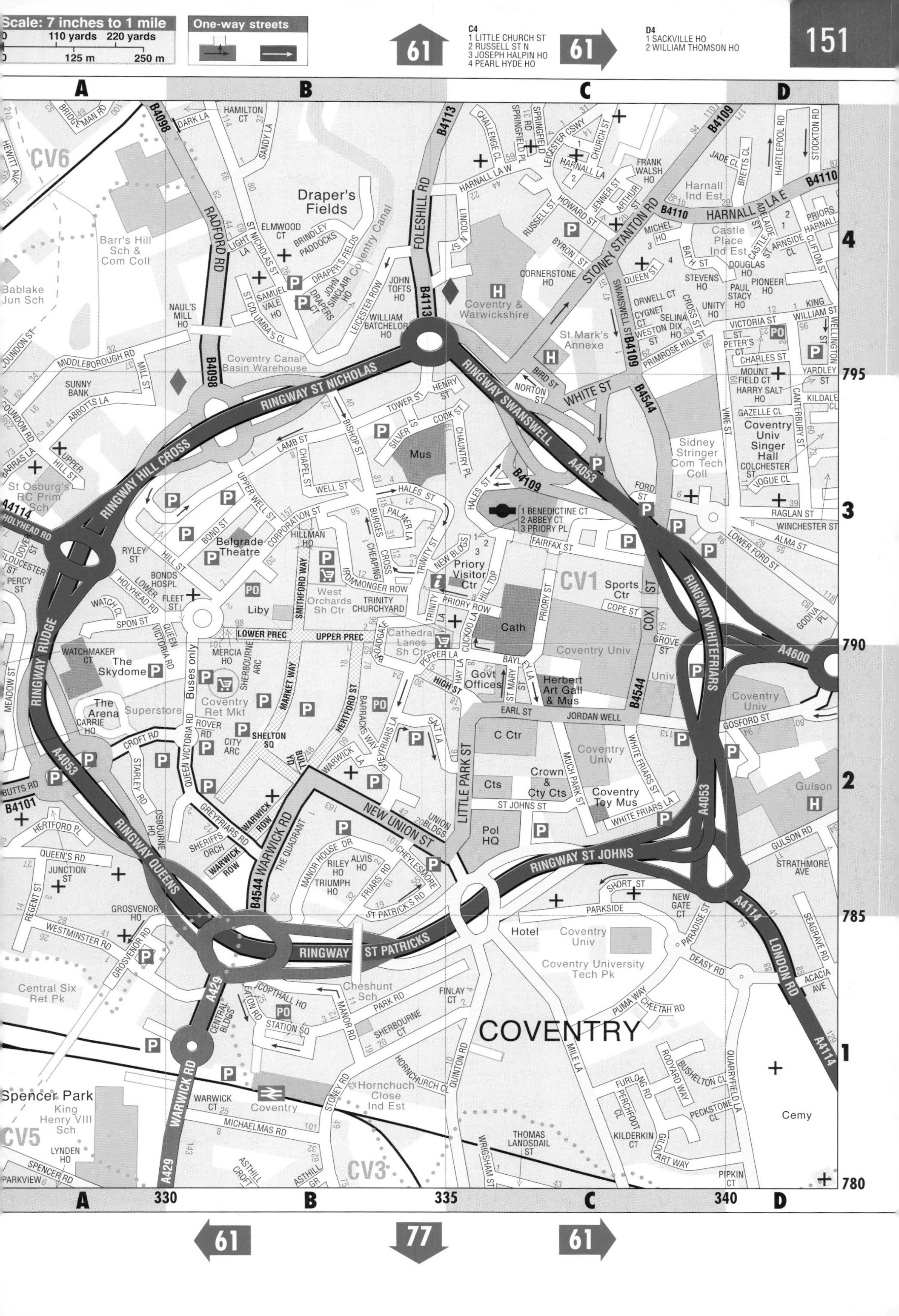

Scale: 7 inches to 1 mile
110 yards 220 yards
125 m 250 m
One-way streets
61
C4
1 LITTLE CHURCH ST
2 RUSSELL ST N
3 JOSEPH HALPIN HO
4 PEARL HYDE HO
61
D4
1 SACKVILLE HO
2 WILLIAM THOMSON HO
151
A
B
C
D
CV6
Draper's Fields
Barr's Hill Sch & Com Coll
Bablake Jun Sch
RADFORD RD
B4098
B4113
FOLESHILL RD
Coventry Canal
Coventry Canal Basin Warehouse
Coventry & Warwickshire
St Mark's Annexe
STONEY STANTON RD
HARNALL LA E
B4110
B4109
Harnall Ind Est
Castle Place Ind Est
RINGWAY ST NICHOLAS
RINGWAY HILL CROSS
RINGWAY SWANSWELL
RINGWAY WHITEFRIARS
RINGWAY ST JOHNS
RINGWAY ST PATRICKS
RINGWAY QUEENS
RINGWAY RUDGE
A4053
A4114
HOLYHEAD RD
A4600
B4544
Mus
Belgrade Theatre
Priory Visitor Ctr
Cath
CV1
Sports Ctr
Coventry Univ
Sidney Stringer Com Tech Coll
Coventry Univ Singer Hall
West Orchards Sh Ctr
Cathedral Lanes Sh Ctr
Liby
LOWER PREC
UPPER PREC
SMITHFIELD WAY
MARKET WAY
HERTFORD ST
The Skydome
The Arena
Superstore
Coventry Ret Mkt
SHELTON SQ
CITY ARC
Govt Offices
Herbert Art Gall & Mus
C Ctr
Crown & Cty Cts
Cts
Coventry Toy Mus
Pol HQ
LITTLE PARK ST
JORDAN WELL
NEW UNION ST
WARWICK RD
St Osburg's RC Prim Sch
Gulson
Hotel
Coventry University Tech Pk
Central Six Ret Pk
Cheshunt Sch
COVENTRY
Coventry
Spencer Park
King Henry VIII Sch
CV5
CV3
Hornchurch Close Ind Est
LONDON RD
Cemy
WARWICK RD
A429
795
790
785
780
330
335
340
4
3
2
1
61
77
61

Index

Place name May be abbreviated on the map → **Church Rd** **6** Beckenham BR2.........**53** C6

Location number Present when a number indicates the place's position in a crowded area of mapping

Locality, town or village Shown when more than one place has the same name

Postcode district District for the indexed place

Page and grid square Page number and grid reference for the standard mapping

Public and commercial buildings are highlighted in magenta **Places of interest** are highlighted in blue with a star★

Abbreviations used in the index

Acad	**Academy**	Comm	**Common**	Gd	**Ground**	L	**Leisure**	Prom	**Promenade**
App	**Approach**	Cott	**Cottage**	Gdn	**Garden**	La	**Lane**	Rd	**Road**
Arc	**Arcade**	Cres	**Crescent**	Gn	**Green**	Liby	**Library**	Recn	**Recreation**
Ave	**Avenue**	Cswy	**Causeway**	Gr	**Grove**	Mdw	**Meadow**	Ret	**Retail**
Bglw	**Bungalow**	Ct	**Court**	H	**Hall**	Meml	**Memorial**	Sh	**Shopping**
Bldg	**Building**	Ctr	**Centre**	Ho	**House**	Mkt	**Market**	Sq	**Square**
Bsns, Bus	**Business**	Ctry	**Country**	Hospl	**Hospital**	Mus	**Museum**	St	**Street**
Bvd	**Boulevard**	Cty	**County**	HQ	**Headquarters**	Orch	**Orchard**	Sta	**Station**
Cath	**Cathedral**	Dr	**Drive**	Hts	**Heights**	Pal	**Palace**	Terr	**Terrace**
Cir	**Circus**	Dro	**Drove**	Ind	**Industrial**	Par	**Parade**	TH	**Town Hall**
Cl	**Close**	Ed	**Education**	Inst	**Institute**	Pas	**Passage**	Univ	**University**
Cnr	**Corner**	Emb	**Embankment**	Int	**International**	Pk	**Park**	Wk, Wlk	**Walk**
Coll	**College**	Est	**Estate**	Intc	**Interchange**	Pl	**Place**	Wr	**Water**
Com	**Community**	Ex	**Exhibition**	Junc	**Junction**	Prec	**Precinct**	Yd	**Yard**

Index of localities, towns and villages

A

Abbey Fields 92 E5
Abbots Morton 118 A2
Abbot's Salford 127 E5
Admington 130 A1
Alcester 143 D3
Alderman's Green 50 B3
Alderminster 130 D3
Alkerton 138 F5
Allen End 13 F6
Allesley 60 B7
Alne End 119 D6
Alne Hills 119 D7
Alvecote 4 D6
Alveston 121 D3
Amington 4 B4
Ansley 27 B3
Ansley Common 27 F8
Ansty 51 D4
Appleby Magna 3 E8
Appleby Parva 3 D6
Appletree 134 E4
Ardens Grafton 119 D1
Arlescote 133 B3
Armscote 136 E7
Arrow 118 F3
Ascott 142 A5
Ash Green 49 C6
Ashorne 122 E4
Ashow 93 E1
Aspley Heath 86 D2
Astley 37 E7
Aston Cantlow 119 F6
Aston Flamville 32 E6
Aston le Walls 134 F5
Aston Magna 140 A6
Astwood Bank 102 F1
Atch Lench 127 B5
Atherstone 18 E8
Atherstone on Stour 130 A5
Attleborough 29 F2
Austrey 3 B2
Avon Dassett 133 C5

B

Bacon's End 33 B4
Badby 126 F5
Baddesley Clinton 90 B6
Baddesley Ensor 11 D1
Baginton 77 F2
Ballard's Green 26 D3
Balsall Common 74 A7
Balsall Street 73 E6
Balscote 139 B4
Banbury 139 E3
Barby 101 D1
Barby Nortoft 101 F6
Barcheston 149 F4
Barford 122 B7
Barnacle 51 B6
Barnmoor Green 113 E3
Barston 57 B1
Barton-on-the-Heath 140 F3
Bascote 115 C2
Bascote Heath 115 B1
Baxterley 17 D6
Baylis Green 86 A1
Bearley 120 E7
Bearley Cross 120 D8
Beausale 91 C2
Bedworth 39 B1
Bedworth Heath 38 E1
Beechwood 75 A6
Beechwood Gardens 76 E8
Belgrave 9 E8
Bell Green 62 B8
Bentley 17 E4
Bentley Bar 17 D2
Bentley Heath 71 E5
Benton Green 58 E3
Berkswell 58 D3
Bermuda 39 A8
Bickenhill 44 D1
Bickmarsh 128 C4
Bidford-on-Avon 148 F4
Billesley 120 A3
Bilton 99 C7
Binley 78 E8
Binley Woods 79 C7
Binton 120 A1
Birch Acre 85 D7
Birchley Heath 17 F2
Birchmoor 10 E8
Birdingbury 115 F7
Birmingham 33 D5
Bishopgate Green 61 D5
Bishops Itchington 124 B4
Bishops Tachbrook 122 E7
Bishopton 144 D6
Black Bank 39 A1
Blackdown 105 F6
Blackwell 136 E6
Blunt's Green 112 F7
Blyth End 24 C2
Bodymoor Heath 15 A3
Bond End 53 E3
Botts Green 25 D5
Bourton on Dunsmore 97 E2
Bouts 118 B5
Box Trees 71 B1
Bradley Green 11 F5
Bradnock's Marsh 57 D3
Bramcote 40 E6
Brandon 79 F5
Branson's Cross 86 C2
Braunston 117 E5
Bretford 80 D7
Bridge End 108 F5
Bridge Town 145 C1
Brinklow 64 E4
Broad Marston 128 F1
Broadwell 116 B4
Brockhurst 53 F3
Broom 148 B7
Broughton 139 E1
Brownshill Green 48 C2
Brownsover 83 C8
Bubbenhall 95 D5
Buckley Green 113 B6
Budbrooke 114 F4
Bulkington 40 B1
Burbage 32 B6
Burdrop 142 D8
Burmington 141 B8
Burton Dassett 133 B6
Burton Green 75 C4
Burton Hastings 41 B8
Butlers Marston 131 F5

C

Caldecote 20 A2
Callow Hill 102 A7
Camp Hill 28 E5
Canley 76 C7
Canley Gardens 76 E8
Carol Green 74 F7
Carpenter's Hill 85 F1
Carroway Head 7 C4
Castle Green 92 D6
Castle Vale 22 B3
Catchems Corner 74 E5
Catherine de Barnes 56 B6
Cathiron 66 A1
Catthorpe 68 E1
Cawston 99 B8
Chadbury 127 A1
Chadshunt 132 C8
Chadwick End 90 B7
Chapel End 28 B7
Chapel Fields 60 E3
Chapel Green 125 C7
Charingworth 136 A2
Charlecote 146 B6
Charwelton 126 D2
Chelmsley Wood 33 C2
Cherington 141 D7
Chessetts Wood 89 D8
Chesterton 123 D5
Chesterton Green 123 C5
Cheswick Green 70 E4
Cheylesmore 77 E7
Chilvers Coton 29 A1
Chipping Campden 135 B2
Chipping Warden 134 F3
Church Charwelton 126 E2
Church End Coleshill 25 C2
Coventry 62 C4
Hook Norton 142 A2
Nuneaton 27 A5
Church Lawford 81 B5
Church Lench 127 A6
Churchover 67 C6
Cladswell 118 C5
Clarke's Green 112 B4
Clattercote 134 B3
Claverdon 113 F3
Claybrooke Magna 43 D6
Claybrooke Parva 43 F4
Claydon 134 B5
Cleeve Prior 128 A4
Cliff 9 C1
Cliff Hill 108 F8
Clifford Chambers 129 F6
Clifton upon Dunsmore 84 A6
Coalpit Field 39 D1
Cock Bevington 127 D7
Cole End 33 E8
Coleshill 23 F2
Coleshill Heath 44 C8
Collycroft 39 A5
Combrook 131 E6
Cookhill 118 D5
Copston Magna 42 C5
Copt Green 113 D8
Copt Heath 72 B8
Corley 48 B7
Corley Ash 48 A8
Corley Moor 47 E6
Cornets End 58 B6
Cornwell 150 E3
Cosford 66 F3
Coughton 118 F7
Coundon 60 F6
Coundon Green 60 E8
Coventry 151 C1
Cowpasture 142 B5
Crabbs Cross 102 E6
Crackley 93 B7
Cranhill 128 E8
Crimscote 130 D2
Cropredy 134 C1
Cross Green 124 A4
Cubbington 106 D6
Curdworth 23 B6

D

Dadlington 21 F8
Dagtail End 102 E3
Danzey Green 112 E8
Darley Green 89 B8
Darlingscott 136 D5
Daventry 117 F1
Dean's Green 112 F7
Deppers Bridge 124 B6
Devitts Green 26 C1
Dickens Heath 70 B6
Dordon 10 F6
Dorridge 71 E3
Dorsington 128 F4
Dosthill 9 C5
Drakes Cross 69 A6
Draper's Fields 151 B4
Draycote 116 A8
Drayton Banbury 139 E4
Stratford-upon-Avon 120 C2
Drayton Bassett 8 D5
Duke End 34 D5
Dunchurch 99 D3
Dunnington 127 E8
Dunsmore 84 C6

E

Earlsdon 61 A1
Earlswood 70 B1
Easenhall 65 E3
Eastcote 56 E3
East End 142 E4
Eastern Hill 102 F3
Eathorpe 115 B8
Eaves Green 46 F2
Ebrington 135 F3
Edgehill 132 F2
Edge Hill 10 C2
Edgiock 118 B7
Edgwick 61 F8
Edstone 120 D8
Emscote 109 B8
Epwell 138 D3
Ettington 131 B4
Exhall Alcester 119 C2
Bedworth 50 B7

F

Falcon Lodge 13 A6
Farnborough 133 F4
Fazeley 8 F8
Fen End 73 E3

Fenny Compton 133 D7
Fenny Drayton 20 A6
Fillongley 36 E3
Finham 77 C3
Finwood 113 F7
Five Ways 114 C8
Flecknoe 117 C2
Flint's Green 59 B5
Foleshill 50 A2
Fordbridge 33 A3
Forshaw Heath 86 C7
Foul End 16 C2
Four Ashes 71 D3
Four Oaks 58 C6
Foxford 50 A5
Frankton 97 C1
Freasley 10 C4
Fulford Heath 69 D2
Fulready 131 C1
Furnace End 25 E4
Furze Hill 149 D4

G

Galley Common 27 E5
Gaydon 123 E1
Gibbet Hill 76 E2
Gilbert's Green 86 E3
Gilson 23 E1
Goodyers End 49 D8
Gosford Green 61 F2
Grandborough 116 E5
Great Alne 119 E6
Great Heath 61 E6
Great Rollright 142 B1
Great Wolford 140 F5
Green End 36 A2
Greenlands 103 A8
Green Lane Coventry 77 B5
Redditch 103 C6
Grendon 11 D3
Grendon Common 11 C2
Griff 39 B6
Grimes Hill 69 B4
Groom's Hill 118 A1
Grove End
Shipston-on-Stour 137 E2
Sutton Coldfield 13 F3
Gun Hill 36 F7
Guy's Cliffe 105 A2

H

Halford 137 A8
Hall End 10 F5
Hall Green 50 A3
Hampton-in-Arden 57 B8
Hampton Lucy 121 F4
Hampton Magna 114 F4
Hampton on the Hill 114 F3
Hanwell 139 F6
Harborough Magna 66 B4
Harborough Parva 66 B2
Harbury 123 E7
Hartshill 19 A1
Hartshill Green 19 A2
Harvest Hill 47 E2
Harvington 127 C4
Haseley 114 D6
Haseley Green 114 D8
Haseley Knob 91 B3
Haselor 119 E4
Hatton 114 E6
Hawkesbury 50 C5
Hawkes End 48 B2
Headless Cross 102 D8
Heath 99 C4
Heathcote 109 D3
Heath End 28 E2
Heath Green 85 F3
Hellidon 126 B5
Henley Green 62 D8
Henley-in-Arden 113 B5
Hidcote Boyce 135 D5
Higham on the Hill 21 B3
High Cross Claverdon 113 F6
Claybrooke Magna 43 A6
Hill 116 B6
Hillfield 71 C7
Hillfields 61 E4
Hillmorton 101 B8
Hill Top New Arley 27 B1
Nuneaton 29 C1
Hill Wooton 105 C6
Hinckley 31 B8
Hockley Coventry 59 C4
Tamworth 9 E5
Hockley Heath 88 D6
Hoggrill's End 24 E4
Holberrow Green 118 A6
Holbrooks 49 C3
Hollyberry End 47 C4
Hollyhurst 50 F8
Hollywood 69 B8
Holywell 113 F5
Honiley 91 D5
Honington 137 A5
Hook Norton 142 D4
Hopsford 52 C5
Horeston Grange 29 F5
Horley 139 D6
Hornton 139 B8
Hungerfield 65 D2
Hunningham 107 F5
Hunt End 102 C5
Hunts Green 14 C7
Hurley 16 C4

I

Idlicote 137 C7
Illshaw Heath 70 E1
Ilmington 136 B6
Ingon 145 D7
Iron Cross 127 E7

K

Kemps Green 88 A1
Kenilworth 93 D5
Keresley 48 F5
Keresley Newlands 49 B6
Kilsby 101 F3
Kineton 132 C6
Kingsbury 15 E5
King's Coughton 143 A7
Kingshurst 33 A5
King's Newnham 81 C7
Kingswood 89 D3
Kingswood Brook 89 E3
Kinwalsey 46 F7
Kinwarton 143 E5
Kitebrook 140 E2
Kite Green 113 C5
Kites Hardwick 116 C7
Kixley Wharf 72 D7
Knightcote 124 B1
Knighton 118 B3
Knowle 72 B6
Knowle Fields 118 C4
Knowle Grove 72 B3

L

Ladbroke 124 D5
Ladyes Hills 93 A7
Langley 113 E2
Langley Green 113 F1
Lapworth 88 E3
Lark Stoke 135 F6
Lawford Heath 98 C7
Lea Marston 24 A8
Leamington Hastings 116 B6
Leek Wootton 104 F7
Lenchwick 127 A2
Lighthorne 123 B2
Lighthorne Heath 123 C2
Lillington 106 C3
Lime Tree Park 60 A2
Little Alne 119 F8
Little Braunston 117 E5
Little Britain 119 D1
Little Compton 141 A1
Little Heath 49 F1
Little Kineton 132 B5
Little Lawford 81 F7
Little Morrell 122 F3
Little Orton 6 F8
Little Packington 45 C6
Little Rollright 141 D1
Little Shreweley 114 C6
Little Walton 54 E3
Little Warton 5 F3
Little Wolford 141 A6
Littlewood Green 103 D2
Littleworth 135 A2
Lodge Green 46 E3
Longbridge 108 C2
Long Compton 141 C3
Longford 49 F4
Long Itchington 115 E4
Long Lawford 82 A4
Long Marston 129 B3
Lower Boddington 134 E7
Lower Brailes 137 F2
Lower Catesby 126 B6
Lower Eastern Green 60 A3
Lower Green 117 A7
Lower Lemington 140 C5
Lower Norton 114 D2
Lower Quinton 129 D2
Lower Shuckburgh 116 F1
Lower Stoke 62 A1
Lower Tysoe 138 C8
Lowsonford 113 E6
Loxley 130 F8
Luddington 129 C7
Lye Green 113 F4

M

Major's Green 69 D8
Mancetter 19 A6
Manor House 50 C2
Mappleborough Green 112 A4
Market End 38 D2
Marlcliff 148 D2
Marston Kingsbury 15 B3
Wolston 80 B4
Marston Doles 125 C5
Marston Green 44 A8
Marston Jabbett 39 E5
Marton 115 C7
Maxstoke 35 B2
Meer End 74 D1
Meriden 46 D1
Mickleton 135 C6
Middle Bickenhill 45 A3
Middle Littleton 127 F1
Middle Stoke 62 A3
Middleton 8 A1
Middletown 103 D1
Middle Tysoe 138 C7
Mile Oak 8 B8
Mill End 93 A6
Milverton 105 D2
Minworth 22 C5
Minworth Greaves 22 D6
Mollington 134 A2
Monks Kirby 53 F2
Monks Park 49 C1
Monkspath 71 B5
Monkspath Street 70 E6
Monwode Lea 26 B3
Moreton Hill 122 F2
Moreton-in-Marsh 140 B3
Moreton Morrell 122 F3
Moreton Paddox 122 F1
Morton Bagot 112 D3
Morton Spirt 118 C1
Mount Pleasant Bedworth 39 B3
Coventry 63 B8
Mousley End 114 B8

N

Napton on the Hill 125 C8
Neal's Green 49 D5
Nebsworth 135 F5
Nethercote 117 B3
Nether Whitacre 25 A6
New Arley 37 A8
New Bilton 82 E3
Newbold on Avon 82 C7
Newbold-on-Stour 130 E1
Newbold Pacey 122 D4
New End Alcester 119 C7
Redditch 118 C7
Newhall Green 36 A1
Newnham 120 B7
Newton 68 A1
Newton Regis 2 D4
No Man's Heath 2 F6
Northend 133 B7
North Littleton 128 A2
North Newington 139 D2
Norton 127 B2
Norton Green 72 B2
Norton Lindsey 114 C2
Nuneaton 29 C6
Nuthurst 88 C4

O

Oakenshaw 102 E6
Offchurch 111 C8
Offenham 127 D1
Old Arley 26 E2
Oldberrow 112 D4
Oldbury 18 E2
Old Milverton 105 B3
Oldwich Lane 73 C1
Onley 100 C2
Orton-on-the-Hill 6 D4
Over Green 13 F1
Overslade 99 E8
Over Whitacre 25 E2
Oxhill 137 F8

P

Packmores 108 E8
Packwood 89 A7
Packwood Gullet 71 E1
Pailton 66 A8
Paradise 61 F6
Park Farm 103 C8
Park Hill 93 C6
Pathlow 120 D5
Paxford 135 E1
Pebworth 128 F1
Piccadilly 15 F8
Pickford 59 E8
Pickford Green 59 C7
Pillerton Hersey 131 E3
Pillerton Priors 131 D2
Pinkett's Booth 59 C8
Pinley 78 B7
Pinley Gdns 78 A8
Pinley Green 114 B5
Pinwall 12 D5
Plough Hill 28 A6
Polesworth 5 B1
Portway 86 A5
Potter's Green 50 E1
Preston Bagot 113 D5
Preston Fields 113 D5
Preston Green 113 C4
Preston on Stour 130 A4
Princethorpe 96 E2
Priors Hardwick 125 D3
Priors Marston 125 F4

Q

Quarry Hill 10 A7

R

Radford 61 B7
Radford Hill 111 B4
Radford Semele 110 E5
Radway 132 F3
Rainsbrook 100 C6
Ratley 133 A2
Redditch 102 E8
Red Hill 120 A3
Reeves Green 75 A8
Ridge Lane 18 B3
Robinson's End 27 F3
Rotten Row 72 C3
Rowington 114 A8
Rowington Green 90 A1
Rowley's Green 49 F3
Royal Leamington Spa 109 C5
Rugby 83 B1
Rumbush 69 E3
Rushbrook 86 D3
Ryton 40 D2
Ryton-on-Dunsmore 79 B2

S

St Helena 11 A8
St Nicolas Park 30 A7
Salford Priors 127 F6
Salter Street 70 D2
Sambourne 118 D8
Sawbridge 117 A4
Scotland End 142 C4
Seckington 2 A3
Shawell 68 D5
Shelfield 112 E1
Shelfield Green 119 E8
Shelford 41 C6
Shenington 138 F5
Sherbourne 121 F8
Sheriff's Lench 127 A4
Shilton 51 F5
Shipston-on-Stour 149 B6
Shirley Heath 70 C7
Shottery 144 C2
Shotteswell 139 E8
Shrewley 114 B6
Shurnock 118 A7
Shustoke 24 F2
Shutford 139 A3
Shuttington 4 F7
Sibford Ferris 142 D7
Sibford Gower 142 D8
Sketchley 31 C6
Sketchley Hill 31 E7
Smockington 42 D8
Snitterfield 121 B6
Solihull 71 B7
Southam 147 B4
South Littleton 127 F1
Southrop 142 D3
Spencer Park 151 A1
Spernal Ash 103 F1
Spernall 112 A1
Spon End 61 A3
Springfield 39 C2
Stareton 94 D3
Staverton 126 D7
Stivichall 77 D5
Stockingford 28 C3
Stockton 147 E8
Stoke 62 C2
Stoke Aldermoor 78 B8
Stoke End 13 F7
Stoke Golding 21 E8
Stoke Heath 62 A6
Stoke Park 62 A2
Stonebridge 45 D3
Stoneleigh 94 B6
Stoneton 125 C1
Stourton 141 D7
Stourton Hill 141 E6
Stratford-upon-Avon 145 B3
Street Ashton 53 E1
Stretton-on-Dunsmore 97 A5
Stretton on Fosse 136 B1
Stretton under Fosse 65 C8
Studley 103 F4
Studley Common 103 C4
Sutton Coldfield 13 B3
Sutton-under-Brailes 141 E8
Swalcliffe 142 F8
Swerford 142 F1
Sydenham 110 D5

T

Tamworth 9 C6
Tanner's Green 69 B1
Tanworth-In-Arden 87 B2
Tatchbrook Mallory 110 A1
Tattle Bank 113 E3
Temple Balsall 73 B5
Temple Grafton 119 E1
Temple Herdewyke 132 E7
Terry's Green 86 F7
The Cape 108 D8
The Hollows 141 C2
The Moors 143 B4
Thimble End 13 A1
Thomas Town 103 E3
Thorpe Constantine 1 E6
Three Maypoles 70 A7
Thurlaston 98 E3
Tidbury Green 69 E4
Tiddington 145 F4
Tidmington 149 D1
Tile Hill 59 E1
Tilehouse Green 71 F6
Tipper's Hill 36 E6
Todenham 140 E6
Toft 99 B2
Tollbar End 78 C4
Tomlow 116 B2
Tredington 136 E6
Trueman's Heath 69 C7
Turner's Green 113 F8
Two Gates 9 D8
Twyford 127 B1

U

Ufton 111 F1
Ullenhall 112 D6
Upper Boddington 134 D8
Upper Brailes 137 E2
Upper Catesby 126 C6
Upper Eastern Green 59 D4
Upper Quinton 129 D1
Upper Stoke 62 B4
Upper Tysoe 138 B6
Upton 119 E4

W

Walcote 119 F5
Walkwood 102 B6
Wall Hill 48 A4
Walsal End 57 A3
Walsgrave on Sowe 63 B7
Walton 131 C8
Wapping 103 E5
Wardington 134 F1
Waring's Green 70 D1
Warmington 133 D2
Warton 5 E4
Warwick 108 E7
Washford 103 E7
Wasperton 122 A5
Water Orton 23 C3
Weavers Hill 102 C4
Weddington 29 D7
Weethley 118 D2
Weethley Bank 118 D1
Weethley Gate 118 D1
Welford-on-Avon 129 B6
Wellesbourne 146 D3
Westington 135 A1
Weston in Arden 40 A3
Weston-on-Avon 129 B6
Weston under
Wetherley 107 C8
Westwood Gardens 76 D8
Westwood Heath 75 E6
Whatcote 137 D7
Whateley 9 F3
Whichford 141 F5
Whitacre Fields 25 E5
Whitacre Heath 24 D6
Whitemoor 93 B5
Whitemore Park 49 C1
White Stitch 46 C3
Whitestone 40 B7
Whitlock's End 69 E6
Whitnash 110 C3
Whittington 12 B3
Whittleford 28 C5
Whoberley 60 D2
Wibtoft 43 B4
Wigston Parva 42 F8
Willenhall 78 D6
Willey 54 E6
Willington 149 F3
Willoughby 117 B6
Wilmcote 120 C4
Wilnecote 9 F8
Wimpstone 130 B3
Winderton 138 A3
Windy Arbour 93 B3
Wirehill 103 B5
Wishaw 14 B2
Witherley 19 B7
Withybrook 52 F5
Wixford 119 B1
Wolfhamcote 117 C4
Wolston 80 B4
Wolverton 114 B1
Wolvey 41 D4
Wolvey Heath 41 E5
Wood Bevington 127 D8
Wood End Coventry 50 C1
Fillongley 37 A4
Tamworth 10 C1
Tanworth-in-Arden 86 F3
Woodloes Park 104 D2
Woodrow 103 B7
Woodshires Green 49 E5
Woodway Park 62 E8
Woolscott 116 F6
Wootton Green 58 A1
Wootton Wawen 113 B1
Wormleighton 134 A8
Wroxall 90 E3
Wroxton 139 D5
Wyken 62 D5
Wyken Green 62 C6
Wykin 21 F4
Wythall 69 B3

Y

Yew Green 114 D5
Yew Tree 74 A6

Index of streets, hospitals, industrial estates, railway stations, schools, shopping centres, universities and places of interest

1st Ave GL56 140 B4
2nd Ave GL56 140 B4
3rd Ave GL56 140 B3
5 Houses The CV23 67 C6
5th Ave GL56 140 C4
6th Ave GL56 140 B4
7th Ave GL56 140 B3
8th Ave GL56 140 B3

A

Abberley B77 4 C2
Abberton Gr B90 71 B7
Abberton Way CV4 76 E3
Abbey CE Inf Sch CV11 29 B5
Abbey Cl
 Alcester B49 143 A5
 Southam CV47 147 B3
Abbey Croft B78 5 A2
Abbey Ct
 Coventry CV1 151 C3
 Coventry,Pinley CV3 78 B6
Abbeydale Cl CV3 62 F2
Abbey End CV8 92 F4
Abbeyfields Dr B80 103 E6
Abbey Gate CV11 29 C4
Abbey Gate Sh Ctr CV11 29 C4
Abbey Gn CV11 29 B5
Abbey Green Ct B78 5 A1
Abbey Hill CV8 92 F5
Abbey Ind Est CV2 62 F5
Abbey La CV47 147 B3
Abbey Mews B49 143 B3
Abbey Rd CV3 78 A6
Abbey St
 Nuneaton CV11 29 B5
 Rugby CV21 83 C4
Abbey The CV8 92 F5
Abbey View B78 11 B8
Abbey Way CV3 77 F6
Abbotsbury Cl CV2 63 A4
Abbotsbury Way CV11 39 E7
Abbots Cl B93 72 A7
Abbots Farm Jun & Inf Schs CV21 83 F1
Abbotsford Rd CV11 29 E1
Abbotsford Sch CV8 92 F6
Abbots Way CV34 108 D6
Abbots Wlk CV8 80 B4
Abbots Wood Cl B98 112 A6
Abbotts Gn LE10 31 F5
Abbotts La CV1 151 A3
Abbotts St 4 CV31 109 F7
Abbotts Way CV21 83 F2
Abbotts Wlk CV3 79 C7
Abeles Way CV9 12 C2
Abelia B77 4 A3
Abercorn Rd CV5 60 E2
Aberdeen Cl CV5 60 A5
Aberdeen Rd CV11 29 E1
Aberfoyle Rd CV35 132 D4
Abergavenny Wlk CV3 78 F6
Abingdon Way
 Birmingham B35 22 A3
 Nuneaton CV11 29 F7
Ab Lench Rd WR11 127 A6
Abu Sultan Rd CV47 132 F5
Acacia Ave CV1 61 E1
Acacia Ct CV6 60 E5
Acacia Gr CV21 83 A4
Acacia Rd
 Nuneaton CV10 28 E5
 Royal Leamington Spa CV32 105 D1
Achal Cl CV6 49 F2
Achilles Cl CV34 109 F2
Achilles Rd CV6 62 A7
Achray Cotts CV23 97 E1
Acklan Gdns B95 113 B2
Acorn Cl
 Bedworth CV12 49 C8
 Stoneleigh CV8 94 B7
Acorn Ct
 1 Royal Leamington Spa CV32 106 A2
 Coventry CV2 62 C2
Acorn Dr CV22 82 B1
Acorn St CV3 78 B8
Acre Cl CV31 110 A4
Acre Ditch OX15 142 D8
Acton Ho CV4 59 F3
Adam Rd 1 CV6 61 F7
Adams St CV21 82 E3
Adams Way B49 143 B5
Adare Dr CV3 77 C8
Adcock Dr CV8 93 B5
Addenbrooke Rd CV7 49 A6
Adderley St CV1 61 E4
Addingham Cl 2 CV34 104 E1
Addison Cl CV10 28 A5
Addison Dr 4 CV37 130 B8
Addison Pl B46 23 B3
Addison Rd
 Coventry CV6 61 A8
 Rugby CV22 82 D2
Adelaide Ct 3 CV12 39 A2
Adelaide Rd CV31,CV32 109 E8
Adelaide St CV1 151 D4
Adkins Croft CV7 36 E3
Adkinson Ave CV22 99 C4
Admington Dr CV35 114 F5
Admington La CV36 135 E7
Admiral Gdns CV8 93 C6
Admirals Way CV11 40 E6
Adrians' Cl CV9 18 F6
Adrians Ct 6 CV37 145 A4
Advanced Tech Unit CV4 76 C6
Agincourt Rd CV3 77 E7
Aikman Gn CV23 116 F5
Ainsbury Rd CV5 76 E8
Ainsdale Cl CV6 50 B4
Aintree Cl
 Bedworth CV12 39 B4
 Coventry CV6 61 E5
Aintree Dr CV32 106 C3
Aintree Rd CV37 144 D1
Airport Way B26 44 C3
Ajax Cl CV21 83 C6
Akon Ho CV6 48 F2
Alan Bray Cl LE10 30 D7
Alandale Ave CV5 59 E4
Alandale Ct CV12 49 C8
Alan Higgs Way CV4 75 C8
Alauna Ave B49 143 C5
Albany Ct CV1 61 A2
Albany Rd
 Coventry CV5 61 A1
 Stratford-u-A CV37 144 F2
Albany Terr CV32 105 E1
Albert Bean Cl CV31 110 A4
Albert Cl B80 103 E4
Albert Cres CV6 49 B3
Albert Fearn Gdns CV6 49 F1
Albert Rd
 Allesley CV5 59 A8
 Fazeley B78 9 A8
Albert Sq CV21 83 B3
Albert St
 Coventry CV1 61 E4
 Nuneaton CV10 28 E3
 Royal Leamington Spa CV32 105 C1
 Rugby CV21 83 B3
 Warwick CV34 108 D7
Albion Cotts B46 23 B3
Albion Ct CV11 29 D3
Albion Ind Est CV6 61 D7
Albion St CV8 93 A5
Albion Terr
 Broom B50 148 C7
 Water Orton B46 23 B3
Albrighton Wlk CV11 30 A2
Albury Rd B80 103 E4
Alcester Gram Sch B49 143 B4
Alcester Heath B49 118 E6
Alcester High Sch Tech Coll B49 143 D5
Alcester Highway B98 102 F8
Alcester Hospl B49 143 C4
Alcester Rd
 Hollywood B47 69 A8
 Portway B47,B48 86 B3
 Stratford-u-A CV37 144 C3
 Studley B80 103 E3
 Wootton Wawen B95 113 A1
Alcocks Rd B49 143 D4
Alcott Cl B93 71 F2
Alcott Hall Prim Sch B37 33 B1
Aldbourne Rd CV1 61 C5
Aldbury Rise CV5 60 C4
Alderbrooke Dr CV11 30 A1
Alder Carr Cl B98 102 F8
Alder Cl B47 69 B6
Alder Ct CV9 12 D1
Alder Dr B37 33 B1
Alderhanger La B94,B98 112 B8
Alder Ho 12 CV34 109 D8
Alder La CV7 74 C5
Alderman Callow Sch & Com Coll CV4 76 A6
Alderman Gee Hall CV12 39 A4
Alderman's Green Com Prim Sch CV2 50 C3
Alderman's Green Ind Est CV2 50 D2
Alderman's Green Rd CV2 50 B3
Alderman Smith Sch CV10 28 D2
Alderman Way CV33 107 D7
Alder Meadow Cl CV6 49 D4
Aldermill Bsns Pk CV9 12 D3
Alderminster Cl B97 102 E4
Alderminster Gr CV35 114 F5
Alderminster Rd
 Coventry CV5 60 A4
 Solihull B91 71 C8
Aldermoor Farm Prim Sch CV3 78 B8
Aldermoor La CV3 62 A1
Alderney Cl
 Bramcote CV11 40 F6
 Coventry CV6 49 B2
Alder Rd CV6 50 A2
Alders Dr B98 112 A6
Aldersgate
 Kingsbury B78 15 D7
 Nuneaton CV11 29 C3
Alders Gr CV34 108 D4
Aldershaws B90 70 A5
Alders La CV10 28 A7
Alders The CV12 38 E2
Alderton Mews 16 CV31 110 C6
Aldrich Ave CV4 59 E2
Aldridge Cl B78 10 F8
Aldridge Rd LE10 31 D6
Aldrin Way CV4 76 D5
Aldwick Cl CV32 106 A4
Alesworth Dr LE10 31 F4
Alexander Ct 1 CV34 108 F7
Alexander Rd CV12 39 C3
Alexandra Ct
 5 Rugby CV21 83 B3
 Atherstone CV9 18 E8
 Kenilworth CV8 93 A4
Alexandra Hospl The B98 103 C6
Alexandra Rd
 Coventry CV1 61 F4
 Royal Leamington Spa CV31 110 B6
 Rugby CV21 83 B4
Alexandra St CV11 29 B4
Alexandra Terr CV6 49 E2
Alexandra Wlk 7 CV21 83 B3
Alex Grierson Cl CV3 78 E7
Alex Stewart Ho CV11 29 E1
Alfall Rd CV2 62 B5
Alfreda Ave B47 69 A8
Alfred Green Cl CV22 83 A2
Alfred Rd CV1 61 F4
Alfred St CV21 82 F3
Alfreton Cl LE10 31 F5
Alfriston Rd CV3 77 C4
Algate Cl CV6 49 C3
Alice Arnold Ho 1 CV2 50 B1
Alice Cl CV12 38 F1
Alice Stevens Sch CV3 78 A6
Alicia Cl CV22 99 A8
Alison Sq CV6 50 B4
Allan Rd CV6 60 F4
Allans Cl CV23 84 A5
Allans Dr CV23 84 A5
Allans La CV23 84 A5
Allard Ho CV3 78 B6
Allard Way CV3 78 C7
Allen Cl B80 103 E3
Allendale Ave B80 103 E3
Allendale Cres B80 103 E3
Allendale Ct B80 103 E3
Allens Cl CV9 17 C8
Allens Orch OX17 134 F3
Allerton Cl CV2 62 E2
Allesley Croft CV5 60 A6
Allesley Ct CV5 60 A6
Allesley Hall Dr CV5 60 C5
Allesley Hall Prim Sch CV5 60 B4
Allesley Old Rd CV5 60 D3
Allesley Prim Sch CV5 60 A7
Allesley Rd CV21 82 F6
Alliance Cl CV11 29 F3
Alliance Way CV2 62 A5
Allibone Cl CV31 110 A4
Allied Cl CV6 49 D2
Allimore La B49 143 A4
Allitt Gr CV8 93 B5
All Saints CE Inf Sch CV12 39 C2
All Saints' CE Jun Sch CV34 105 A1
All Saints CE Prim Sch
 Coventry CV1 61 E1
 Leek Wootton CV35 105 A5
 Nuneaton CV10 29 C1
All Saints Cl CV7 52 F5
All Saints La CV1 61 F3
All Saints Rd
 Bedworth CV12 38 F1
 Warwick CV34 109 B8
All Saints Sq CV12 39 B3
All Souls RC Prim Sch CV5 60 E2
Allwood Cl B49 143 A4
Alma Ct CV11 40 F6
Alma St CV1 151 D3
Almond Ave
 Nuneaton CV10 28 C6
 Royal Leamington Spa CV32 105 F3
Almond Cl CV23 101 C1
Almond Gr
 Rugby CV21 82 E7
 Warwick CV34 105 A1
Almond Tree Ave CV2 50 C2
Almshouses
 2 Warwick CV34 108 E6
 8 Stratford-u-A CV37 145 A2
 Chipping Campden GL55 135 B2
 Leamington Hastings CV23 116 A6
 Rowington Green CV35 90 A1
 Stoneleigh CV8 94 C6
Alne Bank Rd B49 143 D4
Alne Cl B95 113 B4
Alpha Bsns Pk CV2 50 D1
Alpha Ho CV2 62 A4
Alpine Ct CV8 93 A6
Alpine Rise CV3 77 A5
Alspath La CV5 59 F4
Alspath Rd CV7 46 C1
Althorpe Dr B93 71 E3
Althorpe Ho CV31 110 A6
Althorpe Ind Est 15 CV31 110 A7
Althorpe St CV31 110 A7
Alton Cl CV2 50 D2
Alum Cl CV6 61 D8
Alvecote Cotts B79 4 D6
Alvecote La B79 4 D6
Alvecote Pools Nature Reserve* B79 4 E6
Alverley Rd CV6 61 C6
Alverstone Rd CV2 62 A4
Alverton Cl B77 9 C4
Alveston CE Prim Sch CV37 145 E3
Alveston Grange GL55 135 B6
Alveston Gr B93 72 B7
Alveston La CV37 121 D3
Alveston Pastures Cotts CV37 121 E1
Alveston Pl 19 CV32 105 F1
Alveston Rd B47 69 A7
Alvin Cl CV3 62 F1
Alvis Gate 1 OX16 139 F4
Alvis Ho CV1 151 B2
Alvis Ret Pk CV5 61 A3
Alvis Way NN11 117 F2
Alvis Wlk B36 22 F1
Alwynne Freeman Ct CV7 49 A6
Alwyn Rd CV22 99 C6
Alwyn B77 9 E7
Ambassador Ct CV32 105 F3
Ambassador Rd B26 44 C4
Amber Bsns Village B77 4 B3
Amber Cl B77 4 B3
Amber Ct B77 4 B3
Amberley Ave CV12 40 C2
Amberley Ho CV8 93 A3
Ambien Rd CV9 18 D7
Ambler Gr CV2 62 C3
Ambleside CV2 50 E2
Ambleside Rd CV10 39 A2
Ambleside CV21 83 D7
Ambleside Way CV11 29 E6
Ambrose Cl CV21 83 C6
Amelia Cl CV12 40 C3
Amersham Cl CV5 60 B4
Amery Lodge Farm WR11 128 A2
Amherst Rd CV8 92 E6
Amhurst Bsns Ctr CV34 108 B7
Amicombe B77 4 C1
Amington Hall B79 4 A8
Amington Heath Com Sch B77 4 A4
Amington Ind Est B77 4 B3
Amington Pk B77 4 A6
Amington Rd B90 70 A8
Amis Way CV37 145 C1
Amos Ave CV10 29 B2
Amos Jacques Rd CV12 39 A4
Amroth Mews CV31 110 C6
Amy Cl CV6 49 F4
Anchor La
 Harvington WR11 127 D3
 Harvington WR11 127 E3
Anchorway Rd CV3 77 B4
Anderson Ave CV22 100 A8
Anderson Dr CV31 110 A2
Anderton Rd
 Bedworth CV12 38 C1
 Coventry CV6 50 B4
Andertons Yd CV36 149 D6
Andrew Cl CV13 21 D7
Andrews Cl CV8 77 F2
Angela Ave CV2 50 E1
Angel Mews 8 B46 33 F7
Anglesey Ave B36 33 B6
Anglesey Cl CV5 60 B7
Angless Way CV8 92 F3
Angus Cl
 Coventry CV5 60 A4
 Kenilworth CV8 93 C6
Anker Dr CV23 82 B5
Ankerside B78 5 A3
Anker St CV11 29 D3
Anker View B78 11 A8
Anley Way CV6 61 C6
Annandale B77 4 B1
Anne Cres CV3 78 C5
Anne Hathaway's Cott* CV37 144 C2
Annie Osborn Prim Sch CV2 62 D7
Ann Rd B47 69 A3
Anns La CV23 65 C7
Ansell Dr CV6 50 A5
Ansell Way CV34 108 D7
Ansley Comm CV10 28 A7
Ansley Hall CV10 27 D7
Ansley La CV7 26 F3
Ansley Rd CV10 27 E3
Anson Cl
 Rugby CV22 82 C2
 Wellesbourne CV35 146 C1
Anson Ct B78 9 B8
Anson Way CV2 62 F8
Anstey Croft B37 33 A4
Ansty Rd
 Brinklow CV23 64 D5
 Coventry CV2 62 E5
Antelope Gdns CV34 108 C8
Anthony Way CV2 62 C2
Anton Dr B76 22 A6
Antony Gardner Cres 5 CV31 110 A4
Antrim Cl CV5 60 B7
Antrobus Cl CV35 114 C5
Apollo Way CV34 109 D5
Appian Cl B77 9 D7
Appian Way B90 70 D4
Applebee Rd LE10 31 D6
Applebees Mdw LE10 30 E6
Applebees Wlk LE10 30 F6
Appleby Cl
 Banbury OX16 139 F4
 Great Alne B49 119 D6
Appleby Gr B90 71 B6
Appleby Hill CV9 3 B3
Applecross Cl CV4 75 F6
Appledore Dr CV5 59 F5
Apple Gr CV22 82 B2
Apple Pie La CV10 19 B3
Appletree Cl B91 56 B5
Appletree Cotts CV35 89 F1
Appletree Ind Est OX17 134 F4
Appletree La
 Aston le W NN11 134 F5
 Cookhill WR7 118 A3
Appletree Rd OX17 134 F3
Appleyard Cl CV12 39 B2
Approach The CV31 109 F6
Apsley Gr B93 71 F2
Aqua Ho CV32 106 A1
Aqua Pl CV21 83 C5
Aragon Dr CV34 109 D6
Aragon Ho CV3 77 C8
Arboretum The CV4 76 D3
Arborfields Cl CV8 93 B8
Arbor Way B37 33 C1
Arbour Cl
 Kenilworth CV8 93 B3
 Mickleton GL55 135 B6
 Rugby CV22 99 D7
Arbours The CV22 83 C2
Arbour Tree La B93 89 F7
Arbury Ave
 Bedworth CV12 39 A3
 Coventry CV6 49 F2
Arbury Banks OX17 134 F3
Arbury Cl CV32 106 A4
Arbury Ct CV10 28 C3
Arbury Garth CV10 28 C3
Arbury Hall Park & Gdns* CV10 38 D7
Arbury Hall Rd B90 70 D8
Arbury Rd CV10 28 D2
Arbury Wlk B76 22 D5
Arcade The
 Atherstone CV9 18 D8
 Coventry CV3 62 B2
Archer Ave NN11 117 E5
Archer Cl B80 103 D4
Archer Rd CV8 92 E3
Archers Spinney CV21 101 B8
Archery Fields CV34 108 F6
Archery Rd
 Meriden CV7 46 B1
 Royal Leamington Spa CV31 109 E8
Arches Bsns Ctr CV21 83 C5
Arches Ind Est CV21 83 C5
Arches Ind Est The CV5 61 A3
Arches La CV21 83 C5
Arch Rd CV2 62 E5
Arden Ave CV9 18 E8
Arden Bldgs B93 71 F3
Arden Bsns Ctr B49 143 B6
Arden Cl
 Balsall Common CV7 74 B7
 Drayton OX15 139 E4
 Henley-in-A B95 113 B4
 Meriden CV7 46 C1
 Rugby CV22 99 E6
 Warwick CV34 105 A1
 Whitnash CV31 110 B5
 Wilmcote CV37 120 C5
Arden Craft Ctr The B95 119 F8
Arden Croft B46 23 F1
Arden Ct
 Alcester B49 143 B6
 Binley Woods CV3 79 D6
 Hampton-in-A B92 57 A7
 Stratford-u-A CV37 144 F3
Ardendale 6 B90 70 C8
Arden Dr
 Dorridge B93 72 A1
 Sutton Coldfield,Falcon Lodge B75 13 B5
Arden Forest Est CV10 18 B2
Arden Forest Ind Est B49 143 C6
Arden Forest Inf Sch CV12 40 B3
Arden Hill Inf Sch CV9 18 E7
Arden Lawn Sch B95 113 A4
Arden Leys B94 86 D2
Arden Meads B94 88 C6
Arden Mews CV37 120 C5
Arden Rd
 Alcester B49 143 B6
 Bulkington CV12 40 C2
 Dorridge B93 71 F2
 Henley-in-A B95 113 B4
 Hollywood B47 69 A6

Arden Rd *continued*
Kenilworth CV8 . . . . 93 B3
Nuneaton CV11 . . . . 30 A1
Tamworth B77 . . . . 9 F5
Arden Sch B93 . . . . 72 B5
Ardens Cl B98 . . . . 112 A5
Arden St
Atherstone CV9 . . . . 18 E7
Coventry CV5 . . . . 76 F8
Stratford-u-A CV37 . . . . . . 144 F3
Arden Vale Rd B93 . . . . 72 B7
Arderne Dr B37 . . . . 33 A1
Arena Pk CV6 . . . . 49 F3
Argyle St CV21 . . . . 83 C3
Argyle Way 5 CV33 . . . . . 122 F8
Argyll St CV2 . . . . 62 A3
Ariel Way CV22 . . . . 99 D6
Arkle Dr CV2 . . . . 62 F7
Arkle B77 . . . . 9 D4
Arklet Cl CV10 . . . . 28 C5
Arlescote Cl CV35 . . . . 114 F6
Arleston Way B90 . . . . 70 E8
Arley La CV10 . . . . 27 C3
Arley Mews CV32 . . . . 105 E1
Arlidge Cres CV8 . . . . 93 C5
Arlington Ave CV32 . . . . . 105 F2
Arlington Ct 2 CV32 . . . . 105 F2
Arlington Mews 5 CV32. 105 F2
Arlington Way CV11 . . . . . . 29 F2
Arlon Ave CV10 . . . . 28 D7
Armarna Dr CV5 . . . . 59 B8
Armfield St CV6 . . . . 62 A8
Armorial Rd CV3 . . . . 77 B7
Armour Cl LE10 . . . . 31 D5
Armscote Gr CV35 . . . . . . 114 E6
Armscote Rd
Blackwell CV36 . . . . 136 E6
Ilmington CV36 . . . . 136 B6
Newbold-on-S CV37 . . . . . . 136 E8
Armscott Rd CV2 . . . . 62 C6
Armson Rd CV7 . . . . 39 A1
Armstrong Ave CV3 . . . . . . 62 B1
Armstrong Cl
Rugby CV22 . . . . 82 E1
Whitnash CV31 . . . . 110 A2
Armstrong Dr B36 . . . . 22 F1
Arna Ho CV3 . . . . 78 B6
Arncliffe Cl CV11 . . . . 30 A2
Arncliffe Way 4 CV34 . . . 104 F1
Arne Rd CV2 . . . . 63 A6
Arnhem Cnr CV3 . . . . 78 D6
Arnold Ave CV3 . . . . 77 C5
Arnold Cl CV22 . . . . 83 A2
Arnold Lodge Sch CV32 . 105 F2
Arnold Rd CV13 . . . . 21 D6
Arnolds La B46 . . . . 34 E3
Arnold St CV21 . . . . 83 B3
Arnold Villas 9 CV21 . . . . 83 B3
Arnside Cl CV1 . . . . 151 D4
Arran Cl CV10 . . . . 29 A3
Arran Dr B77 . . . . 9 F7
Arran Way B36 . . . . 33 B7
Arras Bvd CV35 . . . . 108 A7
Arrow Cl B93 . . . . 72 A6
Arrow Cres B49 . . . . 143 C5
Arrow End WR11 . . . . 128 A2
Arrow La WR11 . . . . 127 F2
Artemis Dr CV34 . . . . 109 E5
Arthingworth Cl CV3 . . . . . 62 E1
Arthur Alford Ho CV12 . . . 38 D1
Arthur Rd CV37 . . . . 145 A4
Arthur St
Coventry CV1 . . . . 151 C4
Kenilworth CV8 . . . . 93 A5
Artillery Rd CV11 . . . . 40 F6
Arundel Cl 2 CV34 . . . . . . 108 F8
Arundel Pl OX16 . . . . 139 F3
Arundel Rd
Bulkington CV12 . . . . 40 C3
Coventry CV3 . . . . 77 D6
Arundel B77 . . . . 9 C7
Arun Way B76 . . . . 13 A1
Asbury Rd CV7 . . . . 74 B5
Ascot Cl
Bedworth CV12 . . . . 39 B4
Coventry CV3 . . . . 78 C6
Stratford-u-A CV37 . . . . . . 144 D1
Ascot Dr B77 . . . . 9 D4
Ascote La B90 . . . . 70 A5
Ascote Way CV47 . . . . 147 C3
Ascot Rd CV35 . . . . 132 D3
Ascot Ride CV32 . . . . 106 C3
Ascott Hill CV36 . . . . 142 A5
Ascott Rd CV36 . . . . 141 F5
Asfare Bsns Pk LE10 . . . . . 31 E1
Ashborough Dr B91 . . . . . . 71 C8
Ashbourne Way B90 . . . . . . 70 E8
Ashbridge Rd CV5 . . . . 60 C4
Ashbrook Cres B91 . . . . . . 71 C8
Ashbrook Rise CV10 . . . . . . 19 B2
Ashburton Cl LE10 . . . . 32 A6
Ashburton La OX15 . . . . . 142 D3
Ashburton Rd CV2 . . . . 62 E8
Ashbury Ct B95 . . . . 113 B5
Ashby Cl CV3 . . . . 78 F8
Ashby Ct CV11 . . . . 29 D3
Ashby Rd NN11 . . . . 117 E5
Ash Cl CV35 . . . . 114 C5
Ashcombe Dr CV4 . . . . 59 F3
Ash Cres B47 . . . . 85 F8
Ashcroft Cl CV2 . . . . 63 A8
Ashcroft Way CV2 . . . . 63 B8
Ash Ct
Balsall Common CV7 . . . . . . 74 C5
Rugby CV22 . . . . 99 E7
Ashdale Cl CV3 . . . . 79 E7
Ashdene Gdns CV8 . . . . 93 B4
Ashdown Cl CV3 . . . . 78 D8
Ashdown Dr CV10 . . . . 28 F2
Ash Dr
Hartshill CV10 . . . . 28 A8
Kenilworth CV8 . . . . 93 A4
Ash End House Farm★
B78 . . . . 14 B8
Ashe Rd CV10 . . . . 28 B3
Ashfield Ave CV4 . . . . 59 D1
Ashfield Rd CV8 . . . . 93 B4
Ashford Dr CV12 . . . . 39 A3
Ashford Gdns CV31 . . . . . 109 F3
Ashford La B94 . . . . 88 B7
Ashford Rd
Hinckley LE10 . . . . 31 B7
Whitnash CV31 . . . . 109 F2
Ashfurlong Cl CV7 . . . . 74 B6
Ash Gr CV7 . . . . 49 C7
Ash Green La CV7 . . . . 49 D6
Ash Green Mobile Home Pk
CV7 . . . . 49 C7
Ash Green Sch CV7 . . . . . . 49 D6
Ash Gr
Kingsbury B78 . . . . 15 D7
Old Arley CV7 . . . . 26 E2
Ashgrove CV36 . . . . 149 D4
Ash Gr
Southam CV47 . . . . 147 B5
Stratford-u-A CV37 . . . . . . 144 E5
Tamworth B77 . . . . 9 F5
Ashington Gr CV3 . . . . 78 A5
Ashington Rd CV12 . . . . 38 C1
Ash La
Bearley CV37 . . . . 120 E7
Newton Regis B79 . . . . 2 F6
Ash Lawn Ho 8 CV31 . . . 110 A7
Ashlawn Rd CV22 . . . . 100 D7
Ashlawn Sch CV22 . . . . . . 100 E7
Ashlea B78 . . . . 10 F5
Ashleigh Cl CV23 . . . . 101 C2
Ashleigh Dr
Nuneaton CV11 . . . . 29 F1
Tamworth B77 . . . . 9 E8
Ashleigh Mews Cotts B76 23 C6
Ashley Cres CV34 . . . . 109 B6
Ashley Way CV7 . . . . 74 B7
Ashman Ave CV23 . . . . 82 B5
Ashmead Rd 13 OX16 . . . . 139 F5
Ashmore Rd CV6 . . . . 61 B4
Ashmores Cl B97 . . . . 102 D5
Ashorne Cl
Coventry CV2 . . . . 50 C2
Redditch B98 . . . . 103 D8
Ashorne Hall Nickelodeon★
CV33 . . . . 122 F5
Ashorne Hill Management
Coll CV33 . . . . 122 E5
Ashow Cl CV8 . . . . 93 B4
Ash Priors Cl CV4 . . . . 60 B1
Ashridge Cl CV11 . . . . 39 F8
Ashstead Cl B76 . . . . 22 B6
Ash Tree Ave CV4 . . . . 60 A2
Ash Tree Cl CV35 . . . . 146 E3
Ash Tree Gr CV7 . . . . 51 E5
Ashurst Cl CV6 . . . . 50 B5
Ash Way NN11 . . . . 117 D5
Ashwood Ave CV6 . . . . 60 F5
Ashwood Ct CV21 . . . . 82 F3
Ashwood Dr B37 . . . . 33 D3
Ashwood Rd CV10 . . . . 28 E5
Aspbury Croft B36 . . . . 22 D1
Aspects Park Gate CV11 . . 29 F7
Aspen Cl
Alcester B49 . . . . 143 B5
Coventry CV4 . . . . 59 D1
Aspen Ct B95 . . . . 113 B5
Aspen Dr
Bedworth CV6 . . . . 50 C6
Birmingham B37 . . . . 44 C8
Aspen Gr B47 . . . . 69 B5
Aspens The B78 . . . . 15 C7
Asplen Ct CV8 . . . . 93 C4
Aspley Ct CV35 . . . . 114 F6
Aspley Heath La B94 . . . . . 86 D2
Aspley Heath B94 . . . . 86 D2
Assheton Cl CV22 . . . . 99 C8
Aster Cl
Hinckley LE10 . . . . 31 E6
Nuneaton CV11 . . . . 30 A1
Aster Way LE10 . . . . 31 D6
Aster Wlk CV10 . . . . 39 A8
Asthill Croft CV3 . . . . 77 C8
Asthill Gr CV3 . . . . 77 C8
Astley Ave CV6 . . . . 49 E2
Astley Cl
Redditch B98 . . . . 103 A7
Royal Leamington Spa
CV32 . . . . 105 D2
Astley La
Astley CV10 . . . . 37 F6
Bedworth CV12 . . . . 38 C4
Fillongley CV7 . . . . 37 B3
Nuneaton CV10 . . . . 28 B1
Astley Pl CV21 . . . . 101 B7
Astley Wlk CV47 . . . . 133 A7
Aston Cantlow Rd CV37,
B95 . . . . 120 B5
Aston Flamville Rd LE10 . . 32 C7
Aston Hill CV37 . . . . 120 B5
Aston La
Aston Flamville LE10 . . . . . . 32 D7
Hinckley LE10 . . . . 32 A6
Aston Pk Ind Est CV11 . . . . 29 B5
Aston Rd
Chipping Campden GL55 . . 135 B3
Coventry CV5 . . . . 60 F1
Nuneaton CV11 . . . . 29 B5
Astwood Bank Fst Sch
B96 . . . . 102 E2
Astwood La B96 . . . . 102 C2
Atcheson Cl B80 . . . . 103 E4
Atch Lench Rd WR11 . . . . 127 A6
Athena Dr CV34 . . . . 109 E5
Athena Gdns CV6 . . . . 50 A1
Atherstone Ind Est CV37 130 C6
Atherstone La CV9 . . . . 17 B5
Atherstone Rd
Appleby Magna DE12 . . . . 3 E5
Atherstone CV9 . . . . 12 D4
Fenny Drayton CV10,CV13 . . 20 A6
Furnace End B46 . . . . 25 F5
Hartshill Green CV10 . . . . . . 19 B2
Hurley CV9 . . . . 16 D4
Atherstone Sta CV9 . . . . . . 18 C8
Atherstone St B77,B78 . . . . . 9 B8
Atherston Pl CV4 . . . . 76 D6
Atholl Cres CV10 . . . . 28 E2
Atholl Ct CV10 . . . . 28 E2
Athol Rd CV2 . . . . 63 A6
Atkins Way LE10 . . . . 31 E7
Atkins Wlk B78 . . . . 11 A8
Atterton La CV9 . . . . 19 C8
Attleborough Fields Ind Est
CV11 . . . . 29 E3
Attleborough La B46 . . . . . 23 A1
Attleborough Rd CV11 . . . . 29 D3
Attoxhall Rd CV2 . . . . 62 E4
Attwood Cres CV2 . . . . 62 C7
Atworth Cl B98 . . . . 103 B5
Auckland Dr B36 . . . . 33 B7
Auden Cl CV10 . . . . 27 F4
Augusta Pl CV32 . . . . 109 F8
Augustine Ave B80 . . . . . . 103 D4
Augustus Cl B46 . . . . 23 F1
Augustus Dr B49 . . . . 143 B3
Augustus Rd CV1 . . . . 61 F4
Austcliff Cl B97 . . . . 102 D6
Austcliff Dr B91 . . . . 71 C8
Austen Cl CV10 . . . . 27 F5
Austen Ct CV32 . . . . 106 E5
Austen Rd 11 CV37 . . . . . . 130 B8
Austin Cl CV9 . . . . 18 D7
Austin Croft B36 . . . . 22 E1
Austin Dr
Banbury OX16 . . . . 139 F4
Coventry CV6 . . . . 62 A7
Austin Edwards Dr CV34. 109 B8
Austin's Way OX15 . . . . . . 142 E4
Austin Way NN11 . . . . 117 F2
Austrey CE Prim Sch CV9 . . 3 B2
Austrey Cl B93 . . . . 72 A6
Austrey La
Newton Regis B79 . . . . 2 E3
No Man's Heath B79 . . . . 2 F6
No Man's Heath B79 . . . . 3 A5
Orton-on-t-H CV9 . . . . 6 C6
Austrey Rd
Appleby Magna DE12 . . . . 3 D5
Warton B79 . . . . 5 E5
Austwick Cl CV34 . . . . 104 E1
Auxerre Ave B98 . . . . 103 B8
Auxerre Ho B98 . . . . 103 B8
Avebury Cl CV11 . . . . 29 F2
Aventine Way CV21 . . . . . . 82 F7
Avenue Cl B93 . . . . 72 A3
Avenue Farm Ind Est
CV37 . . . . 144 E5
Avenue Farm CV37 . . . . . . 144 E5
Avenue Field Ind Est
CV37 . . . . 144 E4
Avenue Ho CV37 . . . . 144 D5
Avenue Rd
Astwood Bank B96 . . . . . . 102 E1
Dorridge B93 . . . . 72 A3
Kenilworth CV8 . . . . 92 D6
Nuneaton CV11 . . . . 29 D2
Royal Leamington Spa
CV31 . . . . 109 F7
Rugby CV21 . . . . 82 E4
Stratford-u-A CV37 . . . . . . 145 A4
Avenue The
Coventry CV3 . . . . 78 A6
Rowington Green CV35 . . . . 90 A1
Stratford-u-A CV37 . . . . . . 144 D5
Avery Ct 6 CV34 . . . . 108 F7
Aviemore Cl CV10 . . . . 29 A2
Avill B77 . . . . 10 A5
Avocet Cl
Coventry CV2 . . . . 50 B3
Rugby CV23 . . . . 67 C1
Avon Ave CV35 . . . . 138 B6
Avonbank 7 CV37 . . . . 145 A3
Avonbank Cl B97 . . . . 102 C6
Avonbank Dr CV37 . . . . . . 129 E8
Avonbank Paddocks 9
CV37 . . . . 145 A2
Avonbrook Cl CV37 . . . . . 144 D4
Avon Carrow CV47 . . . . . . 133 D4
Avon Cl
Barford CV35 . . . . 122 B8
Bulkington CV12 . . . . 40 B6
Ettington CV37 . . . . 131 B3
Avoncliffe CV37 . . . . 145 F5
Avon Cres
Alcester B49 . . . . 143 C5
Stratford-u-A CV37 . . . . . . 145 D1
Avoncroft Ho B37 . . . . 33 A2
Avoncroft WR11 . . . . 127 D1
Avon Ct
Kenilworth CV8 . . . . 92 F5
Offenham WR11 . . . . 127 D1
Rugby CV21 . . . . 83 A4
Avondale Rd
Brandon CV8 . . . . 79 F5
Coventry CV5 . . . . 77 A8
Royal Leamington Spa
CV32 . . . . 106 C4
Avon Dassett Rd CV47 . . . 133 D6
Avonfields Cl CV37 . . . . . . 121 D3
Avon Fields CV37 . . . . 131 B3
Avon Ho CV4 . . . . 76 C6
Avonhurst CV37 . . . . 145 E4
Avon Ind Est
Rugby CV21 . . . . 83 C5
Stratford-u-A CV37 . . . . . . 144 F4
Avonlea Rise CV32 . . . . . . 105 D2
Avon Lodge CV11 . . . . 29 A5
Avonmeadow Cl 8 CV37 144 F1
Avon Meadows Cvn Site
B50 . . . . 148 F4
Avonmere CV21 . . . . 82 E7
Avon Mill 21 CV37 . . . . 145 A3
Avon Park Cvn Pk B92 . . . . 44 D1
Avon Rd
Coventry CV4 . . . . 76 B6
Kenilworth CV8 . . . . 92 E3
Lighthorne Heath CV33 . . . 123 D2
Whitnash CV31 . . . . 110 A3
Avonside Cvn Pk CV37 . . . 129 A7
Avonside CV37 . . . . 145 A1
Avon St
Clifton u D CV23 . . . . 83 E4
Coventry CV2 . . . . 62 B5
Rugby CV21 . . . . 83 A4
Warwick CV34 . . . . 109 A7
Avon B77 . . . . 10 A5
Avon Terr CV8 . . . . 95 C6
Avon Valley Sch The CV21. 82 E6
Avon Way CV35 . . . . 138 B6
Avon Wlk LE10 . . . . 31 A8
Avro Way B35 . . . . 22 B2
Awson St CV6 . . . . 61 F6
Axholme Rd CV2 . . . . 62 E4
Axminster Cl CV11 . . . . 29 F5
Aylesbury Cl B94 . . . . 88 C6
Aylesbury Rd B94 . . . . 88 D7
Aylesdene Ct CV5 . . . . 76 F8
Aylesford Ct 7 CV31 . . . . 110 A6
Aylesford Dr B37 . . . . 44 A7
Aylesford Sch & Language
Coll CV34 . . . . 108 C4
Aylesford St
Coventry CV1 . . . . 61 E4
Royal Leamington Spa
CV31 . . . . 110 A6
Aylstone Cl CV37 . . . . 129 D2
Aynho Cl CV5 . . . . 60 A3
Aysgarth Cl CV11 . . . . 30 A2
Azalea Cl LE10 . . . . 31 E5
Azalea Dr LE10 . . . . 31 E6
Azalea Wlk LE10 . . . . 31 E5

B

Babbacombe Rd CV3 . . . . . 77 D5
Bablake Cl CV6 . . . . 60 F8
Bablake Jun Sch CV1 . . . 151 A4
Bablake Sch CV1 . . . . 61 B4
Bachelors Bench CV9 . . . . 18 D7
Back Ends GL55 . . . . 135 B2
Back Hill OX17 . . . . 139 E8
Back La
Birdingbury CV23 . . . . 115 F7
Claverdon CV35 . . . . 114 A6
Claybrooke Magna LE17 . . . 43 E6
Cleeve Prior WR11 . . . . . . 128 A4
Harborough Magna CV23 . . 66 B3
Henley-in-A B95 . . . . 113 B5
Long Compton CV36 . . . . . 141 D3
Long Lawford CV23 . . . . 82 A4
Lower Quinton CV37 . . . . . 129 E2
Meriden CV7 . . . . 58 E5
Mickleton GL55 . . . . 135 B6
Middle Tysoe CV35 . . . . . . 138 B7
Oxhill CV35 . . . . 137 F8
Pebworth CV37 . . . . 128 E1
Shustoke B46 . . . . 24 F2
Sibford Ferris OX15 . . . . . 142 D8
Solihull B90 . . . . 70 A5
Warwick CV34 . . . . 108 E6
Backside La OX15 . . . . 142 D8
Back St
Ilmington CV36 . . . . 136 B6
Nuneaton CV11 . . . . 29 C5
Badbury Cl B80 . . . . 103 D4
Badbury Gdns B80 . . . . . . 103 D4
Badby Leys CV22 . . . . 99 F7
Badby Sch NN11 . . . . 126 F6
Baddesley Clinton★ B93 . . 89 F4
Baddesley Cl CV31 . . . . . . 110 C5
Badger Brook La B96 . . . 102 D1
Badger Cl B90 . . . . 70 D4
Badger Rd CV3 . . . . 78 D8
Badgers Cres CV36 . . . . . . 149 D7
Badgers Field GL55 . . . . . 135 B2
Badgers La CV35 . . . . 138 C8
Baffin Cl CV22 . . . . 82 E1
Baginton Fields Sch CV3 . 78 B4
Baginton Rd
Birmingham B35 . . . . 22 B4
Coventry CV3 . . . . 77 C5
Bagot Way CV34 . . . . 109 E3
Bagshaw Cl CV8 . . . . 79 A1
Bailey Ave B77 . . . . 9 F5
Bailey Rd CV37 . . . . 129 B1
Bailey's La CV23 . . . . 82 A4
Bakehouse La
Chadwick End B93 . . . . 90 B6
Nether Whitacre B46 . . . . . . 24 F6
Rugby CV21 . . . . 82 F3
Shotteswell OX17 . . . . 139 E8
Baker Ave
Royal Leamington Spa
CV31 . . . . 109 F6
Baker Ave *continued*
Stratford-u-A CV37 . . . . . . 144 D3
Baker Dr CV35 . . . . 146 C3
Bakers Croft CV9 . . . . 11 C1
Bakers Ct CV9 . . . . 18 D8
Baker's Hill GL55 . . . . 135 C5
Bakers La
Coventry CV5 . . . . 60 E2
Dorridge B93 . . . . 72 D1
Swalcliffe OX15 . . . . 142 F8
Bakers Mews B93 . . . . 90 B6
Baker St CV6 . . . . 50 B6
Bakers Wlk 1 B77 . . . . 9 F6
Bakewell Cl CV3 . . . . 78 F8
Balcombe Ct CV22 . . . . . . 100 E8
Balcombe Rd CV22 . . . . . . 100 D8
Balding Cl CV23 . . . . 101 C1
Baldwin Croft CV6 . . . . 50 B1
Baldwins La CV35 . . . . 138 B6
Balfour Cl LE10 . . . . 31 E7
Ballantine Rd CV6 . . . . 61 B6
Ballards Cl GL55 . . . . 135 B6
Ballards La CV36 . . . . 136 B6
Ballard Wlk B37 . . . . 33 A6
Ballingham Cl CV4 . . . . 60 A2
Balliol Rd
Coventry CV2 . . . . 62 C4
Hinckley LE10 . . . . 31 F6
Balmoral Ave
Banbury OX16 . . . . 139 F2
Banbury OX16 . . . . 139 F3
Balmoral Cl CV2 . . . . 62 E6
Balmoral Ct CV10 . . . . 28 E5
Balmoral Rd B36 . . . . 33 A7
Balmoral Way CV32 . . . . . 106 C6
Balsall Common Prim Sch
CV7 . . . . 74 B5
Balsall St E CV7 . . . . 74 B5
Balsall St B93,CV7 . . . . 73 D7
Balthazar Cl CV34 . . . . 109 E4
Bamburgh Gr CV32 . . . . . . 105 E3
Bamburgh B77 . . . . 9 C7
Ban Brook Copse WR11 . 127 F6
Ban Brook Rd WR11 . . . . . 127 F6
Banbury Rd
Chipping Warden OX17 . . . 134 F3
Ettington CV37 . . . . 131 B3
Kineton CV35 . . . . 132 C5
Ladbroke CV47 . . . . 124 D3
Lighthorne Heath CV35 . . . 123 C3
Lower Boddington NN11 . . 134 E7
North Newington OX15 . . . 139 E2
Shutford OX15 . . . . 139 A3
Southam CV47 . . . . 147 B1
Stratford-u-A CV37 . . . . . . 130 D7
Swerford OX7 . . . . 142 E1
Warmington OX17 . . . . 133 D1
Warwick CV34 . . . . 109 A3
Banbury St CV35 . . . . 132 B5
Bancroft Pl CV37 . . . . 145 A3
Bangley La
Drayton Bassett B78 . . . . 7 E6
Mile Oak B78 . . . . 8 A8
Bangor Ho B37 . . . . 33 B4
Banister Way CV36 . . . . . . 149 D4
Bank Cl CV35 . . . . 131 F5
Bank Croft CV31 . . . . 110 C5
Bank Farm Ct CV37 . . . . . 128 E1
Bankfield Dr CV32 . . . . . . 105 C1
Bank Rd CV9 . . . . 18 E8
Bankside Cl CV3 . . . . 78 A6
Banks Rd CV6 . . . . 61 A5
Bank St CV21 . . . . 83 A3
Bank The
Bidford-on-A B50 . . . . 148 D4
Bidford-on-A B50 . . . . 148 D5
Lighthorne CV35 . . . . 123 B2
Marlcliff B50 . . . . 148 D2
Stoneleigh CV8 . . . . 94 C6
Bank View CV35 . . . . 131 F5
Banky Mdw LE10 . . . . 32 A7
Banner La CV4 . . . . 59 D2
Banners La B97 . . . . 102 E5
Banning Cnr CV37 . . . . 129 D2
Banquo App CV34 . . . . 109 F3
Bantam Gr CV6 . . . . 49 A3
Bantock Rd CV4 . . . . 59 E2
Barbers La B91 . . . . 56 C6
Barber Wlk CV35 . . . . 114 F4
Barbican Rise CV2 . . . . 62 E2
Barbourne Cl B91 . . . . 71 B7
Barbridge Cl CV12 . . . . 40 C2
Barbridge Rd CV12 . . . . 40 C3
Barby CE Prim Sch CV23 117 E8
Barby La
Braunston NN11 . . . . 117 E5
Rugby CV22,CV23 . . . . 101 B4
Barby Rd
Kilsby CV23 . . . . 101 F3
Rugby CV22 . . . . 100 B7
Barcheston Dr CV35 . . . . . 114 E6
Barcheston Mews CV37 . . 114 F6
Barcheston Rd B93 . . . . 72 A4
Barcombe Cl 7 OX16 . . . 139 F5
Bardley Dr CV6 . . . . 61 C6
Bardon View Rd B78 . . . . . 11 A7
Bardswell Ct
Stratford-u-A CV37 . . . . . . 144 F4
Stratford-u-A CV37 . . . . . . 144 F4
Bards Wlk 16 CV37 . . . . . . 145 A3
Barford App CV31 . . . . 110 B2
Barford Cl CV3 . . . . 78 D8
Barford Rd CV8 . . . . 93 B3
Barford St Peter's CE Prim
Sch CV35 . . . . 122 B7

Barham Cl B90 71 A5
Bari Rd CV35 132 E5
Barker's Butts La CV6 61 A4
Barkers' Butts La CV6 61 A5
Barkers La B47 69 A1
Barkus Cl CV47 147 C4
Barle Gr B36 33 A7
Barley Cl
Henley-in-A B95 113 B4
Rugby CV21 101 A8
Sibford Gower OX15 142 D8
Barley Ct CV32 105 F2
Barley Lea Ho CV3 78 B8
Barley Lea The CV3 78 C8
Barlichway B49 143 D4
Barling Way CV10 29 B1
Barlow Ct B78 15 D6
Barlow Rd CV2 50 D2
Barnack Ave CV3 77 B5
Barnack Dr CV34 104 E1
Barnacle La CV12 40 C1
Barnard Cl
Birmingham B37 33 D1
Royal Leamington Spa CV32 106 C3
Barnbrook Rd B93 72 A7
Barn Cl
Clifford Chambers CV37 129 F7
Coventry CV5 60 C5
Dordon B78 10 F6
Whitnash CV31 110 B3
Barncroft CV36 141 C3
Barne Cl CV11 40 B7
Barn End Rd B79 5 E3
Barnfield Ave CV5 60 B6
Barn La CV23 96 E1
Barn Leigh Dr CV4 75 D6
Barnsley Cl CV9 18 D7
Barnsley Ct CV6 61 D8
Barnstaple Cl CV5 59 F5
Barnwell Cl CV22 99 C4
Baron's Croft CV3 77 E7
Barons Croft CV10 28 C4
Baron's Field Rd CV3 77 E8
Barpool Rd CV10 28 F4
Barrack Cl B75 13 A6
Barracks Gn CV35 130 F7
Barracks La CV35 91 C2
Barrack St CV34 108 E7
Barracks Way CV1 151 B2
Barra Croft B35 22 B4
Barras Ct CV2 62 A4
Barras Gn CV2 62 A4
Barras La CV1 61 B3
Barrats Hill CV36 141 F5
Bar Rd CV3 77 E8
Barrels Pitch GL55 135 B2
Barretts La CV7 74 C6
Barrie Cl CV37 145 C1
Barrington Rd CV22 82 C1
Barr La
Brinklow CV23 64 F4
Higham on t H CV13 21 B3
Barrow Cl CV2 63 B6
Barrowfield Ct CV8 92 F4
Barrowfield La CV8 92 F4
Barrow Rd CV8 92 F4
Barr's Hill Sch & Com Coll CV1 151 A4
Barry Ho CV2 50 D1
Barsby Cl CV9 18 D7
Barston Cl CV6 50 A2
Barston La
Balsall Common CV7 73 D8
Barston B92 57 C1
Catherine de B B91 56 B2
Eastcote B92 56 D3
Bartholomew Ct CV3 78 A6
Bartleet Rd B98 103 E8
Bartlett Cl
3 Warwick CV34 108 F7
Coventry CV6 49 E2
Barton Cres CV31 110 C6
Barton Dr B93 72 B4
Barton Fields CV37 129 A6
Barton Rd
Bedworth CV12 39 A4
Coventry CV6 49 F2
Long Compton CV36 141 B4
Nuneaton CV10 29 C1
Rugby CV22 99 D8
Welford-on-A CV37 129 A6
Barton's Mdw CV2 62 B6
Barwell Cl
Dorridge B93 71 E4
Royal Leamington Spa CV32 105 F3
Basant Cl CV34 109 A7
Bascote Chase CV47 115 C2
Bascote Rd CV47 115 C3
Bascote Rise CV47 147 A5
Baseley Way CV6 49 D4
Basford Brook Dr CV6 49 F4
Basildon Wlk 3 CV2 63 A7
Basin Bridge La CV13 21 C4
Bassett Rd CV6 61 A5
Bateman Rd B46 23 F1
Bateman's Acre S 1 CV6 61 A4
Bates Cl B76 22 B8
Bates La B94 86 F1
Bates Rd CV5 76 E8
Bath Pl 3 CV31 109 F7
Bath Rd
Atherstone CV9 18 E7
Nuneaton CV11 29 C5
Bath St CV1 151 C4
Bath Street Mews 1 CV21 83 B3
Bath St
Royal Leamington Spa CV31 109 F7
Rugby CV21 83 B3
Bathurst Cl CV22 82 E1
Bathurst Rd CV6 61 A6
Bathway Rd CV3 77 A4
Batsford Cl B98 103 B5
Batsford Rd CV6 60 F4
Battalion Ct CV6 49 A1
Battlebrook Dr GL55 135 C2
Battle Ct 8 CV35 132 B6
Baulk La CV7 58 D1
Bawnmore Ct CV22 99 D8
Bawnmore Inf Sch CV22 99 E7
Bawnmore Pk CV22 99 E7
Bawnmore Rd CV22 99 D7
Baxter Cl
Atherstone CV9 18 E7
Coventry CV4 60 A2
Baxter Ct 10 CV31 110 A7
Baxters Gn B90 70 B8
Baxters Rd B90 70 B8
Bayley La CV1 151 C2
Bayliss Ave CV6 50 A4
Bayton Rd CV7 50 B7
Bayton Road Ind Est CV7 50 B8
Bayton Way CV7 50 C7
Bay Tree Cl CV2 50 D1
Bay Tree Farm WR11 128 A4
Baywell Cl B90 71 A7
Bazzard Rd CV11 41 B5
Beacon Cl B49 143 C5
Beacon Rd CV6 49 D3
Beaconsfield Ave CV22 83 A1
Beaconsfield Ct CV11 29 D5
Beaconsfield Rd CV2 62 B2
Beaconsfield St W CV31 110 B8
Beaconsfield St CV31 110 B7
Beake Ave CV6 61 B7
Beale Cl
10 Bishops Tachbrook CV33 122 F8
Birmingham B35 22 A2
Beamish Cl CV2 63 A6
Beanacre OX15 142 D3
Beanfield Ave CV3 76 F4
Bear Cl B95 113 B5
Bearcroft Gdns GL55 135 C6
Bear La B95 113 A5
Bear Lane Cl B78 5 A2
Bearley Croft B90 70 C8
Bearley Gn CV37 120 E7
Bearley Grange CV37 120 D7
Bearley Halt B95 120 D7
Bearley Rd
Aston Cantlow B95 120 A7
Snitterfield CV37 121 A7
Beatty Dr CV22 82 D2
Beaty's Gdns CV32 106 A4
Beauchamp Ave CV32 105 F1
Beauchamp Cl
1 Birmingham B37 33 B2
Sutton Coldfield B76 22 B7
Beauchamp Ct
1 Royal Leamington Spa CV32 105 F1
Alcester B49 143 A6
Beauchamp Gdns CV34 109 B6
Beauchamp Hill CV32 105 E1
Beauchamp Ind Pk B77 9 D8
Beauchamp Rd
Alcester B49 143 C5
Kenilworth CV8 92 F2
Royal Leamington Spa CV32 105 F1
Tamworth B77 9 F5
Warwick CV34 109 B8
Beaudesert Cl
Henley-in-A B95 113 B4
Hollywood B47 69 A6
Beaudesert Ho B95 113 B6
Beaudesert La B95 113 B5
Beaudesert Pk B95 113 A5
Beaudesert Rd
Coventry CV5 61 A1
Hollywood B47 69 A6
Beaufell Cl CV34 104 E1
Beaufort Ave CV32 106 C5
Beaufort Cl
Hinckley LE10 31 E4
Wellesbourne CV35 146 C2
Beaufort Dr CV3 78 F7
Beaulieu Pk CV31 110 D6
Beaumaris Cl
Banbury OX16 139 F4
Coventry CV5 59 F5
Beaumont Ave LE10 31 A7
Beaumont Cl CV47 133 A7
Beaumont Cres CV6 61 A4
Beaumont Ct
8 Royal Leamington Spa CV31 110 A6
9 Coventry CV6 61 A4
Beaumont Pl CV11 29 A4
Beaumont Rd
Keresley CV7 49 A6
Nuneaton CV11 29 A4
Beaurevoir Way CV34 109 A8
Beausale Croft CV5 60 A3
Beausale Dr B93 72 C7
Beausale La CV35 114 E7
Beceshore Cl 2 GL56 140 A3
Beche Way CV5 60 B5
Beckbury Rd CV2 62 F6
Becket Cl GL56 140 E7
Beckfoot Cl CV21 83 D8
Beckfoot Dr CV2 50 F1
Beckford Croft B93 71 F3
Beck's Cl CV47 147 F8
Becks Croft B95 113 B4
Becks La CV7 47 A5
Beck's La CV47 147 F8
Beconsfield Cl B93 71 F2
Bedale Rd CV35 132 D4
Bede Arc 2 CV12 39 B3
Bede Rd
Bedworth CV12 39 A4
Coventry CV6 61 B6
Nuneaton CV10 28 D3
Bedford Cl 7 OX16 139 F4
Bedford Ho B36 33 B6
Bedford Pl 5 CV32 109 F8
Bedford St
Coventry CV1 61 A2
Royal Leamington Spa CV32 109 F8
Bedlam La CV6 49 E2
Bedworth Cl CV12 40 B2
Bedworth La CV12 38 D4
Bedworth Rd
Bedworth CV12 39 F2
Bulkington CV12 40 A2
Coventry CV6,CV7 50 A5
Bedworth Sta CV12 39 C2
Beecham Ind Est CV37 130 C5
Beecham Rd CV36 149 D7
Beecham Wlk CV37 144 C4
Beech Ave B37 33 B1
Beech Cl
Alcester B49 143 D2
Hartshill CV10 28 A8
Hurley CV9 16 C5
Beech Cliffe CV34 108 F8
Beech Cl
Kingsbury B78 15 C7
Rowington CV35 114 A8
Southam CV47 147 A3
Stratford-u-A CV37 145 C2
Beechcroft
Bedworth CV12 38 F1
Long Itchington CV47 115 D4
Beechcroft Rd B36 22 C1
Beech Ct
Royal Leamington Spa CV34 109 E2
Rugby CV22 100 F8
Stratford-u-A CV37 145 B2
Beech Dr
Kenilworth CV8 93 B5
Rugby CV22 99 C8
Thurlaston CV23 98 F3
Beecher's Keep CV8 79 F5
Beeches The
Bedworth CV12 38 E2
Clifton u D CV23 83 F5
Harbury CV33 123 E7
Hartshill Green CV10 19 B2
Polesworth B78 11 A8
Beeches Wlk CV37 145 E4
Beech Gr
Old Arley CV7 26 E2
Warwick CV34 105 B1
Beech Hill NN11 126 B5
Beech Ho
6 Warwick CV34 109 D8
Redditch B98 102 F8
Beechnut Cl CV4 59 D2
Beech Rd
Coventry CV6 61 B5
Hollywood B47 69 B6
Oxhill CV35 137 F8
Beech Tree Ave CV4 60 B2
Beechtree Pk B50 148 E6
Beechwood Ave
Coventry CV5 76 F8
Hinckley LE10 31 D3
Beechwood Cl B90 70 D4
Beechwood Croft CV8 92 F2
Beechwood Ct
Coventry CV5 76 F8
Rugby CV21 82 F4
Beechwood Rd
Bedworth CV12 39 D4
Nuneaton CV10 28 D6
Beehive Hill CV8 92 E7
Beehive La B76 23 C6
Beekes Croft B78 9 A8
Beeston Cl CV3 78 F8
Begonia Cl LE10 31 E5
Begonia Dr LE10 31 E5
Belcony GL56 136 C1
Beldesert Cl B95 113 B4
Belfry Cl LE10 31 D4
Belgrade Theatre CV1 151 B3
Belgrave Dr CV21 83 D6
Belgrave Rd
Coventry CV2 62 E4
Tamworth B77 9 E8
Belgrave Sq CV2 62 E4
Belgravia Ct B37 33 A5
Bellairs Ave CV12 38 E1
Bellam Rd CV35 114 F4
Bellbrooke Cl CV6 50 B1
Bell Brook CV37 121 B6
Bell Cl B36 33 B6
Bell Ct CV32 105 F2
Bell Dr CV7 49 E7
Belle Cotts B94 88 D5
Bellemere Rd B92 57 B6
Belle Vue CV10 28 E3
Belle Vue Terr B92 57 A6
Bellfield B94 87 A2
Bell Green Rd CV6 62 A8
Bell Hill OX15 142 D4
Bellingham B77 4 D1
Bellington Croft 5 B90 71 A6
Bell La
Monks Kirby CV23 53 E2
Snitterfield CV37 121 B6
Stratford-u-A CV37 144 D2
Studley B80 103 E4
Bell Mead B80 103 E4
Bell's La OX15 142 D4
Bells La OX15 137 E3
Bell St
Claybrooke Magna LE17 43 E6
Hornton OX15 139 B7
Bell Tower Mews CV32 105 F3
Bellview Way CV6 50 B1
Bell Wlk CV21 101 A8
Belmont Ct CV32 106 A4
Belmont Dr CV32 106 A4
Belmont Mews CV8 92 F4
Belmont Rd
Coventry CV6 62 A7
Rugby CV22 83 A1
Tamworth B77 9 E7
Belton Cl B94 88 C5
Belvedere Rd CV5 77 A8
Belvoir B77 9 C7
Benches Furlong CV23 67 D1
Benedictine Ct CV1 151 C3
Benedictine Rd CV3 77 C8
Benedict Sq CV2 62 C8
Bengrove Cl B98 103 A7
Benjamins Ctyd CV36 149 D5
Bennet Cl CV13 21 D7
Bennett Ct CV8 79 F3
Bennett Dr CV34 109 C7
Bennett Pl CV36 136 B6
Bennetts Hill Bsns Pk WR11 127 E1
Bennetts Hill WR11 127 E1
Bennett's Rd CV7 48 F4
Bennett's Road N CV7 48 E7
Bennett's Road S CV6 48 F2
Bennett St CV21 82 F3
Bennett Way 9 CV37 130 B8
Bennfield Rd CV21 83 A3
Benn Rd CV12 40 B2
Benn St CV22 83 C2
Benson Rd
Coventry CV6 49 A1
Stratford-u-A CV37 145 A4
Benthall Rd CV6 49 F2
Bentley Cl
2 Banbury OX16 139 F4
Royal Leamington Spa CV32 106 B3
Bentley Comm CV9 17 E5
Bentley Ct
Coventry CV6 49 C4
Nuneaton CV11 29 A4
Bentley Farm Cl B93 71 E4
Bentley Heath CE Prim Sch B93 71 F5
Bentley Heath Cotts B93 71 F5
Bentley La B46 35 C3
Bentley Rd
Bedworth CV7 39 A1
Nuneaton CV11 29 A4
Bentley Way NN11 117 F2
Benton Green La CV7 58 F2
Bentree The CV3 78 B8
Beoley Hall B98 85 C1
Beoley La B98 86 B1
Berenska Dr CV32 106 A2
Beresford Ave CV6 49 E1
Bericote Rd CV32 105 E8
Berkeley Cl
Banbury OX16 139 F4
Nuneaton CV11 29 B3
Redditch B98 112 A6
Berkeley Rd CV8 92 E6
Berkeley Rd N CV5 61 A1
Berkeley Rd S CV5 77 A8
Berkett Rd CV6 49 B2
Berkshire Cl CV10 28 E3
Berkswell CE Prim Sch CV7 58 C3
Berkswell Hall CV7 58 C3
Berkswell Mus* CV7 58 C3
Berkswell Rd
Coventry CV6 50 B2
Meriden CV7 58 C7
Berkswell Sta CV7 74 C8
Berkswell Windmill* CV7 74 D4
Bermuda Bsns Pk CV10 39 A7
Bermuda Ind Est CV10 39 B8
Bermuda Rd CV10 29 A1
Berners Cl CV4 59 E2
Berrills La CV36 141 D7
Berrington Rd
Chipping Campden GL55 135 C2
Nuneaton CV10 28 D7
Royal Leamington Spa CV31 110 B6
Berrow Cottage Homes B93 72 C6
Berry Ave CV36 149 C6
Berry Cl CV36 149 C6
Berryfields CV7 36 E4
Berryfields La CV36,CV37 136 C7
Berry Hall La B91 56 B4
Berry La
Hellidon NN11 126 B5
Southam CV47 147 A3
Berry Mdw CV47 133 E7
Berrymound View B47 69 C7
Berry St CV1 61 E4
Bertie Rd CV8 93 A4
Bertie Terr CV32 105 E1
Berwick Cl
Coventry CV5 60 B4
Warwick CV34 104 E2
Berwick Ho CV8 93 A3
Berwicks La B37 33 B1
Berwood Pk B35 22 A2
Berwyn Ave CV6 49 A1
Berwyn Way CV10 28 C4
Besbury Cl B93 71 E2
Besford Gr B90 71 B6
Best Ave CV8 93 C7
Beswick Gdns CV22 99 D7
Betjeman Rd 10 CV37 130 B8
Bettina Cl CV10 28 B5
Bettman Cl CV3 77 E6
Bettridge Pl CV35 146 D4
Bevan Ct CV3 77 D7
Beverley Ave CV10 28 B4
Beverley Cl
Astwood Bank B96 102 E2
Balsall Common CV7 74 C7
Beverley Rd CV32 105 D1
Beverly Dr CV4 76 D2
Bevington Cres CV6 60 E5
Bexfield Cl CV5 60 A6
Beyer Cl B77 4 A2
Biart Pl CV21 83 D4
Bicester Sq B35 22 B4
Bickenhill Green Ct B92 44 D1
Bickenhill La
Birmingham B37 44 C6
Birmingham B40 44 D4
Catherine de B B92 56 C6
Bickenhill Parkway B37 44 D6
Bickenhill Rd B37 44 B7
Bickmarsh La B50 148 D1
Bickmarsh Lodge Cotts WR11 128 D2
Bidavon Ind Est B50 148 E6
Biddles Hill B94 86 C6
Biddulph Terr CV23 97 D1
Bideford Rd CV2 62 C7
Bidford-on-Avon CE Prim Sch B50 148 D5
Bidford Rd B50 148 C7
Bigbury Cl CV3 77 E5
Biggin Cl B35 22 A3
Biggin Hall Cres CV3 62 B2
Biggin Hall La CV23 98 E2
Bignolds Cl OX17 134 B4
Bigwood Dr B75 13 A5
Bilberry Rd CV2 50 D2
Bilbury Cl B97 102 C6
Billesden Cl CV3 78 E8
Billesley La B48 85 E6
Billesley Rd CV37 120 C4
Billingham Cl B91 71 B8
Billing Rd CV5 60 D3
Billinton Cl CV2 62 E2
Bills La B90 69 F8
Bilton CE Jun Sch CV22 99 D6
Bilton Grange Sch CV22 99 E4
Bilton High Sch CV22 82 B1
Bilton Ind Est CV3 61 F1
Bilton Inf Sch CV22 99 C7
Bilton La
Dunchurch CV22 99 D4
Long Lawford CV22,CV23 82 B3
Bilton Rd CV22 82 E2
Binley Ave CV3 78 F7
Binley Bsns Pk CV3 63 A1
Binley Cl B90 70 A8
Binley Gr CV3 78 F7
Binley Ind Est CV3 79 A8
Binley Rd CV2,CV3 62 D1
Binley Woods Prim Sch CV3 79 E7
Binns Cl CV4 75 F8
Binswood Ave CV32 105 F2
Binswood Cl CV2 50 D2
Binswood Ct 9 CV32 105 F2
Binswood End CV33 123 E7
Binswood Mans 12 CV32 105 F2
Binswood St CV32 105 E1
Binton Bridges Cvn Pk CV37 129 A8
Binton Hill CV37 120 A1
Binton Rd
Coventry CV2 50 D2
Welford-on-A CV37 129 A7
Binton View CV37 144 A4
Birbeck Ho B36 33 B6
Birch Abbey B49 143 B3
Birch Cl
Bedworth CV12 39 D4
Coventry CV5 59 F6
Kingsbury B78 15 D7
Birch Coppice Distribution Ctr B78 10 E4
Birch Croft B37 33 C1
Birch Ct CV34 109 E2
Birch Dr CV22 82 B2
Birch End CV34 109 B8
Birches La CV8 93 B3
Birches The CV12 40 B4
Birchfield Cl CV9 10 C1
Birchfield Rd
Coventry CV6 60 F8
Stratford-u-A CV37 145 A5
Birchgrave Cl CV6 62 A7
Birch Gr
Balsall Common CV7 74 B8
Birchmoor B78 10 D7
Wellesbourne CV35 146 E3
Birch Ho B98 102 F8
Birchley Heath Rd CV10 17 F1

Birch Meadow Cl CV34 . . 108 D7
Birchmoor Rd B78 . . . . 10 F8
Birchtree Rd CV10 . . . . 28 C6
Birchway Cl CV32 . . . . 105 C1
Birchwood Ave B78 . . . . . . 10 F7
Birchwood Prim Sch B78. 10 F7
Birchwood Rd CV3 . . . . 79 C7
Birchy Cl B90 . . . . 69 F6
Birchy Leasowes La B90 . . 69 E5
Bird Grove Ct CV1 . . . . 61 D5
Birdhaven Cl CV33 . . . . . . 123 D2
Birdhope B77 . . . . 4 C1
Birdingbury La CV23 . . . . 115 E8
Birdingbury Rd
Birdingbury CV23 . . . . 115 F8
Marton CV23 . . . . 115 D7
Bird Rd
Lighthorne Heath CV33 . . . 123 D2
Royal Leamington Spa
CV34 . . . . 109 D4
Birds Bush Prim Sch B77 . . 9 E8
Birds Bush Rd B77 . . . . 9 F8
Birds La OX15 . . . . 138 D3
Bird St CV1 . . . . 151 C3
Birkdale Cl
Coventry CV6 . . . . 49 B4
Nuneaton CV11 . . . . 30 A1
Birmingham Bsns Pk B37 44 E8
Birmingham Int Airport
B40 . . . . 44 B4
Birmingham Int Sta B40 . . 44 D4
Birmingham Rd
Alcester B49 . . . . 143 B4
Alcester,King's Coughton
B49 . . . . 143 A8
Allesley CV5 . . . . 59 E7
Ansley CV10 . . . . 27 B4
Burton Green CV8 . . . . 75 A1
Coleshill B46 . . . . 33 E5
Henley-in-A B95 . . . . 113 B6
Kenilworth CV8 . . . . 92 C8
Little Packington CV7 . . . . . 45 E3
Shrewley CV35 . . . . 114 D6
Stoneleigh CV8 . . . . 94 B6
Stratford-u-A CV37 . . . . . . 144 E5
Studley B80,B98 . . . . 103 E7
Water Orton B46 . . . . 23 A3
Whitacre Heath B46,B76 . . . 24 C7
Wilmcote CV37,B95 . . . . . . 120 D6
Wroxall B93,CV35 . . . . 90 D3
Birstall Dr CV21 . . . . 83 D6
Birvell Ct CV12 . . . . 39 D3
Bishop Carpenter CE Prim
Sch Ox15 . . . . 139 D2
Bishopgate Bsns Pk CV1 . 61 D5
Bishopgate Ind Est CV1 . . 61 D5
Bishops Bowl Lakes Water
Sports Ctr* CV47 . . . . . . 124 A5
Bishops Cl 16 CV33 . . . . . . 122 F8
Bishops Cleeve CV9 . . . . 3 A1
Bishops Cl CV37 . . . . 144 C4
Bishop's Ct B37 . . . . 44 E8
Bishops Gate CV47 . . . . . . 124 B5
Bishop's Hill CV35 . . . . . . 123 B2
Bishop's Itchington Prim Sch
CV47 . . . . 124 B4
Bishop's Tachbrook CE Prim
Sch CV33 . . . . 122 F8
Bishop St CV1 . . . . 151 B3
Bishops Wlk CV5 . . . . 77 B8
Bishopton Cl CV5 . . . . 60 B3
Bishopton Hill CV37 . . . . . 144 D8
Bishopton La CV37 . . . . . . 144 C5
Bishopton Prim Sch
CV37 . . . . 144 C4
Bishop Ullathorne RC Sch
CV3 . . . . 76 F4
Bishop Wilson CE Prim Sch
B37 . . . . 33 C3
Bishop Wulstan RC Sch
CV22 . . . . 83 A1
Bisset Cres 12 CV31 . . . . . 110 C6
Bitham Hall CV47 . . . . 133 D5
Bitham Rd CV33 . . . . 123 D3
Bixhill La B46 . . . . 25 A3
Black-a-Tree Ct CV10 . . . . . 28 F5
Black-A-Tree Rd CV10 . . . . 28 E4
Blackbades Bvd CV34 . . . . 108 B4
Black Bank CV7 . . . . 39 B1
Blackberry Ave B94 . . . . . . 88 C6
Blackberry Cl CV23 . . . . 83 D8
Blackberry La
Coventry,Neal's Green
CV7 . . . . 49 C5
Coventry,Wyken Green CV2 . 62 C6
Blackbird Croft B36 . . . . . . 33 A7
Blackburn Rd CV6 . . . . 49 F3
Blackcat Cl B37 . . . . 33 A3
Blackdown Hall CV32 . . . . 105 F6
Blackdown Rd B93 . . . . 72 B6
Blackdown B77 . . . . 4 C1
Blackfirs La B37,B46 . . . . . . 44 D7
Blackford Cl B95 . . . . 113 B4
Blackford Hill B95 . . . . 113 B4
Blackford Rd B90 . . . . 70 C8
Blackford Way CV35 . . . . . 137 F8
Blackgreaves La B76 . . . . . . 14 F1
Black Hall La CV7 . . . . 36 C4
Black Horse Hill DE12 . . . . . 3 F8
Black Horse Rd CV6,CV7 . . 50 B6
Black La CV32 . . . . 106 C2
Blacklow Rd CV34 . . . . 105 A1
Blackman Way CV21 . . . . . . 82 F4
Black Prince Ave CV3 . . . . . 77 E6
Blackshaw Dr CV2 . . . . 62 F6
Blacksmiths Cl WR11 . . . . 127 F1
Blacksmith's La NN11 . . . . 134 F5
Blacksmiths La
Hockley Heath B94 . . . . 88 C6
Mollington OX17 . . . . 134 A2
Northend CV47 . . . . 133 B7
South Littleton WR11 . . . . 127 F1
Blackthorn Cl CV4 . . . . 76 D5
Blackthorn Ct B95 . . . . 113 B5
Blackthorne Rd CV8 . . . . . . 93 A3
Blackthorn Gr CV11 . . . . 29 F2
Blackthorn Rd CV37 . . . . . 145 A5
Blackthorn Way B49 . . . . . 143 B5
Blackwatch Rd CV6 . . . . 61 C8
Blackwell La CV35 . . . . . . 114 F5
Blackwell Rd
Coventry CV6 . . . . 61 E8
Tredington CV36 . . . . 136 F6
Blackwood Ave CV22 . . . . . 82 D2
Blackwood Rd B77 . . . . 9 C7
Blacon Way CV37 . . . . 144 C3
Bladon Cl CV11 . . . . 29 F8
Bladon Wlk 6 CV31 . . . . . . 110 C6
Blair Dr CV12 . . . . 38 D1
Blair Gr B37 . . . . 33 D1
Blake Cl
Nuneaton CV10 . . . . 28 A5
Rugby CV22 . . . . 82 C2
Blakelands Ave CV31 . . . . 110 B6
Blakenhurst WR11 . . . . . . 127 C4
Blake's Hill WR11 . . . . 128 B1
Blandford Ave B36 . . . . 22 E1
Blandford Dr CV2 . . . . 62 F5
Blandford Rd CV32 . . . . . . 105 C1
Blandford Way CV35 . . . . 108 A7
Blanning Ct B93 . . . . 71 E3
Blaze La B96,B97 . . . . 102 A3
Bleaberry CV21 . . . . 83 C7
Bleachfield St B49 . . . . . . 143 B3
Blenheim Ave CV6 . . . . 49 C2
Blenheim Cl
Bidford-on-A B50 . . . . 148 D5
Nuneaton CV11 . . . . 29 F2
Blenheim Cres CV31 . . . . 110 C5
Blenheim Way
1 Moreton-in-M GL56 . . . . 140 A3
Birmingham,Castle Vale B35 22 B2
Blenheim Wlk
Coventry CV6 . . . . 49 B4
Wellesbourne CV35 . . . . . . 146 C1
Bletchley Dr
Coventry CV5 . . . . 60 B4
Tamworth B77 . . . . 9 C8
Blew Gates OX15 . . . . 137 F2
Blewitt Cl B36 . . . . 22 D2
Blick Rd CV34 . . . . 109 C4
Blind La
Berkswell CV7 . . . . 58 D4
Chipping Campden GL55 . . 135 A1
Kenilworth CV8 . . . . 75 F1
Tanworth-In-A B94 . . . . 86 D1
Blindpit La B76 . . . . 23 B8
Bliss Cl CV4 . . . . 59 E3
Blockley Rd CV12 . . . . 39 C4
Blockley's Yd 4 LE10 . . . . . 31 D8
Blondvil St CV3 . . . . 77 D7
Bloxam Gdns CV22 . . . . 82 F2
Bloxam Pl 6 CV21 . . . . 83 A3
Bloxham Rd OX16 . . . . 139 F1
Bluebell Cl CV23 . . . . 83 D8
Bluebell Dr
Bedworth CV12 . . . . 38 E2
Birmingham B37 . . . . 33 E2
Bluebell Wlk CV4 . . . . 59 F1
Bluebellwood Cl B76 . . . . . 13 A3
Blue Cap Rd CV37 . . . . 145 A5
Blue Lake Rd B93 . . . . 72 B2
Blue La CV35,CV37 . . . . . . 130 E6
Blue Lias Ind Est CV47 . . 115 F4
Blundells Croft CV37 . . . . 129 A7
Blundells The CV8 . . . . 93 A5
Blyth Ave CV7 . . . . 74 C5
Blyth Cl
Bedworth CV12 . . . . 38 C1
Cawston CV22 . . . . 99 A8
Blyth Ct CV11 . . . . 29 C3
Blythe Cl B97 . . . . 102 D7
Blythe Ct B46 . . . . 34 A7
Blythe Gate B90 . . . . 70 F3
Blythe Rd
Coleshill B46 . . . . 34 B8
Coventry CV1 . . . . 61 E4
Blythe Sch B46 . . . . 34 A4
Blythe Valley Pk B90 . . . . . 70 F2
Boar Croft CV4 . . . . 59 F2
Boat La CV37 . . . . 129 A7
Bockendon Rd CV4 . . . . 75 E5
Boddington CE Sch
OX17 . . . . 134 E8
Boddington Cl CV32 . . . . . 106 E5
Boddington Cotts CV37 . . 129 D7
Boddington Rd OX17 . . . . 134 B5
Bodmin Rd CV2 . . . . 62 F5
Bodnant Way CV8 . . . . 93 C6
Bodymoor Heath La B76 . . 15 A4
Bohun St CV4 . . . . 59 F1
Boleyn Cl CV34 . . . . 109 C6
Bolingbroke Dr CV34 . . . . 109 E3
Bolingbroke Rd CV3 . . . . . . 62 A1
Bolton Cl CV3 . . . . 77 E5
Bolyfant Cres CV31 . . . . . . 110 A2
Bond Dr B35 . . . . 22 A3
Bond End CV23 . . . . 53 E3
Bond Gate CV11 . . . . 29 C4
Bonds End La OX15 . . . . . 142 D8
Bonds Hospl CV1 . . . . 151 A3
Bond St
Coventry CV1 . . . . 151 B3
Nuneaton CV11 . . . . 29 C5
Rugby CV21 . . . . 82 F3
Boningale Way B93 . . . . . . 71 E3
Bonington Dr CV12 . . . . . . 39 A4
Bonneville Cl CV5 . . . . 59 B8
Bonniksen Cl 7 CV31 . . . 109 F5
Bonnington Cl CV21 . . . . . . 84 B1
Boot Hill CV9 . . . . 11 C2
Booths Fields CV6 . . . . 49 E2
Bordesley Ct CV32 . . . . . . 106 A3
Bordon Hill CV37 . . . . 144 C1
Bordon Pl CV37 . . . . 144 E1
Borough The LE10 . . . . 31 D8
Borrowdale Cl CV6 . . . . 61 A8
Borrowdale Dr CV32 . . . . 105 D2
Borrowdale CV21 . . . . 83 C8
Borrowell La CV8 . . . . 92 E4
Borrowell Terr CV8 . . . . . . 92 E4
Boscobel Rd B90 . . . . 70 D5
Bosley Cl CV36 . . . . 149 D4
Bostock Cres CV33 . . . . . . 107 C7
Boston Pl CV6 . . . . 61 D8
Boswell Dr CV2 . . . . 63 A7
Boswell Gr CV34 . . . . 104 D1
Boswell Rd CV22 . . . . 99 E7
Bosworth Cl CV8 . . . . 77 E2
Bosworth Dr B37 . . . . 33 A2
Bosworth Wood Prim Sch
B36 . . . . 22 F1
Boteler Cl B49 . . . . 143 B3
Botham Ho CV11 . . . . 29 E1
Botoner Rd CV1 . . . . 61 F2
Bottom St CV47 . . . . 133 B7
Bott Rd CV5 . . . . 76 D8
Bottrill St CV11 . . . . 29 B5
Botts Green La B46 . . . . . . 25 C5
Bott's La DE12 . . . . 3 F7
Boucher Cl CV37 . . . . 144 D1
Boughton Leigh Inf Sch
CV21 . . . . 83 C7
Boughton Leigh Jun Sch
CV21 . . . . 83 C7
Boughton Rd CV21 . . . . 83 C6
Boughton Road Ind Est
CV21 . . . . 83 B6
Boulters La CV9 . . . . 10 D1
Boultons La B97 . . . . 102 D6
Boundary La B90 . . . . 70 A6
Boundary Rd E CV37 . . . . 129 C2
Boundary Rd N CV37 . . . . 129 C2
Boundary Rd CV21,CV22 . . . 83 D2
Boundary Rd W CV37 . . . . 129 B2
Bournebrook CE Prim Sch
CV7 . . . . 36 E3
Bourne Brook Cl CV7 . . . . . 36 E3
Bournebrook View CV7 . . . 26 E1
Bourne Cl CV9 . . . . 12 E2
Bourne End CV47 . . . . 147 A3
Bourne La OX15 . . . . 142 D4
Bourne Rd CV3 . . . . 62 C1
Bourne The OX15 . . . . 142 D4
Bourton Dr CV31 . . . . 110 B5
Bourton La CV23 . . . . 115 F8
Bourton Rd
Frankton CV23 . . . . 97 D1
Moreton-in-M GL56 . . . . . . 140 A3
Bouts La WR7,B96 . . . . 118 B5
Bovey Croft B76 . . . . 22 A7
Bovingdon Rd B35 . . . . 22 A3
Bowbrook Ave B90 . . . . 71 A5
Bow Ct CV5 . . . . 76 D8
Bowden Way CV3 . . . . 62 F1
Bowen Rd CV22 . . . . 83 D1
Bowers Croft CV32 . . . . . . 106 A5
Bowes Lyon Cl GL56 . . . . 140 A2
Bowfell Cl CV5 . . . . 60 B4
Bow Fell CV21 . . . . 83 D7
Bow La CV7,CV23 . . . . 53 B4
Bowleys La DE12 . . . . 3 E8
Bowling Green Ave B77 . . . . 9 F7
Bowling Green Ct GL56 . . 140 A3
Bowling Green La CV7,
CV12 . . . . 49 E8
Bowling Green St CV34 . . 108 D6
Bowls Ct CV5 . . . . 60 F3
Bowman Gn LE10 . . . . 31 F6
Bowness Cl CV6 . . . . 61 A8
Bowshot Cl B36 . . . . 22 D1
Box Cl CV31 . . . . 110 B3
Boxhill The CV3 . . . . 62 B1
Box Rd B37 . . . . 44 C8
Box Trees Rd B93,B94 . . . . 71 C1
Boyce Way CV23 . . . . 82 B5
Boyd Cl CV2 . . . . 63 A8
Boyslade Rd LE10 . . . . 31 F6
Boyslade Road E LE10 . . . . 31 F5
Bracadale Cl CV3 . . . . 63 A2
Bracebridge Cl CV7 . . . . . . 74 B6
Bracebridge Rd
Atherstone CV9 . . . . 18 D7
Kingsbury B78 . . . . 15 C6
Bracebridge St CV11 . . . . . . 29 B3
Bracken Cl CV22 . . . . 82 E1
Bracken Croft 1 B37 . . . . . 33 C3
Brackendale Dr
Barby CV23 . . . . 101 C1
Nuneaton CV10 . . . . 28 F3
Bracken Dr
Rugby CV22 . . . . 82 E1
Sutton Coldfield B75 . . . . . . 13 A5
Wolvey LE10 . . . . 41 D4
Brackenhurst Rd CV6 . . . . 61 A7
Bracklesham Way B77 . . . . 4 A6
Brackley Cl CV6 . . . . 60 F7
Bracknell Wlk 1 CV2 . . . . . 63 A7
Braddock Cl CV3 . . . . 63 A1
Brade Dr CV2 . . . . 63 B7
Bradestone Rd CV11 . . . . . 29 D1
Bradewell Rd B36 . . . . 22 D1
Bradfield Cl CV5 . . . . 60 C5
Bradford Cl 6 CV33 . . . . . 122 E8
Brading Rd CV10 . . . . 29 D6
Bradley Arc 12 OX16 . . . . 139 F3
Bradley Croft CV7 . . . . 74 B6
Bradmore Cl B91 . . . . 71 A8
Bradney Gn CV4 . . . . 75 E7
Bradnick Pl CV4 . . . . 59 F1
Bradnock's Marsh La B92 57 E2
Braemar Cl CV2 . . . . 62 E6
Braemar Rd CV32 . . . . 106 B4
Braemar Way CV10 . . . . 29 A2
Braeside Croft B37 . . . . 33 D2
Brafield Leys CV22 . . . . . . 100 A6
Braggington La CV37 . . . . 128 F5
Braggs Farm La B90 . . . . . 70 A4
Braids Cl CV21 . . . . 83 D4
Brailes CE Prim Sch
OX15 . . . . 137 E2
Brailes Ind Est OX15 . . . . 138 A2
Brain St B77 . . . . 4 A2
Brakesmead CV31 . . . . 109 F5
Bramber Cl 13 OX16 . . . . 139 F4
Bramble Cl
6 Coleshill B46 . . . . 33 F7
Nuneaton CV11 . . . . 29 F2
Bramble Ho B98 . . . . 102 F8
Bramble St CV1 . . . . 61 E2
Brambles The B76 . . . . 22 A8
Brambling CV23 . . . . 83 C8
Brambling B77 . . . . 10 A7
Bramcote Cl CV12 . . . . 40 D2
Bramcote Hospl CV11 . . . . 40 E7
Bramdene Ave CV10 . . . . . . 29 D8
Bramley Dr B47 . . . . 69 B6
Bramley Rd CV35 . . . . 132 E6
Bramley Way B50 . . . . 148 D5
Brampton Way CV12 . . . . . . 40 B3
Bramshall Dr B93 . . . . 71 E3
Bramston Cres CV4 . . . . 59 F1
Bramwell Gdns CV6 . . . . . . 49 F5
Brancaster Cl B77 . . . . 4 A5
Brandfield Rd CV6 . . . . 60 F8
Brandheath La B96 . . . . . . 118 D6
Brandon Ct CV3 . . . . 79 A7
Brandon La CV3,CV8 . . . . . . 79 C5
Brandon Marsh Nature
Reserve* CV3 . . . . 79 A4
Brandon Marsh Visitor Ctr*
CV3 . . . . 79 B4
Brandon Par CV32 . . . . 110 A8
Brandon Rd
Bretford CV23 . . . . 80 D6
Coventry CV3 . . . . 79 A8
Hinckley LE10 . . . . 31 B7
Brandon Wood Farm*
CV8 . . . . 79 D5
Branksome Rd CV6 . . . . 60 E6
Bransdale Ave CV6 . . . . 49 D3
Bransford Ave CV4 . . . . 76 D5
Bransford Rise B91 . . . . 56 B5
Branstree Dr CV6 . . . . 49 D2
Brascote Rd LE10 . . . . 30 F8
Bratches The GL55 . . . . . . 135 B3
Brathay Cl CV3 . . . . 77 D6
Braunston CE Prim Sch
NN11 . . . . 117 E5
Braunston Cl B76 . . . . 13 A2
Braunston La NN11 . . . . . . 126 E8
Braunston Pl CV22 . . . . . . 100 D8
Braunston Rd NN11 . . . . . 117 F3
Bray Bank B46 . . . . 25 D3
Brayford Ave CV3 . . . . 77 C6
Brays Cl CV23 . . . . 64 E3
Bray's La CV2 . . . . 62 A3
Braytoft Cl CV6 . . . . 49 C2
Brazil St CV4 . . . . 59 E2
Breaches La B98 . . . . 103 D8
Breach La CV35 . . . . 113 F3
Breach Oak La CV7 . . . . 37 D3
Bream Cl B37 . . . . 33 C2
Bream B77 . . . . 9 D7
Brechin Cl LE10 . . . . 31 A8
Bredon Ave CV3 . . . . 78 F8
Bredon Ho B98 . . . . 103 B7
Bredon View B97 . . . . 102 D8
Bree Cl CV5 . . . . 60 A7
Breeden Dr B76 . . . . 23 B6
Bree's La CV8 . . . . 74 A1
Brendan Cl B46 . . . . 34 A5
Brendon B77 . . . . 4 B1
Brendon Way CV10 . . . . 28 A3
Brenfield Dr LE10 . . . . 31 A8
Brent B77 . . . . 9 E7
Brentwood Ave CV3 . . . . . . 77 C3
Brentwood Gdns CV3 . . . . . 77 C3
Brese Ave CV34 . . . . 104 F1
Bretch Hill OX16 . . . . 139 F3
Bretford Rd CV2 . . . . 50 C1
Bretshall Cl B90 . . . . 70 F5
Bretts Cl CV1 . . . . 151 D4
Bretts Hall Est CV10 . . . . . . 28 A7
Brewer Rd CV12 . . . . 40 D2
Brewers Cl CV3 . . . . 63 A1
Brewery La OX15 . . . . 142 C4
Brewery Row GL56 . . . . . . 140 F1
Brewery St CV37 . . . . 144 F3
Brewster Cl CV2 . . . . 62 E2
Briansway CV6 . . . . 49 E3
Briar Cl
Hinckley LE10 . . . . 31 F6
Royal Leamington Spa
CV32 . . . . 106 B2
Briar Coppice B90 . . . . 70 D4
Briar Croft CV37 . . . . 144 F3
Briardene Ave CV12 . . . . . . 39 B2
Briar Hill Inf Sch CV31 . . 110 B3
Briarmead LE10 . . . . 31 E4
Briars Cl
Coventry CV2 . . . . 62 C2
Long Lawford CV23 . . . . 82 B4
Nuneaton CV11 . . . . 29 E5
Briar B77 . . . . 4 A3
Briarwood Cl B90 . . . . 70 D4
Brickall The CV37 . . . . 129 B3
Brickhill Cl CV36 . . . . 149 C6
Brickhill Dr B37 . . . . 33 A2
Brick Hill OX15 . . . . 142 D3
Brick Hill La CV5 . . . . 59 E8
Brickkiln La CV9 . . . . 16 B4
Brick Kiln La
Middleton B78 . . . . 14 D6
Solihull B91 . . . . 70 F8
Brick Kiln St LE10 . . . . 31 C8
Brick Kiln Way CV12 . . . . . 39 D3
Brick Row OX15 . . . . 142 F8
Brickyard Cl CV7 . . . . 74 C7
Brickyard Cotts WR11 . . . 127 D5
Brickyard La B80 . . . . 103 C4
Brickyard Rd CV47 . . . . . . 125 B8
Bridal Path The CV5 . . . . . 60 B6
Bridgeacre Gdns CV3 . . . . 62 F2
Bridgecote CV3 . . . . 78 E6
Bridge Ct CV47 . . . . 147 B3
Bridge End
Southam CV47 . . . . 147 B4
Warwick CV34 . . . . 108 F5
Bridge Foot CV37 . . . . 145 A2
Bridge Hill OX15 . . . . 142 D4
Bridge Ho CV31 . . . . 110 A8
Bridge La
Ladbroke CV47 . . . . 124 D5
Witherley CV9 . . . . 19 B7
Bridgeman Rd CV6 . . . . 61 B4
Bridge Meadow Dr B93 . . . 71 F6
Bridge Rd
Butlers Marston CV35 . . . . 131 F5
Hinckley LE10 . . . . 31 D7
Bridge St
Barford CV35 . . . . 122 A7
Coventry CV6 . . . . 62 A7
Fenny Compton CV47 . . . . 133 D7
Hampton Lucy CV35 . . . . . 121 F4
Hurley CV9 . . . . 16 C4
Kenilworth CV8 . . . . 92 F5
Kineton CV35 . . . . 132 B5
Nuneaton,Chilvers Coton
CV11 . . . . 29 C2
Nuneaton CV11 . . . . 29 C4
Polesworth B78 . . . . 5 A1
Rugby CV21 . . . . 83 C3
Stratford-u-A CV37 . . . . . . 145 A2
Warwick CV34 . . . . 109 C8
Wellesbourne CV35 . . . . . . 146 D3
Bridge Town Prim Sch
CV37 . . . . 145 B1
Bridgetown Rd CV37 . . . . 145 B1
Bridget St CV21 . . . . 82 F3
Bridge View
3 Coleshill B46 . . . . 33 F7
Baginton CV8 . . . . 77 D3
Bridgeway CV37 . . . . 145 B3
Bridle Brook La CV5,CV7 . . 48 A3
Bridle Rd
Lighthorne Heath CV33 . . . 123 D2
Rugby CV21 . . . . 82 E3
Bridport Cl CV2 . . . . 63 A4
Brierley Rd CV2 . . . . 62 C8
Briggs Cl OX16 . . . . 139 F2
Brightmere Rd CV6 . . . . . . 61 B4
Brighton St CV2 . . . . 61 F3
Bright St CV6 . . . . 61 E6
Brightwalton Rd CV3 . . . . . 77 D7
Brightwell Cres B93 . . . . . . 71 E3
Brill Cl CV4 . . . . 76 C5
Brindle Ave CV3 . . . . 62 C2
Brindles Alley CV36 . . . . . 149 D6
Brindley Cl
Atherstone CV9 . . . . 12 C1
Daventry NN11 . . . . 117 F3
Brindley Ct NN11 . . . . 117 D4
Brindley Paddocks CV1 . . 151 B4
Brindley Quays NN11 . . . . 117 D4
Brindley Rd
Bedworth CV7 . . . . 50 B8
Hinckley LE10 . . . . 30 E8
Rugby CV21 . . . . 84 B1
Brinklow Cl B98 . . . . 103 D8
Brinklow Rd
Coventry CV3 . . . . 63 A2
Easenhall CV23 . . . . 65 E4
Brisbane Cl CV3 . . . . 77 E6
Brisbane Ct 2 CV12 . . . . . . 39 A2
Briscoe Rd CV6 . . . . 49 D4
Bristol Rd CV5 . . . . 60 F2
Bristol Way CV35 . . . . 146 C1
Britannia Rd LE10 . . . . 32 A5
Britannia St CV2 . . . . 61 F3
Briton Rd CV2 . . . . 62 A4
Brittania Sh Ctr 3 LE10 . . 31 D8
Britten Cl CV11 . . . . 40 A7
Brittons La CV35 . . . . 114 C2
Brixfield Way B90 . . . . 70 B5
Brixham Cl CV11 . . . . 29 F5
Brixham Dr CV2 . . . . 62 C7
Brixworth Cl CV3 . . . . 78 E8
Broad Cl CV33 . . . . 123 F8
Broadfern Rd B93 . . . . 72 B8
Broadgate CV1 . . . . 151 B3
Broadhaven Cl CV31 . . . . . 110 C7
Broad Heath Com Prim Sch
CV6 . . . . 61 E6

Broad La
Coventry CV5 59 D4
Fillongley CV7 36 A4
Broadlands Cl CV5 60 C2
Broad La B98 86 E3
Broadlee B77 4 C1
Broad Marston Rd
Mickleton CV37,GL55 135 B7
Pebworth CV37 128 F1
Broadmead Ct CV5 60 C2
Broadmeadow La CV37 144 C4
Broadmere Rise CV5 60 A2
Broadmoor La CV36 141 A6
Broad Oaks B76 13 A1
Broad Park Rd CV2 62 D8
Broad St
Brinklow CV23 64 F3
Coventry CV6 61 E7
Long Compton CV36 141 C3
Broad Street Jetty CV6 61 E7
Broad St
Stratford-u-A CV37 144 F2
Warwick CV34 108 F7
Broadsword Way LE10 31 D4
Broadwater CV5 77 A8
Broadway
Coventry CV5 61 A1
Cubbington CV32 106 E5
Broadway Mans CV5 61 A1
Broadway Rd GL55 135 B6
Broadwell Ct CV4 75 F6
Broadwells Cres CV4 76 A5
Broad Wlk CV37 144 F2
Brockenhurst Way CV6 50 B6
Brockhill La B98 85 F2
Brockhurst Ave LE10 31 D4
Brockhurst Dr CV4 59 D2
Brockhurst La
Carroway Head B75 7 B7
Monks Kirby CV23 53 F4
Solihull B90 70 B5
Brodick Cl LE10 31 A8
Brodick Rd LE10 30 F8
Brodick Way CV10 28 F3
Bromage Ave B78 15 C6
Brome Hall La B94 89 D2
Bromford Way CV37 144 D4
Bromhurst Way CV34 108 B4
Bromleigh Dr CV2 62 C2
Bromleigh Villas CV8 77 F2
Bromley Cl CV8 92 E6
Bromsgrove Highway
B98 102 E8
Bromsgrove Rd B80 103 D2
Bromwich Cl CV3 78 F8
Bromwich Rd CV21 83 F1
Bromyard Ave B76 22 A8
Bronte Cl
Galley Common CV10 27 F5
Rugby CV21 83 D3
Bronze Cl CV11 39 E8
Brook Ave B77 10 A7
Brook Bsns Pk CV35 132 A6
Brook Cl
Coventry CV1 61 E4
Kingsbury B78 15 D5
Shipston-on-S CV36 149 D6
Brook Cottage Cl B46 25 D3
Brook Cottage Gdn*
OX15 138 F5
Brook Cotts CV36 149 F3
Brook Croft B37 44 B7
Brookdale
Harvington WR11 127 C4
Hinckley LE10 31 B7
Brookdale Rd CV10 29 E7
Brooke Cl
12 Stratford-u-A CV37 130 B8
Warwick CV34 108 F5
Brooke Ct CV21 82 F3
Brooke Mews 8 CV34 108 F7
Brook End Cl B95 113 A4
Brook End Dr B95 113 A4
Brook End B78 9 B8
Brooke Rd CV8 93 B4
Brooke Sch CV22 99 E7
Brooke Specl Sch CV22 82 F1
Brook Farm Ind Est B94 70 B2
Brook Farm Wlk B37 33 D2
Brookfield Cl B97 102 D4
Brookfield Ct CV37 144 C3
Brookfield Dr LE10 41 D4
Brookfield Rd
Cubbington CV32 106 E5
Hinckley LE10 31 C6
Brookford Ave CV6 49 A3
Brook Green La B92 57 A1
Brookhampton Cl B97 102 E4
Brookhampton La CV35 132 A5
Brookhurst Ct CV32 105 D1
Brookhurst Prim Sch
CV32 105 C1
Brookhus Farm Rd B76 22 A8
Brook La CV35 122 F3
Brooklands Ho 8 CV34 109 D8
Brooklands Way B37 44 A8
Brook La
Newbold-on-S CV37 130 E1
Nuneaton CV10 29 C6
Brooklea CV12 38 F2
Brooklime Dr CV23 83 E8
Brooklyn Rd CV1 61 D6
Brook Piece Wlk B35 22 B3
Brook Rd B95 119 F6
Brooksby Gr B93 72 A2
Brooks Cl CV23 117 B6
Brooks Croft B35 22 A2
Brookshaw Way CV2 62 F8
Brookside Ave
Coventry CV5 60 C3
Kenilworth CV8 92 E4
Pailton CV23 66 A8
Wellesbourne CV35 146 E3
Brookside B90 70 D3
Brookside Cl
Rugby CV22 83 A2
Stratford-u-A CV37 144 D3
Brookside
Hinckley LE10 31 E7
Hook Norton OX15 142 D4
Brookside Rd CV37 144 D3
Brookside
Snitterfield CV37 121 B7
Stretton-on-D CV23 96 F6
Brookside Way B77 10 A6
Brookside B95 113 B2
Brook St
Bedworth CV12 39 B5
Fenny Compton CV47 133 D7
Brookstray Flats CV5 60 B3
Brook St
Warwick CV34 108 E6
Wolston CV8 80 A3
Brook Turn Cotts CV47 115 D4
Brookvale Ave CV3 62 E1
Brookvale Rd CV37 144 E2
Brook View CV22 99 C3
Brookweed B77 4 A3
Brook Wlk CV9 18 F7
Broom Cl CV22 82 E1
Broome Croft CV6 49 B3
Broomey Croft Childrens
Farm* B76 15 B7
Broomfield Ave B78 9 A8
Broomfield Pl CV5 61 A2
Broomfield Rd CV5 61 A1
Broomfield Rise CV10 28 F2
Broom La B90 70 A6
Broomybank CV8 93 B6
Broughton Castle*
OX15 139 D1
Broughton Rd OX15,OX16 139 F2
Browett Rd CV6 61 A5
Brown Ave B77 9 C8
Browning Ave CV34 108 C5
Browning Cl
7 Stratford-u-A CV37 130 B8
Nuneaton CV10 28 A5
Browning Rd
Coventry CV2 62 C3
Rugby CV21 101 B8
Brownley Rd B90 70 E7
Brownlow Dr CV37 144 E1
Brownlow St 7 CV32 106 A2
Brown's Bridge Rd CV47 147 B3
Brownshill Ct CV6 60 F8
Brownshill Green Rd CV6 48 E1
Brown's La
Brownshill Green CV5 48 C1
Dordon CV9 11 A5
Browns La B93 71 E6
Brownsover Cl B36 22 B1
Brownsover Com Inf Sch
CV23 83 D8
Brownsover La CV21 83 B8
Brownsover Rd
Rugby CV21 82 F7
Rugby CV21 83 A7
Browns Rd NN11 117 F1
Broxell Cl CV34 104 C1
Bruce Rd
Bedworth CV7 49 F7
Coventry CV6 61 B8
Bruces Way CV37 144 B3
Bruce Williams Way CV22 83 B2
Brudenell Cl CV22 99 A8
Brunel Cl
Coventry CV2 61 F3
Daventry NN11 117 F2
Whitnash CV31 110 B2
Brunel Rd LE10 31 C8
Brunel Wlk B78 5 A3
Brunes Ct CV21 83 D7
Brunswick Cl CV21 83 C6
Brunswick Ct CV31 110 A5
Brunswick Rd CV1 61 B2
Brunswick St CV31 110 A5
Bruntingthorpe Way CV3 78 E8
Brunton Cl CV3 63 B1
Brutus Dr B46 23 E1
Bryan Mews B50 148 E4
Bryanston Cl CV2 63 A4
Bryant Rd CV7 50 A7
Brymbo Cotts OX15 142 E4
Brympton Rd CV3 62 C2
Bryn Jones Cl CV3 78 F7
Bryn Rd CV6 61 F7
Bryony Cl CV12 38 E1
Bubbenhall Rd CV8 77 F1
Buccaneer Way LE17 55 D6
Buccleuch Cl CV22 99 C4
Buchanan Rd CV22 82 E1
Buchan Cl
Galley Common CV10 27 F4
Stratford-u-A CV37 130 B8
Buckbury Croft B90 71 B6
Buckden Cl 2 CV34 104 F1
Buckden B77 4 C1
Buckfast Cl CV3 77 E5
Buckhold Dr CV5 60 B5
Buckingham Cl CV10 29 B1
Buckingham Rd CV47 132 F5
Buckingham Rise CV5 60 B4
Buckland Rd CV6 49 B2
Buckler's Yd 5 CV12 39 A2
Buckle St WR11,B50 128 C3
Buckley Ho CV5 60 F1
Buckley Rd CV32 106 C2
Buckminster Dr B93 71 E4
Bucknill Cres CV21 101 B7
Buckridge La B90 70 A5
Bucks Hill CV10 28 C6
Buckwell La CV23 84 B6
Budbrooke Cl CV2 50 D2
Budbrooke Ind Est CV34 108 B7
Budbrooke Prim Sch
CV35 114 F4
Budbrooke Rd CV34 108 B7
Bufferys Cl B91 71 B8
Bulkington La CV11 40 A7
Bulkington Rd
Bedworth CV12 39 D2
Shilton CV7 51 E6
Wolvey LE10 41 D4
Bullaces La LE17 68 C4
Bullfield Ave CV4 59 E1
Bullfurlong La LE10 31 F4
Bullimore Gr CV8 93 A2
Bullivents Cl B93 71 F5
Bull Ring Farm Rd CV33 123 F7
Bull Ring CV10 29 B2
Bull Ring The CV33 123 F6
Bull's Head La CV3 62 B2
Bulls Head Yd B49 143 B3
Bull's La B76 13 E1
Bull St
Nuneaton CV11 29 D2
Southam CV47 147 B4
Stratford-u-A CV37 144 F1
Bull Yd CV1 151 B2
Bull Yd The 5 CV47 147 B4
Bulwer Rd CV6 61 A6
Bulwick Cl CV3 63 B1
Bungalows The CV37 129 B7
Bunkers Hill NN11 126 F5
Bunkers Hill La CV23 80 E5
Bunneys Mdw LE10 30 E6
Burbage Ave CV37 144 F5
Burbage CE Inf Sch LE10 32 A5
Burbage Jun Sch LE10 31 F6
Burbage Rd LE10 32 A7
Burbages La CV6 49 D4
Burberry Gr CV7 74 A6
Burbury Cl
Bedworth CV12 39 C4
Royal Leamington Spa
CV32 106 C2
Burbury Ct CV34 109 B8
Burford La B49,B80 112 C1
Burford Mews 13 CV31 110 C6
Burford Rd
Hollywood B47 69 A6
Stratford-u-A CV37 145 D2
Burgage Pl CV11 29 C4
Burgage Wlk CV11 29 C4
Burges CV1 151 B3
Burges Gr CV34 104 F1
Burghley Cl CV11 29 F2
Burhill Way B37 33 B5
Burleigh Cl CV7 74 B7
Burlington Ct B78 9 B8
Burlington Rd
Coventry CV2 61 F4
Nuneaton CV10 39 B7
Burman Dr B46 34 A5
Burnaby Cl CV10 28 B5
Burnaby Rd CV6 49 B1
Burnaston Cres B90 71 C6
Burnell Cl B50 148 C5
Burnett Rd CV33 123 D2
Burnham Rd CV3 78 A6
Burnham Rise CV11 30 A6
Burnsall Gr CV5 76 D8
Burnsall Rd CV5 76 D8
Burns Ave CV34 108 C5
Burns Cl
10 Stratford-u-A CV37 130 B8
Redditch B97 102 C8
Burnside
Coventry CV3 63 A2
Rugby CV22 82 F2
Stratford-u-A CV37 144 C2
Burns Rd
Coventry CV2 62 B3
Royal Leamington Spa
CV32 106 B4
Burns Wlk CV12 39 C1
Burnthurst Cres B90 71 A7
Burnthurst La CV23 96 B3
Burrow Hill La CV7 48 D7
Burrows Cl CV31 110 B3
Burrows The CV37 130 E1
Burton Cl CV5 48 C2
Burton Dassett Hills Ctry Pk*
CV47 133 B7
Burton Green CE Prim Sch
CV8 75 B3
Burton La CV11 40 F7
Burton Rd CV9 3 F1
Bury Court La OX17 139 E8
Burycroft Rd OX15 142 D3
Bury Ho CV4 59 F3
Bury Rd CV31 109 F7
Bury The CV36 149 D6
Buryway La CV36 141 C3
Busby Cl CV3 78 F7
Busbys Piece CV23 53 F3
Bushbery Ave CV4 59 F2
Bushbury Croft B37 33 C3
Bush Cl CV4 59 F3
Bush Ct CV2 62 B6
Bushelton Cl CV1 151 C1
Bush Heath La CV33 123 F6
Bush Heath Rd CV33 123 F6
Bush Hill La CV23 117 B2
Bushley Cl B98 103 A7
Bushley Croft B91 71 B8
Bushwood Dr B93 72 B3
Bushwood La B94,B95 113 C8
Bushy End CV34 109 E4
Butchers Cl
Bishops Itchington CV47 124 A4
Brinklow CV23 64 F3
Butcher's La CV5 60 C6
Butchers La OX15 137 F2
Butchers Rd B92 57 A6
Butler Cl CV8 93 C7
Butlers Cl
Aston le W NN11 134 F5
Long Compton CV36 141 D3
Butlers Cres CV7 39 A1
Butlers End CV35 91 C2
Butlers La
Baddesley Ensor CV9 11 C2
Long Compton CV36 141 C3
Butlers Leap Ind Est CV21 83 D4
Butlers Leap CV21 83 D5
Butlers Rd CV36,OX7 141 E3
Butler St B96 102 E1
Butlin Rd
Coventry CV6 49 C4
Rugby CV21 83 D3
Buttercup Way CV12 38 D2
Buttermere Ave CV11 30 A6
Buttermere Cl CV3 78 F7
Buttermere
Rugby CV21 83 D7
Tamworth B77 10 B7
Buttermilk La CV35 113 F5
Butter St B49 143 C3
Butterworth Dr CV4 76 A6
Butt Hill CV47 125 C8
Butt La
Allesley CV5 60 B7
Harbury CV33 123 F6
Butts Ct CV9 3 A2
Butts CV1 61 A2
Butts La B94 87 B2
Butts Rd CV1 61 B2
Butts The
Long Compton CV36 141 C3
Napton on t H CV47 125 C8
Warwick CV34 108 E7
Buxton Ave B78 9 B8
Byefield Rd OX17 134 F4
Byfield Pl CV7 74 D5
Byfield Rd
Coventry CV6 60 E5
Priors Marston CV47 125 F4
Byford Ct CV10 28 F4
Byford St CV10 28 F4
Byford Way B37 44 B8
Bygones Mus* OX17 134 B4
By Pass Rd B77 4 A5
Byres The GL56 140 D6
Byron Ave
Bedworth CV12 39 D2
Warwick CV34 108 C4
Byron Ct B93 72 A6
Byron Rd
Redditch B97 102 D8
Stratford-u-A CV37 145 C1
Byron St CV1 151 C4
Byron Wlk CV47 132 F7
Bywater Cl CV3 77 B5

C

Cadbury Dr B35 22 A2
Cadden Dr CV4 60 B2
Cadman Cl CV12 39 C3
Cadogan Rd B77 9 D5
Caen Cl CV35 108 A7
Caernarfon Dr CV11 29 D3
Caernarvon Way 3
OX16 139 F3
Caesar Rd CV8 92 E3
Caesar Way B46 23 E1
Caister B77 4 A6
Caistor Cl B78 8 B8
Caithness Cl CV5 60 A4
Calcott Ho CV3 78 B5
Calcutt Mdw CV47 147 D4
Calcutt Way B90 70 A6
Caldecote Cl CV10 29 C8
Caldecote Hall CV10 19 F2
Caldecote Hall Dr CV10 19 F3
Caldecote Rd CV6 61 C5
Caldecott Pl CV21 83 C2
Caldecott St CV21,CV22 83 C2
Caldeford Ave B90 71 A7
Calder Cl
Bulkington CV12 40 B2
Coventry CV3 77 E7
Calder Dr B76 22 A7
Calder B77 4 B2
Calder Wlk CV31 110 C6
Caldon Cl LE10 31 B8
Caldwell Ct CV11 29 D1
Caldwell Rd CV11 29 D1
Calf's La GL55 135 B2
Calgary Cl CV3 63 A2
Calias La CV23 116 A3
Caliban Mews CV34 109 E3
Callaways Rd CV36 149 D5
Callendar Cl CV11 30 A7
Callier Cl CV22 99 B8
Callis Wlk 2 B77 9 F6
Callow Hill La B97 102 B6
Calmere Cl CV2 62 F8
Calpurnia Ave CV34 109 E2
Caludon Castle Sch CV2 62 E4
Caludon Lodge CV2 62 E5
Caludon Park Ave CV2 62 E5
Caludon Rd CV2 62 A4
Calvert Cl
Coventry CV3 77 D6
Rugby CV21 83 E7
Calvestone Pl CV22 99 A7
Calvestone Rd CV22 99 B8
Calvestone Sq CV22 99 B8
Camberwell Terr CV31 110 A7
Camborne Dr CV11 29 F5
Cambourne Rd LE10 32 A6
Cambria Cl B90 69 E7
Cambrian B77 4 A2
Cambridge Ct CV21 83 C3
Cambridge Dr
Birmingham B37 33 A1
Nuneaton CV10 28 E3
Cambridge Gdns CV32 106 A1
Cambridge St
Coventry CV1 61 E5
Rugby CV21 83 C3
Camden Cl GL56 140 F3
Camden St CV2 62 A4
Camellia Rd 1 CV2 50 B2
Camelot Gr CV8 93 C5
Cameron Cl
Allesley CV5 60 A7
Royal Leamington Spa
CV32 106 A4
Camhouses B77 4 B1
Campbell Cl CV10 28 A4
Campbell St CV21 82 E3
Campden Ave CV36 135 F5
Campden Cl B97 102 D6
Campden Gr CV35 114 F6
Campden Hill CV36 136 A6
Campden Lawns CV37 130 D3
Campden Pitch CV36 136 A6
Campden Rd
Ebrington GL55 135 D3
Lower Quinton CV37 129 D4
Mickleton GL55 135 B4
Shipston-on-S CV36 149 A5
Camp Hill Dr CV10 28 D7
Camp Hill Prim Sch CV10 28 E6
Camp Hill Rd CV10 28 C7
Campion Cl CV3 77 D6
Campion Gn CV32 106 A2
Campion Rd CV32 106 A2
Campion Sch & Com Coll
CV31 110 C5
Campion Terr CV32 106 A1
Campion Way
3 Bedworth CV12 38 D2
Rugby CV23 83 D8
Solihull B90 70 A5
Camp La
Henley-in-A B95 113 B6
Warmington OX17 133 B2
Camplea Croft B37 33 A2
Campling Cl CV12 40 B2
Campriano Dr CV34 109 A8
Campton Cl LE10 31 E7
Camville CV3 63 A2
Canada La CV35 114 D1
Canal Rd
Coventry CV6 61 F8
Hatton CV35 114 E5
Canalside
Bedworth CV6 50 B6
Kingswood B94 89 D3
Canal Way LE10 30 F7
Canberra Cl CV35 146 C1
Canberra Ct 2 CV12 38 F2
Canberra Rd CV2 50 C4
Canberra Way LE10 31 E4
Canford Cl CV3 77 C3
Canley Ford CV4,CV5 76 E7
Canley Rd CV5 76 D8
Canley Sta CV5 60 D1
Cannes Ct CV4 76 D6
Cannocks La CV4 76 D6
Cannon Cl CV4 76 F6
Cannon Hill Rd CV4 76 D5
Cannon Park District Ctr
CV4 76 C6
Cannon Park Prim Sch
CV4 76 D5
Cannon Park Rd CV4 76 E5
Canon Dr CV7 49 D6
Canon Evans CE Inf Sch
CV12 39 A2
Canon Hudson Cl CV3 78 C6
Canon Maggs CE Jun Sch
CV12 39 B2
Canon Young Rd CV31 110 B3
Canterbury Cl
Kenilworth CV8 93 C3
Studley B80 103 C4
Canterbury Dr B37 44 A7
Canterbury St CV1 151 D3
Canterbury Way CV11 30 A8
Cantlow Cl CV5 60 A3
Canton La B46 24 A5
Canwell Dr B75 7 B5
Cape Ind Est CV34 108 E7
Cape Rd CV34 108 D8
Capmartin Rd CV6 61 C7
Captain's Hill B49 143 D5
Capulet Cl
Coventry CV3 78 C6
Rugby CV22 99 E6
Capulet Dr CV34 109 E3

Capulet Ho 12 CV37 145 A3
Caradoc Cl CV2 62 D7
Caradoc Hall CV2 62 D7
Caradoc B77 4 A2
Cardale Croft 1 CV3 78 F8
Cardiff Cl CV3 78 D5
Cardigan Rd CV12 38 C1
Cardinal Newman RC Sch & Com Coll CV6 48 F2
Cardinal Wiseman RC Sch CV2 50 E1
Carding Cl CV5 59 F4
Carew Cl CV37 144 E5
Carew Wlk CV22 82 C1
Carey St CV6 62 B8
Carey B77 10 A5
Cargill Cl CV6 49 F5
Carhampton Rd B75 13 A5
Carisbrooke Ave B37 33 C2
Carisbrooke B77 4 A2
Carisbrook Rd CV10 29 D6
Carlcroft B77 4 B2
Carlton Cl CV12 40 B3
Carlton Ct CV5 60 F2
Carlton Gdns CV5 77 A8
Carlton Ho 8 CV32 109 F8
Carlton Rd
Coventry CV6 49 F1
Rugby CV22 82 D1
Carlyle Cl CV10 27 F5
Carlyon Rd CV9 18 F8
Carlyon Road Ind Est CV9 12 F1
Carmelite Rd CV1 61 E2
Carnation Way CV10 39 A8
Carnbroe Ave CV3 78 F7
Carnegie Cl CV3 78 B5
Carnoustie Cl CV11 40 C8
Carnoustie B77 4 C5
Caroline Cl CV11 39 F7
Carolyn Lane Ct CV21 82 F4
Carpenters Cl LE10 31 F5
Carrie Ho CV1 151 A2
Carroll Cl 16 CV37 130 B8
Carroway Head Hill B78 7 D4
Carsal Cl CV7 49 D5
Carson Cl GL56 136 C1
Carter Dr CV35 122 A7
Carter Rd CV3 78 A8
Carters Cl B37 44 A7
Carters La CV37 145 E4
Carters Leaze CV36 140 E5
Carthusian Rd CV3 77 C7
Cartmel Cl CV5 60 A4
Cart's La CV9 11 C2
Carvell Cl CV5 48 B1
Carver Cl CV2 62 E2
Cascade Cl CV3 77 E6
Case La CV35 114 B8
Casern View B75 13 A6
Cashmore Ave CV31 109 F5
Cashmore Rd
Bedworth CV12 38 E1
Kenilworth CV8 93 C4
Cash's Bsns Ctr CV1 61 D5
Cash's La CV1 61 D6
Casita Gr CV8 93 C4
Caspian Way CV2 63 A8
Cassandra Cl CV4 76 D3
Cassandra Gr CV34 109 D4
Castello Dr B36 22 D1
Castle Bromwich Bsns Pk B35 22 A1
Castle Cl
Coventry CV3 77 D6
Fillongley CV7 36 E2
Henley-in-A B95 113 B4
Warwick CV34 108 E6
Castle Cres CV35 132 B5
Castle Ct
Hinckley LE10 31 D6
Kenilworth CV8 93 A6
Castleditch La B98 102 E7
Castle Dr
Astley CV10 37 E7
Coleshill B46 33 F5
Castlegate Mews 5 CV34 108 F7
Castle Gdns GL55 135 C2
Castle Gn CV8 92 D5
Castle Gr CV8 92 E4
Castlehall B77 4 A2
Castle Hill CV8 92 E5
Castle Hill La OX15 137 E2
Castle Hill
Upper Brailes OX15 137 E3
Warwick CV34 108 E6
Castle La
Grandborough CV23 116 F6
Maxstoke B46 34 F7
Warwick CV34 108 E6
Castle Mews 6 CV34 108 E6
Castle Mound CV23 101 C2
Castle Mound Way CV23 67 D2
Castle Nurseries GL55 135 C2
Castle Place Ind Est CV1 151 D4
Castle Rd
1 Kineton CV35 132 B6
Alcester B49 143 C5
Hartshill CV10 19 B1
Henley-in-A B95 113 B4
Kenilworth CV8 92 E5
Nuneaton CV10 29 C7
Studley B80 103 F4
Tamworth B77 9 F5
Castle St
Astwood Bank B96 102 E2
Coventry CV1 151 D4
Hinckley LE10 31 D8
Castle St *continued*
Rugby CV21 83 B3
Warwick CV34 108 E6
Castle Vale Ent Pk B76 22 C4
Castle Vale Ind Est B76 22 A5
Castle Vale Sch B35 22 B3
Castle View CV10 19 B1
Caswell Rd CV31 110 B6
Catbrook Cl GL55 135 B1
Catbrook Gdns GL55 135 A1
Catesby End NN11 126 B5
Catesby La B94 89 B2
Catesby Rd
Coventry CV6 61 B8
Rugby CV22 83 D1
Cathedral Lanes Sh Ctr CV1 151 B3
Catherine de Barnes La
Bickenhill B92 44 D1
Catherine de B B92 56 C7
Catherines Cl B91 56 B4
Catherine St CV2 61 F3
Catherine Ward Hall CV12 39 B5
Cathiron La
Cathiron CV23 66 A1
Easenhall CV23 65 C1
Harborough Magna CV23 66 B1
Cattell Dr B75 13 B5
Cattell Rd CV34 108 E7
Catthorpe Manor LE17 68 F1
Catthorpe Rd LE17 68 C4
Cavalier Cl CV11 29 E2
Cavans Cl CV3 79 A8
Cavans Way CV3 79 A8
Cave Cl CV22 99 A8
Cavendish Cl CV22 82 A1
Cavendish Ct B93 72 A3
Cavendish Rd CV4 59 E2
Cavendish Wlk CV11 40 C8
Caversham Cl CV11 30 A7
Cawdon Gr B93 71 F3
Cawnpore Rd CV6 49 B2
Cawston Grange Dr CV22 99 A8
Cawston Grange Prim Sch CV22 99 B8
Cawston Ho
Hampton Magna CV35 114 F4
Rugby CV22 99 B6
Cawston La CV22 99 B5
Cawston Way CV22 99 C8
Cawthorne Cl 1 CV1 61 E4
Cecil Ct CV31 110 A8
Cecil Leonard Knox Cres CV11 40 F6
Cecily Rd CV3 77 E7
Cedar Ave CV8 79 B1
Cedar Cl
Royal Leamington Spa CV32 106 A4
Stratford-u-A CV37 145 B4
Cedar Cres B78 15 D6
Cedar Ct
Allesley CV5 60 A6
Hinckley LE10 32 A6
Tamworth B77 9 E6
Cedar Dr CV37 121 B7
Cedar Gr CV34 105 A1
Cedar Ho
7 Royal Leamington Spa CV32 109 E8
Barford CV35 122 A7
Cedar Rd
Mickleton GL55 135 C6
Nuneaton CV10 28 D6
Cedars Ave CV6 60 F5
Cedars Mews The 3 CV32 109 D8
Cedars Rd CV7 39 B1
Cedars The
Dorridge B93 72 A4
Shipston-on-S CV36 149 D6
Cedar Tree Farm CV31 111 C3
Cedar Wlk 6 B37 33 B2
Cedar Wood Dr CV7 74 B6
Cedric Cl CV3 78 C5
Celandine Rd CV2 50 D2
Celandine CV23 83 E8
Celandine Way CV12 38 E2
Cemetery La CV10 19 B1
Centaur Rd CV5 60 F2
Centenary Bsns Ctr CV11 29 E3
Centenary Rd CV4 76 D7
Central Ave
Coventry CV2 62 A2
Nuneaton CV11 29 B5
Royal Leamington Spa CV31 109 F6
Central Bldgs
8 Rugby CV21 83 B3
Coventry CV3 151 B1
Central Bvd
Cheswick Green B90 71 A3
Coventry CV6,CV7 49 A5
Central City Ind Est CV6 61 F5
Central Dr CV47 124 B4
Central Park Dr CV23 67 D2
Central Six Ret Pk CV1 151 A1
Centrovell Ind Est CV11 29 C2
Centurion Cl B46 23 F1
Centurion Pk B77 10 B6
Centurion Way B77 10 B6
Century Pk B26 44 C6
Ceolmund Cres B37 33 B2
Chace Ave CV3 78 C6
Chaceley Cl CV2 63 A8
Chaceley Ct B97 102 D8
Chace Prim Sch CV3 78 C6
Chadbury Croft 1 B91 71 B8
Chadbury Rd WR11 127 A1
Chadshunt Cl B36 22 D2
Chadstone Cl B90 71 B6
Chadwick Cl CV5 60 B3
Chadwick La
Chadwick End B93 90 B8
Temple Balsall B93 73 B2
Chadwick Manor B93 73 A1
Chadwick Mews
Chadwick End B93 90 B6
Redditch B98 103 A7
Chadworth Ave B93 71 E3
Chaffinch Dr B36 33 B7
Chalfont Cl
Bedworth CV12 39 A4
Coventry CV5 60 B4
Chalford way 7 B90 70 C8
Challenge Bsns Pk CV1 61 D5
Challenge Cl CV1 151 C4
Chamberlain Cl CV32 106 E5
Chamberlaine St CV12 39 B3
Chamberlain La B49 118 D5
Chamberlain Rd CV21 101 B8
Chamberlain's Gn CV6 60 F7
Chamberlain Wlk 10 B46 33 F7
Chance Fields CV31 110 F6
Chancellors Cl CV4 76 D4
Chancery Ct CV10 28 A7
Chancery La CV10 28 B7
Chanders Rd CV34 104 D1
Chandlers Cl B97 102 D7
Chandlers Dr B77 4 B5
Chandlers Rd CV31 110 A2
Chandlers CV31 109 D7
Chandos Ct 15 CV32 105 F1
Chandos St
Coventry CV2 62 A3
Nuneaton CV11 29 A4
Royal Leamington Spa CV32 105 F1
Change Brook Cl CV11 29 F8
Channel Way CV6 50 B6
Chantries The CV1 61 E5
Chantry Cl B47 69 A7
Chantry Cres B49 143 B3
Chantry Heath Cres B93 72 C7
Chantry Ind Est B76 23 B7
Chantry The CV34 105 A1
Chapel Cl
Bidford-on-A B50 148 D4
Welford-on-A CV37 129 B6
Chapel Ct
13 Royal Leamington Spa CV32 109 F8
Astwood Bank B96 102 E1
Chapel Dr
Balsall Common CV7 74 B8
Wythall B47 69 A3
Chapel End OX7 142 A2
Chapel Farm Cl CV3 78 C6
Chapel Gdns GL56 136 C1
Chapel Gn CV47 125 C7
Chapel Hill OX7 142 F2
Chapelhouse Rd B37 33 A1
Chapel La
Aston Cantlow B95 119 F7
Barnacle CV7 51 B6
Bidford-on-A B50 148 D4
Cropredy OX17 134 C1
Kingswood B94 89 D7
Mickleton GL55 135 B6
Napton on t H CV47 125 C8
Newbold-on-S CV37 130 E1
Pillerton Priors CV35 131 D2
Ratley OX15 133 A2
Ryton-on-D CV8 79 B2
Shotteswell OX17 139 E8
Stratford-u-A CV37 145 A2
Ullenhall B95 112 E6
Witherley CV9 19 C7
Chapel Mews B77 4 A5
Chapelon B77 4 A2
Chapel Rd
Astwood Bank B96 102 E1
Pebworth CV37 128 F1
Chapel Row
Cropredy OX17 134 C1
Warwick CV34 108 E7
Chapel St
5 Royal Leamington Spa CV31 110 A7
Astwood Bank B96 102 E1
Bedworth CV12 39 C3
Bishops Itchington CV47 124 A4
Charwelton NN11 126 D2
Coventry CV1 151 B3
Harbury CV33 123 F6
Hook Norton OX15 142 D4
Long Lawford CV23 82 A4
Nuneaton CV11 29 C4
Rugby CV21 83 A3
Stratford-u-A CV37 145 A2
Warmington OX17 133 D2
Warwick CV34 108 E7
Welford-on-A CV37 129 B6
Wellesbourne CV35 146 D3
Chapel Wlk B50 148 D4
Chapman Cl CV31 110 E5
Chapman Ct CV34 109 C8
Chapman Way B49 143 C5
Chard Rd CV3 78 D8
Charingworth Dr CV35 114 F5
Chariot Way CV21 83 A7
Charity Hos The CV23 67 C6
Charity Rd CV7 49 A7
Charlbury Mews CV31 110 C6
Charlecote Cl CV37 145 E3
Charlecote Croft B90 70 C8
Charlecote Fields CV35 146 D4
Charlecote Gdns CV31 110 D5
Charlecote Pk* CV35 121 F3
Charlecote Rd
Charlecote CV35 146 A6
Coventry CV6 49 A2
Wellesbourne CV35 146 D4
Charlecote Wlk CV11 39 F8
Charles Ct
14 Royal Leamington Spa CV31 110 A6
1 Warwick,Emscote CV34 109 B8
Warwick CV34 108 C7
Charles Eaton Rd CV12 38 F3
Charlesfield Rd CV22 100 A8
Charles Gardner Rd 6 CV31 109 F6
Charles Lakin Cl CV7 51 C5
Charles Rd CV9 18 F7
Charles St
Coventry CV1 151 D4
Hurley CV9 16 C5
New Arley CV7 37 A8
Nuneaton CV11 29 A5
Rugby CV21 82 F3
Warwick CV34 109 A8
Charles Warren Cl CV21 83 B3
Charles Watson Ct 4 CV32 106 A2
Charlesworth Ave B90 71 B6
Charlewood Rd CV6 49 B2
Charlotte Cl CV10 28 C6
Charlotte St
Royal Leamington Spa CV31 109 F6
Rugby CV21 83 B3
Charlton Terr GL56 140 B3
Charminster Dr CV3 77 D4
Charnwood Ave CV10 28 E2
Charnwood Dr CV10 19 B2
Charnwood Way CV32 106 C3
Charter App CV34 108 D5
Charter Ave CV4 76 B7
Charter Ho CV4 76 A7
Charterhouse Rd CV1 61 E2
Charter Prim Sch (Harris Site) CV4 75 F7
Charter Prim Sch (Parkes Site) CV4 76 C8
Charter Rd CV22 100 E8
Chartley Cl B93 71 E3
Chartwell Cl CV11 29 F1
Chartwell Dr B90 70 D5
Charwelton Dr CV21 83 E6
Charwelton La NN11 126 B4
Chase Cl CV11 29 E6
Chase La CV8 92 B7
Chater Dr B76 13 A1
Chaters Orch CV47 115 D4
Chatham Cl CV3 78 C8
Chatillon Cl CV34 109 E3
Chatsworth Cl
Cheswick Green B90 70 E5
Hinckley LE10 31 F6
Chatsworth Dr CV11 29 F2
Chatsworth Gdns CV31 110 D6
Chatsworth Gr CV8 93 C5
Chatsworth Rise CV3 77 E6
Chattaway Dr CV7 74 B6
Chattle Hill B46 23 E2
Chaucer Cl 5 CV37 130 B8
Chaucer Dr CV10 28 A4
Chaucer Rd CV22 99 F6
Chauntry Pl CV1 151 C3
Chauson Gr B91 71 A8
Chaytor Dr CV10 28 B6
Chaytor Rd B78 11 A8
Cheadle Cl CV2 50 A4
Cheam Cl CV6 50 A1
Cheapside B50 128 C4
Cheatle Ct B77 9 D5
Cheedon Cl B93 71 E2
Cheetah Rd CV1 151 C1
Chelmarsh CV6 61 C6
Chelmsley Ave B46 33 F6
Chelmsley Circ B37 33 B2
Chelmsley La B37 44 A8
Chelmsley Rd B37 33 C2
Chelmsley Wood Ind Est B37 33 B4
Chelney Wlk CV3 63 A1
Chelsea Cl CV11 29 F7
Chelsey Rd CV2 62 E8
Cheltenham Cl CV12 39 B4
Cheltenham Croft CV2 62 F7
Cheltondale 3 B90 70 C8
Chelveston Rd CV6 60 E5
Chelwood Gr CV2 50 F1
Chenies Cl CV5 60 B3
Chepstow Cl
Coventry CV3 78 C5
Stratford-u-A CV37 144 E1
Chepstow Gdns 9 OX16 139 F3
Chequer St CV12 40 C2
Cheriton Cl CV5 60 D4
Cherry Blossom Gr CV31 110 B2
Cherry Blossom Ho 6 CV37 144 F1
Cherrybrook Way CV2 50 C1
Cherry Cl
Coventry CV6 49 D2
Ettington CV37 131 A3
Hurley CV9 16 C4
Offenham WR11 127 D1
Cherryfield Cl CV10 19 B2
Cherry Fields OX17 134 C1
Cherry Gr CV22 99 E8
Cherry La
Bearley CV37 120 E7
Hampton Magna CV35 114 F4
Cherry Orchard Cl GL55 135 B1
Cherry Orchard Est CV13 20 F3
Cherry Orch
Henley-in-A B95 113 B5
Kenilworth CV8 93 A5
Shipston-on-S CV36 149 D5
Stratford-u-A CV37 144 E1
Wellesbourne CV35 146 D4
Cherry Pit La B98 86 A1
Cherry Rd 17 OX16 139 F4
Cherry St
4 Stratford-u-A CV37 144 F1
Warwick CV34 108 F7
Cherry Tree Ave CV10 28 E6
Cherry Tree Cres WR11 127 F6
Cherry Tree La CV23 97 E2
Cherry Tree Wlk CV47 147 B5
Cherry Way CV8 93 A5
Cherry Wlk B47 69 B5
Cherrywood Cres 3 B91 71 C8
Cherrywood Gr CV5 59 F5
Cherwell Cl LE10 31 A8
Cherwell The NN11 117 F1
Cherwell Way CV23 82 B4
Chesford Cres
Coventry CV6 50 B2
Warwick CV34 105 B1
Chesford Gr CV37 144 D4
Chesham St CV31 110 B7
Cheshire Cl CV22 99 C8
Chesholme Rd CV6 49 B2
Cheshunt Ho 3 B37 33 B2
Cheshunt Sch CV1 151 B1
Chesils The CV3 77 D6
Chessetts Wood Rd B94 89 C7
Chester Cl B37 33 A2
Chester Ct 4 B37 33 D2
Chester Rd
3 Birmingham B36,B37 33 C3
Birmingham,Chelmsley Wood B37 44 F8
Hampton-in-A B46,B92,CV7 45 B5
Chester St
Coventry CV1 61 B3
Rugby CV21 83 C4
Chesterton Cl B97 102 D4
Chesterton Dr
18 Stratford-u-A CV37 130 B8
Nuneaton CV10 28 A5
Royal Leamington Spa CV31 110 C5
Chesterton Hill CV35 123 B4
Chesterton Rd
Coventry CV6 61 A7
Lighthorne CV35 123 C3
Chester Way 5 OX16 139 F3
Chesterwood B47 69 A6
Chestnut Ave CV8 92 F3
Chestnut Cl
Ettington CV37 131 B3
Kingsbury B78 15 D6
Chestnut Cres CV10 28 E6
Chestnut Ct
Alcester B49 143 C3
Coventry CV3 78 B8
Royal Leamington Spa CV34 109 E2
Chestnut Dr CV11 29 E3
Chestnut Field CV21 83 A3
Chestnut Gr
Coleshill B46 34 A7
Coventry CV4 60 A2
Moreton Morrell CV35 122 E3
Wolston CV8 80 A3
Chestnut Pl CV47 147 B5
Chestnut Rd
Astwood Bank B96 102 E1
Bedworth CV12 39 D4
Mollington OX17 134 A2
Chestnut Sq
Royal Leamington Spa CV32 106 B2
Wellesbourne CV35 146 D3
Chestnuts The CV12 38 E2
Chestnut Tree Ave CV4 60 A2
Chestnut Wlk
2 Birmingham B37 33 B2
Henley-in-A B95 113 A5
Stratford-u-A CV37 144 F2
Cheswick Cl
Coventry CV6 62 A7
Redditch B98 112 A6
Cheswick Green Prim Sch B90 70 E4
Cheswick Way B90 70 D4
Cheswood Dr B76 22 B6
Chetton Ave CV6 61 C6
Chetwode Cl CV5 60 B4
Chetwynd Ave B78 11 A8
Chetwynd Dr CV11 40 B7
Chetwynd Jun Sch CV11 40 A7
Cheveral Ave CV6 61 B6
Cheveral Rd CV12 39 A3
Cheverel Pl CV11 29 B2
Cheverel St CV11 29 B3
Cheviot Cl CV10 28 B3
Cheviot Rise CV32 106 C3
Cheviot B77 4 C1
Cheviot The CV4 76 D6
Cheviot Way 22 OX16 139 F5
Cheylesmore CV1 151 B2
Chichester Cl CV11 30 A7

Chichester Gr B37 33 B1
Chichester La CV35 114 F3
Chickabiddy La [10] CV47 147 B4
Chicory Dr CV23 83 D8
Chideock Hill CV3 77 A6
Chiel Cl CV5 59 F4
Chigwell Cl B35 22 A3
Childs Cl CV37 144 E5
Childs Oak Cl CV7 74 A6
Chilham Dr B37 33 C2
Chillaton Rd CV6 49 B2
Chillingham B77 9 C7
Chiltern Ct [2] CV6 61 A5
Chiltern Ho CV5 59 D4
Chiltern Leys [2] CV6 61 A4
Chiltern Rd B77 4 C1
Chilterns The CV5 60 B4
Chilvers Coton Com Inf Sch CV11 29 B3
Chilvers Coton Craft Ctr CV11 29 C2
Chilvers Ct CV11 29 C3
Chilworth Cl CV11 39 E8
Chines The CV10 29 D7
Chingford Rd CV6 50 A4
Chingley Bank B95 113 B4
Chipping Campden Bsns Pk GL55 135 C2
Chipping Campden Sch GL55 135 B2
Chipping Norton Rd OX15 142 D4
Chipstone Cl B91 71 C8
Chiswick Wlk B37 33 E2
Chivenor Ho B35 22 A2
Chivenor Jun & Inf Sch B35 22 A2
Chivington Cl B90 71 B6
Chorley Way CV6 61 C6
Choyce Cl CV9 12 D2
Christchurch Cl CV10 28 F1
Christchurch Rd CV6 61 A5
Christie Way [20] CV37 130 B8
Christine Ledger Sq [9] CV31 110 A6
Christopher Hooke Ho CV6 61 E8
Christ the King RC Inf Sch CV6 60 F6
Christ the King RC Jun Sch CV6 60 F7
Chub B77 9 D7
Chudleigh Rd CV2 62 E7
Church Ave B46 23 B3
Church Bank
Binton CV37 129 A8
Temple Grafton B49 119 E1
Church Cl
Birmingham B37 33 A6
Bishops Itchington CV47 124 A4
Drayton Bassett B78 8 E5
Ebrington GL55 135 E3
Harborough Magna CV23 66 B3
Hartshill CV10 28 B8
Hinckley LE10 32 A5
Luddington CV37 129 C7
Old Arley CV7 26 E2
Ryton-on-D CV8 79 B2
Stoke Golding CV13 21 D7
Wardington OX17 134 F1
Whitnash CV31 110 B4
Wolvey LE10 41 E4
Wood End CV9 10 C1
Church Cotts
Astley CV10 37 E7
Church End B46 25 C3
Church Ct
Astwood Bank B96 102 E2
Coventry CV6 48 F1
Churchdale Cl CV10 28 C4
Church Down Cl B97 102 D6
Church Dr
Cookhill B49 118 D5
Kenilworth CV8 92 F5
Church End
Great Rollright OX7 142 A2
Radford Semele CV31 110 E6
Church Farm Ct CV35 138 C7
Church Farm La GL56 140 A6
Church Fields
Staverton NN11 126 E8
Wixford B49 119 A1
Churchfield CV37 129 A7
Church Hill
[15] Bishops Tachbrook CV33 122 F8
Badby NN11 126 F5
Coleshill B46 34 A7
Combrook CV35 131 E6
Church Hill Ct CV35 123 B2
Church Hill
Cubbington CV32 106 E5
Royal Leamington Spa CV32 109 E8
Stretton-on-D CV23 96 F6
Ullenhall B95 112 E6
Warmington OX17 133 D2
Wolvey LE10 41 E4
Church Hos CV35 132 B5
Churchill Ave
Coventry CV6 61 E8
Kenilworth CV8 93 A6
Churchill Cl CV37 131 A4
Churchill Ho [11] CV32 109 F8
Churchill Par B75 13 A5
Churchill Rd
Rugby CV22 83 A1
Sutton Coldfield,Falcon Lodge B75 13 A5
Church La
Alveston CV37 121 D3
Ash Green CV7 49 E7
Aston Cantlow B95 119 F6
Austrey CV9 3 B1
Barford CV35 122 B7
Bearley CV37 120 E7
Berkswell CV7 58 C3
Bickenhill B92 44 E2
Claydon OX17 134 B5
Cookhill B49 118 D5
Corley CV7 48 B7
Coventry,Middle Stoke CV2 62 B3
Coventry,Upper Eastern Green CV5 59 C5
Cropredy OX17 134 C1
Cubbington CV32 106 E5
Curdworth B76 23 B6
Ettington CV37 131 A3
Fenny Drayton CV13 19 F6
Fillongley CV7 36 E3
Gaydon CV35 132 E8
Hanwell OX17 139 F6
Hellidon NN11 126 B5
Hornton OX15 139 B7
Kingsbury B78 15 D5
Lapworth B94 88 E3
Lea Marston B76 24 A7
Leek Wootton CV35 104 F6
Lighthorne CV35 123 B2
Maxstoke B46 35 A2
Meriden CV7 58 E8
Middleton B78 8 C1
Mollington OX17 134 A2
Churchlands Bsns Pk CV33 123 F7
Church La
Newbold-on-S CV37 130 E1
No Man's Heath B79 3 A6
Norton WR11 127 C2
Nuneaton CV10 29 C7
Old Arley CV7 26 F2
Oxhill CV35 137 F8
Radford Semele CV31 110 E6
Royal Leamington Spa CV32 106 A3
Shawell LE17 68 C4
Shotteswell OX17 139 E8
Shutford OX15 139 A3
Shuttington B79 4 E7
Snitterfield CV37 121 B7
South Littleton WR11 127 F1
Stoneleigh CV8 94 C6
Stratford-u-A CV37 144 C3
Thurlaston CV23 98 F2
Welford-on-A CV37 129 A7
Church Lawford Bsns Ctr CV23 81 A5
Church La
Whatcote CV36 137 D7
Whitnash CV31 110 B4
Wigston Parva LE10 42 F8
Willey CV23 54 F6
Wishaw B76 14 A2
Churchlea OX17 134 A2
Church Lees [7] CV33 122 F8
Church Lench CE Fst Sch WR11 127 A6
Church Mews [3] CV35 132 B6
Church Park Cl CV6 48 F1
Church Path CV35 114 F3
Church Rd
Astwood Bank B96 102 E2
Baginton CV8 77 F2
Barford CV35 122 A8
Braunston NN11 117 D5
Bubbenhall CV8 95 C6
Church Lawford CV23 81 C5
Claverdon CV35 113 F3
Dordon B78 11 A5
Gaydon CV35 132 E8
Grandborough CV23 116 F5
Hartshill CV10 28 B8
Ladbroke CV47 124 D5
Long Itchington CV47 115 D4
Newbold-on-S CV37 130 E1
Norton Lindsey CV35 114 C2
Nuneaton,Stockingford CV10 28 C3
Ryton-on-D CV8 79 B2
Shilton CV7 51 E5
Shustoke B46 25 B2
Snitterfield CV37 121 B6
Tamworth B77 9 C4
Ullenhall B95 112 D5
Upper Boddington NN11 134 E8
Warton B79 5 E3
Wilmcote CV37 120 C4
Witherley CV9 19 B7
Church Row
Cherington CV36 141 D7
Middleton B78 8 B1
Church St
Alcester B49 143 C3
Appleby Magna DE12 3 E8
Atherstone CV9 18 D8
Barford CV35 122 B7
Bidford-on-A B50 148 E4
Bulkington CV12 40 C2
Charwelton NN11 126 D2
Chipping Campden GL55 135 B2
Churchover CV23 67 B6
Clifton u D CV23 84 A5
Coventry CV1 151 C4
Church St *continued*
Fenny Compton CV47 133 D7
Hampton Lucy CV35 121 F4
Harbury CV33 123 F6
Harvington WR11 127 D3
Hinckley LE10 32 A5
Marton CV23 115 C7
Moreton-in-M GL56 140 A3
Nuneaton CV11 29 C4
Offenham WR11 127 D1
Royal Leamington Spa CV31 110 A7
Rugby CV21 83 A3
Shipston-on-S CV36 149 D6
Staverton NN11 126 D8
Stockton CV47 147 F8
Stratford-u-A CV37 145 A2
Studley B80 103 E3
Warwick CV34 108 E6
Welford-on-A CV37 129 A7
Wellesbourne CV35 146 D3
Wroxton OX15 139 D4
Church Terr
[1] Royal Leamington Spa CV31 110 A7
Cubbington CV32 106 E5
Harbury CV33 123 F7
Newbold-on-S CV37 130 E1
Church View
Aston Magna GL56 140 A6
Tamworth B77 9 F7
Warton B79 5 E4
Church Way CV12 39 B2
Church Wlk
[1] Royal Leamington Spa CV31 109 F7
Allesley CV5 60 C6
Atherstone CV9 18 F7
Barby CV23 101 C1
Hinckley LE10 31 D8
Norton WR11 127 C2
Rugby,Bilton CV22 99 D8
Rugby CV21,CV22 83 A2
Church Wlks CV13 21 D7
Church Wlk
Thurlaston CV23 98 F3
Wellesbourne CV35 146 D3
Chylds Ct CV5 60 A5
Cicero App CV34 109 E2
Cicester Terr [19] GL56 140 A3
Cicey La CV11 41 A8
Cidermill La GL55 135 B2
Cinder La CV9 6 A8
Circle The CV10 28 F4
Circuit The CV37 129 C8
Circus Ave B37 33 C2
City Arc CV1 151 B2
City Coll Coventry (Butts Ctr) CV1 61 A2
City Coll Coventry (Maxwell Ctr) CV1 61 B1
City College Coventry (Tile Hill Ctr) CV4 59 F1
City Tech Coll The B37 33 A4
Cladswell Cl B49 118 D5
Cladswell La B49,B96 118 C6
Clapham Sq CV31 110 B7
Clapham St CV31 110 B6
Clapham Terrace Com Prim Sch CV31 110 B7
Clapham Terr CV31 110 B7
Clara St CV2 62 A2
Clare Cl CV32 106 C2
Clare Ct CV21 82 F3
Claremont Cl CV12 40 B4
Claremont Rd
Royal Leamington Spa CV31 109 F6
Rugby CV21 83 C3
Claremont Wlk CV5 60 C6
Clarence Ct [5] LE10 31 E8
Clarence Ho [7] CV32 105 F1
Clarence Rd
Hinckley LE10 31 E8
Rugby CV21 82 E3
Stratford-u-A CV37 144 D3
Clarence St
[5] Coventry CV1 61 E4
Nuneaton CV11 29 A4
Royal Leamington Spa CV31 110 A6
Clarence Terr [6] CV32 105 F1
Clarendon Ave CV32 105 F1
Clarendon Cres CV32 105 E1
Clarendon Ct [10] CV21 83 B3
Clarendon Ho LE10 31 B7
Clarendon Pl CV32 105 E1
Clarendon Rd
Hinckley LE10 31 C7
Kenilworth CV8 93 A3
Clarendon Sq CV32 105 F1
Clarendon St
Coventry CV5 60 F1
Royal Leamington Spa CV32 106 A1
Clarewell Ave B91 71 B8
Clark Cl CV36 149 D5
Clarke Ave GL56 140 C3
Clarke's Ave CV8 93 A3
Clarks La CV36 141 D3
Clarksland Gr B37 44 A8
Clarks La B90 70 A6
Clarkson Dr CV31 110 A4
Clark St CV6 50 A1
Clark Wlk CV37 131 B4
Claverdon Cl B97 102 D4
Claverdon Ho CV34 109 B8
Claverdon Prim Sch CV35 113 F3
Claverdon Rd CV5 60 B3
Claverdon Sta CV35 114 A3
Clay Ave CV11 29 F7
Clay Bank OX15 142 D4
Claybrook Dr B98 103 F7
Claybrooke Prim Sch LE17 43 E4
Claydon Gr CV35 114 F6
Claydon Rd OX17 134 C2
Clay Hall Farm B50 128 C4
Clayhill La CV23 81 F6
Clay La
Coventry CV2 62 A4
Harvest Hill CV5 47 E3
Claylands CV35 123 E1
Claymore B77 9 E7
Clay Pit La B90 70 A5
Clayton Rd CV6 60 E5
Clayton Wlk B35 22 A2
Cleasby B77 4 C1
Cleaver Gdns CV10 29 C6
Clebe Rd CV35 113 F3
Cleeve Ct B50 148 D2
Cleeve Prior CE Fst Sch WR11 128 A4
Cleeve Rd
Marlcliff B50 148 D2
Middle Littleton WR11 127 F2
Cleeves Ave CV34 109 D6
Cleeve View WR11 127 F5
Clematis B77 4 A3
Clemens St CV31 110 A7
Clement Ho CV8 93 A5
Clements Cl CV8 93 A5
Clements St CV2 62 A3
Clement St CV11 29 B3
Clement Way CV22 99 A8
Clennon Rise CV2 62 D8
Clent Ave B97 102 D7
Clent Dr CV10 28 B3
Cleobury La B94 70 A3
Cleopatra Gr CV34 109 E4
Clevedon Gn WR11 128 A1
Cleveland Ct [1] CV32 105 F2
Cleveland Rd
Bulkington CV12 40 B3
Coventry CV2 62 A4
Hinckley LE10 31 C8
Cleveley Dr CV10 28 D7
Clews Rd B98 102 F7
Clifden Gr CV8 93 C6
Cliffe Ct CV32 105 D1
Cliffe Rd CV32 105 D1
Cliffe Way CV34 109 A8
Cliff Hall La B78 9 C1
Clifford Bridge Prim Sch CV3 63 A3
Clifford Bridge Rd CV3 62 F4
Clifford La CV37 130 A8
Clifford Mill CV37 129 F7
Clifford Rd B93 71 F4
Clifton Cl B98 103 E8
Clifton Ct [5] CV31 110 B7
Clifton La B79 1 B3
Clifton Rd
Nuneaton CV10 28 F4
Rugby CV21 83 D3
Clifton St CV1 151 D4
Clifton-upon-Dunsmore CE Prim Sch CV23 83 F5
Clinic Dr CV11 29 C3
Clinton Ave
Hampton Magna CV35 108 A7
Kenilworth CV8 92 D6
Clinton La CV8 92 D6
Clinton Prim Sch CV8 92 E3
Clinton Rd
Coleshill B46 33 F6
Coventry CV6 49 F2
Solihull B90 70 D8
Clinton St [2] CV31 110 A7
Clipstone Rd CV6 60 E6
Cliveden Wlk CV11 39 E8
Clive Rd CV7 74 C5
Clock La B92 44 D2
Clock Towers Sh Ctr The CV21 83 A3
Cloister Croft CV2 62 F6
Cloister Crofts CV32 105 F3
Cloisters The
Atherstone CV9 18 E8
Priors Hardwick CV47 125 D3
Royal Leamington Spa CV32 105 F3
Southam CV47 147 C4
Studley B80 103 D4
Cloister Way CV32 105 F3
Clopton Cres B37 33 C4
Clopton Ct [2] CV37 144 F3
Clopton Ho CV37 145 A6
Clopton Rd CV37 144 F4
Closers Bsns Ctr CV11 29 D2
Close The
Brandon CV8 79 F5
Chipping Warden OX17 134 F3
Cleeve Prior WR11 128 A4
Clifford Chambers CV37 129 F7
Epwell OX15 138 D3
Halford CV36 137 A8
Hampton Lucy CV35 121 F4
Hollywood B47 69 A5
Kenilworth CV8 93 A6
Lower Quinton CV37 129 E2
Stratford-u-A CV37 145 A1
Whitnash CV31 110 A5
Wilmcote CV37 120 C5
Closters Gn CV35 132 B6
Cloud Gn CV4 76 D5
Cloudsley Bush La LE10 42 A5
Clovelly Gdns CV2 62 C5
Clovelly Rd CV2 62 B5
Clovelly Way CV11 29 E5
Clover Ave B37 33 D2
Clover Cl
Rugby CV23 83 D8
Stratford-u-A CV37 144 E5
Cloverdale Cl CV6 49 B4
Clover Way CV12 38 D2
Cloweswood La B94 86 F8
Clumber Park Rd CV35 132 D3
Clunes Ave CV11 29 E6
Clyde Rd
Bulkington CV12 40 A2
Dorridge B93 72 A2
Coach Ho The CV35 131 F7
Coach House Ct CV36 149 D5
Coach House Mews [2] CV34 108 F7
Coach House Rise B77 9 F7
Coalpit Fields Rd CV12 39 C1
Coal Pit La CV23 54 C6
Coalpit La CV8 80 D2
Coal Pit La LE10 41 D1
Coat Of Arms Bridge Rd CV3 77 A6
Cobalt Ctr CV47 147 A3
Cobbs Rd CV8 92 D6
Cobden Ave CV31 110 C5
Cobden St CV6 61 E5
Cobham Gn [3] CV31 110 A4
Cobia B77 9 D7
Coburg Ho CV5 60 E3
Cockerills Mdw CV21 101 A8
Cockermouth Cl CV32 105 D2
Cocksfoot Cl CV37 144 E5
Cocksparrow St CV34 108 D7
Cockspur St B78 10 E7
Coffee Pot La CV35 114 C6
Colbek Ct CV10 27 E4
Colbourne Gr CV32 105 D2
Cold Comfort La B49 143 A4
Coldfield Dr B98 102 E7
Coldicott Leys GL55 135 E3
Coldicotts Cl GL55 135 B2
Coldwells Ct CV22 83 A2
Colebridge Cres B46 33 F8
Colebrook Cl
Alcester B49 143 C3
Coventry CV3 62 F2
Coleby Cl CV4 75 D7
Cole Ct B37 33 B2
Coleford Dr B37 33 A2
Colehaven B46 34 A6
Colehurst Croft B90 70 F6
Coleman St CV4 59 F3
Colemeadow Rd B46 33 F7
Coleridge Cl
[8] Stratford-u-A CV37 130 B8
Redditch B97 102 C8
Coleridge Rd CV2 62 C3
Coleshill CE Prim Sch B46 33 F6
Coleshill Cl B97 102 C5
Coleshill Heath Rd
Birmingham B37 44 C7
Coleshill B37,B46 33 E2
Coleshill Heath Sch B37 33 C1
Coleshill Ind Est B46 23 F2
Coleshill Rd
Ansley Common CV10 27 D8
Atherstone CV9 18 C6
Birmingham,Marston Green B37 44 B8
Church End B46 25 C3
Curdworth B76 23 C5
Fazeley B78 9 A7
Hartshill CV10 28 A7
Maxstoke B46 34 E5
Shustoke B46 24 E2
Water Orton B46 23 B2
Coleshill Sch The B46 34 A4
Coleshill St
Atherstone CV9 18 D8
Fazeley B78 9 A8
Colesleys The B46 34 A6
Coleville Rd B76 22 B6
Coley Cl LE10 31 D7
Colina Cl CV3 78 C5
Colledge Cl CV23 64 E3
Colledge Rd CV6 49 D1
College Dr CV32 105 F2
College La
Balsall Common CV8 73 E1
Long Compton CV36 141 D2
Stratford-u-A CV37 144 F1
College Mews CV37 144 F1
College Rd CV23 117 C6
College St
Nuneaton CV10 29 C1
Stratford-u-A CV37 144 F1
Collets Brook B75 7 A2
Collett B77 4 A1
Collett Wlk [2] CV1 61 B3
Colliers Way CV7 36 F8
Colliery La CV7 39 B1
Colliery La N CV7 39 B1
Collingham La CV47 115 E4
Colling Wlk B37 33 A5
Collingwood Ave CV22 82 D1
Collingwood Rd CV5 61 A2
Collins Gr CV4 76 D5
Collins Rd CV34 109 D5
Collins Way B49 143 D4
Colmore Dr B75 13 A5

Colony The OX15 142 C8
Colts Cl LE10 31 D4
Columbia Gdns CV12 39 E2
Columbine Way CV12 38 E1
Colyere Cl CV7 49 A6
Combe Fields Rd CV3 63 F4
Combroke Gr CV35 114 F5
Comet Rd B26 44 C4
Commainge Cl CV34 108 D7
Commander Cl 12 CV33 122 F8
Commanders Cl CV33 123 C3
Commissary Rd B26 44 A3
Common La
  Claverdon CV35 113 F4
  Corley Moor CV7 47 E7
  Kenilworth CV8 93 B7
  Mappleborough Green B80 112 A6
  Polesworth B78 11 A8
Common The CV9 11 C1
Common Way CV2 62 A6
Compass Ct 4 CV1 61 B3
Compton Cl CV32 106 C2
Compton Croft B37 33 D1
Compton Ct
  Coventry CV6 49 D2
  Long Compton CV36 141 C4
  Rugby CV22 99 B6
  Shipston-on-S CV36 149 D6
Compton District Prim Sch The CV36 141 C3
Compton Hill CV35 131 E7
Compton Rd
  Coventry CV6 49 D2
  Lighthorne Heath CV33 123 D2
Compton Verney* CV35 131 F7
Comrie Cl CV2 62 F6
Comyn St CV32 106 B1
Concorde Rd B26 44 C4
Conduit Hill GL55 135 A1
Coneybury Wlk B76 22 D5
Congleton Cl CV6 49 E2
Congreve Cl CV34 104 F2
Congreve Way 14 CV37 130 B8
Congreve Wlk 3 CV12 39 B3
Conifer Cl CV12 39 C4
Conifer Gr 3 CV31 109 F5
Conifer Paddock CV3 62 E1
Conifers The CV8 93 B3
Coningsby Cl 3 CV31 110 C6
Coniston Cl
  Bulkington CV12 40 C3
  Rugby CV21 83 D6
Coniston Ct
  2 Royal Leamington Spa CV32 105 D1
  Nuneaton CV11 29 F7
Coniston Dr CV5 59 D4
Coniston Grange CV8 92 F5
Coniston Rd
  Coventry CV5 60 F1
  Royal Leamington Spa CV32 105 D1
Coniston B77 10 B7
Coniston Way CV11 29 F7
Conrad Cl CV22 99 F6
Conrad Rd CV6 61 A7
Constable Cl CV12 39 A5
Constable Rd CV21 84 B1
Constance Cl CV12 49 F8
Constance Dr CV33 123 F6
Constance Harris Cl CV35 146 D3
Constantine La B46 23 F1
Consul Rd CV21 83 A6
Convent Cl
  Atherstone CV9 18 F7
  Kenilworth CV8 93 A7
Convent La CV9 18 E7
Conway Ave CV4 75 D8
Conway Croft B49 127 E8
Conway Dr 7 OX16 139 F3
Conway Rd
  Birmingham B37 33 B3
  Royal Leamington Spa CV32 109 D8
Conwy Cl CV11 29 D3
Cook Cl
  Knowle B93 72 C6
  Rugby CV21 83 C7
Cooke Cl
  Coventry CV6 50 A4
  Warwick CV34 104 F2
Cooks Cl CV9 18 D8
Cook's Hill OX15 139 A3
Cooks La
  Baddesley Ensor CV9 11 C2
  Birmingham B37 33 A4
  Frankton CV23 97 C1
Cook St CV1 151 B3
Coombe Abbey Ctry Pk* CV3 63 E3
Coombe Abbey Visitor Ctr* CV3 63 E4
Coombe Ave CV3 78 F7
Coombe Ct CV3 63 A2
Coombe Dr
  Binley Woods CV3 79 E7
  Nuneaton CV10 28 B4
Coombe Park Rd CV3 62 F2
Coombe St CV3 62 B2
Co-Operative St CV2 50 B3
Coopers Cl CV37 144 D6
Cooper St CV11 29 D4
Cooper's Way CV47 132 F6
Coopers Wlk CV8 95 C5
Cope Arnolds Cl CV6 49 F4
Copeland Cl B79 5 E4
Copeland CV21 83 C7
Cope St CV1 151 C3
Copland Pl CV4 59 E1
Coplow Cl CV7 74 A6
Copperas St CV2 50 B2
Copper Beech Cl CV6 49 E1
Copperfield Rd CV2 62 B3
Coppice Cl
  Cheswick Green B90 70 C4
  Ryton-on-D CV8 96 B8
  Stratford-u-A CV37 145 A5
Coppice Dr B78 11 A6
Coppice Gdns B47 69 A7
Coppice La
  Middleton B78 7 D2
  Newton Regis B79 2 A8
Coppice Prim Sch The B47 69 A6
Coppice Rd CV31 110 B2
Coppice The
  Atherstone CV9 19 A6
  Coventry CV3 78 B8
  Hinckley LE10 31 F8
  Nuneaton CV10 29 C7
Coppice Way 7 B37 33 B2
Coppice Wlk B90 70 D4
Copps Rd CV32 109 D8
Copse Dr CV5 59 B8
Copse The CV7 50 A8
Copsewood Ave CV11 40 B7
Copsewood Terr CV3 62 C2
Copstone Dr B93 71 F3
Copston La LE10 42 B5
Copthall Ho CV1 151 B1
Copt Heath Croft B93 72 B8
Copt Heath Dr B93 72 A7
Copthorne Lo CV6 60 F8
Copthorne Rd CV6 60 F8
Copt Oak Cl CV4 75 C6
Coral Cl
  Coventry CV5 60 C2
  Hinckley LE10 31 F4
Coralin Cl B37 33 C2
Corbet Rd CV6 61 C7
Corbett Ho CV37 129 D2
Corbett Rd B47 69 A7
Corbetts Cl B92 57 B7
Corbett St CV21 83 C4
Corbin Rd B78 11 A6
Corbison Cl CV34 104 D1
Corbizum Ave B80 103 D4
Cordelia Gn CV34 109 D4
Cordelia Way CV22 99 E6
Corders Cl 9 GL56 140 A3
Corder's La 6 GL56 140 A3
Cord La CV23 65 F4
Corfe Cl CV2 62 F5
Corinne Croft B37 33 A4
Corinthian Ct B49 143 B3
Corinthian Pl CV2 62 D6
Coriolanus Sq CV34 109 F3
Corley (Coventry) Sch CV7 48 B6
Corley View CV7 49 C6
Corncrake Dr B36 33 A7
Cornel Cl B37 44 C8
Cornelius St CV3 77 D8
Cornel B77 4 A4
Corner Ho The 9 CV32 105 F1
Cornerstone Ho CV1 151 C4
Cornet's End La CV7 58 B6
Cornets End La CV7 57 E7
Cornfield Croft B37 33 D3
Cornfield The CV3 62 C1
Cornflower Dr CV23 83 D8
Cornhill Gr CV8 93 C5
Cornish Cl CV10 27 F8
Cornish Cres CV10 29 A2
Cornish Hos GL56 140 B3
Corn Mdws CV12 39 C2
Cornwall Cl 3 CV34 108 F8
Cornwall Ho CV32 105 D1
Cornwallis Rd CV22 82 C2
Cornwall Pl CV32 105 D1
Cornwall Rd CV1 61 E1
Cornwell Cl B98 103 B5
Cornwell OX7 150 E3
Coronation Ave B78 5 B2
Coronation Cl GL55 135 A2
Coronation Cres B79 4 F7
Coronation Ct CV11 29 B4
Coronation La OX17 139 E8
Coronation Rd
  Church Lawford CV23 81 B5
  Coventry CV1 61 F4
  Hurley CV9 16 C5
Coronel Ave CV6 49 E4
Corporation St
  Coventry CV1 151 B3
  Nuneaton CV11 29 B5
  Rugby CV21 83 A3
Corpus Christi RC Sch CV3 78 D7
Correen B77 4 C1
Corsham Rd CV47 132 F6
Corston Mews CV31 110 C6
Corunna Rd CV34 108 C7
Cosford Cl CV32 106 B3
Cosford Cres B35 22 A3
Cosford La
  Rugby CV21 67 A2
  Rugby CV21 82 F8
Costard Ave
  Royal Leamington Spa CV34 109 E3
  Shipston-on-S CV36 149 D5
Costock Cl B37 44 B8
Coten End Prim Sch CV34 108 F7
Coten End CV34 108 F7
Cotes Rd LE10 31 F5
Cotheridge Cl B90 71 C6
Cotman Cl CV12 39 A4
Coton Park Dr CV23 83 C8
Coton Rd
  Churchover CV23 67 C5
  Nether Whitacre B46 15 C1
  Nuneaton CV11 29 C3
  Rugby CV21 84 A1
Cotsmore Cl GL56 140 B3
Cotswold Bsns Village GL56 140 B3
Cotswold Cl
  Sibford Ferris OX15 142 D8
  Tredington CV36 136 F6
Cotswold Cnr OX7 142 A2
Cotswold Cres CV10 28 B3
Cotswold Dr CV3 77 C3
Cotswold Edge GL55 135 B6
Cotswold Gdns 26 GL56 140 A3
Cottage Cl
  Nuneaton CV11 29 D4
  Royal Leamington Spa CV31 110 C6
Cottage Farm Ct GL56 136 C1
Cottage Farm Lodge CV6 49 A1
Cottage Farm Rd
  Coventry CV6 49 A2
  Tamworth B77 9 D7
Cottage Gdns CV10 19 B2
Cottage La
  Minworth B76 22 D6
  Stratford-u-A CV37 144 C2
  Whitacre Heath B46 24 D6
Cottage Leap CV21 83 D5
Cottage Sq CV31 110 C6
Cottage Wlk 4 B77 9 F6
Cotterell Rd CV21 82 F6
Cotterill's Cl CV31 110 B3
Cotters Croft CV47 133 D7
Cottesbrook Cl CV3 62 E1
Cotton Dr CV8 93 C6
Cotton Mill Spinney CV32 106 E6
Cotton Park Dr CV23 67 C1
Cottrells Mews B46 23 B2
Coughton CE Prim Sch B49 118 F7
Coughton Ct* B49 119 A7
Coughton Dr CV31 110 D5
Coughton Fields La B49 143 C8
Coughton La B49 118 F7
Council Hos
  Gaydon CV35 123 E1
  Harvest Hill CV5 47 D1
Council Hos The OX17 139 F6
Coundon Court Sch & Com Coll CV6 60 E7
Coundon Gn CV6 60 E8
Coundon Prim Sch CV6 60 E5
Coundon Rd CV1 61 B3
Coundon St CV1 151 A4
Coundon Wedge Dr CV5, CV6 60 D7
Countess Rd CV11 29 A4
Countess's Croft The CV3 77 D7
Countryside NN11 117 D5
Courtaulds Way CV6 61 D6
Court Cl
  7 Bishops Tachbrook CV33 122 E8
  Warmington OX17 133 D2
Courthouse Croft CV8 93 C4
Courthouse Green Prim Sch CV6 62 A8
Courtland Ave CV6 60 F5
Court La WR11 127 D1
Court Leet CV3 79 D7
Court Leet Rd CV3 77 E7
Courtney Cl CV11 29 F7
Court of Lady Katherine Leveson The B93 73 B5
Court St CV31 110 A7
Court Way B50 148 D4
Courtyard The B46 23 F2
Court Yard The CV35 132 B5
Courtyard The
  Stoke Golding CV13 21 C7
  Warwick CV34 108 F5
Coventry Airport CV8 78 B2
Coventry Blue Coat CE Sch The CV1 61 F1
Coventry Bsns Pk CV5 60 D1
Coventry Canal Basin Warehouse CV1 151 B4
Coventry Cath Church of St Michael* CV1 151 C3
Coventry Gram Sch CV5 60 F1
Coventry Highway B98 112 A7
Coventry Muslim Sch CV6 61 E8
Coventry Prep Sch CV3 77 B8
Coventry Railway Ctr CV8 78 A3
Coventry Rd
  Aston Flamville LE10 32 F1
  Baginton CV8 77 F2
  Barnacle CV7,CV12 51 A8
  Bedworth CV12 39 B2
  Bedworth,Hawkesbury CV2 50 E6
  Berkswell CV7 58 E3
  Bickenhill B26,B92 44 C2
  Brinklow CV23 64 C4
  Bulkington CV12 40 B1
  Cawston CV22 99 A7
  Church Lawford CV23 80 E6
  Coleshill B46 34 A5
  Cubbington CV32 106 E7
  Dunchurch CV22 99 B3
Coventry Rd continued
  Fillongley CV7 36 F2
  Hampton-in-A B92 45 B3
  Hinckley LE10 31 B7
  Hinckley,Sketchley Hill LE10 31 F5
  Kenilworth CV8 93 A7
  Kingsbury B78 15 D5
  Kingsbury B78 15 E2
  Long Lawford CV23 81 E4
  Marton CV23 115 C8
  Nether Whitacre B46 24 F7
  Nuneaton CV10 39 C7
  Pailton CV23 66 A8
  Southam CV47 147 B5
  Stoneleigh CV8,CV3 94 C7
  Thurlaston CV23 98 E4
  Warwick CV34 108 F8
  Willey LE17 55 D5
  Wolvey LE10 41 D4
Coventry Ret Mkt CV1 151 B2
Coventry Road Exhall CV7 50 A8
Coventry Sta CV1 151 B1
Coventry St
  Coventry CV2 62 A4
  Nuneaton CV11 29 C4
  Southam CV47 147 B5
Coventry Toy Mus* CV1 151 C2
Coventry Univ CV1 151 C2
Coventry University Tech Pk CV1 151 C1
Coventry Walsgrave Triangle Bsns Pk CV2 51 A1
Coventry & Warwickshire Hospl CV1 151 C4
Cove Pl CV2 62 C7
Cover Croft B76 13 A1
Coverley Pl CV22 82 E3
Covers The B80 103 E6
Cowan Cl CV22 82 C1
Cowdray Cl CV31 110 C7
Cow La
  Lower Brailes OX15 137 F2
  Whateley B78 9 F3
Cowley Cl B36 22 F1
Cowley Rd CV2 62 D4
Cowley Way CV23 101 F2
Cowper Cl CV34 104 E1
Cowper Rd LE10 31 D6
Cox Cl B50 148 E5
Cox Cres CV22 99 C4
Cox's Cl CV10 29 B3
Cox's La
  Hellidon NN11 126 B5
  Napton on t H CV47 125 C7
Cox's Orch 4 CV31 110 A4
Cox St CV1 151 C3
Cozens Cl CV12 39 A4
Crabbs Cross La B97 102 E5
Crabmill Cl B93 72 C7
Crabmill La CV6 61 F7
Crabtree Gr CV31 110 C6
Crackley Cotts CV8 93 B8
Crackley Cres CV8 93 B8
Crackley Hall Sch CV8 93 B7
Crackley La
  Coventry CV4 75 F3
  Kenilworth CV8 93 A7
Crackthorne Dr CV23 67 D1
Craddock Ct CV10 28 C7
Craddock Dr CV10 28 C7
Craig Cl CV31 110 B6
Craig Croft B37 33 D2
Craigends Ave CV3 78 E6
Crakston Cl CV2 62 E2
Crammond Cl LE10 31 B8
Cramper's Field CV6 61 A5
Cranborne Chase CV2 63 A5
Cranebrook Hill B78 7 E5
Crane Cl
  Stratford-u-A CV37 144 C5
  Warwick CV34 104 D1
Craner's Rd CV1 61 F4
Cranford Rd CV5 60 D4
Cranham Cl B97 102 B8
Cranmer Gr CV34 109 D3
Cranmore Ave B90 70 E8
Cranmore Bvd B90 70 D8
Cranmore Rd
  Birmingham B36 22 E1
  Solihull B90 70 D8
Crantock Way CV11 29 F4
Cranwell Dr CV35 146 C1
Cranwell Rise B78 8 B8
Cranwell Way B35 22 A3
Crathie Cl CV2 62 F6
Craven Arms Rd CV35 132 D3
Craven Ave CV3 79 D7
Craven Ct
  7 Southam CV47 147 B4
  Coventry CV3 62 F2
Craven La CV47 147 B4
Craven Rd CV21 83 C4
Craven St CV5 60 F2
Craven B77 4 B1
Crawford Cl
  Bidford-on-A B50 148 C4
  Royal Leamington Spa CV32 106 B5
Crawshaws Rd B36 22 C1
Creampot Cl OX17 134 D1
Creampot Cres OX17 134 C1
Creampot La OX17 134 C1
Crecy Rd CV3 77 E7
Crediton Cl CV11 29 F5
Crendon Cl B80 103 E5
Crescent Ave CV3 62 C2
Crescent Sch CV22 99 D8
Crescent The
  Baddesley Ensor CV9 11 C3
  Bidford-on-A B50 148 D4
  Birmingham,Coleshill Heath B37 44 E8
  Brinklow CV23 64 F4
  Cawston CV22 99 B8
  Charlecote CV35 146 C7
  Hampton-in-A B92 57 B7
  Harborough Magna CV23 66 A3
  Keresley CV7 48 F6
  Lawford Heath CV23 98 C6
  Napton on t H CV47 125 C7
  Wootton Wawen B95 120 C7
Cressage Rd CV2 63 A6
Cressida Cl CV34 109 F3
Cresswell Cl CV10 29 C8
Cresswell Ho CV6 61 B7
Crest Hill WR11 127 D3
Crest The CV32 106 D3
Crestwood B77 4 A5
Creswell Pl CV22 82 A1
Crew La CV8 93 E6
Creynolds Cl B90 70 D3
Creynolds La B90 70 E4
Cricket Cl CV5 60 F3
Crick Rd CV23 101 D7
Crigdon B77 4 C1
Crimscote Cl B90 70 F6
Crimscote Sq CV35 114 F6
Cringlebrook B77 9 D8
Cripplegate CV36 149 D7
Critchley Dr CV22 99 D3
Crockwell St CV36 141 C4
Croft Cl
  6 Bishops Tachbrook CV33 122 F8
  Stretton-on-D CV23 96 F6
  Warwick CV34 109 C7
  Wolvey LE10 41 E4
Croft Field CV47 125 C7
Croft Fields CV12 39 B2
Croft Holm GL56 140 B3
Croft Ind Est B37 33 D2
Croft Jun Sch CV10 28 F3
Croft La
  Shrewley CV35 114 C6
  Staverton NN11 126 D8
  Temple Grafton B49 119 E2
Croft Mead CV10 27 C3
Croft Mews CV10 29 A4
Croft Pool CV12 38 F2
Croft Rd
  Atherstone CV9 12 D1
  Bedworth CV12 38 F2
  Coventry CV1 151 A2
  Leek Wootton CV35 105 A7
  Middle Littleton WR11 127 F2
  Nuneaton CV10 28 F3
Croft Sch CV37 121 D1
Crofts La B96 102 B2
Croft's La OX15 142 D3
Crofts The B76 22 A8
Croft The
  Bulkington CV12 40 B2
  Church Lench WR11 127 A6
  Coventry CV6 49 F4
  Henley-in-A B95 113 B4
  Meriden CV7 46 C1
  Rugby CV21 101 A8
  Warton B79 5 E4
Cromarty Cl CV5 60 A5
Cromarty Dr LE10 21 F1
Cromdale Cl CV10 28 A3
Cromdale B77 4 C1
Cromer Rd CV32 106 B2
Cromes Wood CV4 59 D1
Crompton Ave B50 148 E5
Crompton Ct CV34 108 D6
Crompton St CV34 108 D6
Cromwell La CV4,CV8 75 C6
Cromwell Pl CV33 123 D2
Cromwell Rd CV22 83 C1
Cromwell St CV6 61 F6
Crondal Rd CV7 50 B7
Crook House Yd CV23 64 F4
Crooks La
  Alcester B49 143 C5
  Studley B80 103 D3
Croome Cl CV6 60 F4
Cropredy CE Prim Sch OX17 134 C1
Cropthorne Cl B98 103 B7
Cropthorne Dr B47 69 B7
Crosbie Rd CV5 60 E3
Cross Cheaping CV1 151 B3
Cross Cotts B49 118 F7
Crossfell B77 4 B1
Cross Fields Rd 4 CV34 108 F8
Crossgate Rd B98 103 C7
Cross In Hand LE17 55 B4
Crosskirk Rd LE10 21 F1
Cross La
  Braunston NN11 117 E5
  Cubbington CV32 106 E4
Crossland Row LE10 32 A6
Crosslands CV35 146 C1
Crossley Ct CV6 61 F7
Cross Leys CV36 136 B6
Cross Point Bsns Pk CV2 63 B8
Cross Rd
  4 Royal Leamington Spa CV32 105 D1
  Alcester B49 143 B3
  Coventry CV6 61 F8

Cross Rd *continued*
Keresley CV7 48 F6
Cross Road Ind Est CV6 61 F7
Cross St
11 Warwick CV34 108 F7
Coventry CV1 151 C4
Long Lawford CV23 82 A5
Nuneaton CV10 28 D3
Royal Leamington Spa CV32 106 A1
Rugby CV21 83 C4
Crossway Rd CV3 77 B4
Crossways Cotts CV7 37 A4
Crossways LE10 31 F5
Cross Wlk B78 11 A6
Crowberry La B78 14 C8
Crowden Rd B77 4 A1
Crow Hill CV9 11 C1
Crowhill Rd CV11 30 A1
Crow La CV9 12 E6
Crowley's Barns B95 112 D6
Crowleys Cl B95 112 E6
Crowmere Rd CV2 62 F7
Crown Cl CV33 123 F7
Crown Gn CV6 49 E2
Crown Hill Cl CV13 21 D7
Crownhill Rd LE10 31 D4
Crown Ho CV5 60 E3
Crown St CV33 123 F7
Crown Terr CV31 109 F7
Crown Way CV32 106 B3
Crowsfurlong CV23 67 D1
Crow Thorns CV21 83 D6
Croxall Dr B46 25 A2
Croxhall St CV12 39 C3
Croydon Cl CV3 77 E6
Croy Dr B35 22 B4
Crucible Ho 5 CV37 144 F3
Crummock Cl CV6 49 D3
Crutchley Way CV31 110 A2
Cryersoak Cl B90 71 B7
Cryfield Grange Rd CV4, CV8 76 C2
Cryfield Hts CV4 76 D2
Cryfield Village CV4 76 B4
Cubbington CE Prim Sch CV32 106 F5
Cubbington Rd
Coventry CV6 50 A2
Royal Leamington Spa CV32 106 B3
Cuckoo La CV1 151 C3
Culey Wlk B37 33 D2
Culpepper Cl CV10 28 E4
Culverley Cres B93 71 F6
Culworth Cl
Rugby CV21 83 E7
Whitnash CV31 109 F5
Culworth Ct
Coventry CV6 61 E7
Whitnash CV31 110 A5
Culworth Rd OX17 134 F3
Culworth Row CV6 61 E8
Cumberland Cres CV32 106 C3
Cumberland Dr CV10 28 E3
Cumberland Wlk B75 13 B5
Cumbernauld Wlk 7 CV2 63 A7
Cumbria Cl CV1 61 A3
Cumming St 14 CV31 110 A7
Cumsey The CV35 114 A5
Cundall Cl CV31 110 B6
Cunnery The CV8 94 A3
Cunningham Way N CV22 82 C1
Cunningham Way S CV22 82 C1
Cup & Saucer OX17 134 C1
Curdworth La B76 23 A8
Curdworth Prim Sch B76 23 B3
Curie Cl CV21 83 D3
Curlew Cl
Stratford-u-A CV37 144 C4
Warton B79 5 E4
Curlew B77 10 A7
Curlieu Cl CV35 108 A7
Curlieu La CV35 114 C2
Curran Cl CV31 110 B4
Curriers Cl CV4 75 D7
Curtis Rd CV2 62 D6
Curzon Ave CV6 61 E8
Curzon Cl LE10 31 F7
Curzon Gr CV31 110 C6
Cut Throat La B94 87 D7
Cuttle Mill La B76 14 D3
Cuttle Pool La B93 72 F4
Cutworth Cl B76 13 A3
Cygnet Ct CV1 151 C4
Cymbeline Way
Royal Leamington Spa CV34 109 E4
Rugby CV22 99 D6
Cypress Croft CV3 78 F8
Cypress La CV31 110 B3
Cypress Way CV10 28 D6
Cyprus Ave B96 102 D2

D

Dace B77 9 D7
Dadglow Rd CV47 124 B4
Daffern Ave CV7 37 A8
Daffern Rd CV7 39 A1
Daffodil Dr 4 CV12 38 D2
Dagtail La B97 102 D3
Dahlia Cl LE10 31 E6
Dahlia Wlk CV10 39 A8
Daimler Ave 5 OX16 139 F4
Daimler Cl B36 22 F1
Daimler Rd CV6 61 C5
Daintree Croft CV3 77 C7
Dairyground The OX15 139 A3
Daisy Croft CV12 38 D2
Dalby Cl CV3 78 E8
Dale Ave CV37 145 D1
Dale Cl
Long Itchington CV47 115 C4
Warwick CV34 109 A8
Dale End Cl LE10 31 A7
Dale End CV10 28 E5
Dalehouse Flats CV8 93 B6
Dalehouse La CV8 93 D7
Dale Meadow Cl CV7 74 B6
Dales Com Jun Sch B77 10 B8
Dales Inf Sch The B77 10 B8
Dale St
Royal Leamington Spa CV32 109 E8
Rugby CV21 83 A4
Dale The B95 113 B2
Daleway Rd CV3 77 B4
Dalkeith Ave CV22 99 D7
Dallington Rd CV6 60 E6
Dalmahoy Cl CV11 40 C8
Dalmeny Rd CV4 75 D7
Dalton Cl CV23 81 B6
Dalton Gdns CV2 62 F4
Dalton Rd
Bedworth CV12 39 A2
Coventry CV5 61 B1
Dalwood Way CV6 50 B4
Daly Ave CV35 114 F3
Dama Rd B78 8 F8
Dame Agnes Gr CV6 62 B8
Damson Cl B97 102 C6
Damson Ct LE10 31 B7
Damson Rd CV35 114 F3
Danbury Cl B76 13 A2
Dancers Dr CV35 130 F7
Dane Ct NN11 117 E5
Dane Rd CV2 62 B4
Danesbury Cres CV31 110 D6
Daneswood Rd CV3 79 E7
Daniel Ave CV10 28 C3
Daniell Rd CV35 146 D4
Daniel Rd CV9 18 F7
Danvers Cl OX15 139 E1
Danvers Rd OX15 139 E1
Danzey Cl B98 103 B5
Danzey Green La B94 87 B1
Danzey Green Rd B36 22 B1
Danzey Sta B94 112 E8
Daphne Cl CV2 50 C3
Darfield Ct CV8 95 C5
Dark La
Astwood Bank B96 102 D1
Bedworth CV12 38 D1
Birchmoor B78 10 E8
Braunston NN11 117 E5
Coventry CV1 151 B4
Hollywood B47 69 A8
Tiddington CV37 145 E4
Wroxton OX15 139 D4
Darlaston Ct CV7 46 D1
Darley Green Rd B93 72 B1
Darley Rd LE10 31 E6
Darlingscote Rd CV36 149 C7
Darlow Dr CV37 144 D3
Darlston Row CV7 46 B1
Darnbrook B77 4 C1
Darnford Cl CV2 62 F7
Darnley Cl CV36 149 D7
Darrach Cl CV2 50 E1
Dart Cl LE10 31 A8
Dartington Way CV11 39 F8
Dartmouth Rd CV2 62 C5
Dartmouth Sch CV2 62 D5
Dart B77 10 A5
Darwell Pk B77 4 B2
Darwin Cl CV2 63 A6
Darwin Ct 1 CV12 39 A2
Darwin Ho 3 B37 33 C1
Dasset Rd OX17 133 F4
Dassett CE Prim Sch The CV47 133 D7
Dassett Cl CV35 114 F5
Dassett Rd B93 71 F4
Datchet Cl CV5 60 C4
D'aubeny Rd CV4 76 C8
Davenport Dr B35 22 C3
Davenport Lodge Sch CV5 77 B8
Davenport Rd CV5 77 B8
Davenport Terr LE10 31 E8
Daventry Rd
Barby CV23 101 C1
Coventry CV3 77 D7
Rugby CV22 99 E2
Southam CV47 147 D4
Staverton NN11 126 D8
Daventry St 3 CV47 147 B4
David Rd
Bedworth CV7 49 F8
Coventry CV1 61 F2
Rugby CV22 99 D8
Davidson Ave CV31 110 A7
Davies Rd
Bedworth CV7 49 F7
Moreton-in-M GL56 140 B3
Davis Cl CV32 105 D2
Davy Ct CV23 67 C2
Dawes Cl CV2 62 A3
Dawley Cres B37 33 B1
Dawley Wlk 9 CV2 63 A7
Dawlish Cl CV11 29 E5
Dawlish Dr CV3 77 D5
Dawson Cl CV31 110 A2
Dawson Rd CV3 62 A1
Days Cl CV1 61 E3
Day's La CV1 61 F3
Daytona Dr CV5 59 B8
Deacon Cl CV22 83 C1
Deacon St CV11 29 C3
Deanbrook Cl B90 71 A6
Deane Par CV21 101 A8
Deane Rd CV21 101 B8
Dean St CV2 62 A3
Deanston Croft CV2 50 F1
Deans Way CV7 49 D6
Deansway CV34 104 E1
Deasy Ho CV3 78 B5
Deasy Rd CV1 151 C1
Debden Cl
Dorridge B93 71 E2
Wellesbourne CV35 146 C1
De-Compton Cl CV7 49 A7
Deedmore Rd CV2 50 D1
Deedmore Sch CV2 62 C8
Deegan Cl CV2 62 A5
Deeley B77 4 A1
Deepdale B77 4 D2
Deep La B46 24 F6
Deepmore Rd CV22 99 D8
Deerdale Terr 8 CV3 78 F8
Deerdale Way CV3 78 F8
Deerhill B77 4 C1
Deerhurst Cl GL56 140 F1
Deerhurst Mews CV22 99 C3
Deerhurst Rd CV6 49 B2
Deerings Rd CV21 101 A8
Deer Leap The CV8 93 B6
Deerpark Dr CV34 108 E8
Dee Wlk
Birmingham B36 33 A7
Birmingham B36 33 A8
Daventry NN11 117 F1
Dehavilland Cl CV11 29 B5
De Havilland Dr B35 22 A2
De Havilland Way LE10 31 E4
Deighton Gr CV3 78 C6
De-La-Bere Cres LE10 32 A6
Delage Cl CV6 50 B4
Delamere Cl B36 22 D1
Delamere Rd CV12 38 F2
Delamere Way CV32 106 C4
Delancey Keep B75 13 A5
Delaware Rd CV3 77 C5
Delf Ho CV2 50 D1
Delhi Ave CV6 49 D1
Delius St CV4 59 E3
Dell Cl CV3 78 C5
Dell Ct B95 113 B5
Dell Farm Cl B93 72 B6
Dell The B95 113 B2
Delmore Way B76 22 B6
Delphi Cl CV34 109 E4
Deltic La B77 9 F8
Deltic B77 4 A1
Delves Cres CV9 10 C1
De Mohun Cres CV36 141 F5
De Montfort Ct B95 113 B4
De Montfort Mews 1 B46 34 A6
De Montfort Rd CV8 92 E6
De Montfort Way CV4 76 D5
Dempster Ct CV11 29 C4
Dempster Rd CV12 39 A4
Denbigh Cl OX16 139 F2
Denbigh Cnr B46 45 A6
Denbigh Rd CV6 60 E5
Denby Bldgs 17 CV32 109 F8
Denby Cl CV32 106 C3
Denby Croft B90 71 B6
Dencer Dr CV8 93 C4
Dene Cl CV35 132 B5
Denegate Cl B76 22 B6
Denehurst Way CV10 28 F3
Denemoor Ct CV8 93 B5
Dene Valley Bsns Pk CV35 132 A6
Denewood Way CV8 93 C6
Dengate Dr CV7 74 B7
Denham Ave CV5 60 C4
Denham Ct CV9 18 E8
Denis Rd LE10 31 D5
Denne Cl CV37 145 A5
Dennett Cl CV34 104 F2
Dennis Rd CV2 62 B6
Denshaw Croft CV2 63 A8
Denton Cl CV8 92 D6
Denton Croft B93 71 D3
Denville Rd CV32 106 A3
Deppers Bridge CV33, CV47 124 B6
Derby Dr B37 33 B2
Dereham Ct CV32 106 A2
Derek Ave B78 11 A6
Dering Cl CV2 62 D8
Deronda Cl CV12 39 A3
Derry Cl CV8 80 A3
Dersingham Dr CV6 50 B2
Derwent Cl
Coventry CV5 59 E4
Royal Leamington Spa CV32 105 D1
Rugby CV21 83 C6
Derwent Rd
Bedworth CV12 39 A2
Coventry CV6 49 A2
Derwent Way CV11 29 F6
Desdemona Ave CV34 109 E4
Despard Rd CV5 59 D4
Devere Ct 1 CV37 144 F3
Devereux Cl CV4 59 C1
Devitts Cl B90 70 F7
Devon Cl CV10 28 F3
Devon Gr CV2 62 B6
Devonish Cl B49 143 C5
Devon Ox Rd CV23 101 F2
Devonshire Cl CV22 82 B1
Devonshire Terr 7 GL56 140 A3
Devoran Cl CV7 50 B8
Dewar Gr CV21 83 E2
Dew Cl CV22 99 C3
Dewis Ho 4 CV2 50 B1
Dewsbury Ave CV3 77 B5
Dewsbury Cl B96 102 E1
Dexter Ct CV9 16 C4
Dexter La CV9 16 C3
Dexter Way B78 10 F8
Dey Croft CV34 108 B4
Dial House La CV5 59 F4
Diana Dr CV2 50 E1
Dickens Cl CV10 28 A4
Dickens Heath Prim Com Sch B90 70 A6
Dickens Heath Rd
Solihull B90 70 A5
Solihull B90 70 A6
Solihull B90 70 B6
Dickens Rd
Coventry CV6 61 A8
Harbury CV33 123 E6
Rugby CV22 99 F6
Dickinson Ct CV22 83 A1
Dickins Rd CV34 105 B1
Dick's La B94 113 E8
Didcot Cl B97 102 C5
Didcott Way DE12 3 F8
Diddington La B92,CV7 45 C1
Didgley Gr B37 33 A5
Didgley La CV7 36 C4
Didsbury Rd CV7 39 A1
Digbey Cl CV5 60 B6
Digby Cres B46 23 B3
Digby Dr B37 44 B6
Digby Pl CV7 46 C1
Digby Rd B46 33 F6
Dighton Cl CV37 129 F7
Dilcock Way CV4 75 F7
Dillam Cl CV6 50 A4
Dillington Ho 8 B37 33 B2
Dillon Ct CV11 29 B5
Dillotford Ave CV3 77 D6
Dingle Cl CV6 61 A6
Dingle La
Appleby Magna B79,DE12 3 C6
Nether Whitacre B46 24 F5
Dingleside Mid Sch B98 103 B8
Dingles Way CV37 145 A5
Dingle The
Cheswick Green B90 70 D5
Nuneaton CV10 28 E6
Dingley Rd CV12 40 B2
Discovery Way CV3 79 B7
Ditchford Cl B97 102 D4
Ditton Cl CV22 82 C1
Dixon Cl B35 22 A2
Dobbie Rd CV37 129 D1
Dobson La CV31 110 A4
Dockers Cl CV7 74 C7
Doctors Cl B94 87 A2
Doctors Hill B94 87 A2
Doctors La B95 113 B5
Dodd Ave CV34 109 C7
Dodgson Cl CV6 50 A4
Dodwell Pk CV37 129 C8
Dodwells Bridge Ind Est LE10 30 E8
Dodwells Rd LE10 30 E8
Dodwell Trad Est CV37 129 C8
Doe Bank La CV1 61 A3
Dogberry Cl CV3 78 C6
Dogberry Way CV34 109 F2
Dog Kennel La B90 70 D7
Dog La
Fenny Compton CV47 133 D7
Napton on t H CV47 125 C8
Doglands The CV31 110 B4
Dog La
Nether Whitacre B46 25 A7
Tamworth B77 4 B6
Doily Cl OX15 142 D4
Dolomite Ave CV4 60 D1
Donalbain Cl CV34 109 F3
Doncaster Cl CV2 62 D7
Done Cerce Cl CV22 99 C3
Donegal Cl CV4 76 A7
Dongan Rd CV34 108 E7
Donibristle Croft B35 22 A4
Donnington Ave CV6 60 E5
Donnington Rd CV36 149 D7
Donnithorne Ave CV10, CV11 29 D1
Doone Cl CV2 62 E6
Dorado B77 9 D7
Dorcas Cl CV11 40 C8
Dorchester Ave CV35 114 F3
Dorchester Gr OX16 139 F2
Dorchester Rd LE10 32 B7
Dorchester Way
Coventry CV2 63 A4
Nuneaton CV11 30 A7
Dordon Com Prim Sch B78 11 A6
Dordon Rd B78 10 F8
Doris Rd B46 33 F8
Dorlecote Ct CV10 29 C1
Dorlecote Pl CV10 39 C8
Dorlecote Rd CV10 39 C8
Dormer Harris Ave CV4 59 F1
Dormer Ho 15 CV32 105 F2
Dormer Pl CV32 109 F8
Dormston Cl B91 71 C8
Dorney Cl CV5 76 E8
Dorn GL56 140 A5
Dorothy Powell Way CV2 50 F1
Dorridge Croft B93 71 F2
Dorridge Jun & Inf Schs B93 72 A4
Dorridge Rd B93 72 A2
Dorridge Sta B93 71 F2
Dorset Cl
Nuneaton CV10 28 F3
Rugby CV22 82 B1
Dorset Rd CV1 61 C5
Dorsington Cl CV35 114 F6
Dorsington Manor CV37 128 E5
Dorsington Rd CV37 128 E2
Dosthill Prim Sch B77 9 D5
Dosthill Rd (Two Gates) B77 9 D7
Douglas Ho CV1 151 D4
Douglas Rd
Hollywood B47 69 A7
Rugby CV21 83 C6
Doulton Cl CV2 50 E1
Dove Cl
Bedworth CV12 38 E3
Hinckley LE10 31 A8
Dovecote Cl CV6 60 D5
Dovecotes The CV5 60 B5
Dovedale Ave CV6 49 F2
Dovedale CV21 83 C7
Dovehouse Dr CV35 146 C1
Dovehouse La CV33 123 F7
Dover Ave OX16 139 F3
Doverdale Cl B98 103 B7
Dover Farm Cl B77 10 B8
Dover St CV1 151 A3
Dovestone B77 4 D1
Dovey Dr B76 22 A7
Dowler's Hill Cres B98 103 A8
Dowley Croft CV3 63 B1
Downderry Way CV6 62 A6
Down End OX15 142 D4
Downing Cl B93 72 A4
Downing Cres CV12 39 C4
Downing Ho B37 33 B1
Downton Cl CV2 63 A8
Dowty Ave CV12 38 D1
Doyle Dr CV6 49 F3
Drakes Cl B97 102 C6
Drakes Cross Par B47 69 A5
Drake St CV6 61 D7
Draper Cl CV8 93 C4
Drapers Ct CV1 151 B4
Draper's Fields CV1 151 B4
Drawbridge Rd B90 69 E8
Draycote Water Ctry Pk* CV23 116 C8
Draycote Water* CV23 116 B8
Draycott Rd CV2 62 C7
Drayton Ave CV37 144 D4
Drayton Cl
Bidford-on-A B50 148 C5
Fenny Drayton CV13 19 F6
Hartshill CV10 28 A8
Redditch B98 103 D8
Stratford-u-A CV37 144 D4
Drayton Cres CV5 59 D5
Drayton Ct
Hartshill Green CV10 19 B2
Warwick CV34 104 E2
Drayton Fields Ind Est NN11 117 F3
Drayton La
Drayton Bassett B78 8 C5
Fenny Drayton CV13 19 E6
Drayton Leys CV22 100 A7
Drayton Manor Dr
Drayton Bassett B78 8 F7
Fazeley B78 8 F8
Stratford-u-A CV37 120 C2
Drayton Manor Pk* B78 8 E7
Drayton Rd
Bedworth CV12 39 D2
Solihull B90 70 E8
Drayton Sch OX16 139 F4
Drayton Way
Daventry NN11 117 F2
Nuneaton CV10 28 C7
Drem Croft B35 22 A2
Drew Cres CV8 93 A4
Dreyer Cl CV22 82 C2
Drift La OX15 139 D4
Driftway The CV36 149 D6
Drinkwater Cl CV33 123 F6
Drinkwater Ho 7 CV1 61 B2
Drivers La GL56 141 A1
Drive The
Coleshill B46 34 A6
Coventry CV2 62 E3
Dunchurch CV22 99 E4
Dronfield Rd CV2 62 B3
Drovers Way CV47 147 C4
Droylsdon Park Rd CV3 77 B3
Dr Phillips Sh Ctr The CV2 50 D1
Druid Rd CV2 62 B3
Drummond Cl CV6 60 F7
Drummond Way B37 33 C2
Drury La CV21 83 A3
Drybrooks Cl CV7 74 B6
Dryden Cl
Galley Common CV10 27 F5
Kenilworth CV8 92 F3
Dryden Pl CV22 82 E3
Dryden Way 17 CV37 130 B8

Dryden Wlk CV22 82 E3
Drymen Rd CV35 132 D3
Duck Lake DE12 3 F8
Duck La CV37 129 B7
Dudley Gn CV32 106 B2
Dudley Rd CV8 92 F2
Dudley Rise LE10 31 D6
Dudley St
Atherstone CV9 18 D7
Coventry CV6 50 A1
Dudley Terr CV8 94 B6
Duffus Hill CV35 122 F3
Duffy Pl CV21 101 A8
Dugard Pl CV35 122 B7
Dugdale Ave
Bidford-on-A B50 148 C5
Stratford-u-A CV37 145 A5
Dugdale Ct 5 CV31 110 A6
Dugdale Ho CV11 29 C3
Dugdale Rd CV6 61 B6
Dugdale St CV11 29 C4
Duggins La CV4,CV7 75 B8
Duke Barn Field CV2 62 A5
Duke's Ct 10 CV37 145 A3
Dukes Jetty 8 CV21 83 A3
Dukes Rd B78 11 A6
Duke St
2 Rugby CV21 83 A4
Coventry CV5 60 F2
Nuneaton CV11 29 B4
Royal Leamington Spa CV32 106 A1
Dulverton Ave CV5 60 D4
Dulverton Ct CV5 60 D4
Dulverton Pl GL56 140 B3
Dumble Pit La B47,B48 85 F7
Dumphouse La B48 85 C3
Dunblane Dr CV32 106 C5
Duncan Dr CV22 99 D6
Dunchurch Boughton CE Jun Sch CV22 99 C3
Dunchurch Cl CV7 74 B7
Dunchurch Hall CV22 99 C3
Dunchurch Highway CV5 60 A4
Dunchurch Inf Sch CV22 99 C3
Dunchurch Rd CV22 99 F7
Dunchurch Trad Est CV23 98 D5
Duncombe Gn 12 B46 33 F7
Dun Cow Cl CV23 64 E3
Duncroft Ave CV6 60 F7
Duncumb Rd B75 13 A5
Dunedin B77 4 A1
Dunham Croft B93 71 D3
Dunhill Ave CV4 59 E3
Dunkirk Pl CV3 78 F7
Dunley Croft B90 70 F6
Dunlop Rd B97 102 D5
Dunnerdale CV21 83 D7
Dunnington CE Prim Sch B49 127 E8
Dunnose Cl CV6 61 E8
Dunn's La B78 11 B6
Dunrose Cl CV2 62 E2
Dunsmore Ave
Coventry CV3 78 C6
Rugby CV22 100 E8
Dunsmore Bsns Ctr CV21 83 B3
Dunsmore Heath CV22 99 C3
Dunstall Cres 2 CV33 122 E8
Dunstall Ho 22 GL56 140 A3
Dunstan Croft B90 70 C8
Dunster Pl CV6 49 D3
Dunster Rd B37 33 D2
Dunster B77 9 C7
Dunsville Dr CV2 62 F8
Dunton Hall Rd B90 70 A8
Dunton La B76 14 C1
Dunton Pk B76 23 C7
Dunvegan Cl
Coventry CV3 63 A2
Kenilworth CV8 93 C4
Duport Rd LE10 31 F7
Durbar Ave CV6 61 D8
Durham Cl CV7 48 F4
Durham Cres CV5 60 B7
Durham Croft B37 33 B2
Durlston Cl B77 4 A5
Durrell Dr CV22 99 A7
Dursley La B98 112 A6
Dutton Rd CV2 50 D3
Duttons Cl CV37 121 B7
Duxford Cl
Redditch B97 102 B8
Wellesbourne CV35 146 C2
Dwarris Wlk CV34 104 E2
Dyas Rd B47 69 A7
Dyce Cl B35 22 A4
Dyer's La GL55 135 A2
Dyers La B94 87 D8
Dyer's La CV8 80 B3
Dyers Rd CV11 40 F6
Dymond Rd CV6 49 D3
Dysart Cl CV1 61 E4
Dyson Cl CV21 83 F1
Dyson St CV4 59 E3

E

Eacott Cl CV6 49 A3
Eadie St CV10 28 D4
Eagle Cl CV11 40 B8
Eagle Dr B77 4 C4
Eagle Gr B36 33 A8
Eagle Ho CV1 61 D5
Eagle La CV8 92 F3
Eagle St E CV1 61 D5
Eagle St
Coventry CV1 61 D5
Royal Leamington Spa CV31 110 A6
Ealingham B77 4 B1
Earles Cl CV47 147 F8
Earl Place Bsns Pk CV4 60 B1
Earl's Croft The CV3 77 D7
Earlsdon Ave CV5 77 A8
Earlsdon Ave N CV5 60 F1
Earlsdon Ave S CV5 77 A8
Earlsdon Ho CV5 77 A8
Earlsdon Prim Sch CV5 61 A1
Earlsdon St CV5 76 F8
Earlsmere B94 70 B1
Earls Rd CV11 29 A5
Earls Rivers Ave CV34 109 D3
Earl St
Bedworth CV12 39 C2
Coventry CV1 151 C2
Royal Leamington Spa CV32 106 A1
Rugby CV21 83 B3
Earl's Wlk CV3 79 D7
Earlswood Comm B94 87 A6
Earlswood Rd B93 71 D2
Earlswood Sta B94 69 D1
Earlswood Trad Est B94 86 C6
Easedale Cl
Coventry CV3 77 B6
Nuneaton CV11 30 A6
Easenhall Cl B93 72 A4
Easenhall Rd CV23 66 A2
Easingwold Rd CV35 132 D4
East Ave
Bedworth CV12 39 D2
Coventry CV2 62 A2
Eastboro Ct CV11 29 E2
Eastboro Fields CV11 30 A4
Eastboro Way CV11 29 F2
Eastbourne Cl CV6 60 E6
East Car Park Rd B40 44 F4
East Cl LE10 31 D7
Eastcote La B92 56 F4
Eastcotes CV4 60 B1
East Dene CV32 106 B2
East End OX15 142 D4
Eastern Green Jun Sch CV5 59 D5
Eastern Green Rd CV5 59 F4
Eastern Hill B96 102 F2
Eastfield Cl CV37 144 F5
Eastfield Pl CV21 83 A3
Eastfield Rd
Nuneaton CV10 29 D6
Royal Leamington Spa CV32 110 A8
Eastfields NN11 117 E5
Eastgate Ho 4 CV34 108 E6
Eastgate OX15 139 B8
Eastgate Mews 3 CV34 108 E6
East Green Dr CV37 144 C3
East Gr CV31 110 A6
East House Dr CV9 16 D4
Eastlands Gr CV5 60 E4
Eastlands Pl CV21 83 D3
Eastlands Prim Sch CV21 83 D2
Eastlands Rd CV21 83 D2
Eastlang Rd CV7 36 E3
Eastleigh Ave CV5 76 F7
Eastleigh Croft B76 22 A7
Eastley Cres CV34 108 B8
Eastnor Gr CV31 110 B7
Easton Gr B47 69 B7
East Side WR11 128 A2
East St
Coventry CV1 61 E3
Long Compton CV36 141 C3
Moreton-in-M GL56 140 A3
Rugby CV21 83 D4
Tamworth B77 9 D5
East Union St CV22 83 A2
East View B79 4 F7
East Way B92 45 B3
Eastway B40 44 F3
Eastwood Cl CV31 110 D6
Eastwood Ct B96 102 E1
Eastwood Gr CV21 101 C8
Easy La CV21 82 F3
Eathorpe Cl
Coventry CV2 50 C1
Redditch B98 103 E8
Eathorpe Pk CV33 115 B8
Eaton Cl CV32 105 D2
Eaton Ct CV32 105 D1
Eaton Rd CV1 151 B1
Eaves Green La CV7 46 E1
Eaves Green Mobile Home Pk CV7 46 F2
Ebbw Vale Terr CV3 77 D7
Eborall Cl CV34 104 E2
Eborne Croft CV7 74 C8
Ebourne Cl CV8 93 A4
Ebrington Dr CV35 114 F5
Ebrington GL55 135 E3
Ebro Cres CV3 62 F1
Ebsdorf Cl B50 148 E5
Eburne Rd CV2 50 C3
Eccles Cl CV2 62 C8
Eckington Cl B98 103 B8
Eclipse Rd B49 143 A4
Ecton Leys CV22 100 A7
Edale Gn LE10 31 F6
Edale B77 4 B1
Edale Way CV6 62 A7
Eddens Wood Cl B78 8 E5
Eddie Miller Ct CV12 39 B2
Eden Cl B80 103 D3
Eden Croft CV8 93 B3
Eden Ct
Nuneaton CV10 28 C7
Royal Leamington Spa CV32 106 D3
Edenfield Pl B77 4 B1
Eden Gr B37 33 D1
Eden Rd
Coventry CV2 63 A8
Rugby CV21 83 F1
Eden St CV6 61 F7
Edgecote Cl CV21 83 F1
Edgefield Rd CV2 63 A8
Edgehill Ctry Pk* OX17 133 B3
Edgehill Pl CV4 59 C1
Edgehill Rd CV33 123 C2
Edge Hill CV9 10 B2
Edge La B95 113 C5
Edgewick Com Prim Sch CV6 61 E8
Edgioake La B96 118 C7
Edgwick Park Ind Est CV6 61 F8
Edgwick Rd CV6 61 F7
Edinburgh Cl OX16 139 F4
Edinburgh Cres CV31 109 F6
Edinburgh Rd
Hurley CV9 16 C5
Nuneaton CV10 28 D6
Edinburgh Villas CV8 77 F2
Edinburgh Way
Banbury OX16 139 F3
Long Lawford CV23 82 B5
Edingale Rd CV2 62 F8
Edison Rd
Coleshill B46 24 A3
Curdworth B46,B76 23 F4
Edkins Cvn Site CV37 120 B5
Edmondes Cl CV34 104 F1
Edmonds Cl CV37 129 D1
Edmondscote Rd CV32 109 D8
Edmondson Cl CV22 99 D4
Edmund Rd CV1 61 D5
Edmunds Rd OX16 139 F3
Edstone Cl B93 71 F4
Edward Bailey Cl CV3 78 E7
Edward Ct
2 Rugby CV21 83 B3
Nuneaton CV11 29 C3
Edward Mews CV34 108 E7
Edward Rd
Bedworth CV12 39 C3
Coventry CV6 49 A3
Water Orton B46 23 C3
Edwards Ctr 7 LE10 31 D8
Edwards Gr CV8 93 C5
Edward St
Coventry CV6 61 E5
Nuneaton CV11 29 C3
Royal Leamington Spa CV32 105 C1
Rugby CV21 82 F3
Warwick CV34 108 D7
Edward Tyler Rd CV7 39 A1
Edwin Cl CV22 99 B7
Edyth Rd CV2 62 E4
Edyvean Cl CV22 99 E6
Edyvean Walker Ct CV11 29 B5
Egerton Cl CV21 82 F6
Eglamour Way CV34 109 F3
Egret Wlk CV2 50 B3
Eileen Gdns B37 33 A4
Elan Cl CV32 106 C3
Elborow St 5 CV21 83 A3
Elbury Croft B93 71 F5
Elderberry Way CV2 62 B6
Elder Cl
Kingsbury B78 15 D7
Rugby CV22 82 B1
Eldersfield Gr B91 71 B7
Eldorado Cl B80 103 D4
Eld Rd CV6 61 E7
Elford Gr B37 33 B1
Elgar Cl
Nuneaton CV11 40 A7
Redditch B97 102 C8
Elgar Rd CV6 62 B8
Eliot Cl
15 Stratford-u-A CV37 130 B8
Warwick CV34 104 E2
Eliot Ct CV22 82 E3
Eliot Way CV10 29 B2
Elisabeth Ct CV31 110 B8
Elizabeth Ave B78 5 A2
Elizabeth Ct
8 Coventry CV6 61 A4
Warwick CV34 109 B6
Elizabeth Rd CV31 109 F6
Elizabeth Way
Coventry CV2 62 F7
Kenilworth CV8 92 E5
Long Lawford CV23 82 B5
Elkington Croft B90 71 A5
Elkington La CV23 101 B1
Elkington St CV6 61 F8
Ellacombe Rd CV2 62 D8
Ellen Badger Hospl CV36 149 E6
Ellerbeck B77 4 B1
Ellerdene Cl B98 102 D8
Ellerman Gdns CV6 49 F3
Ellesmere Rd CV12 39 A2
Ellice Dr B36 33 B7
Elliot Ct CV36 149 D6
Elliot Dr CV35 146 C3
Elliott Cl B50 148 C5
Elliott Ct CV5 60 C1
Elliott's Field Ret Pk CV21 83 A6
Elliotts Orch CV35 122 A7
Ellison Dr 16 OX17 139 F5
Ellis Park Dr CV3 63 B1
Elliston Gr CV31 110 C6
Ell La CV23 64 F4
Ellys Rd CV1 61 C5
Elm Bank Cl CV32 106 A4
Elmbank Rd CV8 92 E6
Elmbank CV47 147 B3
Elmbridge Dr B90 71 B6
Elm Cl
Binley Woods CV3 79 C7
Ilmington CV36 136 B6
Pebworth CV37 128 F1
Southam CV47 147 B3
Elm Ct
7 Stratford-u-A CV37 144 F3
Allesley CV5 59 B8
Elmdene Cl
Hatton CV35 114 C5
Wolston CV8 80 A4
Elmdene Rd CV8 93 B4
Elmdon Ct B37 44 A7
Elmdon La
Birmingham B37 44 A6
Solihull B26 44 A3
Elmdon Rd B37 44 A7
Elmdon Trad Est B37 44 C5
Elm Dr B49 143 D3
Elmfield Rd CV10 29 C7
Elm Gr
Balsall Common CV7 74 C6
Ebrington GL55 135 F3
Hurley CV9 16 C4
Old Arley CV7 26 E2
Elmhurst Cl B97 102 D4
Elmhurst Rd CV6 50 A4
Elm La CV23 68 E1
Elm Lodge B92 57 A7
Elmore Cl
Birmingham B37 33 A4
Coventry CV3 78 D8
Elmore Rd CV22 82 F1
Elm Rd
Royal Leamington Spa CV32 106 B3
Shipston-on-S CV36 149 D4
Stratford-u-A CV37 144 F5
Elm Row CV47 115 F3
Elms Ct CV9 3 A2
Elmsdale Ave CV6 49 F2
Elms Dr
Austrey CV9 3 A2
Rugby CV22 100 F8
Elms Paddock The CV23 83 F5
Elms The
Bedworth CV12 38 E2
Kingswood B94 89 D3
Leek Wootton CV35 104 F6
Stratford-u-A CV37 145 A4
Elmstone Cl B97 102 C5
Elm Tree Ave CV4 60 B2
Elm Tree Cl B78 15 D6
Elm Tree Dr LE10 31 F8
Elm Tree Rd CV12 40 D2
Elm Tree Rise B92 57 B6
Elm Way CV10 28 A8
Elmwood Ave CV6 60 F5
Elmwood Cl CV7 74 C7
Elmwood Ct CV1 151 B4
Elmwood Gr B47 69 A6
Elphin Cl CV6 49 A4
Elsee Rd CV21 83 B3
Elstop Ave CV23 67 D1
Elter Cl CV21 83 D7
Eltham Rd CV3 77 E7
Elton Cl CV32 106 C2
Elton Croft B93 71 F4
Elva Croft B36 22 F1
Elvers Green La B92,B93 72 E7
Elwy Circ CV7 49 C6
Ely Cl
Birmingham B37 33 B2
Coventry CV2 63 A6
Ely Gdns CV37 144 F2
Ely St CV37 145 A2
Embassy Wlk CV2 62 D8
Emerald Way CV31 109 F5
Emerson Rd CV2 62 C3
Emery Cl CV2 62 E7
Emily Smith Ho 2 CV2 50 B1
Emmerson Ave CV37 144 D3
Emmott Dr CV31 110 B5
Emperor Way CV21 82 F7
Empire Rd CV4 59 E2
Emscote Inf Sch CV34 109 B8
Emscote Rd
Coventry CV3 62 C2
Warwick CV34 109 B8
Ena Rd CV1 61 D5
Endemere Rd CV6 61 D7
Enderby Cl B93 71 F4
Endsleigh Gdns CV31 110 B6
Enfield Rd
Coventry CV2 62 B3
Redditch B97 102 D5
Engine La B77 4 A2
England Cres CV31 109 E7
England Ho 10 CV32 105 F2
Engleton Rd CV6 61 A6
English Martyrs RC Prim Sch CV21 101 A7
Ennerdale Cl CV32 105 D2
Ennerdale Cres CV11 29 F6
Ennerdale La CV2 62 F4
Ennerdale CV21 83 C7
Ennersdale Bglws B46 23 F1
Ennersdale Cl B46 23 F1
Ennersdale Rd B46 23 F1
Enright Cl CV32 105 E2
Ensign Bsns Ctr CV4 75 F6
Ensign Cl CV4 59 D1
Ensor Cl CV11 30 A6
Ensor Dr B78 4 F1
Enterprise Ho B92 57 A6
Enville Cl B37 33 B1
Epperston Ct CV31 109 F7
Epping Way CV32 106 C4
Epsom Cl
Bedworth CV12 39 B4
Redditch B97 102 C8
Tamworth B77 9 C4
Epsom Dr CV3 78 C6
Epsom Rd
Royal Leamington Spa CV32 106 C4
Rugby CV22 82 D1
Epwell Rd
Shutford OX15 138 F3
Upper Tysoe CV35 138 B6
Erdington Rd CV9 18 D7
Erica Ave CV12 38 F2
Erica Dr CV31 110 B2
Eric Grey Cl CV2 62 A5
Eringden B77 4 B1
Erithway Rd CV3 77 B4
Ernesford Grange Prim Sch CV3 62 E1
Ernesford Grange Sch & Com Coll CV3 78 D8
Ernest Richards Rd CV12 39 B4
Ernsford Ave CV3 62 B1
Ernsford Cl B93 71 F2
Errington GL56 140 B3
Esher Dr CV3 77 E7
Eskdale Rd LE10 31 A7
Eskdale CV21 83 C8
Eskdale Wlk CV3 78 D7
Essen La CV23 101 F3
Essex Cl
Coventry CV5 60 B3
Kenilworth CV8 92 E2
Essex Ct CV34 108 E8
Essex Gn CV47 132 F7
Essex St CV21 83 A4
Esterton Cl CV6 49 C2
Ethelfield Rd CV2 62 B3
Ethelfleda Rd B77 9 F5
Etone Com Sch CV11 29 D5
Etone Ct CV11 29 B5
Eton Rd CV37 145 C1
Ettingham Cross Rds CV37 131 A4
Ettingham Grange CV37 131 A4
Ettingley Cl B98 103 B5
Ettington CE Prim Sch CV37 131 B3
Ettington Cl
Dorridge B93 71 D2
Wellesbourne CV35 146 D2
Ettington Rd
Coventry CV5 60 A3
Wellesbourne CV35 146 D1
Wellesbourne CV35 146 D2
Eunal Ct B97 102 E5
Europark Ind Est CV23 68 B2
Europa Way CV34 109 D5
Eustace Rd CV12 40 D1
Euston Cres CV3 78 C6
Euston Pl CV32 109 F8
Euston Sq 1 CV32 109 F8
Evans Cl
Bedworth CV12 39 C3
Stratford-u-A CV37 144 D1
Evans Gr CV31 110 A2
Evans Rd CV22 82 C2
Evelyn Ave CV6 49 F2
Evenlode Cl CV37 145 C1
Evenlode Cres CV6 60 F5
Evenlode Gdns GL56 140 B3
Evenlode Rd GL56 140 B3
Everard Cl CV23 84 A5
Everard Ct CV11 29 E2
Everdon Cl CV22 100 E8
Everdon Rd CV6 49 B2
Everest Rd CV22 99 E8
Everglade Rd CV9 10 C2
Evergreens The CV10 28 F6
Everitt Dr B93 72 A6
Eversleigh Rd CV6 60 E7
Evesham Country Park Visitor Ctr* WR11 127 C1
Evesham Pl CV37 144 F2
Evesham Rd
Bidford-on-A B50,CV37 128 E8
Church Lench WR11 127 A6
Cookhill B49 118 D5
Harvington WR11 127 D4
Middle Littleton WR11 127 F3
Redditch B96,B97 102 E3
Salford Priors WR11 127 F5
Stratford-u-A CV37 144 D1
Evesham St B49 143 B3
Evesham Wlk CV4 76 D5
Evreux Way CV21 83 A3
Exbury Way CV11 39 E8
Exeter Cl CV3 78 D8
Exhall Cedars Inf Sch CV7 50 A8
Exhall Cl CV37 145 D1
Exhall Gn CV7 49 F7
Exhall Grange Sch & Science Coll CV7 49 C5
Exhall Rd CV7 49 A6
Exham Cl CV34 104 E1

- Exhibition Way B40 44 D4
- Exis Ct CV11 29 E2
- Exminster Rd CV3 77 E5
- Exmoor Dr CV32 106 C4
- Exmouth Cl CV2 62 C7
- Exton Cl CV7 49 C6
- Eydon Cl CV21 83 E6
- Eyffler Cl CV34 108 D7

F

- Fabian Cl CV3 78 D7
- Fabius Cl LE10 31 C7
- Fairbanks Cl CV2 63 A7
- Fairbourne Gdns B97 102 C7
- Fairbourne Way CV6 60 E8
- Fair Cl CV23 97 D1
- Faircroft CV8 92 F3
- Faircroft Rd B36 22 D1
- Fairfax Cl CV35 122 A7
- Fairfax Ct 7 CV34 108 F7
- Fairfax St CV1 151 C3
- Fairfield Ct CV3 78 A7
- Fairfield Rise CV7 46 C1
- Fairfields Hill B78 10 F8
- Fairfields Wlk CV37 144 D4
- Fairhurst Dr CV32 105 E3
- Fair Isle Dr CV10 28 F2
- Fairlands Pk CV4 76 E5
- Fairlawn Cl CV32 105 D1
- Fairlawns B76 22 A8
- Fairmile Cl CV3 78 C8
- Fairview Ind Est B76 23 B7
- Fairview Mews 9 B46 33 F7
- Fairview Wlk CV6 49 E2
- Fairwater Cres B49 143 D4
- Fairway Ct
  - Rugby CV21 83 D4
  - Tamworth B77 4 B3
- Fairway CV11 40 B8
- Fairway Rise CV8 93 C6
- Fairways Cl CV5 60 A6
- Fairways B93 72 A8
- Fairways The CV32 105 D2
- Fairway B77 9 F5
- Fairway The
  - 16 Banbury OX16 139 F4
  - Hinckley LE10 31 F7
- Falcon Ave CV3 78 F8
- Falcon Cl CV11 40 B8
- Falcon Cres B50 148 E5
- Falcon Ct 6 CV47 147 B4
- Falconers Gn LE10 31 F6
- Falcon Lodge Cres B75 13 A6
- Falcon Pk B77 9 E7
- Falcons The B75 13 B5
- Falcon B77 10 A6
- Falkener Ho CV6 61 E7
- Falkland Cl CV4 75 D7
- Falkland Pl CV47 133 A7
- Falkland Way B36 33 B5
- Falkwood Gr B93 71 F6
- Fallowfields CV6 49 C4
- Fallow Hill CV31 110 C6
- Falmouth Cl CV11 30 A5
- Falstaff Ave B47 69 A6
- Falstaff Cl
  - Nuneaton CV11 30 A1
  - Sutton Coldfield B76 22 B7
- Falstaff Ct
  - 18 Stratford-u-A CV37 145 A3
  - Sutton Coldfield B75 13 C5
- Falstaff Dr CV22 99 D6
- Falstaff Gr CV34 109 E3
- Falstaff Rd CV4 59 E1
- Fancott Dr CV8 92 F6
- Fant Hill OX15 137 E3
- Faraday Ave
  - Coleshill B46 24 A4
  - Curdworth B46,B76 23 F5
- Faraday Rd
  - Hinckley LE10 30 E7
  - Rugby CV22 83 C1
- Farber Rd CV2 63 A6
- Farbury End OX7 142 A2
- Farcroft Ave CV5 59 D4
- Fareham Ave CV22 100 E8
- Far Gosford St CV1 61 E2
- Faringdon B77 4 A1
- Far Lash LE10 31 F7
- Farley Ave CV33 123 E6
- Farley St CV31 110 B7
- Farlow Cl CV6 62 A6
- Farman Rd CV5 61 A2
- Farm Cl
  - Coventry CV6 49 B3
  - Harbury CV33 123 E6
  - Shipston-on-S CV36 149 C6
- Farmcote Cl B97 102 D4
- Farmcote Lodge CV2 50 B4
- Farmcote Rd CV2 50 B4
- Farmer Ward Rd CV8 93 A3
- Farm Gr CV22 83 C1
- Farmhouse Way B90 71 B7
- Farmhurst CV22 83 D1
- Farm La
  - Easenhall CV23 65 E4
  - Grendon CV9 11 F6
  - South Littleton WR11 127 F1
- Far Moor La B98 112 A6
- Farm Rd
  - Hinckley LE10 31 E6
  - Kenilworth CV8 92 E2
- Farm Rd *continued*
  - Royal Leamington Spa CV32 106 B3
- Farmside CV3 78 D5
- Farmstead The CV3 78 B8
- Farm St CV33 123 E6
- Farm Stile NN11 134 E8
- Farm Wlk 2 CV33 122 F8
- Farnborough Dr B90 70 F6
- Farnborough Hall* OX17 133 F4
- Farnborough Rd
  - Birmingham B35 22 B3
  - Radway CV35 132 F3
- Farndale Ave CV6 49 D3
- Farndon Ave B37 44 B7
- Farndon Cl CV12 40 B3
- Farnell Dr CV37 144 D3
- Farnworth Gr B36 22 E1
- Far Pool Mdw CV35 113 F3
- Farr Dr CV4 60 B2
- Farren Rd CV2 62 E5
- Farriers Ct
  - Stretton u F CV23 65 C7
  - Wasperton CV35 122 A5
- Farriers Way
  - Hinckley LE10 31 F6
  - Nuneaton CV11 29 F2
- Farrington Cl CV35 146 C2
- Farrington Ct CV35 146 D2
- Farther Sand Cl CV35 121 F4
- Farthing La B76 23 C6
- Farthing Wlk CV4 75 D6
- Farvale Rd B76 22 C6
- Farzens Ave CV34 108 B3
- Faseman Ave CV4 59 F3
- Fasson Cl B77 9 C8
- Faulconbridge Ave CV5 59 E4
- Faulconbridge Way CV34 109 E3
- Faultlands Cl CV11 39 F8
- Fawley Cl CV3 78 C6
- Fawsley Leys CV22 100 A7
- Faygate Cl CV3 62 F3
- Fearnings Cotts B97 102 D5
- Featherbed La
  - Bascote CV47 115 B1
  - Cherington CV36 141 D7
  - Coventry CV4 76 A5
  - Redditch B97 102 C5
  - Rugby CV21 84 A1
  - Wilmcote CV37 120 D5
  - Withybrook CV7 52 F6
- Featherston Dr LE10 31 E6
- Featherstone Cl CV10 29 C2
- Feckenham Rd
  - Astwood Bank B96 102 E2
  - Redditch,Headless Cross B97 102 C8
  - Redditch,Hunt End B97 102 C4
- Feilding Cl CV2 63 A6
- Feilding Way CV10 28 A5
- Fein Bank CV4 59 C2
- Feldon Edge CV36 137 A8
- Felgate Cl B90 71 A6
- Fell Gr CV32 106 C3
- Fell Mill La
  - Honington CV36 149 F7
  - Shipston-on-S CV36 149 E6
- Fellmore Gr CV31 110 D7
- Fellows Way CV21 100 F8
- Fell's La CV47 125 C8
- Felspar Rd B77 4 B3
- Felstead Cl B77 9 C4
- Felton Cl CV2 50 E1
- Fencote Ave B37 33 A4
- Fen End Rd CV8 73 E4
- Fennell Ho 10 CV1 61 B2
- Fennis Cl B93 71 F3
- Fenn Lanes CV13 20 D8
- Fenny Compton Rd OX17 134 B5
- Fennyland La CV8 93 B7
- Fenside Ave CV3 77 D4
- Fentham Cl B92 57 B6
- Fentham Gn B92 57 A7
- Fentham Rd B92 57 A6
- Fenton Rd B47 69 A7
- Fenwick Cl B49 143 D5
- Fenwick Dr CV21 101 A8
- Ferguson Cl CV37 131 B3
- Fern Cl
  - Coventry CV2 50 C2
  - Rugby CV23 83 D8
  - Salford Priors WR11 127 D6
- Ferncumbe CE Prim Sch The CV35 114 D6
- Ferndale Cl CV11 29 E5
- Ferndale Ct B46 34 A5
- Ferndale Dr CV8 93 A2
- Ferndale Gr LE10 31 A7
- Ferndale Mews B46 34 A5
- Ferndale Rd 15 OX16 139 F4
- Fern Dale Rd CV7 73 F6
- Ferndale Rd
  - Binley Woods CV3 79 D7
  - Coleshill B46 34 A5
- Ferndown Cl CV4 60 A3
- Ferndown Ct CV22 82 E1
- Ferndown Rd CV22 82 E1
- Ferndown Terr CV22 82 E1
- Fern Gr CV12 38 E2
- Fernhill Cl CV8 92 E6
- Fernhill Dr CV32 106 B1
- Fernhill La CV7,CV8 73 F5
- Fern Hill Way LE10 41 D4
- Fernwood Cl B98 103 B5
- Ferrers Cl CV4 59 F2
- Ferrieres Cl CV22 99 C3
- Ferry La CV37 121 D3
- Fetherston Cres CV8 79 B1
- Fetherston Ct 4 CV31 109 F6
- Fetherston Grange B94 88 F5
- Fiddlers Gn B92 57 A7
- Field Barn Rd CV35 108 A7
- Field Cl
  - Harbury CV33 123 F8
  - Kenilworth CV8 93 B5
  - Warwick CV34 109 B7
- Field Ct CV2 62 D7
- Fieldfare Cl CV23 83 C8
- Fieldfare Croft B36 33 A8
- Fieldgate La
  - Fenny Compton CV47 133 E7
  - Kenilworth CV8 92 F6
  - Whitnash CV31 110 B2
- Fieldgate Lawn CV8 92 F6
- Field Head La CV34 109 B6
- Field Ho CV8 92 F5
- Fieldhouse Cl B95 113 B4
- Fielding Cl CV9 12 D2
- Field La B91 56 A5
- Field March CV3 78 E5
- Fields Ct CV34 108 F8
- Fieldside La CV3 62 F3
- Fields Park Dr B49 143 D4
- Field View
  - Binton CV37 120 A1
  - Braunston NN11 117 D5
  - Cawston CV22 99 B8
- Field View Cl CV7 50 A8
- Field View
  - Shrewley CV35 114 C6
  - Whitnash CV31 110 B3
- Field Way B94 88 C6
- Fieldways Cl B47 69 A7
- Fife Rd CV5 60 F2
- Fife St CV11 29 A4
- Fifield Cl CV11 29 D2
- Fighting Cl 7 CV35 132 B6
- Fillingham Cl B37 33 D1
- Fillongley Rd
  - Lodge Green CV7 46 E3
  - Maxstoke B46 35 D4
- Filton Croft B35 22 A4
- Finch Cl CV6 49 C2
- Finch Croft CV7 74 B7
- Finch La WR11 127 D3
- Findley Cl CV9 18 F6
- Findon Cl CV12 40 C3
- Fineacre La CV8,CV23 96 D5
- Finford Croft CV7 74 B6
- Fingal Cl CV3 78 C6
- Fingest Cl CV5 60 B4
- Finham Cres CV8 93 B6
- Finham Flats CV8 93 B6
- Finham Gr CV3 77 C3
- Finham Green Rd CV3 77 B3
- Finham Park Sch CV3 77 A4
- Finham Prim Sch CV3 77 B3
- Finham Rd CV8 93 B6
- Finings Ct 7 CV32 105 F2
- Finlay Ct CV1 151 C1
- Finmere CV21 83 D6
- Finnemore Cl CV3 77 B5
- Finwood Rd CV35 113 F8
- Fircroft Ho B37 33 A2
- Fircroft B78 15 D7
- Firedrake Croft CV1 61 F2
- Fire Service Coll The GL56 140 B3
- Firethorn Cres CV31 110 A2
- Fir Gr CV4 60 A2
- Firleigh Dr CV12 40 D2
- Firs Dr CV22 82 F2
- First Ave
  - Birmingham B35 22 A5
  - Coventry CV3 62 C1
- First Exhibition Ave B40 44 D4
- Firs The
  - Bedworth CV12 38 E2
  - Coventry CV5 77 B8
  - Kingsbury B78 15 D7
  - Lower Quinton CV37 129 E2
  - Meriden CV7 46 B1
  - Wroxton OX15 139 D4
- Firth Ave GL56 140 C3
- Fir Tree Ave CV4 60 B2
- Firtree Cl 17 OX16 139 F5
- Fir Tree Gr CV11 39 D8
- Firtree La CV7 37 A8
- Fisher Ave CV22 100 E8
- Fisher Rd
  - Bishops Itchington CV47 124 A4
  - Coventry CV6 61 E8
- Fishers Cl CV23 101 F2
- Fisher's Ct CV34 108 D4
- Fishers Dr B90 69 F5
- Fishponds Rd CV8 92 E3
- Fishpool La CV7 45 B5
- Fitton St CV11 29 B3
- Fitzalan Cl CV23 81 B6
- Fitzroy Cl CV2 63 B6
- Fivefield Rd CV7 48 E5
- Five Lane Ends LE10 41 F6
- Five Ways Rd CV35 114 C7
- Five Ways
  - Shutford OX15 139 B3
  - Wroxall CV35 90 F1
- Fladbury Cl B98 103 B8
- Flamboro' Cl CV3 78 F8
- Flamville Rd LE10 32 B5
- Flats La CV9 3 B1
- Flaunden Cl CV5 60 B4
- Flavel Cres CV31 109 F7
- Flavel Ct CV9 3 A1
- Flax Cl B47 69 A5
- Flaxley Cl B98 112 A6
- Flecknoe Cl B36 22 C1
- Flecknose St CV3 78 C6
- Fleet Cres CV21 83 E2
- Fleet St CV1 151 B3
- Fleming Rd LE10 30 F7
- Fletchamstead Highway CV5 76 D7
- Fletcher Gr B93 72 B4
- Fletcher Rd LE10 31 E7
- Fletchers Way CV35 146 C3
- Fletchworth Gate CV5 76 D8
- Fletchworth Gate Ind Est CV4 76 D8
- Fleur de-lys Ct CV34 109 B8
- Flint Cl CV9 12 E2
- Florence Cl
  - Atherstone CV9 12 D1
  - Bedworth CV12 49 F8
- Florence Rd CV3 63 A2
- Florendine St B77 4 A5
- Florian Way LE10 21 F1
- Florin Cl CV4 75 E6
- Florin Pl CV21 101 A8
- Flower Ct 3 CV37 144 F1
- Flowerdale Dr CV2 62 B6
- Flower Rd CV37 144 F6
- Floyd Gr CV7 74 C7
- Flude Rd CV7 49 C6
- Flying Fields Rd CV47 147 C4
- Flynt Ave CV5 60 B6
- Focus Pk B90 70 E8
- Fold The 9 CV37 145 A3
- Foldyard Cl B76 22 A8
- Foleshill CE Prim Sch CV6 50 A2
- Foleshill Rd CV1,CV6 61 D6
- Folkland Gn CV6 61 A7
- Follager Rd CV21 82 F4
- Folly Ct OX15 142 E8
- Folly La
  - Baddesley Ensor CV9 17 D8
  - Napton on t H CV47 125 B7
- Folly The B97 102 D8
- Fontmell Cl CV2 63 A4
- Fordbridge Inf Sch B37 33 A5
- Fordbridge Rd B37 33 A5
- Ford Cotts CV33 106 F2
- Forde Hall La B94,B95 112 D7
- Fordham Ave CV37 145 A4
- Fordington Pl 6 CV35 132 B6
- Ford La CV37 113 F1
- Fordrift The B37 44 A6
- Fordrough The B90 69 C7
- Fords Rd B90 69 E7
- Ford St
  - Coventry CV1 151 C3
  - Nuneaton CV10 28 E4
- Fordway The CV37 129 D2
- Fordwell Cl CV5 60 F3
- Foredraught B80 103 E4
- Foregate St B96 102 E1
- Foreland Way CV6 49 A3
- Forest Ct
  - Coventry CV5 60 A4
  - Dorridge B93 71 F3
- Foresters Pl CV21 101 B7
- Forester's Rd CV3 77 E6
- Forest Oak Sch B36 22 E1
- Forest Rd
  - Dorridge B93 71 F3
  - Hinckley LE10 31 F8
- Forest View B97 102 E6
- Forest Way
  - Hollywood B47 69 B6
  - Nuneaton CV10 28 E2
- Forfield Pl CV31 110 A7
- Forfield Rd CV6 60 E5
- Forge Croft B76 22 B6
- Forge La
  - Farnborough OX17 133 F4
  - Sutton Coldfield B76 22 B5
- Forge Rd
  - Kenilworth CV8 93 A6
  - Shustoke B46 25 A2
- Forge Way CV6 49 C3
- Forknell Ave CV2 62 C5
- Fornside Cl CV21 83 D7
- Forresters Cl LE10 31 F6
- Forresters Rd LE10 31 F6
- Forrest Rd CV8 92 E4
- Forryan Rd LE10 31 F7
- Forshaw Heath La B94 86 A7
- Forshaw Heath Rd B94 69 C1
- Forth Dr B37 33 B4
- Forties B77 9 E7
- Forum Dr CV21 83 A6
- Forum Rd B40 44 E3
- Forward Rd B26 44 A3
- Fosberry Cl CV34 109 B8
- Fossdale Rd B77 10 A8
- Fosse Cl LE10 32 A5
- Fosse Cotts CV23 80 E8
- Fosse Cres CV23 96 E3
- Fosseway Ave GL56 140 A2
- Fosse Way Bsns Ctr GL56 140 A3
- Fosseway Cl GL56 140 A2
- Fosseway Cres CV36 136 F6
- Fosseway Dr GL56 140 A2
- Fosse Way
  - Eathorpe CV33 115 A7
  - Ettington CV35,CV37 131 C5
- Fosseway Gdns LE17 43 E6
- Fosse Way
  - Harbury CV33 123 C7
  - Moreton Morrell CV35 123 A3
- Fosseway Rd CV3 77 B4
- Fosse Way
  - Shipston-on-S CV36 149 A8
  - Stretton-o-D CV23 97 A6
  - Stretton u F CV23 65 B7
  - Ufton CV31,CV33 111 C5
- Foster Ave B80 103 E3
- Fosterd Rd CV21 82 F6
- Foster Rd CV6 61 B7
- Founder Cl CV4 75 F7
- Foundry Ct 8 CV37 144 F3
- Fountain Gdns CV35 146 D4
- Fountain Way 1 CV37 145 A2
- Four Ashes Rd B93 71 E4
- Four Crosses CV23 117 C6
- Fourfields Way CV7 36 F7
- Four Lanes End CV10 37 E7
- Four Oaks Cl B98 102 D8
- Four Pounds Ave CV5 60 F3
- Fourways CV9 18 F8
- Fowey Cl B76 22 A7
- Fowler Rd
  - Coventry CV6 61 B4
  - Sutton Coldfield B75 13 B5
- Fow Oak CV4 59 C2
- Fox Ave CV10 29 D7
- Foxbury Dr B93 72 B3
- Fox Cl
  - Harbury CV33 123 F6
  - Rugby CV21 84 B1
  - Tamworth B77 9 C8
- Foxcote Cl B90 70 D8
- Foxcote Dr B90 70 D8
- Foxcote Hill CV36 136 A6
- Foxcovert La CV13 21 A8
- Foxdale Wlk 8 CV31 110 C6
- Foxes La CV37 120 C5
- Foxes Mdw B76 22 A8
- Foxes Way
  - Balsall Common CV7 74 B6
  - Warwick CV34 108 D4
- Foxfield CV23 66 A8
- Foxford Cl B36 22 D1
- Foxford Cres CV2 50 B4
- Foxford Sch & Com Arts Coll CV6 50 A5
- Foxglove Cl
  - Bedworth CV12 38 E1
  - Coventry CV6 49 C2
  - Rugby CV23 83 E8
- Foxglove B77 4 A4
- Fox Hill Rd B75 7 A2
- Foxhills Cl CV11 30 C1
- Foxholes La B97 102 A6
- Fox Hollies Rd
  - Sutton Coldfield B76 13 A1
  - Sutton Coldfield B76 13 B2
- Fox la B95 113 C4
- Foxland Cl
  - Birmingham B37 33 D2
  - Cheswick Green B90 70 D4
- Foxley Dr B91 56 B5
- Foxons Barn Rd CV21 83 C6
- Foxon's Cnr CV23 53 C4
- Fox's Covert CV13 19 F6
- Foxtail Cl CV37 144 D5
- Foxton Ct LE10 31 B7
- Foxton Rd CV3 62 E1
- Foxwood Dr CV3 79 D7
- Foxwood Rd B78 10 F8
- Framlingham Gr CV8 93 C6
- Frampton Cl B37 33 D3
- Frampton Wlk CV2 62 F4
- Frances Ave CV34 109 A7
- Frances Cres CV12 39 A3
- Frances Havergal Cl 2 CV31 109 F6
- Frances Rd
  - Baginton CV8 77 F3
  - Harbury CV33 123 F6
- Franciscan Rd CV3 77 D8
- Francis Cl B78 5 A2
- Francis Dr CV22 99 A8
- Francis Gibbs Gdns 1 CV31 110 A4
- Francis St CV6 61 E7
- Frankholmes Dr B90 71 A6
- Frankland Rd CV6 50 A1
- Franklin Ct CV11 29 D1
- Franklin Gr CV4 59 E1
- Franklin Rd
  - Nuneaton CV11 29 D1
  - Whitnash CV31 110 A3
- Franklins Gdns CV3 63 B1
- Franklin's La WR11 127 B7
- Frankpledge Rd CV3 77 E7
- Frank St CV11 29 B3
- Frankton Ave CV3 77 C5
- Frankton Cl B98 103 E8
- Frankton La CV23 97 A5
- Frankton Rd CV23 97 E2
- Frank Walsh Ho CV1 151 C4
- Frankwell Dr CV2 50 E1
- Fraser Cl CV10 28 B6
- Fraser Rd CV6 49 A1
- Fraser Way CV37 129 B6
- Frederick Bird Prim Sch CV2 61 F5
- Frederick Eary Ho B98 103 B7
- Frederick Johnson Almshouses B95 113 B5
- Frederick Neal Ave CV5 59 D4
- Frederick Press Way CV21 82 F3
- Frederick Rd CV7 37 A8
- Frederick St CV21 82 F3
- Fred Lee Gr CV3 77 D4
- Freeboard La CV23 96 E7

Freeburn Cswy CV4 . . . . . . **76** C7
Freehold St CV1 . . . . **61** F4
Freeman Cl CV10 . . . . **28** D4
Freeman Ct 3 CV37 . . . . . **145** A4
Freemans Cl CV32 . . . . . . **105** E2
Freeman's La LE10 . . . . **32** A5
Freeman St CV6 . . . . **61** F6
Freemantle Rd CV22 . . . . . **82** C2
Freers Mews CV34 . . . . . . **108** B4
Freer St CV11 . . . . **29** E2
Freesland Rise CV10 . . . . . **28** B6
Frensham Cl B37 . . . . **33** C2
Frensham Dr CV10 . . . . **28** B5
Freshfield Cl CV5 . . . . **48** C1
Freshwater Gr 1 CV31 . . **110** C6
Freswick Cl LE10 . . . . **21** F1
Fretton Cl CV6 . . . . **61** F7
Frevill Rd CV6 . . . . **62** B8
Friars Cl CV3 . . . . **79** E7
Friar's Gate CV9 . . . . **18** D8
Friars Gate B90 . . . . **70** E7
Friars Hill OX15 . . . . **139** C5
Friars La OX15 . . . . **137** F2
Friars' Rd CV1 . . . . **151** B2
Friars St CV34 . . . . **108** D6
Friars Wlk B37 . . . . **33** D2
Friary Ave B90 . . . . **71** A6
Friary Cl CV35 . . . . **114** F3
Friary Rd CV9 . . . . **12** D1
Friary St CV11 . . . . **29** B5
Friday Cl B50 . . . . **148** D5
Friday Furlong B50 . . . . . **148** D6
Friday La B92 . . . . **56** D4
Friday St
Lower Quinton CV37 . . . . . **129** E2
Pebworth CV37 . . . . **128** F1
Frilsham Way CV5 . . . . **60** B4
Frisby Ct CV11 . . . . **29** E2
Frisby Rd CV4 . . . . **59** E2
Friswell Dr CV6 . . . . **61** F8
Friswell Ho 3 CV2 . . . . **62** D8
Friz Hill CV35 . . . . **131** D8
Frobisher Rd
Coventry CV3 . . . . **77** C5
Rugby CV22 . . . . **82** C2
Frog La
Balsall Common CV7 . . . . . . **74** A5
Ilmington CV36 . . . . **136** A6
Froglands La WR11 . . . . . **128** A4
Frog La
Upper Boddington NN11 . . **134** E8
Welford-on-A CV37 . . . . . . **129** B6
Frogmere Cl CV5 . . . . **60** C6
Frogmore La CV8 . . . . **73** F2
Frogmore Rd CV37 . . . . . . **121** B6
Frolesworth La LE17 . . . . . **43** F7
Front St
Ilmington CV36 . . . . **136** B6
Pebworth CV37 . . . . **128** E1
Frost Rd CV35 . . . . **146** D4
Froxmere Cl B91 . . . . **71** C8
Fryer Ave CV32 . . . . **105** E3
Frythe Cl CV8 . . . . **93** C6
Fuchsia Cl 3 CV2 . . . . **50** B2
Fulbrook La CV35 . . . . **121** F8
Fulbrook Rd CV2 . . . . **50** C2
Fulford Dr B76 . . . . **22** B5
Fulford Hall Rd B90,B94 . . **69** D3
Fullbrook Cl B90 . . . . **71** A5
Fuller Pl CV35 . . . . **122** F3
Fullers Cl CV6 . . . . **60** F7
Fullwood Cl CV2 . . . . **50** E2
Fulwell Mews B37 . . . . **44** B8
Furlong Mdw CV36 . . . . . . **149** D4
Furlong Rd CV1 . . . . **151** C1
Furnace Cl CV12 . . . . **39** D3
Furnace Rd CV12 . . . . **39** D4
Furness Cl CV21 . . . . **83** D7
Furr Marsh The CV34 . . . . **108** B4
Furrow Cl CV21 . . . . **83** D4
Furrows The CV47 . . . . . . **147** C5
Furze Hill Rd CV36 . . . . . . **149** D4
Furze La
Chipping Campden GL55 . . **135** C4
Redditch B98 . . . . **112** A6
Fylde Ho CV2 . . . . **62** D4
Fynford Rd CV6 . . . . **61** B5

G

Gable Cl CV22 . . . . **99** D8
Gables The B78 . . . . **5** A2
Gabor Cl CV21 . . . . **83** C6
Gadsby Ct CV11 . . . . **29** E3
Gadsby St CV11 . . . . **29** E3
Gadshill CV34 . . . . **109** E4
Gainford Rise CV3 . . . . **63** A3
Gainsborough Cres
Dorridge B93 . . . . **72** A6
Rugby CV21 . . . . **84** B1
Gainsborough Dr
Bedworth CV12 . . . . **39** A4
Mile Oak B78 . . . . **8** B8
Royal Leamington Spa
CV31 . . . . **110** D6
Gainsborough Ho GL55 . . **135** C2
Gainsborough Rd CV37 . . **144** D1
Gainsborough Terr GL55 **135** A1
Gainsborough Trad Est
CV47 . . . . **147** A3
Galena Cl B77 . . . . **4** B2
Galey's Rd CV3 . . . . **77** D8
Gallagher Bsns Pk CV6 . . . . **49** E5
Gallagher Rd CV12 . . . . **39** A2
Gallagher Ret Pk CV6 . . . . **61** F8
Galley Common Inf Sch
CV10 . . . . **27** F5
Galliards The CV4 . . . . **76** D4
Galliers Cl B77 . . . . **9** F5
Gallows Hill CV34 . . . . **109** B4
Galmington Dr CV3 . . . . . . **77** B6
Gannaway B93 . . . . **72** A4
Gannaway Rd CV35 . . . . . **114** B3
Garard Ct 3 CV22 . . . . **99** A8
Garard Pl 1 CV22 . . . . **99** A8
Garard Row 2 CV22 . . . . . **99** A8
Garden Cl
Hinckley LE10 . . . . **31** D6
Knowle B93 . . . . **71** F6
Mickleton GL55 . . . . **135** B6
Garden Ct
Warwick,Emscote CV34 . . . **109** C8
Warwick,Packmores CV34 . **108** E7
Garden Flats CV5 . . . . **59** D5
Garden Gr CV12 . . . . **49** F8
Gardenia Dr CV5 . . . . **60** B6
Gardens The
Kenilworth CV8 . . . . **93** A3
Radford Semele CV31 . . . . **110** E5
Rugby CV22 . . . . **99** C7
Thurlaston CV23 . . . . **98** F3
Garden Terr CV35 . . . . **146** D3
Gardner Ho 8 CV1 . . . . **61** B2
Gardner Way CV8 . . . . **93** A2
Garlands Croft CV7 . . . . . . **49** A6
Garlick Dr CV8 . . . . **93** C6
Garnette Cl CV10 . . . . **28** B5
Garrard Cl WR11 . . . . **127** F6
Garratt Cl CV23 . . . . **82** B5
Garrett St CV11 . . . . **29** E2
Garrick Cl CV5 . . . . **59** C4
Garrick Way CV37 . . . . **144** E1
Garrigill B77 . . . . **4** B1
Garth Cres CV3 . . . . **78** D8
Garth Ho CV3 . . . . **78** D8
Garton Cl DE12 . . . . **3** F8
Garway Cl CV32 . . . . **105** F4
Garyth Williams Cl CV22 . . **99** E8
Gas House La B49 . . . . **143** C3
Gas St
Royal Leamington Spa
CV31 . . . . **109** F7
Rugby CV21 . . . . **83** B3
Gate Farm Dr CV23 . . . . **53** F3
Gatehouse Cl CV21 . . . . . . **101** A8
Gatehouse La CV12 . . . . **39** A2
Gatehouse CV31 . . . . **109** D7
Gate La
Dorridge B93,B94 . . . . **71** C3
Nether Whitacre B46 . . . . . . **24** F6
Gateley Cl B98 . . . . **112** A6
Gateside Rd CV6 . . . . **49** E2
Gatwick Rd B35 . . . . **22** B4
Gaulby Wlk CV3 . . . . **63** A1
Gaveston Cl 7 CV34 . . . . **108** F8
Gaveston Rd
Coventry CV6 . . . . **60** F6
Royal Leamington Spa
CV32 . . . . **105** E1
Gaydon Cl CV6 . . . . **62** A8
Gaydon Rd CV47 . . . . **124** A3
Gayer St CV6 . . . . **50** A1
Gayhurst Cl CV3 . . . . **78** E8
Gayle B77 . . . . **4** A1
Gaza Cl CV4 . . . . **60** A1
Gazelle Cl CV1 . . . . **151** D3
Geeson Cl B35 . . . . **22** B4
Gentian Way CV23 . . . . **83** E8
Gentlemans La B94 . . . . . . **112** E7
Geoffrey Cl
Coventry CV2 . . . . **62** B5
Sutton Coldfield B76 . . . . . . **22** B7
George Birch Cl CV23 . . . . **64** E3
George Eliot Ave CV12 . . . **39** D2
George Eliot Com Sch
Nuneaton CV11 . . . . **29** D1
Nuneaton CV11 . . . . **39** D8
George Eliot Hospl CV10 . **29** B2
George Eliot Rd CV1 . . . . . . **61** D5
George Eliot St CV11 . . . . . **29** C2
George Fentham Endowed
Sch B92 . . . . **57** B6
George Fox La CV13 . . . . . . **20** A6
George Hodgkinson Cl
CV4 . . . . **59** F3
George La GL55 . . . . **135** B1
George Marston Rd CV3 . . **62** E1
George Park Cl CV2 . . . . **50** C1
George Poole Ho 6 CV1 . . **61** B2
George Rd
Warwick CV34 . . . . **109** A8
Water Orton B46 . . . . **23** C3
George Robertson Cl CV3 **78** E7
George's Elm La B50 . . . . **148** E8
George St
Coventry CV1 . . . . **61** E5
Hinckley LE10 . . . . **31** D8
New Arley CV7 . . . . **37** A8
Nuneaton CV11 . . . . **29** E2
George Street Ringway
CV12 . . . . **39** B3
George St
Royal Leamington Spa
CV31 . . . . **110** A7
Rugby CV21 . . . . **82** F3
Stockton CV47 . . . . **115** F3
Georgian Cl B49 . . . . **143** B4
Gerandria Ct CV22 . . . . . . **100** E8
Gerard Ave CV4 . . . . **76** B8
Gerard Rd
Alcester B49 . . . . **143** D4
Cawston CV22 . . . . **99** A8
Gerrards Rd CV36 . . . . **149** D5
Gerrard St 1 CV34 . . . . . . **108** E6
Gibbet Hill LE17 . . . . **67** F6
Gibbet Hill Rd CV4 . . . . **76** B3
Gibbet La LE17 . . . . **68** B6
Gibbons Cl CV4 . . . . **59** F2
Gibbs Cl CV2 . . . . **63** B6
Gibbs Ct CV37 . . . . **145** E4
Gibbs La WR11 . . . . **127** D1
Gibson Cres CV12 . . . . **39** A1
Gibson Dr CV21 . . . . **84** A1
Gielgud Way CV2 . . . . **63** B8
Giffard Terr B95 . . . . **113** E7
Giffard Way CV34 . . . . **104** E1
Gifford Rd CV33 . . . . **123** D3
Gifford Wlk CV37 . . . . **144** C4
Gigg La B76 . . . . **14** B3
Gilberry Cl B93 . . . . **72** A4
Gilbert Ave CV22 . . . . **82** D2
Gilbert Cl
3 Coventry CV1 . . . . **61** E3
Bedworth CV12 . . . . **39** B2
Stratford-u-A CV37 . . . . . . **144** F6
Gilberts Rugby Football
Mus★ CV21 . . . . **83** A3
Giles Cl CV6 . . . . **49** C2
Gilfil Rd CV10 . . . . **29** B1
Gilkes La CV35 . . . . **137** F8
Gillet Cl CV11 . . . . **29** B3
Gillett's La OX15 . . . . **137** E2
Gillians Wlk CV2 . . . . **63** A8
Gillows Croft B90 . . . . **71** A7
Gilquart Way CV1 . . . . **151** C1
Gilson Dr B46 . . . . **33** D8
Gilson Rd B46 . . . . **33** E8
Gilson Way B37 . . . . **33** A5
Gingles Ct CV21 . . . . **101** A8
Ginkgo Wlk 2 CV31 . . . . . **109** F5
Gipsy Cl CV7 . . . . **74** B5
Gipsy La
Balsall Common CV7 . . . . . . **74** C5
Nuneaton CV10,CV11 . . . . . . **39** D7
Wolvey LE10 . . . . **41** E7
Girdlers Cl CV3 . . . . **77** B5
Girtin Cl CV12 . . . . **39** A4
Girvan Gr CV32 . . . . **106** C5
Gisburn Cl CV34 . . . . **104** F1
Givens Ho 9 CV1 . . . . **61** B2
Glade The CV5 . . . . **59** F3
Gladiator Way CV21 . . . . . . **82** F7
Gladstone Ct 22 CV32 . . . **105** F1
Gladstone Rd B93 . . . . **72** A2
Gladstone St CV21 . . . . **82** F4
Gladstone Terr LE10 . . . . . . **31** E8
Glaisdale Ave CV6 . . . . **49** E3
Glamis Pl 2 OX16 . . . . **139** F3
Glamorgan Cl CV3 . . . . **78** D5
Glaramara Cl CV21 . . . . **83** D7
Glascote Heath Prim Sch
B77 . . . . **4** A2
Glascote La B77 . . . . **9** F8
Glascote Rd B77 . . . . **4** B2
Glasshouse La
Hockley Heath B94 . . . . **88** F6
Kenilworth CV8 . . . . **93** D4
Gleave Rd CV31 . . . . **110** A3
Glebe Ave CV12 . . . . **38** E1
Glebe Cl
Bidford-on-A B50 . . . . **148** D4
Coventry CV4 . . . . **76** A7
Stockton CV47 . . . . **147** F8
Glebe Cotts WR11 . . . . **127** D3
Glebe Cres
Kenilworth CV8 . . . . **93** A3
Rugby CV21 . . . . **82** E3
Glebe Ct CV31 . . . . **110** A3
Glebe Est CV37 . . . . **120** B5
Glebefarm Gr CV3 . . . . **62** F3
Glebe Farm Ind Est CV21 . **82** F7
Glebe Farm (Mus)★
CV37 . . . . **120** C5
Glebe Farm Rd CV21 . . . . . . **82** F7
Glebe Fields B76 . . . . **23** B6
Glebe Fold GL55 . . . . **135** B2
Glebe La
Nuneaton CV11 . . . . **29** F6
Staverton NN11 . . . . **126** E8
Glebe Pl CV31 . . . . **110** B7
Glebe Rd
Hinckley LE10 . . . . **31** F8
Nuneaton CV11 . . . . **29** D4
Southam CV47 . . . . **147** A5
Stratford-u-A CV37 . . . . . . **144** C4
Glebe Rise CV9 . . . . **3** B1
Glebe The
Corley CV7 . . . . **48** C7
Hook Norton OX15 . . . . **142** D4
Wootton Wawen B95 . . . . . **113** B2
Glebe Way CV7 . . . . **74** A7
Gleeson Dr CV34 . . . . **104** E1
Glenbarr Cl LE10 . . . . **31** A8
Glenbarr Dr LE10 . . . . **31** A8
Glen Cl CV36 . . . . **149** D6
Glencoe Rd CV3 . . . . **62** B1
Glendale Ave CV8 . . . . **93** A6
Glendale Ct B77 . . . . **10** B6
Glendale Inf Sch CV10 . . . **28** F2
Glendale Way CV4 . . . . **59** C2
Glendon Gdns CV12 . . . . . . **40** C3
Glendon Way B93 . . . . **71** E3
Glendower 4 CV37 . . . . . . **145** A3
Glendower App CV34 . . . . **109** E3
Glendower Ave CV5 . . . . **60** D3
Gleneagles Cl
Hinckley LE10 . . . . **31** D4
Nuneaton CV11 . . . . **30** C1
Gleneagles Rd CV2 . . . . **62** E6
Gleneagles B77 . . . . **4** B5
Glenfern Gdns CV8 . . . . **78** E2
Glenfield Ave CV10 . . . . **29** D7
Glenfield Cl
2 Solihull B91 . . . . **71** C8
Redditch B97 . . . . **102** D6
Glenhurst Rd B95 . . . . **113** A4
Glenmore Dr CV6 . . . . **49** F5
Glenmount Ave CV6 . . . . **49** F5
Glenn St CV6 . . . . **49** D3
Glenridding Cl CV6 . . . . **49** F5
Glenrosa Wlk CV4 . . . . **76** A7
Glenroy Cl CV2 . . . . **62** E6
Glentworth Ave CV6 . . . . . . **49** A2
Glentworth B76 . . . . **13** A2
Glenville Ave CV9 . . . . **10** C1
Glenwood Dr B90 . . . . **70** D4
Glenwood Gdns
Bedworth CV12 . . . . **39** A5
Tamworth B77 . . . . **10** B6
Gloster Dr CV8 . . . . **92** F6
Gloster Gdns CV35 . . . . . . **146** C1
Gloucester Cl CV11 . . . . . . **30** A7
Gloucester La GL55 . . . . . **135** B6
Gloucester St
3 Royal Leamington Spa
CV31 . . . . **110** A7
Coventry CV1 . . . . **61** B3
Gloucester Way B37 . . . . . **33** A1
Glover Cl CV34 . . . . **108** B4
Glover Rd B75 . . . . **13** A5
Glover's Cl CV9 . . . . **18** F7
Glovers Cl CV7 . . . . **46** C1
Glover St CV3 . . . . **77** D8
Godfrey Cl CV31 . . . . **110** E5
Godiva Pl CV1 . . . . **151** D3
Godiva Trad Est CV6 . . . . . . **61** F8
Godson Cotts OX15 . . . . . **137** F2
Godsons La CV47 . . . . **125** C8
Gofton B77 . . . . **10** A8
Goldacre Cl CV31 . . . . **109** F4
Gold Ave CV22 . . . . **99** B8
Gold Cl CV11 . . . . **39** E8
Goldcrest Croft B36 . . . . . . **33** A8
Goldcrest B77 . . . . **10** A6
Golden Acres La CV3 . . . . . **78** F7
Golden End Dr B93 . . . . **72** D6
Goldicote Bsns Pk CV37 . **130** E5
Goldicote Hall CV37 . . . . . **130** E6
Goldicote Mews CV37 . . . **130** E6
Goldicote Rd CV35 . . . . . . **130** F7
Goldsborough B77 . . . . **4** A1
Goldsmith Ave
Rugby CV22 . . . . **99** F6
Warwick CV34 . . . . **108** C5
Goldthorn Cl CV5 . . . . **59** D4
Golf Dr CV11 . . . . **30** B1
Golf La CV31 . . . . **110** B2
Goodacre Cl CV23 . . . . **84** A5
Goode Cl CV34 . . . . **108** C7
Goode Croft CV4 . . . . **59** F2
Goodere Ave B78 . . . . **11** A8
Goodere Dr B78 . . . . **5** A2
Goodeve Wlk B75 . . . . **13** B5
Goodfellow St CV32 . . . . . **105** C1
Goodman Way CV4 . . . . **59** C1
Good Shepherd RC Sch
CV6 . . . . **49** F1
Goodway Ct 9 CV34 . . . . **108** F7
Goodway Ho
5 Royal Leamington Spa
CV32 . . . . **109** D8
Kenilworth CV8 . . . . **93** A5
Goodwood Cl CV3 . . . . **78** C6
Goodyers End La CV12 . . . **49** D8
Goodyers End Prim Sch
CV12 . . . . **49** E8
Goosehills Rd LE10 . . . . **31** E5
Goose La CV37 . . . . **129** D1
Gorcott Hill B98 . . . . **112** B7
Gorcott La B90 . . . . **70** A5
Gordon Cl CV12 . . . . **39** C4
Gordon Rd CV37 . . . . **129** C2
Gordon St
Coventry CV1 . . . . **61** B2
Royal Leamington Spa
CV31 . . . . **110** A7
Goring Rd CV2 . . . . **62** A4
Gorse Cl CV22 . . . . **82** E1
Gorse Farm Rd CV11 . . . . . **40** B8
Gorse La B95 . . . . **113** A2
Gorse Lea CV47 . . . . **147** A5
Gorseway CV5 . . . . **60** C3
Gorsey Cl B96 . . . . **118** C8
Gorsey La
Coleshill B46 . . . . **23** F2
Wythall B47 . . . . **69** A3
Gorsey Way B46 . . . . **23** E2
Gorsy Bank Rd B77 . . . . **9** F5
Gorsy Way CV10 . . . . **28** D5
Gorton Croft CV7 . . . . **74** B7
Gosford Ind Est CV1 . . . . . . **61** F2
Gosford Park Prim Sch
CV1 . . . . **61** F2
Gosford St CV1 . . . . **151** D2
Gospel Oak La CV37 . . . . **120** F5
Gospel Oak Rd CV6 . . . . **49** B4
Gosport Rd CV6 . . . . **61** E8
Gossett La CV8 . . . . **79** F7
Gould Cl NN11 . . . . **117** D5
Gould Rd CV35 . . . . **108** A7
Governor's Ct CV34 . . . . . **108** D8
Grace Rd CV5 . . . . **59** A8
Grafton Cl B98 . . . . **103** B7
Grafton Ct
Coventry CV4 . . . . **76** B7
Temple Grafton B49 . . . . . . **119** E1
Grafton La B50 . . . . **148** F6
Grafton St CV1 . . . . **61** F2
Graham Cl CV6 . . . . **50** B1
Graham Rd CV21 . . . . **83** C4
Graham St CV11 . . . . **29** C5
Gramer Cotts CV9 . . . . **19** A6
Granborough Cl CV3 . . . . . . **78** F8
Granborough Ct CV32 . . . **106** A3
Granbrook La GL55 . . . . . **135** C7
Granby Cl LE10 . . . . **31** C7
Granby Rd
Hinckley LE10 . . . . **31** C7
Honington CV36 . . . . **137** A5
Nuneaton CV10 . . . . **28** F3
Grandborough Fields Rd
CV23 . . . . **116** E5
Grand Depot Rd CV11 . . . . **40** F6
Grange Ave
Coventry,Binley CV3 . . . . **78** F7
Coventry,Finham CV3 . . . . . **77** C3
Kenilworth CV8 . . . . **92** E7
Grange Cl
Nuneaton CV10 . . . . **28** C7
Ratley OX15 . . . . **132** F2
Southam CV47 . . . . **147** B5
Tamworth B77 . . . . **9** C8
Warwick CV34 . . . . **109** C8
Grange Ct CV37 . . . . **129** B3
Grange Dr LE10 . . . . **31** E5
Grange Education Unit The
CV6 . . . . **48** E1
Grange Farm Dr CV47 . . . **147** F8
Grange Farm Prim Sch
CV3 . . . . **77** B5
Grange Gdns CV35 . . . . . . **146** D3
Grangehurst Prim Sch
CV6 . . . . **50** B4
Grange La
Harvington WR11 . . . . **127** D3
Sibford Ferris OX15 . . . . . . **142** E8
Grange Mews The 1
CV32 . . . . **105** D1
Grangemouth Rd CV6 . . . . . **61** B7
Grange Pk CV37 . . . . **145** A4
Grange Rd
Balsall Common CV7 . . . . . . **73** F7
Bearley CV37 . . . . **120** E7
Bidford-on-A B50 . . . . **148** E4
Coventry CV6 . . . . **50** B5
Dorridge B93 . . . . **71** E2
Hartshill Green CV10 . . . . . . **19** C2
Hockley Heath B94 . . . . **88** E8
Royal Leamington Spa
CV32 . . . . **106** B3
Rugby CV21 . . . . **82** E6
Grangers La B98 . . . . **102** F5
Grange The
4 Moreton-in-M GL56 . . . **140** A3
Cubbington CV32 . . . . **106** F5
Royal Leamington Spa
CV32 . . . . **106** B1
Warwick CV34 . . . . **109** C7
Grange Wlk CV6 . . . . **50** B5
Granhill Cl B98 . . . . **103** A8
Granleigh Ct CV32 . . . . . . **106** E5
Granoe Cl CV3 . . . . **78** E8
Grantham St CV2 . . . . **61** F3
Grantley Dr B37 . . . . **33** B3
Grant Rd
Bedworth CV7 . . . . **39** A1
Coventry CV3 . . . . **62** B2
Grants Cl CV47 . . . . **133** D7
Granville Ct CV36 . . . . **149** D6
Granville Gdns LE10 . . . . . . **31** C8
Granville Rd
Dorridge B93 . . . . **72** A2
Hinckley LE10 . . . . **31** C8
Wellesbourne CV35 . . . . . . **146** C3
Granville St CV32 . . . . **106** A2
Grapes Cl CV6 . . . . **61** B5
Grasmere Ave CV3 . . . . **76** F6
Grasmere Cl CV21 . . . . **83** D6
Grasmere Cres CV11 . . . . . . **29** F7
Grasmere Ct 2 CV37 . . . . **145** A3
Grasmere Rd CV12 . . . . **39** B2
Grasscroft Dr CV3 . . . . **77** E6
Grassholme B77 . . . . **10** A8
Grassington Ave CV34 . . . **104** F1
Grassington Dr CV11 . . . . . **30** A2
Gratton Ct CV3 . . . . **76** F6
Gravel Hill CV4 . . . . **59** F1
Gravel The B76 . . . . **14** B2
Graylands The CV3 . . . . **77** C4
Grayling B77 . . . . **9** D6
Grayling Wlk B37 . . . . **33** C3
Gray's La 23 GL56 . . . . . . **140** A3
Grays Orch CV23 . . . . **98** F2
Grayswood Ave CV5 . . . . . . **60** D4
Grazier Ave B77 . . . . **9** C8
Great Alne Prim Sch
B49 . . . . **119** D6
Great Balance CV23 . . . . . . **64** E3
Great Borne CV21 . . . . **83** C7
Great Central Walk Nature
Trail★ CV22 . . . . **100** D7
Great Central Way CV21 . . **83** D5
Great Central Wlk★ CV23 . **67** F2
Greatheed Rd CV32 . . . . . **105** E2
Great Pinley Barns CV35 . **114** B5
Great Rollright CE Prim Sch
OX7 . . . . **142** A2
Great William St CV37 . . . **145** A3
Greaves Cl CV34 . . . . **109** C7
Greaves Cotts CV47 . . . . . **115** E3
Greaves The B76 . . . . **22** F6
Greaves Way The CV47 . . **124** B4
Greenacre Cl B77 . . . . **4** B5
Greenacres Prim Sch B77 . . **4** B5
Greenacres B76 . . . . **22** A8

Greenbank Rd CV7 .... 73 F6
Green Cl
Long Lawford CV23 .... 81 F4
Studley B80 .... 103 E3
Whitnash CV31 .... 110 B4
Wythall B47 .... 69 A3
Green Ct CV21 .... 83 D4
Greendale Cl CV9 .... 18 E7
Greendale Rd
Atherstone CV9 .... 18 E7
Coventry CV5 .... 60 D3
Green End CV47 .... 115 D4
Green Farm End CV35 ... 132 B6
Greenfield Ave CV7 ...... 74 A7
Greenfields Cl CV36 ..... 149 D5
Green Field The CV3 ...... 78 B8
Greenfinch Cl B36 .... 33 A7
Greenfinch Rd B36 .... 33 A7
Green Gables B47 .... 69 A7
Green Gates B95 .... 113 B5
Greenheart B77 .... 4 A4
Greenhill Cl B77 .... 9 C5
Greenhill Cotts WR11 ... 127 E1
Greenhill Farm CV47 .... 124 A6
Greenhill Rd
Rugby CV22 .... 82 F1
Stoke Golding CV13 .... 21 D7
Whitnash CV31 .... 110 B4
Greenhill St CV37 .... 144 F3
Green La
Balsall Common CV7 ...... 74 B7
Birchmoor B77,B78 .... 10 D7
Bouts B96 .... 118 A6
Bradley Green CV9 .... 11 F5
Brinklow CV23 .... 64 D3
Church Lawford CV23 ..... 81 C5
Coleshill B46 .... 33 F5
Corley Moor CV7 .... 47 D6
Coventry CV3 .... 77 B4
Grendon CV9 .... 11 F3
Middleton B78 .... 14 B6
Greenland Ave CV5 .... 59 F5
Greenland Ct CV5 .... 59 F5
Greenlands Ave B98 .... 103 A8
Greenlands Dr B98 ...... 102 F8
Greenlands Rd B37 ...... 33 C1
Green Lane Cl CV36 ..... 149 D5
Green La
Nuneaton CV10 .... 28 C7
Old Arley CV10 .... 26 E8
Oxhill CV35 .... 137 F8
Redditch B97 .... 102 A7
Shipston-on-S CV36 ...... 149 D5
Shrewley CV35 .... 114 C6
Studley B80 .... 103 B5
Swalcliffe OX15 .... 139 A1
Tamworth B77 .... 10 C6
Warwick CV34 .... 108 F8
Wibtoft LE17 .... 43 B3
Wolvey LE10 .... 42 C5
Greenleaf Cl CV5 .... 60 A3
Greenlea B77 .... 10 A8
Greenmoor Rd
Hinckley LE10 .... 31 D5
Nuneaton CV10 .... 29 A3
Greenodd Dr CV6 .... 49 F5
Green's Cl CV23 .... 67 C6
Greenside B90 .... 70 D4
Greenside Cl CV11 .... 30 C1
Greensleeves Cl CV6 ..... 49 B2
Greens Rd CV6 .... 49 A1
Greensward Cl CV8 .... 93 B6
Greensward The
Coventry CV3 .... 63 A2
Wardington OX17 .... 134 F1
Greenswood CV37 .... 120 E7
Greens Yd CV12 .... 39 C3
Green The
13 Moreton-in-M GL56 ... 140 A3
Atherstone CV9 .... 19 A6
Austrey CV9 .... 3 B1
Barby CV23 .... 101 C1
Braunston NN11 .... 117 E5
Broadwell CV23 .... 116 B4
Chipping Campden GL55 . 135 B1
Churchover CV23 .... 67 C6
Claverdon CV35 .... 113 F4
Cleeve Prior WR11 ...... 128 A4
Dadlington CV13 .... 21 E8
Dunchurch CV22 .... 99 C3
Freasley B78 .... 10 C4
Great Rollright OX7 ..... 142 A2
Great Wolford CV36 ...... 140 E5
Harborough Magna CV23 .. 66 B3
Hellidon NN11 .... 126 B5
Hook Norton OX15 .... 142 D4
Hornton OX15 .... 139 B7
Kingsbury B78 .... 15 C6
Lighthorne CV35 .... 123 B2
Little Wolford CV36 ..... 141 A6
Long Itchington CV47 .... 115 D4
Long Lawford CV23 .... 82 A4
Long Marston CV37 ...... 129 B3
Meriden CV7 .... 46 B1
Middle Tysoe CV35 ...... 138 B7
Nuneaton CV11 .... 29 E2
Orton-on-t-H CV9 .... 6 C4
Priors Marston CV47 ..... 125 E4
Ratley CV35 .... 132 F3
Rugby CV22 .... 99 C8
Seckington B79 .... 2 A3
Shrewley CV35 .... 114 D6
Shustoke B46 .... 24 F2
Shutford OX15 .... 139 A3
Snitterfield CV37 .... 121 B6

Green The *continued*
Stoneleigh CV8 .... 94 C6
Swalcliffe OX15 .... 142 F8
Tamworth B77 .... 4 B5
Tamworth-In-A B94 .... 87 A2
Wigston Parva LE10 ...... 42 E8
Greenway NN11 .... 117 D5
Greenway Cl CV36 ...... 149 D6
Greenway Nature Trail The
CV37 .... 129 C5
Greenway
Nuneaton CV11 .... 40 B8
Polesworth B78 .... 5 A3
Greenway Rd CV36 ...... 149 D6
Greenways CV4 .... 59 C2
Greenways Ct CV36 ..... 149 C6
Greenways The CV32 .... 106 B3
Greenway The B37 .... 44 A6
Greenway CV34 .... 104 E1
Greenwood Cl CV23 ...... 82 A5
Greenwood Ct
Nuneaton CV11 .... 29 E3
Royal Leamington Spa
CV32 .... 106 B1
Greenwood Rd CV13 ..... 21 E7
Greenwood Sq 5 B37 .... 33 B2
Greenwood Way B37 ..... 33 B2
Gregory Ave CV3 .... 77 A6
Gregory Hood Rd CV3 .... 77 E4
Grenden Hall Rd CV35 ... 132 D3
Grendon Cl CV4 .... 59 C1
Grendon Dr CV21 .... 83 E7
Grendon Rd B78 .... 11 A8
Grenfell Cl CV31 .... 110 D6
Grenville Ave CV2 .... 62 B3
Grenville Cl CV22 .... 82 C1
Gresham Ave CV32 ...... 106 B2
Gresham Pl CV32 .... 106 B2
Gresham Rd CV10 .... 39 B8
Gresham St CV2 .... 62 A2
Gresley Rd CV2 .... 62 D7
Greswold Cl CV4 .... 59 F1
Greswoldes The CV31 ... 110 F6
Gretna Rd CV3 .... 76 F4
Grevel La GL55 .... 135 B2
Greville Ho 13 CV34 ..... 108 F7
Greville Rd
Alcester B49 .... 143 A5
Kenilworth CV8 .... 92 F4
Warwick CV34 .... 105 B1
Greville Smith Ave CV31 . 110 B4
Grewcock Cl LE17 .... 43 E6
Greycoat Rd CV6 .... 49 A2
Greyfriars Ct CV6 .... 61 A7
Greyfriars La CV1 .... 151 B2
Greyfriars Rd CV1 .... 151 B2
Greygoose La GL56 ..... 150 D6
Greyhurst Croft 5 B91 ... 71 B8
Grey Mill Cl B90 .... 70 F6
Grey Mill La B95 .... 120 A8
Greyrick Ct GL55 .... 135 B6
Greys Cl OX16 .... 139 F3
Grey's Rd B80 .... 103 E3
Grey Tree Cres B93 ...... 71 E3
Griffin Bsns Pk B37 ...... 33 C3
Griffin Rd CV34 .... 109 C7
Griffins La B90 .... 70 A5
Griffiths Ho CV21 .... 83 C7
Griff La
Nuneaton CV10 .... 39 A6
Nuneaton CV10 .... 39 B6
Griggs Cl GL55 .... 135 B2
Grimshaw Villas B93 ..... 72 D8
Grimston Cl CV3 .... 63 A2
Grindle Rd CV6 .... 49 F4
Grindley Ho 5 CV1 ...... 61 D2
Grindsbrook B77 .... 10 A8
Grizebeck Dr CV5 .... 60 A5
Grizedale CV21 .... 83 C7
Grosvenor Cres LE10 ..... 32 A6
Grosvenor Ct 2 CV32 ... 105 F1
Grosvenor Ho CV1 ...... 151 A2
Grosvenor Rd
Coventry CV1 .... 151 A1
Rugby CV21 .... 83 C3
Whitnash CV31 .... 110 A5
Grouse Cl CV37 .... 144 C5
Grove Croft CV35 .... 114 F3
Grove Ct
Coventry CV5 .... 77 B8
Nuneaton CV11 .... 29 E2
Grovefield Cres CV7 ..... 74 C8
Grove Fields CV10 .... 29 D8
Grove Ho CV37 .... 144 F2
Grovehurst Pk CV8 .... 94 B2
Grove La
Keresley CV7 .... 48 F7
Lapworth B94 .... 88 F4
Grovelands Ind Est CV7 .. 50 A6
Grove La B76 .... 13 F2
Grove Pk
Hampton Magna CV35 .... 114 F3
Hinckley LE10 .... 32 A6
Grove Pl
2 Royal Leamington Spa
CV31 .... 110 A6
Nuneaton CV10 .... 28 D3
Grove Rd
Ansty CV7 .... 51 D3
Atherstone CV9 .... 18 D8
Dorridge B93 .... 72 B3
Hinckley LE10 .... 32 A6
Nuneaton CV10 .... 28 D3
Stratford-u-A CV37 ..... 144 F2
Grove St
Coventry CV1 .... 151 C3
Royal Leamington Spa
CV32 .... 109 E8

Grove The
Bedworth CV12 .... 39 C3
Coleshill B46 .... 33 F4
Hampton-in-A B92 .... 45 A1
Hinckley LE10 .... 31 C8
Moreton-in-M GL56 ...... 140 B3
Studley B80 .... 103 D3
Grump St CV36 .... 136 A6
Guardhouse Rd CV6 ...... 61 B8
Guernsey Dr B36 .... 33 B6
Guernsey Way 5 OX16 .. 139 F5
Guild Cotts The CV34 .... 108 D6
Guildford Ct CV6 .... 61 D7
Guild Rd
Aston Cantlow B95 ...... 119 F6
Coventry CV6 .... 61 D7
Guild St CV37 .... 145 A3
Guillemard Ct B37 .... 33 B1
Guilsborough Rd CV3 .... 78 E8
Guinea Cres CV4 .... 75 E6
Guinness Cl B98 .... 102 D8
Gulistan Ct 6 CV32 ..... 105 E1
Gulistan Rd CV32 .... 105 E1
Gullet The B78 .... 4 F1
Gullicote La OX17 .... 139 F6
Gulliman's Way CV31 .... 110 D7
Gulliver's Cl OX15 .... 139 D6
Gulson Hospl CV1 .... 151 D2
Gulson Rd CV1 .... 61 E2
Gundry Cl CV31 .... 110 A7
Gun Hill Inf Sch CV7 ..... 37 A8
Gun Hill CV7 .... 37 A8
Gun La CV2 .... 62 A5
Gunn Ct B49 .... 119 E6
Gunn End CV36 .... 149 D7
Gunner Gr B75 .... 13 A6
Gunners La B80 .... 103 E4
Gunnery Terr 3 CV32 ... 105 D1
Gunnings Rd B49 .... 143 C4
Gunton Ave CV3 .... 78 C6
Guphill Ave CV5 .... 60 D2
Guphill La CV5 .... 60 D3
Gurnard B77 .... 9 D6
Gurney Cl CV4 .... 59 E3
Gutteridge Ave CV6 ...... 49 A2
Guy Pl E 13 CV32 .... 105 F1
Guy Pl W 12 CV32 .... 105 F1
Guy Rd CV8 .... 92 F2
Guy's Cliffe Ave CV32 ... 105 D2
Guy's Cliffe Rd CV32 .... 109 E8
Guy's Cliffe Terr CV34 ... 108 F7
Guy's Cl CV34 .... 109 A8
Guy's Cross Park Rd
CV34 .... 108 F8
Guy St
Royal Leamington Spa
CV32 .... 105 F1
Warwick CV34 .... 108 F7
Gypsy La
Atherstone CV9 .... 12 D2
Dordon CV9 .... 11 A4
Kenilworth CV8 .... 92 F2
Water Orton B46 .... 23 D2

H

Hack La CV36 .... 141 C5
Hackwell St CV47 .... 125 C8
Haddon End CV3 .... 77 E6
Haddon Rd CV32 .... 106 B2
Haddon St CV6 .... 62 A8
Hadfield Cl CV23 .... 84 A5
Hadfield Way B37 .... 33 A4
Hadleigh Croft B76 ...... 22 A6
Hadleigh Rd CV3 .... 77 C4
Hadley Cl B47 .... 69 A5
Hadley Mews CV11 .... 29 D1
Hadleys Croft B78 .... 15 D5
Hadrian Cl
Hinckley LE10 .... 21 F1
Royal Leamington Spa
CV32 .... 106 B4
Hadrian Dr B46 .... 23 F1
Hadrians Cl B77 .... 9 D8
Hadrians Way CV21 .... 82 F7
Hadrians Wlk B49 .... 143 B3
Haig Ct CV22 .... 82 E1
Halberd Cl LE10 .... 31 D5
Hales Cl CV37 .... 121 B7
Hales Park Ind Est CV6 ... 49 E4
Hales St CV1 .... 151 C3
Halford Gr CV35 .... 114 F5
Halford La CV6 .... 49 A2
Halford Lodge CV6 .... 49 A2
Halford Rd
Ettington CV37 .... 131 A3
Idlicote CV36 .... 137 C7
Stratford-u-A CV37 ..... 144 E1
Halfpenny Field Wlk B35 . 22 A3
Halfway La CV22 .... 99 B3
Halifax Cl
Allesley CV5 .... 60 A7
Wellesbourne CV35 ...... 146 B1
Hallam Rd CV6 .... 49 B2
Hallams Cl CV8 .... 79 F5
Hall Brook Rd CV6 .... 49 A4
Hall Cl CV8 .... 94 B6
Hall Cl The CV22 .... 99 C2
Hallcroft Way B93 .... 72 A6
Hall Ct B78 .... 5 A1
Hall Dr
Baginton CV8 .... 77 E3
Birmingham B37 .... 44 A7
Stoke Golding CV13 ...... 21 E7
Hall End CV11 .... 29 D2
Hall End Pl CV11 .... 29 D2
Hallfields CV31 .... 110 E5

Hall Gr CV23 .... 64 F4
Hall Green Rd CV2,CV6 ... 50 B2
Hall La
Coventry CV2 .... 62 F6
Harbury CV33 .... 123 F7
Witherley CV9 .... 19 B8
Wolvey LE10 .... 41 D4
Hall Rd
Hinckley LE10 .... 31 D5
Royal Leamington Spa
CV32 .... 105 F1
Wolvey LE10 .... 41 D4
Hall's Cl CV31 .... 110 B3
Hall's Croft Mus★ CV37 . 145 A2
Hallway Dr CV7 .... 51 E6
Hall Wlk B46 .... 33 F4
Halstead Gr B91 .... 71 A8
Haltonlea B77 .... 10 A8
Hamar Way B37 .... 33 B1
Hambridge Rd CV47 ..... 124 C3
Hames La B79 .... 2 D3
Hamilton Cl CV12 .... 38 C1
Hamilton Ct
Coventry CV1 .... 151 B4
Nuneaton CV10 .... 28 D4
Hamilton Dr B80 .... 103 D3
Hamilton Rd
Coventry CV2 .... 62 A3
Radford Semele CV31 .... 110 E5
Redditch B97 .... 102 C8
Tiddington CV37 .... 145 F3
Hamilton Terr CV32 ..... 109 F8
Hamlet Cl
Nuneaton CV11 .... 30 B1
Rugby CV22 .... 99 D6
Hamlet The
Leek Wootton CV35 ...... 105 A7
Marlcliff B50 .... 148 D2
Hammersley St CV12 ..... 38 E1
Hammerton Way CV35 .. 146 C1
Hammond Bsns Ctr CV11 . 29 E3
Hammond Cl CV11 .... 29 E3
Hammond Gn CV35 ..... 146 D4
Hammond Rd CV2 .... 61 F4
Hammonds Terr CV8 ..... 92 D5
Hampden Cl 11 OX16 .... 139 F3
Hampden Ct CV47 .... 133 A7
Hampden Way CV22 ...... 99 C7
Hampdon Way CV35 ..... 146 C2
Hampshire Cl CV3 .... 78 F8
Hampstead Norreys Rd
CV35 .... 132 D4
Hampton Ave CV10 .... 28 B4
Hampton Cl
Coventry CV6 .... 61 F6
Redditch B98 .... 103 B7
Hampton Croft CV35 .... 114 F2
Hampton Ct B92 .... 57 B6
Hampton Grange CV7 .... 46 B1
Hampton Gr CV32 .... 106 B1
Hampton-in-Arden Sta
B92 .... 57 B7
Hampton La
Catherine de B B91 .... 56 B5
Meriden CV7 .... 57 E8
Hampton Lucy CE Prim Sch
CV35 .... 121 F4
Hampton Rd
Coventry CV6 .... 61 F6
Knowle B93 .... 72 C8
Warwick CV34 .... 108 B5
Hampton St CV34 .... 108 D6
Hams La B76 .... 23 F6
Hanbury Cl 13 CV35 ..... 132 B6
Hanbury Rd
Bedworth CV12 .... 39 C4
Dorridge B93 .... 71 F4
Hancock Gn CV4 .... 75 F8
Hancox Cl CV33 .... 107 D7
Handcross Gr CV3 .... 77 A5
Handley Gr CV34 .... 104 D1
Handley's Cl CV8 .... 79 A1
Hands Paddock CV37 .... 130 E1
Handsworth Cres CV5 .... 59 E4
Hanford Cl CV6 .... 61 E6
Hanford Close Ind Est
CV6 .... 61 E6
Hanger Rd B26 .... 44 A3
Hangmans La B79 .... 2 A2
Hanley Ct B49 .... 143 C4
Hanlith B77 .... 10 A8
Hanover Ct
Hinckley LE10 .... 31 E6
Redditch B97 .... 102 D8
Hanover Gdns
8 Royal Leamington Spa
CV32 .... 106 A1
Rugby CV21 .... 83 B4
Hanover Glebe CV11 ..... 29 C2
Hans Cl CV2 .... 61 F4
Hansell Dr B93 .... 71 E2
Hansom Ct 2 LE10 .... 31 D8
Hanson Ave CV36 .... 149 C5
Hanson Farm Cotts
CV36 .... 149 C5
Hanson's Bridge Rd B24,
B35 .... 22 A4
Hanson Way CV6 .... 50 A4
Hanwell Cl B76 .... 22 B7
Hanwell Ct OX17 .... 139 F6
Hanwood Cl CV5 .... 59 D4
Hanworth Cl CV32 .... 106 C2
Hanworth Rd CV34 ...... 108 D8
Harbet Dr B40 .... 44 E4
Harborough Cotts B94 .... 89 D3
Harborough Dr B36 ...... 22 D1
Harborough Rd
Coventry CV6 .... 49 B2

Harborough Rd *continued*
Rugby CV23 .... 82 C8
Harbour Cl B50 .... 148 C4
Harbourne Cl CV8 .... 93 A5
Harbury CE Prim Sch
CV33 .... 123 F6
Harbury Cl B76 .... 22 B6
Harbury La
Harbury CV33 .... 123 B7
Royal Leamington Spa CV33,
CV34 .... 109 E2
Harbury Rd CV47 .... 124 C6
Harby Cl B37 .... 44 B8
Harcourt CV3 .... 78 E5
Harcourt Gdns CV11 ..... 29 C3
Hardingwood La CV7 ..... 35 F3
Hardwick Cl CV5 .... 60 A4
Hardwick La B80 .... 112 B3
Hardwick Pk 18 OX16 ... 139 F5
Hardwick Rd CV47 ...... 125 E4
Hardwyn Cl CV3 .... 63 A1
Hardy Cl
Nuneaton CV10 .... 28 A4
Rugby CV22 .... 82 C2
Hardy Rd CV6 .... 61 A8
Harebell B77 .... 4 A4
Harebell Way CV23 .... 83 D8
Harebell Wlk 1 B37 ..... 33 D2
Harefield Ho CV2 .... 62 B3
Harefield La CV12 .... 38 F8
Harefield Rd
Coventry CV2 .... 62 B3
Nuneaton CV11 .... 29 C4
Hare & Hounds La CV10 .. 29 A2
Haresfield B90 .... 70 A5
Hareway La CV35 .... 122 C7
Harewood Rd CV5 .... 60 C2
Harger Ct CV8 .... 92 F4
Harger Mews CV8 .... 92 F4
Hargrave Cl
Coventry CV3 .... 63 A1
Grandborough CV23 ..... 116 F5
Water Orton B46 .... 23 B3
Harington Rd CV6 .... 61 A5
Harlech Cl
10 Banbury OX16 .... 139 F3
Kenilworth CV8 .... 93 C5
Harley St CV2 .... 62 A3
Harlow Wlk 8 CV2 .... 63 A7
Harmar Cl CV34 .... 104 D1
Harmer Cl CV2 .... 63 A7
Harmony Ct CV10 .... 29 B2
Harnall Cl B90 .... 70 E7
Harnall Ind Est CV1 ..... 151 C4
Harnall La CV1 .... 151 C4
Harnall La E CV1 .... 61 E4
Harnall La W CV1 .... 151 C4
Harnall Row
Coventry CV1 .... 61 E2
Coventry CV1 .... 61 E3
Harold Cox Pl CV22 ...... 99 E5
Harold Rd CV2 .... 62 D2
Harold's Orch GL56 ..... 136 B1
Harold St CV11 .... 29 C3
Harpenden Dr CV5 .... 60 A5
Harper Rd CV1 .... 61 E2
Harpers La CV9 .... 19 A7
Harrier Parkway LE17 .... 55 D7
Harrington Ct CV3 .... 62 F2
Harrington Way CV10 .... 39 A7
Harriott Dr CV34 .... 109 D4
Harris Cl
Henley-in-A B95 .... 113 B4
Redditch B98 .... 102 F8
Harris Dr CV22 .... 99 F8
Harris Mews B95 .... 113 B4
Harrison Cl CV21 .... 101 B8
Harrison Cres CV12 ...... 39 A2
Harrison Rd B97 .... 102 C8
Harrison Way CV31 ..... 109 F5
Harris Rd
Coventry CV3 .... 62 B2
Warwick CV34 .... 108 C8
Harris Sch CV22 .... 82 F1
Harrowbrook Ind Est
LE10 .... 30 E7
Harrowbrook Rd LE10 .... 30 E7
Harrow Cl CV6 .... 50 A4
Harrow Rd CV31 .... 110 B3
Harry Caplan Ho CV5 ..... 60 B6
Harry Edwards Ho 2 CV2 62 D8
Harry Rose Rd CV2 .... 62 E3
Harry Salt Ho CV1 ...... 151 D3
Harry Stanley Ho CV6 .... 62 A8
Harry Taylor Fst Sch The
B97 .... 102 E6
Harry Truslove Cl CV6 .... 61 A7
Harry Weston Rd CV3 .... 63 A1
Hart Cl CV21 .... 83 D2
Hartington Cl B93 .... 71 E3
Hartington Cres CV5 ..... 60 F1
Hartington Gn LE10 ...... 31 E6
Hartland Ave CV2 .... 62 B5
Hartlebury Cl B93 .... 71 F3
Hartlepool Rd CV1 ...... 151 D4
Hartleyburn B77 .... 10 A8
Hartley Gdns CV47 ...... 147 A3
Hartridge Wlk CV5 .... 60 B4
Hartshill Hayes Ctry Pk★
CV10 .... 18 F1
Hartshill Hayes Cty Pk
Woodland★ CV10 .... 19 A1
Hartshill Hayes Visitors Ctr★
CV10 .... 18 F1
Hartshill Sch CV10 .... 28 B8
Harvard Cl
Moreton-in-M GL56 ...... 140 B3
Wellesbourne CV35 ...... 146 C1

Harvesters Cl CV3 63 A2
Harvest Hill Cl 7 CV31 110 C6
Harvest Hill Cotts CV5 47 D1
Harvest Hill La CV5,CV7 47 C4
Harvest Hill Pk CV5 47 D1
Harvey Cl CV5 60 A7
Harvington CE Fst Sch WR11 127 D4
Harvington Cross WR11 127 D4
Harvington Dr B90 71 B6
Harvington Way B76 22 A8
Harvon Garth CV21 83 C4
Harwood Dr B77 9 D4
Harwood Gr 1 B90 70 C8
Haselbech Rd CV3 62 F1
Haselbury Cnr CV10 28 F1
Haseley Bsns Ctr CV35 114 D7
Haseley Cl CV31 110 B5
Haseley Ct
Five Ways CV35 114 D8
Lower Quinton CV37 129 D2
Haseley Hall CV35 114 D8
Haseley Rd CV2 50 C1
Haselor Cl B49 143 D4
Haselor Sch B49 119 D4
Hasilwood Sq CV3 62 B2
Haslucks Green Rd B90 69 E7
Hassall Cl 9 CV33 122 F8
Hastang Fields CV31 110 C5
Hastings Cl
1 Banbury OX16 139 F3
Tamworth B77 9 F6
Hastings High Sch LE10 31 F7
Hastings Rd
Banbury OX16 139 F4
Coventry CV2 62 A4
Wellesbourne CV35 146 D4
Haswell Cl CV22 83 C2
Hatchford Wlk B37 33 B1
Hathaway Cl
Balsall Common CV7 74 B7
South Littleton WR11 127 F1
Hathaway Dr
Nuneaton CV11 30 A1
Warwick CV34 104 E2
Hathaway Green La CV37 144 B3
Hathaway Hamlet CV37 144 C2
Hathaway La CV37 144 D1
Hathaway Rd CV4 59 D1
Hatherden Dr B76 13 A2
Hatherell Rd CV31 110 E5
Hatters Ct CV12 39 D2
Hatters Dr CV9 12 D2
Hatton Bank La CV37 121 D5
Hatton Cl CV35 114 E5
Hatton Ctry World★ CV35 114 D5
Hatton Gn CV35 114 D6
Hatton Sta CV35 114 C5
Hatton Terr CV35 114 F5
Haunch La B76 24 A8
Haunchwood Park Dr CV10 27 E4
Haunchwood Park Ind Est CV10 27 E4
Haunchwood Rd CV10 28 D4
Havendale Cl CV6 61 B5
Hawbridge Cl B90 71 B6
Hawfinch B77 10 A6
Hawk Cl CV11 40 B8
Hawkesbury Fields Sch CV2 50 C3
Hawkesbury La CV2 50 D5
Hawkes Dr CV34 109 D4
Hawkeshead CV21 83 D7
Hawkes Mill La CV5 48 B2
Hawkeswell La B46 34 B3
Hawkesworth Dr CV8 93 A6
Hawke Way LE17 55 C7
Hawkinge Dr B35 22 A4
Hawkins Cl CV22 82 E1
Hawkins Rd CV5 61 A2
Hawkshead Dr B93 71 F6
Hawkside B77 10 B8
Hawk's La OX15 142 E8
Hawkswood Dr CV7 74 B7
Hawksworth Cres B37 33 D3
Hawksworth Dr 1 CV1 61 B3
Hawlands CV21 83 D6
Hawley Rd LE10 31 D7
Hawnby Gr B76 13 A2
Hawthorn Ave CV9 16 C5
Hawthorn Cl B49 143 B5
Hawthorn Cres LE10 31 E4
Hawthorn Ct CV4 59 E1
Hawthorn Dr CV7 74 B8
Hawthorne Ave CV7 37 B8
Hawthorne Cl CV8 80 A4
Hawthorne Dr B47 69 B6
Hawthorne Terr CV10 28 F5
Hawthorn La CV4 59 E1
Hawthorn Rd CV31 109 F6
Hawthorns The B78 15 C7
Hawthorn Terr CV23 66 B3
Hawthorn Way
Hartshill CV10 28 A8
Rugby CV22 82 B2
Shipston-on-S CV36 149 D4
Haybarn The B76 22 A8
Haydock Cl
Coventry CV6 50 B4
Stratford-u-A CV37 144 E1
Tamworth B77 9 D4
Haydon Cl B93 71 F2
Haydons Cl GL55 135 B2
Haydon Way B49 118 F8
Haye La B80 112 A5
Hayes Cl CV21 83 D7
Hayes Green Rd CV12 49 F8
Hayes La CV7 50 A8
Hayes Rd CV10 28 A8
Hayes The CV35 104 F5
Hay La
Coventry CV1 151 C2
Solihull B90 71 A6
Hayle Ave CV34 104 F1
Hayle Cl CV11 30 A5
Hay Mdw CV36 149 C6
Haynestone Rd CV6 60 E6
Haynes Way CV21 82 F8
Hay Pool OX17 133 F5
Hays La LE10 31 B7
Haysum's Cl GL55 135 B1
Hayton Gn CV4 75 F8
Haytor Rise CV2 62 C7
Hayward Cl CV35 114 F3
Hayward's Gn CV6 61 A7
Hayway La CV23 116 B4
Hay Wood La B93,CV35 90 A3
Hazel Cl
Hartshill CV10 28 A8
Royal Leamington Spa CV32 106 A2
Hazel Croft
Birmingham,Chelmsley Wood B37 33 B1
Braunston NN11 117 E5
Hazelcroft B78 15 C7
Hazel Dr B47 69 B5
Hazelgarth B77 10 B8
Hazel Gr
Bedworth CV12 39 D3
Hockley Heath B94 88 C6
Hazell Way CV10 29 A1
Hazel Rd
Coventry CV6 50 B1
Nuneaton CV10 28 D5
Hazeltree Gr B93 71 E3
Hazelwood Cl CV22 99 C3
Hazlemere Cl CV5 60 B4
Headborough Rd CV2 62 A5
Headington Ave CV6 49 A2
Headland Cl CV37 129 A6
Headland Rd CV37 129 A6
Headland Rise CV37 129 A6
Headlands The CV5 60 D4
Headley Ct B97 102 D8
Healey Cl CV21 83 C7
Healey Ct CV34 108 F7
Health Centre Rd CV4 76 C4
Heanley La CV9 16 D5
Hearsall Comm CV5 60 F2
Hearsall Com Prim Sch CV5 60 F2
Hearsall Ct CV4 60 D2
Hearsall La CV5 60 F2
Heart of England Sch CV7 74 C6
Heart of England Way CV11 29 F3
Heath Ave CV12 38 E1
Heathcote Cl B77 10 B7
Heathcote Ct CV6 61 A7
Heathcote Ind Est CV34 109 D4
Heathcote La
Royal Leamington Spa CV34 109 D4
Warwick CV34 109 A5
Heathcote Rd CV31 110 A4
Heathcote St CV6 61 A7
Heathcote Way CV34 109 D4
Heath Cres CV2 62 A6
Heath Ct OX15 142 D4
Heath End La CV37 121 D7
Heath End Rd CV10 28 F2
Heather Cl
Birmingham B36 33 A8
Nuneaton CV10 28 F3
Rugby CV22 82 E1
Southam CV47 147 B5
Stratford-u-A CV37 144 D3
Heather Ct CV9 12 D1
Heather Dr CV12 38 E2
Heather Rd
Binley Woods CV3 79 D7
Coventry CV2 50 C2
Heath Farm La CV35 123 C2
Heathfield Cl B93 72 A5
Heathfield Rd
Coventry CV5 60 C2
Norton WR11 127 B2
Heathfields Inf Sch B77 9 F6
Heathgreen Cl B37 33 D3
Heath Green Way CV4 75 F6
Heath La CV23 64 E2
Heathley La B78 8 E5
Heath Rd
Bedworth CV12 38 F1
Coventry CV2 62 A4
Hollywood B47 69 A7
Heath Terr
Beausale CV35 91 C2
Royal Leamington Spa CV32 105 E1
Heath The CV22 99 C4
Heath Way CV22 100 D8
Hebden Ave CV34 104 F1
Hebden B77 10 B8
Hebden Way CV11 30 A2
Heber Dr CV33 123 E6
Heckley Rd CV7 50 A7
Heddle Gr CV6 62 B8
Hedera Rd B98 112 A7
Hedgefield Way CV4 75 F8
Hedgerows The
Nuneaton CV10 28 F6
Tamworth B77 9 F8
Hedgerow Wlk CV6 49 B4
Hedges Cl CV47 124 D6
Hedges The OX15 139 A4
Hedgetree Croft B37 33 C2
Hedge Way CV10 28 C7
Hedging Lane Ind Est B77 9 E5
Hedging La B77 9 E5
Hedingham Gr B37 33 D2
Hedley Croft B35 22 B4
Heemstede La CV32 106 A2
Heera Cl CV6 61 D8
Helena Cl CV10 28 F3
Helen St CV6 61 F6
Hele Rd CV3 77 D6
Hellidon Cl 6 CV32 106 A2
Hellidon Rd CV47 125 F4
Helmdon Cl CV21 83 D6
Helmsdale Rd CV32 106 B5
Helmswood Dr B37 44 C8
Helston Cl CV11 30 A5
Helvellyn Way CV21 83 D7
Hemdale Bsns Pk CV11 30 A4
Hemdale CV11 30 A4
Hemingford Rd CV2 63 A8
Heming Rd B98 103 E8
Hemlingford Croft B37 44 A7
Hemlingford Rd
Kingsbury B78 15 D4
Sutton Coldfield B76 22 A6
Hemmings Cl CV31 110 E5
Hemmings Mill CV35 122 A7
Hemplands OX7 142 A2
Hemsby Cl CV4 76 A7
Hemsworth Dr CV12 40 B2
Henbrook La OX15 137 E2
Henderson Cl CV5 60 C7
Hendre Cl CV5 60 D2
Hen La CV6 49 D3
Henley Cl CV11 29 F8
Henley Coll CV2 62 C8
Henley Ct CV2 62 D7
Henleydale 4 B90 70 C8
Henley-in-Arden Com Prim Sch B95 113 B4
Henley-in-Arden Her Ctr★ B95 113 B4
Henley-in-Arden High Sch B95 113 B4
Henley-in-Arden Sta B95 113 A4
Henley Mill La CV2 62 C7
Henley Park Ct B95 113 B4
Henley Park Ind Est CV2 62 E7
Henley Rd
Claverdon CV35 113 E4
Coventry CV2 62 D7
Lowsonford B95 113 D6
Mappleborough Green B80 112 A5
Norton Lindsey CV35 114 D3
Whitnash CV31 110 B5
Henley St
Alcester B49 143 C4
Stratford-u-A CV37 145 A3
Henley Wlk CV2 62 D8
Henrietta St CV6 61 E5
Henry Boteler Rd CV4 76 B7
Henry Hinde Inf Sch CV22 82 C1
Henry Hinde Jun Sch CV22 82 B2
Henry St
Coventry CV1 151 B3
Kenilworth CV8 93 A5
Nuneaton CV11 29 C2
Rugby CV21 83 A3
Henry Tanday Ct 4 CV32 105 E1
Hensborough B90 70 A5
Henson Rd CV12 38 E1
Henwood La B91 56 B4
Henwoods Ct CV36 149 D7
Hepworth Rd CV3 63 B1
Herald Ave CV5 60 D1
Herald Bsns Pk CV3 78 F7
Herald Rd B26 44 C4
Heralds Ct 6 CV34 109 B8
Herald Way
Coventry CV3 79 A7
Hinckley LE10 31 D4
Herbert Art Gall & Mus★ CV1 151 C2
Herbert Fowler Jun Sch CV7 26 F2
Herbert Gray Coll CV21 83 A3
Herbert's La CV8 93 A5
Herbert St CV10 28 E3
Hercules La CV35 113 F4
Herdwycke Cl CV47 147 D4
Hereford Cl CV10 28 E4
Hereford Rd CV11 40 F6
Hereford Way 4 OX16 139 F5
Hereward Coll CV4 59 F1
Herford Way LE10 31 F6
Heritage Ct
Coventry CV4 76 D3
Kenilworth CV8 93 B7
Heritage Dr CV6 50 C6
Heritage Motor Ctr★ CV35 123 D1
Hermes Cl CV34 109 E5
Hermes Cres CV2 62 E6
Hermes Ct CV34 109 E5
Hermes Rd B26 44 C4
Hermione Cl CV34 109 F3
Hermitage Cl
Catthorpe CV23 68 E1
Hermitage Cl continued
Polesworth B78 4 F1
Hermitage Dr B76 13 A4
Hermitage Rd CV2 62 D4
Hermitage Way CV8 93 A3
Hermit's Croft CV3 77 D8
Heronbank CV4 59 C2
Heron Cl
Alcester B49 143 B5
Cheswick Green B90 70 D4
Heron Ho CV3 62 B2
Heron La CV37 144 C5
Herons Ct LE10 31 A7
Heron Way CV37 130 E1
Herrick Rd CV2 62 D3
Herring Rd CV9 18 E7
Hertford Pl CV1 151 A2
Hertford Rd
Alcester B49 143 C5
Stratford-u-A CV37 144 F1
Hertford St CV1 151 B2
Hertford Way B93 72 B4
Hesleden B77 10 B8
Heslop Cl CV3 78 F8
Hetton Cl 1 CV34 104 F1
Hewitt Ave CV6 61 B4
Hexby Cl CV2 63 A6
Hexworthy Ave CV3 77 B5
Heybrook Cl CV2 62 C7
Heycroft CV4 76 D4
Heydons Terr OX17 133 F4
Heyford Cl CV2 50 D3
Heyford Gr B91 71 C8
Heyford Leys CV22 99 F6
Heyford Way B35 22 B5
Heyville Croft CV8 93 C3
Heywood Cl CV6 62 A7
Hibberd Ct CV8 92 F4
Hibbert Cl CV22 83 A1
Hickman Ho CV10 27 E4
Hickman Rd CV10 27 F5
Hicks Cl CV34 104 E2
Hidcote Ave B76 22 A8
Hidcote Cl
Nuneaton CV11 39 F8
Royal Leamington Spa CV31 110 C5
Hidcote Gr B37 44 A7
Hidcote Manor Gdn★ GL55 135 D5
Hidcote Rd
Ebrington GL55 135 D3
Kenilworth CV8 93 C6
Higham Fields Ct CV13 21 A6
Higham Fields La CV13 21 A6
Higham Lane Sch CV10 29 D6
Higham La
Nuneaton CV11 29 E7
Stoke Golding CV13 21 C6
Wykin LE10 21 F3
Higham on the Hill CE Prim Sch CV13 21 A4
Higham Way LE10 31 E7
Higham Way Ho LE10 31 E7
High Ash Cl CV7 49 F7
High Beech CV5 60 A6
High Brink Rd B46 33 F7
Highbury Gn CV10 28 C7
Highclere Gdns OX16 139 F3
Highcliffe Rd B77 9 D8
Highcroft CV35 113 F3
Highcroft Cres CV32 105 C1
High Cross La CV35 113 F6
High Cross Rd LE17 43 C6
Highdown Cres 3 B90 71 A6
Highdown Rd CV31 110 B6
Highfield Ave
Redditch B97 102 D8
Tamworth B77 4 A5
Highfield Cl
Kenilworth CV8 92 E4
Snitterfield CV37 121 B7
Highfield CV35 114 F6
Highfield La CV7 37 C1
Highfield CV7 46 C1
Highfield Rd
Coventry CV2 61 F4
Nuneaton CV11 29 E2
Redditch B97 102 D8
Stratford-u-A CV37 144 E5
Studley B80 103 D4
Highfield Terr CV32 105 D1
Highgrove
Coventry CV4 75 F5
Rugby CV22 99 D7
Highland Rd
Coventry CV5 60 F1
Kenilworth CV8 93 C7
Royal Leamington Spa CV32 106 B4
Highlands 19 OX16 139 F5
Highlands Cl CV34 109 A8
Highlands Ct B90 70 E8
Highlands Rd B90 70 F8
Highland Way B98 103 A7
High La OX15 137 E1
High Mdw OX15 138 D1
High Meadow Inf Sch B46 33 F8
High Park Cl CV5 59 F3
High St
Alcester B49 143 B3
Astwood Bank B96 102 E1
Barford CV35 122 B8
Bedworth CV12 39 B2
Bidford-on-A B50 148 D4
Bidford-on-A B50 148 E4
Birmingham,Castle Vale B35 22 B4
Bishops Itchington CV47 124 A4
High St continued
Braunston NN11 117 D5
Broom B50 148 B7
Charwelton NN11 126 D2
Chipping Campden GL55 135 B2
Coleshill B46 33 F7
Coventry CV1 151 C2
Coventry,Keresley CV6 48 F1
Cropredy OX17 134 C1
Cubbington CV32 106 E5
Fenny Compton CV47 133 D7
Great Rollright OX7 142 A2
Hampton-in-A B92 57 A7
Harbury CV33 123 F6
Henley-in-A B95 113 B5
Hook Norton OX15 142 D4
Hurley CV9 16 C5
Kenilworth CV8 92 E5
Knowle B93 72 C6
Lower Brailes OX15 137 F2
Marton CV23 115 C7
Mickleton GL55 135 C6
Moreton-in-M GL56 140 A3
Napton on t H CV47 125 C8
Nuneaton CV11 29 B4
Polesworth B78 5 B2
Ratley OX15 133 A2
Royal Leamington Spa CV31 110 A7
Rugby CV21 83 A3
Rugby,Hillmorton CV21 101 A8
Ryton-on-D CV8 79 B1
Shipston-on-S CV36 149 D6
Shutford OX15 139 A3
Southam CV47 147 B4
Stockton CV47 147 F8
Stoke Golding CV13 21 D7
Stratford-u-A CV37 145 A2
Studley B80 103 E4
Tamworth B77 9 C5
Warwick CV34 108 E6
Welford-on-A CV37 129 A7
High Trees Cl B98 102 E7
High Trees Rd B93 72 A7
High View Dr CV7 49 C7
High View CV9 16 C4
High View Rd CV32 106 C5
Highwaymans Croft CV4 76 D5
Hijaz Coll CV11 21 C2
Hiker Gr 3 B37 33 D2
Hilary Bevins Cl CV13 20 F4
Hilary Dr B76 13 A3
Hilary Rd
Coventry CV4 76 E6
Nuneaton CV10 28 F5
Hilditch Way CV11 29 E2
Hillary Rd CV22 99 F8
Hillborough La B50 128 E7
Hill Cl
Northend CV47 133 B7
Royal Leamington Spa CV32 106 A3
Hill Cres CV23 96 F6
Hill Crest CV32 106 E5
Hill Crest Farm Cl B79 5 E4
Hill Crest Hosp B98 103 C6
Hillcrest Pk B47 85 F8
Hillcrest Rd
Nuneaton CV10 28 E5
Polesworth B78 11 A7
Hill Farm Ave CV11 30 B1
Hill Farm Prim Sch CV6 61 B7
Hillfield Mews 3 B91 71 B8
Hillfield Rd
Rugby CV22 82 C1
Solihull B91 71 B8
Hillfields Ho 1 CV1 61 E3
Hill Fray Dr CV3 78 A5
Hill Ho CV37 145 B4
Hillhurst Gr B36 22 D1
Hilliard Cl CV12 39 B4
Hill La
Middleton B75 7 B2
Upper Brailes OX15 137 E3
Upper Quinton CV37 129 D1
Hillman Gr B36 22 F1
Hillman Ho CV1 151 B3
Hillman Way CV37 131 B3
Hillmorton La
Clifton u D CV23 84 A4
Dunsmore CV23 84 F5
Hillmorton Prim Sch CV21 101 B8
Hillmorton Rd
Coventry CV2 50 C1
Dorridge B93 72 A5
Rugby CV22 83 C2
Hill Rd
Grandborough CV23 116 E6
Keresley CV7 48 F6
Lower Boddington NN11 134 E7
Hill Rise OX7 142 A2
Hillrise LE10 31 F8
Hill Row NN11 117 E4
Hillside DE12 3 F8
Hill Side CV2 62 A6
Hillside Croft CV47 125 C8
Hillside Dr CV10 28 C7
Hillside
Harbury CV33 123 E7
Hartshill CV10 28 A8
Hill Side B78 15 D4
Hillside CV47 125 C8
Hillside N CV2 62 A6

Hillside Rd
Hinckley LE10 31 D6
Stratford-u-A CV37 144 C4
Hillside CV37 144 A4
Hill St
Bedworth CV12 39 B5
Coventry CV1 151 B3
Hinckley LE10 31 E8
Nuneaton CV10 28 D4
Royal Leamington Spa CV32 106 A1
Rugby CV21 83 A4
Warwick CV34 109 B8
Hill The CV37 145 B4
Hill Top CV9 11 B2
Hilltop Cl
Honiley CV8 90 E8
Southam CV47 147 A5
Hill Top
Coventry CV1 151 C3
Hill Top CV7 27 B1
Loxley CV35 130 F7
Hilltop Pk CV23 96 F2
Hill View CV47 124 A4
Hill View Cl GL55 135 C7
Hill View Rd B50 148 E5
Hill View CV37 144 A4
Hillwood Ave B90 71 A6
Hill Wootton Rd CV32, CV35 105 C6
Hillyard Rd CV47 147 A5
Hilmore Way B77 9 E8
Hilton Ave CV10 28 B6
Hilton Ct CV5 60 F2
Himbleton Croft 1 B90 71 A6
Himley Rd 2 CV12 38 D2
Himley Rise B90 70 E4
Hinchwick Ct B93 71 F3
Hinckley Bsns Pk LE10 30 F8
Hinckley & District Hospl LE10 31 D8
Hinckley La CV13 21 C3
Hinckley Rd
Ansty CV2,CV7 51 C2
Aston Flamville LE10 32 E6
Burbage LE9 32 D8
Burton Hastings CV11,LE10 41 C8
Coventry CV2 63 A8
Hinckley LE10 32 A6
Nuneaton CV11 29 E5
Stoke Golding CV13 21 F7
Wolvey LE10 41 E7
Hinckley Sta LE10 31 D7
Hind Cl CV34 104 F2
Hinde Cl CV21 83 C7
Hindlip Cl B98 112 A6
Hintons Coppice B93 71 E6
Hipsley Cl B36 22 C1
Hipsley La CV9 16 E6
Hipswell Highway CV2 62 D3
Hipton Hill WR11 127 B3
Hirdemonsway B90 70 A5
Hiron Croft CV3 77 C8
Hiron The CV3 77 C8
Hiron Way CV34 108 B7
Hirst Cl CV23 82 A5
Hitchman Ct CV31 110 A5
Hitchman Rd CV31 110 A5
Hithersand Cl CV35 121 F4
Hitherside B90 70 B5
HM Prison Rye Hill CV23 100 D1
HM Young Offender Institution CV23 100 C1
Hoarestone Ave CV11 40 A7
Hobbins The CV36 149 C5
Hob La
Balsall Common CV7 74 E4
Burton Green CV8 75 A3
Temple Balsall B92 73 A8
Hobley Cl CV22 99 D7
Hockett St CV3 77 D8
Hocking Rd CV2 62 E4
Hockley Cl CV23 116 F5
Hockley Ct B94 88 C7
Hockley Heath Prim Sch B94 88 C6
Hockley La
Coventry CV5 59 C5
Ettington CV37 131 B3
Hockley Rd
Shrewley CV35 114 C6
Tamworth B77 9 F5
Hoden La WR11 128 B3
Hodge La B77 4 B6
Hodgett's La
Balsall Common CV7 74 F7
Coventry CV7,CV8 75 A6
Hodgson Rd CV37 144 F5
Hodnell Cl B36 22 C1
Hodnell Dr CV47 147 C3
Hodnet Cl CV8 93 B5
Hogarth Cl CV12 39 A4
Hogarth Rd CV37 144 D1
Hogg End OX17 134 F3
Hoggrills End La B46 25 A4
Holbeche Cres CV7 36 E3
Holbeche Rd
Dorridge B93 72 A7
Sutton Coldfield B75 13 B5
Holbein Cl CV12 39 A4
Holborn Ave CV6 49 C2
Holbrook Ave CV21 83 B4
Holbrook Gr B37 33 A1
Holbrook La CV6 49 D2
Holbrook Park Est CV6 61 D8
Holbrook Prim Sch CV6 49 E1
Holbrook Rd
Long Lawford CV23 82 B5
Stratford-u-A CV37 144 C3
Holbrook Way CV6 49 D1
Holcot Leys CV22 100 A7
Holder Cl B50 148 D5
Hole House La B94 88 F1
Holioak Dr CV34 109 B6
Holland Ave B93 72 B8
Holland Cl B50 148 D4
Holland Croft B76 15 B2
Holland Rd CV6 61 A6
Hollick Cres CV7 37 A8
Hollicombe Terr CV2 62 D8
Hollies Rd B78 11 B8
Hollies The CV23 67 F1
Hollin Brow Cl B93 72 B3
Hollings Gr B91 71 B8
Hollington Way B90 71 C7
Hollinwell Cl CV11 40 C8
Hollis La CV8 92 E8
Hollis Rd CV3 62 A2
Holloway Field CV6 61 A6
Holloway Hill OX15 138 A1
Holloway La OX15 138 A1
Holloway The
Mollington OX17 134 A2
Priors Marston CV47 125 E4
Warwick CV34 108 D6
Hollow Cres CV6 61 B5
Hollowell Way CV21 83 C7
Hollows The CV11 29 F1
Hollow Way CV47 125 C8
Holly Bank CV5 77 A8
Holly Bank Est CV9 3 A2
Hollyberry Ave B91 71 A8
Hollyberry Cl B98 112 A6
Hollybush La CV6 50 A4
Holly Bush La CV47 125 E4
Hollybush Rd OX15 142 D4
Holly Cl LE10 31 E5
Holly Ct CV7 74 B3
Holly Dr
Hollywood B47 69 B7
Hurley CV9 16 D4
Ryton-on-D CV8 79 B1
Holly Farm Bsns Pk CV8 91 B7
Hollyfast La CV7 48 C4
Hollyfast Prim Sch CV6 60 E7
Hollyfast Rd CV6 60 E6
Holly Gr
Church Lawford CV23 81 B5
Coventry CV4 60 B2
Hollyhurst CV12 38 F1
Hollyhurst Gr B90 70 B8
Hollyhurst B46 23 C2
Holly La
Atherstone CV9 12 C2
Atherstone CV9 12 D2
Balsall Common CV7 74 B3
Hollyland B46 24 F1
Holly Lane Ind Est CV9 12 C2
Holly La
Portway B48 85 F5
Wishaw B76 13 D4
Holly Lodge CV35 146 D3
Holly Lodge Wlk B37 33 A2
Holly Marie Ct CV5 60 F1
Holly Orch 5 CV37 145 A4
Holly Rd CV36 149 D4
Hollystitches Rd CV10 28 E6
Holly St CV32 106 B1
Holly Tree Wlk LE17 43 E6
Hollywell Rd B93 72 A5
Holly Wlk
Baginton CV8 77 E2
Nuneaton CV11 29 F2
Royal Leamington Spa CV32 106 A1
Stratford-u-A CV37 144 C4
Hollywood Gdns B47 69 A8
Hollywood La B47 69 B7
Hollywood Motor Pk B47 69 A8
Hollyword Dr B47 69 A8
Holman Way CV11 29 D3
Holmcroft CV2 62 F8
Holme Cl CV21 83 C6
Holmes Ct CV8 92 F5
Holmes Dr CV5 59 D5
Holmes Rd CV31 110 B3
Holme Way CV23 101 D1
Holmewood Cl CV8 93 B5
Holmewood Ct CV8 93 B5
Holmfield Rd CV2 62 B3
Holmsdale Rd CV6 61 E7
Holroyd Ho CV4 59 F2
Holsworthy Cl CV11 29 E5
Holt Ave CV33 122 E8
Holte Rd CV9 18 D8
Holt Gdns B80 103 E2
Holt Leys CV47 147 C4
Holtom St CV37 144 F1
Holt Rd
Hinckley LE10 31 E6
Studley B80 103 E2
Holt The
Mollington OX17 133 F2
Royal Leamington Spa CV32 106 B3
Holwick B77 10 B8
Holy Cross Ct CV2 62 E4
Holy Cross RC Prim Sch B76 13 A3
Holy Family RC Prim Sch CV6 49 B3
Holyhead Rd CV5 60 E5
Holyoak Cl
Bedworth CV12 38 F1
Rugby CV22 99 C8
Holyoke Gr CV31 110 B2
Holyrood Ct CV10 28 D5
Holywell Cl CV4 59 D1
Holywell CV35 113 F5
Holywell Rd CV47 147 A4
Home Cl
Bubbenhall CV8 95 C6
Staverton NN11 126 E8
Home Farm Barns CV35 138 B7
Home Farm CV36 141 C7
Home Farm Cl
Pailton CV23 66 A8
Witherley CV9 19 B8
Home Farm Cres CV31 110 B4
Home Farm Dr OX15 138 E8
Home Farm
Leek Wootton CV35 104 F6
Stoneleigh CV8 94 A3
Homefield La CV22 99 E4
Home Furlong CV35 146 C1
Home Mdw CV35 113 F3
Home Park Rd CV11 29 C3
Homer Cl CV34 109 E5
Homestalls Mdw CV35 131 D2
Homeward Way CV3 63 A1
Honeybourne Cl CV5 60 B3
Honeybourne Rd B50 148 E3
Honeyfield Rd CV1 61 D5
Honeysuckle Cl CV23 83 D8
Honeysuckle Dr CV2 50 B2
Honiley Ct CV2 50 D1
Honiley Rd
Honiley CV8 91 B6
Meer End CV8 74 A1
Honiley Way CV2 50 D1
Honington Cl CV35 114 F5
Honington Hall* CV36 137 A5
Honiton Rd CV2 62 C5
Honiwell Cl CV33 123 E6
Hood St CV1 61 E3
Hood's Way CV22 82 D2
Hook Norton Brewery* OX15 142 C4
Hook Norton CE Prim Sch OX15 142 D4
Hook Norton Rd
Great Rollright OX7 142 A2
Sibford Ferris OX15 142 D8
Hoo La GL55 135 A2
Hoopers La B96 102 E1
Hope Aldridge Bsns Ctr CV10 29 C6
Hope Cl CV7 49 A7
Hopedale Cl CV2 62 E3
Hope St CV1 61 B2
Hopkiln Cotts WR11 127 D3
Hopkins Field CV37 129 B3
Hopkins Prec The B49 143 C4
Hopkins Rd CV6 61 A4
Hopkins Way CV35 146 D5
Hopper's La CV35 146 D4
Hopton Cl CV5 60 A4
Hopton Crofts CV32 105 C2
Horeston Grange Sh Ctr CV11 30 A5
Horley Path Rd OX15 139 D5
Hornbeam Dr CV4 59 D1
Hornbeam Gr CV31 110 C6
Hornbeam B77 4 A4
Hornchurch Close Ind Est CV1 151 B1
Hornchurch Cl CV1 151 B1
Horndean Cl CV6 61 E8
Horne Cl CV21 101 B8
Horninghold Cl CV3 78 E8
Hornsby Cl CV36 149 E7
Hornsey Cl CV2 62 E7
Hornton Gr CV35 114 E6
Hornton Prim Sch OX15 139 B7
Horsefair CV36 149 D6
Horsefair The 8 LE10 31 D8
Horsepool LE10 32 A5
Horsepool Hollow CV31 110 C5
Horse Shoe Rd CV6 50 A4
Horsewell 1 CV47 147 B4
Horsfall Rd B75 13 A5
Horsford Rd CV3 77 E6
Horsham Cl 20 OX16 139 F5
Horton Cl
Alcester B49 143 D5
Bedworth CV7 49 F7
Horton Cres CV22 83 B2
Horton Gr B90 71 A5
Hosiery St CV12 39 C2
Hoskyn Cl CV21 100 F8
Hospital La CV12 38 B1
Hospital of St Cross CV22 83 B1
Hospital Rd GL56 140 A3
Hotchkiss Cl CV35 146 C2
Hotchkiss Way CV3 79 A7
Hothorpe Cl CV3 62 F1
Houldsworth Cres CV6 49 C4
Houndsfield Cl B47 69 C6
Houndsfield Farm B47 69 B5
Houndsfield Gr B47 69 A5
Houndsfield La B47 69 C6
Houston Rd CV21 83 C6
Houting B77 9 D5
Hove Ave CV5 59 E4
Hovelands Cl CV2 62 C8
Howard Cl
Bidford-on-A B50 148 C4
Coventry CV5 59 E4
Dunchurch CV22 99 D4
Howard Rd
Nuneaton CV10 29 A3
Redditch B98 103 C8
Howard St CV1 151 C4
Howard Wlk CV31 109 D6
Howat Rd CV7 48 F7
Howcombe La CV47 125 C7
Howcotte Gn CV4 75 E8
Howe Green La CV7,CV10 37 D4
Howells Cl CV12 38 D1
Howes Com Prim Sch CV3 77 E5
Howes Croft B35 22 A2
Howes La CV3 77 D3
Howkins Rd CV21 83 C6
Howlette Rd CV4 59 E2
Hoylake Cl CV11 30 B1
Hoylake B77 4 B4
Huckson Rd CV47 124 B4
Huddesford Dr CV7 74 C8
Huddisdon Cl 5 CV34 104 F1
Hudson Ave B46 33 F6
Hudson Rd CV22 82 E1
Huggins Cl CV7 74 C7
Hughes Cl
Harvington WR11 127 D4
Warwick CV34 104 D2
Whitnash CV31 110 A2
Hughes Hill CV35 114 B6
Hughes La WR11 127 D4
Hughes The CV34 108 E6
Hugh Rd CV3 62 A2
Hulme Cl CV3 63 B1
Humber Ave
Coventry CV1 61 F1
Sutton Coldfield B76 22 A7
Humber Cl NN11 117 F2
Humber Gr B36 22 F1
Humber Rd CV3 78 A8
Humberstone Rd 4 CV6 61 A5
Humber Wlk 8 OX16 139 F4
Humphrey Burton's Rd CV3 77 C8
Humphrey-Davy Rd CV12 49 D8
Humphris St CV34 109 B8
Hungerfield Rd B36 22 C1
Hunningham Gr 6 B91 71 B8
Hunscote La CV35 121 F1
Hunt Cl CV35 114 F3
Hunt End Ind Est B97 102 C5
Hunt End La B97 102 C5
Hunter Bvd LE17 55 C7
Hunters Cl CV3 63 A2
Hunters La CV13 20 A6
Hunters Lane Ind Est CV21 83 A5
Hunters La CV21 83 A5
Hunters Moon CV23 117 B2
Hunters Pk CV9 11 C1
Hunter St CV21 83 C4
Hunters Wlk CV9 19 B7
Hunter Terr CV5 76 D8
Hunt Hall La CV37 129 A6
Huntingdon Rd CV5 77 A8
Huntingdon Way CV10 28 E3
Huntington Ct CV35 146 E3
Hunt La CV9 19 B7
Hunt Paddocks CV8 92 E1
Hunts Rd CV37 145 C1
Hunt Terr CV4 76 B7
Hurdlers La CV37 121 B6
Hurlbutt Rd CV34 109 C4
Hurley Cl CV32 106 A2
Hurley Comm CV9 16 C6
Hurley La B46 25 D6
Hurley Prim Sch CV9 16 D4
Hurn Way CV6 50 B4
Hurricane Way B35 22 A2
Hurst Green Rd
Bentley Heath B93 71 F4
Minworth B76 22 D6
Hurst Rd
Bedworth CV12 39 B3
Coventry CV6 50 A4
Hinckley LE10 31 D8
Southam CV47 147 A3
Hurst The B47 69 A6
Hurst Wlk CV6 50 A4
Husbandmans Cl CV36 149 D6
Hutchings La B90 70 B5
Hyacinth Way LE10 31 D5
Hyde Pl CV32 109 E8
Hyde Rd
Coventry CV2 62 E4
Kenilworth CV8 93 A5
Hydes La LE10 30 E4
Hypericum Gdns CV2 62 C4

I

Ibex Cl CV3 62 F1
Ibstock Rd CV6 50 A5
Icknield Cl B50 148 E4
Icknield Ct B50 148 E4
Icknield Row B49 143 B4
Icknield St
Bidford-on-A B50 148 E4
Carpenter's Hill B48,B98 85 C2
Portway B48 85 B6
Icknield Street Dr B98 103 D7
Iden Rd CV1 61 E4
Idlicote Rd CV36 137 B8
Ilam Pk CV8 93 C5
Ilex Ct CV34 109 A7
Ilford Cl CV12 39 A3
Ilford Ct CV3 79 D7
Ilford Dr CV3 77 B5
Ilfracombe Gr CV3 77 A5
Iliffe Ho LE10 31 B7
Illshaw Cl B98 112 A6
Illshaw Heath Rd B90,B94 70 D2
Ilmer Cl CV21 83 E7
Ilmington CE Prim Sch CV36 136 A6
Ilmington Cl
Coventry CV3 77 B5
Hatton CV35 114 E6
Ilmington Rd
Blackwell CV36 136 E6
Ilmington CV36,CV37 136 D7
Ilminster Cl LE10 32 B7
Imogen Gdns CV34 109 E3
Imperial Rise B46 23 E2
Inca Cl CV3 78 F8
Inchbrook Rd CV8 93 C7
Inchcape Cl CV22 99 B8
Inchford Ave CV34 104 E2
Inchford Cl CV11 29 F1
Infantry Pl B75 13 A6
Ingle Ct CV31 109 E7
Ingleton Cl CV11 30 A2
Inglewood Cl CV32 106 A3
Ingon La CV37 121 B5
Ingram Cl CV36 140 E5
Ingram Pit La B77 4 A5
Ingram Rd CV5 76 D8
Innage Cl CV31 110 B8
Innage Park Small Ind Units CV9 12 C1
Innage Terr CV9 18 D8
Innage The B47 69 A5
Innis Rd CV5 76 E8
Innsworth Dr B35 22 A4
Instone Rd CV6 49 A1
Inveraray Cl CV8 93 C4
Inverlea Ct GL55 135 B6
Inverness Cl CV5 60 A4
Invicta Rd CV3 78 F8
Io Ctr The B98 103 C8
Ipswich Wlk B37 33 B2
Irelands La B94,B95 113 D7
Ireton Cl CV4 59 C1
Iris Cl LE10 31 E5
Ironbridge Way CV6 50 B6
Iron Cross NN11 126 A1
Ironmonger Row CV1 151 B3
Ironstone Hollow OX15 142 E4
Irving Rd CV1 61 E2
Isambard Dr CV6 49 F5
Isis Gr B36 33 A8
Islington Cres CV9 10 C1
Ivanhoe Ave CV11 29 E1
Ivor Rd
Atherstone CV9 18 F7
Coventry CV6 49 F2
Ivybridge Rd CV3 77 D6
Ivy Cl CV13 21 D7
Ivycroft Rd B79 5 E4
Ivy Farm La CV4 76 D6
Ivy Gr CV10 28 D6
Ivy Grounds CV36 141 A8
Ivyhouse Wlk 6 B77 9 F6
Ivy La
Ettington CV37 131 A3
Harbury CV33 123 F6
Mollington OX17 134 A2
Shutford OX15 139 A3
Ivy Lodge Cl B37 44 A7
Ivy Way B90 70 A6
Izod's Cl GL55 135 A1

J

Jack Cade Way CV34 109 E4
Jackdaw Dr B36 33 A8
Jacker's Rd CV2 50 B4
Jacklin Dr CV3 77 C4
Jacknell Rd LE10 30 D8
Jack O'Watton Bsns Pk B46 23 D3
Jackson Cl
Hampton Magna CV35 114 F3
Keresley CV7 49 A7
Jackson Gr CV8 93 C4
Jackson La CV47 125 C7
Jackson Rd
Coventry CV6 49 D1
Rugby CV21 84 A1
Jacksons Mdw B50 148 C6
Jacksons Orch CV37 129 B3
Jackson Wlk B35 22 A2
Jack Thomson Croft WR11 127 F6
Jackwood Gn CV12 49 C8
Jacob Dr CV4 76 D6
Jacobean La B93 56 B1
Jacox Cres CV8 93 C5
Jacquard Cl CV3 77 D4
Jacquard Ho 3 CV1 61 E4
Jade Cl CV1 151 D4
Jago La CV37 121 C7
Jamescroft CV3 78 E6
James Ct
4 Rugby CV21 83 B3
Warwick CV34 108 F7
James Dawson Dr CV5 59 B8
James Diskin Ct CV11 29 E2
James Galloway Cl CV3 78 E7
James Green Rd CV4 59 F2
James Ho CV2 62 C8
James Moore Ho 11 CV47 147 B4
Jameson Ct 27 GL56 140 A3
James Rd B46 33 F8

James St
New Arley CV7 37 A8
Nuneaton CV11 29 A5
Rugby CV21 83 B3
James Watt Cl NN11 117 F2
James Wlk 6 CV21 83 B3
Jaques Cl B46 23 B2
Jardine Cres CV4 59 F2
Jasmine Gr
Coventry CV3 78 C8
Royal Leamington Spa CV32 106 A2
Jasmine Rd B77 4 A4
Javelin Ave B35 22 B2
Jays Cl B98 112 A6
Jean St CV9 11 C1
Jedburgh Gr CV3 77 A4
Jeffrey Cl CV12 49 D8
Jeffrey Woods Cross CV1 61 F4
Jeff's Cl OX15 137 F2
Jeffs Cl CV35 138 B6
Jeliff St CV4 59 F2
Jenkins Ave CV5 59 F4
Jenkins Rd CV21 84 A1
Jenner St CV1 151 C4
Jenton Rd CV31 110 B6
Jephcott Cl B49 143 A4
Jephcott Ho 2 CV1 61 E3
Jephson Ct CV2 50 C4
Jephson Pl 3 CV31 110 B7
Jephsons The CV47 115 C5
Jerome Ct CV21 83 C3
Jersey Croft B36 33 B6
Jersey Dr 6 OX16 139 F5
Jervis Rd B77 9 F5
Jesmond Rd CV1 61 F4
Jesson Rd B75 13 A5
Jetty The OX17 134 F1
Jill La B96 103 B2
Jim Forrest Cl 4 CV3 78 F8
Joanna Dr CV3 77 C3
Joan of Arc Ho CV3 77 E6
Joan's Cl CV31 110 C6
Joan Ward St CV3 77 D8
Job's La CV4 60 A2
Jodrell St CV11 29 B6
Joe OBrien Cl CV3 78 C6
Joe Williams Cl 7 CV3 78 F8
John Black Day Hospl B37 44 C8
Johndory B77 9 D6
John Grace St CV3 77 D8
John Gulson Prim Sch CV1 61 D5
John Haynes Ct CV7 50 A7
John Knight Rd CV12 39 B5
John McGuire Cres CV3 78 E7
John Nash Sq CV8 92 F3
John Nichols St LE10 31 B7
John of Gaunt Ho CV3 77 E6
John O'Gaunt Rd CV8 92 E3
John Rous Ave CV4 76 B7
John's Cl LE10 31 D5
Johns Cl B80 103 C4
John Shelton Com Prim Sch CV6 49 D4
John Shelton Dr CV6 49 D4
John Simpson Cl CV8 80 A3
John Sinclair Ho CV1 151 B4
Johnson Ave CV22 82 E2
Johnson Pl B95 113 B5
Johnson Rd
Bedworth CV12 39 C3
Coventry CV6 62 A8
Johnson St CV9 10 C1
John St
11 Stratford-u-A CV37 145 A3
Bedworth CV12 39 A2
Nuneaton CV11 29 C2
Nuneaton,Stockingford CV10 28 E3
Royal Leamington Spa CV32 109 F8
John Taylor Way CV35 122 E3
John Thwaites Cl CV22 83 A2
John Tofts Ho CV1 151 B4
Jolyffe Ct CV37 144 F4
Jolyffe Park Rd CV37 145 A4
Jonathan Rd CV2 62 F8
Jon Baker Ct LE10 31 E8
Jones Rd CV37 39 A1
Jones Wood Cl B76 22 A7
Jonkel Ave B77 10 A5
Jordan Cl CV8 93 B2
Jordans Cl B97 102 D6
Jordans The CV5 60 C4
Jordan Well CV1 151 C2
Joseph Cash Prim Sch CV6 61 C7
Joseph Creighton Cl CV3 78 E7
Joseph Halpin Ho 3 CV1 151 C4
Joseph Latham Ho 3 CV2 50 B1
Joseph Luckman Rd CV12 39 B4
Joseph Way CV37 144 E5
Jourdain Pk CV34 109 E3
Joyce Pool CV34 108 E7
Joyce Way CV22 99 A8
Jubilee Ave
Lower Shuckburgh NN11 116 E1
Redditch B97 102 D7
Jubilee Cl
Bidford-on-A B50 148 E5
Chipping Campden GL55 135 A2
Jubilee Cres CV6 61 B7
Jubilee Ct
Alcester B49 143 C4
Jubilee Ct continued
Kingsbury B78 15 D5
Jubilee St CV21 82 E4
Jubilee Terr CV12 39 B4
Judd Cl CV12 38 F3
Judds La CV6 49 E4
Judge Cl CV23 82 A5
Judith Way CV22 99 A8
Juggins La B94 86 B7
Julian Cl CV2 62 F8
Juliet Cl CV11 30 A1
Juliet Dr
Royal Leamington Spa CV34 109 F3
Rugby CV22 99 D6
Julius Dr B46 23 F1
Junction One Ret Pk CV21 83 B6
Junction St CV1 151 A2
Junewood Cl CV21 83 D7
Juniper Cl CV12 38 E2
Juniper Dr
Coventry CV5 59 F5
Sutton Coldfield B76 22 A7
Juniper B77 4 A4
Juno Dr CV31 109 F5
Jury St CV34 108 E6
Justice Cl CV31 110 A4
Justins Ave CV37 144 F5

K

Kalfs Dr CV22 99 B8
Kanzan Rd CV2 50 B4
Kareen Gr CV3 79 C7
Karen Cl CV10 28 E7
Karlingford Cl CV5 76 D8
Kathleen Ave CV12 38 E1
Katrine Cl CV10 28 C5
Kay Cl CV21 83 C7
Kaysbrook Dr CV23 97 A6
Keats Cl CV10 28 A4
Keats Ho B97 102 C8
Keats Rd
Coventry CV2 62 D2
Stratford-u-A CV37 145 B1
Keble Ho B37 33 A2
Keble Rd GL56 140 A2
Kebull Gn CV4 75 E8
Keele Ho B37 33 B4
Keeling Rd CV8 93 B5
Keenan Dr CV12 38 D1
Keepers Cl B46 34 A4
Keepers Wlk CV12 38 D1
Keetley Cl CV36 149 D4
Kegworth Cl CV6 50 A4
Keir Cl CV32 106 A2
Keith Rd CV32 106 B4
Kele Rd CV4 76 A7
Kelmscote Rd CV6 60 F8
Kelsey Cl CV11 29 E3
Kelsey La CV7 74 D5
Kelsey's Cl CV8 79 F3
Kelsull Croft B37 33 A2
Kelvin Ave CV2 62 D5
Kelvin Rd CV32 106 C5
Kelway CV3 63 A2
Kemble Dr B35 22 A3
Kemerton Way B90 70 F6
Kemp Cl CV34 109 A7
Kempley Ave CV2 62 C2
Kempsey Cl B98 103 B7
Kempsford Cl B98 102 F6
Kemps Green Rd
Balsall Common CV7 74 B6
Kemps Green B94 88 A1
Kempton Cl CV37 129 F8
Kempton Cres CV32 106 C4
Kempton Dr B77 9 D4
Kem St CV11 29 E2
Kendal Ave
Coleshill B46 33 F7
Royal Leamington Spa CV32 105 C2
Kendal Cl
Nuneaton CV11 30 A6
Redditch B98 112 A6
Kendall Ave CV37 145 A3
Kendal Rise CV5 60 C4
Kenderdine Montessori Sch CV5 77 A8
Kendon Ave CV6 60 E6
Kendrick Cl CV6 50 A4
Kenelm Ct CV3 78 C5
Kenhill Rd OX15 138 F5
Kenilcourt CV8 92 D6
Kenilworth Castle* CV8 92 D5
Kenilworth Cl
Balsall Common CV7 74 A6
Redditch B97 102 D6
Kenilworth Ct CV3 77 C8
Kenilworth Dr CV11 29 B3
Kenilworth Hall Mews CV8 92 F5
Kenilworth Rd
Balsall Common CV7,CV8 74 D4
Blackdown CV32 105 E5
Bradnock's Marsh B92 57 E5
Coventry CV4 76 E3
Kenilworth CV8 93 C8
Knowle B93 72 E5
Lighthorne Heath CV33 123 D2
Meriden CV7 45 D1
Royal Leamington Spa CV32 106 C6
Kenilworth Sch Castle Hall Sixth Form CV8 92 F2
Kenilworth Sch CV8 93 C5
Kenilworth St 20 CV32 105 F1
Kenilworth Way 8 OX16 139 F3
Kennan Ave CV31 109 F6
Kennedy Dr CV22 82 C2
Kennedy Sq 3 CV32 106 A1
Kennel La CV9 19 B7
Kennet Cl CV2 62 C8
Kenneth Vincent Cl B97 102 E4
Kenning Cl CV47 115 C4
Kenpas Highway CV3 77 A5
Kenrick Croft B35 22 A2
Kensington Ct
Coventry CV5 61 A1
Nuneaton CV10 28 C6
Kensington Rd CV5 61 A1
Kent Cl CV3 77 E6
Kenthurst Cl CV5 59 C4
Kentmere Cl CV2 50 E2
Kent Rd CV47 132 F5
Kents La CV37 131 A4
Kent The CV21 84 A2
Kenway B47 69 A7
Kenwyn Gn CV7 50 B8
Keppel Cl CV22 82 C1
Keppel St CV1 61 E5
Keresley Brook Rd CV6 49 A2
Keresley Cl CV6 49 A2
Keresley Grange Prim Sch CV6 48 F1
Keresley Green Rd CV6 48 F1
Keresley Newland Prim Sch CV7 48 F7
Keresley Rd CV6 61 A8
Kerns Terr 22 CV37 145 A3
Kerria Ctr B77 4 A4
Kerria Rd B77 4 B4
Kerris Way CV3 63 A1
Kerr La B90 70 A6
Kerr Way GL56 140 C3
Kerry Croft B97 102 E5
Kerry's Ho 4 CV1 61 B2
Kerswell Dr B90 71 A5
Kestrel Cl
Birmingham,Castle Vale B35 22 B3
Hinckley LE10 31 F6
Stratford-u-A CV37 145 A5
Kestrel Croft 2 CV3 78 F8
Kestrel B77 10 A6
Keswick Cl CV11 30 A6
Keswick Dr CV21 83 C8
Keswick Gn CV32 105 D1
Keswick Wlk CV2 62 F4
Kettlebrook Rd B90 71 C6
Kettlewell Cl CV34 104 E1
Keviliok St CV3 77 D6
Kew Cl CV8 93 C5
Kew Ho CV4 59 F3
Kew Rd CV21 83 B4
Keyes Dr CV22 82 C2
Keys Hill CV9 11 C1
Keys La CV47 125 F4
Keyte Rd CV36 136 B6
Keytes Acre GL55 135 E3
Keytes La CV35 122 B7
Kiblers La CV35 131 D2
Kielder Dr CV10 28 E2
Kiftsgate Court Gdns* GL55 135 C6
Kilburn Dr CV5 60 F3
Kilby Ct CV31 110 A6
Kilbye Cl B77 9 F5
Kilby Gn LE10 31 F6
Kilby Gr CV31 110 C5
Kildale Cl CV1 151 D3
Kilderkin Ct CV1 151 C1
Kildwick Way 5 CV34 104 E1
Kiln Cl
Nuneaton CV10 28 E3
Royal Leamington Spa CV32 106 A1
Studley B80 103 C4
Kiln La B90 70 A5
Kilnsey Gr CV34 104 E1
Kiln Way B78 4 F1
Kilsby Gr B91 71 C8
Kilsby La CV21 101 C7
Kilsby Rd CV23 101 C1
Kilworth Ho 8 CV32 105 F1
Kilworth Rd CV21 101 B7
Kimberley Cl CV5 59 F4
Kimberley Rd
Baginton CV8 77 F2
Bedworth CV12 39 C4
Rugby CV21 83 B4
Kimberley B77 9 F7
Kimberley Wlk B76 22 D6
Kimble Cl
Coventry CV5 60 B4
Knightcote CV47 124 B1
Kimmond Ct 21 CV32 105 F1
Kinchford Cl B91 71 B8
Kineton CE Prim Sch CV35 132 B6
Kineton High Sch CV35 132 C6
Kineton La B90,B94 71 A1
Kineton Rd
Coventry CV2 62 C6
Kenilworth CV8 93 C4
Southam CV47 147 A3
Wellesbourne CV35 146 E2
Kineton Road Ind Est CV47 147 A3
King Charles Ct CV37 129 E2
Kingcomb La GL55 135 A2
King Edward Rd
Coventry CV1 61 F4
King Edward Rd continued
Nuneaton CV11 29 D4
Rugby CV21 83 B4
King Edward's Ct CV35 114 F5
King Edwards Terr CV36 141 F5
King Edward VI Coll CV11 29 D4
King Edward VI Sch CV37 145 A2
Kingfield Ind Est CV1 61 C6
Kingfield Rd CV1,CV6 61 D7
Kingfisher Ave CV10 28 C5
Kingfisher Ct LE10 30 F6
Kingfisher Dr B36 33 A8
Kingfisher Prim Sch B36 33 A8
Kingfisher B77 10 A6
Kingfisher Way B49 143 B5
King George's Ave
Bedworth CV12 39 B5
Coventry CV6 49 F2
King George's Ct CV23 82 A5
King George's Way LE10 31 B7
Kingham Cl B98 112 A6
Kingham Hill Sch OX7 150 D1
King Henry VIII Sch CV3 151 A1
King John's La CV35 132 E2
King John's Rd CV35 132 B6
Kingland Dr CV32 105 C1
Kingley Ave B49 143 C5
King Richard St CV2 61 F3
Kings Ave CV9 18 E8
Kingsbridge Rd CV10 29 D6
Kingsbrook Dr B91 71 B8
Kingsbury Bsns Pk B76 22 E6
Kingsbury Cl B76 22 D5
Kingsbury Inf Sch B78 15 C6
Kingsbury Jun Sch B78 15 D6
Kingsbury Rd
Birmingham B35,B76 22 B5
Coventry CV6 60 E5
Curdworth B76 23 B6
Marston B76 23 B4
Minworth B76 22 D5
Kingsbury Sch B78 15 D6
Kingsbury Water Park Visitor Ctr* B76 15 B5
Kingsbury Water Pk* B76 15 B5
Kingscote Gr CV3 77 A4
Kingscote Rd B93 71 E2
Kings Coughton La B49 143 A6
King's Ct CV11 29 B4
Kingsford Cl B36 22 D1
Kingsford Rd CV6 61 C7
Kingsgate Ho B37 33 A2
Kings Gdns CV12 39 C2
Kings Gr CV2 62 B3
King's High Sch for Girls The CV34 108 E7
King's Hill La CV3 77 B2
Kingsholm Cl CV3 63 B1
Kingshurst Inf Sch B37 33 A6
Kingshurst Jun Sch B37 33 A6
Kingshurst CV31 110 E6
King's La B50 148 B6
Kingsland Ave CV5 60 F2
Kingsland Dr B93 71 E4
King's La
Newton Regis B79 2 D5
Norton WR11 127 B2
Snitterfield CV37 121 B6
Stratford-u-A CV37 144 F8
Kingsleigh Dr B36 22 B1
Kingsley Ave CV21 83 F1
Kingsley Coll B98 103 C6
Kingsley Cres CV12 40 B3
Kingsley Ct
18 Bishops Tachbrook CV33 122 F8
Binley Woods CV3 79 D6
Kingsley Orch CV21 83 E1
Kingsley Prep Sch B93 72 A4
Kingsley Rd 11 CV33 122 F8
Kingsley Sch The CV32 105 F1
Kingsley Terr CV2 62 E8
Kingsley Wlk CV2 62 F7
Kings Mdw CV10 28 A3
Kingsmead Mews CV3 78 D6
Kings Newnham La CV23 80 E7
Kings Newnham Rd CV23 81 B6
Kings Park Dr CV3 63 B1
King St CV12 39 C2
Kingston Ho CV12 49 C8
Kingston Mews CV31 110 C6
Kingston Rd CV5 60 F2
King St
Royal Leamington Spa CV32 106 A1
Rugby CV21 83 A4
Kingsway Com Prim Sch CV31 109 F6
Kingsway CV2 62 A3
Kingsway Ho CV12 39 C2
Kingsway
Kingsbury B78 15 C6
Lighthorne Heath CV33 123 D2
Nuneaton CV11 29 B4
Royal Leamington Spa CV31 109 F6
Rugby CV22 83 A1
Kingswood Ave CV7 48 B8
Kingswood Cl
Coventry CV6 49 D1
Kingswood B94 89 E5
Kingswood Cotts B94 89 D3
Kingswood Gdns CV10 28 B4
Kingswood Rd CV10 28 B4
Kington La CV35 113 E3
Kington Rise CV35 113 E2
King William St CV1 61 E4
Kinman Way CV21 83 C6
Kinross Cl CV10 28 F2
Kinross Rd CV32 106 B4
Kinross Way LE10 21 F1
Kinsall Gn B77 10 C6
Kinsham Dr B91 71 B8
Kintyre The CV2 63 B7
Kinver Cl CV2 50 E1
Kinver Croft B76 22 A8
Kinwalsey La CV7 46 F6
Kinwarton Dovecote* B49 143 F6
Kinwarton Farm Rd B49 143 D5
Kinwarton Rd B49 143 C4
Kinwarton Workshops B49 143 C6
Kipling Ave CV34 108 C4
Kipling Cl CV10 28 A5
Kipling Rd
Coventry CV6 61 A8
Stratford-u-A CV37 130 A8
Kirby Ave CV34 104 F1
Kirby Cl
Brandon CV8 79 F5
Coventry CV1 61 D6
Kirby Cnr CV4 76 B5
Kirby Corner Rd CV4 76 B6
Kirby La CV7 52 F5
Kirby Rd CV5 60 F2
Kirigushi Rd CV35 132 E5
Kirkby Cl CV21 83 E6
Kirkby Rd CV21 83 F1
Kirkdale Ave CV6 49 D3
Kirkland Way B78 8 B8
Kirkstone Rd CV12 39 A2
Kirkstone CV21 83 D7
Kirkstone Wlk CV11 30 A6
Kirkwall CV47 147 B4
Kirtland Cl CV9 3 B1
Kirton Cl
Coventry CV6 48 F1
Whitnash CV31 110 B3
Kissing Tree La CV37 121 D3
Kitchener Rd
Coventry CV6 61 E8
Long Marston CV37 129 C2
Kitebrook Cl B90 71 A7
Kites Cl CV34 104 E2
Kites Nest La CV35 114 E8
Kittermaster Rd CV7 46 C1
Kitwood Ave B78 10 F6
Kixley La B93 72 C6
Klevedon Cl CV11 30 A1
Knebley Cres CV10 29 C1
Knibbs The CV34 108 E7
Knight Ave CV1 61 E1
Knightcote Dr
Royal Leamington Spa CV32 109 E8
Solihull B91 71 B8
Knight Ct B75 13 C5
Knightley Cl CV32 106 E5
Knightlow Ave CV3 78 C6
Knightlow CE Prim Sch CV23 96 F7
Knightlow Cl CV8 93 C3
Knightlow Way CV35 123 F6
Knightsbridge Ave CV12 39 C4
Knights Cl LE10 31 D4
Knights Ct
1 Stratford-u-A CV37 144 F2
Birmingham B37 44 E8
Hinckley LE10 30 E8
Warwick CV34 108 D6
Knights La CV37 145 E3
Knights Templar Way CV4 60 A1
Knob Hill CV23 96 F6
Knoll Croft
Cheswick Green B90 70 D4
Coventry CV3 77 C6
Knoll Dr
Coventry CV3 77 C6
Warwick CV34 104 E1
Knottesford Cl B80 103 C3
Knotting Way CV3 62 C1
Knowlands Rd B90 71 A7
Knowle CE Prim Sch B93 72 C6
Knowle Hill
Hurley CV9 16 C4
Kenilworth CV8 93 C6
Knowle Rd B92 56 E2
Knowles Ave CV10 28 C4
Knowle Wood Rd B93 72 B3
Knox Cres CV11 29 F8
Kranji Rd CV47 132 F5
Kurtus B77 9 D6
Kwikform Bldg CV6 49 E4
Kyetts Cnr OX17 134 C1
Kynner Way CV3 79 B8
Kyter La B36 22 B1

L

Laburnum Ave
Coventry CV6 60 F5
Kenilworth CV8 93 A4
Laburnum Cl
Bedworth CV12 38 E2
Hollywood B47 69 A5
Kingsbury B78 15 D6
Laburnum Dr
Sutton Coldfield B76 13 A3
Whitnash CV31 110 B3

Laburnum Gr
Nuneaton CV10 28 D6
Rugby CV22 99 E8
Warwick CV34 105 B1
Lacell Cl CV34 104 E1
Ladbroke By-Pass CV47 124 D5
Ladbroke Hall CV47 124 D5
Ladbroke Pk CV34 104 E1
Ladbroke Rd CV47 124 B4
Ladbrook Cl B98 102 E7
Ladbrook Rd CV5 60 A4
Lady Byron La
Knowle B93 56 A1
Knowle B93 71 F8
Ladycroft CV32 106 E5
Ladyfields Way CV6 49 B4
Lady Grey Ave CV34 109 E3
Ladygrove Cl B98 103 A8
Lady Katherine Leveson CE Sch B93 73 B5
Lady La
Coventry CV6 49 F4
Earlswood B90,B94 70 B3
Kenilworth CV8 92 F4
Lady Lane Mobile Home Pk CV6 49 F4
Ladymead Dr CV6 49 B2
Ladysmock CV23 83 D8
Lady Warwick Ave CV12 39 D2
Laertes Gr CV34 109 F2
Laggan Cl CV10 28 C5
Lairhillock Pk CV23 115 D7
Lair The B78 10 F8
Lakeland Dr B77 10 B7
Lakeland Ho CV34 109 A7
Lakeside CV12 39 A2
Lakeside Dr B90 70 F7
Lakeside B95 113 B2
Lakes The B94 86 F8
Lake View Rd CV5 60 F4
Lakin Ct CV34 108 F8
Lakin Dr CV47 124 A4
Lakin Ho CV34 108 F8
Lakin Rd CV34 108 F8
Lambert Ct
Barford CV35 122 A7
Bidford-on-A B50 148 C5
Warwick CV34 108 D6
Lambeth Cl
Birmingham B37 33 B4
Coventry CV2 62 E7
Lambourn Cres CV31 110 C6
Lambourne Cl
Bidford-on-A B50 148 D5
Coventry CV5 60 A4
Lamb St CV1 151 B3
Lamerton Cl CV2 62 C6
Lamintone Dr CV32 105 D2
Lammas Croft CV31 110 A3
Lammas Ct
Warwick CV34 108 D6
Wolston CV8 80 A3
Lammas Ho 6 CV6 61 A4
Lammas Rd CV6 60 F4
Lammas Wlk CV34 108 D7
Lamorna Cl CV11 29 F4
Lampitts Gn OX15 139 D4
Lamp La CV7 36 F6
Lamprey B77 9 D6
Lancaster Cl
Atherstone CV9 12 E1
Wellesbourne CV35 146 C2
Lancaster Dr B35 22 B2
Lancaster Pl CV8 92 E2
Lancaster Rd
Hinckley LE10 31 D8
Rugby CV21 83 A4
Lance Cl LE10 31 D5
Lanchester Dr 9 OX16 139 F4
Lanchester Rd CV6 61 B6
Lanchester Way
Birmingham B36 22 F1
Daventry NN11 117 F2
Lancia Cl CV6 50 B4
Lancing Rd CV12 40 C2
Lancut Hill CV23 67 D1
Land La B37 44 A7
Landor Ho CV31 110 A2
Landor Rd
Dorridge B93 72 A6
Redditch B98 103 A8
Warwick CV34 108 D8
Whitnash CV31 110 A3
Landrail Wlk B36 33 A8
Landseer Cl CV21 84 B1
Lane Cl OX15 139 D6
Lane Croft B76 22 A8
Laneside CV3 78 E6
Lane The
Burmington CV36 149 E1
Little Wolford CV36 141 A6
Lanfear Ct LE10 31 C7
Langbank Ave CV3 78 D7
Langbay Ct CV2 62 F6
Langcliffe Ave CV34 104 F1
Langcomb Rd B90 70 A8
Langdale Ave CV6 49 D3
Langdale Cl
Royal Leamington Spa CV32 106 D3
Rugby CV21 83 C7
Langdale Ct B77 4 A6
Langdale Dr CV11 30 A6
Langdale Rd LE10 31 A8
Langdon La CV35 132 E3
Langfield Rd B93 72 A7
Langlands The CV35 121 F4
Langley Croft CV4 60 A2
Langley Dr B35 22 A1
Langley Hall Dr B75 13 B5
Langley Hall Rd B75 13 B5
Langley Heath Dr B76 13 A3
Langley Rd
Claverdon CV35 113 E3
Whitnash CV31 110 A4
Langley Specl Sch B75 13 A6
Langley Wlk B37 33 D2
Langlodge Rd CV6 49 B2
Langnor Rd CV2 62 C6
Langton Cl
Birmingham B36 33 B6
Coventry CV3 78 E8
Langton Rd CV21,CV22 83 E1
Langwood Cl CV4 76 B7
Lankett The CV47 133 D7
Lansbury Cl CV2 62 E7
Lansdowne Cir CV32 106 A1
Lansdowne Cl CV12 39 A3
Lansdowne Cres
6 Royal Leamington Spa CV32 106 A1
Studley B80 103 D3
Tamworth B77 9 D8
Lansdowne Pl CV21 83 D2
Lansdowne Rd
2 Royal Leamington Spa CV32 106 A1
Studley B80 103 D3
Lansdowne St
Coventry CV2 61 F3
Royal Leamington Spa CV32 106 A1
Lansdown Ho B46 24 F4
Lant Cl CV7 75 B7
Lapwing Dr B92 57 B7
Lapwing B77 10 A6
Lapworth CE Prim Sch B94 89 D3
Lapworth Cl B98 102 F7
Lapworth Oaks B94 89 D3
Lapworth Rd CV2 50 C1
Lapworth Sta B94 89 D4
Lapworth St B94 89 B2
Larch Cl
Alcester B49 143 B5
Rugby CV22 82 B2
Stratford-u-A CV37 145 A4
Larch Croft B37 33 B2
Larches The
Bedworth CV7 50 B8
Kingsbury B78 15 D7
Larchfields CV8 80 A4
Larch Gr CV34 105 A1
Larch Tree Ave CV4 60 A2
Larchwood Rd CV7 39 B1
Larkfield Way CV5 60 A6
Larkin Cl CV12 40 B3
Larkin Gr CV2 62 F6
Larkspur Ct CV12 49 C8
Larkspur Gr 5 CV12 38 D2
Larkspur
Rugby CV23 83 E8
Tamworth B77 9 D4
Latham Rd CV5 61 A2
Latimer Cl CV8 92 F2
Lattimore Rd CV37 144 E5
Latymer Cl B76 22 A7
Lauderdale Ave CV6 49 D3
Lauderdale Cl CV23 82 B4
Launce Gr CV34 109 F2
Launceston Dr CV11 29 F4
Laundry Cotts CV35 90 E4
Laurel Ave B78 11 A8
Laurel Cl CV2 50 E2
Laurel Ct CV5 60 F1
Laurel Dr
Hartshill CV10 28 A7
Rugby CV22 82 B1
Stockton CV47 147 E8
Laurel Fields LE17 43 E6
Laurel Gdns CV22 99 F8
Laurels Cres CV7 74 C6
Laurels The
Bedworth CV12 38 E2
Coventry CV4 76 F6
Kingsbury B78 15 D7
Portway B47 85 F8
Lavender Ave CV6 60 F5
Lavender Cl
Bedworth CV12 38 E1
Rugby CV23 83 E8
Lavender Hall La CV7 58 C2
Lavenham Cl CV11 40 C8
Lawford Cl CV3 62 E1
Lawford Heath Ind Est CV23 98 C7
Lawford Heath La CV23 98 C6
Lawford La CV22 82 B1
Lawford Rd
Rugby CV21,CV22 82 E3
Whitnash CV31 110 B5
Lawley Cl CV4 60 A2
Lawns Bsns Ctr The LE10 31 E8
Lawnsdale Cl B46 33 F7
Lawns The
Bedworth CV12 38 C2
Hinckley LE10 31 E8
Portway B47 85 F7
Wootton Wawen B95 113 B2
Lawnswood
Hinckley LE10 31 A8
Sutton Coldfield B76 22 A8
Lawrence Dr B76 22 D6
Lawrence Gdns CV8 93 A6
Lawrence Mackie Gdns CV35 146 E4
Lawrence Mackie Ho CV35 146 E4
Lawrence Rd
Bedworth CV7 50 A8
Rugby CV21 83 D3
Lawrence Saunders Rd CV6 61 B5
Lawrence Sheriff Sch CV21 83 B3
Lawrence Sheriff St CV22 83 A2
Lawson Ave CV37 145 E4
Lawton Cl LE10 30 F8
Laxford Cl LE10 21 F1
Laxton Way 14 OX16 139 F5
Lay Gdns CV31 110 E5
Lea Cl
Alcester B49 143 C5
Stratford-u-A CV37 144 B4
Lea Cres CV21 82 D6
Leacrest Rd CV6 49 A2
Lea Croft Rd B97 102 D5
Lea Ct 11 CV37 144 F1
Leaf Ct CV3 77 D4
Leafield Cl CV2 62 F8
Leaf La CV3 77 E5
Leagh Cl CV8 93 B7
Lea Green Dr B47 69 C4
Lea Green La B47 69 C5
Lealholme Ct CV5 76 F8
Leam Cl CV11 29 F1
Leam Gn CV4 76 D5
Leamington Hastings CE Inf Sch CV23 116 B6
Leamington Hastings Rd CV23 115 F7
Leamington Rd
Coventry CV3 77 C6
Kenilworth CV8 93 B2
Long Itchington CV47 115 C4
Princethorpe CV23 96 D2
Ryton-on-D CV8 96 A8
Southam CV47 124 C8
Leamington Spa Art Gallery & Mus* CV32 109 F8
Leamington Spa Sta CV31 109 F7
Leamington Way NN11 117 F1
Leam Rd
Lighthorne Heath CV33 123 D2
Royal Leamington Spa CV31 109 D7
Leam Side Ho 9 CV34 109 D8
Leam St CV31 110 B7
Leam Terr CV31 110 B8
Leam The NN11 117 F1
Lear Gr CV34 109 E4
Leas Cl CV12 39 A3
Leasowe's Ave CV3 76 F4
Leasows The
Chipping Campden GL55 135 A1
Mickleton GL55 135 C6
Leathermill La CV10 19 D4
Leather St CV47 115 D4
Leaward Cl CV10 28 E2
Lea Wlk CV8 79 B1
Ledbrook Rd CV32 106 E5
Ledbury Rd CV31 110 C6
Ledbury Way B76 22 A8
Ledwell B90 70 A5
Lee Cl CV34 104 E2
Leeder Cl CV6 49 C2
Lee Meadowe CV34 108 B4
Leeming Cl CV4 76 C6
Lee Rd
Hollywood B47 69 A7
Royal Leamington Spa CV31 109 E6
Lees The CV33 122 E8
Lee The CV5 60 C4
Le Hanche Cl CV7 49 A7
Leicester Cres CV9 12 E1
Leicester Cswy CV1 61 D5
Leicester Ct CV12 40 C2
Leicester La
Cubbington CV32 94 E1
Royal Leamington Spa CV32 106 C6
Leicester Rd
Bedworth CV12 39 B4
Nuneaton CV11 29 D5
Rugby CV21 83 B6
Shilton CV7 51 F6
Wolvey LE10 41 E5
Leicester Row
Coventry CV1 151 B4
Long Itchington CV47 115 D4
Leicester St
Bedworth CV12 39 B3
Bulkington CV12 40 C2
Royal Leamington Spa CV32 106 A1
Leigh Ave CV3 77 C3
Leigh CE Prim Sch CV4 75 D8
Leigh Cres CV47 115 D3
Leigh Rd
Rugby CV21 82 F8
Sutton Coldfield B75 13 B5
Leigh St 4 CV1 61 E4
Leigh Terr CV33 107 F5
Leighton Cl
Coventry CV4 76 D2
Royal Leamington Spa CV32 106 C4
Leisure Wlk 7 B77 9 F6
Lennon Cl CV21 101 C7
Lennox Cl CV3 78 E6
Lenton's La CV2 50 E4
Leofric St CV6 61 A5
Leonard Parkins Ho CV12 40 D2
Leontes Mdws CV34 109 E3
Leopold Rd CV1 61 F4
Lesingham Dr CV4 59 E1
Lesley Souter Ho CV21 83 B2
Lestock Cl CV22 82 C2
Letchlade Cl CV2 62 C8
Level The OX15 138 F5
Leven Cl LE10 31 B8
Leven Croft B76 22 A7
Leven Way CV2 63 A8
Lever Rd CV21 84 A1
Leveson Cres CV7 74 B6
Levett Rd B77 4 B5
Levy Cl CV21 82 F3
Lewis Ct CV9 18 F6
Lewis Rd
Coventry CV1 61 D5
Radford Semele CV31 110 F5
Lexington Ct CV11 29 B5
Leyburn Cl
3 Warwick CV34 104 F1
Coventry CV6 49 E2
Nuneaton CV11 30 A2
Leycester Cl CV33 123 E7
Leycester Ct 13 CV34 108 E6
Leycester Pl 12 CV34 108 E6
Leycester Rd CV8 93 A2
Leyes La CV8 93 C5
Leyfields Cres CV34 108 D4
Leyland Rd
Bulkington CV12 40 B2
Coventry CV5 60 D4
Nuneaton CV11 29 E1
Leylands Way CV34 108 B4
Leymere Cl CV7 46 C1
Leysbourne GL55 135 B2
Leys Cl
Northend CV47 133 B7
Wroxton OX15 139 D4
Leysfield WR11 127 C4
Leyside CV3 78 E5
Leys La CV7 46 C1
Leysmill Cl LE10 21 F1
Leys Rd
Church Lench WR11 127 B5
Rugby CV21 101 C7
Leys The
Bidford-on-A B50 148 E5
Halford CV36 137 A8
Hinckley LE10 32 A6
Newton CV23 68 A1
Upper Boddington NN11 134 E8
Whatcote CV36 137 E7
Ley's The OX15 139 D4
Libbards Gate 4 B91 71 C8
Libbards Way B91 71 B8
Liberty Rd B77 9 F5
Liberty Way CV11 29 F3
Library Cl LE10 32 A5
Library Rd CV4 76 B5
Lichen Gn CV4 76 D5
Lichfield Cl
New Arley CV7 37 A8
Nuneaton CV11 30 A7
Lichfield Cotts B78 15 D5
Lichfield Rd
Coventry CV3 77 D8
Water Orton B46,B76 23 D4
Wishaw B76,B78 14 B3
Lichfield St B78 9 A8
Lifford Way CV3 79 A7
Light Hall Sch B90 70 B8
Lighthorne Heath Prim Sch CV33 123 C2
Lighthorne Rd CV35 132 B6
Light La CV1 151 B4
Lightoak Cl B97 102 C6
Lightwood Cl B93 72 B8
Lilac Ave CV6 60 F5
Lilac Cl LE10 31 E6
Lilac Dr CV22 82 B2
Lilac Gr CV34 105 A1
Lilac Rd CV12 39 D5
Lilacvale Way CV4 76 D5
Lilbourne Rd CV23 84 C5
Lilleburne Dr CV10 28 B7
Lilley Cl CV6 49 C2
Lilley Green Rd B48 85 D5
Lillington Ave CV32 105 F2
Lillington Cl
Royal Leamington Spa CV32 106 A3
Sutton Coldfield B75 13 A4
Lillington Prim Sch CV32 106 B3
Lillington Rd
Coventry CV2 50 D1
Royal Leamington Spa CV32 106 A3
Solihull B90 70 B8
Limbrick Ave CV4 60 A1
Limbrick Wood Prim Sch CV4 59 F3
Lime Ave CV32 106 A4
Lime Cl B47 69 A5
Lime Gr
Birmingham,Chemsley Wood B37 33 B1
Coventry CV4 60 B2
Hurley CV9 16 B4
Kenilworth CV8 93 A4
Nuneaton CV10 28 E5
Limekiln La B94 70 D1
Lime Kilns B78 11 A8
Lime Rd CV47 147 B5
Limes Ave CV37 144 D1
Limes Coppice CV10 27 E7
Limes The
Bedworth CV12 38 E2
Coventry CV6 60 E5
Tiddington CV37 145 E4
Limestone Hall La CV23 81 A4
Lime Tree Ave
Coventry CV4 60 A2
Rugby CV22 99 B7
Lime Tree Dr CV35 122 E2
Linaker Rd CV3 78 C5
Lincoln Ave CV10 28 B7
Lincoln Cl
Warwick CV34 104 E1
Wellesbourne CV35 146 C1
Lincoln Ct CV32 110 A8
Lincoln Gr B37 33 A1
Lincoln St CV1 151 C4
Lincroft Cres CV5 60 E4
Lindale CV21 83 D8
Linden Ave CV35 146 E3
Linden Cl CV34 104 E2
Linden Lea CV12 39 B3
Lindera B77 4 A4
Lindfield The CV3 78 C8
Lindhurst Dr B94 88 C6
Lindisfarne Dr CV8 93 C4
Lindley Rd
Bedworth CV12 38 D2
Coventry CV3 62 B2
Lindop Cl CV32 106 D5
Lindridge Cl B98 112 A6
Lindridge Dr B76 22 D6
Lindridge Rd B75,B76 13 B6
Lindsay Wlk CV47 132 F7
Lindsey Cres CV8 93 A1
Lineholt Cl B98 103 A6
Linen St CV34 108 D6
Linford Wlk CV2 50 F1
Lingard Rd B75 13 A5
Lingfield Cres CV37 129 F8
Lingfield Ct CV6 50 B4
Lingwood Dr CV10 28 F3
Links Rd CV6 61 B8
Linkway CV31 109 E6
Linley Rd CV47 147 B5
Linnell Rd CV21 83 F2
Linnet Cl
Coventry CV3 78 D5
Rugby CV23 67 C1
Linstock Way CV6 50 B4
Linthouse Wlk 3 B77 9 F6
Lintly B77 4 B1
Linwood Dr CV2 50 F1
Lion Fields Ave CV5 60 B6
Liskeard Cl CV11 30 A5
Liskeard Rd CV35 132 D3
Lisle Ct 4 CV31 110 A6
Lisle Gdns 4 CV33 122 F8
Lismore Croft CV2 63 B7
Lister Rd CV9 12 E1
Lister St CV11 29 D3
Little Acre B97 102 D6
Little Back La NN11 126 B5
Little Brum CV9 11 C2
Little Church St
1 Coventry CV1 151 C4
Rugby CV21,CV22 83 A3
Little Cryfield CV4 76 C2
Little Duke St CV11 29 B4
Little Elborow St CV21 83 A3
Little Farm CV3 78 D5
Little Field CV2 62 A5
Little Forge Rd B98 103 C8
Little Gr CV22 83 C1
Little Heath Ind Est CV6 50 A2
Little Heath Prim Sch CV6 49 F1
Little La OX15 139 D6
Little Lawford La
Little Lawford CV23 81 F7
Rugby CV23 82 B7
Little London La CV23 68 A1
Little Mdw CV37 128 E1
Littlemead Rd B90 69 E8
Little Park St CV1 151 C2
Little Pennington St CV21 82 F3
Little Pittern CV35 132 B6
Little Pk CV47 147 B4
Littleshaw Croft B47 69 C4
Littleshaw La B47 69 C4
Little South St CV1 61 E3
Littlethorpe CV3 78 D6
Littleton Cl
Kenilworth CV8 93 A7
Sutton Coldfield B76 13 A2
Littleton Croft 6 B91 71 C8
Littletons CE Fst Sch The WR11 127 F1
Little Warton Rd B79 5 F3
Littlewood Cl 2 B91 71 B8
Littlewood Gn B80 103 D3
Little Woods B97 102 E6
Littleworth GL55 135 A2
Littleworth Croft CV31 110 C5
Littleworth B95 113 B4
Litton B77 4 C1
Liveridge Cl B93 71 F6
Liveridge Hill B95 113 B7
Livery St CV32 109 F8
Livia Cl LE10 21 F1
Livingstone Ave CV23 81 F4
Livingstone Rd CV6 61 E7
Liza Ct CV21 83 C8
Llewellyn Rd CV31 110 A6
Lloyd Cl
Hampton Magna CV35 114 F3

Lloyd Cl *continued*
Norton WR11 127 C2
Nuneaton CV11 29 D2
Lloyd Cres CV2 62 E3
Lloyd Rd CV21 83 C6
Lloyds Way CV37 144 D5
Loach Dr CV2 50 B4
Lobelia Cl LE10 31 E5
Lochmore Cl LE10 31 A8
Lochmore Dr LE10 31 A8
Lochmore Way LE10 31 A8
Lochsong Cl B77 9 D4
Loch St CV3 62 C1
Lock Cl CV37 145 A3
Locke Cl CV6 49 A1
Lockhart Cl CV8 93 A4
Lockheed Cl [8] CV31 109 F5
Lockhurst La CV6 61 D7
Locking Croft B35 22 B3
Lock La CV34 108 D8
Locks The
Royal Leamington Spa CV31 109 D7
Rugby CV21 84 B1
Loder Cl CV4 59 F3
Lodge Cl
Atherstone CV9 19 A6
Hinckley LE10 32 A5
Lodge Cres CV34 108 D4
Lodge Croft B93 72 B6
Lodge Ct CV37 144 E3
Lodge Farm Cotts CV35 132 A7
Lodge Farm OX15 142 F6
Lodge Green La CV7 46 F2
Lodge Green La N CV7 46 E3
Lodge Rd
Coventry CV3 62 B1
Knowle B93 72 B6
Rugby CV21 83 B4
Stratford-u-A CV37 144 E3
Logan Rd CV2 62 E7
Lole Cl CV6 50 A4
Lollard Croft CV3 77 D8
Lomita Cres B77 9 D8
Lomond Cl LE10 31 B8
Lomond Way CV10 28 C5
Lomsey Cl CV4 60 A1
London End NN11 134 E8
London Rd
Coventry,Cheylesmore CV3 77 E8
Coventry,Willenhall CV3 78 B5
Hinckley LE10 31 E8
Middleton B75,B78 13 D7
Moreton-in-M GL56 140 B3
Ryton-on-D CV8 79 B1
Shipston-on-S CV36 149 D4
Stretton-on-D CV23 97 C6
Sutton Coldfield B75 7 A4
Thurlaston CV23 98 C5
Willoughby CV23 117 C6
London Road Terr GL56 140 B3
Long Barrow NN11 134 F4
Longborough Cl B97 102 B6
Long Brook La CV7,CV8 73 E5
Long Cast Park Homes CV37 129 A6
Long Close Ave CV5 60 B6
Long Close Wlk B35 22 A3
Long Cl The CV36 141 D7
Longcroft Cl B35 22 A3
Longdon Cl B98 103 B7
Longdon Croft B93 72 A8
Longdon Rd B93 72 A6
Longdown La CV23 117 D7
Longfellow Ave CV34 108 C4
Longfellow Cl B97 102 C7
Longfellow Rd
[3] Stratford-u-A CV37 130 B8
Coventry CV2 62 C3
Longfield Ho CV6 62 A8
Longfield Rd CV31 110 B6
Longford Cl
Bidford-on-A B50 148 E5
Dorridge B93 72 B3
Longford Park Prim Sch CV6 50 A3
Longford Rd
Bedworth CV7 50 A6
Coventry CV6 50 A4
Longford Sq CV6 50 A4
Long Furlong CV22 99 F7
Long Hassocks CV23 67 E1
Longhope Cl B98 112 A6
Long Hyde Rd WR11 127 F1
Long Itchington CE Prim Sch CV47 115 E3
Long La CV5,CV7 48 D2
Long Lawford Prim Sch CV23 82 B5
Longleat Dr B90 70 E5
Longleat Gr [17] CV31 110 C6
Longley Ave B76 22 D5
Long Leys Croft B46 23 B2
Long Leys Ct B46 23 B2
Longley Wlk B37 33 C2
Long Marston Rd
Mickleton CV37,GL55 135 B8
Pebworth CV37 128 F2
Welford-on-A CV37 129 B5
Long Meadow Dr LE10 30 F7
Longrood Pl CV22 99 D7
Longrood Rd CV22 99 D7
Long Shoot The CV11 30 C6
Long St
Atherstone CV9 18 D8
Bulkington CV12 40 D2
Dordon B78 11 A5
Longstock Rd CV23 67 D1
Longstone Cl B90 71 B6
Longville Ct CV3 78 A6
Longwood Cl CV4 75 F6
Lonscale Dr CV3 77 B5
Lonsdale Ct OX7 142 A2
Lonsdale Rd CV32 106 B4
Lord Leycester Hospl & Knot Gdn* CV34 108 E6
Lord Lytton Ave CV2 62 D2
Lords La B80 103 E2
Lord St CV5 60 F2
Lorenzo Cl CV3 78 D6
Lossiemouth Rd LE10 21 F1
Lothersdale B77 10 C8
Loudon Ave CV6 61 A5
Loudon Gate CV11 29 F1
Loughshaw B77 4 C1
Louisa Ward Cl CV23 115 C7
Loveday Cl CV9 12 D2
Loveday Dr CV32 105 E2
Lovelace Ave B91 71 D8
Love La LE10 32 A6
Lovell Cl CV7 50 A8
Lovell Rd CV12 39 A3
Love Lyne B97 102 B5
Loverock Cres CV21 83 E2
Lovetts Cl LE10 30 F8
Lowbrook La B90 69 D4
Lowdham B77 4 C1
Lower Ave CV31 109 F7
Lower Cape CV34 108 D8
Lower Cladswell La B49 118 C5
Lowe Rd CV6 49 A2
Lower Eastern Green La CV5 59 F4
Lower End CV8 95 C6
Lower End Cotts CV47 133 C4
Lower End OX15 139 A3
Lower Farm CV35 114 E6
Lower Farm La OX17 133 F2
Lower Ford St CV1 151 D3
Lower Grinsty La B97 102 A8
Lower High St GL55 135 A2
Lower Hillmorton Rd CV21 83 D2
Lower Holyhead Rd CV1 151 A3
Lower House La
Baddesley Ensor CV9 11 A3
Wood End CV9 10 F2
Lower Ladyes Hills CV8 93 A6
Lower Leam St CV31 110 B7
Lower Prec CV1 151 B3
Lower Rd CV7 51 C6
Lower St
Rugby CV21 101 B8
Willoughby CV23 117 B6
Lower Villiers St [1] CV32 106 A1
Lowes Ave CV34 104 E1
Lowes La CV35 146 D2
Loweswater Cl CV11 30 A6
Loweswater Rd CV3 62 E1
Lowfield Rd CV3 62 C1
Lowforce B77 4 C1
Low Rd WR11 127 A6
Lowry Cl CV12 39 A4
Lowther St CV2 61 F4
Loxley CE Com Prim Sch CV35 130 F7
Loxley Cl
Coventry CV2 50 D2
Wellesbourne CV35 146 C2
Loxley Ct CV2 50 D2
Loxley Fields CV35 130 F7
Loxley Rd
Alveston CV37 121 D1
Wellesbourne CV35 146 C2
Loxley Way CV32 106 A2
Lucas Ct
Royal Leamington Spa CV32 109 D8
Rugby CV21 83 B4
Lucas Ho CV32 105 F2
Lucas Rd LE10 31 D6
Luce Cl B35 22 B4
Lucerne Cl CV2 50 C3
Lucian Cl CV2 63 B7
Lucy's Mill CV37 145 A1
Luddington Rd CV37 129 E8
Ludford Cl
Ansley CV10 27 B4
Stratford-u-A CV37 144 C4
Ludford Rd CV10 28 C6
Ludgate Cl B46 23 B3
Ludlow Cl B37 33 C2
Ludlow Dr OX16 139 F4
Ludlow Rd CV5 61 A2
Ludlow's La CV35 114 C7
Ludworth Ave B37 44 B8
Luff Cl CV3 78 B8
Lugtrout La B91 56 A6
Lulworth Pk CV8 93 C6
Lumley Gr B37 33 D2
Lumsden Cl CV2 62 F8
Lunar Cl CV4 76 D5
Lundy View B36 33 B6
Lunn Ave CV8 92 E3
Lunn Poly Ho [3] CV32 105 F1
Lunt The* CV8 77 E3
Lupin Cl LE10 31 D5
Lupton Ave CV3 77 C7
Luscombe Rd CV2 62 E8
Luther Way CV5 59 F4
Lutterworth Rd
Brinklow CV23 64 F5
Churchover CV23,LE17 67 D5
Coventry CV2 62 C5
Lutterworth Rd *continued*
Hinckley LE10 32 C3
Nuneaton CV11 40 C8
Pailton CV23,LE17 54 D2
Shawell LE17 68 D6
Wolvey LE10 41 E6
Luxor La CV5 59 B8
Lychgate Cl LE10 32 A5
Lychgate La LE10 32 C5
Lydd Croft B35 22 B4
Lydford Cl CV2 62 C7
Lydgate Ct
Bedworth CV12 39 A4
Nuneaton CV11 29 C3
Lydgate Rd CV6 61 B5
Lydstep Gr CV31 110 C7
Lyecroft Ave B37 33 D2
Lye Green Rd CV35 113 F4
Lymesy St CV3 77 D7
Lymington Cl CV6 61 D8
Lymington Dr CV6 50 B6
Lymore Croft CV2 63 A8
Lynbrook Cl B47 69 A7
Lynbrook Rd CV5 76 D8
Lynchgate Ct CV4 76 C6
Lynchgate Ho CV4 76 C6
Lynchgate Rd CV4 76 C6
Lynch The
Nuneaton CV11 29 D2
Polesworth B78 4 F1
Lyndale Cl CV5 60 C3
Lyndale Rd CV5 60 C3
Lyndale B77 9 F6
Lynden Ho CV5 77 B8
Lyndhurst Cl
Bedworth CV6 50 B6
Hinckley LE10 32 A7
Lyndhurst Croft CV5 59 C4
Lyndhurst Rd CV21 83 F1
Lyndon Croft B37 44 B7
Lyndon Ct CV32 109 E8
Lyneham Gdns B76 22 B6
Lyne Ho [1] CV2 62 D8
Lyng Cl CV5 60 A4
Lyng Hall Sch CV2 62 C6
Lynmouth Cl CV11 29 E5
Lynmouth Rd CV2 62 E8
Lynnon Field CV34 108 B4
Lynton Cl CV34 104 E1
Lynton Rd CV6 49 F1
Lynwood Wlk [10] CV31 110 C6
Lysander Cl
Hinckley LE10 31 E4
Wellesbourne CV35 146 C2
Lysander Ct [7] CV37 145 A2
Lysander Way B35 22 B2
Lyster Cl CV34 108 B8
Lythall Cl CV31 110 F5
Lythalls La CV6 49 E2
Lythalls Lane Ind Est CV6 49 E1
Lytham Cl B76 22 B6
Lytham Rd CV22 82 E1
Lytham B77 4 C5
Lyttelton Rd CV34 108 E8
Lyttleton Cl CV3 63 A1

M

M40 Distribution Pk CV35 146 B2
MacAdam Cl NN11 117 F3
MacAulay Rd
Coventry CV2 62 D4
Rugby CV22 99 E7
Macbeth App CV34 109 D4
Macbeth Cl CV22 99 E6
MacDonald Rd CV2 62 D3
McDonnell Dr CV6,CV7 49 F6
Macefield Cl CV2 50 D2
Mackenzie Cl CV5 60 A7
McKinnell Cres CV21 83 E2
Mackley Way CV33 123 E6
McMahon Rd CV12 49 E8
Madam's Hill Rd B90 70 D7
Madden Pl CV22 82 C2
Madeira Croft CV5 60 E2
Madrona B77 4 B4
Maffey Ct CV22 83 A2
Magdalen Cl CV37 129 D2
Magdalen Rd CV23 117 C6
Magna Pk LE17 55 C6
Magnet La CV22 99 C8
Magnolia Cl CV3 77 B5
Magnolia B77 4 A4
Magnus B77 9 E6
Magpie Ho CV5 59 D5
Magpie La CV7 73 E6
Maguire Ind Est CV4 75 F8
Magyar Cres CV11 40 A8
Maidavale Cres CV3 77 C4
Maidenhair Dr CV23 83 D8
Maidenhead Cl CV37 145 A4
Maidenhead Rd CV37 145 A4
Maidwell Dr B90 70 E8
Main Rd
Ansty CV7 51 D3
Austrey CV9 3 B1
Baxterley CV9 17 B7
Binton CV37 120 A1
Broughton OX15 139 E1
Claybrooke Magna LE17 43 E5
Kilsby CV23 101 F3
Lower Quinton CV37 129 E2
Meriden CV7 58 D8
Newton Regis B79 2 C2
Main St
Aston le W NN11 134 F5
Main St *continued*
Badby NN11 126 F5
Birdingbury CV23 115 F7
Bourton on D CV23 97 F1
Burmington CV36 141 A8
Church Lench WR11 127 A6
Claydon OX17 134 B5
Cleeve Prior WR11 128 A4
Clifton u D CV23 83 F5
Easenhall CV23 65 E4
Frankton CV23 97 D1
Grandborough CV23 116 F6
Hanwell OX17 139 F6
Harborough Magna CV23 66 B3
Higham on t H CV13 21 A3
Long Compton CV36 141 C3
Long Lawford CV23 82 A5
Middle Tysoe CV35 138 B7
Mollington OX17 134 A2
Monks Kirby CV23 53 E3
Newton CV23 68 A1
North Newington OX15 139 D2
Norton Lindsey CV35 114 C2
Offenham WR11 127 D1
Orton-on-t-H CV9 6 D4
Oxhill CV35 137 F8
Rugby CV22 99 C8
Rugby,Newbold on A CV21 82 D7
Shawell LE17 68 C5
Sibford Gower OX15 142 D8
South Littleton WR11 127 F1
Stoke Golding CV13 21 D7
Stretton u F CV23 65 B7
Thurlaston CV23 98 F3
Tiddington CV37 145 E4
Willey CV23 54 F6
Willoughby CV23 117 C6
Withybrook CV7 52 E5
Wolston CV8 80 A4
Wroxton OX15 139 D4
Makepeace Ave CV34 104 F1
Malam Cl CV4 60 A1
Maldale B77 4 C1
Maldens The CV36 149 D5
Malham Cl CV11 30 A2
Malham Rd
Tamworth B77 10 C8
Warwick CV34 104 F1
Malin Ct B49 143 B4
Malins The CV34 109 B6
Mallaby Cl B90 70 A8
Mallard Ave CV10 28 C6
Mallard Cl CV37 144 C5
Mallard Dr LE10 31 A7
Mallard Rd B80 103 F4
Mallender Dr B93 71 F6
Mallerin Croft CV10 28 B5
Malletts Cl CV35 138 B6
Mallory Dr CV34 108 D7
Mallory Rd
Bishops Tachbrook CV33 122 E8
Lighthorne Heath CV33 123 D2
Mallory Way CV6 49 E4
Mallow Croft CV12 38 E2
Mallow Way CV23 83 C8
Malmesbury Rd CV6 49 A3
Malthouse Cl CV10 27 B4
Malt House Cl B50 148 C7
Malthouse Cl WR11 127 D3
Malt House Cl CV47 133 B7
Malt House La WR11 127 A6
Malthouse La
Earlswood B94 86 E7
Kenilworth CV8 92 E6
Long Compton CV36 141 C3
Malt House La CV47 133 B7
Malthouse La OX15 139 A3
Malthouse Row B37 44 A8
Maltings Ct [4] CV37 144 F3
Maltings The
[4] Stratford-u-A CV37 145 A2
Nuneaton CV11 29 E5
Royal Leamington Spa CV32 105 F2
Studley B80 103 D4
Maltmill La B49 143 C3
Malvern Ave
Nuneaton CV10 28 B3
Rugby CV22 83 D1
Malvern Dr B76 22 A8
Malvern Ho CV5 59 D4
Malvern Rd
Balsall Common CV7 74 C6
Coventry CV5 60 F4
Redditch B97 102 D8
Manby Rd B35 22 A4
Mancetter Rd
Atherstone CV9 19 A6
Nuneaton CV10 28 D7
Manchester Ct [8] GL56 140 A3
Mandale Cl CV47 124 A4
Mandarin Cl LE10 31 A6
Mander Gr CV34 108 C4
Manderley Cl CV5 59 C5
Mandrake Cl CV6 49 D4
Manfield Ave CV2 63 A7
Mannings Cl OX15 142 D8
Manning Wlk [3] CV21 83 A3
Mann's Cl CV8 96 B8
Manor Barns CV36 136 B6
Manor Cl
Baddesley Ensor CV9 11 B2
Charwelton NN11 126 D2
Hinckley LE10 31 C5
Manor Cotts GL56 136 C1
Manor Court Ave CV11 29 B5
Manor Court Mews CV11 29 A5
Manor Court Rd CV11 29 A5
Manor Ct
Cleeve Prior WR11 128 A4
Dorridge B93 71 F2
Ettington CV37 131 A3
Fenny Compton CV47 133 D7
Kenilworth CV8 93 A6
Royal Leamington Spa CV31 109 F7
Stretton on F GL56 136 C1
Manor Dr
Stretton-on-D CV23 96 F5
Ullenhall B80 112 D4
Wilmcote CV37 120 C4
Manor Est CV8 79 F3
Manor Farm Cl CV23 101 C2
Manor Farm Cotts
Church Lench WR11 127 B5
Luddington CV37 129 C7
Stretton on F GL56 136 C1
Manor Farm Craft Ctr* B94 69 F2
Manor Farm Ct CV35 123 E1
Manor Farm Rd CV36 136 F6
Manor Farm WR11 127 F1
Manor Gn CV37 145 C2
Manor Hall Mews CV3 78 D6
Manor Ho The CV31 109 F7
Manor House Cl
Aston Flamville LE10 32 E6
Rugby CV21 82 D7
Manor House Dr CV1 151 B2
Manor House La
Astwood Bank B96 102 E3
Water Orton B46 23 B3
Manor La
Claverdon CV35 114 A4
Clifton u D CV23 84 A6
Ettington CV37 131 A3
Honiley CV8,CV35 91 A5
Kineton CV35 132 B5
Loxley CV35 130 F7
Shipston-on-S CV36 149 D6
Wroxall CV35 90 F4
Manor Mews B80 103 E4
Manor Orch
Harbury CV33 123 E6
Horley OX15 139 D6
Manor Park Com Sch CV11 29 A5
Manor Park Prim Sch CV3 77 D7
Manor Park Rd CV11 29 A5
Manor Pk
Claydon OX17 134 B5
Harvington WR11 127 D3
Manor Prim Sch B78 8 E5
Manor Rd
Atherstone CV9 18 F6
Bishops Itchington CV47 124 A4
Claybrooke Magna LE17 43 D6
Coventry CV1 151 B1
Dorridge B93 71 F3
Harbury CV33 123 F6
Manor Rd Ind Est CV9 18 E7
Manor Rd
Kenilworth CV8 92 F6
Middle Littleton WR11 127 F1
Royal Leamington Spa CV32 106 B3
Rugby CV21 83 B4
Staverton NN11 126 D8
Stockton CV47 147 F8
Stratford-u-A CV37 145 C2
Studley B80 103 E4
Wythall B47 69 A3
Manor Terr CV8 93 A6
Manor View CV8 79 F3
Manor Way LE10 31 D5
Mansard Ct B46 34 A7
Manse Cl CV7 39 A1
Manse Gdns B80 103 E3
Mansell Rd B97 102 D7
Mansell St CV37 144 F3
Mansel St CV6 61 E8
Mansfield Ho B37 33 D3
Mansion Ho The CV35 132 B5
Mansions Cl CV47 124 A4
Mansion St [1] LE10 31 D8
Mansley Bsns Ctr The CV37 144 D5
Manston Dr CV35 146 D2
Manta Rd B77 9 D6
Mantilla Dr CV3 77 A5
Manton Croft B93 71 E3
Mantua [5] CV37 145 A3
Maple Ave CV7 39 B1
Maplebeck Cl CV5 61 A3
Maple Cl
Braunston NN11 117 E5
Hinckley LE10 31 E5
Maple Dr B78 15 D7
Maple Gr
Rugby CV21 83 A4
Stratford-u-A CV37 144 F5
Warwick CV34 105 A1
Maple Ho B98 102 F8
Maple Leaf Dr B37 44 B8
Maple Rd
Nuneaton CV10 28 E5
Royal Leamington Spa CV31 109 F6
Maple Rise B77 4 A4
Maples The CV12 38 E2
Mapleton Rd CV6 60 F8

Maple Wlk
4 Birmingham B37 33 B2
Coventry CV6 49 F5
Maplewood B76 22 A8
Mapperley Cl CV2 63 A8
Mappleborough Green CE Prim Sch B80 112 A5
Marble Alley B80 103 E4
Marchant Rd LE10 31 C8
March Ct CV22 83 A1
Marchfont Cl CV11 30 A1
March Rd
Mollington OX17 133 F2
Warmington OX17 133 E2
March Way CV3 78 D7
Marcian Cl LE10 21 F1
Marcos Dr B36 22 F1
Marcroft Pl CV31 110 D6
Mardol Cl CV2 62 D7
Marfield Cl B76 22 A6
Margaret Ave CV12 39 B3
Margaret Cl CV33 123 F6
Margaret Rd CV9 18 E7
Margeson Cl CV2 62 E2
Margetts Cl CV8 92 F4
Marie Brock Cl CV4 60 B1
Marie Cl CV9 19 A7
Marigold Dr LE10 31 E5
Marigold Wlk CV10 39 A8
Marina Cl CV4 75 E7
Marion Rd CV6 61 D7
Mark Antony Dr CV34 109 D4
Market Cnr
7 Royal Leamington Spa CV31 109 F6
Baginton CV8 77 F2
Market End Cl CV12 38 C2
Market Hill CV47 147 B4
Market Mall 4 CV21 83 A3
Market Pl
Alcester B49 143 B3
Hinckley LE10 31 D8
Nuneaton CV11 29 C4
Rugby CV21 83 A3
Shipston-on-S CV36 149 D6
Warwick CV34 108 E6
Market Sq 4 CV35 132 B6
Market St
Atherstone CV9 18 D8
Polesworth B78 5 A1
Rugby CV21 83 B4
Warwick CV34 108 D6
Market Way CV1 151 B2
Markham Dr CV31 110 B3
Marks Mews 7 CV34 108 E6
Marlborough Cl LE10 32 B7
Marlborough Ct B75 13 A6
Marlborough Dr CV31 110 D5
Marlborough Mews B80 103 E4
Marlborough Rd
Coventry CV2 62 A3
Nuneaton CV11 29 B3
Rugby CV22 99 E8
Marlcroft CV3 78 E5
Marleigh Rd B50 148 D5
Marlene Croft B37 33 C1
Marler Rd CV4 75 F7
Marlin B77 9 D6
Marlissa Dr CV6 49 E2
Marloes Wlk CV31 110 C6
Marlow Cl CV5 60 B4
Marlowe Cl
6 Banbury OX16 139 F3
Galley Common CV10 27 F5
Marlowe Rd 21 CV37 130 B8
Marlow Rd CV9 16 C5
Marlston Wlk CV5 60 B4
Marlwood Cl CV6 49 F4
Marne Cl CV34 109 A8
Marner Cres CV6 61 B5
Marner Rd
Bedworth CV12 39 A3
Nuneaton CV10 29 B1
Marnhull Cl CV2 62 F4
Marram Ct CV37 144 E4
Marrick B77 4 C1
Marriners La CV5 60 B5
Marriott Rd
Bedworth CV12 38 D2
Coventry CV6 61 A4
Marsdale Dr CV10 28 E3
Marsett B77 10 C8
Marshall Ave CV36 149 D5
Marshall Lake Rd B90 70 D8
Marshall Rd CV7 49 F8
Marshalls Cl OX15 138 F5
Marsham Cl CV34 109 B8
Marshbrook Cl CV2 50 E3
Marsh Cl WR11 127 D4
Marsh Ct 5 GL56 140 A3
Marshdale Ave CV6 49 E3
Marshfield Dr CV4 76 D2
Marshfield B90 70 B5
Marsh Ho CV2 63 A7
Marsh House Farm La B92 57 D3
Marsh La
Bradnock's Marsh B92 57 D5
Curdworth B76 23 D5
Hampton-in-A B92 57 B6
Stratford-u-A CV37 144 E5
Water Orton B46 23 C3
Marsh Rd CV37 120 B5
Marston Ave CV33 123 D2
Marston Camping & Cvn Pk B76 15 A2
Marston Cl CV32 106 B2
Marston Dr B37 33 A5
Marston Green Inf Sch B37 44 A7
Marston Green Jun Sch B37 44 A7
Marston Hill CV47 125 F4
Marston La
Bedworth CV12 39 D5
Nuneaton CV11 39 E8
Wishaw B76 14 E1
Marten Cl CV35 108 A7
Martin Cl
Coventry CV5 59 E4
Stratford-u-A CV37 145 A5
Martindale Rd CV7 50 C8
Martinique Sq CV34 108 D6
Martin La CV22 99 D7
Martins Dr CV9 12 E2
Martins Rd CV12 38 E1
Martlesham Sq B35 22 A4
Martley Cl B98 103 B7
Martley Croft B91 71 B8
Marton Hill CV47 115 D4
Marton Rd
Birdingbury CV23 115 E7
Long Itchington CV47 115 D5
Martyrs' Cl The CV3 77 D8
Marwood Cl CV11 39 E7
Mary Arden's House & Shakespeare Mus★ CV37 120 C5
Mary Herbert St CV3 77 D7
Mary Slessor St CV3 78 D7
Marystow Cl CV5 60 B8
Marywell Cl LE10 21 F1
Masefield Ave CV34 108 C4
Masefield Rd CV37 145 B1
Maseley Ct CV37 129 D2
Mason Ave CV32 106 C3
Mason Cl
Bidford-on-A B50 148 E5
Redditch B97 102 D7
Mason Ct LE10 31 B8
Mason Gr CV8 93 B5
Mason La B94 69 F1
Mason Rd
Coventry CV6 49 F1
Redditch B97 102 D8
Masons Cl CV37 120 C5
Masons Rd CV37 144 E4
Masons Way CV37 144 D4
Masser Rd CV6 49 D4
Massey Sham Ave GL56 140 C3
Masters Ct CV23 115 F7
Masters Rd CV31 110 A4
Master's Yd CV23 115 F7
Matchborough Way B98 103 E8
Mathe Croft CV31 110 C5
Matlock Cl CV21 83 C7
Matlock Rd CV1 61 D6
Matterson Rd CV6 61 A5
Matthews Cl CV37 145 A4
Maud Rd B46 23 D3
Maudslay Rd CV5 60 E2
Maureen Cl CV4 59 C1
Maurice Mead Ct 12 CV31 110 A6
Mavor Dr CV12 38 D1
Mawby's La DE12 3 F8
Mawnan Cl CV7 50 B8
Max Rd CV6 60 F5
Maxstoke Cl
Meriden CV7 46 B1
Tamworth B77 9 C4
Maxstoke Croft B90 70 C8
Maxstoke Ct B46 34 A4
Maxstoke Gdns CV31 109 F6
Maxstoke La
Coleshill B46 34 B6
Meriden CV7 46 B2
White Stitch CV7 46 B3
Mayama Rd B78 8 F8
Maybird Ctr CV37 144 F4
Maybridge Dr B91 71 B8
Maybrook Ind Est CV37 144 F4
Maybrook Rd
Stratford-u-A CV37 144 F4
Sutton Coldfield B76 22 A5
Maycock Rd CV6 61 D7
Mayfair Dr
Fazeley B78 9 A7
Galley Common CV10 27 F4
May Farm Cl B47 69 A6
Mayfield Ave CV37 145 A4
Mayfield Cl
9 Royal Leamington Spa CV31 110 C6
Bedworth CV12 39 B3
Mayfield Ct CV37 145 A4
Mayfield Dr
Henley-in-A B95 113 A5
Kenilworth CV8 93 C4
Mayfield Rd
Coventry CV5 61 A1
Nuneaton CV11 29 E2
Southam CV47 147 B5
Mayfield B77 10 C8
Mayflower Dr CV2 62 E2
Mayhurst Cl B47 69 C6
Mayhurst Rd B47 69 B6
May La
Ebrington GL55 135 E2
Hollywood B47 69 A7
Rugby CV22 82 D1
Maynard Ave
Bedworth CV12 49 D8
Warwick CV34 109 A7
Mayne Cl CV35 114 F3
Mayo Dr CV8 93 A4
Mayo Rd CV36 149 D7
Mayor's Croft CV4 76 B7
Maypole La CV9 11 C1
Maypole Rd B79 5 E4
May's Hill B95 113 A4
May St CV6 61 E8
Mayswood Rd B95 113 A3
Maythorn Ave B76 22 A6
Maythorn Gr 4 B91 71 B8
Maytree Cl B37 33 A2
Mead Cl 20 GL56 140 A3
Meadfoot Rd CV3 78 E6
Meadowbank Dr B46 23 D1
Meadowbrook Ct DE12 3 F8
Meadow Cl
Ansty CV7 51 D3
Hockley Heath B94 88 C6
Kingsbury B78 15 D5
Lighthorne CV35 123 B4
Royal Leamington Spa CV32 106 C4
Solihull B90 70 D8
Stratford-u-A CV37 144 D3
Stretton-on-D CV23 97 A6
Wolvey LE10 41 D4
Meadow Cotts CV23 116 F5
Meadowcroft Cl CV4 75 F8
Meadow Croft CV7 26 E1
Meadow Crofts CV47 124 B5
Meadow Croft B47 69 A3
Meadow Ct CV11 29 B4
Meadow Dr
Hampton-in-A B92 57 B7
Hinckley LE10 32 A7
Meadow Farm CV37 114 A1
Meadow Gdns CV9 17 C8
Meadow Green Prim Sch B47 69 A3
Meadow Ho 5 CV1 61 B3
Meadow La B94 89 D3
Meadow Lea CV37 144 D3
Meadow Pleck La B90 70 A6
Meadow Rd
Alcester B49 143 B5
Coventry CV6 49 B4
Hartshill CV10 28 A8
Henley-in-A B95 113 B4
Hurley CV9 16 C5
Rugby CV21 82 E6
Southam CV47 147 B5
Warwick CV34 109 A7
Wolston CV8 80 A4
Wythall B47 69 A3
Meadow Rise
Balsall Common CV7 74 C7
Ullenhall B95 112 E6
Meadowside CV11 40 B8
Meadows Sch The CV4 59 E3
Meadow St
Atherstone CV9 18 D7
Coventry CV1 151 A2
Meadows The
Bidford-on-A B50 148 C5
Hinckley LE10 32 A7
Leek Wootton CV35 105 A7
Meadow St CV11 29 B5
Meadow Sweet Rd CV37 144 E5
Meadowsweet CV23 83 C8
Meadow View Cl B49 143 D4
Meadow View WR11 127 F6
Meadow Way
Fenny Compton CV47 133 E7
Harborough Magna CV23 66 B3
Meadow CV37 129 A6
Mead The OX17 133 F2
Meadway CV2 62 B6
Meadway N CV2 62 B6
Meadway The
Hinckley LE10 31 F7
Redditch B97 102 D8
Meakins Cl CV34 108 B4
Mearse La WR7 118 B5
Medhurst Cl CV22 99 C3
Medina Rd CV6 49 E1
Medland Ave CV3 76 F5
Medley Gr CV31 109 F3
Meer End Rd CV8 74 D1
Meerhill Ave B90 71 A6
Meer St CV37 145 A3
Meeting House La CV7 74 C6
Meeting La B49 143 C4
Meir Rd B98 103 C8
Melbourne Cl CV11 39 E8
Melbourne Ct 3 CV12 38 F2
Melbourne Rd CV5 61 A2
Meldrum Ct CV47 132 F7
Meldrum Rd CV10 28 D4
Melfort Cl
Coventry CV3 62 F2
Nuneaton CV10 28 C5
Melksham Sq B35 22 A3
Mellish Ct CV22 82 E1
Mellish Rd CV22 82 E1
Mellor Rd CV21 101 B8
Mellowdew Rd CV2 62 C4
Mellowship Rd CV5 59 D5
Mellwaters B77 10 C8
Melmerby B77 10 C8
Melrose Ave CV12 49 D8
Melrose Cl LE10 31 B8
Melrose Ct 12 OX16 139 F5
Melton Rd CV32 106 B4
Melville Cl
Bedworth CV7 50 A8
Rugby CV22 82 E1
Melville Ho 7 CV37 144 F1
Melville Rd CV1 61 A3
Memorial Rd CV47 133 D7
Menai Wlk B37 33 B4
Mendip Dr CV10 28 B3
Mendip Way B77 4 C1
Meon Cl CV37 129 D1
Meon Rd GL55 135 C7
Mercer Ave
Coventry CV2 62 A5
Water Orton B46 23 A3
Mercer Ct 2 CV22 100 F8
Mercers Mdw CV7 49 A6
Merchants Ct 5 CV32 106 A1
Mercia Ave CV8 92 F4
Mercia Bsns Village CV4 75 F6
Mercia Ho CV1 151 B3
Mercian Pk B77 4 A3
Mercian Way B77 4 B3
Mercia Way CV34 109 B7
Mercot Cl B98 103 A6
Mercury Pk B77 4 B3
Mere Ave B35 22 B3
Meredith Rd CV2 62 D2
Mere La LE10 42 C3
Merestone Cl CV47 147 B6
Merevale Ave
Hinckley LE10 31 C7
Nuneaton CV11 29 A4
Merevale Cl
Hinckley LE10 31 C7
Redditch B98 103 D8
Merevale Ct CV11 29 A4
Merevale La CV9 17 F7
Merevale Rd CV9 12 C1
Merevale View CV9 18 C7
Mereways B90 70 A5
Merganser B77 10 A6
Meriden Bsns Pk CV5 59 B8
Meriden CE Prim Sch CV7 46 C1
Meriden Cl B98 112 A6
Meriden Cross★ CV7 46 B1
Meriden Dr B37 33 A6
Meriden Hill CV7 58 E8
Meriden Park Homes CV7 58 C8
Meriden Rd
Berkswell CV7 58 C4
Fillongley CV7 36 C2
Hampton-in-A B92 57 C7
Meriden St CV1 61 B3
Merlin Ave CV10 28 B6
Merlin Cl
Birmingham B35 22 A3
Rugby CV23 83 C8
Tamworth B77 10 A6
Merrick Ct LE10 31 F5
Merrifield Gdns LE10 31 E5
Merrington Cl 5 B91 71 C8
Merrivale Rd CV5 60 E3
Merryfields Way CV2 50 F1
Merry Hurst Pl LE10 30 E7
Merry La WR11 127 E1
Mersey Rd CV12 40 A3
Merstone Sch B37 33 A1
Merttens Dr CV22 82 F2
Merynton Ave CV4 76 E5
Meschines St CV3 77 D6
Metalloys Ind Est B76 22 B5
Metcalfe Cl OX15 139 E4
Metchley Croft B90 70 F6
Mews Rd CV32 109 D8
Mews The
3 Rugby CV21 84 A1
Atherstone CV9 18 E8
Bedworth CV12 39 B2
Kenilworth CV8 92 E3
Mica Cl B77 4 B2
Michael Banning Pl CV7 74 B7
Michael Blanning Gdns B93 71 E3
Michael Drayton Jun Sch CV10 28 B8
Michaelmas Rd CV3 151 B1
Michel Ho CV1 151 C4
Michell Cl CV3 78 B8
Micklehill Dr B90 70 B8
Mickle Mdw B46 23 B3
Mickleton Cl B98 102 E7
Mickleton Dr CV35 114 F5
Mickleton Prim Sch GL55 135 B6
Mickleton Rd
Coventry CV5 77 A8
Ilmington CV36 136 A7
Mickleton B77 10 C8
Middelburg Cl CV11 30 A1
Middle Bickenhill La B92 45 A4
Middleborough Rd CV1 151 A4
Middlecotes CV4 60 B1
Middlefield Ave B93 72 B4
Middlefield Dr CV3 63 B1
Middlefield La CV37 130 E1
Middlefleld Dr CV3 63 A1
Middle Hill OX15 142 D4
Middle La
Balscote OX15 139 B4
Nether Whitacre B46 24 E6
Shotteswell OX17 139 E8
Middle Littleton Tithe Barn★ WR11 127 F2
Middle Lock La CV35 114 E5
Middlemarch Bsns Pk CV3 78 C2
Middlemarch Rd
Coventry CV6 61 C7
Nuneaton CV10 29 C1
Middlemarch Sch CV10 29 B1
Middlemore Cl B80 103 D3
Middle Rd CV33 123 D7
Middle Ride CV3 78 E5
Middle Row OX7 142 A2
Middlesex CV37 128 E1
Middlesmoor B77 10 C8
Middle St
Armscote CV37 136 E7
Ilmington CV36 136 B6
Middleton Cl CV35 138 B6
Middleton Hall★ B78 8 E1
Middleton La B78 13 F6
Middletown La B96,B80 103 D1
Middletown
Moreton Morrell CV35 122 F3
Studley B80 103 D1
Midland Air Mus★ CV8 78 B3
Midland Oak Trad Est CV6 49 E2
Midland Rd
Coventry CV6 61 E5
Nuneaton CV11 29 A5
Midland Trad Est CV21 83 A6
Midpoint Park Ind Est B76 22 C5
Milburn Hill Rd CV4 76 B6
Milburn B77 10 C8
Milby Ct CV11 29 C2
Milby Dr CV11 30 A7
Milby Prim Sch CV11 29 F8
Milcote Cl B98 103 A7
Milcote Manor Cotts CV37 129 C6
Milcote Rd CV37 129 C6
Mildmay Cl CV37 144 E1
Mile End B94 87 A2
Mile La CV1 151 C1
Mile Post La B96 118 A7
Milesbush Ave B36 22 D1
Miles Mdw
Coventry CV6 50 B1
Newbold-on-S CV37 130 E1
Milestone Dr CV22 99 F8
Milestone Ho 2 CV1 61 B2
Milestone Rd 2 CV37 130 B8
Mile Tree La CV2 50 F7
Milfoil Cl LE10 30 F7
Milford Cl
Allesley CV5 60 B6
Redditch B97 102 C6
Milford Ct CV31 110 A8
Milford Gr B90 71 C7
Milford St CV10 29 B2
Milking La B95 113 B4
Millais Cl CV12 39 A4
Mill Bank B46 25 D3
Mill Bank Mews CV8 93 B6
Millbank CV34 105 B1
Millbeck CV21 83 D7
Mill Cl
Braunston NN11 117 D5
Broom B50 148 B7
Coventry CV2 50 B3
Hollywood B47 69 A7
Norton Lindsey CV35 114 C2
Nuneaton CV11 29 F1
Southam CV47 147 A5
Wolston CV8 79 F3
Mill Cotts B50 148 B7
Mill Cres
11 Kineton CV35 132 B6
Kingsbury B78 15 D4
Southam CV47 147 A5
Mill Ct CV36 149 D5
Mill End CV8 93 A6
Millennium Way CV8 79 F3
Millers Bank B50 148 B7
Millers Cl CV22 99 A3
Miller's Cl CV22 99 A4
Millers Cl
Lower Boddington NN11 134 E6
Welford-on-A CV37 129 B6
Millers Dale Cl CV21 83 C7
Millers Gn LE10 31 F6
Millers La
Hornton OX15 139 B8
Monks Kirby CV23 53 D3
Millers Rd CV34 108 E8
Millers Wharf B78 4 F1
Mill Farm Cl CV22 99 C3
Mill Farm Pk CV12 40 B6
Millfield Cl CV37 129 D2
Millfield Ct B95 113 B5
Mill Field CV37 128 F2
Millfield Prim Sch B78 9 A8
Millfield CV31 110 A8
Millfields Ave CV21 100 F8
Mill Furlong CV23 67 D1
Mill Hill CV8 77 D3
Millholme Cl CV47 147 C4
Mill House Cl CV32 109 C8
Millhouse Ct CV6 61 F7
Mill House Dr CV32 109 C8
Mill House Terr CV32 109 C8
Mill Ind Pk The B49 143 B7
Milliners Ct CV9 18 D8
Millison Gr B90 71 A7
Mill La
10 Kineton CV35 132 B6
Alcester B49 143 B2
Aston Cantlow B49,B95 119 F6
Atherstone CV9 19 A6
Barford CV35 122 A7
Bentley Heath B93 71 F4

Mill La *continued*
Bramcote CV11 .... 40 F8
Broom B50 .... 148 B7
Bulkington CV12 .... 40 A3
Chipping Warden OX17 .... 134 F3
Cleeve Prior WR11 ...... 128 A4
Clifton u D CV23 .... 83 E5
Coventry CV3 .... 62 F2
Cubbington CV32 .... 106 F5
Drayton OX15 .... 139 E4
Earlswood B94 .... 86 B8
Fazeley B78 .... 9 A8
Fenny Compton CV47 ..... 133 D7
Fillongley CV7 .... 36 C5
Great Alne B49 .... 119 E6
Harbury CV33 .... 123 F7
Kingswood B94 .... 89 C4
Lowsonford,Finwood CV35 113 E7
Lowsonford,Turner's Green CV35 .... 113 F8
Mickleton GL55 .... 135 B6
Newbold-on-S CV37 ...... 136 F8
Shenington OX15 .... 138 F5
Shrewley CV35 .... 114 C6
Stratford-u-A CV37 ...... 145 A1
Tredington CV36 .... 136 F6
Welford-on-A CV37 ...... 129 A7
Witherley CV9 .... 19 A8
Wolvey LE10 .... 41 F5
Wythall B47,B94 .... 69 B1
Mill Pleck B80 .... 103 E3
Mill Pool La B93 .... 89 A8
Mill Race La CV6 .... 50 B3
Mill Race View CV9 ...... 12 D2
Mill Rd
Napton on t H CV47 ...... 125 C8
Royal Leamington Spa CV31 .... 110 A8
Rugby CV21 .... 83 C5
Southam CV47 .... 147 A5
Mill Row LE10 .... 41 F5
Mills La OX15 .... 139 D4
Mill St
Bedworth CV12 .... 39 B3
Coventry CV1 .... 151 A3
Harbury CV33 .... 123 E7
Kineton CV35 .... 132 B6
Nuneaton CV11 .... 29 C4
Royal Leamington Spa CV31 .... 110 A7
Shipston-on-S CV36 ...... 149 D5
Warwick CV34 .... 108 F6
Mill Terr CV12 .... 39 B5
Millway Dr [1] CV33 ...... 122 F8
Mill Wlk CV11 .... 29 C4
Milner Cl CV12 .... 40 D2
Milner Cres CV2 .... 50 E1
Milner Dr B79 .... 4 E7
Milrose Way CV4 .... 75 F8
Milton Ave CV34 .... 108 C5
Milton Cl
Bedworth CV12 .... 39 D1
Bentley Heath B93 .... 71 F4
Redditch B97 .... 102 C8
Milton Rd
Bentley Heath B93 .... 71 F4
Stratford-u-A CV37 ...... 130 B8
Milton St CV2 .... 62 A4
Milverton Cres [1] CV32 .. 105 E1
Milverton Cres W [3] CV32 .... 105 E1
Milverton Ct CV32 .... 109 E8
Milverton Hill CV32 ...... 109 E8
Milverton House Prep Sch CV11 .... 29 D3
Milverton Lodge [2] CV32 .... 105 E1
Milverton Prim Sch CV32 .... 105 E1
Milverton Rd
Coventry CV2 .... 50 D2
Knowle B93 .... 72 C5
Milverton Terr CV32 ...... 109 E8
Miners Wlk B78 .... 4 F1
Minerva Mews B49 ...... 143 B4
Minions Cl CV9 .... 18 D8
Miniva Dr B76 .... 13 A2
Minster Cl
Hampton Magna CV35 .... 114 F3
Knowle B93 .... 72 B8
Minster Rd CV1 .... 61 B3
Minton Rd CV2 .... 50 E1
Minworth Ind Pk B76 ...... 22 B5
Minworth Jun & Inf Sch B76 .... 22 D5
Minworth Rd B46 .... 23 A3
Mira Dr CV10 .... 20 D3
Miranda Cl CV3 .... 78 D7
Miranda Dr CV34 .... 109 E2
Mistral Cl LE10 .... 31 F8
Mitcheldean Cl B98 ...... 102 E7
Mitchell Ave CV4 .... 76 A7
Mitchell Ct CV23 .... 67 C2
Mitchell Ho
Coventry CV4 .... 76 A7
Warwick CV34 .... 108 E7
Mitchell Rd CV12 .... 39 C2
Mitchison Cl CV23 .... 117 E8
Mitford Villas GL56 ...... 140 A3
Moat Ave CV3 .... 76 F5
Moat Cl
Bubbenhall CV8 .... 95 C6
Thurlaston CV23 .... 98 F2
Moat Croft
Birmingham B37 .... 33 A2
Sutton Coldfield B76 ...... 22 B7
Moat Dr B78 .... 8 E5
Moat Farm Cotts WR11 .. 127 E5
Moat Farm Dr
Bedworth CV12 .... 49 C8
Rugby CV21 .... 101 A7
Moat Farm La B95 .... 112 E6
Moat Gn CV35 .... 108 A1
Moat House La
Coventry CV4 .... 76 C7
Shustoke B46 .... 25 B1
Moat House Prim Sch CV2 .... 50 D1
Moat La LE10 .... 41 F6
Mobbs La OX15 .... 142 D4
Mockley Wood Rd B93 ... 72 B7
Modbury Cl CV3 .... 77 D5
Model Village The CV47 . 115 D3
Molesworth Ave CV3 ...... 62 A1
Mollington Gr CV35 ...... 114 F6
Mollington La OX17 ...... 133 D2
Mollington Rd
Claydon OX17 .... 134 B4
Shotteswell OX17 .... 139 E8
Whitnash CV31 .... 110 A3
Momus Bvd CV2 .... 62 C2
Moncrieff Dr CV31 ...... 110 C5
Monks Cl CV22 .... 99 A8
Monk's Croft The CV3 .... 77 C7
Monks Dr B80 .... 103 D4
Monks Field Cl CV4 ...... 60 A1
Monks Kirby La CV23 ...... 53 F6
Monkspath Bsns Pk B90 .. 70 F8
Monkspath Cl B90 .... 70 D7
Monkspath Hall Rd B90, B91 .... 71 B7
Monkspath Jun & Inf Sch B90 .... 71 B6
Monkspath B90 .... 71 A6
Monks Rd
Binley Woods CV3 .... 79 C7
Coventry CV1 .... 61 F2
Monks Way CV34 .... 108 D6
Monkswood Cres CV2 .... 62 D8
Monmouth Cl
Coventry CV5 .... 60 B3
Kenilworth CV8 .... 92 F6
Monmouth Gdns CV10 .... 28 E3
Monnington Ho CV8 ...... 93 B7
Montague Ho
[13] Stratford-u-A CV37 ... 145 A3
Warwick CV34 .... 109 A8
Montague Rd
Rugby CV22 .... 99 D5
Warwick CV34 .... 109 A8
Montague's Cnr CV37 ... 129 A6
Montalt Rd CV3 .... 77 E7
Montana Wlk CV10 .... 28 E3
Montfort Rd B46 .... 33 F5
Montgomery Ave CV35 .. 114 F3
Montgomery Cl
Coventry CV3 .... 78 C4
Stratford-u-A CV37 ...... 144 E1
Montgomery Dr CV22 .... 82 C1
Montgomery Rd CV31 ... 109 F4
Montilo La CV23 .... 66 D5
Montjoy Cl CV3 .... 78 D7
Montley B77 .... 10 C8
Montpelier Ho CV8 .... 92 F5
Montpellier Cl CV3 .... 77 C6
Montrose Ave CV32 ...... 106 B5
Montrose Dr
Birmingham B35 .... 22 A4
Nuneaton CV10 .... 28 F3
Montrose Rd CV22 .... 83 A1
Montsford Cl B93 .... 71 F6
Monument View B78 ...... 11 A8
Monument Way CV37 .... 145 A5
Monwode Lea La B46 .... 26 B4
Moorbrooke CV10 .... 28 A7
Moorcroft Cl
Nuneaton CV11 .... 30 B1
Redditch B97 .... 102 B6
Moorcroft Gdns B97 .... 102 B6
Moore Cl
Appleby Magna DE12 .... 3 F8
Coventry CV6 .... 50 A5
Warwick CV34 .... 104 E2
Moorend Ave B37 .... 33 B2
Moore Wlk CV34 .... 109 C7
Moor Farm Cl CV23 ...... 96 F6
Moorfield Ave B93 .... 71 F6
Moorfield Rd B49 .... 143 B4
Moorfield The CV3 .... 78 B8
Moorhill Rd CV31 .... 110 A3
Moorhills Croft B90 ...... 70 B8
Moorings Bsns Pk The CV6 .... 50 A6
Moorings The CV31 ...... 109 D7
Moorlands Ave CV8 ...... 92 F3
Moorlands Lodge CV8 .... 92 F3
Moor La
Tamworth B77 .... 4 A6
Willoughby CV23 .... 117 B6
Moorpark Cl CV11 .... 40 C8
Moor Rd CV10 .... 28 A8
Moors La CV23 .... 84 C1
Moor St CV5 .... 60 F1
Moor The B76 .... 22 A8
Moorwood Cres CV10 .... 28 A8
Moorwood La
Ansley Common CV10 ...... 27 F8
Hartshill CV10 .... 28 A7
Hartshill CV10 .... 28 A8
Morar Cl B35 .... 22 C4
Moray Cl LE10 .... 31 A8
Mordaunt Rd CV35 ...... 146 E4
Moreall Mdws CV4 .... 76 D3
Morecroft Dr CV34 ...... 108 B4
Moreland Croft B76 ...... 22 B6
Moreton Cl CV37 .... 145 D2
Moreton-in-Marsh Hospl GL56 .... 140 A3
Moreton-in-Marsh Sta GL56 .... 140 A3
Moreton Morrell CE Prim Sch CV35 .... 122 F2
Moreton Morrell La CV35 .... 123 B2
Morfa Gdns CV6 .... 60 D5
Morgan Cl
[4] Banbury OX16 .... 139 F4
New Arley CV7 .... 36 F8
Norton Lindsey CV35 .... 114 C2
Studley B80 .... 103 F2
Morgan Gr B36 .... 22 F1
Morgans Rd CV5 .... 59 C4
Morgrove Ave B93 .... 71 F6
Morland Cl CV12 .... 40 D2
Morland Rd CV6 .... 49 C2
Morningside CV5 .... 77 B8
Mornington Ct B46 ...... 34 A7
Morpeth B77 .... 9 C7
Morrell St CV32 .... 105 F1
Morris Ave CV2 .... 62 D4
Morris Cl CV21 .... 82 F6
Morris Croft B36 .... 22 F1
Morris Dr
[10] Banbury OX16 .... 139 F4
Nuneaton CV11 .... 29 D1
Whitnash CV31 .... 110 B2
Morris Hill B78 .... 11 A8
Morris Rd NN11 .... 117 F2
Morse Rd CV31 .... 110 B3
Morson Cres CV21 .... 83 E2
Morston B77 .... 9 D4
Mortimer Rd CV8 .... 92 F2
Morton Cl CV6 .... 49 A1
Morton Ct
[1] Stratford-u-A CV37 ... 145 A3
Rugby CV22 .... 100 F8
Morton Gdns CV21 .... 83 C2
Morton Hall La B96 ...... 118 A6
Morton La B97 .... 102 B7
Morton St CV32 .... 105 F1
Morton Wood La WR7 .... 127 B8
Morville Cl B93 .... 71 D3
Mosedale
Moreton-in-M GL56 ...... 140 B3
Rugby CV21 .... 83 C7
Moseley Ave CV6 .... 61 A4
Moseley Prim Sch CV6 ... 61 A4
Moseley Rd CV8 .... 93 B3
Moss Cl CV22 .... 82 E1
Mossdale Cl CV6 .... 61 B6
Mossdale Cres CV10 ...... 28 F2
Mossdale B77 .... 10 C8
Moss Gr CV8 .... 93 B7
Moss La
Newbold-on-S CV37 ...... 130 E1
Redditch B98 .... 112 A8
Mossop Ct CV34 .... 144 E3
Mosspaul Cl CV32 .... 105 D2
Moss St [12] CV31 .... 110 A7
Mottistone Cl CV3 .... 77 D6
Mott's Way B46 .... 34 A5
Moultrie Rd CV21,CV22 ... 83 B3
Mountbatten Ave CV8 .... 93 C3
Mountbatten Cl CV37 .... 144 D1
Mount Cres CV37 .... 144 C3
Mount Dr CV12 .... 39 A3
Mount Field Ct CV1 ...... 151 D4
Mountfield Gdns [4] CV47 .... 147 B4
Mountford Cl CV35 ...... 146 E3
Mountford Rise CV35 .... 123 B2
Mount Gdns CV5 .... 77 B8
Mount Nod Prim Sch CV5 60 A3
Mount Nod Way CV5 ...... 60 B3
Mount Pleasant CV47 .... 124 A4
Mount Pleasant Cl CV47 . 147 F8
Mount Pleasant Cotts CV2 .... 63 A7
Mount Pleasant La B95 .. 112 E6
Mount Pleasant Rd CV12 . 39 A3
Mount Pleasant
Stockton CV47 .... 147 F8
Stratford-u-A CV37 ...... 144 C3
Tamworth B77 .... 9 C8
Mount Pleasant Terr CV10 .... 28 F6
Mount Pleasant OX17 ... 134 F1
Mount Rd
Henley-in-A B95 .... 113 B4
Hinckley LE10 .... 31 D8
Mount St
Coventry CV5 .... 60 F2
Nuneaton CV11 .... 29 B4
Mount Street Pas CV11 ... 29 B4
Mount The
Coventry CV3 .... 77 E8
Curdworth B76 .... 23 C6
Mowbray St CV2 .... 61 F3
Mowe Croft B37 .... 44 B7
Mows Hill Rd B94,B95 ... 113 A8
Moxhull Rd B37 .... 33 A5
Moyeady Ave CV22 .... 100 E8
Moyle Cres CV5 .... 59 D4
Much Park St CV1 .... 151 C2
Muirfields Cl CV11 .... 40 C8
Muirfield B77 .... 4 C5
Mulberry Cl CV32 .... 106 A2
Mulberry Ct
[19] Stratford-u-A CV37 ... 145 A3
Kenilworth CV8 .... 92 F4
Mulberry Dr [5] CV34 .... 108 F8
Mulberry Rd
Coventry CV6 .... 62 A7
Rugby CV22 .... 82 B2
Mulberry St [20] CV37 .... 145 A3
Mulberry Tree Ctr The CV37 .... 145 A3
Mulberry Way CV10 ...... 28 A8
Mullard Dr CV31 .... 110 B3
Mull Croft B36 .... 33 B7
Mullensgrove Rd B37 .... 33 A5
Mulliners Cl [2] B37 ...... 33 D2
Mulliner St CV6 .... 61 F5
Muntz Cres B94 .... 88 C6
Murcott Ct CV31 .... 110 A3
Murcott Rd E CV31 ...... 110 A3
Murcott Rd W CV31 ...... 110 A3
Murrayfield Way CV3 .... 63 B1
Murrayian Cl CV21 .... 83 B3
Murray Rd
Coventry CV6 .... 61 A7
Rugby CV21 .... 83 B4
Murton B77 .... 10 C8
Musborough Cl B36 ...... 22 C1
Museum of Arms & Armour★ CV37 .... 145 A2
Mus of British Road Transport★ CV1 ...... 151 B3
Mus of Country Bygones★ CV23 .... 115 C7
Myatt Rd WR11 .... 127 D1
Myatt's Field WR11 ...... 127 D4
Myers Rd CV21 .... 101 C8
Mylgrove CV3 .... 77 D3
Mynors Cres B47 .... 69 A6
Myrtle Gr CV5 .... 60 F1
Mythe La CV9 .... 19 A8
Mythe View CV9 .... 12 E1
Myton Cres CV34 .... 109 C6
Myton Crofts CV31 ...... 109 D7
Myton Gdns CV34 .... 109 A6
Myton La CV34 .... 109 C6
Myton Rd CV31,CV34 ...... 109 B6
Myton Sch CV34 .... 109 B6
Mytton Rd B46 .... 22 F3

N

Nailcote Ave CV4 .... 75 C8
Nailcote La CV7 .... 75 A7
Nailsworth Rd B93 .... 71 D2
Nairn Cl CV10 .... 29 A2
Napier St CV1 .... 61 E3
Naples Rd CV35 .... 132 E5
Napton Ct CV22 .... 99 B6
Napton Dr CV32 .... 106 A2
Napton Gn CV5 .... 60 A3
Napton Ind Est CV47 .... 125 B8
Napton Rd CV47 .... 147 F8
Napton Rise CV47 .... 147 D4
Narberth Way CV2 .... 62 F8
Nares Cl CV22 .... 82 E1
Narrowboat Cl CV6 ...... 50 B6
Narrow Hall Mdw CV34 .. 108 B4
Narrow La
Lowsonford B95,CV35 .... 113 F6
Stratford-u-A CV37 ...... 144 F1
Narrows The [1] LE10 ...... 31 E8
Naseby Cl CV3 .... 78 F8
Naseby Rd CV22 .... 83 C1
Nash Croft B37 .... 44 B8
Nashes The CV37 .... 129 F7
Nash's La GL55 .... 135 E3
Nasmyth Rd NN11 .... 117 F3
Nathaniel Newton Inf Sch CV10 .... 28 B8
National Distribution Pk B46 .... 24 A5
National Ex Ctr B40 ...... 44 E4
National Herb Ctr★ OX17 .... 133 D1
National Motorcycle Mus The★ B92 .... 45 A2
Naul's Mill Ho CV1 ...... 151 B4
Navigation Way CV6 ...... 62 A8
Nayler Cl CV21 .... 83 C6
Neal Ct CV2 .... 63 A8
Neale Ave CV5 .... 60 A6
Neale Cl CV12 .... 40 C1
Neale's Cl CV33 .... 123 F7
Nebsworth La CV36 ...... 135 F5
Needhill Cl B93 .... 71 F6
Needle Cl B80 .... 103 E4
Needlers End La CV7 .... 74 A7
Neilston St [13] CV31 ...... 110 A7
Nellands Cl CV36 .... 136 B6
Nelson Ave CV34 .... 109 A8
Nelson Cl CV37 .... 131 A4
Nelson La CV34 .... 109 A8
Nelson St [7] CV1 .... 61 E4
Nelson Way CV22 .... 82 C1
Nemesia B77 .... 4 B4
Nene Cl CV3 .... 78 D7
Nene Side Cl NN11 ...... 126 F6
Nene Wlk NN11 .... 117 F1
Nesfield Gr B92 .... 57 B7
Nesscliffe Rd CV47 ...... 132 F5
Nethercote CV36 .... 140 F5
Nethercote Mdw CV36 .. 141 C4
Netherfield B98 .... 103 A8
Nethermill Rd [1] CV6 .... 61 A5
Nethersole CE Prim Sch The B78 .... 5 B2
Nethersole St B78 .... 5 A2
Netherwood Ind Est CV9 . 12 F1
Netherwood La B93 ...... 90 A7
Netting St OX15 .... 142 D4
Nevada Way B37 .... 33 C1
Nevill Cl CV31 .... 109 F6
Neville Ct [5] CV34 ...... 108 E6
Neville Gr CV34 .... 104 F1
Neville Rd
Birmingham B36 .... 22 E1
Solihull B90 .... 69 F8
Neville Wlk B35 .... 22 A2
Newall Cl CV23 .... 83 E5
New Ash Dr CV5 .... 59 F5
New Barn OX15 .... 138 F5
New Bldgs CV1 .... 151 C3
Newbold Cl
Bentley Heath B93 .... 71 F5
Coventry CV3 .... 62 F1
Newbold Comyn Pk★ CV32 .... 110 D8
Newbold Lawn CV32 .... 110 A8
Newbold Pl
Royal Leamington Spa CV32 .... 110 A8
Wellesbourne CV35 ...... 146 E4
Newbold Quarry Ctry Pk★ CV21 .... 82 E6
Newbold Rd
Armscote CV37 .... 136 E8
Rugby CV21 .... 83 A4
Rugby,Newbold on A CV21 .. 82 F6
Wellesbourne CV35 ...... 146 F5
Newbold Revel Coll CV23 . 65 C6
Newbold Riverside Prim Sch CV21 .... 82 E6
Newbold St CV32 .... 110 A8
Newbold Terr E CV32 .... 110 B8
Newbold Terr CV32 ...... 110 A8
Newbold & Tredington CE Prim Sch
Newbold-on-S CV37 ...... 130 E1
Tredington CV36 .... 136 F6
Newborough Cl CV9 .... 3 A2
New Broad St CV37 ...... 144 F1
New Brook St [3] CV32 .... 109 E8
Newburgh Cres CV34 .... 108 E8
Newburgh Prim Sch CV34 .... 108 C4
Newbury Cl [4] CV31 ...... 110 C6
Newbury Dr CV37 .... 144 E1
Newby Cl CV3 .... 77 E6
Newby Gr B37 .... 33 B5
Newcastle Croft B35 ...... 22 C3
New Century Pk CV3 ...... 62 C2
New Century Way CV11 .. 29 B4
New Cl CV35 .... 114 F3
New Combe Cl CV22 ...... 99 C3
Newcombe Rd CV5 .... 61 A1
Newcomen Cl CV12 ...... 49 D8
Newcomen Rd CV12 ...... 38 D1
New Coppice Ct B97 .... 102 E6
New Cotts CV37 .... 144 E2
Newdegate Cl CV12 ...... 39 A4
Newdegate Pl CV11 ...... 29 C4
Newdegate Rd CV12 ...... 39 A3
Newdegate St CV11 ...... 29 C4
Newdigate Prim Sch CV12 .... 38 C1
Newdigate Rd
Coventry CV6 .... 61 F6
Sutton Coldfield B75 ...... 13 A5
Newdigate CV31 .... 110 C5
New End Rd B46 .... 35 A4
Newent Cl B98 .... 112 A6
Newey Ave CV12 .... 49 D8
Newey Dr CV8 .... 93 A2
Newey Rd CV2 .... 62 D4
Newfield Ave CV8 .... 93 B3
Newfield Rd CV1 .... 61 C5
Newgale Wlk CV31 ...... 110 C7
New Gate Ct CV1 .... 151 C2
New Green Pk CV2 .... 62 D7
New Hall Inf Sch B75 ...... 13 B5
New Hall Jun Sch B75 .... 13 B5
Newhall Rd CV2 .... 62 D7
Newham Gn CV10 .... 28 C7
Newhaven Cl CV6 .... 60 E6
Newhouse Croft CV7 ...... 74 B6
Newing Ct WR11 .... 127 D4
Newington Cl CV6 .... 60 D6
Newington Rd B37 .... 44 B8
New Inn La WR11 .... 127 D5
Newland Cl B98 .... 103 B7
Newland La CV7 .... 49 B7
Newland Rd
Coventry CV1 .... 61 D5
Royal Leamington Spa CV32 .... 106 C3
Newlands Ct CV3 .... 61 F2
Newlands La B37 .... 44 A6
Newlands Rd
Baddesley Ensor CV9 ...... 11 C1
Bentley Heath B93 .... 71 F4
Newlands The B80 .... 103 D3
Newland St CV22 .... 82 E3
New Leasow B76 .... 22 A7
Newlyn Cl CV11 .... 29 F4
Newman Cl CV12 .... 39 B4
Newmarket Cl
Coventry CV6 .... 50 B4
Stratford-u-A CV37 ...... 129 F8
Newmarsh Rd B76 .... 22 A6
New Mill La B78 .... 9 A7
Newnham Ho B36 .... 33 B5
Newnham La B95 .... 120 C7
Newnham Rd
Coventry CV1 .... 61 F5
Royal Leamington Spa CV32 .... 106 B3
New Park Cotts OX15 ... 137 F2
New Place & Nash's Ho (Mus)★ CV37 .... 145 A2

New Pl OX17 . . . 134 C1
Newport Cl B97 . . . 102 B6
Newport Dr B49 . . . 143 B3
Newport Rd CV6 . . . 49 D1
Newquay Cl CV11 . . . 29 F5
New Rd
11 Moreton-in-M GL56 . . . 140 A3
Alderminster CV37 . . . 130 D3
Appleby Magna DE12 . . . 3 E7
Ash Green CV7 . . . 49 B6
Astwood Bank B96 . . . 118 C8
Corley CV12 . . . 37 F2
Coventry CV6 . . . 48 F1
Ebrington GL55 . . . 135 E3
Henley-in-A B95 . . . 113 A4
Hinckley LE10 . . . 32 A6
Hollywood B47 . . . 69 A8
Lowsonford CV35 . . . 113 E6
Norton Lindsey CV35 . . . 114 C2
Pebworth CV37 . . . 128 F1
Ratley OX15 . . . 133 A2
Shotteswell OX17 . . . 139 E8
Shuttington B79 . . . 1 D2
Studley B80 . . . 103 E3
Tamworth B77 . . . 9 F7
Temple Grafton B49 . . . 119 E1
Temple Herdewyke CV47 . . 133 A6
Water Orton B46 . . . 23 B3
New Row
Drayton Bassett B78 . . . 8 E5
Lower Quinton CV37 . . . 129 D2
Newscut La OX17 . . . 134 C1
Newsholme Cl 1 CV34 . . 104 E1
New St
Baddesley Ensor CV9 . . . 11 C1
Bedworth CV12 . . . 39 C2
Birchmoor B78 . . . 10 E7
Bulkington CV12 . . . 40 D2
Cubbington CV32 . . . 106 E5
Dordon B78 . . . 11 A5
Newstead Ave LE10 . . . 31 D4
Newstead Cl CV11 . . . 29 F2
Newstead Dr CV47 . . . 147 A3
Newstead Way CV3 . . . 63 B1
New St
Fazeley B78 . . . 9 B8
Kenilworth CV8 . . . 92 F6
Napton on t H CV47 . . . 125 C7
Royal Leamington Spa CV31 . . . 110 A7
Rugby CV22 . . . 82 E3
Shipston-on-S CV36 . . . 149 D5
Stratford-u-A CV37 . . . 144 F1
Tiddington CV37 . . . 145 E4
Warwick CV34 . . . 108 E6
Newton Cl
Coventry CV2 . . . 62 F7
Hartshill Green CV10 . . . 19 B2
Redditch B98 . . . 103 A6
Newton La
Newton CV23 . . . 68 A3
Newton Regis CV9 . . . 2 F2
Seckington B79 . . . 2 B3
Newton Manor La CV21, CV23 . . . 83 E7
Newton Rd
Clifton u D CV23 . . . 84 A7
Hinckley LE10 . . . 30 E7
Knowle B93 . . . 72 B7
Newton Regis CE Prim Sch B79 . . . 2 E3
Newtown Bldgs CV12 . . . 39 B3
New Town GL56 . . . 150 B8
Newtown Rd
Bedworth CV12 . . . 39 A2
Nuneaton CV11 . . . 29 C5
Newtown WR11 . . . 127 E1
New Union St CV1 . . . 151 B2
Nibbits La NN11 . . . 117 E5
Nicholas Chamberlaine Tec Coll CV12 . . . 39 D3
Nicholas Cl CV12 . . . 39 C3
Nicholas Everton Cl CV8 . . 80 A5
Nicholls St CV2 . . . 61 F4
Nicholson Cl CV34 . . . 104 F1
Nickson Rd CV4 . . . 59 E1
Nightingale Ave B36 . . . 33 A8
Nightingale Cl
Atherstone CV9 . . . 12 E1
Great Alne B49 . . . 119 D6
Nightingale Ct CV31 . . . 110 B8
Nightingale Gdns CV23 . . . 67 C1
Nightingale La
Cleeve Prior WR11 . . . 128 A4
Coventry CV5 . . . 76 E7
Nightingale B77 . . . 10 A6
Nimbus B77 . . . 9 D4
Nineacres Dr B37 . . . 33 A3
Nine Days La B98 . . . 103 B6
Ninefoot La
Tamworth,Belgrave B77 . . . 9 E8
Tamworth,Wilnecote B77 . . . 9 F7
Ninian Pk B77 . . . 9 D6
Ninian Way B77 . . . 9 E6
Niton Rd CV10 . . . 29 D6
Niven Cl CV5 . . . 60 A6
Noble Cl CV34 . . . 108 D5
Noble Dr CV22 . . . 99 A8
Node Hill Cl B80 . . . 103 D3
Node Hill B80 . . . 103 D3
Nod Rise CV5 . . . 60 B3
Noel Ct
Chipping Campden GL55 . . 135 B2
Redditch B97 . . . 102 C8
Nolan Cl CV6 . . . 49 D4
No Man's Heath La CV9 . . . 3 A3
Nook The CV11 . . . 29 E2
Norcombe Gr B90 . . . 71 A5
Nordic Drift CV2 . . . 63 A6
Norfolk Cl LE10 . . . 31 D4
Norfolk Cres CV10 . . . 28 E4
Norfolk St
Coventry CV1 . . . 61 B3
Royal Leamington Spa CV32 . . . 106 A1
Norluck Ct CV36 . . . 149 D6
Norman Ashman Coppice CV3 . . . 79 C7
Norman Ave
Coventry CV2 . . . 50 F1
Nuneaton CV11 . . . 29 B4
Normanby Mdws CV31 . . 110 A2
Normandy Cl CV35 . . . 108 A7
Normandy Way LE10 . . . 21 F2
Norman Place Rd CV6 . . . 60 F7
Norman Rd CV21 . . . 82 F6
Norsefair The B95 . . . 113 B4
Northampton La CV22 . . . 99 D4
North Ave
Bedworth CV12 . . . 39 D2
Birmingham B40 . . . 44 F5
Coventry CV2 . . . 62 A3
Northbourne Dr CV11 . . . 39 F7
North Brook Rd CV6 . . . 60 D8
North Circular Rd GL56 . . 140 C4
North Cl
Braunston NN11 . . . 117 E5
Cubbington CV32 . . . 106 E5
Hinckley LE10 . . . 31 E6
Northcote Rd CV21 . . . 82 F3
Northcote St 7 CV31 . . . 110 B7
Northcote Wlk CV9 . . . 12 D2
North Dr B95 . . . 113 B2
Northend Rd CV47 . . . 133 C7
Northey Rd CV6 . . . 61 D8
Northfield Rd
Coventry CV1 . . . 61 F2
Hinckley LE10 . . . 31 C7
Southam CV47 . . . 147 A3
Northfolk Terr CV4 . . . 76 B7
Northgate St CV34 . . . 108 E7
Northgate CV34 . . . 108 E7
Northlands Prim Sch CV21 . . . 83 B4
North Leamington Com Sch & Arts Coll CV32 . . . 105 F4
North Leamington Com Sch & Arts Coll (Sixth Form) CV32 . . . 105 F2
Northolt Dr B35 . . . 22 A4
North Rd CV23 . . . 83 F6
Northside Cl B98 . . . 102 E7
North St
Atherstone CV9 . . . 18 E8
Coventry CV2 . . . 62 B5
Kilsby CV23 . . . 101 F3
Marton CV23 . . . 115 C7
Nuneaton CV10 . . . 28 F3
Rugby CV21 . . . 83 A3
Northumberland Ave CV10 . . . 28 F3
Northumberland Lodge CV32 . . . 105 F3
Northumberland Mews CV32 . . . 105 F3
Northumberland Pk CV32 . . . 105 F3
Northumberland Rd
Coventry CV1 . . . 61 A3
Royal Leamington Spa CV32 . . . 105 E2
Northvale Cl CV8 . . . 93 B6
North View CV2 . . . 51 A1
North Villiers St CV32 . . . 106 A1
North Warwickshire & Hinkley Coll (Atherstone Coll) CV9 . . . 18 E8
North Warwickshire & Hinkley Coll
Hinckley LE10 . . . 31 F8
Nuneaton CV11 . . . 29 E6
Northway
2 Rugby CV21 . . . 83 A3
Birmingham B40 . . . 44 F5
Whitnash CV31 . . . 110 A5
Norton Curlieu La CV35 . 114 C3
Norton Dr
Warwick CV34 . . . 104 E2
Wythall B47 . . . 69 C4
Norton Gdns CV37 . . . 128 F1
Norton Grange CV5 . . . 60 C6
Norton Green La B93 . . . 72 C2
Norton Hill Dr CV2 . . . 62 E6
Norton La
Austrey CV9 . . . 3 D1
Orton-on-t-H CV9 . . . 6 D6
Tidbury Green B47,B90,B94 69 E3
Norton Lea CV35 . . . 114 C2
Norton Leys CV22 . . . 99 F6
Norton Rd B46 . . . 33 F8
Nortons Cl CV47 . . . 133 B7
Norton's La CV35 . . . 132 F3
Norton St CV1 . . . 151 C3
Norton View GL55 . . . 135 B6
Norval Cres WR11 . . . 127 D1
Norwich Cl CV11 . . . 30 A8
Norwich Dr CV3 . . . 77 B5
Norwood Gr CV2 . . . 50 E2
Norwood Ho 13 CV32 . . . 105 F2
Nova Croft CV5 . . . 59 C4
Nova Lodge CV32 . . . 105 E3
Nuffield Ho B36 . . . 33 A8
Nuffield Rd
Coventry CV6 . . . 62 A7
Hinckley LE10 . . . 30 E7
Nugent Gr B90 . . . 70 D3
Nuneaton Borough Football Club CV11 . . . 29 A4
Nuneaton La CV13 . . . 20 F2
Nuneaton Mus & Art Gal* CV11 . . . 29 C3
Nuneaton Rd
Ansley Common CV10 . . . 27 B6
Atherstone CV9,CV10 . . . 19 B4
Bedworth CV12 . . . 39 B4
Bulkington CV12 . . . 40 B4
Fillongley CV7 . . . 36 F4
Furnace End B46 . . . 25 E2
Furnace End,Monwode Lea B46 . . . 26 C5
Hartshill Green CV10 . . . 19 B2
Nuneaton Trent Valley Sta CV11 . . . 29 C5
Nunhold Farm Bsns Ctr CV35 . . . 114 D4
Nunts La CV6 . . . 49 B3
Nunts Park Ave CV6 . . . 49 B4
Nunwood La CV23 . . . 96 A2
Nursery Cl
Mickleton GL55 . . . 135 C7
Moreton-in-M GL56 . . . 140 A4
Nursery Gdns B90 . . . 69 E8
Nursery Hill Prim Sch CV10 . . . 27 E8
Nursery La CV31 . . . 110 A5
Nursery Rd
Ansley Common CV10 . . . 27 E8
Atherstone CV9 . . . 18 F7
Nutbrook Ave CV4 . . . 59 E2
Nuthurst Cres CV10 . . . 27 C3
Nuthurst Grange Rd B94 . 88 C4
Nuthurst Gr B93 . . . 72 A4
Nuthurst La CV10 . . . 27 D2
Nuthurst Rd B94 . . . 88 A2
Nuthurst B75 . . . 13 B4
Nutt's La LE10 . . . 31 A7
Nymet B77 . . . 9 E8

O

Oak Ave CV7 . . . 26 E2
Oak Cl
Baginton CV8 . . . 77 F2
Bedworth CV12 . . . 39 C4
Hinckley LE10 . . . 31 E5
Oak Ct
Coventry CV3 . . . 77 F7
Royal Leamington Spa CV34 . . . 109 E2
Oakdale Rd CV3 . . . 79 C7
Oakdene Cl CV35 . . . 113 F3
Oakdene Cres
Hatton CV35 . . . 114 C5
Nuneaton CV10 . . . 29 D7
Oakdene Ct CV37 . . . 144 F4
Oak Dr CV10 . . . 28 A8
Oakenhayes Cres B76 . . . 22 C5
Oakenshaw Rd B98 . . . 102 F8
Oakey Cl CV6 . . . 49 F4
Oak Farm Cl B76 . . . 22 A7
Oak Farm Craft Ctr* B78 . . 8 B5
Oakfield Gdns CV9 . . . 18 E7
Oakfield Ho
12 Royal Leamington Spa CV32 . . . 105 F2
Coventry CV3 . . . 63 A1
Oakfield Jun Sch CV9 . . . 18 E7
Oakfield Prim Sch CV22 . . 82 F2
Oakfield Rd
Coventry CV6 . . . 60 F5
Rugby CV22 . . . 82 F2
Oakfields Way B91 . . . 56 B5
Oakford Dr CV5 . . . 59 F6
Oakhall Dr B93 . . . 71 F4
Oakham Cl B98 . . . 103 A5
Oakham Cres CV12 . . . 40 D2
Oakham La NN11 . . . 126 D8
Oakham Rd GL56 . . . 141 A1
Oak Ho 7 CV34 . . . 109 D8
Oakington Dr B35 . . . 22 A3
Oak La
Barston B92 . . . 57 B2
Harvest Hill CV5 . . . 47 E1
Oaklands Croft B76 . . . 22 B7
Oaklands Ct CV8 . . . 93 A2
Oaklands B76 . . . 23 B6
Oaklands The
Birmingham B37 . . . 44 A7
Coventry CV4 . . . 60 A2
Oak Leigh CV33 . . . 123 D2
Oakleigh Rd CV37 . . . 144 E5
Oakley CV8 . . . 73 F1
Oakley Ct CV12 . . . 38 D1
Oakley Wood Rd CV33 . . . 122 F7
Oakmoor Rd CV6 . . . 50 A4
Oak Rd CV37 . . . 145 E4
Oakridge Rd CV32 . . . 106 C4
Oak Rise B46 . . . 33 F5
Oakroyd Cres CV10 . . . 28 D7
Oaks Pl CV6 . . . 50 A3
Oaks Prec CV8 . . . 92 E3
Oaks Rd CV8 . . . 92 E2
Oaks The
Bedworth CV12 . . . 38 F2
Portway B47 . . . 85 F8
Redditch B98 . . . 102 F7
Royal Leamington Spa CV32 . . . 109 D8
Sutton Coldfield B76 . . . 13 A3
Oak St CV22 . . . 83 A2
Oakthorpe Dr B37 . . . 33 A5
Oak Tree Ave CV3 . . . 77 A6
Oaktree Cl CV37 . . . 120 D7
Oak Tree Cl B93 . . . 71 E4
Oaktree Cl
Kingsbury B78 . . . 15 D6
Moreton Morrell CV35 . . . 122 E3
Oak Tree Cl CV32 . . . 106 A2
Oak Tree Ct CV32 . . . 106 A2
Oaktree Farm Mobile Homes Pk B94 . . . 86 B7
Oak Tree La
Cookhill B49 . . . 118 D5
Hollywood B47 . . . 69 B6
Sambourne B96 . . . 103 B2
Oak Tree Rd
Coventry CV3 . . . 79 A7
Harvington WR11 . . . 127 C4
Oak Trees B47 . . . 69 A7
Oak Way CV4 . . . 59 D2
Oakwood Cl CV9 . . . 11 C1
Oakwood Gr CV34 . . . 105 A1
Oakwood Rd B47 . . . 69 A6
Oakworth Cl CV2 . . . 62 F8
Oaston Rd CV11 . . . 29 D4
Oatlands Cl CV6 . . . 49 C4
Oban Dr CV10 . . . 29 A2
Oban Rd
Coventry CV6 . . . 49 F5
Hinckley LE10 . . . 31 A7
Oberon Cl
Nuneaton CV11 . . . 30 A1
Royal Leamington Spa CV34 . . . 109 E4
Rugby CV22 . . . 99 D6
Occupation Rd CV2 . . . 62 C3
Oddfellows' Terr 17 GL56 . . . 140 A3
Oddicombe Croft CV3 . . . 77 D5
Odingsel Dr CV47 . . . 115 C4
Odstone Dr LE10 . . . 30 F8
Offa Dr CV8 . . . 93 A4
Offa Rd CV31 . . . 110 B5
Offchurch La CV31 . . . 110 F6
Offchurch Rd CV32 . . . 106 E4
Offenham CE Fst Sch WR11 . . . 127 D1
Ogley Dr B75 . . . 13 A5
Okeford Way CV10 . . . 29 A1
Okehampton Rd CV3 . . . 77 E5
Okement Gr CV23 . . . 82 B5
Oken Ct CV34 . . . 108 D7
Oken Rd CV34 . . . 108 D8
Olaf Pl CV2 . . . 63 A7
Oldany Way CV10 . . . 28 F2
Oldberrow Cl 4 B90 . . . 71 A6
Oldborough Dr CV35 . . . 130 E8
Old Bowling Gn The CV36 . . . 149 D5
Old Brewery Cl CV36 . . . 149 E7
Old Budbrooke Rd CV35 . 108 A8
Oldbury Rd CV10 . . . 18 F1
Oldbury View CV10 . . . 19 B1
Oldbutt Rd CV36 . . . 149 C5
Old Chapel Wlk LE17 . . . 43 E6
Old Church Rd
Coventry CV6 . . . 50 A1
Water Orton B46 . . . 23 B3
Old Council Hos The OX15 . . . 139 D6
Old Courtyard The CV33 107 D7
Old Crown Mews CV2 . . . 50 D5
Old Damson La B92 . . . 44 A2
Old Dickens Heath Rd B90 . . . 70 A5
Old Farm La B46 . . . 25 A5
Old Farm Rd CV9 . . . 18 F6
Oldfield Rd CV5 . . . 60 E3
Old Ford Ave CV47 . . . 147 A5
Old Forge Bsns Ctr B98 . 103 C8
Old Forge Dr B98 . . . 103 C8
Old Forge Rd
Fenny Drayton CV13 . . . 20 A6
Great Rollright OX7 . . . 142 A2
Old Forge The OX15 . . . 142 F8
Old Fosse Way CV36 . . . 136 F7
Old Gated Rd The CV33, CV35 . . . 123 C4
Old Gram School Mews GL55 . . . 135 B2
Old Green La CV8 . . . 73 C1
Old Hall Ct B79 . . . 2 D3
Oldham Ave CV2 . . . 62 E4
Oldham Way CV23 . . . 82 B4
Old Hedging La B77 . . . 9 D5
Old Hinckley Rd CV10 . . . 29 D5
Old Holly La CV9 . . . 12 C3
Old House La CV7 . . . 48 A7
Oldington Gr B91 . . . 71 B8
Old Kingsbury Rd B76 . . . 22 C5
Old Langley Hall B75 . . . 13 C4
Old La B48 . . . 85 D4
Old Leicester Rd CV21 . . . 83 A7
Old Manor Cl B78 . . . 8 E5
Old Manor Gdns GL55 . . . 135 C6
Old Market Way 14 GL56 140 A3
Old Meeting Yd 1 CV12 . . 39 B3
Old Mill Ave CV4 . . . 76 D5
Old Mill Rd B46 . . . 33 F7
Old Milverton La CV32 . . . 105 E5
Old Milverton CV32 . . . 105 C3
Old Milverton Rd CV32 . . 105 C2
Old Orchard The
Birdingbury CV23 . . . 115 F7
Ebrington GL55 . . . 135 E3
Old Penns La B46 . . . 33 F7
Old Penn's Yd 4 CV12 . . . 39 A2
Old Pound Cotts CV36 . . . 137 A8
Old Pump Ho The WR11 . 127 E2
Old Rd
Bishops Itchington CV47 . . 124 B4
Braunston NN11 . . . 117 E4
Meriden CV7 . . . 46 E1
Ratley OX15 . . . 132 F2
Shipston-on-S CV36 . . . 149 D5
Southam CV47 . . . 147 B3
Old Rectory Cl CV23 . . . 67 C6
Old Rectory Gdn B49 . . . 143 B4
Old Rectory The CV37 . . . 130 A6
Old Red Lion Ct 5 CV37 . 145 A2
Old School Cl WR11 . . . 127 D1
Old School End OX15 . . . 142 D4
Old School La
Hampton Magna CV35 . . . 114 F3
Lighthorne CV35 . . . 123 C2
Wilmcote CV37 . . . 120 C4
Old School Mews CV32 . . 106 B3
Old School The CV36 . . . 149 D6
Old School Yd The B77 . . . 4 A5
Old Snitterfield Rd CV37 . 120 E7
Old Sq The CV37 . . . 144 D2
Old Sq CV34 . . . 108 E6
Old Station Rd B92 . . . 57 A8
Old Stone Yd CV32 . . . 105 E1
Old Tollgate The CV37 . . 145 D6
Old Town 23 GL56 . . . 140 A3
Old Town Mews CV37 . . . 144 F1
Old Town CV37 . . . 145 A1
Old Tree Cotts GL56 . . . 136 C1
Old Tree La CV35 . . . 138 B6
Old Vicarage Gdns B80 . . 103 E4
Old Walled Gdn The CV35 . . . 131 E7
Old Warwick Rd
Kingswood B94,CV35 . . . 89 D3
Rowington CV35 . . . 114 A7
Royal Leamington Spa CV31 . . . 109 E7
Old Waste La CV7 . . . 74 E6
Old Watling St CV9 . . . 11 E3
Oldwich La E
Balsall Common CV8 . . . 73 D1
Honiley CV8 . . . 90 E8
Oldwich La W B93 . . . 90 C8
Old Winnings Rd CV7 . . . 48 F6
Old Yd The CV2 . . . 62 F7
Olive Ave CV2 . . . 62 D5
Olivers Lock 8 CV37 . . . 145 A3
Oliver St
Coventry CV6 . . . 61 F6
Rugby CV21 . . . 82 F3
Olivier Way CV2 . . . 63 B8
Olney Rd CV35 . . . 132 D3
Olton Ave CV5 . . . 59 E4
Olton Cl CV11 . . . 41 A8
Olton Pl CV11 . . . 28 F4
Olympus Ave CV34 . . . 109 D5
Olympus Cl CV5 . . . 59 B8
Omar Rd CV2 . . . 62 D2
Ombersley Cl B98 . . . 103 C7
Omega Pl CV21 . . . 83 B4
Onley La CV22 . . . 100 D6
Onley Pk CV23 . . . 117 B8
Onley Terr CV4 . . . 76 C7
Onslow Croft CV32 . . . 105 F2
Openfield Croft B46 . . . 23 C2
Ophelia Dr CV34 . . . 109 E3
Oratory Dr CV3 . . . 78 C6
Orchard Cl
Austrey CV9 . . . 3 A2
Badby NN11 . . . 126 F6
Bidford-on-A B50 . . . 148 D4
Bishops Itchington CV47 . . 124 B4
Coleshill B46 . . . 33 F7
Curdworth B76 . . . 23 B7
Hartshill CV10 . . . 28 B7
Hinckley LE10 . . . 32 A5
Hurley CV9 . . . 16 C4
Lower Brailes OX15 . . . 137 F2
Mickleton GL55 . . . 135 C7
Polesworth B78 . . . 5 A3
Shipston-on-S CV36 . . . 149 D5
Tamworth B77 . . . 9 C5
Welford-on-A CV37 . . . 129 B6
Witherley CV9 . . . 19 B8
Wolvey LE10 . . . 41 D4
Orchard Cnr B49 . . . 119 E4
Orchard Cres CV3 . . . 77 C8
Orchard Ct
Atherstone CV9 . . . 18 D7
Coventry CV3 . . . 63 A1
Lower Quinton CV37 . . . 129 D2
Orchard Dr
Alcester B49 . . . 143 B3
Coventry CV5 . . . 59 C4
Orchard Gr
Astwood Bank B96 . . . 118 C8
Stockton CV47 . . . 147 F8
Orchard Ho CV6 . . . 50 A4
Orchard La CV8 . . . 93 C3
Orchard Meadow Wlk B35 . . . 22 B3
Orchard Piece OX17 . . . 134 A2
Orchard Pl
Clifford Chambers CV37 . . 129 F7
Harvington WR11 . . . 127 D4
Redditch B80 . . . 103 F8
Orchard Rd
Hockley Heath B94 . . . 88 C6
Hook Norton OX15 . . . 142 D4
Orchard Ret Pk CV3 . . . 78 D4
Orchard Rise
Baddesley Ensor CV9 . . . 11 C2
Binton CV37 . . . 120 A1
Orchard St CV12 . . . 39 B4

Orchards The
Astwood Bank B96 ...... **102** D1
Cheswick Green B90 ...... **70** D4
Hollywood B47 .... **69** A7
Newton CV23 .... **67** F1
Orchard St
Hinckley LE10 .... **31** E8
Nuneaton CV11 .... **29** D4
Orchard The
Baxterley CV9 .... **17** C7
Lower Quinton CV37 ..... **129** D2
Marton CV23 .... **115** C7
Staverton NN11 .... **126** D8
Upper Boddington NN11 .. **134** E8
Whatcote CV36 .... **137** E7
Orchard View OX17 ..... **134** C1
Orchard Way
Bubbenhall CV8 .... **95** D5
Hollywood B47 .... **69** A8
Long Itchington CV47 .... **115** C4
Nuneaton CV10 .... **28** C6
Rugby CV22 .... **99** D8
Southam CV47 .... **147** B5
Stratford-u-A CV37 ...... **144** E2
Stretton-on-D CV23 .... **96** F6
Studley B80 .... **103** E2
Orchid Cl CV12 .... **38** E2
Orchid Way CV23 .... **83** D8
Ordnance Rd CV6 .... **61** E5
Orford Cl CV35 .... **146** E3
Orford Rise CV10 .... **27** E4
Oriel Gr GL56 .... **140** A2
Oriel Ho B37 .... **33** A3
Orion Cres CV2 .... **50** E2
Orkney Cl CV10 .... **29** A2
Orkney Croft B36 .... **33** B7
Orkney Dr B77 .... **9** F7
Orlando Cl CV22 .... **99** D6
Orlescote Rd CV4 .... **76** E6
Orpington Dr CV6 .... **49** D4
Orrian Cl CV37 .... **144** E5
Orsino Cl CV34 .... **109** E2
Orson Leys CV22 .... **99** F7
Orton Ave B76 .... **22** A6
Orton Cl B46 .... **23** A3
Orton Hill CV9 .... **6** E8
Orton La
Austrey CV9 .... **6** B8
Orton-on-t-H CV9 .... **3** F2
Orton-on-t-H CV9 .... **6** D5
Orton-on-t-H CV9 .... **6** F2
Orton Rd
Coventry CV6 .... **49** D4
Warton B79,CV9 .... **5** E3
Orton Way B35 .... **22** A1
Orwell Cl
Clifton u D CV23 .... **84** A5
Nuneaton CV10 .... **28** A5
Orwell Ct CV1 .... **151** C4
Orwell Rd CV1 .... **61** F1
Osbaston Cl CV5 .... **59** E4
Osborne Ct 7 CV31 ..... **110** A4
Osborne Rd CV5 .... **77** A8
Osbourne Croft B90 ...... **70** D5
Osbourne Ho CV1 .... **151** A2
Oslo Gdns CV2 .... **63** A7
Osney Cl OX15 .... **142** D4
Osprey Cl
Coventry CV2 .... **63** B6
Nuneaton CV11 .... **40** B8
Osprey Ho B80 .... **103** D4
Osprey B77 .... **10** A6
Ossetts Hole La CV35 .... **113** E4
Oswald Rd CV32 .... **109** D8
Oswald Way CV22 .... **82** D3
Oswestry Cl B97 .... **102** C7
Oswin Gr CV2 .... **62** C4
Othello Ave CV34 .... **109** F3
Othello Cl CV22 .... **99** D5
Otter Cl B98 .... **112** A6
Otters Rest CV31 .... **110** C5
Ottery B77 .... **10** B5
Our Lady of the Angels RC Inf Sch CV11 .... **29** C3
Our Lady of the Assumption RC Prim Sch CV4 .... **59** E1
Our Lady Of the Wayside RC Prim Sch B90 .... **70** C8
Our Lady & St Teresa's RC Prim Sch CV32 .... **106** D5
Our Lady's RC Prim Sch
Alcester B49 .... **143** B4
Princethorpe CV23 .... **96** D2
Ousterne La CV7 .... **36** D3
Outermarch Rd CV6 ...... **61** C7
Outlands Dr LE10 .... **21** F1
Outwood Cl B98 .... **102** E7
Outwoods Cl CV9 .... **18** C7
Outwoods The LE10 ...... **31** F8
Oval Rd CV22 .... **100** D8
Overbare Cl B94 .... **87** A1
Overberry Cl CV2 .... **50** D2
Overberry Orch 5 CV33 . **122** E8
Overdale B96 .... **102** E1
Overdale Rd CV5 .... **60** C3
Overell Gr CV32 .... **105** D2
Overslade Cres CV6 ...... **60** E8
Overslade La CV22 .... **99** E8
Overslade Manor Dr CV22 **99** F8
Oversley Ho B49 .... **143** C4
Oversley Mill Pk B49 .... **143** B2
Oversley Rd B76 .... **22** A6
Over St CV6 .... **62** A8
Overstone Rd CV7 .... **52** F5
Overton Dr B46 .... **23** C3
Overtons Cl CV31 .... **110** F5
Overwoods Rd B77 .... **10** A4
Owenford Rd CV6 .... **61** C7
Owen Sq CV9 .... **18** D8
Owen St CV9 .... **18** D8
Owl End La NN11 .... **134** E7
Owl End Way NN11 ...... **134** E7
Owlets End B50 .... **148** F3
Ox Cl CV2 .... **62** A6
Oxendon Way CV3 .... **78** E8
Oxford Cl CV11 .... **29** F8
Oxford Pl 14 CV32 .... **105** F1
Oxford Rd
Marton CV23 .... **115** D7
Princethorpe CV8,CV23 .... **96** D4
Oxford Row 16 CV32 ..... **105** F1
Oxford St
16 Moreton-in-M GL56 ... **140** A3
Coventry CV1 .... **61** E3
Royal Leamington Spa CV32 .... **105** F1
Rugby CV21 .... **83** C3
Southam CV47 .... **147** B4
Oxford Way CV35 .... **146** B1
Oxhayes Cl CV7 .... **74** C6
Oxhey Hill OX17 .... **134** B2
Oxhill Bridle Rd CV35 ... **131** E3
Oxhill Rd CV35 .... **138** B6
Oxley Dr CV3 .... **77** C3
Ox Leys Rd B75,B76 .... **13** D3
Oxstall Cl B76 .... **22** D5
Oxstalls Cotts CV37 ..... **145** D6
Oxway Cl CV36 .... **149** D6

P

Packhorse Rd CV37 ..... **144** B4
Packington Ave CV5 ..... **60** B6
Packington La
Coleshill B46,CV7 .... **34** B2
Little Packington CV7 ..... **45** C6
Maxstoke B46 .... **35** B1
Packington Pl 6 CV31 .. **110** A7
Packmores B90 .... **70** A5
Packmore St CV34 ...... **108** F8
Packsaddle Hill CV37 .... **145** E8
Packwood Ave CV21 .... **101** C8
Packwood Cl
Bentley Heath B93 .... **71** E4
Nuneaton CV11 .... **39** F8
Royal Leamington Spa CV31 .... **110** C5
Packwood Cotts B93 ..... **71** F1
Packwood Gn CV5 .... **60** A3
Packwood Ho* B94 .... **89** A5
Packwood La B94 .... **89** A4
Packwood Mews 5 CV34 .... **109** B8
Packwood Rd B94 .... **89** A7
Paddiford Pl CV10 .... **28** C3
Paddock Cl
Bidford-on-A B50 .... **148** C5
Napton on t H CV47 ..... **125** C8
Paddock Dr B93 .... **72** A2
Paddock La
Redditch B98 .... **102** E7
Stratford-u-A CV37 ...... **144** E1
Paddocks Cl
Polesworth B78 .... **4** F1
Wolston CV8 .... **80** A3
Paddocks The
Bulkington CV12 .... **40** B3
Kenilworth CV8 .... **93** B5
Mollington OX17 .... **133** F2
Norton WR11 .... **127** B2
Stretton-on-D CV23 .... **96** F5
Warwick CV34 .... **108** F7
Paddock The
Claybrooke Magna LE17 ... **43** E6
Lower Boddington NN11 .. **134** E7
Newton CV23 .... **68** A1
Sutton Coldfield B76 ...... **13** A4
Paddock Way LE10 .... **30** E6
Paddox Cl CV22 .... **100** F8
Paddox Prim Sch
Rugby CV22 .... **100** D8
Rugby CV22 .... **100** E8
Padgate Cl B35 .... **22** B3
Padmore Ct CV31 .... **110** B6
Padstow Cl CV11 .... **29** F5
Padstow Rd CV4 .... **75** E8
Padua 3 CV37 .... **145** A3
Page Rd CV4 .... **75** E7
Pages La OX15 .... **139** B7
Paget Ct CV2 .... **50** B3
Paget Mews B76 .... **13** A2
Paget's La CV8 .... **95** D5
Pailton Cl CV2 .... **50** C2
Pailton Rd CV23 .... **66** B3
Painswick Cl B98 .... **102** E6
Pake's Croft 3 CV6 .... **61** A5
Palefield Rd B90 .... **70** F6
Palermo Ave CV3 .... **77** E6
Pallett Dr CV11 .... **29** F7
Palmer La CV1 .... **151** B3
Palmer Rd CV31 .... **110** B4
Palmer's Cl CV21 .... **101** B8
Palmers Leys 5 CV35 ... **132** B6
Palmerston Ave B77 .... **9** E6
Palmerston Ct B77 .... **9** F6
Palmerston Rd CV5 .... **76** F8
Palm Tree Ave CV2 .... **50** C2
Pampas Cl CV37 .... **144** E5
Pancras Cl CV2 .... **50** E1
Pandora Rd CV2 .... **62** E7
Pangbourne Cl CV11 ...... **29** F8
Pangbourne Rd CV2 .... **62** C8
Pangfield Pk CV5 .... **60** C4
Pantolf Pl CV21 .... **82** E7
Papenham Gn CV4 .... **76** A8
Parade CV32 .... **109** F8
Parade The
6 Hinckley LE10 .... **31** D8
Birmingham B37 .... **33** A5
Nuneaton CV11 .... **29** C3
Paradise Ho 4 CV6 ...... **61** F7
Paradise St
Coventry CV1 .... **151** C1
Rugby CV21 .... **83** C3
Warwick CV34 .... **108** F8
Paradise Way CV2 .... **51** B1
Paradise Works CV6 .... **61** F7
Paragon Pk CV1 .... **61** D6
Paragon Way CV7 .... **50** B8
Parbrook Cl CV4 .... **75** E8
Parbury B77 .... **9** D5
Parish End CV31 .... **110** C4
Parisienne Ho CV5 .... **60** E2
Park Ave
Coleshill B46 .... **33** F6
Coventry CV6 .... **49** C3
Nuneaton CV11 .... **29** E3
Polesworth B78 .... **11** B8
Studley B80 .... **103** E3
Park Cl
Avon Dassett CV47 ...... **133** C4
Claverdon CV35 .... **113** F3
Hanwell OX17 .... **139** F6
Hook Norton OX15 .... **142** D3
Kenilworth CV8 .... **93** B5
Wilmcote CV37 .... **120** C4
Park Cotts CV33 .... **115** B8
Park Croft B47 .... **69** A5
Park Ct
Allesley CV5 .... **60** B6
Stratford-u-A CV37 ...... **144** E4
Park Dr
Claverdon CV35 .... **113** F3
Royal Leamington Spa CV31 .... **109** E7
Parkend CV21 .... **83** C7
Parke Row CV35 .... **138** B6
Parkers La GL56 .... **140** A3
Parkes Ct CV34 .... **108** D7
Parkes St CV34 .... **108** D7
Park Farm Cl CV22 .... **82** D2
Park Farm Ind Est B98 .. **103** C7
Parkfield Cl B77 .... **9** C8
Parkfield Cres B77 .... **9** C8
Parkfield Ct 11 B46 ...... **33** F7
Parkfield B93 .... **72** A1
Parkfield Dr
Birmingham B36 .... **22** C1
Kenilworth CV8 .... **93** B5
Parkfield Rd
Coleshill B46 .... **33** F6
Keresley CV7 .... **49** A6
Rugby CV21 .... **82** E5
Parkfields CV47 .... **147** B4
Parkgate Prim Sch CV6 .. **49** B3
Parkgate Rd CV6 .... **49** C3
Park Gates CV33 .... **111** B8
Park Gr B46 .... **23** C2
Park Hall Cres B36 .... **22** C1
Park Hall Mews WR11 ... **127** E6
Park Hall WR11 .... **127** E6
Park Hall Sch B36 .... **22** E1
Parkhill Dr CV5 .... **60** A5
Park Hill OX15 .... **142** D4
Park Hill Jun Sch CV8 ..... **93** C5
Park Hill CV8 .... **93** B5
Park Hill La
Allesley CV5 .... **60** A6
Coventry CV5 .... **60** A5
Park Hill NN11 .... **116** F1
Park Hill Prim Sch CV5 ... **60** A4
Park Ho CV37 .... **121** B6
Parkinson Dr CV9 .... **12** E2
Park La
Astley CV10 .... **37** C5
Berkswell CV7 .... **58** B2
Birmingham,Castle Vale B35 .... **22** C4
Galley Common CV10 ..... **27** F3
Great Alne B49 .... **119** D6
Harbury CV33 .... **123** F6
Ilmington CV36 .... **135** F7
Lower Quinton CV37 ..... **129** D2
Lower Shuckburgh NN11 .. **116** F1
Parkland Cl CV6 .... **49** C3
Parklands Ave CV32 ..... **106** C4
Park Lane Prim Sch CV10 **27** F3
Park Lane Terr CV33 .... **123** F6
Park La
North Newington OX15 ... **139** E2
Snitterfield CV37 .... **121** C6
Southam CV47 .... **147** B4
Swalcliffe OX15 .... **142** F8
Park Paling The CV3 ..... **77** E7
Park Piece 2 CV35 ...... **132** B6
Park Rd
Baddesley Ensor CV9 ...... **11** B1
Bedworth CV12 .... **39** B2
Chipping Campden GL55 .. **135** A1
Coleshill B46 .... **33** F6
Coventry CV1 .... **151** B1
Hinckley LE10 .... **31** E8
Hook Norton OX15 .... **142** D4
Kenilworth CV8 .... **93** A6
Polesworth B78 .... **11** B8
Royal Leamington Spa CV32 .... **106** A4
Rugby CV21 .... **83** A4
Stratford-u-A CV37 ...... **144** F4
Tamworth B77 .... **9** C5
Parkside CV1 .... **151** C2
Parkside Ct LE10 .... **31** E8
Park Sq B37 .... **44** D8
Park St
Coventry CV6 .... **61** E7
Nuneaton CV11 .... **29** D3
Parkstone Rd CV6 .... **49** F2
Park St CV32 .... **105** F1
Park The
Lower Brailes OX15 ...... **137** F2
Stratford-u-A CV37 ...... **129** C8
Park View B96 .... **118** F3
Park View Cl CV7 .... **50** A8
Park View CV3 .... **62** A2
Parkview CV5 .... **151** A1
Park View B94 .... **88** C6
Park View La CV37 ...... **130** E1
Parkville Cl CV6 .... **49** C3
Parkville Highway CV6 ... **49** B3
Parkway CV2 .... **63** B8
Parkwood Ct CV8 .... **93** B5
Park Wood La CV4 .... **75** D7
Parmington Cl B97 ...... **102** B6
Parmiter Ho CV32 .... **105** F2
Parnell Cl CV21 .... **82** F3
Parolles Cl CV34 .... **109** E3
Parr Cl CV34 .... **109** D6
Parrish Cl CV47 .... **124** A4
Parrotts Gr CV2 .... **50** D5
Parry Rd CV2 .... **62** C7
Parsonage Cl 13 CV33 ... **122** F8
Parsons Cl
Shipston-on-S CV36 ...... **149** D5
Willey CV23 .... **54** F6
Parsons Hollow B77 .... **9** E7
Parson's La LE10 .... **31** F8
Parson's Nook CV2 .... **62** A5
Parsons Rd NN11 .... **117** F3
Parson St B77 .... **9** E7
Partridge Cl
Birmingham B37 .... **33** D3
Charwelton NN11 .... **126** D3
Partridge Croft CV6 ...... **50** A1
Partridge La B97 .... **102** A7
Partridge Rd CV37 ...... **144** C4
Pasture Way CV34 .... **108** B4
Patch La B98 .... **102** F6
Paterson Ct B93 .... **72** C6
Patience Gr CV34 .... **109** F3
Patricia Cl CV4 .... **59** C1
Pattens Rd CV34 .... **105** B1
Patterdale CV21 .... **83** D7
Patterton Dr B76 .... **22** A7
Pattison Coll CV3 .... **62** A2
Pauline Ave CV6 .... **50** B2
Paul Stacy Ho CV1 ...... **151** D4
Pavilions The B37 .... **44** E8
Pavilion The B77 .... **4** B3
Pavilion Way CV5 .... **60** F3
Paxmead Cl CV6 .... **49** A2
Paxton Rd CV6 .... **61** A4
Payne Cl CV32 .... **106** A2
Paynell Cl CV6 .... **49** B2
Payne's La CV1 .... **61** F3
Paynes La CV21 .... **82** D3
Payton St CV37 .... **145** A3
Peace Wlk B37 .... **33** B1
Peacock Ave CV2 .... **50** F1
Peacock Ct CV35 .... **146** D3
Peacock La CV35 .... **138** C7
Peacocks The CV34 ...... **108** B2
Peake Ave CV11 .... **29** E7
Pearl Hyde Com Prim Sch CV2 .... **63** A5
Pearl Hyde Ho 4 CV1 ... **151** C4
Pearmans Croft B47 ...... **69** A6
Pears Cl CV8 .... **92** F5
Pearson Ave CV6 .... **50** B2
Peart Dr B80 .... **103** C4
Pear Tree Ave
Kingsbury B78 .... **15** D5
Nuneaton CV10 .... **28** E6
Pear Tree Cl
4 Coventry CV2 .... **50** B2
Chipping Campden GL55 .. **135** B1
Long Marston CV37 ...... **129** B3
Shuttington B79 .... **4** E7
Pear Tree Gdns B95 ..... **119** F7
Peartrees CV47 .... **133** B7
Pear Tree Way CV22 ..... **82** B1
Peat Cl CV22 .... **82** E1
Pebblebrook Way CV12 ... **39** C1
Pebble Cl B77 .... **4** B3
Pebble Island Way CV31 . **110** C5
Pebworth Ave B90 .... **71** B6
Pebworth Cl CV5 .... **60** B3
Pebworth Dr CV35 .... **114** F6
Pebworth Fst Sch CV37 . **128** F1
Peckstone Cl CV1 .... **151** C1
Peddimore La B76 .... **22** C7
Pedmore Cl B98 .... **103** B7
Peel Cl
Coventry CV6 .... **61** E6
Drayton Bassett B78 .... **8** E5
Hampton-in-A B92 .... **57** B6
Peel Ct
Fazeley B78 .... **9** B8
Tamworth B77 .... **9** F6
Peel Dr B77 .... **9** F6
Peel La CV6 .... **61** F5
Peel Rd CV34 .... **108** E8
Peel St CV6 .... **61** E6
Pegasus Prim Sch B35 ... **22** B3
Pegmill Cl CV3 .... **77** F8
Pelham La B49 .... **119** D5
Pembridge Rd B93 .... **71** E3
Pembroke Cl
1 Warwick CV34 .... **108** F8
Bedworth CV12 .... **38** C1
Pembroke Ct 8 CV32 ... **105** F2
Pembroke Gdns CV35 ... **146** C1
Pembroke Way CV11 ..... **29** D3
Pembrook Rd CV6 .... **49** C2
Pembury Ave CV6 .... **50** A3
Penarth Gr CV3 .... **78** F7
Pencraig Cl CV8 .... **93** C5
Pendenis Cl CV6 .... **62** A8
Penderel Ct CV6 .... **49** C3
Pendicke Ct 8 CV47 ..... **147** B4
Pendicke St CV47 .... **147** B4
Pendigo Way
Birmingham B40 .... **44** E3
Birmingham B40 .... **44** F4
Pendine Ct 4 CV32 ..... **109** D8
Pendred Rd CV22 .... **82** E3
Pendrell Cl B37 .... **33** A3
Penelope Cl CV33 .... **123** F6
Penfold Cl 3 CV33 ...... **122** F8
Penmire Cl CV9 .... **11** C3
Pennant Rd LE10 .... **31** D5
Penn Ho CV4 .... **59** F1
Pennine Way
Nuneaton CV10 .... **28** B3
Tamworth B77 .... **10** C8
Pennington Mews CV21 .. **82** F3
Pennington St CV21 ...... **82** F3
Pennington Way CV6 ..... **61** E8
Penn La
Tanworth-In-A B94 .... **86** C4
Wibtoft LE17 .... **43** C2
Penns Cl CV32 .... **106** E5
Pennyford La B95 .... **113** B1
Penny Hapenny La CV9 ... **18** C8
Pennymoor Rd B77 .... **10** B7
Penny Park La CV6 .... **49** A3
Pennystone Cl CV31 ..... **110** D6
Penrhyn Cl 14 OX16 ..... **139** F4
Penrith Cl
Coventry CV6 .... **49** C2
Royal Leamington Spa CV32 .... **105** C2
Penrith Gr B37 .... **33** C2
Penrose Cl CV4 .... **76** A7
Penryhn Cl CV8 .... **93** C5
Penryn Cl CV11 .... **30** A4
Pensham Croft B90 ...... **71** A6
Penshurst Way CV11 ..... **39** F8
Pensilva Way 2 CV1 ..... **61** E4
Pentire Cl CV11 .... **29** F5
Penzance Way CV11 ...... **30** A5
Pepper La CV1 .... **151** B2
Pepys Cnr CV4 .... **59** E3
Perch Ave B37 .... **33** A3
Perchfoot Cl CV1 .... **151** C1
Percival Dr CV33 .... **123** F6
Percival Rd CV22 .... **100** D8
Percy Cres CV8 .... **92** E2
Percy Rd
Kenilworth CV8 .... **92** E2
Warwick CV34 .... **108** E8
Percy St
Coventry CV1 .... **151** A3
Stratford-u-A CV37 ...... **145** A4
Percy Terr 5 CV32 ...... **105** D1
Peregrine Dr CV5 .... **60** A5
Pericles Cl CV34 .... **109** E3
Perimeter Rd
Birmingham B40 .... **44** D4
Birmingham B40 .... **44** E4
Periwinkle Cotts WR11 .. **127** F6
Perkins Cl
Hornton OX15 .... **139** B8
Salford Priors WR11 ..... **127** F6
Perkins Gr CV21 .... **83** F1
Permian Cl CV21 .... **83** C6
Perryfields Cl B98 ...... **102** F6
Perryford Dr B91 .... **71** C8
Perryman Dr B78 .... **15** F8
Perrymill La B96 .... **103** B1
Perry Mill La B95 .... **112** E6
Pershore Pl CV4 .... **76** E6
Perth Rise CV5 .... **60** A4
Petard Cl B77 .... **9** C8
Peterbrook Cl B98 ...... **102** F7
Peterbrook Rd B90 .... **69** E8
Peter Hall La CV2 .... **64** B6
Peterlee Wlk 6 CV2 ...... **63** A7
Peters Wlk CV6 .... **50** A4
Petitor Cres CV2 .... **50** C1
Peto Gr CV34 .... **109** F2
Pettiford La B95 .... **113** C3
Pettiphers Farm CV37 ... **129** A3
Pettiver Cres CV21 .... **83** F1
Pettyfields Cl B93 .... **72** A5
Petunia Cl CV10 .... **39** A8
Peveril Dr CV3 .... **77** B5
Peyto Cl CV6 .... **49** C2
Pheasant Cl
Bedworth CV12 .... **38** D1
Stratford-u-A CV37 ...... **144** C4
Pheasant Croft B36 ...... **33** A8
Pheasant La B98 .... **102** F7
Pheasant Oak CV4 .... **59** C2
Philip Ct
1 Royal Leamington Spa CV31 .... **109** F6
Rugby CV21 .... **83** B4
Phillip Docker Ct CV12 ... **40** B2
Phillippes Rd 6 CV34 ... **104** F1
Phipps Ave CV21 .... **83** F1
Phoebe Cl CV34 .... **109** E3
Phoenix Bsns Pk LE10 .... **30** E8
Phoenix Ct B35 .... **22** A3
Phoenix Pk Ind Est CV7 .. **50** B7
Phoenix Way CV6 .... **49** E3
Piccadilly Cl B37 .... **33** C1

Piccadilly Cres B78 9 F1
Piccadilly B78 9 F1
Pickard Cl CV21 83 E7
Pickard St CV34 109 A7
Pickford Cl CV11 30 A1
Pickford Grange La CV5 59 C7
Pickford Green La CV5 59 C7
Pickford Way CV5 60 B6
Picton Croft 6 B37 33 D2
Piers Cl CV34 108 F8
Pike Cl LE10 31 D5
Pike Dr B37 33 C3
Pikehorne Croft B36 22 D2
Pikers La CV7 48 A3
Pilgrims Gate LE10 32 A6
Pilgrims La CV23 67 F1
Pilgrims Wlk CV6,CV7 49 B6
Pilkington Rd CV5 76 D8
Pillerton Rd CV35 131 F4
Pilling Cl CV2 62 F8
Pill La GL56 140 F1
Pimlico La CV37 121 D2
Pinbury Croft B37 33 B1
Pinchester Cl GL56 141 A1
Pinders Ct 3 CV21 83 B3
Pinders La CV21 83 B4
Pine Cl
Stoke Golding CV13 21 E7
Stratford-u-A CV37 144 D1
Pine Ct
Coventry CV5 59 C4
Royal Leamington Spa CV32 106 B3
Pine Gr CV21 84 A1
Pineham Ave CV33 123 F6
Pinehurst CV32 106 E6
Pine Sq B37 33 B2
Pines The
Bedworth CV12 38 E2
Cheswick Green B90 70 D5
Coventry CV4 75 D7
Pine Tree Ave CV4 60 A2
Pine Tree Cres CV47 147 C5
Pine Tree Ct CV12 39 C4
Pine Tree Rd CV12 39 D4
Pinewood Ave CV9 10 C1
Pinewood Bsns Pk B37 44 B8
Pinewood Dr CV3 79 C7
Pinewood Gr CV5 77 B8
Pinfold Cl LE10 30 F7
Pinfold Gn NN11 126 F6
Pinfold St CV21 82 E3
Pingle Ct CV11 29 D2
Pink Green La B98 112 A8
Pinley Fields CV3 78 B8
Pinnacle Ho B97 102 E5
Pinner's Croft CV2 62 A5
Pinnock Pl CV4 59 F1
Pinwall La CV9 12 E4
Pioneer Ho CV1 151 D4
Pioneer Way B35 22 B2
Pipe La CV9 6 C4
Piper's Bath CV35 123 A2
Pipers Ct CV3 76 F4
Piper's End LE10 41 D4
Pipers La CV10 27 C8
Piper's La CV8 93 A5
Pipers Rd B98 103 D7
Pipewell Cl CV22 82 C1
Pipit Wlk CV23 67 C1
Pipkin Ct CV1 151 D1
Pippin Cl B50 148 D5
Pirie Cl CV33 123 F6
Pit Hill CV8 95 C5
Pitmaston Cl 10 OX16 139 F5
Pitt La B92 44 D2
Pittoms La CV23 101 C1
Pittway Ave CV36 149 C6
Pixhall Wlk B35 22 B3
Plain Rd The OX15 139 A3
Plane Cl CV10 28 E7
Plane Gr B37 33 B1
Plank La B46 23 A2
Plantagenet Dr CV22 99 E6
Plantagenet Pk CV34 109 E3
Plantation The OX17 134 C1
Planter Cl CV22 99 A8
Plants Brook Rd B76 22 A6
Plants Hill Cres CV4 59 E1
Plato Cl CV34 109 E5
Pleasant Way CV32 106 A2
Pleck Cl B50 148 D4
Pleck The B50 148 D4
Plexfield Rd CV22 82 C1
Pleydell Cl CV3 78 C5
Plomer Cl CV22 99 C8
Plot Rd OX15 139 A3
Plott La CV23 96 E6
Plough Hill Rd CV10 28 A6
Plough La CV47 124 A4
Ploughmans Holt CV47 147 B6
Plover Cl
Alcester B49 143 B5
Stratford-u-A CV37 144 D5
Plowden Cl NN11 134 F5
Plowman St CV21 82 F3
Plymouth Cl CV2 62 C7
Plymouth Pl CV31 110 A7
Poins Cl CV34 109 F3
Poitiers Rd CV3 77 D6
Poland Ave CV37 129 D2
Polesworth High Sch B78 10 F7
Polesworth Sta B78 5 A3
Polperro Dr CV5 60 A5
Pomeroy Cl CV4 75 D7
Pond Farm Mews CV5 59 E5
Pondthorpe CV3 78 E6
Pontrilas Rd CV35 132 D4
Pontypool Ave CV3 78 F6
Pool Bank St CV11 29 B4
Pool Cl GL56 140 F1
Pool Close Cotts GL56 140 F1
Pool Cl
Rugby CV22 99 D8
Welford-on-A CV37 129 B6
Pool End Cl B93 71 F6
Poole Rd CV6 61 A6
Pooley Fields Heritage Ctr* B78 5 A3
Pooley La B78 4 F2
Pooley View B78 5 A2
Poolgate CV35 138 B6
Poolhead La
Earlswood B94 86 C7
Tanworth-In-A B94 86 E5
Pool Mdw B76 22 A8
Pool Rd
Nuneaton CV10 28 F5
Studley B80 103 E4
Pool Road Bsns Ctr CV10 28 F5
Poolside Gdns CV3 77 A5
Popes La B96 102 E2
Pope St CV22 82 E3
Poplar Ave
Bedworth CV12 39 D2
Birmingham,Coleshill Heath B37 44 C8
Poplar Cl
Alcester B49 143 D3
Knightcote CV47 124 B1
Poplar Dr B95 113 B2
Poplar Gr
Rugby CV21 83 A4
Ryton-on-D CV8 79 B1
Poplar Ho CV12 39 D2
Poplar N B95 113 B2
Poplar Rd
Bishops Itchington CV47 124 B4
Coventry CV5 60 F1
Dorridge B93 71 F3
Napton on t H CV47 125 C8
Poplars Cl GL55 135 A1
Poplars La B96 102 A1
Poplars The
Bidford-on-A B50 148 E5
Hartshill Green CV10 19 B2
Napton on t H CV47 125 B8
Nuneaton CV10 28 D3
Poplars Trad Est B80 103 D6
Poplar Terr CV37 121 D3
Poplar Trees B47 69 A6
Poplar Way WR11 127 D4
Poppy Cl CV10 39 A8
Poppy Ct CV3 78 D6
Poppy Dr CV23 83 E8
Poppyfield Ct CV4 76 D3
Porchester Cl CV3 63 A2
Porlock Cl CV3 77 E5
Porter Cl CV4 75 E8
Portia Cl CV11 30 A1
Portia Way CV34 109 E3
Portland Ct 9 CV32 109 F8
Portland Dr CV10 28 C4
Portland Mews 10 CV32 109 F8
Portland Pl E CV32 109 F8
Portland Pl CV21 83 D2
Portland Pl W 5 CV32 109 E8
Portland Rd CV21 83 D2
Portland St CV32 109 F8
Portleys La B78 8 D4
Portmanteau Mews B94 88 C6
Portreath Dr CV11 30 A5
Portree Ave CV3 62 F2
Portsea Cl CV3 77 D6
Portway Cl
Coventry CV4 75 E8
Royal Leamington Spa CV31 110 D6
Portwrinkle Ave CV6 62 A6
Poseidon Way CV34 109 F4
Postbridge Rd CV3 77 D5
Post House Gdns CV23 66 A8
Postle Cl CV23 101 F2
Post Office La
Lighthorne CV35 123 B2
Stockton CV47 147 F8
Witherley CV9 19 B7
Post Office Rd CV9 11 C1
Post Office Row CV10 37 E7
Post Office Wlk B96 102 E1
Post Office Yd CV23 64 F4
Potters Cl CV23 64 E3
Potters Green Prim Sch CV2 50 E2
Potters Green Rd CV2 50 E1
Potters La
Darlingscott CV36 136 D5
Polesworth B78 11 A8
Potters Rd CV12 38 E1
Potton Cl CV3 78 E6
Potts Cl CV8 93 C4
Poultney Rd CV6 61 A6
Pound Cl
Berkswell CV7 58 D3
Lapworth B94 89 B3
Shipston-on-S CV36 149 D6
Pound Field B95 113 B2
Pound House La
Nuthurst B94 88 A4
Tanworth-in-A B94 87 F4
Pound La
Badby NN11 126 F6
Coleshill B46 34 A4
Pound La *continued*
Furnace End B46 25 D4
Mickleton GL55 135 B6
Royal Leamington Spa CV32 106 A3
Sibford Gower OX15 138 D1
Pound The
Harbury CV33 123 F7
North Newington OX15 139 D2
Pound Way CV47 147 C4
Poverty B96 102 E2
Powell Cl 17 CV33 122 F8
Powell Rd CV2 62 A4
Powell Way CV11 29 C4
Powers Ct 4 CV32 105 F1
Powis Gr CV8 93 C5
Powys Gr OX16 139 F4
Poyser Rd CV10 39 C8
Pratts La B80 112 A4
Preachers Homes CV7 36 E4
Prebend The CV47 133 B7
Precision Way B49 143 C6
Prentice Cl CV23 82 B5
Prescelly Cl CV10 28 B3
Prescelly Ct CV8 92 F5
Prescott Ave OX16 139 F3
President Kennedy Sch & Com Coll CV6 49 B4
Prestbury Cl B98 112 A6
Preston Cl CV4 75 F7
Preston Fields La B95 113 D6
Preston La CV37 130 A4
Prestwick Rd B35 22 B4
Pretorian Way CV21 83 A7
Prew Cotts OX7 142 A2
Priam Cir CV34 109 F3
Price Cl E CV34 108 B4
Price Cl W CV34 108 B4
Price Rd CV32 106 E5
Pridmore Rd CV6 61 D7
Priestfield Rd B97 102 E5
Priesthills Rd LE10 31 D8
Priest Meadow Cl B96 102 D1
Primary Wlk CV22 99 B8
Primley Ave B77 9 F5
Primrose Cl CV23 83 E8
Primrose Ct
Harborough Magna CV23 66 B3
Moreton-in-M GL56 140 A3
Primrose Dr
Bedworth CV12 38 E1
Hinckley LE10 31 E5
Primrose Hill St CV1 151 C4
Primrose Hill CV34 104 E2
Primrose La
Alcester B49 143 C2
Solihull B90 70 A5
Primsland Cl B90 71 C7
Prince Harry Rd B95 113 B4
Prince Of Wales Rd CV5 60 E3
Prince Regent Ct 3 CV31 109 F6
Prince Rupert Cl CV47 133 A6
Prince's Ave CV11 29 B3
Princes Cl CV3 78 B8
Princes Ct CV21 83 A4
Princes Dr
Coventry CV6 50 B1
Kenilworth CV8 93 B7
Prince's Dr CV31 109 D7
Princes Rd CV9 16 C5
Prince's Rd B78 5 B2
Princess Rd
Atherstone CV9 18 E8
Hinckley LE10 31 E8
Princess St CV6 61 F7
Prince's St
Nuneaton CV11 29 C3
Royal Leamington Spa CV32 106 B1
Princes St CV21 83 A4
Princethorpe Coll CV23 96 C3
Princethorpe Way CV3 78 E8
Prince William Cl CV6 60 E6
Printers Pl CV37 144 F3
Prior Deram Wlk CV4 76 C7
Priors Cl CV7 74 B6
Priors Ct CV47 125 E4
Priors Field Prim Sch CV8 92 D7
Priorsfield Rd
4 Coventry CV6 61 A4
Kenilworth CV8 92 D6
Priorsfield Rd N 3 CV6 61 A4
Priorsfield Rd S CV6 61 A4
Priors Grange WR11 127 F6
Priors Harnall CV1 151 D4
Priors Marston Rd NN11 126 B5
Priors Mdw CV47 147 C4
Priors Sch CV47 125 F4
Priors The CV12 39 C2
Priory Cl
Coleshill B46 34 A5
Kingswood B94 89 D5
Priory Croft CV8 93 A4
Priory Ct
Coventry CV5 61 A1
Nuneaton CV11 29 A4
Solihull B90 71 B7
Studley B80 103 E5
Priory Ho CV8 92 F4
Priory La CV35 131 D2
Priory Mews CV34 108 E7
Priory Pl CV1 151 C3
Priory Rd
Alcester B49 143 B3
Kenilworth CV8 93 A4
Warwick CV34 108 E7
Priory Rd *continued*
Wolston CV8 80 B4
Priory Row CV1 151 C3
Priory Sq B80 103 E5
Priory St
Coventry CV1 151 C3
Nuneaton CV10 28 D3
Royal Leamington Spa CV31 109 F6
Priory Terr CV31 110 A7
Priory Visitors Ctr* CV1 151 C3
Priory Wlk
10 Warwick CV34 108 F7
Atherstone CV9 18 F6
Privet Rd CV2 50 B2
Proctor Way CV37 144 A4
Proffitt Ave CV6 50 A1
Progress Cl CV3 79 A7
Progress Way CV3 79 A8
Projects Dr CV21 83 C6
Prologis Pk CV6 49 B5
Prospect Rd CV31 110 B5
Prospect Way
Daventry NN11 117 F2
Rugby CV21 83 D5
Prospero Dr CV34 109 E3
Prossers Wlk B46 33 F7
Providence St CV5 76 F8
Provost Williams CE Prim Sch CV8 79 A1
Ptarmigan Pl CV11 29 F3
Puckering's La 11 CV34 108 E6
Pudding Bag La CV23 98 F2
Pudlicott La GL55 135 E1
Pughe's Cl LE10 32 A6
Pullman Cl B77 4 A2
Puma Way CV1 151 C1
Pumphouse Cl CV6 50 B6
Pump La CV7 36 C3
Purbrook B77 9 E8
Purcell Ave CV11 40 A7
Purcell Cl CV32 110 A8
Purcell Rd CV6 62 B8
Purefoy Rd CV3 77 D8
Purley Chase La CV9 18 D4
Purley View CV9 18 F6
Purlieu La CV8 92 D5
Purnells Way B93 72 A5
Purser Dr CV34 108 B4
Purton Cl B49 143 C5
Purton Mews CV31 110 C6
Putney Wlk B37 33 B3
Pye Ct CV23 117 B6
Pyeharps Rd LE10 31 E5
Pyree Sq CV34 108 B4
Pytchley Rd CV22 83 C1
Pytman Dr B76 22 A7
Pyt Pk CV5 60 D4

Q

Quadrangle The B90 70 E8
Quadrant The
Coventry CV1 151 B2
Nuneaton CV11 29 E3
Quail Cl CV37 144 C4
Quaker Cl CV13 20 A6
Quantock Dr CV10 28 B3
Quarry Berry La DE12 2 E8
Quarry Cl
Leek Wootton CV35 104 F7
Rugby CV21 82 F7
Quarryfield La CV1 151 D1
Quarry Fields CV35 104 F7
Quarry La
Cleeve Prior WR11 128 A4
Nuneaton CV11 29 F1
Rowington Green CV35 90 C1
Quarry Rd
Atherstone CV9 18 E4
Kenilworth CV8 92 E6
Quarry St CV32 109 C8
Quarrywood Gr CV2 62 A4
Quarry Yd CV10 28 C4
Queen Eleanors Dr B93 72 B8
Queen Elizabeth Rd CV10 28 D5
Queen Elizabeth Sch CV9 18 F7
Queen Isabel's Ave CV3 77 D8
Queen Margaret's Rd CV4 76 C8
Queen Mary's Rd
Bedworth CV12 39 C5
Coventry CV6 61 E8
Queen Philippa St CV3 77 D6
Queens Arc CV11 29 C4
Queens Ave CV36 149 C5
Queens CE Jun Sch CV11 29 A4
Queens Cl CV33 123 F6
Queen's Cl CV8 92 F3
Queens Cl CV36 149 D6
Queen's Cres OX15 139 E4
Queen's Ct 5 CV37 144 F1
Queens Ct CV11 29 A4
Queen's Dr CV35 90 A1
Queensferry Cl CV22 99 C8
Queensland Ave CV5 60 F2
Queensland Gdns 4 CV12 38 F2
Queen's Own Hussars Mus The* CV34 108 E6
Queen's Park Ct 3 LE10 31 E8
Queen's Park Flats 2 LE10 31 E8
Queen's Park Terr 4 LE10 31 E8
Queen's Rd CV9 18 E8
Queens Rd CV23 80 E7
Queen's Rd
Coventry CV1 151 A2
Queen's Rd *continued*
Hinckley LE10 31 E8
Kenilworth CV8 92 F3
Nuneaton CV11 29 B4
Queens Rd CV36 136 F6
Queen's Sq CV34 108 D5
Queens St CV36 136 F8
Queen St
Astwood Bank B96 102 E1
Bedworth CV12 39 C2
Coventry CV1 151 C4
Cubbington CV32 106 E5
Hook Norton OX15 142 D4
Royal Leamington Spa CV32 106 A1
Rugby CV21 83 A3
Queensway B50 148 C5
Queens Way
Dordon B78 10 F6
Hurley CV9 16 C4
Queensway
Nuneaton CV10 29 E6
Royal Leamington Spa CV31 109 E6
Queensway Trad Est CV31 109 E6
Queenswood Ct CV7 48 D4
Queen Victoria Rd
Coventry CV1 151 B2
Coventry CV1 151 B3
Queen Victoria St CV21 83 C3
Quilletts Cl CV6 50 A1
Quince B77 4 B3
Quince Tree Sch B77 4 A3
Quiney's Leys CV37 129 A7
Quiney's Rd CV37 144 D2
Quinn Cl CV3 78 B7
Quinneys Ct B50 148 E4
Quinneys La
Bidford-on-A B50 148 E5
Redditch B98 103 B6
Quinton Cl CV35 114 E6
Quintondale 5 B90 70 C8
Quinton Flats CV3 77 D7
Quinton Grange CV37 129 E1
Quinton Par CV3 77 D7
Quinton Pk CV3 77 D7
Quinton Prim Sch CV37 129 D2
Quinton Rd CV1 151 C1
Quorn Way CV3 78 E7

R

Race Leys Inf Sch CV12 39 B3
Race Leys Jun Sch CV12 39 B4
Racemeadow Prim Sch CV9 12 E1
Racemeadow Rd CV9 12 E1
Radbourne Cl CV47 147 C3
Radbourne La CV47 124 E5
Radbrook Way CV31 110 D6
Radburn Cl GL56 140 B3
Radcliffe Gdns 6 CV31 110 A6
Radcliffe Rd CV5 76 F8
Radford Circ 5 CV6 61 A4
Radford Cl CV9 12 E2
Radford Hall CV31 110 E6
Radford Ho CV6 61 A7
Radford Prim Sch CV6 61 B5
Radford Rd
Coventry CV1,CV6 61 B5
Royal Leamington Spa CV31 110 C7
Radford Semele CE Prim Sch CV31 110 E5
Radley Dr CV10 29 A1
Radlow Cres B37 44 B8
Radnor Dr CV10 28 E2
Radnor Wlk CV2 62 F8
Radway Ind Est B90 70 E7
Radway Rd B90 70 E8
Raglan Cl CV11 29 D4
Raglan Ct 7 CV1 61 E3
Raglan Gr CV8 93 B5
Raglan St CV1 151 D3
Raglan Way B37 33 D1
Ragley Cl B93 72 B7
Ragley Hall* B96 118 F2
Ragley Mill La B49 143 B4
Ragley Rd WR11 127 D4
Ragley Way CV11 29 F2
Railway Cl B80 103 D4
Railway Cres CV36 149 D7
Railway Mews B49 143 B4
Railway St CV23 82 A4
Railway Terr
Atherstone CV9 18 D8
Bedworth CV12 39 C2
Rugby CV21 83 B4
Rainbow Fields CV36 149 D6
Rainsbrook Ave CV22 100 F8
Rainsbrook Cl CV47 147 D4
Rainsbrook Dr
Nuneaton CV11 30 A1
Solihull B90 70 F6
Rainsbrook Secure Training Ctr CV23 100 C1
Rainsbrook Valley Rly* CV22 100 C6
Rainscar B77 10 B7
Rainsford Cl CV37 129 F7
Raison Ave CV11 29 F8
Raleigh Rd CV2 62 B2
Ralph Cres B78 15 C6
Ralph Rd CV6 60 F5
Rambures Cl CV34 109 F3
Ramp Rd B26 44 C5

Ramsay Cres CV5 . . . . 60 B7
Ramsay Gn CV35 . . . . 146 D4
Ramsden Ave CV10 . . . . 28 D6
Ramsden Ct CV10 . . . . 28 C7
Ramsden Rd CV9 . . . . 19 A7
Ramsey Rd CV31 . . . . 110 B7
Ramshill La B94,B95 . . . . . 112 E7
Ranby Rd CV2 . . . . 61 F4
Randall Rd CV8 . . . . 92 F3
Randle Rd CV10 . . . . 28 D4
Randle St CV6 . . . . 61 B5
Randolph Cl 11 CV31 . . . . . 110 C6
Ranelagh St CV31 . . . . 110 A6
Ranelagh Terr CV31 . . . . . 109 F6
Range Meadow Cl CV32 . 105 C3
Rangemoor CV3 . . . . 78 D6
Range Way B78 . . . . 15 D5
Rangeworthy Cl B97 . . . . 102 C7
Rankine Cl CV21 . . . . 82 D7
Rannoch Cl LE10 . . . . 31 B8
Rannoch Dr CV10 . . . . 28 C5
Rannock Cl CV3 . . . . 62 F2
Ransome Rd CV7 . . . . 37 A8
Ransom Rd CV6 . . . . 61 E8
Ran-tan The B97 . . . . 102 E5
Ranulf Croft CV3 . . . . 77 C7
Ranulf St CV3 . . . . 77 C7
Raphael Cl CV5 . . . . 60 C3
Rashwood Cl B94 . . . . 88 B6
Ratcliffe Ct CV10 . . . . 28 C4
Ratcliffe La CV9 . . . . 12 F4
Ratcliffe Rd
Atherstone CV9 . . . . 12 E1
Hinckley LE10 . . . . 31 F6
Ratcliffe St CV9 . . . . 18 D8
Rathbone Cl
Keresley CV7 . . . . 48 F6
Keresley CV7 . . . . 49 A6
Rugby CV21 . . . . 101 A8
Rathlin Croft B36 . . . . 33 B6
Ratliffe Rd CV22 . . . . 99 F7
Rattlecombe Rd OX15 . . . 138 E5
Raveloe Dr CV11 . . . . 29 D1
Raven Cragg Rd CV5 . . . . . 76 E8
Ravenglass CV21 . . . . 83 D7
Ravensdale Ave CV32 . . . 105 C2
Ravensdale Prim Sch CV2 62 D4
Ravensdale Rd CV2 . . . . . . 62 D3
Ravenshaw La B91 . . . . 56 A4
Ravenshaw Way B91 . . . . . 56 A3
Ravensholt CV4 . . . . 76 D6
Ravensthorpe Cl CV3 . . . . . 78 E8
Ravenstone B77 . . . . 10 B8
Ravenswood Hill B46 . . . . . 33 F7
Raven Way CV11 . . . . 29 F2
Rawlins Croft B35 . . . . 22 C3
Rawlinson Rd CV32 . . . . . 106 B2
Rawnsley Dr CV8 . . . . 93 C6
Rawn View CV9 . . . . 18 F6
Raygill B77 . . . . 10 B8
Raymond Cl CV6 . . . . 49 F5
Raynor Cres CV12 . . . . 38 D1
Raynsford Wlk CV34 . . . . 104 D1
Raywoods The CV10 . . . . . . 28 F3
Reading Ave CV11 . . . . 29 F7
Reading Cl CV2 . . . . 50 B3
Readings The CV47 . . . . . 133 E7
Read St CV1 . . . . 61 E3
Reardon Ct CV34 . . . . 104 E1
Recreation Rd CV6 . . . . 50 A3
Rectory Cl
Allesley CV5 . . . . 60 C6
Barby CV23 . . . . 101 C1
Bedworth CV7 . . . . 39 A1
Drayton Bassett B78 . . . . . . 8 E5
Harvington WR11 . . . . . . 127 D3
Stockton CV47 . . . . 147 F8
Warmington OX17 . . . . . . 133 D2
Whitnash CV31 . . . . 110 B4
Rectory Dr CV7 . . . . 39 A1
Rectory Gdns OX15 . . . . . 139 E4
Rectory La
Allesley CV5 . . . . 60 C6
Barby CV23 . . . . 101 C1
Lower Brailes OX15 . . . . . 137 F2
Whatcote CV36 . . . . 137 D7
Rectory Rd
Hook Norton OX15 . . . . . . 142 D4
Old Arley CV7 . . . . 26 E1
Sutton Coldfield B75 . . . . . 13 A6
Redcap Croft CV6 . . . . 49 D4
Redcar Cl CV32 . . . . 106 C4
Redcar Rd CV1 . . . . 61 E5
Red Deeps CV11 . . . . 39 D8
Reddicap Heath Rd B75 . . 13 A4
Reddings La B46 . . . . 25 A5
Reddings The B47 . . . . 69 A5
Redditch Rd B80 . . . . 103 D5
Redditch Wlk 4 CV2 . . . . . . 63 A7
Redesdale Ave CV6 . . . . . . 60 F5
Redesdale Mews 10
GL56 . . . . 140 A3
Redesdale Pl GL56 . . . . . . 140 A2
Redfern Ave CV8 . . . . 93 A6
Redgrave Cl CV2 . . . . 63 B8
Redhill Bank CV37 . . . . . . 130 B3
Red Hill Cl B80 . . . . 103 E6
Redhill Cl CV35 . . . . 146 C1
Redhill Furrows CV31 . . . 110 C5
Red Hill Ho CV37 . . . . 129 F7
Red Hill CV35 . . . . 131 B8
Redhouse Cl B93 . . . . 71 E4
Red La
Astley CV10 . . . . 37 E7
Burton Green CV8 . . . . 75 C2
Coventry CV6 . . . . 61 F5
Kenilworth CV8 . . . . 92 D8
Redlake B77 . . . . 9 E8
Redland Cl CV2 . . . . 50 E2
Redland La CV8 . . . . 79 A2
Redland Rd CV31 . . . . 110 B5
Redlands Cres CV37 . . . . . 144 C3
Redlands Cvn Pk CV35 . . 123 B3
Redlands Row GL56 . . . . . 141 A1
Redliff Ave B36 . . . . 22 D1
Red Lion Cl CV47 . . . . 147 B5
Red Lion St OX17 . . . . 134 C1
Red Lodge Dr CV22 . . . . . . 99 E8
Redmoor Way B76 . . . . 22 D6
Red Poll Cl OX16 . . . . 139 F4
Red Rd CV35 . . . . 132 B5
Redruth Cl
Coventry CV6 . . . . 62 A8
Nuneaton CV11 . . . . 30 A4
Redthorne Gr CV8 . . . . 93 B8
Redwing Cl CV37 . . . . 144 C5
Redwing B77 . . . . 10 A6
Red Wing Wlk B36 . . . . 33 A8
Redwood Croft CV10 . . . . . 29 A1
Redwood Dr B78 . . . . 15 D7
Redwood Pk CV36 . . . . . . 149 D5
Reeds Pk CV33 . . . . 111 F1
Rees Dr CV3 . . . . 77 D4
Reeve Dr CV8 . . . . 93 A4
Reeves Rd LE10 . . . . 31 F6
Regal Cl B77 . . . . 9 C8
Regal Ct CV9 . . . . 18 E8
Regal Ho CV11 . . . . 29 D3
Regal Rd CV37 . . . . 144 F4
Regal Road Trad Est
CV37 . . . . 144 F4
Regan Ct B75 . . . . 13 C5
Regency Arc 6 CV32 . . . . 109 F8
Regency Cl CV10 . . . . 29 D6
Regency Ct
Coventry CV5 . . . . 76 F8
Hinckley LE10 . . . . 32 A7
Regency Dr
Alcester B49 . . . . 143 A6
Coventry CV3 . . . . 76 F5
Kenilworth CV8 . . . . 92 F3
Regency Ho CV32 . . . . 110 A8
Regency Mews CV32 . . . . 110 A8
Regent Ct 5 LE10 . . . . 31 D8
Regent Gr CV32 . . . . 109 F8
Regent Pl
4 Royal Leamington Spa
CV31 . . . . 110 A7
Rugby CV21 . . . . 83 A3
Regent St
Bedworth CV12 . . . . 39 C4
Coventry CV1 . . . . 151 A2
Hinckley LE10 . . . . 31 D8
Nuneaton CV11 . . . . 29 D5
Royal Leamington Spa
CV32 . . . . 109 F8
Rugby CV21 . . . . 83 A3
Reg Hadden Ct CV10 . . . . . 29 D6
Regiment Ct CV6 . . . . 49 A1
Regina Cres CV2 . . . . 63 A7
Regis Wlk CV2 . . . . 62 F7
Reignier Pl CV34 . . . . 109 F2
Reindeer Rd B78 . . . . 8 F8
Relay Dr B77 . . . . 10 C7
Relton Mews CV6 . . . . 61 F6
Rembrandt Cl CV5 . . . . 60 C3
Remburn Gdns CV34 . . . . 108 F8
Remembrance Rd CV3 . . . 78 D6
Renfrew Sq B35 . . . . 22 B4
Renfrew Wlk CV4 . . . . 76 A8
Renison Rd CV12 . . . . 38 E1
Renolds Cl CV4 . . . . 60 C2
Renown Ave CV5 . . . . 60 C1
Renshaw B91 . . . . 56 A3
Renshaw Ind Est B80 . . . . 103 B4
Repington Ave CV9 . . . . . . 12 D2
Repington Rd N B77 . . . . . . 4 A5
Repington Rd S B77 . . . . . . 4 A5
Repington Way B75 . . . . . . 13 B5
Repton Dr CV6 . . . . 50 B2
Reservoir Dr B46 . . . . 24 F2
Reservoir Rd CV21 . . . . 83 C6
Retreat St B96 . . . . 102 E1
Retreat The B95 . . . . 113 B2
Reuben Ave CV10 . . . . 28 B6
Revel CE Prim Sch The
CV23 . . . . 53 F2
Rex Cl CV4 . . . . 75 D8
Reynolds Cl CV21 . . . . 84 B1
Reynolds Rd CV12 . . . . 39 A4
Rhoose Croft B35 . . . . 22 B3
Rhyl Rd CV11 . . . . 40 F6
Ribble Cl CV12 . . . . 40 B2
Ribble Rd CV3 . . . . 61 F2
Ribblesdale B77 . . . . 10 B7
Ribbonbrook CV11 . . . . 29 D3
Ribbonfields CV11 . . . . 29 D3
Richard Joy Cl CV6 . . . . . . 49 C2
Richard Lee Prim Sch
CV2 . . . . 62 E3
Richards Cl CV8 . . . . 92 F5
Richards Gr CV31 . . . . . . 110 A5
Richardson Cl CV34 . . . . 104 F1
Richardson Way CV2 . . . . 63 B8
Rich Cl CV34 . . . . 109 B7
Richman Gdns 3 OX16 . . 139 F4
Richmond Cl B47 . . . . 69 C7
Richmond Ct 6 CV31 . . . . 110 B7
Richmond Ho 2 B37 . . . . . . 33 C1
Richmond Rd
Atherstone CV9 . . . . 18 D7
Nuneaton CV11 . . . . 29 A4
Rugby CV21 . . . . 83 D2
Richmond St CV2 . . . . 62 A3
Richmond Way 2 B37 . . . . 33 C3
Rickard Cl B93 . . . . 71 E6
Rickyard Cl B78 . . . . 5 A1
Rickyard The
Easenhall CV23 . . . . 65 F4
Shutford OX15 . . . . 139 A3
Ricoh Arena (Coventry City
FC) CV6 . . . . 49 E3
Riddell Cl B49 . . . . 143 D4
Ridding Gdns B78 . . . . 11 A8
Riddings Hill CV7 . . . . 74 C8
Riddings La CV9 . . . . 11 C3
Riddings The
Baddesley Ensor CV9 . . . . 11 C2
Coventry CV5 . . . . 76 E7
Sutton Coldfield B76 . . . . . 22 B8
Riddon Dr LE10 . . . . 31 B8
Rideswell Gr CV31 . . . . . . 110 A1
Ridge Ct CV5 . . . . 60 A6
Ridge Dr CV21 . . . . 83 D4
Ridge La CV10 . . . . 18 B2
Ridgeley Cl CV34 . . . . 104 E2
Ridgethorpe CV3 . . . . 78 E6
Ridgeway Ave CV3 . . . . 77 C6
Ridgeway Cl B80 . . . . 103 E2
Ridgeway La CV33 . . . . . . 115 A5
Ridgeway Mid Sch B96 . . 118 C8
Ridgeway Sch The CV34 105 A1
Ridgeway The
Astwood Bank B96 . . . . . 118 D6
Barby CV23 . . . . 117 F8
Hinckley LE10 . . . . 31 D6
Warwick CV34 . . . . 105 A1
Ridgeway Trad Est B96 . . 102 E1
Ridgewood Cl CV32 . . . . . 105 C1
Ridgewood Rise B77 . . . . . . 4 A5
Ridgley Rd CV4 . . . . 75 E8
Ridgway The CV37 . . . . . . 120 C3
Ridley La B46 . . . . 25 A5
Ridsdale Cl WR11 . . . . . . 127 F6
Rigby Cl CV34 . . . . 109 D4
Rigdale Cl CV2 . . . . 62 E2
Riley Cl
Daventry NN11 . . . . 117 F2
Kenilworth CV8 . . . . 93 D4
Riley Ct CV21 . . . . 83 C3
Riley Dr
Banbury OX16 . . . . 139 F4
Birmingham B36 . . . . 23 A1
Riley Ho CV1 . . . . 151 B2
Riley Sq CV2 . . . . 50 B1
Rimell Cl CV37 . . . . 130 E1
Ringway Hill Cross CV1 . 151 A3
Ringway Queens CV1 . . . 151 A2
Ringway Rudge CV1 . . . . . 151 A2
Ringway St Johns CV1 . . 151 C2
Ringway St Nicholas
CV1 . . . . 151 B3
Ringway St Patricks CV1 151 B1
Ringway Swanswell CV1 . 151 C3
Ringway Whitefriars
CV1 . . . . 151 C3
Ringwood Highway CV2 . . 50 E2
Rinhill Gr CV31 . . . . 110 D6
Riplingham 3 CV32 . . . . . 105 F2
Ripon Cl CV5 . . . . 60 B8
Risborough Cl CV5 . . . . 60 C3
Risdale Cl CV32 . . . . 105 D2
Rise The B37 . . . . 44 A7
Rising La
Chadwick End B93 . . . . 90 B5
Kingswood B94,B93 . . . . . . 89 F5
Rising Rd B94 . . . . 89 C5
Riverbank Gdns CV37 . . . 145 B2
River Cl
Bedworth CV12 . . . . 38 F1
Royal Leamington Spa
CV32 . . . . 109 D8
River Ct 3 CV1 . . . . 61 B3
River Dr CV9 . . . . 12 D2
Riverford Croft CV4 . . . . . . 76 D4
River House Sch B95 . . . . 113 B4
Rivermead Ct B50 . . . . . . 148 D4
Rivermead Dr CV37 . . . . . 145 E4
Rivermead CV11 . . . . 29 A4
Riversdale 6 CV32 . . . . . 109 E8
Riversdale Rd CV9 . . . . 19 A8
Riverside
Alcester B49 . . . . 143 D4
Bubbenhall CV8 . . . . 95 B5
Riverside Cl CV3 . . . . 78 A7
Riverside Ct 1 B46 . . . . . . 33 F7
Riverside Dr B95 . . . . 113 B2
Riverside Gdns B95 . . . . . 113 B4
Riverside Ind Est B78 . . . . . 9 B8
Riverside
Royal Leamington Spa
CV32 . . . . 109 E8
Studley B80 . . . . 103 F5
Witherley CV9 . . . . 19 B7
Riverslea Rd CV3 . . . . 62 C1
Riversleigh Rd CV32 . . . . 105 C1
Riversley Rd CV11 . . . . 29 C3
River Way CV36 . . . . 149 E7
River Wlk CV2 . . . . 50 C2
Rivington Glebe GL56 . . . 141 A1
Roach Cl B37 . . . . 33 C3
Roach B77 . . . . 9 D6
Roadway Cl CV12 . . . . 39 B2
Roanne Ringway CV11 . . . 29 B4
Robbins Ct 3 CV22 . . . . . 100 F8
Robert Cl CV3 . . . . 78 C4
Robert Cramb Ave CV4 . . . 75 F8
Robert Hill Cl CV21 . . . . . . 84 A1
Robert Rd CV7 . . . . 49 F8
Roberts Cl CV23 . . . . 96 F6
Roberts La WR11 . . . . 127 F1
Robertson Cl CV23 . . . . 84 A5
Robey's La B78 . . . . 4 D3
Robin Cl
Birmingham B36 . . . . 33 A8
Tamworth B77 . . . . 9 C8
Robin Hood Rd CV3 . . . . . 78 C6
Robinia Cl CV32 . . . . 106 B2
Robinia B77 . . . . 4 A4
Robins Cl OX7 . . . . 142 A2
Robins Gr CV34 . . . . 108 C4
Robinson Rd CV12 . . . . 49 D8
Robinson's Way B76 . . . . . 22 D5
Robinson Way LE10 . . . . . . 31 F4
Robins Way CV10 . . . . 28 A3
Robotham Cl CV21 . . . . 82 F6
Rocheberie Way CV22 . . . . 99 F8
Rochester Cl
Nuneaton CV11 . . . . 29 B3
Redditch B97 . . . . 102 C8
Rochester Rd CV5 . . . . 76 E8
Rochford Cl B76 . . . . 22 A8
Rochford Ct
Royal Leamington Spa
CV31 . . . . 109 E7
Solihull B90 . . . . 71 A6
Rock Cl
Coventry CV6 . . . . 50 B1
Galley Common CV10 . . . . 27 F4
Rocken End CV6 . . . . 61 D8
Rockford Cl B98 . . . . 102 F5
Rockingham Cl B93 . . . . . . 71 D2
Rockingham Dr CV11 . . . . . 39 F7
Rock La CV7 . . . . 48 C7
Rock Mill La CV32 . . . . . . 109 C8
Rock Mill CV32 . . . . 105 C1
Rocky La CV8 . . . . 93 D2
Rodborough Rd B93 . . . . . . 71 E3
Rodhouse Cl CV4 . . . . 59 D1
Rodney Cl CV22 . . . . 82 C1
Rodway Dr CV5 . . . . 59 D4
Rodyard Way CV1 . . . . . . 151 C1
Roebuck Pk B49 . . . . 143 A5
Roe Cl CV34 . . . . 108 F8
Roe House La CV9,DE12 . . . . 3 D4
Rofs Croft B78 . . . . 5 A2
Rogers La CV37 . . . . 131 A3
Rogers Way CV34 . . . . . . 108 B4
Rokeby Ct CV22 . . . . 99 E7
Rokeby Inf Sch CV22 . . . . 100 A8
Rokeby Jun Sch CV22 . . . 100 A8
Rokeby St CV21 . . . . 83 D3
Roland Ave CV6 . . . . 49 C3
Roland Mount CV6 . . . . 49 C3
Rolan Dr B90 . . . . 69 E8
Rollason Cl CV6 . . . . 61 C8
Rollason Rd CV6 . . . . 61 B8
Rollason's Yd CV6 . . . . 50 A3
Rolling Stones GL55 . . . . 135 B2
Rollright Stones* OX7 . . 141 D1
Rolph Ct GL56 . . . . 140 A2
Roman Cl LE17 . . . . 43 E6
Roman Ct B77 . . . . 9 E7
Romani Cl CV34 . . . . 108 D7
Roman Pk B46 . . . . 23 F1
Roman Rd CV2 . . . . 62 B3
Roman Row CV36 . . . . 141 F5
Roman Way
Alcester B49 . . . . 143 B3
Coleshill B46 . . . . 23 F2
Coventry CV3 . . . . 77 D3
Dordon B78 . . . . 11 A6
Halford CV36 . . . . 136 F8
Rugby CV21 . . . . 83 A7
Southam CV47 . . . . 147 C4
Romeo Arbour CV34 . . . . 109 E3
Romford Rd CV6 . . . . 49 B2
Romilly Cl B76 . . . . 13 A4
Romney Rd 23 OX16 . . . . 139 F5
Romney B77 . . . . 9 F8
Romsey Ave CV10 . . . . 29 D8
Romsley Rd CV6 . . . . 61 C6
Ronald Gr B36 . . . . 22 D1
Ro-Oak Rd CV6 . . . . 60 F5
Rookery Cl CV13 . . . . 20 A7
Rookery La
Coventry CV6 . . . . 49 B4
Ettington CV37 . . . . 131 A3
Newbold-on-S CV37 . . . . 130 E1
Preston Bagot B95 . . . . . 113 E5
Rookery The
Birchley Heath CV10 . . . . . 17 F2
Galley Common CV10 . . . . 27 E5
Rookes Ct 3 CV37 . . . . . 144 F3
Rooks Nest CV23 . . . . 64 E3
Roosevelt Dr CV4 . . . . 59 E2
Roper Cl CV21 . . . . 101 A8
Ropewalk B49 . . . . 143 B4
Rope Way OX15 . . . . 142 D3
Rosaville Cres CV5 . . . . . . 60 A6
Rose Ave
Coventry CV6 . . . . 60 F5
Henley-in-A B95 . . . . 113 B5
Roseberry Ave CV2 . . . . . . 50 C1
Rosebery Rd B77 . . . . 9 D4
Rosebriars B90 . . . . 69 E7
Rose Cottage Flats CV5 . . 59 D5
Rosecraddoc 9 CV35 . . . . 132 B6
Rose Cres CV37 . . . . 129 C8
Rose Croft CV8 . . . . 92 E6
Rose Ct CV7 . . . . 74 B8
Rosefield Pl 4 CV32 . . . . 109 F8
Rosefield St CV32 . . . . . . 110 A8
Rosefield Wlk 3 CV32 . . . 109 F8
Rosegreen Cl CV3 . . . . 77 E6
Rosehall Cl B98 . . . . 102 E6
Rose Hill CV9 . . . . 18 F7
Rosehip Dr CV2 . . . . 62 B6
Rose La CV47 . . . . 125 C7
Roseland Rd CV8 . . . . 92 F3
Roselands Ave CV2 . . . . . . 62 D8
Rose La CV11 . . . . 29 C3
Rosemary Cl CV4 . . . . 59 E3
Rosemary Hill CV8 . . . . 92 F5
Rosemary Mews CV8 . . . . . 92 F5
Rosemary Way LE10 . . . . . 31 B7
Rosemont Ho B93 . . . . 71 F3
Rosemount Cl CV2 . . . . 62 E7
Rosemullion Cl CV7 . . . . . . 50 B8
Rose Rd B46 . . . . 33 F8
Roseway CV13 . . . . 21 D7
Rosewood Ave CV22 . . . . 100 A8
Rosewood Cl LE10 . . . . 31 F6
Rosewood Cres CV32 . . . . 106 B2
Rosewood CV11 . . . . 29 F1
Ross Cl CV5 . . . . 60 A5
Ross Ct CV21 . . . . 83 D3
Rossendale Way CV10 . . . . 28 E2
Rosslyn Ave CV6 . . . . 60 E6
Rosslyn Rd B76 . . . . 22 A6
Ross Way CV11 . . . . 40 B7
Roston Dr LE10 . . . . 31 A8
Rothay B77 . . . . 9 F8
Rotherby Gr B37 . . . . 44 B7
Rotherfield Cl CV31 . . . . . 110 B7
Rotherham Rd CV6 . . . . 49 C2
Rotherhams Hill CV9 . . . . . 17 C8
Rotherhams Oak La B94 . . 87 F7
Rother Rd 8 OX16 . . . . . . 139 F5
Rother St CV37 . . . . 144 F2
Rotherwick Ct CV36 . . . . . 149 D6
Rothesay Ave CV4 . . . . 60 B2
Rothesay Cl CV10 . . . . 29 A2
Rothley Dr CV21 . . . . 83 E7
Rothwell Rd CV34 . . . . . . 104 C1
Rotten Row Barns B93 . . . 72 C4
Rough Coppice Wlk B35 . . 22 A2
Rough Farm Ind Est
CV37 . . . . 130 C5
Rough Hill Dr B98 . . . . . . 102 F6
Roughknowles Rd CV4 . . . 75 D6
Rough The B97 . . . . 102 D8
Rouncil La CV8 . . . . 104 C8
Round Ave CV23 . . . . 82 A5
Round Close Rd OX15 . . . 142 D4
Round Cl B90 . . . . 70 A6
Roundhill Rd OX17 . . . . . . 134 A2
Roundhouse Mews 3
GL56 . . . . 140 A3
Round House Rd CV3 . . . . 78 B8
Round Moor Wlk B35 . . . . 22 A3
Round Oak Sch The
CV32 . . . . 106 A3
Rounds Gdns CV21 . . . . . . 82 F4
Rounds Hill CV8 . . . . 92 E2
Round St CV21 . . . . 82 F3
Rouse La CV35 . . . . 137 F8
Rover Dr B36 . . . . 22 F1
Rover Rd CV1 . . . . 151 B2
Rowan Cl
Binley Woods CV3 . . . . 79 D7
Hollywood B47 . . . . 69 B5
Kingsbury B78 . . . . 15 D6
Stratford-u-A CV37 . . . . . 144 F5
Rowan Dr
6 Warwick CV34 . . . . 108 F8
Rugby CV22 . . . . 82 B2
Rowan Gdns B78 . . . . 11 B8
Rowan Gr CV2 . . . . 50 E2
Rowan Rd CV10 . . . . 28 C6
Rowans The
Bedworth CV12 . . . . 38 E2
Harvington WR11 . . . . . . 127 D4
Rowan Way
Birmingham,Chelmsley Wood
B37 . . . . 33 C1
Hartshill CV10 . . . . 28 A8
Rowborough Cl
Astwood Bank B96 . . . . . 102 E2
Hatton CV35 . . . . 114 F5
Rowbrook Cl B90 . . . . 69 E8
Rowcroft Rd CV2 . . . . 63 A6
Rowe Cl CV21 . . . . 101 C7
Rowington Cl CV6 . . . . 60 D5
Rowington Gn CV35 . . . . . . 89 F1
Rowland Ave
Polesworth B78 . . . . 5 A3
Studley B80 . . . . 103 E3
Rowland Ct CV7 . . . . 26 E1
Rowland St CV21 . . . . 82 F3
Rowlands Way CV36 . . . . 137 E7
Rowland Way CV9 . . . . 12 C2
Rowley Cres CV37 . . . . . . 145 A4
Rowley Dr CV3 . . . . 78 B4
Rowley La CV3 . . . . 78 D3
Rowley Rd
Coventry CV3,CV8 . . . . 78 B3
Whitnash CV31 . . . . 110 A2
Rowley's Green La CV6 . . . 49 E4
Rowleys Green Lane Ind Est
CV6 . . . . 49 E4
Rowse Cl CV21 . . . . 83 C7
Row The
Ansty CV7 . . . . 51 D3
Broadwell CV23 . . . . 116 B4
Mollington OX17 . . . . 133 F2
Rowthorn Dr B90 . . . . 71 A6
Roxburgh Croft CV32 . . . . 106 C6
Roxburgh Rd CV11 . . . . 29 E1
Royal Cres CV3 . . . . 78 C5
Royal Ct LE10 . . . . 31 D7
Royal Leamington Spa
Rehabilitation Hospl
CV34 . . . . 109 E4
Royal Meadow Dr CV9 . . . . 12 E2
Royal Oak Ind Est NN11 . . 117 F2

Royal Oak La CV7,CV12 . . . 49 C7
Royal Oak Terr GL55 . . . . 135 A1
Royal Oak Way N NN11 . . 117 F2
Royal Oak Way S NN11 . . 117 F2
Royal Oak Yd CV12. . . . . 39 B4
Royal Priors 18 CV32 . . . . 105 F1
Royal Shakespeare Theatre* CV37. . . . . .145 A2
Royston Cl CV3 . . . . 63 A3
Rubens Cl CV5. . . . . 60 C3
Rudgard Rd CV6 . . . . 50 A4
Rufford Cl
Alcester B49 . . . . 143 C5
Hinckley LE10 . . . . 31 D3
Rugby High Sch CV22 . . . . 99 D6
Rugby La CV23. . . . . 97 B6
Rugby Rd
Barby CV23 . . . . 101 C1
Binley Woods CV3 . . . . 79 D8
Brandon CV8 . . . . 80 A5
Brinklow CV23. . . . . 64 F3
Bulkington CV12 . . . . 40 D2
Church Lawford CV23 . . . . . 81 C5
Clifton u D CV23 . . . . 83 F5
Cubbington CV32. . . . . 106 E6
Dunchurch CV22 . . . . 99 D4
Dunsmore CV23. . . . . 84 F6
Easenhall CV23 . . . . 65 F3
Harborough Magna CV23 . . 66 B2
Hinckley LE10 . . . . 31 D5
Kilsby CV23 . . . . 101 E5
Long Lawford CV23. . . . . . . 82 B4
Pailton CV23 . . . . 66 A8
Princethorpe CV23 . . . . 96 F2
Royal Leamington Spa CV32. . . . . .105 D1
Shawell LE17 . . . . 68 A8
Stockton CV47 . . . . 115 F3
Weston u W CV33 . . . . 107 D7
Wolston CV8 . . . . 80 C4
Rugby Sch CV22 . . . . 83 A2
Rugby Sta CV21. . . . . 83 C4
Ruislip Cl B35 . . . . 22 A4
Rumbush La
Earlswood B90,B94 . . . . 69 F3
Solihull B90 . . . . 70 A5
Rumer Cl CV37. . . . . 129 B4
Runcorn Cl
Birmingham B37 . . . . 33 C4
Redditch B98. . . . . 102 F8
Runcorn Wlk 10 CV2 . . . . . 63 A7
Runneymede Gdns CV10. . 28 F3
Runnymede Dr CV7 . . . . . . 74 C5
Rupert Brooke Rd CV22 . . 99 E7
Rupert Kettle Dr CV47. . . 124 B4
Rupert Rd CV6. . . . . 61 B8
Rushbrook La B94 . . . . 86 D3
Rushbrook Rd CV37 . . . . . 145 C1
Rushford Cl B90 . . . . 71 A7
Rush La B77,B78 . . . . 9 D4
Rushleigh Rd B90. . . . . 69 E8
Rushmoor Dr CV5. . . . . 60 F3
Rushmore St CV31 . . . . . . 110 B7
Rushmore Terr 9 CV31 . 110 B7
Rushock Cl B98. . . . . 103 C7
Rushton Cl CV7. . . . . 74 C7
Rushton Hall Sch CV7. . . . 49 D5
Rushwick Gr B90 . . . . 71 A6
Rusina Ct CV31 . . . . 109 F6
Ruskin Cl
Coventry CV6. . . . . 60 D6
Nuneaton CV10 . . . . 28 A5
Rugby CV22. . . . . 99 F6
Russell Ave CV22 . . . . 99 D4
Russell Cl
Long Itchington CV47 . . . . 115 D4
Tamworth B77. . . . . 9 E6
Russell Ct 7 CV31 . . . . . . 110 A7
Russell St N 2 CV1 . . . . . 151 C4
Russell St
Coventry CV1. . . . . 151 C4
Royal Leamington Spa CV32. . . . . 105 F1
Russell Terr CV31. . . . . . . 110 A7
Russelsheim Way CV22. . . 83 A2
Russet Gr CV4 . . . . 76 D3
Rutherford Glen CV11. . . . 29 F1
Rutherford Way NN11. . . . 117 F2
Rutherglen Ave CV3. . . . . . 78 A6
Rutland Ave
Hinckley LE10 . . . . 31 C7
Nuneaton CV10 . . . . 28 F4
Rutland Croft 3 CV3. . . . . 78 F8
Rydal Ave CV11 . . . . 30 A6
Rydal Cl
Allesley CV5. . . . . 60 B8
Hinckley LE10 . . . . 30 F7
Rugby CV21 . . . . 83 D6
Rydal B77 . . . . 10 A7
Ryde Ave CV10. . . . . 29 D7
Ryder Cl CV35 . . . . 114 F3
Ryder Row CV7 . . . . 37 A8
Ryders Hill Cres CV10 . . . . 28 C7
Rye Cl 9 OX16. . . . . 139 F5
Ryeclose Croft B37 . . . . . . 33 D3
Rye Cl CV37 . . . . 144 E5
Rye Croft B47. . . . . 69 A5
Ryefield La B76. . . . . 14 B2
Rye Fields 1 CV33. . . . . . 122 E8
Ryegrass La B97 . . . . 102 C6
Rye Grass Wlk B35. . . . . . . 22 B3
Rye Hill CV5 . . . . 60 A6
Rye Hill Office Pk CV5 . . . 60 A7
Ryelands The CV23. . . . . . . 98 D7
Rye Piece Ringway CV12 . 39 C3
Ryhope Cl CV12. . . . . 38 C1
Ryknild St B49. . . . . 143 A6
Ryland Cl CV31 . . . . 110 C6
Ryland Rd CV35. . . . . 122 B8
Ryland St CV37 . . . . 144 F1
Ryley St CV1. . . . . 151 A3
Rylston Ave CV6 . . . . 49 A1
Rylstone Way 4 CV34. . . 104 E1
Ryon Hill CV37. . . . . 145 E7
Ryton Cl CV4 . . . . 76 B8
Ryton Organic Gdns* CV8. . . . . 79 E1
Ryton Pools Ctry Pk* CV8 95 E5
Ryton Pools Visitor Ctr* CV8. . . . . 95 E5
Ryton B77 . . . . .9 F8

S

Sabin Cl CV47 . . . . 115 C4
Sabin Dr CV33 . . . . 107 D7
Sackville Cl CV37 . . . . 144 C4
Sackville Ct OX17 . . . . . . 139 F6
Sackville Ho 1 CV1. . . . . 151 D4
Sacred Heart RC Prim Sch CV2. . . . . 62 A3
Saddington Rd CV3 . . . . . . 78 E8
Saddlebow La CV35,CV37 114 B2
Saddlers Cl LE10. . . . . 31 F6
Saddleton St CV35 . . . . . . 138 C7
Sadler Cl CV37. . . . . 144 F6
Sadler Gdns CV12. . . . . 39 C2
Sadler Rd CV6 . . . . 61 A8
Sadlers Ave CV36 . . . . 149 C5
Sadlers Cl CV36. . . . . 149 C6
Sadlers Mdw B46 . . . . 26 A2
Sadlerswell La B94 . . . . . . 88 B6
Saffron Cl CV23. . . . . 83 E8
Saffron Mdw CV37 . . . . . . 144 F1
Saffron B77 . . . . .4 B4
Saffron Wlk 9 CV37 . . . . . 144 F1
Sage Cl 2 OX16 . . . . 139 F5
St Agatha's Rd CV2 . . . . . . 62 A3
St Agnes Cl B80. . . . . 103 C4
St Agnes Way CV11 . . . . . . 29 F4
St Albans Cl CV32. . . . . . . 105 C2
St Andrews Benn CE Prim Sch CV21. . . . . 83 D3
St Andrew's CE Inf Sch CV5. . . . . 59 C5
St Andrews Cres CV22. . . 100 A8
St Andrew's Cres CV37 . . 144 F2
St Andrew's Ct CV21 . . . . . 83 A4
St Andrews Dr CV11. . . . . . 30 B1
St Andrew's Rd
Coventry CV5. . . . . 76 F8
Royal Leamington Spa CV32. . . . . 106 B5
St Andrews B77. . . . . .4 B4
St Annes Gr B93 . . . . 72 A6
St Anne's RC Prim Sch
Birmingham B37 . . . . 33 A2
Coventry CV3. . . . . 78 C6
Nuneaton CV10 . . . . 28 D7
St Anne's Rd CV22 . . . . 82 E1
St Ann's Cl CV31 . . . . 110 C7
St Ann's Rd CV2 . . . . 62 A3
St Anthony's RC Prim Sch CV31. . . . . 110 C7
St Antony's RC Prim Sch B37. . . . . 33 A5
St Asaphs Ave B80 . . . . . . 103 D4
St Athan Croft B35. . . . . . . 22 B3
St Augustine's RC High Sch B97. . . . . 102 D5
St Augustine's RC Prim Sch
Coventry CV6. . . . . 61 A7
Kenilworth CV8 . . . . 92 E7
St Augustine's Wlk CV6 . . 61 A7
St Austell Cl CV11. . . . . 30 A5
St Austell Rd CV2 . . . . 62 E3
St Bartholemews Cl CV3. . 63 A2
St Bartholomew's CE Prim Sch CV3. . . . . 78 E7
St Benedicts Cl CV9. . . . . . 18 D8
St Benedict's RC High Sch B49. . . . . 143 C4
St Benedict's RC Prim Sch CV9. . . . . 18 F7
St Bernard's Wlk CV3 . . . . 78 D6
St Blaise Ave B46 . . . . 23 C2
St Bride's Cl CV31. . . . . . . 110 C6
St Buryan Cl CV11. . . . . 30 A5
Saintbury Cl CV37. . . . . . . 145 D1
Saintbury Dr B91 . . . . 71 C8
St Catharine's RC Prim Sch GL55. . . . . 135 A2
St Catherine's Cl
Coventry CV3. . . . . 78 B8
Hinckley LE10 . . . . 31 F7
St Catherine's Cres CV34 109 F3
St Catherine's Lodge 7 CV6 . . . . 61 A4
St Chads Mews B94. . . . . . . 89 D3
St Chads Rd
3 Bishops Tachbrook CV33. . . . . 122 E8
Studley B80. . . . . 103 C4
St Christian's Croft CV3 . . 77 E8
St Christian's Rd CV3 . . . . 77 E8
St Christopher Prim Sch CV5. . . . . 60 D4
St Christopher's Cl CV34 108 D8
St Clements Ct CV2 . . . . . . 62 D8
St Columba's Cl CV1 . . . . 151 B4
St David's Cl CV31 . . . . . . 110 C7
St David's Ct GL56 . . . . . . 140 A3
St Davids Orch CV3 . . . . . . 78 F7
St David's Sch GL56. . . . . 140 A3
St Davids Way CV10. . . . . . 39 A6
St Davids Wlk CV37 . . . . . 130 E1
St Denis View CV23 . . . . . . 66 A8
St Edithas Rd B78. . . . . 11 A8
St Edith's Cl CV23. . . . . 53 E3
St Edith's Gn 3 CV34 . . . . 109 B8
St Edith's Ho 2 CV34 . . . 109 B8
St Edmonds Rd CV9. . . . . . 16 C5
St Edwards Ct GL56 . . . . . 140 A2
St Edward's RC Prim Sch B46. . . . . 34 A3
St Egwin's Cl WR11 . . . . . 127 B2
St Elizabeth's RC Prim Sch CV6. . . . . 61 E7
St Elizabeth's Rd CV6 . . . . 61 E7
St Faith's Rd B49 . . . . 143 B5
St Francis RC Prim Sch CV12. . . . . 39 C3
St Fremund Way CV31. . . 110 C5
St George & St Teresa RC Prim Sch B93. . . . . 72 A4
St Georges Ave CV22. . . . . 99 F8
St George's Cl
24 Moreton-in-M GL56 . . . 140 A3
Stratford-u-A CV37 . . . . . . 144 D4
St George's Rd
Atherstone CV9. . . . . 12 E1
Coventry CV1. . . . . 61 F2
Royal Leamington Spa CV31. . . . . 109 F6
Solihull B90 . . . . 70 D8
St Georges Way CV10 . . . . 39 B8
St Gerards RC Prim Sch B35. . . . . 22 B4
St Giles Jun Sch CV7. . . . . 49 F8
St Giles Rd
Coventry CV7. . . . . 49 D6
Gaydon CV35. . . . . 132 E8
St Govan's Cl 2 CV31 . . . 110 C6
St Gregory's RC Prim Sch
Coventry CV2. . . . . 62 E3
Stratford-u-A CV37 . . . . . . 145 A3
St Gregory's Rd CV37 . . . 145 A3
St Helena Rd B78 . . . . 11 B8
St Helen's Rd CV31. . . . . . 110 A5
St Helen's Way CV5 . . . . . . 60 B8
St Ives Rd CV2 . . . . 62 E3
St Ives Way CV11. . . . . 29 F5
St James' Ave CV35 . . . . . 146 E4
St James CE Jun Sch CV12. . . . . 40 C2
St James CE Prim Sch CV47. . . . . 147 B5
St James Cl WR11. . . . . . . 127 D3
St James Cres CV47. . . . . 147 B5
St James Ct
Coventry CV3. . . . . 78 E6
Moreton-in-M GL56 . . . . . . 140 A2
St James & Ebrington CE Prim Sch GL55. . . . . 135 B1
St James Gdns CV12 . . . . . 40 C2
St James' La CV3 . . . . 78 D6
St James Meadow Rd CV32 . . . . 105 C2
St James Rd CV47. . . . . . . 147 B5
St James's Cl LE10. . . . . . . 31 D5
St John Fisher RC Prim Sch CV2. . . . . 62 D5
St John's Ave CV8 . . . . 93 A3
St Johns Ave CV22 . . . . . . 100 E8
St John's CE Prim Sch CV5. . . . . 60 C4
St John's Cl
Cherington CV36 . . . . 141 D7
Henley-in-A B95. . . . . 113 A4
St Johns Cl
Knowle B93 . . . . 72 B6
Stratford-u-A CV37 . . . . . . 144 F1
St John's Ct
1 Stratford-u-A CV37 . . . 144 F1
4 Warwick CV34 . . . . 108 F7
St John's Flats CV8 . . . . . . 93 A3
St John's House Mus* CV34. . . . . 108 F7
St John's La CV23. . . . . 82 A5
St John's Prim Sch CV8. . . 92 F2
St Johns Rd CV10 . . . . 27 E7
St John's Rd
Cherington CV36 . . . . 141 D7
Royal Leamington Spa CV31. . . . . 110 A6
St John's St
Coventry CV1. . . . . 151 C2
Kenilworth CV8 . . . . 93 A3
St John's Terr 13 CV31 . . 110 A6
St John St CV21. . . . . 83 A4
St Johns CV34 . . . . 108 F7
St Johns Way B93. . . . . 72 C6
St John the Baptist RC Prim Sch B36. . . . . 33 B7
St John the Divine CE Prim Sch CV3. . . . . 78 C5
St John Vianney RC Prim Sch CV5. . . . . 60 B3
St Joseph B96 . . . . 118 D8
St Joseph's RC Jun Sch CV11. . . . . 29 C3
St Joseph's RC Prim Sch
Banbury OX16 . . . . 139 F3
Whitnash CV31 . . . . 110 A3
St Judes Ave B80 . . . . 103 D4
St Jude's Cres CV3. . . . . . . 78 D7
St Laurence Ave CV34. . . . 108 D5
St Laurence Cl CV35 . . . . 114 A8
St Laurence Way B50 . . . 148 D5
St Lawrence CE Prim Sch CV47. . . . . 125 C7
St Lawrence Cl
Knowle B93 . . . . 72 B5
Napton on t H CV47. . . . . . 125 C8
St Lawrence Rd CV10 . . . . 27 B4
St Lawrence's Rd CV6. . . . 49 F1
St Leonards Cl
Birmingham B37 . . . . 44 A7
Dordon B78 . . . . 11 A6
St Leonards View B78. . . . 10 F8
St Leonard's Wlk CV8 . . . . 79 A1
St Luke's Rd CV6. . . . . 49 D3
St Lukes Way CV10. . . . . . . 28 C4
St Margaret Rd
Coventry CV1. . . . . 61 F2
Stoke Golding CV13. . . . . . . 21 E7
St Margaret's CE Jun Sch CV31. . . . . 110 B3
St Margaret's CE Prim Sch CV13. . . . . 21 D7
St Margaret's Ho CV31 . . 110 B4
St Margaret's Rd CV31 . . 110 B5
St Marie's RC Inf Sch CV22. . . . . 83 A2
St Marie's RC Jun Sch CV22. . . . . 82 F2
St Mark's Annexe (Coventry & Warwickshire Hospl) CV1. . . . . 151 C4
St Mark's Ave CV22 . . . . . . 99 C7
St Mark's Cl CV35. . . . . . . 132 E8
St Marks Cl CV10 . . . . 28 C4
St Mark's Cl B95. . . . . 112 E6
St Mark's Ct CV22. . . . . 99 D8
St Mark's Mews CV32 . . . 105 E1
St Mark's Rd CV32 . . . . . . 105 D1
St Martins Ave B80. . . . . . 103 D4
St Martin's Cl CV37 . . . . . 144 E2
St Martin's LE10 . . . . 31 E6
St Martin's RC Sch CV13 . 21 F7
St Martin's Rd CV3. . . . . . . 77 C2
St Marys Acre CV37 . . . . . 120 E7
St Mary & St Benedict RC Prim Sch CV1 . . . . 61 E4
St Mary's CE Prim Sch LE10. . . . . 31 D8
St Mary's Cl
Priors Hardwick CV47. . . . 125 D3
Southam CV47. . . . . 147 C5
Ullenhall B95 . . . . 112 E6
Warwick CV34. . . . . 108 D8
St Mary's Cres CV31. . . . . 110 B7
St Mary's Ct
Kenilworth CV8 . . . . 92 F2
Nuneaton CV11 . . . . 29 B5
St Marys Gr B79 . . . . 2 D3
St Mary's Immaculate RC Prim Sch CV34. . . . . 108 E8
St Mary's La OX7. . . . . 142 F2
St Mary's RC Prim Sch
Aston le W NN11. . . . . 134 F5
Henley-in-A B95. . . . . 113 B4
Southam CV47. . . . . 147 C4
Studley B80. . . . . 103 E4
St Mary's Rd
Alcester B49 . . . . 143 D4
Atherstone CV9. . . . . 18 E8
Fillongley CV7 . . . . 36 E3
Hinckley LE10 . . . . 31 D8
Nuneaton CV11 . . . . 29 B5
Royal Leamington Spa CV31. . . . . 110 B7
Stratford-u-A CV37 . . . . . . 145 A4
St Mary St CV1. . . . . 151 C2
St Mary's Terr CV31 . . . . . 110 B7
St Matthew's Bloxam CE Prim Sch CV22. . . . . 82 E2
St Matthews Cl
Nuneaton CV10 . . . . 28 C4
Salford Priors WR11 . . . . . 127 E6
St Matthews St 7 CV21 . . 83 A3
St Mawgen Cl B35 . . . . 22 C4
St Michael's CE Prim Sch CV12. . . . . 39 D3
St Michaels Cl CV9. . . . . . . 12 F1
St Michael's Cl
Bishops Itchington CV47. . 124 A4
Claverdon CV35. . . . . 113 F3
New Arley CV7. . . . . 37 A8
South Littleton WR11. . . . . 127 F1
St Michaels Cl CV33. . . . . 111 F1
St Michael's Cl CV33 . . . . 107 C7
St Michaels Cl CV9. . . . . . . 10 C1
St Michael's Cres CV47. . 147 F8
St Michael's Dr DE12. . . . . . .3 F8
St Michael's Hospl CV34 108 D8
St Michael's Rd
Claverdon CV35. . . . . 113 F3
Coventry CV2. . . . . 62 A3
Warwick CV34. . . . . 108 D8
St Michael's Way CV10 . . . 28 C4
St Milburgh Cl WR11 . . . . 127 D1
St Nicholas Ave CV8 . . . . . 92 F3
St Nicholas CE Com Prim Sch CV8. . . . . 92 F5
St Nicholas' CE Prim Sch B49. . . . . 143 C4
St Nicholas Church St CV34 . . . . 108 F6
St Nicholas Cl
Alcester B49 . . . . 143 C4
Austrey CV9. . . . . 3 B2
Coventry CV1. . . . . 61 C5
St Nicholas Ct
3 Coventry,Edgwick CV6 . . 61 F7
Coventry,Radford CV6 . . . . 61 B6
St Nicholas Est CV9 . . . . . . 11 C1
St Nicholas Pk CV34. . . . . 108 F6
St Nicholas Rd
Henley-in-A B95. . . . . 113 B4
Radford Semele CV31 . . . . 110 F5
St Nicholas St CV1 . . . . . . 151 B4
St Nicholas Terr CV31 . . . 110 E4
St Nicholas Wlk B76 . . . . . . 23 B6
St Nicolas CE Prim Sch CV11. . . . . 29 F6
St Nicolas Park Dr CV11. . 29 F7
St Nicolas Rd CV11. . . . . . . 29 D5
St Osburg's RC Prim Sch CV1. . . . . 151 A3
St Osburg's Rd CV2 . . . . . . 62 A3
St Oswalds CE Prim Sch CV22. . . . . 82 D3
St Patrick's CE Jun & Inf Sch B94. . . . . 70 C2
St Patrick's RC Prim Sch
Birmingham B37 . . . . 33 C2
Coventry CV2. . . . . 50 D1
St Patricks RC Prim Sch CV31. . . . . 109 F6
St Patrick's Rd CV1 . . . . . 151 B2
St Paul's CE Prim Sch
Nuneaton CV10 . . . . 28 C3
Royal Leamington Spa CV32. . . . . 106 B1
St Paul's Cl CV34 . . . . 108 D6
St Paul's Cres 5 B46 . . . . 33 F7
St Pauls Ct GL56 . . . . 140 A2
St Paul's Ct B77 . . . . 9 C4
St Pauls Ct B46 . . . . 23 B3
St Paul's Rd
Coventry CV6. . . . . 61 E6
Nuneaton CV10 . . . . 28 D3
St Paul's Sq 4 CV32 . . . . 106 A1
St Paul's Terr CV34 . . . . . 108 D6
St Peter's Ave CV9 . . . . 19 B7
St Peter's Cl
Redditch B97 . . . . 102 E5
Water Orton B46. . . . . 23 B2
Witherley CV9 . . . . 19 B7
St Peters Ct 15 CV35 . . . . 132 B6
St Peter's Ct CV1 . . . . 151 D4
St Peters Ct GL56 . . . . 140 A2
St Peter's Dr CV10 . . . . 27 F4
St Peters La B92 . . . . 44 D1
St Peter's Pl B78. . . . . 15 D5
St Peter's RC Prim Sch CV32. . . . . 109 F8
St Peters Rd 12 CV35. . . . 132 B6
St Peter's Rd 7 CV32 . . . 109 F8
St Peters Rd
Atherstone CV9. . . . . 19 A7
Rugby CV21 . . . . 83 C3
St Peter's Rd CV35 . . . . . . 146 D4
St Peters Way CV37 . . . . . 144 D5
St Philip's Ct B46 . . . . 34 A7
Saint's Peter & Paul RC Prim Sch CV2. . . . . 62 F7
Saints Way CV10. . . . . 29 D5
St Swithin's Dr CV37 . . . . 129 D2
St Thomas More RC Fst Sch B98. . . . . 103 B7
St Thomas More RC Prim Sch CV3. . . . . 77 D5
St Thomas More RC Sch CV10. . . . . 29 A3
St Thomas' Rd CV6. . . . . . . 50 A3
St Thomas's Cl CV10 . . . . . 28 C3
St Thomas's Ct 13 CV1 . . . 61 B2
St Thomas's Ho 12 CV1. . . 61 B2
St Wulstan Way CV47 . . . 147 C5
Salcombe Cl
Coventry CV3. . . . . 78 D6
Nuneaton CV11 . . . . 29 F5
Salemorton Ct CV22. . . . . . 99 B6
Salem Rd LE10. . . . . 31 F5
Salford Cl
Coventry CV2. . . . . 62 A5
Redditch B98. . . . . 103 B6
Salford Priors CE Prim Sch WR11 . . . . 127 F6
Salford Rd B50 . . . . 148 C4
Salisbury Ave CV3 . . . . 77 C6
Salisbury Cl CV8 . . . . 79 F3
Salisbury Dr
Nuneaton CV10 . . . . 28 B7
Water Orton B46. . . . . 23 C3
Salisbury Rd LE10. . . . . 32 B7
Salters La B95 . . . . 120 C7
Salter St B94 . . . . 70 C2
Saltisford Canal Ctr* CV34. . . . . 108 C8
Saltisford Gdns CV34. . . . 108 C8
Saltisford CV34 . . . . 108 D7
Salt La CV1. . . . . 151 B2
Salts La B78. . . . . .8 E5
Salt St B79,CV9. . . . . .3 B5
Salt Way B96 . . . . 118 B7
Salt Way La OX15 . . . . 137 F2
Sambourne La
Astwood Bank B96 . . . . . . 102 F1
Coughton B49,B96. . . . . . . 118 F7
Sambourne Park La B96. 103 A1
Sambourne Pk B96 . . . . . 118 D8
Sam Gault Cl CV3 . . . . 78 E7
Sammons Way CV4 . . . . . . 59 D1
Sampson Cl CV2 . . . . 62 C8
Samuel Hayward Ho 5 CV2 . . . . 50 B1
Samuel Vale Ho CV1 . . . . 151 B4
Sanby Cl CV12 . . . . 39 A4
Sanctus Ct 2 CV37 . . . . . 144 F1
Sanctus Dr CV37. . . . . 144 F1
Sanctus Rd CV37. . . . . 144 F1
Sanctus St CV37 . . . . 144 F1

Sanda Croft B36 33 B6
Sandbarn Cl B90 70 F6
Sand Barn La CV37 121 D6
Sandel Cl CV37 144 E3
Sanders Cl
Atherstone CV9 12 E1
Braunston NN11 117 D5
Sanders Ct CV34 109 C8
Sanders Rd
Bedworth CV6 50 B6
Salford Priors WR11 127 F6
Sandfield Cl B90 70 B8
Sandfield Ct 12 CV37 144 F1
Sandfield La CV37 130 E1
Sandfield Rd CV37 144 F1
Sandfine Rd OX15 139 D1
Sandford Cl CV2 50 E3
Sandford Gn OX16 139 F4
Sandford Way CV22 99 C3
Sandgate Cres CV2 62 E2
Sandhills Cres B91 71 B8
Sandhurst Gr CV6 61 B5
Sandilands Cl CV2 62 E4
Sandon Rd CV11 29 B5
Sandown Ave CV6 49 F2
Sandown Cl
Royal Leamington Spa CV32 106 C4
Stratford-u-A CV37 144 D1
Sandown Rd CV21 83 C4
Sandpiper Cl
Rugby CV23 67 C1
Stratford-u-A CV37 144 D5
Sandpiper Rd CV2 50 B3
Sandpiper B77 10 A5
Sandpits Cl
Curdworth B76 23 C6
Upper Tysoe CV35 138 B6
Sandpits La CV6 48 F2
Sandpits Rd CV35 138 B7
Sandpits The CV12 40 C2
Sandringham Cl CV4 75 F5
Sandringham Ct CV10 28 F6
Sandstone Ct B77 10 A7
Sandwick Cl CV3 78 F8
Sandy La
Blackdown CV32 105 F6
Coventry CV1 61 C5
Fillongley CV7 37 A3
Furnace End B46 25 E3
Marton CV23 115 D7
Monks Kirby CV23 53 F4
Sandy Lane Bsns Pk CV1 61 C5
Sandy La
Newton Regis B79 2 D6
Royal Leamington Spa CV32 105 D4
Rugby CV21 82 E3
Sandythorpe CV3 78 E6
Sandy Way CV35 122 B7
Sandy Way La B78 11 C7
Sandy Way B77 4 B3
Sankey Gr GL56 140 A2
Santos Cl CV3 78 F8
Sapcote Gr CV2 50 B4
Sapcote Rd LE10 32 B7
Saplings The B76 22 A8
Sapphire Dr CV31 109 F5
Sapphire Gate CV2 62 C2
Saracen Dr
Balsall Common CV7 73 E6
Sutton Coldfield B75 13 A6
Sarawak Pl CV22 99 B8
Sargeaunt St CV31 109 F7
Sark Dr B36 33 B6
Satchwell Ct 15 CV32 109 F8
Satchwell Wlk 16 CV32 109 F8
Saumur Way CV34 109 C6
Saunders Ave CV12 39 B2
Saunders Ho 11 CV32 105 F2
Saunton Cl CV5 60 B8
Saunton Rd CV22 82 F1
Savages Cl CV33 122 F8
Savernake Rd CV35 132 C4
Saville Gr CV8 93 C5
Sawbridge Rd CV23 116 F5
Sawlcliffe Lea OX15 139 A1
Saxon Cl
4 Cawston CV22 99 A8
Binley Woods CV3 79 D7
Polesworth B78 4 F1
Stratford-u-A CV37 145 C2
Studley B80 103 E5
Tamworth B77 9 F6
Saxon Ct B50 148 D4
Saxonfields B50 148 D4
Saxon Mdws CV32 105 C2
Saxon Rd CV2 62 B4
Saxon Wood Rd B90 70 D5
Scafell Cl CV5 60 A4
Scafell CV21 83 D7
Scammerton B77 10 B7
Scar Bank CV34 104 E1
Scarborough Way CV4 75 F7
Scarman Rd CV4 76 B5
Schofield Rd B37 33 A5
Scholars Ct CV37 144 F3
Scholars Dr CV22 99 B8
Scholars La CV37 144 F2
Scholfield Rd CV7 49 A6
School Ave WR11 127 F6
School Bell Mews CV8 94 B6
School Cl
Birmingham,Castle Vale B35 22 B3
Birmingham,Kingshurst B37 33 A6
Braunston NN11 117 E5
Coventry CV3 61 F2

School Cl *continued*
Great Alne B49 119 D6
Hinckley LE10 32 A6
Long Compton CV36 141 C3
School Cotts CV35 90 F3
School Croft CV35 91 C2
School Dr B47 69 A3
Schoolfield Gr 1 CV21 83 A3
School Gdns CV21 84 A1
School Hill
Hartshill CV10 28 A8
Mollington OX17 133 F2
Napton on t H CV47 125 C8
Offchurch CV33 111 B8
Wootton Wawen B95 113 A3
School House La CV2 63 A6
School House Mews B95 113 B4
School La
Badby NN11 126 F6
Bearley CV37 120 E7
Bedworth CV7 49 F7
Galley Common CV10 27 E5
Kenilworth CV8 92 F5
Ladbroke CV47 124 D5
Lea Marston B76 24 A7
Little Packington CV7 45 D7
Lower Brailes OX15 137 F2
Middle Littleton WR11 127 F1
North Newington OX15 139 E2
Priors Marston CV47 125 E4
Radford Semele CV31 110 E5
Shuttington B79 4 F7
Stretton-on-D CV23 96 F6
Tamworth B77 9 D5
Tiddington CV37 145 E4
Warmington OX17 133 D2
Weston u W CV33 107 E5
Wolvey LE10 41 E4
Wroxall CV35 90 E4
School Rd
Alcester B49 143 B4
Bulkington CV12 40 C2
Great Alne B49 119 D6
Henley-in-A B95 113 B4
Hockley Heath B94 88 B7
Pebworth CV37 128 F1
Salford Priors WR11 127 F6
Snitterfield CV37 121 B6
Wellesbourne CV35 146 E3
School St
Church Lawford CV23 81 B5
Churchover CV23 67 C6
Dunchurch CV22 99 C3
Long Lawford CV23 82 A4
Rugby CV21 84 A1
Southam CV47 147 C4
Stockton CV47 147 F8
Wolston CV8 80 B4
School Wlk CV11 29 E2
Scotchill The CV6 49 A1
Scotland End OX15 142 D4
Scots Cl CV22 99 C7
Scots La CV6 60 F6
Scott Ave CV10 29 D8
Scott Cl
13 Stratford-u-A CV37 130 B8
Bidford-on-A B50 148 C5
Scott Rd
Kenilworth CV8 92 E2
Redditch B97 102 C8
Royal Leamington Spa CV31 110 B6
Scowcroft Dr CV47 124 A4
Seabroke Ave CV22 82 F3
Seafield La
Carpenter's Hill B98 86 A2
Portway B48,B98 85 E4
Seaford Cl CV6 50 B4
Seagrave Rd CV1 151 D1
Sealand Dr CV12 39 A3
Sear Hills Cl CV7 74 B6
Seathwaite CV21 83 C7
Seaton Cl
Hinckley LE10 32 B7
Nuneaton CV11 29 F5
Seaton B77 9 F8
Sebastian Cl CV3 78 B5
Seckington La B79 2 C3
Second Ave CV3 62 C1
Second Exhibition Ave B40 44 D4
Sedgemere Gr CV7 74 C5
Sedgemoor Rd CV3 78 B5
Sedlescombe Lodge CV22 99 E7
Sedlescombe Pk CV22 99 F8
Seed Field Croft CV3 77 E7
Seekings Dr CV8 93 B4
Seekings The CV31 110 B3
Seeney La B76 15 B2
Seeswood Cl CV10 28 C2
Sefton Rd
Coventry CV4 76 E6
Tamworth B77 9 D4
Seggs La B49 143 B3
Segrave Cl 14 CV35 132 B6
Selborne Rd CV22 99 D8
Selby Way CV10 28 B5
Selco Way B76 22 A5
Selina Dix Ho CV1 151 C4
Selsdon Cl B47 69 C5
Selsey Cl CV3 78 C4
Selside CV21 83 D7
Selworthy Rd CV6 49 E3
Selwyn Cl CV35 146 D4
Selwyn Ho B37 33 D3
Semele Cl CV31 110 E5
Seneschal Rd CV3 77 E7
Sennen Cl CV11 30 A5

Sentry Way B75 13 A6
Sephton Dr CV6 50 C6
Servite Ho
2 Coleshill B46 33 F7
Kenilworth CV8 92 F3
Sett The CV35 137 F8
Seven Acre Cl 4 CV33 122 E8
Seven Ho CV37 145 E4
Seven Meadows Rd CV37 144 F1
Seven Stars Ind Est CV3 78 A7
Severn Ave LE10 31 A8
Severn Cl CV32 106 C3
Severn Rd
Bulkington CV12 40 A3
Coventry CV1 61 F1
Sevilla Cl CV3 63 A2
Sevincott Cl CV37 144 C4
Sevington Cl B91 71 C8
Sewall Ct CV6 62 A8
Sewall Highway CV2 62 B6
Seymour Cl
Coventry CV3 78 C5
Hampton Magna CV35 114 F3
Seymour Gate GL55 135 B2
Seymour Gr CV34 109 D6
Seymour Ho CV3 77 C8
Seymour Homes B95 113 B2
Seymour Rd
Alcester B49 143 C5
Nuneaton CV11 29 D3
Rugby CV21 83 C6
Stratford-u-A CV37 144 D1
Shackelton Way LE17 55 D5
Shackleton Dr LE10 31 E4
Shadowbrook La B92 56 E7
Shadowbrook Rd CV6 61 A5
Shaftesbury Ave CV7 49 A7
Shaftesbury Rd CV5 76 F8
Shaft La CV7 47 A4
Shakels Cl B97 102 E4
Shakers La CV47 115 C5
Shakesfield Cl CV36 136 F6
Shakespeare Ave
Bedworth CV12 39 D2
Warwick CV34 108 C4
Shakespeare Ct 14 CV37 145 A3
Shakespeare Ctr Mus The★ CV37 145 A3
Shakespeare Dr CV11 30 A1
Shakespeare Gdns CV22 99 E7
Shakespeare La WR11 127 D3
Shakespeare Rd B90 70 D8
Shakespeares Birthplace Mus★ CV37 145 A3
Shakespeare's Grave★ CV37 145 A1
Shakespeare St
Coventry CV2 62 B4
Stratford-u-A CV37 145 A3
Shakleton Rd CV5 61 A2
Shanes Castle Rd CV35 132 D3
Shanklin Dr CV10 29 D6
Shanklin Rd CV3 78 B4
Shannon B77 9 F8
Shap Fell CV21 83 D7
Sharnford Rd LE10 32 F6
Sharp Cl CV6 49 C2
Sharpe Cl CV34 108 E8
Sharpe St B77 4 A5
Sharpless Rd LE10 31 F7
Sharpley Ct CV2 63 A8
Sharratt Rd CV12 39 A2
Sharries The GL56 136 C1
Sharry La CV37 129 C1
Shawberry Ave B35 22 B4
Shawbury Cotts B46 35 E7
Shawbury La
Fillongley CV7 36 A5
Shustoke B46 35 C7
Shawbury Village B46 35 E6
Shawe Ave CV10 29 C7
Shawell Rd
Shawell LE17 68 D8
Shawell LE17 68 F4
Shawfield B47 69 A5
Shawhurst Croft B47 69 A7
Shawhurst Gdns B47 69 B7
Shawhurst La B47 69 A6
Shaw's La CV35 114 C8
Shearings The OX15 142 D4
Shearwater Dr CV23 67 C1
Sheen Ho CV2 62 D8
Sheepclose Dr B37 33 A3
Sheepcote Cl CV32 106 A1
Sheep Dip La CV23 96 E2
Sheep St
Chipping Campden GL55 135 A1
Rugby CV21 83 A3
Shipston-on-S CV36 149 D6
Stratford-u-A CV37 145 A2
Sheepy La CV9 6 E3
Sheepy Rd
Atherstone CV9 12 D2
Atherstone,Pinwall CV9 12 E6
Shefford Rd CV35 132 D3
Shelbourne Rd CV37 144 B4
Shelby La CV37 121 C7
Sheldon Gr CV34 104 F2
Sheldon Rd B98 103 A8
Sheldons The CV36 149 D7
Sheldrake Cl CV3 63 A1
Shelfield Cl
Coventry CV5 60 B3
Hockley Heath B94 88 C6
Shelley Ave CV34 108 C4
Shelley Cl
Bedworth CV12 39 D1

Shelley Cl *continued*
Redditch B97 102 C8
Shelley Rd
Coventry CV2 62 C3
Stratford-u-A CV37 145 B1
Shellon Cl CV3 78 F8
Shelly Cres B90 71 B6
Shelly La B90 71 B6
Shelton Sq CV1 151 B2
Shelton St B77 9 F7
Shelwick Gr B93 71 F4
Shenington CE Prim Sch OX15 138 E5
Shenington Kart Club★ OX15 138 E5
Shenstone Ave CV22 83 E1
Shenstone Dr CV7 74 A6
Shenton Cl CV13 21 E7
Shepheards La CV7 46 A3
Shepherd Cl
Coventry CV4 59 F3
Long Itchington CV47 115 D3
Shepherd Pl CV35 132 B5
Shepherds Cl OX15 142 D8
Shepherds Hill CV47 147 D4
Shepherd St CV23 115 C7
Shepperton Bsns Pk CV11 29 C1
Shepperton Ct CV11 29 C1
Shepperton St CV11 29 C2
Sheppey Dr B36 33 B5
Sherard Croft B36 33 B6
Sherborne Cl B46 34 A4
Sherborne Rd LE10 32 B7
Sherbourne Arc CV1 151 B2
Sherbourne Ave CV10 28 B4
Sherbourne Cres CV5 60 E4
Sherbourne Ct CV1 151 B1
Sherbourne Fields Sch CV6 60 D5
Sherbourne St CV1 61 A2
Sherbrooke Ave B77 9 E6
Sherdmore Croft B90 70 F6
Sheridan Cl CV22 99 F7
Sheridan Dr CV10 27 F5
Sheridan Wlk B35 22 A3
Sheriff Ave CV4 76 B7
Sheriff Rd CV21 83 D3
Sheriffs Orch CV1 151 B2
Sheringham Cl CV11 29 F2
Sherington Ave CV5 60 C4
Sherlock Rd CV5 60 D3
Sherwell Dr B49 143 B4
Sherwood Cl CV9 10 C1
Sherwood Jones Cl CV6 61 B6
Sherwood Rd CV13 21 E7
Sherwood Wlk CV32 106 C4
Shetland Ave B77 9 F7
Shetland Cl CV5 60 A4
Shetland Dr CV10 29 A2
Shetland Wlk B36 33 B6
Shevlock Way CV6 62 A6
Shillingstone Cl CV2 63 A4
Shillingstone Dr CV10 29 A1
Shilton & Ansty CE Fst Sch CV7 51 E5
Shilton Cl B90 70 F6
Shilton Ind Est CV7 51 E7
Shilton La
Barnacle CV2,CV7 51 B4
Bulkington CV12 40 D1
Coventry CV2 50 F3
Shilton CV7,CV12 51 D8
Shinehill La WR11 128 A1
Shipston High Sch CV36 149 C6
Shipston Ind Est CV36 149 C7
Shipston Rd
Alderminster CV37 130 B5
Coventry CV2 62 C6
Long Compton CV36 141 C4
Upper Tysoe CV35 138 B6
Shipston-on-Stour Prim Sch CV36 149 D6
Shirebrook Cl CV2 50 D2
Shire Cl CV6 50 B1
Shires Gate Ret Pk CV31 109 E6
Shires Gate Trad Est CV31 109 E6
Shires Ret Pk CV34 109 D6
Shires The CV23 81 B6
Shirland Rd B37 33 A1
Shirlett Cl CV2 50 B4
Shirleydale 2 B90 70 C8
Shirley La CV7 59 A5
Shirley Rd CV2 63 A7
Shirrall Dr B78 7 E4
Shopping Ctr The CV31 110 B5
Shopping Prec The CV34 105 A1
Shorncliffe Rd CV6 60 E6
Shortacres CV35 132 C6
Shortfield Cl CV7 74 B7
Short La CV47 115 C4
Shortland Cl B93 72 A7
Shortlands CV7 49 D6
Shortley Rd CV3 77 F8
Short St
Coventry CV1 151 C2
Nuneaton CV10 28 D4
Solihull B90 70 A5
Shortwoods The B78 11 A6
Shottery Cl CV5 60 B3
Shottery Rd CV37 144 E2
Shottery St Andrew's CE Prim Sch CV37 144 D2
Shottery CV37 144 D2
Shotteswell Rd B90 70 B8
Shoulderway La CV36 149 D2
Showell La CV7 47 A1

Shreres Dyche CV34 108 C4
Shrewley Comm CV35 114 B6
Shrieve's Wlk 6 CV37 145 A2
Shrubberies The CV4 76 E4
Shrubland Street Com Prim Sch CV31 110 A6
Shrubland St CV31 110 A6
Shuckburgh Cres
Bourton on D CV23 97 E2
Rugby CV22 100 D8
Shuckburgh Gr 5 CV32 106 A2
Shuckburgh Rd
Napton on t H CV47 125 C8
Priors Marston CV47 125 E4
Shulman's Wlk CV2 62 D7
Shultern La CV4 76 D6
Shuna Croft CV2 63 B7
Shurnock Court Barns B96 118 A7
Shustoke CE Prim Sch B46 25 A2
Shustoke Resrs★ B46 24 F3
Shutford Rd
North Newington OX15 139 D2
Shutford OX15 139 B1
Shuttington Rd B77,B79 4 B6
Shutt La B94 70 B1
Shuttle St CV6 62 B8
Shuttleworth Rd CV23 83 F5
Shylock Gr CV34 109 E2
Sibford Gower Prim Sch OX15 142 D8
Sibford Rd
Hook Norton OX15 142 D4
Shutford OX15 138 F2
Sibford Sch OX15 142 D8
Sibree Rd CV3 78 B4
Sibton Cl CV2 50 C1
Sidbury Gr B93 71 E3
Sidbury Rd CV6 61 C6
Siddaway Ho CV21 83 C7
Siddeley Ave
Coventry CV3 62 B1
Kenilworth CV8 92 E3
Siddeley Way NN11 117 F2
Sidelands Rd CV37 144 C3
Sidenhill Cl B90 70 B8
Sidings Ind Est The CV23 115 D7
Sidings The
Rugby CV21 83 B4
Shipston-on-S CV36 149 D7
Sidmouth Cl
Coventry CV2 62 C7
Nuneaton CV11 29 F5
Sidney Rd CV22 100 D8
Sidney Stringer Com Tech Coll CV1 151 C3
Signal Hayes Rd B76 13 A2
Signal Rd CV36 149 D7
Signal Wlk B77 4 A2
Silica Rd B77 4 B2
Silken Ct CV11 29 B4
Silksby St CV3 77 D8
Silver Birch Ave CV12 38 E2
Silver Birch Cl CV3 79 D7
Silverbirch Cl CV10 28 A7
Silver Birch Dr B47 69 B6
Silver Birch Gr 5 CV31 109 F5
Silverdale Cl CV2 50 B4
Silver Link Rd B77 4 A2
Silver St
Coventry CV1 151 B3
Newton CV23 68 A1
Silverstone Dr CV6 49 E5
Silver St OX15 139 D4
Silverton Rd CV6 61 F7
Silver Trees Dr CV12 40 B4
Silver Wlk CV10 28 F3
Simmonds Way CV9 12 D2
Simmons Cl B78 8 B1
Simmons Ct CV35 146 D3
Simms La B47 69 A5
Simon Cl CV11 29 D2
Simon Ct CV7 50 A8
Simon Rd B47 69 A7
Simon Stone St CV6 61 F8
Simpkins Cl CV33 107 D7
Simpson Gr CV3 78 C6
Simpson Rd CV36 149 D5
Sinclair Ave 11 OX16 139 F4
Sinclair Dr CV6 50 C6
Singer Cl CV6 62 B8
Singer Croft B36 22 F1
Sir Frank Whittle Bsns Ctr CV21 83 D5
Sir Frank Whittle Prim Sch CV2 62 F8
Sir Henry Parkes Rd CV5 76 D7
Sir John Moore CE Prim Sch DE12 3 E7
Sir Thomas White's Rd CV5 60 F2
Sir Toby Belch Dr CV34 109 F3
Sir William Lyons Rd CV4 76 C6
Sir Winston Churchill Pl CV3 79 C7
Siskin Cl CV23 83 C8
Siskin Dr CV3 78 C4
Siskin Parkway E CV3 78 C1
Siskin Parkway W CV3 78 C2
Sitwell Ave CV47 115 D3
Sixteen Acres La B50 148 E1
Skelwith Rise CV11 30 A6
Sketchley Hall Gdns LE10 31 C5

Sketchley Hill Prim Sch LE10 . . . 31 E5
Sketchley La LE10 . . . 31 C5
Sketchley La Ind Est LE10 31 B5
Sketchley Manor La LE10 . 31 D5
Sketchley Mdws LE10 . . . 31 C5
Sketchley Meadows Bsns Pk LE10 . . . 31 C4
Sketchley Old Village LE10 . . . 31 C5
Sketchley Rd LE10 . . . 31 E5
Skey Dr CV10 . . . 28 B6
Skiddaw CV21 . . . 83 C7
Skidmore Ave B77 . . . 9 C5
Skilts Sch B98 . . . 112 B6
Skipton Gdns CV2 . . . 62 B6
Skipton Lodge CV2 . . . 62 B6
Skipwith Cl CV23 . . . 64 D3
Skipworth Rd CV3 . . . 63 A1
Sky Blue Way CV1 . . . 61 E3
Skydome The CV1 . . . 151 A2
Skye Cl
Birmingham B36 . . . 33 B6
Nuneaton CV10 . . . 28 F2
Tamworth B77 . . . 9 F7
Slack's Ave CV9 . . . 18 D7
Slade Cl CV11 . . . 40 C8
Slade Gr B93 . . . 71 F6
Slade Hill CV35 . . . 114 F4
Slade La
Sutton Coldfield B75 . . . 7 A3
Tamworth B77 . . . 9 C4
Slade Mdw CV31 . . . 110 E5
Slade Rd
Rugby CV21,CV22 . . . 83 C2
Sutton Coldfield B75 . . . 7 A4
Slade The OX17,CV47 . . . 133 E6
Slateley Cres B90 . . . 70 F6
Slater Rd B93 . . . 71 F4
Sleath's Yd CV12 . . . 39 B3
Sledmere Cl CV2 . . . 50 B3
Sleets Yd CV12 . . . 39 A2
Slimbridge Cl
2 Solihull B90 . . . 71 A6
Redditch B97 . . . 102 E5
Slingates Rd CV37 . . . 145 A4
Slingsby Cl CV11 . . . 29 F2
Slingsby B77 . . . 9 C7
Slough The B97,B80 . . . 103 B4
Slowley Hill CV7 . . . 36 A8
Smallbrook Bsns Ctr B50 . . . 148 E6
Smalley Pl CV8 . . . 92 F4
Small Ho OX15 . . . 142 D8
Small La B94 . . . 86 E6
Smallman Rd CV10 . . . 28 A7
Smarts La CV35 . . . 138 B6
Smarts Rd CV12 . . . 38 F1
Smeaton La CV23 . . . 64 E6
Smercote Cl CV12 . . . 38 D1
Smite Cl CV23 . . . 53 F3
Smithford Way CV1 . . . 151 B3
Smiths Cl B50 . . . 148 E5
Smiths La B93 . . . 71 E7
Smith's La CV37 . . . 121 B6
Smiths Orch CV21 . . . 83 C3
Smith St
2 Royal Leamington Spa CV31 . . . 109 F7
Bedworth CV12 . . . 38 E1
Coventry CV6 . . . 61 F5
Warwick CV34 . . . 108 F7
Wood End CV9 . . . 10 C1
Smith's Way B49 . . . 143 C5
Smiths Way B46 . . . 23 A3
Smiths Wood Sch B36 . . . 33 A6
Smithy La
Aston Flamville LE9 . . . 32 C8
Aston Flamville LE9 . . . 32 D8
Baxterley CV9 . . . 17 D6
Church Lawford CV23 . . . 81 B6
Tamworth B77 . . . 9 F7
Smockington La LE10 . . . 42 B7
Smorrall La
Bedworth CV12 . . . 38 C2
Corley CV7,CV12 . . . 37 E1
Smythe Gr CV34 . . . 104 E1
Snape Rd CV2 . . . 62 F5
Snarestone Rd DE12 . . . 3 F8
Snitterfield La
Norton Lindsey CV37 . . . 114 C1
Snitterfield CV37 . . . 121 C7
Snitterfield Prim Sch CV37 . . . 121 B6
Snitterfield Rd CV37 . . . 120 E7
Snitterfield St CV35 . . . 121 F4
Snowdon Cl CV10 . . . 28 B3
Snowdrop Cl CV12 . . . 38 E1
Snowford Hill CV33,CV47 . 115 A5
Snows Drive Hill B90 . . . 70 D5
Snowshill Cl CV11 . . . 39 F8
Snuff La OX17 . . . 139 E8
Soar Way LE10 . . . 31 A8
Soden Cl CV3 . . . 78 D6
Soden's Ave CV8 . . . 79 A1
Solent Dr CV2 . . . 50 F1
Solihull Coll (Chelmsley Campus) B37 . . . 33 C4
Solihull Parkway B37 . . . 44 E8
Solihull Rd B92 . . . 56 E6
Solihull Ret Pk B90 . . . 70 C8
Solway Cl CV31 . . . 110 C6
Somerby Dr B91 . . . 71 A8
Somerly Cl CV3 . . . 78 F8
Somerset Dr CV10 . . . 28 E4
Somerset Pl CV22 . . . 82 B1
Somerset Rd CV1 . . . 61 C5
Somers Pl 4 CV32 . . . 109 E8
Somers Rd
Keresley CV7 . . . 49 A6
Meriden CV7 . . . 45 F1
Rugby CV22 . . . 82 D3
Somerton Dr B37 . . . 44 B7
Somerville Ho B37 . . . 33 D3
Sommerville Rd CV2 . . . 62 C4
Soot La OX17 . . . 133 D2
Sopwith Croft B35 . . . 22 A2
Sorbus B77 . . . 4 B4
Soredale Croft CV3 . . . 63 A1
Sorrel Cl CV4 . . . 75 E8
Sorrel Dr
Kingsbury B78 . . . 15 D7
Rugby CV23 . . . 83 D8
Sorrell Pl CV10 . . . 39 D8
Sorrell Rd CV10 . . . 39 D8
Sorrel B77 . . . 4 B5
Southam Cl CV4 . . . 75 E7
Southam Coll CV47 . . . 147 A5
Southam Cres CV33 . . . 123 D2
Southam Dr CV47 . . . 147 A2
Southam Prim Sch CV47 147 B5
Southam Rd
Dunchurch CV22 . . . 99 B2
Kineton CV35 . . . 132 B6
Ladbroke CV47 . . . 124 D6
Long Itchington CV47 . . . 115 D3
Mollington OX17 . . . 134 A2
Priors Marston CV47 . . . 125 E4
Southam CV33,CV47 . . . 124 B8
Ufton,Radford Hill CV31,CV33, CV47 . . . 111 D3
Southam St CV35 . . . 132 B6
South Ave CV2 . . . 62 A2
Southbank Ct CV8 . . . 92 F4
Southbank Ho 10 CV34 . . 109 D8
Southbank Rd
Coventry CV6 . . . 60 E5
Kenilworth CV8 . . . 92 F4
Southborough Terr 1 CV31 . . . 110 A6
Southbrook Rd CV22 . . . 83 A1
South Car Park Rd B40 . . . 44 E3
South Cl NN11 . . . 117 E5
Southcott Way CV2 . . . 50 F1
South Dr B46 . . . 33 E6
South End OX7 . . . 142 A2
Southern La CV37 . . . 145 A2
Southey Cl B91 . . . 71 B8
Southey Rd CV22 . . . 99 E7
Southfield Cl CV10 . . . 29 D5
Southfield Dr CV8 . . . 93 A6
Southfield Rd
Hinckley LE10 . . . 31 E7
Rugby CV22 . . . 83 C1
Southam CV47 . . . 147 A2
Southfields Cl B46 . . . 34 A4
Southfields Prim Sch CV1 61 E3
Southfields CV32 . . . 106 A3
South Green Dr CV37 . . . 144 C3
Southlands
8 Royal Leamington Spa CV31 . . . 110 B7
Atherstone CV9 . . . 18 E7
Southlea Ave CV31 . . . 109 E6
Southlea Cl CV31 . . . 109 E6
Southleigh Ave CV5 . . . 76 F7
South Lynn Gdns CV36 . . 149 D5
Southmead Gdns B80 . . . 103 E3
South Par CV33 . . . 123 F6
Southport Cl CV3 . . . 78 B5
South Rd CV23 . . . 84 A5
South Ridge CV5 . . . 60 B4
Southrop Rd OX15 . . . 142 D3
South St
Atherstone CV9 . . . 18 E8
Coventry CV1 . . . 61 E3
Rugby CV21 . . . 83 D3
South Terr CV31 . . . 110 B3
South View
Hampton Magna CV35 . . . 108 A6
Kingsbury B78 . . . 15 D4
South View Rd
Long Lawford CV23 . . . 81 F4
Royal Leamington Spa CV32 . . . 106 C5
South Way B40 . . . 44 F3
Southway CV31 . . . 110 A5
Sovereign Cl CV8 . . . 92 F1
Sovereign Ct 9 CV47 . . . 147 B4
Sovereign Rd CV5 . . . 61 A2
Sovereign Row CV5 . . . 61 A2
Sowe Valley Prim Sch CV3 . . . 78 D7
Sparkbrook St CV1 . . . 61 F3
Sparkbrook Workshops CV1 . . . 61 F3
Sparrow Cock La B93 . . . 73 C1
Sparrowdale Sch CV9 . . . 11 D4
Sparta Cl CV21 . . . 83 A6
Spartan Cl CV34 . . . 109 E4
Spa View CV31 . . . 110 B4
Speedway La CV8 . . . 79 F7
Speedwell Cl
6 Bedworth CV12 . . . 38 D2
Rugby CV23 . . . 83 E7
Speedwell Dr CV7 . . . 74 A6
Speedwell La CV9 . . . 11 B1
Spencer Ave CV5 . . . 61 A1
Spencer Ct 10 CV37 . . . 144 F1
Spencer Rd CV5 . . . 151 A1
Spencer's La CV7 . . . 58 E1
Spencer St CV31 . . . 109 F7
Spencer Yd CV31 . . . 109 F7
Spernal Ash B80 . . . 103 F1
Spernal La
Great Alne B80 . . . 119 C7
Spernall B80 . . . 112 A1
Spetchley Cl B97 . . . 102 C6
Sphinx Dr CV3 . . . 62 B1
Spicer Pl CV22 . . . 82 D1
Spiers Cl B93 . . . 72 A6
Spiers Ct B50 . . . 148 D5
Spillers Cl CV37 . . . 144 D5
Spilsbury Cl CV32 . . . 105 E2
Spilsbury Croft B91 . . . 71 A8
Spindle La B90 . . . 70 A6
Spindle St CV1 . . . 61 D6
Spindles The LE10 . . . 31 F5
Spinners Bridge CV36 . . . 149 D6
Spinney Cl
Binley Woods CV3 . . . 79 E7
Lighthorne CV35 . . . 123 B3
New Arley CV7 . . . 36 E8
Polesworth B78 . . . 10 F8
Spinney Dr B90 . . . 70 D4
Spinney Hill
Braunston NN11 . . . 117 E5
Warwick CV34 . . . 105 A1
Spinney La CV10 . . . 28 C4
Spinney Rd LE10 . . . 31 C6
Spinney The
Atherstone CV9 . . . 19 A7
Bishops Itchington CV47 . . 124 B4
Coventry CV4 . . . 76 D3
Long Lawford CV23 . . . 82 A5
Royal Leamington Spa CV32 . . . 105 D1
Solihull B91 . . . 71 C8
Wythall B47 . . . 69 B4
Spire Bank CV47 . . . 147 B3
Spires The CV10 . . . 28 C4
Spitfire Cl CV5 . . . 60 C1
Spitfire Way B35 . . . 22 A2
Spon End CV1,CV5 . . . 61 A3
Spon Gate Ho CV1 . . . 61 A2
Spon Gate Prim Sch CV1 . 61 A3
Spon La
Bradley Green CV9 . . . 11 E5
Grendon CV9 . . . 11 D4
Spon St CV1 . . . 151 A3
Spottiswood Cl CV22 . . . 99 A8
Springbrook Cl B36 . . . 22 D1
Springbrook La B94 . . . 87 A7
Spring Cl
6 Coventry CV1 . . . 61 E3
Ettington CV37 . . . 131 A3
Spring Coppice Dr B93 . . 72 A3
Spring Ct CV8 . . . 95 C5
Springdale Ct CV11 . . . 29 D3
Springfield Bsns Pk B49 . 143 B5
Springfield Cl CV36 . . . 149 C5
Springfield Cres
Bedworth CV12 . . . 39 B2
Sutton Coldfield B76 . . . 13 A4
Springfield Ct B75 . . . 13 C5
Springfield Gr CV47 . . . 147 B5
Springfield OX17 . . . 139 F6
Springfield House Com Specl Sch B93 . . . 73 A5
Springfield Pl CV1 . . . 151 C4
Springfield Rd
Coventry CV1 . . . 151 C4
Hinckley LE10 . . . 31 D7
Nuneaton CV11 . . . 29 E2
Shipston-on-S CV36 . . . 149 D4
Sutton Coldfield B75,B76 . . . 13 A4
Tamworth B77 . . . 9 D8
Springfields B46 . . . 33 F5
Springfields Rd B49 . . . 143 B5
Spring Hill
Bubbenhall CV8 . . . 95 C5
Combrook CV35 . . . 131 F7
Springhill CV10 . . . 28 A8
Springhill Houses CV22 . 100 C8
Springhill Ind Pk CV7 . . . 36 F8
Spring Hill CV7 . . . 36 F7
Spring Hill Rd CV10 . . . 28 C6
Spring La
Combrook CV35 . . . 131 E6
Hockley Heath B94 . . . 88 B5
Kenilworth CV8 . . . 93 A5
Lapworth B94 . . . 88 D3
Radford Semele CV31 . . . 110 E5
Spring Pool CV34 . . . 108 E7
Spring Rd
Barnacle CV7 . . . 51 B6
Coventry CV6 . . . 49 F1
Springs Cres CV47 . . . 147 B5
Springside B98 . . . 103 C8
Spring St CV21 . . . 83 B3
Springwell Rd CV31 . . . 110 D6
Spruce Gr 4 CV31 . . . 109 F5
Spruce Rd
5 Coventry CV2 . . . 50 B2
Nuneaton CV10 . . . 28 E7
Spruce B77 . . . 4 B4
Squadron Cl B35 . . . 22 C4
Square La CV7 . . . 37 B2
Square The
Clifford Chambers CV37 . . 129 F7
Coventry CV2 . . . 63 A7
Dunchurch CV22 . . . 99 D3
Ettington CV37 . . . 131 A3
Fazeley B78 . . . 9 A8
Kenilworth CV8 . . . 92 F4
Long Itchington CV47 . . . 115 D4
Middle Tysoe CV35 . . . 138 B7
Nuneaton CV11 . . . 29 E2
Stockton CV47 . . . 147 F8
Swalcliffe OX15 . . . 142 F8
Wolvey LE10 . . . 41 D4
Square The *continued*
Wootton Wawen B95 . . . 113 A3
Squire Pl CV47 . . . 133 D7
Squires Croft
Coventry CV2 . . . 50 F1
Sutton Coldfield B76 . . . 13 A2
Squires Gate Wlk B35 . . . 22 A3
Squires Gn LE10 . . . 31 F6
Squires Rd CV23 . . . 96 F6
Squires Way CV4 . . . 76 D6
Squirhill Pl 1 CV31 . . . 110 B7
Squirrel Hollow B76 . . . 13 A2
Stableford Cl B97 . . . 102 D7
Stables The
Berkswell CV7 . . . 58 C4
Hinckley LE10 . . . 31 D5
Longbridge CV35 . . . 114 F1
Royal Leamington Spa CV32 . . . 105 C1
Stable Wlk CV11 . . . 29 F2
Stable Yd The CV13 . . . 21 D7
Stacey Ct CV22 . . . 99 C5
Stadium Cl CV6 . . . 49 D2
Stafford Cl CV12 . . . 40 C2
Stafford St CV9 . . . 18 E8
Staines Cl CV11 . . . 29 F7
Stainforth Cl CV11 . . . 30 A2
Stainsby Croft B90 . . . 71 B5
Staircase La CV5 . . . 60 C7
Stamford Ave CV3 . . . 77 C6
Stamford Gdns CV32 . . . 105 E1
Stanbrook Rd B90 . . . 71 A5
Standard Ave CV4 . . . 60 B1
Standedge B77 . . . 10 B7
Standish Cl CV2 . . . 62 E2
Standlake Mews 14 CV31 . . . 110 C6
Stand St CV34 . . . 108 D5
Stanford Cl B97 . . . 102 B6
Stanier Ave CV1 . . . 61 B4
Stanley Ct CV31 . . . 110 C7
Stanley Rd
Atherstone CV9 . . . 18 D7
Coventry CV5 . . . 76 F8
Nuneaton CV11 . . . 29 A5
Rugby CV21,CV22 . . . 83 E1
Stannells Cl CV37 . . . 129 E8
Stansfield Gr CV8 . . . 93 D4
Stanton Bridge Prim Sch CV6 . . . 61 F6
Stanton Rd CV31 . . . 110 C6
Stanton Wlk CV34 . . . 104 D1
Stanway Rd CV5 . . . 77 A8
Stan Williams Ct CV11 . . . 29 D4
Stapenhall Rd B90 . . . 71 A5
Stapledon Gn CV47 . . . 132 F7
Staple Hill Ho CV35 . . . 122 D2
Staples Cl CV12 . . . 40 C3
Stapleton Cl
Studley B80 . . . 103 D3
Sutton Coldfield B76 . . . 22 B6
Stapleton Dr B37 . . . 33 A4
Stapleton La CV13 . . . 21 F8
Stapleton Rd B80 . . . 103 D4
Starbold Cres B93 . . . 72 B5
Starbold Ct B93 . . . 72 A6
Starbold Rd CV47 . . . 124 A4
Star Cnr CV23 . . . 101 C1
Starcross Cl CV2 . . . 62 C7
Stare Gn CV4 . . . 76 D5
Stareton Cl CV4 . . . 76 F6
Star Ind Pk CV2 . . . 62 F5
Starkey Croft B37 . . . 33 D2
Star La CV35 . . . 114 A4
Starley Ct CV3 . . . 79 A7
Starley Pk CV7 . . . 50 B8
Starley Rd CV1 . . . 151 A2
Starley Way B37 . . . 44 C6
Starmer Pl CV35 . . . 114 D6
Startin Cl CV7 . . . 49 F7
Station App
Dorridge B93 . . . 71 F2
Royal Leamington Spa CV31 . . . 109 F7
Station Ave
Coventry CV4 . . . 75 D8
Warwick CV34 . . . 108 F8
Station Bldgs B46 . . . 23 B3
Station Cotts
Chipping Campden GL55 . . 135 D2
Long Itchington CV47 . . . 115 D3
Station Dr B94 . . . 69 D1
Station La B94 . . . 89 D3
Station Link Rd B26 . . . 44 D4
Station Rd
12 Moreton-in-M GL56 . . . 140 A3
Alcester B49 . . . 143 B4
Balsall Common CV7 . . . 74 B7
Birmingham,Marston Green B37 . . . 44 A8
Bishops Itchington CV47 . . 124 A4
Chipping Campden GL55 . . 135 C2
Claverdon CV35 . . . 114 A3
Clifton u D CV23 . . . 83 F5
Coleshill B46 . . . 23 F1
Cropredy OX17 . . . 134 C1
Dorridge B93 . . . 72 B4
Dunsmore CV23 . . . 84 F8
Fenny Compton CV47 . . . 133 E7
Hampton-in-A B92 . . . 57 B7
Harvington WR11 . . . 127 D3
Hatton CV35 . . . 114 C5
Henley-in-A B95 . . . 113 A5
Higham on t H CV13 . . . 20 F4
Hinckley LE10 . . . 31 D8
Hook Norton OX15 . . . 142 E4
Kenilworth CV8 . . . 92 F4
Kingswood B94 . . . 89 D4
Station Rd *continued*
Long Marston CV37 . . . 129 C2
Old Arley CV7 . . . 36 D8
Polesworth B79 . . . 5 A2
Salford Priors WR11 . . . 127 F6
Shipston-on-S CV36 . . . 149 D6
South Littleton WR11 . . . 127 F1
Stockton CV47 . . . 116 A3
Stoke Golding CV13 . . . 21 C7
Stratford-u-A CV37 . . . 144 F3
Studley B80 . . . 103 D4
Warwick CV34 . . . 108 F7
Whitacre Heath B46 . . . 24 D4
Wilmcote CV37 . . . 120 C5
Wythall B47 . . . 69 B3
Station St E CV6 . . . 61 E7
Station St W CV6 . . . 61 E7
Station Sq CV1 . . . 151 B1
Station St CV9 . . . 18 D8
Station Street W Bsns Pk CV6 . . . 61 D7
Staunton Rd CV31 . . . 110 A5
Staveley Way CV21 . . . 83 E6
Staverton CE Prim Sch NN11 . . . 126 E8
Staverton Cl CV5 . . . 60 A3
Staverton Leys CV22 . . . 100 A7
Staverton Rd NN11 . . . 126 F8
Staverton Sports Ctr NN11 . . . 117 F1
Steeds Ct CV35 . . . 122 A7
Steele St CV22 . . . 82 E3
Steels La CV36 . . . 141 D7
Steeping Rd CV23 . . . 82 B5
Steeplefield Rd CV6 . . . 61 A5
Steeples The CV23 . . . 116 F5
Stefen Way NN11 . . . 126 F8
Stella Croft B37 . . . 33 C2
Stennels Cl CV6 . . . 60 F8
Stephanie Gr B77 . . . 4 A6
Stephenson Cl
Daventry NN11 . . . 117 F2
Royal Leamington Spa CV32 . . . 105 C1
Tamworth B77 . . . 4 A2
Stephenson Ct CV23 . . . 101 F2
Stephenson Dr B37 . . . 33 B2
Stephenson Rd
Bedworth CV7 . . . 50 C7
Hinckley LE10 . . . 30 E7
Stephens Rd B76 . . . 13 A4
Stephen St CV21 . . . 82 F3
Stepney Rd CV2 . . . 62 A4
Steppes Piece B50 . . . 148 C5
Stepping Stones B50 . . . 148 C5
Stepping Stones Rd CV5 . . 60 F4
Sterling Pk
Hinckley LE10 . . . 30 D8
Tamworth B77 . . . 9 E7
Sterling Way CV11 . . . 39 E8
Stevenage Wlk 2 CV2 . . . 63 A7
Stevens Ho CV1 . . . 151 C4
Stevenson Rd CV6 . . . 61 A8
Stewart Cl CV4 . . . 60 D2
Stewart Ct CV7 . . . 37 A8
Stewart St CV11 . . . 29 C3
Stidfall Gr CV31 . . . 110 D6
Stileman Cl CV37 . . . 129 D2
Stiper's Hill B78 . . . 5 B2
Stirling Ave CV32 . . . 106 B6
Stirling Cl CV3 . . . 78 F8
Stirling Ct 4 OX16 . . . 139 F3
Stirling Pk B90 . . . 70 E8
Stirling Rd B90 . . . 70 E8
Stivichall Croft CV3 . . . 77 B6
Stivichall Prim Sch CV3 . . 77 A6
Stockingford Inf & Jun Schs CV10 . . . 28 D3
Stocking La OX15 . . . 138 E5
Stocking Leys LE10 . . . 32 A7
Stocking Mdw CV23 . . . 53 F3
Stockley Rd CV6 . . . 50 C6
Stocks Ct CV22 . . . 99 D8
Stocks La CV23 . . . 98 F3
Stockton Cl
Dorridge B93 . . . 72 B4
Sutton Coldfield B76 . . . 22 C5
Stockton Gr 2 CV32 . . . 106 A2
Stockton Prim Sch CV47 147 F8
Stockton Rd
Coventry CV1 . . . 151 D4
Long Itchington CV47 . . . 115 E3
Stockwell La NN11 . . . 126 B5
Stockwells GL56 . . . 140 A3
Stoke Gn CV3 . . . 62 A2
Stoke Green Cres CV3 . . . 62 B1
Stoke Heath Prim Sch CV2 . . . 62 A6
Stoke La
Higham on t H CV13 . . . 21 A4
Stoke Golding CV13 . . . 21 E8
Stoke Park Mews CV2 . . . 62 A3
Stoke Park Sch & Com Tech Coll CV2 . . . 62 B4
Stoke Prim Sch CV2 . . . 62 A4
Stoke Rd CV13 . . . 21 F6
Stoke Row CV2 . . . 62 A4
Stokesay Cl CV11 . . . 29 A3
Stone Ave B75 . . . 13 A5
Stonebow Ave B91 . . . 71 B8
Stonebridge Highway CV3 . . . 77 E4
Stonebridge La CV47 . . . 115 B4
Stonebridge Rd
Birmingham B46 . . . 45 A7
Coleshill B46 . . . 33 F5
Lighthorne Heath CV33 . . . 123 C3
Stone Bridge GL56 . . . 140 D7

Stonebridge Trad Est CV3 78 B4
Stonebrook Way CV6 49 F3
Stonebury Ave CV5 59 E4
Stonechat Rd CV23 67 D1
Stone Cross B46 23 B3
Stone Ct OX7 142 A2
Stonefern Ct 21 GL56 140 A3
Stonefield Cl CV2 63 A8
Stonehall Rd CV22 99 A8
Stonehaven Dr CV3 77 C3
Stonehill Croft B90 70 F6
Stonehills CV21 83 C7
Stonehill Wlk 5 B77 9 F6
Stonehouse Cl CV32 106 D5
Stone House La CV7 47 F6
Stonehouse La
Coventry CV3 78 C4
New Arley CV7 36 E7
Stoneleigh Abbey★ CV8 93 F3
Stoneleigh Ave
Coventry CV5 76 F7
Kenilworth CV8 93 A6
Stoneleigh Cl
Hartshill Green CV10 19 B2
Redditch B98 102 F6
Stoneleigh CV8 94 B6
Stoneleigh Ct CV11 29 C3
Stoneleigh Deer Park Bsns Village CV8 94 D4
Stoneleigh Gdns CV11 29 C3
Stoneleigh Park National Ag Ctr★ CV8 94 A4
Stoneleigh Rd
Baginton CV8 77 F1
Blackdown CV32 106 A7
Coventry CV4 76 E2
Kenilworth CV8 93 A6
Stoneleigh CV8 94 B3
Stoneley Rd CV13 21 D6
Stone Mdw CV7 49 A6
Stonepits La B97 102 D4
Stone Pits Mdw CV37 120 C5
Stoneton Cl CV47 147 C3
Stoneton Cres CV7 74 A6
Stoneway NN11 126 F5
Stoneway Gr CV31 110 D6
Stonewell Cres CV11 40 B8
Stoney Ct CV3 79 A7
Stoneydelph Prim Sch B77 4 A1
Stoney La CV35 114 C6
Stoneymoor Dr B36 22 D1
Stoney Rd
Coventry CV1,CV3 151 B1
Nuneaton CV10,CV11 29 B6
Stoney Stanton Rd CV1, CV6 61 E5
Stoneywood Rd CV2 62 F8
Stonydelph La B77 10 A7
Stoop The CV3 63 B1
Stornoway Rd B35 22 B4
Storrage La B48 85 A3
Stour Ct CV36 149 D5
Stour B77 10 A5
Stourton Cl B93 72 B7
Stour View CV36 137 A8
Stowe Dr CV47 147 B3
Stowe Pl CV4 59 C1
Stow Rd GL56 140 A2
Strachey Ave CV32 105 E2
Stradey Cl CV3 63 B1
Straight Mile CV23 98 A4
Stratford Ave CV9 18 C7
Stratford Bsns & Tech Pk CV37 130 C8
Stratford Butterfly Farm★ CV37 145 B2
Stratford Coll CV37 144 E3
Stratford Prep Sch CV37 144 F2
Stratford Rd
Alcester B49 143 D3
Banbury OX15,OX16 139 E4
Bidford-on-A B50 128 D7
Dorridge B94 71 B3
Hampton Lucy CV35,CV37 121 E4
Harvington WR11 127 D3
Henley-in-A B95 113 A3
Ilmington CV36 136 B8
Lighthorne Heath CV33 123 D2
Longbridge CV34 108 C3
Loxley CV35 130 F8
Mickleton GL55 135 B7
Newbold-on-S CV37 130 E1
Nuthurst B94 88 C5
Shenington OX15 138 F7
Shipston-on-S CV36 149 D7
Solihull B90 70 D7
Temple Grafton B49 119 E3
Wellesbourne CV35 146 B3
Wroxton OX15 139 B5
Stratford St
Coventry CV2 62 A4
Nuneaton CV11 29 C4
Stratford-upon-Avon Gram Sch For Girls CV37 144 D2
Stratford-upon-Avon High Sch CV37 144 E3
Stratford-upon-Avon Hospl CV37 144 F3
Stratford-upon-Avon Prim Sch CV37 144 F2
Stratford-upon-Avon Shire Horse Ctr★ CV37 129 F7
Stratford-upon-Avon Sta CV37 144 F3
Strath Cl CV21 101 A7
Strathearn Rd CV32 105 E1
Strathmore Ave CV1 61 E1
Strathmore Rd LE10 31 A7
Stratton St CV9 18 E7
Strawberry Fields CV7 46 B1
Strawberry Wlk CV2 50 D2
Streamside Cl CV5 60 A8
Stretton Ave CV3 78 C6
Stretton Cl LE10 31 D6
Stretton Cres CV31 110 B5
Stretton Ct
Hinckley LE10 31 D3
Rugby CV21 83 D7
Stretton Rd
Nuneaton CV10 29 A3
Solihull B90 70 B8
Wolston CV8 80 A2
Stroma Way CV10 28 F2
Strutt Rd LE10 32 A5
Stuart Cl CV34 108 D5
Stuart Ct
7 Royal Leamington Spa CV32 105 E1
Coventry CV6 62 A8
Stuart Gdns CV47 132 F7
Stubbs Cl CV12 39 A4
Stubbs Gr CV2 62 B5
Stud Farm Cl OX17 134 F1
Studland Ave CV21 83 F1
Studland Gn CV2 63 A4
Studley High Sch B80 103 E3
Studley Inf Sch B80 103 E4
Studley Rd B98 103 B8
Studley St Mary's CE Jun Sch B80 103 E3
Sturley Cl CV8 93 B6
Sturminster Cl CV2 63 A4
Styles Cl
Hampton Magna CV35 114 F4
Royal Leamington Spa CV31 110 A7
Styvechale Ave CV5 77 A8
Sudbury Cl CV32 106 C3
Sudeley Cl B36 22 B1
Sudeley Rd CV10 39 C8
Sudeley B77 9 C8
Suffolk Cl
Bedworth CV12 39 A3
Coventry CV5 60 B3
Nuneaton CV10 28 E3
Suffolk St CV32 106 A1
Sugarswell La OX15 138 D7
Sugarswell Cotts OX15 138 E8
Sulgrave Cl CV2 62 E7
Sullivan Ct CV6 62 B7
Sullivan Rd CV6 62 B7
Sumburgh Croft B35 22 A3
Summerhouse Cl B97 102 A6
Summer La B76 22 D6
Summerton Rd CV31 110 A3
Sumner Cl CV35 114 F3
Sumner Rd B46 34 A6
Sunart Way CV10 28 C5
Sunbeam Cl
Birmingham B36 22 F1
Rugby CV21 83 C3
Sunbridge Terr CV21 83 C3
Sunbury Rd CV3 78 C5
Suncliffe Dr CV8 93 A2
Sunderland Pl CV35 146 C1
Sundew St CV2 50 D2
Sundorne Cl CV5 60 A4
Sunfields Cl B78 11 B8
Sunningdale Ave
Coventry CV6 49 D2
Kenilworth CV8 93 B4
Sunningdale Cl CV11 30 A1
Sunningdale B77 4 C5
Sunnybank Ave CV3 78 B5
Sunny Bank
Coventry CV1 151 A3
Great Rollright OX7 142 A2
Sunnydale Cres LE10 31 A7
Sunnydale Rd LE10 30 F7
Sunnyhill LE10 31 F7
Sunnyhill S LE10 31 F6
Sunnyside B95 119 F7
Sunnyside Cl
Balsall Common CV7 74 C7
Coventry CV5 60 F3
Sunnyside Ct CV10 28 F3
Sunnyside La CV7 74 C7
Sun Rising Hill OX15 132 D1
Sunset Cl B78 11 A8
Sunset Dr CV37 129 C8
Sunshine Cl CV8 93 A2
Sun St CV21 83 C3
Sunway Gr CV3 77 B6
Surrey Cl
Hinckley LE10 31 E4
Nuneaton CV10 28 E3
Surrey Ct CV34 108 E8
Sussex Cl CV10 28 E3
Sussex Ct CV34 108 E8
Sussex Dr 21 OX16 139 F5
Sussex Rd CV5 60 F4
Sutcliffe Ave CV37 130 D3
Sutcliffe Dr CV33 123 E6
Sutherland Ave CV5 60 A4
Sutherland Cl CV34 104 E1
Sutherland Dr CV12 39 A4
Sutton Ave CV5 59 D4
Sutton Cl NN11 134 F6
Sutton Ct CV6 50 C6
Sutton Ho CV22 82 C1
Sutton La OX15 137 E1
Sutton Pk CV10 28 B7
Sutton Rd B78 8 A8
Sutton Sq B76 22 E6
Sutton Stop CV6 50 B5
Swadling St CV31 109 F6
Swain Crofts CV31 110 B6
Swains Gn LE10 31 F6
Swalcliffe Barn Mus★ OX15 142 F8
Swalcliffe Park Sch Trust OX15 142 F8
Swaledale CV4 76 D6
Swale Rd B76 13 A1
Swallow Ave B36 33 A8
Swallow Cl CV37 145 A5
Swallow Ct
Bedworth CV12 49 C8
Hinckley LE10 30 F6
Swallowdean Rd CV6 60 E8
Swallowgate Bsns Pk CV6 49 D1
Swallow Rd CV6 49 C1
Swallows Ind Est The B90 70 D8
Swallows' Mdw B90 70 D8
Swanage Gn CV2 63 A4
Swan Cl GL56 140 A3
Swan Croft B95 113 A5
Swancroft Rd CV2 62 A5
Swan Ct
Alcester B49 143 B3
Stratford-u-A CV37 145 B2
Swanfold CV37 120 C5
Swan La CV2 61 F4
Swans Cl CV37 120 C5
Swan's Nest CV37 145 B2
Swan St
Alcester B49 143 B3
Royal Leamington Spa CV32 106 A1
Warwick CV34 108 E6
Swanswell St CV1 151 C4
Swanswood Gr 3 B37 33 C3
Swedish Houses CV23 116 B6
Sweet Knowle Farm Cotts CV37 130 A2
Swerford Rd OX15,OX7 142 D3
Swift Cl
Birmingham B36 33 A8
Kenilworth CV8 93 A2
Swift Pk CV21 83 A7
Swift Point CV21 66 F1
Swift Rd CV37 145 A5
Swift's Cnr CV3 77 E8
Swift Valley Ind Est CV21 82 F8
Swillington Rd CV6 61 B5
Swinburne Ave CV2 62 D2
Swinburne Cl CV10 28 A5
Swinburne Rd B97 102 C7
Swindale Croft CV3 78 F8
Swindale B77 10 B7
Swinford Gr B93 71 E3
Swinford Rd LE17 68 F8
Swiss Lodge Dr B78 8 F8
Sycamore Ave B78 11 A8
Sycamore Cl
Hinckley LE10 31 E5
Sibford Gower OX15 142 D8
Stockton CV47 147 E8
Stratford-u-A CV37 144 F5
Wellesbourne CV35 146 E3
Sycamore Cres
Birmingham,Marston Green B37 44 A8
New Arley CV7 37 B8
Sycamore Ct
Allesley CV5 59 F7
Kineton CV35 132 B5
Sycamore Dr B47 69 B6
Sycamore Gr
Rugby CV21 83 A4
Southam CV47 147 B6
Warwick CV34 105 A1
Sycamore Ho B98 102 F8
Sycamore Rd
Coventry CV2 50 B2
Kingsbury B78 15 D7
Nuneaton CV10 28 D6
Sycamores The CV12 38 E2
Sycamore B77 9 E7
Sydenham Dr CV31 110 B6
Sydenham Ind Est CV31 110 B6
Sydenham Prim Sch CV31 110 C6
Sydnall Fields CV6 49 F4
Sydnall Rd CV6 49 F4
Sydney Ct 1 CV12 38 F2
Sykes Cotts CV37 129 B6
Sykesmoor B77 10 B7
Sylvan Dr CV3 76 F6
Synkere Cl CV7 49 A6
Sywell Leys CV22 99 F6

T

Table Oak La CV8 74 B1
Tachbrook Cl CV2 50 C2
Tachbrook Link CV34 109 E4
Tachbrook Park Dr CV34 109 E5
Tachbrook Rd CV31 109 F4
Tachbrook St CV31 110 A6
Tackford Cl B36 22 D1
Tackford Rd CV6 62 A8
Tackley Cl B90 70 B8
Tailor's La CV37 129 D1
Tainters Hill CV8 93 A6
Talbot Cl 6 OX16 139 F4
Talbot Ct
Royal Leamington Spa CV32 106 A1
Wellesbourne CV35 146 E3
Talbot Rd CV37 145 A4
Talisman Cl CV8 92 F3
Talisman Sq CV8 92 F4
Talland Ave CV6 62 A6
Tallants Cl CV6 62 A8
Tallants Rd CV6 62 A8
Talton Cl B90 71 A5
Tamar Cl CV23 82 B5
Tamar Dr B76 22 B7
Tamar Rd
Bulkington CV12 40 B2
Tamworth B77 10 A5
Tame Bank B78 15 C6
Tame Ct B78 9 B8
Tameside Dr B35 22 A1
Tame Valley Bsns Pk B77 9 E6
Tame Valley Ind Est B77 9 E6
Tame Way LE10 31 A8
Tamora Cl CV34 109 D3
Tamworth Bsns Ctr B77 4 B3
Tamworth Bsns Pk B77 4 B3
Tamworth Rd (Amington) B77 4 A5
Tamworth Rd B78 9 C2
Tamworth Rd (Dosthill) B77 9 C6
Tamworth Rd
Fillongley,Corley Ash CV7 37 A1
Fillongley CV7 36 C6
Keresley CV6,CV7 48 D5
Kingsbury B78 15 C7
Polesworth B78 4 E1
Sutton Coldfield B75 7 A2
Tamworth,Two Gates B77 9 D8
Wood End CV9 10 C1
Tancred Cl CV31 109 F5
Tangmere Dr B35 22 A3
Tanhill B77 10 B7
Tankards Hill GL56,GL55 136 B1
Tanners Ctyd CV34 108 D5
Tanners Gr CV6 49 D4
Tanners Green La B47,B94 69 B2
Tanners' La CV4,CV7 55 B1
Tannery Cl CV9 18 E8
Tannery Ct CV8 92 F4
Tannery The CV36 149 C6
Tanser Ct CV22 99 C3
Tansley Cl B93 71 F4
Tanwood Cl
Redditch B97 102 A6
Solihull B91 71 B8
Tanworth-in-Arden CE Prim Sch B94 87 A2
Tanworth La
Henley-in-A B95 113 A7
Redditch B98 112 B8
Solihull B90 70 C5
Tanyard Cl CV4 59 D1
Tanyard The B95 113 B5
Tapcon Way CV2 62 F5
Tappinger Gr CV8 93 C5
Tapster La B94 88 F2
Tara Ct CV2 62 B4
Tarlington Rd CV6 60 E6
Tarn Cl CV12 39 A2
Tarquin Cl CV3 78 D7
Tarragon Cl CV2 50 D1
Tarrant B77 9 F8
Tarrant Wlk CV2 63 A5
Taskers Way 3 CV37 145 A2
Tatchbrook Ct 5 CV31 109 F6
Tatnall Gr CV34 108 E8
Tattle Bank CV47 147 B3
Taunton Way CV6 49 A2
Taverners La CV9 18 D7
Tavern La CV37 144 D2
Tavistock St CV32 105 F1
Tavistock Way CV11 29 E5
Tavistock Wlk CV2 62 C7
Tay Croft B37 33 C4
Taylor Ave CV32 106 B2
Taylor Cl CV8 93 B6
Taylor Ct CV34 108 D7
Tay Rd CV6 61 B6
Teachers Cl CV6 61 A5
Tea Gdn The CV12 49 E8
Teal Bsns Ctr LE10 30 D7
Teal Cl CV37 144 C5
Teal Dr LE10 31 A6
Teal Rd B80 103 F4
Teasel Cl CV23 83 D8
Teddy Bear Mus The★ CV37 144 F3
Ted Pitts La CV5 48 B2
Teign B77 10 A5
Telegraph St CV36 149 D6
Telephone Rd CV3 62 C2
Telfer Rd CV6 61 B7
Telford Ave CV32 106 B5
Telford Inf & Jun Schs CV32 106 C5
Telford Rd CV7 50 C8
Templar Ave CV4 60 A1
Templar Ct CV11 29 C3
Templars' Fields CV4 76 B7
Templars Prim Sch CV4 60 A1
Templars The CV34 108 F5
Temple Ave CV7 73 F6
Temple Ct
Coleshill B46 23 F1
Rugby CV22 83 C2
Temple End CV33 123 E6
Temple Grafton CE Prim Sch B49 119 E1
Temple Gr CV34 108 D5
Temple Herdewyke Prim Sch CV47 133 A7
Temple Hill Rd OX15 142 D8
Temple Hill LE10 41 E5
Temple La B93 73 A4
Temple Rd B93 72 A3
Temple St CV21,CV22 83 C2
Templeton Cl B93 72 A3
Temple Way B46 23 F1
Ten Acres B49 143 D4
Tenby Cl CV12 38 C1
Tenby Ct CV32 109 E8
Teneriffe Rd CV6 49 F1
Tenlons Rd CV10 28 F2
Tennant Cl CV21 83 E1
Tennant St CV11 29 E3
Tennyson Ave
Rugby CV22 99 E7
Warwick CV34 108 C4
Tennyson Cl CV8 93 C4
Tennyson Rd
Coventry CV2 62 C3
Redditch B97 102 C8
Stratford-u-A CV37 130 A8
Ten Shilling Dr CV4 75 E6
Tenter St CV9 18 D8
Terrace Rd CV9 18 D8
Terrace The
Moreton Morrell CV35 122 F2
Snitterfield CV37 121 B6
Welford-on-A CV37 129 B6
Terrett Ct 2 CV37 145 A2
Terry Ave CV32 105 C1
Terry Rd CV1 61 F1
Tewkesbury Dr CV12 39 C3
Thackeray Cl
Lower Quinton CV37 129 D2
Nuneaton CV10 28 A4
Rugby CV22 99 F7
Thackhall St CV2 61 F4
Thames Cl CV12 40 A3
Thames Rd NN11 117 F1
Thamley Rd CV6 61 A4
Thane Cl B80 103 F4
Thatchers Cl OX15 138 D3
Thatchings The CV22 99 D3
The Archbishop Grimshaw RC Sch B37 33 A3
Theatre Ct CV34 108 D6
Theatre St CV34 108 D7
Thebes Cl CV5 59 B8
Theddingworth Cl CV3 78 E8
Thickthorn Cl CV8 93 B2
Thickthorn Mews CV8 93 B2
Thickthorn Orchs CV8 93 B2
Thimble End Rd B76 13 A2
Thimbler Rd CV4 76 C7
Third Exhibition Ave B40 44 D4
Thirlestane Cl CV8 93 C6
Thirlmere Ave CV11 29 F6
Thirlmere Cl CV4 59 E3
Thirlmere Rd
Bedworth CV12 39 A2
Hinckley LE10 31 A7
Thirlmere CV21 83 C7
Thirsk Rd CV3 77 C5
Thistle Way CV23 83 D8
Thistlewood Gr B93 90 B6
Thistley Field E CV6 61 A7
Thistley Field N CV6 61 A7
Thistley Field S CV6 60 F6
Thistley Field W CV6 60 F7
Thomas Jolyffe Prim Sch CV37 145 A5
Thomas King Ho 6 CV1 61 E4
Thomas Landsdail St CV3 77 D8
Thomas Lane St CV6 50 A1
Thomas Naul Croft CV4 59 F3
Thomas Sharp St CV4 76 A7
Thomas St
Bedworth CV12 39 A2
Royal Leamington Spa CV32 106 A1
Thomas Way CV23 82 A5
Thomas Wlk B35 22 B3
Thompson's La CV7 48 E6
Thompson's Rd CV7 48 F6
Thomson Cl CV21 83 B6
Thornbury Ho CV8 93 A3
Thornbury Rise OX16 139 F3
Thornby Ave
Kenilworth CV8 93 B3
Tamworth B77 9 E8
Thorncliffe Cl B97 102 A6
Thorncliffe Way CV10 27 F8
Thorn Cl CV21 83 C6
Thorney Rd CV2 62 B6
Thornfield Ave CV13 21 E7
Thornfield Way LE10 31 E8
Thorngrove Ave 7 B91 71 C8
Thornhill Dr CV11 40 C8
Thornhill Rd CV1 61 D5
Thornley Cl CV31 110 F5
Thornley Gr B76 22 C6
Thorns Com Inf Sch CV8 93 B4
Thorn Stile Cl CV32 106 E6
Thornton Cl
Coventry CV5 59 C4
Warwick CV34 104 F1
Thornton Rd B90 70 F6
Thorntons La CV47 125 C7
Thorntons Way CV10 28 A3
Thornton Way B77 9 C8
Thorn Way CV47 115 D4
Thornycroft Rd LE10 31 E8
Thorpe Rd OX17 134 F1
Threadneedle St CV1 61 D6
Three Acres La B90 69 F6
Three Cocks La WR11 127 D1
Three Corner Cl B90 69 E8

Three Cornered Cl CV32 106 E6
Three Oaks Rd B47 69 B4
Three Pots Rd LE10 31 E4
Three Spires Ave CV6 61 A6
Three Spires Ind Est CV6 50 A5
Three Spires Jct CV6 49 E1
Three Spires Sch CV6 60 D6
Throckmorton Cl CV35 114 C8
Throckmorton Rd
Alcester B49 143 D4
Redditch B98 103 A8
Thruppence Cl CV4 75 E6
Thurlaston Dr CV22 99 B6
Thurlestone Rd CV6 60 F8
Thurlow Cl CV9 12 D2
Thurne B77 9 F8
Thurnmill Rd CV23 82 C4
Thursfield Rd CV32 106 B3
Tibberton Cl B91 71 A8
Tibbets Cl B49 143 C4
Tibbits Ct 8 CV34 108 E6
Tibblestone B90 70 A5
Tiber Cl CV5 59 F4
Tiberius Cl B46 23 F1
Tiber Way CV21 82 F7
Tidbury Cl B97 102 C6
Tidbury Green Sch B90 69 E4
Tiddington Cl B36 22 B1
Tiddington Ct CV37 145 E4
Tiddington Rd CV37 145 C3
Tideswell Cl CV3 63 A1
Tidmarsh Cl CV7 74 A6
Tidmarsh Rd CV35 105 A7
Tidmington Cl CV35 114 F5
Tile Gr B37 33 A5
Tile Hill La
Coventry,Allesley CV4, CV5 60 D2
Coventry,Tile Hill CV4 60 B1
Tile Hill Sta CV4 75 C8
Tile Hill Wood Sch & Language Coll CV4 59 D2
Tilehouse Green La B93 71 F6
Tilehouse La B90 69 E6
Tilehurst Dr CV4 59 D1
Tilemans La CV36 149 D7
Tilesford Cl B90 71 A6
Tilewood Ave CV5 59 F4
Tilia Rd B77 4 B5
Tilton Rd LE10 31 E6
Timber Ct CV22 83 C2
Timberlake Cl B90 71 B6
Timon View CV34 109 E3
Timothy Gr CV4 60 B1
Timothy's Bridge Rd CV37 144 D4
Timsa Rd CV35 132 E5
Tink-A-Tank CV34 108 E6
Tinker's Cl 28 GL56 140 A3
Tinkers Green Rd B77 9 F6
Tinkers La
Earlswood B94 87 E7
Lapworth B94 88 E1
Mollington OX17 133 F2
Tintagel Cl CV3 78 D5
Tintagel Gr CV8 93 B4
Tintagel Way CV11 30 A5
Tintern Way CV12 39 C3
Tipper's Hill La CV7 36 E6
Tippett Cl CV11 40 A7
Tipping's Hill B97 102 C5
Tisdale Rise CV8 93 B6
Titan Bsns Ctr CV34 109 E4
Tite La OX15 142 D4
Tithe Barn Cl CV35 114 F4
Tithe Barn La B94 87 C6
Tithe Cl CV13 21 D6
Tithe Ct WR11 127 F2
Titheway WR11 127 F2
Tithings The OX15 142 F8
Tiverton Dr CV11 29 F5
Tiverton Gr CV2 62 D5
Tiverton Rd CV2 62 D5
Tiverton Sch CV6 60 D5
Tiveycourt Rd CV6 50 A3
Tocil Croft CV4 76 D4
Todenham Way CV35 114 F6
Toft Hill CV23 99 B1
Tokchong Rd CV35 132 E5
Toledo Cl CV5 60 C1
Toler Rd CV11 29 B5
Tollard Cl CV2 62 F5
Toll Gate Cl CV37 144 B3
Toll Gate Rd CV47 147 B5
Tolson Ave B78 9 B8
Tolson Cl B77 9 D5
Tom Brown St CV21 83 C3
Tom Ellis Ct CV7 50 A8
Tom Henderson Cl CV3 78 F7
Tom Hill B94 87 B3
Tomkinson Rd CV10 28 F4
Tomlinson Rd B36 22 D1
Tommy's Turn La OX15 137 E1
Tompson Cl NN11 117 E5
Tomson Ave CV6 61 B4
Toms Town La B80 103 E3
Tom Ward Cl CV3 78 E7
Tomwell Cl CV47 147 B5
Tom Williams Way B77 9 C8
Tonbridge Rd CV3 78 A6
Tongue Ave B78 9 A8
Tookeys Dr B96 118 C8
Topcliffe Prim Sch B35 22 A3
Topp's Dr CV12 38 E1
Topp's Heath CV12 38 E1
Top Rd CV7,CV12 51 B7
Top St
Appleby Magna DE12 3 F7
Northend CV47 133 B7
Torbay Rd CV5 60 C4
Torcastle Cl CV6 61 F7
Torcross Ave CV2 62 C6
Torpoint Cl CV2 62 C7
Torrance Rd CV21 82 F3
Torres Cl CV34 108 B4
Torridge B77 10 A5
Torrington Ave CV4 75 E8
Torside B77 10 B7
Torwood Cl CV4 75 F6
Totnes Cl CV2 62 C7
Touchstone Rd CV34 109 F2
Tove Ct CV23 82 B5
Towbury Cl B98 102 F5
Tower Cl
Bidford-on-A B50 148 E5
Stratford-u-A CV37 145 A5
Tower Croft
Bidford-on-A B50 148 E5
Birmingham B37 33 B4
Tower Hill B50 148 E5
Tower Rd
Bedworth CV12 39 B2
Rugby CV22 83 C1
Towers Cl CV8 92 F2
Tower St
16 Royal Leamington Spa CV31 110 A7
Coventry CV1 151 B3
Tower View Cres CV10 28 B3
Townesend Cl CV34 104 F1
Town Feilds Cl CV5 60 B7
Town Ground CV35 131 F5
Townhill OX15 133 A2
Townsend Cl
Binton CV37 120 A1
Newton Regis B79 2 D4
Townsend Croft CV3 77 C7
Townsend Dr CV11 29 F3
Townsend La
Long Lawford CV23 82 B4
Upper Boddington NN11 134 E8
Townsend Rd
Coventry CV3 77 C8
Rugby CV21 83 D3
Tiddington CV37 145 E3
Townsends Cl CV11 31 A1
Town Sq CV37 145 A2
Towpath Cl CV6 50 B6
Trafalgar Ct B50 148 D4
Trafalgar Ho 3 CV1 61 B2
Trafford Cl CV9 12 D2
Trafford Dr CV10 28 C6
Trafford Lodge 4 CV31 110 B7
Traitor's Ford La OX15,CV36, OX7 142 B6
Trajan Hill B46 23 F1
Tramway Ct CV37 145 B2
Travellers Way B37 33 D3
Tredington Cl B98 103 B7
Tredington Pk CV35 114 F6
Tredington Rd CV5 59 F4
Treedale Cl CV4 75 D8
Trefoil B77 4 B5
Treforest Rd CV3 78 C8
Tregaron 4 CV37 145 A4
Tregorrick Rd CV7 50 A8
Tregullan Rd CV7 50 B8
Trehern Cl B93 72 A5
Treherne Rd CV6 61 B8
Trelawney Rd CV7 50 A7
Tremelling Way CV7 36 F8
Trenance Rd CV7 50 A8
Trench La B49 143 F3
Treneere Rd CV7 50 B8
Trensale Ave CV6 60 F4
Trentham Cl CV11 39 F8
Trentham Gdns CV8 93 C5
Trentham Rd
Coventry CV1 61 F4
Hartshill Green CV10 19 B2
Trent Rd
Bulkington CV12 40 A2
Hinckley LE10 31 A8
Nuneaton CV11 29 D5
Trent Wlk NN11 117 F1
Tresillian Rd CV7 50 B8
Tressel Croft CV34 109 E2
Trevelyan Cl
Claverdon CV35 113 F3
Stratford-u-A CV37 144 C4
Trevelyan Cres CV37 144 C4
Trevelyan Ho 1 B37 33 C1
Treviscoe Cl CV7 50 A7
Trevor Cl CV4 75 D8
Trevor White Dr CV22 83 B1
Trevose Ave CV7 50 B8
Trewint Cl CV7 50 A8
Triangle The CV5 60 B4
Tribune Trad Est CV21 83 A6
Trident Bsns Pk CV11 29 D3
Trident Bvd B35 22 B2
Trident Ct B37 44 E8
Trident Rd B26 44 C4
Trimpley Cl B93 71 E3
Trimpley Dr CV6 61 C6
Trinculo Gr CV34 109 F2
Trinity Churchyard CV1 151 B3
Trinity Cl
Banbury OX16 139 F4
Stratford-u-A CV37 145 A1
Warton B79 5 E4
Trinity Coll 2 CV37 144 F2
Trinity Ct
Hinckley LE10 31 C8
Rugby CV21 83 B3
Trinity La
Coventry CV1 151 B3
Hinckley LE10 31 C8
Trinity Pk B40 44 D3
Trinity RC Sch CV32 105 D2
Trinity RC Sch The CV34 109 C6
Trinity Rd
Freasley B78,CV9 10 B3
Kingsbury B78 15 E7
Trinity St
Coventry CV1 151 B3
Royal Leamington Spa CV32 105 F1
Stratford-u-A CV37 145 A1
Trinity Vicarage Rd LE10 31 C8
Trinity Way CV37 130 B8
Trinity Wlk CV11 29 E3
Tripontium Bsns Ctr CV23 68 A4
Triton Pk CV21 82 F8
Triumph Cl CV2 62 E3
Triumph Ho CV1 151 B2
Triumph Wlk B36 23 A1
Troilus Ct CV34 109 F3
Troon B77 4 C4
Troon Way LE10 31 D4
Trossachs Rd CV5 59 F3
Troubridge Wlk CV22 82 C2
Troughton Cres CV6 61 A5
Troutbeck Ave CV32 105 C2
Troutbeck Rd CV5 59 F4
Troyes Cl CV3 77 E7
Troy Ind Est B96 103 A3
Trueman Cl CV34 108 E8
Truemans Heath La B47, B90 69 C7
Truggist La CV7 74 E8
Trundalls La B90 70 A5
Truro Cl CV11 29 F5
Truro Wlk B37 33 B2
Trussell Way CV22 99 A8
Trust Cotts B49 118 D8
Trusteel Hos CV23 67 C5
Tryan Rd CV10 28 E4
Tuckwell Cl CV47 147 E8
Tudman Cl B76 22 A7
Tudor Ave CV5 59 F4
Tudor Cl CV7 74 A6
Tudor Cres CV9 12 D1
Tudor Ct
Bedworth CV7 49 E7
Coventry CV3 77 C8
Warwick CV34 108 D5
Tudor La CV47 147 B3
Tudor Rd CV10 28 C6
Tuer The WR11 127 A6
Tulip Tree Ave CV8 93 B5
Tulip Tree Ct CV8 93 B4
Tulip Wlk B37 44 C8
Tulliver Cl CV12 39 B3
Tulliver Rd CV10 29 C1
Tulliver St CV6 61 B5
Tunnel Rd CV10 27 D4
Turchil Dr B76 22 B8
Turchil Rd CV22 99 A8
Turchil Wlk CV22 99 A8
Turlands Cl CV2 63 A7
Turnberry Dr CV11 40 C8
Turnberry B77 4 C5
Turner Cl
Bedworth CV12 39 A4
Rugby CV21 101 B8
Warwick CV34 108 B4
Turner Rd CV5 60 D3
Turnhouse Rd B35 22 B4
Turnpike Cl
18 Moreton-in-M GL56 140 A3
Balsall Common CV7 74 B7
Turnpike Dr
Lower Quinton CV37 129 D2
Water Orton B46 23 C2
Turnstone Cl CV23 83 C8
Turpin Ct CV31 109 F6
Turpin Ho CV21 83 C7
Turton Way CV8 93 C4
Turville Cl LE10 31 F5
Turvins Mdw CV47 125 E4
Tutbury Ave CV4 76 E6
Tutbury B77 9 C7
Tutehill B77 10 B7
Tuthill Furlong CV23 67 D1
Tutnall Dr B94 88 B6
Tuttle Hill CV10 28 F6
Tweed Cl NN11 126 F8
Twenty One Oaks CV9 17 E6
Twickenham Way CV3 63 B1
Two Gates Com Prim Sch B77 9 C8
Two Gates Ind Est B77 9 D7
Twycross La CV9 6 F6
Twycross Rd LE10 31 F6
Twycross Way CV34 104 D1
Twycross Zoo* CV9 3 F1
Tybalt Cl
Coventry CV3 78 C5
Royal Leamington Spa CV34 109 D4
Tylers Gr B90 70 F6
Tyler St 15 CV37 145 A3
Tylney Cl CV3 63 B2
Tyne Cl B37 33 C4
Tynemouth Cl CV2 50 D5
Tyne Rd NN11 126 F8
Tynward Cl CV3 77 B5
Tysoe CE Prim Sch CV35 138 C7
Tysoe Cl B94 88 C6
Tysoe Croft CV3 78 F8
Tysoe Rd
Kineton CV35 132 B4
Oxhill CV35 137 F8
Radway CV35 132 E3
Tyte End OX7 142 A2
Tythe Barn Cotts WR11 127 B2
Tythe Barn La B90 70 A6
Tything Rd B49 143 C6

U

Ufton Croft CV5 60 A3
Ufton Fields CV33 123 F8
Ufton Hill CV33 111 F1
Ullapool Cl B97 102 D5
Ullenhall La B95 112 D6
Ullenhall Rd
Dorridge B93 72 A6
Ullenhall B95 112 E5
Ullenhall St B95 112 E6
Ullswater Ave
Nuneaton CV11 29 F6
Royal Leamington Spa CV32 105 C2
Ullswater Rd
Bedworth CV12 39 A2
Coventry CV3 62 E1
Ullswater B77 10 B7
Ulverscroft Rd CV3 77 D7
Ulverston CV21 83 D7
Umberslade Children's Farm* B94 87 C2
Umberslade Rd
Earlswood B94 87 C7
Tanworth-In-A B94 87 E3
Underhill Cl
Coventry CV3 77 D3
Redditch B98 102 F6
Underpass The B40 44 E4
Underwood Cl B97 102 A7
Unicorn Ave CV5 59 E4
Unicorn La CV5 59 F4
Union Bldgs CV1 151 B2
Union Pl CV6 49 F4
Union Rd CV32 105 E1
Union St
Rugby CV22 83 A2
Stratford-u-A CV37 145 A3
Unity Ho CV1 151 C4
University Farm 15 GL56 140 A3
University Hospl-Walsgrave CV2 63 A5
University Rd CV4 76 C5
Univ of Birmingham (The Shakespeare Inst) CV37 144 F2
Univ of Warwick CV4 76 C4
Univ of Warwick (Gibbet Hill) CV4 76 D3
Univ of Warwick Science Pk CV4 76 C5
Univ of Warwick (Westwood) CV4 76 B6
Upavon Cl B35 22 A4
Uplands CV2 62 A5
Upleadon Cl B97 102 A6
Upper Abbey St CV11 29 B5
Upper Cape CV34 108 D8
Upper Crossgate Rd B98 103 C8
Upper Eastern Green La CV5 59 E5
Upper Farm Mdw CV35 123 E1
Upperfield Way CV3 63 A1
Upper Grove St 8 CV32 105 E1
Upper Hill St
Coventry CV1 151 A3
Royal Leamington Spa CV32 106 A1
Upper Holly Wlk CV32 106 A1
Upper Ladyes Hills CV8 93 A6
Upper Pk CV3 78 D6
Upper Prec CV1 151 B3
Upper Ride CV3 78 D5
Upper Rosemary Hill CV8 92 F5
Upper Spon St CV1 61 A3
Upper Spring La CV8 92 F7
Upper Well St CV1 151 B3
Upper York St CV1 61 B2
Upton Dr CV11 39 F8
Upton Ho* OX15 138 E8
Upton La CV13 21 B7
Upton Rd CV22 82 D3
Usher Dr 11 OX16 139 F5
Utrillo Cl CV5 60 C3
Uxbridge Ave CV3 62 C2

V

Valanders La CV36 136 B6
Vale Cl CV21 101 A8
Valencia Croft B35 22 B4
Valencia Rd CV3 63 A2
Valentine Cl CV37 129 F8
Vale The CV3 78 C8
Vale View CV10 28 E4
Valiant Cl LE10 31 E4
Vallet Ave B49 143 B5
Valletta Way CV35 146 C2
Valley Cl B97 102 A6
Valley Dr CV21 83 A8
Valley La
Kingswood B94 89 E7
Tamworth B77 9 E7
Valley Rd
Coventry CV2 62 A6
Valley Rd *continued*
Earlswood B94 70 A1
Galley Common CV10 27 F4
Radford Semele CV31 110 E4
Royal Leamington Spa CV32 106 C3
Valley The CV31 110 E4
Van Dyke Cl CV5 60 C3
Vanguard Ave CV5 60 C1
Vanguard Ctr CV4 76 C6
Vanguard Rd B26 44 C4
Vanguard B77 9 D6
Vardon Dr CV3 77 D4
Vauxhall Cl 4 CV1 61 E3
Vauxhall Cres B36 22 F1
Vauxhall La B49 119 D1
Vauxhall St CV1 61 E3
Vaynor Dr B97 102 D8
Vaynor Fst Sch The B97 102 C7
Veasey Cl CV11 29 E3
Vecqueray St CV1 61 E2
Ventnor Cl CV2 62 E3
Ventnor St CV10 29 D6
Venture Ct LE10 30 E8
Verbena Cl CV2 50 B1
Verden Ave CV34 108 B4
Verdon Pl CV35 122 B8
Verdun Cl CV31 110 B2
Vere Rd CV21 83 F1
Vermont Gr CV31 110 D6
Verney Cl
Butlers Marston CV35 131 F4
Lighthorne CV35 123 B2
Verney Dr CV37 144 F5
Verney Gdns CV37 144 F5
Verney Rd
Lighthorne Heath CV33 123 C3
Temple Herdewyke CV47 133 A6
Vernon Ave CV22 100 E8
Vernon Cl
5 Coventry CV1 61 E3
Royal Leamington Spa CV32 105 E3
Vernon Ct 9 CV1 61 E4
Vernons Ct CV10 28 F4
Vernons La CV10,CV11 28 F4
Vernons Mews CV10 28 F4
Verona 6 CV37 145 A3
Verona Cl CV11 30 A1
Vesey Cl B46 23 B2
Viaduct Cl CV21 83 D4
Vicarage Cl
Atherstone CV9 18 E7
Dordon B78 10 F5
Vicarage Cotts GL55 135 B2
Vicarage Field CV34 109 B8
Vicarage Flats OX17 134 C1
Vicarage Gdns OX17 134 C1
Vicarage Hill
Badby NN11 126 F5
Clifton u D CV23 83 E5
Middleton B78 8 B1
Tanworth-In-A B94 86 F3
Vicarage La
Coventry CV7 49 D7
Dunchurch CV22 99 D3
Harbury CV33 123 F6
Longbridge CV35 108 A1
Long Compton CV36 141 C3
Priors Marston CV47 125 F4
Water Orton B46 23 B2
Vicarage Rd
Cheswick Green B90,B94 70 C3
Flecknoe CV23 117 B2
Hockley Heath B94 88 F7
Napton on t H CV47 125 C8
Royal Leamington Spa CV32 106 B3
Rugby CV22 82 F3
Stoneleigh CV8 94 B6
Vicarage Rise 8 CV33 122 F8
Vicarage St CV11 29 C4
Victor Hodges Ho 2 CV47 147 B4
Victoria Ave CV21 82 F4
Victoria Bsns Ctr 11 CV31 110 A7
Victoria Cl 23 CV37 145 A3
Victoria Colonnade 5 CV31 109 F7
Victoria Ct CV5 60 D4
Victoria Dr B78 9 A8
Victoria Mews
Coventry CV3 62 E2
Warwick CV34 108 D7
Victoria Rd
Atherstone CV9 18 F6
Bidford-on-A B50 148 C6
Hartshill CV10 28 B8
Hinckley LE10 31 F5
Royal Leamington Spa CV31 109 E8
Victoria St
Coventry CV1 151 D4
Nuneaton CV11 29 C4
Royal Leamington Spa CV31 109 E8
Rugby CV21 82 E3
Warwick CV34 108 D7
Victoria Terr
Royal Leamington Spa CV31 109 F7
Stockton CV47 147 F8
Victoria Way B50 148 C5
Victory Rd CV6 49 E1
Victory Terr B78 9 B8
Vienna Ho CV5 60 E2
Viking B77 9 D7

Vilia Cl LE10 31 F4
Villa Cl CV12 40 C2
Villa Cres CV12 40 C1
Village Hall Yd CV47 115 D4
Village Mews CV22 99 C7
Village Rd OX17 133 D2
Village St
Harvington WR11 127 D4
Offchurch CV33 111 B8
Villa Rd CV6 61 B6
Villebon Way CV31 110 A2
Villiers Rd CV8 93 B5
Villiers St
Coventry CV2 62 A3
Nuneaton CV11 29 B3
Royal Leamington Spa CV32 106 A1
Vincent Ave CV37 145 A4
Vincent Ct 2 CV37 145 A4
Vincent St
Coventry CV1 61 B2
Royal Leamington Spa CV32 106 A1
Vincent Wyles Ho CV2 62 E3
Vinecote Rd CV6 49 F4
Vine Cottage Est CV35 121 F4
Vine Ct CV34 108 F8
Vine La CV34 108 F8
Vinery Ct CV37 144 F2
Vine St CV1 151 C3
Vineyard The LE17 43 E6
Violet Cl
Bedworth CV12 38 E2
Coventry CV2 50 C3
Rugby CV23 83 E8
Virginia Pl CV10 28 E3
Virginia Rd CV1 61 E3
Viscount Cl
Birmingham B35 22 A2
Royal Leamington Spa CV31 109 F6
Viscount Dr B35 22 B2
Vittle Dr CV34 108 D7
Vodena Ct 5 CV32 105 E1
Vogue Cl CV1 151 D3
Vulcan Way LE17 55 C7

W

Wackrill Dr CV32 106 C3
Wadbarn B90 70 A5
Wade Ave CV3 77 B5
Wadebridge Dr CV11 29 F5
Wade Gr CV34 104 E2
Wade La CV33 123 D2
Wadham Ho B37 33 D3
Wadleys Cl B50 148 D5
Waggestaff Dr CV10 28 A7
Waggoners Cl CV8 95 C5
Waggoner's La B78 7 E8
Wagstaffe Cl CV33 123 E6
Wagstaff Way B37 44 A8
Wainbody Ave N CV3 77 A6
Wainbody Ave S CV3 76 F5
Wainbody Wood Sch CV4 76 D2
Wain Cl B49 143 D5
Wainrigg B77 10 B7
Wakefield Cl
Coventry CV3 78 F7
Hurley CV9 16 B4
Wakefield Gr B46 23 B3
Wakeford Cl CV10 18 A3
Wake Gr CV34 108 B5
Wakehurst Cl CV11 39 F8
Wakelin Rd B90 70 B7
Walcote Cl LE10 30 F8
Walcot Gn B93 72 A2
Waldron Ct 17 CV37 145 A3
Walford Gr CV34 104 F1
Walford Pl CV22 100 F8
Walford Rd OX15 142 D8
Walkers Orch CV8 94 B6
Walkers Rd CV37 145 A5
Walker's Terr CV23 64 D5
Walkers Way
Bedworth CV12 38 F1
Coleshill B46 34 A6
Kenilworth CV8 92 F2
Walkwood CE Mid Sch B97 102 C8
Walkwood Cres B97 102 C6
Walkwood Rd B97 102 D6
Wallace Ho CV34 108 D7
Wallace Rd CV6 61 A8
Wall Ave B46 33 F5
Waller Cl CV35 104 F7
Waller St CV32 106 A2
Wall Hill Rd CV5,CV7 48 B3
Wallingford Ave CV11 29 F7
Wallsgrove Cl CV32 106 B3
Wallwin Ct CV34 108 D6
Walmer Way B37 33 C3
Walmley Ash La B76 22 C6
Walmley Ash Rd B76 22 A7
Walmley Jun & Inf Schs B76 22 A7
Walnut Cl
Birmingham B37 33 B1
Braunston NN11 117 E5
Hartshill CV10 28 A8
Harvington WR11 127 D3
Nuneaton,Camp Hill CV10 28 E6
Walnut Croft CV9 17 C8
Walnut Dr
Atherstone CV9 18 F7
Royal Leamington Spa CV32 106 B3
Walnut Gdns OX17 134 B5
Walnut St CV2 50 B2
Walnut Tree Cl CV8 93 A3
Walnut Way CV22 82 B1
Walsal End La B92 56 F3
Walsall St CV4 76 B7
Walsgrave CE Prim Sch CV2 63 A6
Walsgrave Gdns 5 CV2 63 A7
Walsgrave Rd CV2 62 B3
Walsgrave Ret Pk CV2 63 B7
Walsh La CV7 46 E2
Walsingham Dr CV10 39 A7
Walter Scott Rd CV12 39 C1
Waltham Cres CV10 28 B5
Walton Cl
Coventry CV3 78 E7
Nuneaton CV11 40 A7
Walton Cotts CV35 132 C6
Walton Fields CV35 132 C5
Walton Rd CV35 146 E2
Walton W ay CV35 146 C1
Walton Way CV35 146 D2
Wandsbeck B77 9 E8
Wanley Rd CV3 77 D6
Wansfell Cl CV4 76 A7
Wantage Rd B46 23 E1
Wappenbury Cl CV2 50 C2
Wappenbury Rd CV2 50 D2
Wapping La B98 112 A7
Warden Rd CV6 61 B6
Wardens Ave The CV5 60 B6
Wardens The CV8 93 C5
Ward Gr CV34 109 C7
Wardour Dr B37 33 C2
Wareham Gn CV2 63 A5
Ware Orch CV23 101 C2
Ware Rd CV23 101 C2
Warings Green Rd B94 70 D1
Waring Way CV22 99 D4
Warkworth Cl OX16 139 F4
Warmington Cl CV3 78 E8
Warmington Gr CV34 108 B8
Warmington Rd B47 69 A6
Warmwell Cl CV2 62 F4
Warneford Mews 9 CV31 110 A7
Warneford Pl 23 GL56 140 A3
Warner Cl CV34 104 D1
Warner Row 2 CV6 61 F7
Warren Cl
Earlswood B94 87 A8
Royal Leamington Spa CV32 106 A3
Ryton-on-D CV8 79 A1
Warren Dr B93 72 A3
Warren Field CV8 79 A1
Warren Gn CV4 75 F7
Warren Rd CV22 83 D1
Warrington Cl B76 13 A1
Warton Cl CV8 93 C4
Warton La
Austrey CV9 3 A1
Orton-on-t-H CV9 6 C4
Warton B79 5 F8
Warton Nethersole's CE Prim Sch B79 5 E4
Warwick Ave CV5 77 A8
Warwick By-Pass
Hampton Magna CV34, CV35 108 A5
Warwick CV34 109 A1
Warwick Castle* CV34 108 E6
Warwick Cl B80 103 D3
Warwick Cres CV37 145 B3
Warwick Ct
5 Birmingham,Chelmsley Wood B37 33 D2
Coventry CV3 151 B1
Stratford-u-A CV37 145 A3
Warwick Dr CV9 12 D2
Warwick Gdns CV10 28 E4
Warwick Gn CV12 40 C1
Warwick Highway
Mappleborough Green B80 112 A5
Redditch B98 102 F8
Warwick Hospl CV34 108 E8
Warwick House Ind Pk CV47 147 B2
Warwick La CV1 151 B2
Warwick Mews CV37 145 B3
Warwick New Rd CV32 109 C8
Warwick Parkway CV35 108 A7
Warwick Pl
Royal Leamington Spa CV32 105 E1
Shipston-on-S CV36 149 C6
Southam CV47 147 B4
Warwick Race Course CV34 108 C6
Warwick Rd
Chadwick End B93 90 A7
Coventry CV3 151 B1
Ettington CV37 131 A4
Hanwell OX16,OX17 139 F5
Henley-in-A B95 113 C4
Kenilworth CV8 93 A1
Kineton CV35 132 B6
Knowle B93 72 D3
Leek Wootton CV35 104 F7
Norton Lindsey CV35 114 C2
Sherbourne CV35 121 E7
Snitterfield CV37 121 C5
Southam CV47 147 A3
Stratford-u-A CV37 145 C5
Tiddington CV37 145 E7
Upper Boddington NN11 134 E8
Warwick Rd *continued*
Wellesbourne CV35 146 D4
Wolston CV8 80 A3
Warwick Row CV1 151 B2
Warwick Sch CV34 109 A6
Warwickshire Ave CV37 129 D4
Warwickshire Coll (Moreton Morrell Ctr) CV35 122 E2
Warwickshire Coll
Royal Leamington Spa CV32 109 D8
Rugby CV21 83 D2
Warwickshire Ex Ctr CV31 111 C4
Warwickshire Mus* CV34 108 E6
Warwickshire Nuffield Hospl The CV32 105 E5
Warwick Sta CV34 108 F7
Warwick St CV5 60 F1
Warwicks The CV35 114 F3
Warwick St
Royal Leamington Spa CV32 105 F1
Rugby CV21 83 A2
Southam CV47 147 B4
Warwick Tech Pk CV34 109 B5
Warwick Terr CV32 105 E1
Wasdale Cl CV32 105 C2
Washbourne Rd CV31 110 A2
Washbrook La CV5 48 A1
Washbrook Pl CV36 136 B6
Washford Dr B98 103 D7
Washford Ind Est B98 103 E8
Washford La B98 103 D8
Wasperton Cl 6 CV3 78 F8
Wasperton La CV35 122 C7
Waste La
Baddesley Ensor CV9 11 E1
Balsall Common CV7 74 F5
Coventry CV6 48 F1
Watchbury Cl B36 22 C1
Watch Cl CV1 151 A3
Watchmaker Ct CV1 151 A2
Watcombe Rd CV2 62 E8
Watercall Ave CV3 77 C6
Waterdale B90 70 D5
Waterfall Cl CV7 46 C1
Waterfield Gdns CV31 110 C7
Waterfield Way LE10 31 C5
Waterford Way CV3 62 C1
Watergall Cl CV47 147 C3
Water Lily Way CV10 39 A8
Waterloo Ave B37 33 B4
Waterloo Cl CV35 146 C2
Waterloo Cres B50 148 E5
Waterloo Ct CV34 109 A8
Waterloo Dr CV37 145 D1
Waterloo Ind Est
Bidford-on-A B50 148 E6
Birmingham B37 33 B5
Waterloo Pk B50 148 E6
Waterloo Pl 5 CV32 105 F1
Waterloo Rd
Bidford-on-A B50 148 E6
Hinckley LE10 31 D8
Waterloo Rise 1 CV37 130 B8
Waterloo St
8 Coventry CV1 61 E4
Royal Leamington Spa CV31 110 B7
Waterman Rd CV6 61 F6
Water Orton La B46,B76 22 E4
Water Orton Prim Sch B46 23 B2
Water Orton Rd B36 22 E1
Water Orton Sta B46 23 A3
Watersbridge Gdns CV10 29 C1
Waterside CV6 50 C6
Waterside Cl B24 22 A5
Waterside Ct
Hinckley LE10 30 F7
Royal Leamington Spa CV31 110 B6
Waterside Dr CV21 83 C5
Waterside
Polesworth B78 5 A1
Royal Leamington Spa CV31 109 D7
Stratford-u-A CV37 145 A2
Watersmeet Gr CV2 62 B6
Watersmeet Ho B78 9 B8
Watersmeet Rd CV2 62 B6
Waterson Croft B37 33 D3
Watery La
Baddesley Ensor CV9 11 B2
Cheswick Green B90 70 D4
Corley Moor CV7 47 D5
Coventry CV6 49 A4
Hook Norton OX15 142 D4
Keresley CV7 48 F4
Kineton CV35 132 C7
Knowle B93 72 E4
Longbridge CV35 108 A1
Pillerton Hersey CV35 131 E3
Portway B47,B48 85 D7
Shipston-on-S CV36 149 D6
Shustoke B46 24 D2
Ullenhall B95 112 E6
Wathen Rd
Royal Leamington Spa CV32 106 A2
Warwick CV34 108 E8
Watling Cl LE10 31 C4
Watling Cres CV23 68 C1
Watling Ct CV11 29 F3
Watling Dr LE10 31 C4
Watling La CV9 11 B2
Watling Rd CV8 93 B6
Watling St
Dordon B77,B78 10 D6
Grendon B78,CV9 11 C4
Hinckley CV11,LE10 30 C8
Tamworth,Wilnecote B77 9 E7
Watson Cl 3 CV34 104 E1
Watson Rd CV5 60 D2
Watson Way CV7 74 C8
Wattisham Sq B35 22 A4
Watton Gn B35 22 A2
Watton La B46 23 D2
Watton's La CV47 147 B4
Watton's Lodge CV47 147 B4
Watts La CV21 101 B8
Watts Rd B80 103 E2
Waugh Cl B37 33 B2
Wavebeck Ct CV23 82 B5
Waveley Rd CV1 61 A3
Wavendon Cl CV2 50 F1
Waveney Cl LE10 31 A8
Waveney B77 9 E8
Wavere Ct CV21 83 D7
Waverley Ave CV11 29 F1
Waverley Edge CV8 95 B3
Waverley Rd
Kenilworth CV8 93 A4
Royal Leamington Spa CV31 110 B6
Rugby CV21 84 A1
Waverley Sq CV11 29 F1
Wavers Marston B37 44 A8
Waverton Ave B79 5 E4
Waverton Mews 15 CV31 110 C6
Wavytree Cl CV34 108 D7
Wawensmere Rd B95 113 A2
Wayside B37 44 A8
Weale Gr CV34 104 F2
Weatheroak Rd B49 143 D4
Weaver Ave B76 13 A1
Weaver Dr CV23 82 C4
Weavers Cl
Redditch B97 102 D4
Shipston-on-S CV36 149 D6
Weavers Cotts CV36 141 C3
Weavers Hill B97 102 D4
Weavers Row OX15 139 A3
Weavers Wlk CV6 62 B8
Webb Dr CV23 83 D8
Webb Ellis Bsns Pk CV21 83 B4
Webb Ellis Rd CV22 82 E2
Webb St CV10 28 D3
Webster Ave CV8 93 B5
Webster St CV6 61 E7
Webster Way B76 22 B8
Weddington Country Wlk* CV10 20 C1
Weddington Ctry Wlk* CV10 29 B8
Weddington La CV10 20 A3
Weddington Prim Sch CV10 29 D7
Weddington Rd CV10 29 C7
Weddington Terr CV10 29 D5
Wedgewood Cl CV2 62 E8
Wedgewood Ho B37 33 B4
Wedge-Woods CV5 76 F8
Wedgnock Gn CV34 108 D8
Wedgnock Ind Est CV34 108 C8
Wedgnock La CV34 104 C1
Wedon Cl CV4 75 E7
Weigh Bridge Ct GL55 135 B2
Weilerswist Dr CV31 109 F4
Weland Cl B46 23 B2
Weland Ct B46 23 B2
Welbeck Ave LE10 31 D4
Welby Gate CV7 74 B5
Welchman Pl CV35 138 C6
Welcombe Ct 1 CV37 145 A4
Welcombe Hills Ctry Pk (Nat Res)* CV37 145 B7
Welcombe Hills Sch CV37 145 A5
Welcombe Rd CV37 145 B4
Welcome St CV9 18 E8
Welford Cl B98 102 F5
Welford Gr CV35 114 E6
Welford-on-Avon Prim Sch CV37 129 A6
Welford Pl CV6 61 D7
Welford Rd
Bidford-on-A B50,CV37 128 D6
Long Marston CV37 129 B4
Rugby CV21 83 C4
Tamworth B77 9 C5
Welgarth Ave CV6 60 F6
Welham Croft B90 71 A6
Welland Cl
Long Lawford CV23 82 C5
Staverton NN11 126 F8
Welland Rd CV1 61 F1
Welland Way B76 22 A7
Well Bank OX15 142 D4
Well Cl B97 102 E5
Wellesbourne CE Prim Sch CV35 146 E3
Wellesbourne Farm CV35 146 E3
Wellesbourne Gr CV37 144 F2
Wellesbourne Ho CV35 146 D2
Wellesbourne Rd
Alveston CV37 121 D3
Barford CV35 122 B7
Coventry CV5 60 A3
Lighthorne CV35 123 B2
Loxley CV35 130 F8
Wellesbourne Sch (Annexe) CV35 146 E4
Wellesbourne Water Mill* CV35 146 E1
Wellfield Cl CV7 74 D5
Wellington Aviation Mus The* GL56 140 A3
Wellington Cl
Hinckley LE10 31 E4
Wellesbourne CV35 146 C1
Wellington Dr CV37 145 D1
Wellington Gdns 1 CV1 61 B2
Wellington Parkway LE17 55 D6
Wellington Rd
Moreton-in-M GL56 140 B3
Royal Leamington Spa CV32 106 C2
Wellington St CV1 151 D4
Wellington Terr GL56 140 B3
Wellington Way B35 22 B2
Well La
Shenington OX15 138 F5
Staverton NN11 126 D8
Tanworth-In-A B94 87 A1
Wellmeadow Gr B92 57 A7
Wells Cl CV10 27 F4
Wells Ct CV3 77 F7
Well Spring Cl CV9 18 F8
Wells St CV21 83 B3
Well St CV1 151 B3
Wells Wlk B37 33 A1
Welsh Cl CV34 104 E2
Welsh Rd
Aston le W NN11 134 F6
Bascote CV47 115 B2
Coventry CV2 62 B4
Cubbington CV32,CV33 106 F2
Welsh Rd E CV47 147 D2
Welsh Rd
Lower Boddington NN11 134 E7
Napton on t H CV47 125 C5
Offchurch CV33 111 E6
Welsh Rd W CV47 147 A5
Welton Cl B76 13 A2
Welton Pl CV22 100 D8
Welton Rd
Braunston NN11 117 E5
Warwick CV34 104 D1
Wembrook Cl CV11 29 D2
Wembrook Ho CV11 29 E2
Wembrook Prim Sch CV11 29 C2
Wendiburgh St CV4 76 B7
Wendover Rise CV5 60 C4
Wenlock Way CV10 28 B3
Wensum Cl LE10 31 B8
Wentworth Ave CV47 133 A6
Wentworth Dr
Coventry CV6 49 B4
Nuneaton CV11 30 A1
Wentworth Rd
Royal Leamington Spa CV31 110 D6
Rugby CV22 82 F1
Wesley Rd CV21 101 A8
Wessenden B77 10 B7
Wessex Cl CV12 39 A4
Wessex Ct B79 4 F7
Wessons Rd B50 148 E5
West Ave
Bedworth CV12 39 D2
Coventry CV6,CV7 49 A5
Coventry,Middle Stoke CV2 62 A2
Westbourne Gr CV22 82 F1
Westbrook Ct CV5 60 A4
Westbury Ct
Coventry CV2 62 A3
Warwick CV34 109 A7
Westbury Rd
Coventry CV5 60 D5
Nuneaton CV10 28 D3
West Cl LE10 31 D7
Westcliff Dr CV34 104 E2
Westcliffe Dr CV3 77 B5
Westcotes CV4 60 B1
West Dr B95 113 B2
West End WR11 128 A4
West End Cres CV37 144 F1
West End Ct CV34 108 D6
West End
Hornton OX15 139 B7
Radway CV35 132 E2
Westend Terr GL55 135 A2
Westerham Cl B93 71 F6
Western Dr LE17 43 E5
Western Hill Cl B96 102 E1
Western Rd CV37 144 F3
Western Road Ind Est CV37 144 F3
Westfield Barns CV47 125 E4
Westfield Cl
Dorridge B93 71 F2
Nuneaton CV10 29 D5
Stratford-u-A CV37 144 F5
Westfield Cres CV35 146 D3
Westfield Ct LE10 31 C7
Westfield Ho B36 33 A7
Westfield Inf Sch LE10 31 B7
Westfield Jun Sch LE10 31 B7
Westfield Rd
Hinckley LE10 31 B7
Rugby CV22 82 F2
Southam CV47 147 A3
Westfields B78 10 D8
Westgate Cl CV34 108 D6
Westgate Ho 10 CV34 108 E6

Westgate Prim Sch CV34 108 D6
Westgate Rd CV21 83 E1
West Green Dr CV37 144 B3
Westgrove Ave 6 B90 71 A6
Westgrove Terr 1 CV32 109 D8
Westham Ho
Barford CV35 122 A7
Birmingham B37 33 B4
Westham La CV35 122 A7
Westhill Rd
Blackdown CV32 106 A6
Coventry CV6 60 F6
Westholme Ct B50 148 D4
Westholme Rd B50 148 D5
West Hyde LE10 30 F7
Westlea Rd CV31 109 E6
Westleigh Ave CV5 76 F7
West Leyes CV21 83 A3
Westmead Ave B80 103 E4
Westmede Ctr CV5 60 C4
Westminster Dr
Hinckley LE10 31 F4
Nuneaton CV10 28 B7
Westminster Rd CV1 151 A1
Westmoreland Ave CV10 28 E4
Westmorland Rd CV2 62 F4
West of St Laurence CV35 114 A8
Westonbirt Cl CV8 93 C6
Weston Cl
5 Royal Leamington Spa CV31 110 C6
Dorridge B93 72 A2
Dunchurch CV22 99 C4
Warwick CV34 108 F7
Weston Ct
Long Compton CV36 141 D3
Rugby CV21 83 C4
Weston Hall Stables CV12 40 A3
Weston La
Bubbenhall CV8,CV33 95 B3
Bulkington CV12 40 B3
Weston St CV1 151 C4
West Orchards Sh Ctr CV1 151 B3
West Park Cl CV37 144 B3
West Ridge CV5 60 A5
West Rock CV34 108 D7
West Side Bsns Ctr CV4 75 F8
West Side WR11 128 A2
West St
17 Royal Leamington Spa CV31 110 A7
Coventry CV1 61 E3
Long Lawford CV23 82 A4
Shipston-on-S CV36 149 D6
Shutford OX15 139 A3
Stratford-u-A CV37 144 F1
Warwick CV34 108 D5
West View CV10 27 E8
West View Rd
Royal Leamington Spa CV32 106 C5
Rugby CV22 82 E2
Westway CV21 83 A3
Westwood Bsns Pk CV4 75 F6
Westwood Cl CV10 28 E3
Westwood Cres CV9 18 D7
Westwood Heath Rd CV4 75 E6
Westwood Rd
Atherstone CV9 18 D7
Coventry CV5 61 A1
Rugby CV22 100 F7
Westwood Way CV4 76 A6
Wetherby Way CV37 144 E1
Wetherell Way CV21 83 C7
Wexford Rd CV2 50 D1
Weymouth Cl CV3 78 D5
Whaley's Croft CV6 61 B8
Wharf Ind Est The CV23 65 A7
Wharf La B94 88 D4
Wharf Lodge CV31 109 D7
Wharf Rd
Coventry CV6 61 F5
Stratford-u-A CV37 144 F4
Wharf St CV34 109 A8
Wharf The
Shipston-on-S CV36 149 D7
Wilmcote CV37 120 C5
Wharf Yd LE10 31 A7
Wharrage Rd B49 143 D4
Wharrington Cl B98 103 A8
Wharrington Hill B98 103 A8
Whatcote Rd CV35 137 F8
Whateley Ct CV11 29 B4
Whateley Hall Cl B93 72 C7
Whateley Hall Rd B93 72 B7
Whateley La B77,B78 9 F4
Whateley's Dr CV8 93 A5
Whateley Villas CV9 10 A2
Wheatcroft Dr B37 33 C1
Wheate Croft CV4 59 F2
Wheaten Cl B37 33 D3
Wheatfield Cl B36 33 A7
Wheatfield Ct GL55 135 B6
Wheatfield Rd CV22 82 D1
Wheathill Cl CV32 105 E2
Wheatley Grange B46 33 F6
Wheatmoor Rd B75 13 A6
Wheatsheaf La B94 113 C8
Wheat St CV11 29 D4
Wheelbarrow La CV35 114 A3
Wheeler Cl B93 90 B7
Wheeley Moor Rd B37 33 A5
Wheelwright Ct 6 CV37 144 F3
Wheelwright La CV6,CV7 49 C4
Wheelwright Lane Prim Sch CV7 49 D5
Wheler Rd CV3 78 A7
Whernside CV21 83 C7
Whetstone Dr CV21 83 E7
Whichcote Ave CV7 46 C1
Whiley Cl CV23 83 F5
Whimbrel Cl CV23 83 C8
Whitacre Rd 3 CV32 106 A2
Whitacre Rd Ind Est CV11 29 E4
Whitacre Rd
Knowle B93 72 B7
Nuneaton CV11 29 E4
Whitaker Rd CV5 60 C3
Whitburn Rd CV12 38 C1
Whitchurch Cl B98 102 F6
Whitchurch Way CV4 75 F8
Whitebeam Cl CV4 59 D1
White Beam Rd B37 44 D8
Whitebeam Way CV10 28 D7
Whitefield Cl CV4 75 D6
Whitefriars Dr CV22 82 A1
White Friars La CV1 151 C2
White Friars St CV1 151 C2
Whitehall Cl CV10 19 A2
Whitehall Rd CV21 83 B2
White Hart La CV33 111 F1
Whitehead Dr
Kenilworth CV8 93 C7
Minworth B76 22 D6
Wellesbourne CV35 146 E4
Whitehead Gr CV7 74 B7
Whiteheads Ct 17 CV32 105 F1
Whitehorse Cl CV6 50 B6
White Horse Hill CV37 121 B6
White Ho The B95 113 B4
Whitehouse Cres CV10 28 D3
White House Hill B95 120 B7
Whitehouse Rd B78 11 A7
Whitelaw Cres CV5 60 C6
Whitemoor Dr B90 71 A7
Whitemoor La B96 118 D8
Whitemoor Rd CV8 93 B5
Whitemoors Cl CV13 21 E7
Whitemoors Rd CV13 21 E7
Whitepits La B48 85 F4
Whitepump La B95 112 E7
White Rose Ho 4 CV32 105 F2
Whiteside Cl CV3 78 F8
Whiteslade Cl B93 72 A7
Whites Row CV8 93 A3
White St CV1 151 C3
Whitestitch La CV7 46 C3
Whitestone Inf Sch CV11 40 A8
Whitestone Rd CV11 40 B7
Whitethorn Dr CV32 106 B2
Whiteway OX17 133 F2
Whitfield Cl CV37 145 E4
Whitford Dr B90 71 C7
Whiting B77 9 D7
Whitley Abbey Com Sch CV3 77 F6
Whitley Abbey Prim Sch CV3 78 A6
Whitley Ct CV3 77 F7
Whitley Rd B95 113 B4
Whitley Village CV3 77 F7
Whitlocks End Halt B90 69 E7
Whitmore Park Prim Sch CV6 49 A1
Whitmore Park Rd CV6 49 D3
Whitmore Rd CV31 110 A3
Whitnash Cl CV7 74 A6
Whitnash Gr CV2 62 D5
Whitnash Prim Sch CV31 110 A4
Whitnash Rd CV31 110 B4
Whittington Cl 4 CV34 109 B8
Whittington La CV9 12 B2
Whittle Cl
Coventry CV3 78 F8
Daventry NN11 117 F3
Rugby CV22 99 D7
Whittle Ct 9 CV32 106 A1
Whittleford Gr B36 22 C1
Whittleford Rd CV10 28 C4
Whittle Rd LE10 30 E7
Whittons Cl OX15 142 D4
Whitwell Cl B90 71 A6
Whitworth Ave
Coventry CV3 62 B1
Hinckley LE10 30 F7
Whitworth Cl CV35 146 C2
Whoberley Ave CV5 60 D2
Whoberley Hall Prim Sch CV5 60 C3
Wickham Cl CV6 48 F2
Wickham Ct CV32 106 B3
Wickham Rd B80 103 F4
Wickmans Dr CV4 59 C2
Wiclif Way CV10 28 B3
Widdecombe Cl CV2 62 D7
Widdrington Rd CV1 61 C5
Widney Cl B93 71 F5
Widney La B91 71 B8
Widney Manor Rd B91, B93 71 D7
Widney Manor Sta B91 71 C8
Widney Rd B93 71 F5
Wigford Rd B77 9 C5
Wiggins Cl CV21 101 B8
Wiggins Hill Rd B76 22 F7
Wight Croft B36 33 B6
Wigston Hill CV9 17 D5
Wigston Rd
Coventry CV2 50 F1
Wigston Rd continued
Rugby CV21 101 A8
Wike La B96 118 E8
Wilcox Cl CV47 124 A4
Wilcox Leys CV35 122 F2
Wildcroft Rd CV5 60 C3
Wilderness B95 113 B2
Wildey Rd 1 CV12 38 D2
Wild Goose La B98 103 D8
Wildmoor Cl CV2 50 B4
Wilford Gr B76 22 B6
Wilhelmina Cl CV32 109 E8
Wilkes Way B50 148 D5
Wilkins Cl CV35 122 A7
Wilkinson Way B46 25 A2
Willday Dr CV9 12 D2
Willenhall La CV3 78 F7
Willenhall Wood Prim Sch CV3 78 D6
Willes Ct 2 CV31 110 B7
Willes Rd CV31,CV32 110 A8
Willes Terr CV31 110 B8
Willett Gdns CV35 146 D4
Willett Ho CV35 146 D4
William Arnold Cl CV2 62 A4
William Batchelor Ho CV1 151 B4
William Beesley Cres CV11 40 E6
William Bree Rd CV5 59 C5
William Bristow Rd CV3 77 E7
William Cl 12 OX16 139 F4
William Cree Cl CV8 79 F3
William Groubb Cl CV3 78 D7
William Iliffe St LE10 31 B7
William Kirby Cl CV4 60 A1
William McCool Cl CV3 78 F7
William McKee Cl CV3 78 E7
William Malcolm Ho CV2 62 E3
William Morris Sch OX16 139 F4
William Sheriden Ho CV2 62 E3
Williams Rd CV31 110 E4
William St
Bedworth CV12 39 D2
Nuneaton CV11 29 E3
Royal Leamington Spa CV32 110 A8
Rugby CV21 83 B3
William Tarver Cl CV34 109 A7
William Thomas Ho 7 CV32 106 A1
William Thomson Ho 2 CV1 151 D4
William Tolson's Ind Est B78 9 A8
Willington St CV11 29 B5
Willis Croft B79 5 E4
Willis Gr CV12 39 C3
Willis Ho CV11 29 E1
Willoughby Ave CV8 92 E3
Willoughby Cl
Alcester B49 143 A6
Coventry CV3 78 E8
Willoughby Pl CV22 100 D7
Willowbank Rd LE10 31 C7
Willow Bank Rd B93 71 F6
Willow Bank CV37 129 A7
Willow Brook Rd CV8 80 A4
Willowbud Ho B98 102 F8
Willow Cl
Alcester B49 143 B2
Bedworth CV12 39 A5
Hinckley LE10 31 E5
Kingsbury B78 15 D7
Nuneaton CV10 28 A7
Whitnash CV31 110 B2
Willow Ctyd CV2 62 D7
Willowdale LE10 31 A7
Willowdene Cvn Site CV37 120 B5
Willow Dr
Cheswick Green B90 70 D4
Wellesbourne CV35 146 E3
Willow End GL56 141 A1
Willowfields Rd CV11 30 A1
Willow Gdns CV47 147 B4
Willow Gr
Coventry CV4 60 B2
Long Itchington CV47 115 D4
Willowherb Cl 5 CV3 78 F8
Willowherb Way B90 70 A5
Willow Ho 11 CV34 109 D8
Willow La
Fillongley CV7 36 C5
Rugby CV22 83 C2
Willow Meer CV8 93 B5
Willow Park Ind Est CV13 21 C7
Willow Rd CV10 28 F5
Willows CE Prim Sch The CV37 144 E2
Willows Dr N CV37 144 E3
Willow Sheets Mdw CV32 106 E6
Willows The
Atherstone CV9 12 E2
Bedworth CV12 38 E2
Hollywood B47 69 A6
Portway B47 85 F7
Stratford-u-A CV37 144 E2
Willow Tree Gdns CV21 101 B8
Willow Way
Birmingham B37 33 B1
Studley B80 103 E2
Willow Wlk CV7 26 E1
Wilmcote CE Prim Sch CV37 120 C4
Wilmcote Gn CV5 60 A3
Wilmcote La B95 120 A5
Wilmcote Sta CV37 120 C5
Wilmhurst Rd CV34 108 C8
Wilmot Ave B46 33 F6
Wilmot Cl CV7 74 B8
Wilnecote Gr CV31 110 B5
Wilnecote High Sch B77 9 F6
Wilnecote Jun Sch B77 9 F7
Wilnecote La B77 9 E8
Wilnecote Sta B77 9 D7
Wilson Cl CV22 82 C2
Wilson Dr B75 13 A5
Wilson Gn CV3 62 F1
Wilson Gr CV8 93 C4
Wilson Rd CV37 144 E3
Wilsons La CV7 50 A6
Wilson's La CV6 49 F6
Wilsons Rd B93 72 C6
Wilton Rd CV7 74 B5
Wiltshire Cl
Bedworth CV12 39 A3
Coventry CV5 60 B3
Wimborne Dr CV2 63 A4
Wimbourne Cl CV10 28 B5
Wimbourne Rd B76 13 A4
Wimpstone La CV37 130 B4
Winceby Pl CV4 59 D1
Winchat Cl CV3 62 F1
Winchcombe Rd B49 143 D4
Winchelsea Cl 3 OX16 139 F5
Winchester Ave CV10 29 C7
Winchester Ct CV22 99 C3
Winchester Dr
Birmingham B37 33 A2
Hinckley LE10 32 B7
Winchester St CV1 61 E3
Wincott Cl CV37 145 C1
Windermere Ave
Coventry,Binley CV3 62 E1
Coventry,Upper Eastern Green CV5 59 E4
Nuneaton CV11 29 F6
Windermere Cl CV21 83 C7
Windermere Dr CV32 105 D2
Windermere B77 10 A7
Winderton Ave CV35 114 E5
Winding House La CV6, CV7 49 C4
Windmill Ave 4 B46 33 F7
Windmill Cl
Ilmington CV36 136 B6
Kenilworth CV8 93 A6
Warton B79 5 E3
Windmill Croft CV32 106 D5
Windmill Ct CV6 50 A3
Windmill Dr B97 102 C6
Windmill Gdns
Redditch B97 102 B6
Staverton NN11 126 E8
Windmill Hill
Bidford-on-A B50 128 E8
Cubbington CV32 106 D5
Windmill Hill La CV33, CV35 123 C5
Windmill Hill The CV5 60 A7
Windmill Ind Est CV5 59 F7
Windmill La
Astley CV10 37 E6
Austrey CV9 3 C3
Balsall Common CV7 74 D4
Baxterley CV9 17 D6
Corley Moor CV7 47 D6
Dorridge B93 71 F1
Dunchurch CV22 99 A4
Ladbroke CV47 124 D6
Ladbroke CV47 124 E5
Staverton NN11 126 E8
Tanworth-in-A B94 89 A8
Windmill Rd
Atherstone CV9 12 D1
Bedworth CV7 50 A8
Coventry CV6 50 A3
Nuneaton CV10 28 D7
Whitnash CV31 109 F5
Windmill Way
Southam CV47 147 A5
Upper Tysoe CV35 138 B6
Windridge Cl CV3 78 C6
Windrush Cl B97 102 D6
Windrush Dr LE10 31 A8
Windrush Rd B47 69 B7
Windrush Way CV23 82 B5
Windsor Ct
12 Royal Leamington Spa CV32 109 F8
9 Stratford-u-A CV37 144 F3
Coventry CV4 60 B2
Hinckley LE10 32 A5
Nuneaton CV10 28 E6
Windsor Gdns CV10 28 E4
Windsor Pl 10 CV32 105 F1
Windsor Rd B78 5 A3
Windsor St
Coventry CV1 61 B2
Hinckley LE10 32 A5
Nuneaton CV11 29 B4
Royal Leamington Spa CV32 109 F8
Rugby CV21 83 C3
Stratford-u-A CV37 144 F3
Windward Way B36 33 B6
Windy Arbor Prim Sch B37 33 D2
Windy Arbour CV8 93 B4
Windyridge Rd B76 22 A6
Winfield Rd CV11 29 B5
Winfield St CV21 83 D3
Wingfield Rd B46 33 F5
Wingfield Way CV6 49 A2
Wingrave Cl CV5 60 A6
Winifred Ave CV5 61 A1
Winnallthorpe CV3 78 E6
Winsford Ave CV5 60 B4
Winsford Cl CV7 74 A6
Winsford Ct CV5 60 C4
Winsham Wlk CV3 77 C3
Winslow Cl
Coventry CV5 60 B3
Royal Leamington Spa CV32 105 C1
Winslow Ho 11 CV1 61 B2
Winspear Cl CV7 46 B1
Winster Ave B93 71 E4
Winster Cl CV7 49 A7
Winston Ave CV2 62 D8
Winston Cl
Coventry CV2 62 D8
Stratford-u-A CV37 144 D1
Winston Dr 15 OX17 139 F5
Winterborne Gdns CV10 29 A2
Winterdene CV7 74 B7
Winter Gardens Way 1 OX16 139 F5
Winterton Rd CV12 40 C2
Winthorpe Dr B91 71 C8
Winton Gr B76 22 A6
Winwick Pl CV22 99 C8
Winyates Rd CV33 123 D2
Wise Gr
Rugby CV21 83 F2
Warwick CV34 104 E2
Wise St CV31 109 F7
Wise Terr CV31 109 F7
Wishaw Cl B98 103 A8
Wishaw La
Curdworth B76 23 A7
Middleton B76,B78 14 C6
Minworth B76 22 E7
Wisley Gr CV8 93 C5
Wistaria Cl 2 CV2 50 B2
Witham Cl B76 13 A1
Witham The NN11 117 F1
Witherley CE Prim Sch CV9 19 B7
Witherley Rd
Atherstone CV9 18 F7
Witherley CV9 19 B6
Withington Gr B93 71 E4
Withybrook Cl CV2 50 D2
Withybrook La CV7 51 F5
Withybrook Rd
Bulkington CV12 40 D2
Solihull B90 70 B8
Withycombe Dr OX16 139 F3
Withy Hill Rd B75 13 B8
Witnell Rd CV6 61 C6
Wixford Lodge B50 148 D8
Wixford Rd B49,B50 119 B1
Woburn Cl CV31 110 C6
Woburn Dr CV10 29 A2
Wolds End Cl GL55 135 B2
Wolds La LE10 41 E4
Wolfe Rd CV4 75 F8
Wolford Rd GL56 140 D6
Wolseley Cl B36 23 A1
Wolsey Rd CV22 99 D6
Wolston La CV8 79 E2
Wolston St Margaret's CE Prim Sch CV8 80 A4
Wolston Way CV3 78 C6
Wolverton Prim Sch CV35 114 B2
Wolverton Rd
Birmingham,Marston Green B37 44 B7
Coventry CV5 60 A3
Norton Lindsey CV35 114 C2
Snitterfield CV37 121 B7
Wolvey CE Prim Sch LE10 41 D4
Wolvey Rd
Bulkington CV12 40 E2
Hinckley LE10 31 E4
Woodbank LE10 32 A7
Woodberrow La B97 102 D6
Woodberry Dr B76 13 A2
Woodbine Cotts
2 Royal Leamington Spa CV32 109 E8
Kingswood CV35 89 D3
Woodbine St 1 CV32 109 E8
Woodbine Wlk B37 33 D2
Woodbridge Ct CV21 83 A3
Woodbridge Pk CV9 16 C4
Woodbrook Ho 9 B37 33 B2
Woodburn Cl CV5 60 B4
Woodbury Cl B97 102 A6
Woodby La LE17 55 E8
Woodchester Rd B93 71 E2
Wood Cl B46 33 F7
Woodclose Ave CV6 60 F6
Woodclose Rd B37 33 A3
Woodcock Cl B94 86 E3
Woodcote Ave
Kenilworth CV8 92 D6
Nuneaton CV11 29 F8
Woodcote Dr
Dorridge B93 72 B2
Leek Wootton CV35 104 F7
Woodcote La CV8,CV35 104 F7
Woodcote Rd
Royal Leamington Spa CV32 105 F3
Warwick CV34 108 F8
Woodcot Park Dr CV37 120 B5
Woodcot Park Homes Est CV37 120 B5

Woodcraft Cl CV4........ **60** A2
Wood Croft B47......... **69** B6
Wood Ct CV2............ **62** D7
Woodend Croft CV4...... **75** E8
Wood End La
Fillongley CV7........... **37** A3
Tanworth-In-A B94........ **86** F5
Wood End Prim Sch CV9. **10** C1
Wood End Sta B94....... **86** F4
Woodfield Rd
Coventry CV5............ **76** E8
Hinckley LE10........... **31** C6
Woodford Cl
Coventry CV7............ **49** D5
Nuneaton CV10.......... **28** D4
Woodford La CV10....... **19** C4
Woodgate Rd LE10....... **32** A8
Woodgreen Cl B97...... **102** B7
Woodhall Cl CV11........ **30** A2
Woodhams Rd CV3....... **78** C3
Wood Hill Rise CV6...... **49** D2
Woodhouse Cl CV3....... **78** E8
Woodhouse La B77....... **4** A5
Woodhouse St CV34..... **108** D6
Woodington Rd B75...... **13** B5
Wood La
Aston Cantlow B49,B95... **119** F5
Birmingham,Marston Green B37.................. **44** A8
Cherington CV36........ **141** D7
Cookhill B96............ **118** C6
Earlswood B94........... **69** E1
Eastcote B92............ **56** F2
Hartshill CV10........... **28** A8
Higham on t H CV13...... **20** E3
Woodland Ave
Claybrooke Magna LE17... **43** E6
Coventry CV5............ **76** F7
Hinckley LE10........... **32** A7
Woodland Rd
Kenilworth CV8.......... **93** B7
Tamworth B77............ **4** A4
Woodlands Ave B46...... **23** B2
Woodlands Cl B78....... **11** A5
Woodlands Ct
Binley Woods CV3........ **79** D7
Coventry CV5............ **77** A8
Woodlands Farm Rd B24. **22** A4
Woodlands Inf Sch B90.. **70** B8
Woodlands La
Bedworth CV12.......... **38** E4
Solihull B90............. **70** B8
Woodlands Rd
Bedworth CV12.......... **38** F3
Binley Woods CV3........ **79** D7
Stratford-u-A CV37...... **144** F5
Woodlands Sch The CV5.. **59** D3
Woodlands Terr B78..... **11** A5
Woodlands The
Hartshill CV10........... **19** A1
Staverton NN11......... **126** D8
Sutton Coldfield B75...... **13** A6
Wood End CV9........... **10** C1
Woodlands Way B37..... **33** D3
Woodland Way B78...... **10** F8
Wood La
Old Arley CV7........... **26** D2
Shilton CV7............. **51** D5
Woodleigh Rd CV4....... **75** F5
Woodloes Ave N CV34... **104** F2
Woodloes Ave S CV34... **104** F1
Woodloes Inf Sch CV34.. **104** E1
Woodloes Jun Sch CV34. **104** E1
Woodloes La CV34,CV35. **104** F2
Woodloes Rd B90........ **70** B7
Woodman Ct CV37...... **144** F4
Woodmill Mdw CV8...... **93** B6
Woodpecker Gr B36..... **33** A7
Woodridge Ave CV5...... **60** A6
Woodroffe Wlk CV6...... **50** A4
Woodrow Cres B93...... **72** A5
Woodrow Ctr B98....... **103** B8
Woodrow Dr B98....... **103** B6
Woodrow Fst Sch B98... **103** B7
Woodrow N B98........ **103** A7
Woodrow S B98........ **103** B7
Woodrow Wlk B98...... **103** A7
Woodrush Com High Sch The B47.................... **69** A6
Woodrush Dr B47........ **69** A5
Woodshires Rd CV6...... **49** F5
Woodsia Cl CV23......... **83** C8
Woodside Ave N CV3..... **76** F6
Woodside Ave S CV3..... **76** F5
Woodside CV9........... **11** D1
Woodside Bsns Pk CV21.. **83** A4
Woodside CE Prim Sch CV9.................... **11** D1
Woodside Cl CV9........ **10** C1
Woodside Cotts CV9..... **18** A5
Woodside Cres B93...... **72** B4
Woodside CV7........... **26** D1
Woodside Park Cvn Pk CV8.................... **96** B6
Woodside Pk Mobile Homes Pk B94................ **86** B7
Woodside Pk CV21....... **83** B5
Woods Piece CV7........ **48** F6
Wood St
Bedworth CV12.......... **39** B5
Nuneaton CV10.......... **28** F4
Woodstock Cl LE10...... **32** A5
Woodstock Cres B93..... **71** F3
Woodstock Rd
Coventry CV3............ **77** D7
Nuneaton CV11.......... **29** E1
Woodston Gr B91........ **71** C8
Wood St
Royal Leamington Spa CV32................. **110** A8
Rugby CV21............. **83** B4
Southam CV47.......... **147** B4
Stratford-u-A CV37...... **145** A2
Wood End CV9........... **10** C1
Wood Terr B96......... **118** D8
Woodview Rd CV9........ **18** E7
Woodville Ct CV34...... **108** F7
Woodville Rd CV34...... **108** E8
Woodward Cl CV31...... **110** A2
Woodward Ct CV37..... **121** B6
Woodway Ave CV35..... **114** F3
Woodway Cl CV2......... **62** F8
Woodway CV35......... **114** F3
Woodway La
Claybrooke Parva LE17.... **43** D4
Coventry CV2............ **50** F1
Woodway Park Sch & Com Coll CV2................ **50** F1
Woodway Rd OX15...... **142** D8
Woodway Wlk CV2....... **62** E8
Woolaston Rd B98...... **103** C8
Woolaway Bglws GL56.. **140** A6
Woolgrove St CV6....... **50** A3
Wooll St 9 CV21......... **83** A3
Woolpack The 9 CV34.. **108** E6
Woolpack Way CV9...... **18** D8
Woolscott Rd CV23...... **117** B6
Woolwich Rd CV11....... **40** F6
Wootton Cl CV37........ **145** D2
Wootton Ct
6 Royal Leamington Spa CV32................. **105** F2
Coventry CV2............ **62** D7
Wootton Green La CV7... **74** A8
Wootton Hall B95....... **113** B2
Wootton La CV7......... **57** E1
Wootton St CV12........ **39** D3
Wootton Wawen CE Prim Sch B95............... **113** A2
Wootton Wawen Sta B95.................. **113** A2
Worcester Cl CV5........ **60** B7
Worcester Ct CV6........ **50** B4
Worcester Ho B36....... **33** A8
Worcester Pl CV36...... **149** C6
Worcester Rd CV8....... **93** B3
Worcester St CV21....... **83** A4
Worcester Wlk B37...... **33** A1
Wordsworth Ave
Redditch B97........... **102** C8
Stratford-u-A CV37...... **130** B8
Warwick CV34.......... **108** D5
Wordsworth Dr CV8...... **93** C4
Wordsworth Rd
Bedworth CV12.......... **39** D1
Coventry CV2............ **62** C4
Rugby CV22............. **99** E6
Workhouse La LE10...... **32** A4
Works Rd B26........... **44** A3
World of Shakespeare (Mus)* CV37........... **145** A2
Worsdell Cl CV1......... **61** B4
Worsfold Cl CV5......... **60** A7
Worths Way CV37...... **144** D6
Worthy Down Wlk B35... **22** B3
Wortley Cl
Cawston CV22........... **99** A8
Cawston CV22........... **99** A8
Wrenbury Dr CV6........ **50** A4
Wren Cl DE12.............. **3** E8
Wren's Nest Cl B90...... **70** A5
Wren St CV2............ **61** F3
Wright Cl B78........... **15** D5
Wrighton Gr B78.......... **9** A8
Wright St CV1........... **61** E4
Wrigsham St CV3........ **77** D8
Wroxall Dr CV3.......... **78** D5
Wroxton CE Prim Sch OX15................... **139** D4
Wroxton Coll OX15...... **139** D4
Wroxton Ct OX15....... **139** D4
Wroxton Ho OX15...... **139** D4
Wr Twr La CV8........... **92** F6
Wulfstan Dr CV47....... **115** D4
Wyatt Ho CV2............ **62** D7
Wyatt Rd B75............ **13** B5
Wyatts Ct CV12.......... **39** B3
Wychbold Cl B97....... **102** A6
Wychbury B76........... **13** A1
Wych-Elm Cl CV22....... **82** B1
Wych Elm Dr 6 CV31... **109** F5
Wychwood Ave
Coventry CV3............ **77** C3
Knowle B93............. **72** B8
Wychwood Cl 14 CV33... **122** F8
Wychwood Dr B97...... **102** D6
Wycliffe Gr CV2......... **62** B5
Wycliffe Rd W CV2....... **62** C5
Wye Cl
Bulkington CV12......... **40** B2
Hinckley LE10........... **31** A8
Royal Leamington Spa CV32................. **106** C3
Sutton Coldfield B76...... **22** B7
Wyegate Cl B36.......... **33** A8
Wykeham Ho CV21....... **83** C7
Wykeley Rd CV2......... **62** C4
Wyken Ave CV2.......... **62** D5
Wyken Cl B93............ **71** E2
Wyken Croft CV2......... **62** D6
Wyken Croft Nature Pk* CV2..................... **62** D6
Wyken Croft Prim Sch CV2..................... **62** E5
Wyken Grange Rd CV2... **62** C5
Wyken Way CV2......... **62** B5
Wyke Rd CV2............ **62** C4
Wykham La OX15,OX16... **139** F1
Wykin La CV13,LE10...... **21** E5
Wykin Rd LE10........... **21** F3
Wyld Ct CV5............. **60** B5
Wyley Rd CV6............ **61** B5
Wynbrook Gr B90........ **71** A6
Wyncote Cl CV8.......... **93** A4
Wyndshiels B46.......... **34** A6
Wynter Rd CV22......... **82** D3
Wyre La CV37........... **129** B3
Wythall Sta B47.......... **69** C4
Wythburn Way CV21..... **83** D7
Wythwood Gr B47....... **69** C6
Wythwood Rd B47....... **69** C6
Wyver Cres CV2.......... **62** C3
Wyvern Cl
Hinckley LE10........... **31** E4
Wellesbourne CV35...... **146** C2

Y

Yardley Chase Rd CV35.. **132** D4
Yardley Cl CV34......... **104** F2
Yardley St CV1........... **61** E4
Yard The CV37.......... **120** E7
Yarmouth Gn CV4........ **75** E8
Yarn Cl B47............. **69** A5
Yarningale Cl B98...... **102** F6
Yarningale La CV35..... **113** E5
Yarningale Rd CV3....... **78** D5
Yarningdale 7 B90...... **70** C8
Yarn La B90............. **70** A6
Yarranton Cl CV37...... **144** E5
Yarrow Cl CV23.......... **83** D8
Yates Ave CV21.......... **82** F6
Yatesbury Ave B35....... **22** A3
Yeats Rd 6 CV37....... **130** B8
Yelverton Rd CV6........ **61** D8
Yeomanry Cl
12 Warwick CV34....... **108** F7
Sutton Coldfield B75...... **13** A6
Yew Cl CV3.............. **62** C1
Yewdale Cres CV2....... **50** E1
Yewdale Ct CV2.......... **50** F1
Yews The CV12.......... **38** E2
Yew Tree Cl B94......... **89** D3
Yew Tree Ct
1 Royal Leamington Spa CV31................. **109** F5
Austrey CV9.............. **3** A2
Yew Tree Farm Craft Ctr* B95.................. **113** B2
Yew Tree Gdns B95..... **113** A4
Yew Tree Hill CV23....... **64** E3
Yew Tree La B94........ **113** D8
Yew Trees The B95..... **113** B4
Yew Wlk B37............ **33** B2
York Ave
Atherstone CV9.......... **12** E1
Bedworth CV12.......... **39** D2
York Cl
Coventry CV3............ **78** C5
Studley B80............ **103** C4
Yorkminster Dr B37..... **33** D3
York Rd CV31........... **109** F8
Yorksand Rd B78.......... **8** F8
York St
Coventry CV1............ **61** B2
Nuneaton CV11.......... **29** A4
Rugby CV21............. **82** F4
Young Cl CV34.......... **108** B5
Yule Rd CV2............. **62** D5
Yvonne Rd B97......... **102** D7

Z

Zorrina Cl CV10.......... **28** B5

Notes

Name and Address	Telephone	Page	Grid reference

Addresses

Name and Address	Telephone	Page	Grid reference

Using the Ordnance Survey National Grid

Any feature in this atlas can be given a unique reference to help you find the same feature on other Ordnance Survey maps of the area, or to help someone else locate you if they do not have a Street Atlas.

The grid squares in this atlas match the Ordnance Survey National Grid and are at 500 metre intervals. The small figures at the bottom and sides of every other grid line are the National Grid kilometre values (**00** to **99** km) and are repeated across the country every 100 km (see left).

To give a unique National Grid reference you need to locate where in the country you are. The country is divided into 100 km squares with each square given a unique two-letter reference. Use the administrative map to determine in which 100 km square a particular page of this atlas falls.

The bold letters and numbers between each grid line (**A** to **F**, **1** to **8**) are for use within a specific Street Atlas only, and when used with the page number, are a convenient way of referencing these grid squares.

Example *The railway bridge over DARLEY GREEN RD in grid square B1*

Step 1: Identify the two-letter reference, in this example the page is in **SP**

Step 2: Identify the 1 km square in which the railway bridge falls. Use the figures in the southwest corner of this square: Eastings **17**, Northings **74**. This gives a unique reference: **SP 17 74**, accurate to 1 km.

Step 3: To give a more precise reference accurate to 100 m you need to estimate how many tenths along and how many tenths up this 1 km square the feature is (to help with this the 1 km square is divided into four 500 m squares). This makes the bridge about **8** tenths along and about **1** tenth up from the southwest corner.

This gives a unique reference: **SP 178 741**, accurate to 100 m.

Eastings (read from left to right along the bottom) come before Northings (read from bottom to top). If you have trouble remembering say to yourself "Along the hall, THEN up the stairs"!

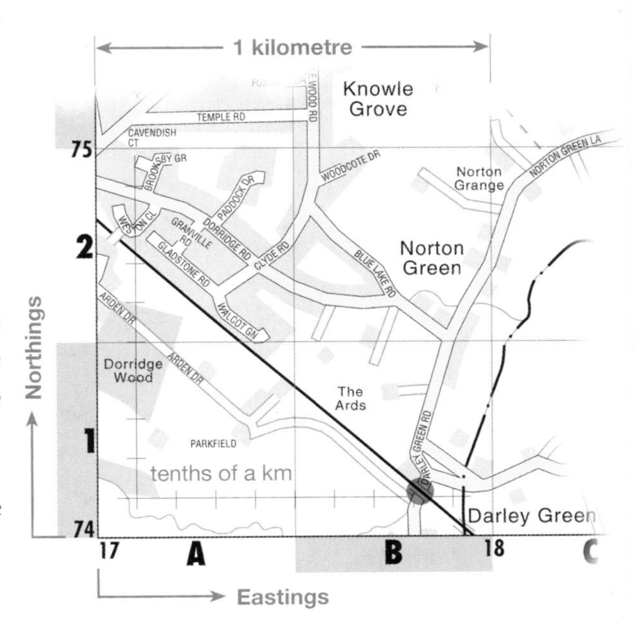